PUBLICATIONS

OF THE

SCOTTISH HISTORY SOCIETY

VOLUME X.

———————

JOHN MAJOR'S GREATER BRITAIN

FEBRUARY 1892

A HISTORY OF
GREATER BRITAIN

AS WELL ENGLAND AS SCOTLAND

COMPILED FROM THE ANCIENT AUTHORITIES
BY JOHN MAJOR, BY NAME INDEED A
SCOT, BUT BY PROFESSION A THEOLOGIAN

1521

Translated from the original Latin and Edited
with Notes by

ARCHIBALD CONSTABLE

to which is prefixed a Life of the Author by

ÆNEAS J. G. MACKAY

LL.D. ADVOCATE.

EDINBURGH

Printed at the University Press by T. and A. CONSTABLE
for the Scottish History Society

1892

CONTENTS

PAGE

EDITOR'S PREFACE, ... xvii

LIFE OF THE AUTHOR, by Æneas J. G. Mackay, . xxix

Appendix to the Life.

    i. Notice of Major in French and Scottish Records, . . cxvi
    ii. Note on the School of the Terminists, . . . cxxii

HISTORY OF GREATER BRITAIN

Author's Preface to King James v. . . . cxxx

BOOK I.

Chap. I.—A short Preface by John Major, theologian of Paris, and Scotsman by birth, to his work concerning the rise and gests of the Britons. Likewise concerning the name and the first inhabitants of Greater Britain, ... 1

Chap. II.—Of the description of Britain and its extent : that is, its breadth, length, and circumference ; also of its fruitfulness, alike in things material and in famous men, . . . 5

Chap. III.—Concerning things that are lacking in Britain, and what the country possesses in their stead ; and concerning the length of the day in that land, ... 12

Chap. IV.—Of those who have possessed Britain, how the peoples of Wales are Aremoric Britons, and the Scots are Irish Britons, and of the threefold language of the Britons, . . . 17

Chap. V.—Of the situation of Britain, that is, of England and Scotland, and of their rivers, and, in special, of the wealth of London, ... 19

Chap. VI.—Of the boundaries of Scotland, its cities, towns and villages ; of its customs in war, and in the church ; of its abundance of fish, its harbours, woods, islands, etc., . . 27

Chap. VII.—Concerning the Manners and Customs of the Scots, 40

CONTENTS

BOOK I—(*continued.*)

PAGE

CHAP. VIII.—Something further concerning the manners and customs of the Scots, that is, of the peasantry, as well as of the nobles, and of the Wild Scots, as well as the civilised part, . 47

CHAP. IX.—Concerning the various origin of the Scots, and the reason of the name. For the Scots are sprung from the Irish, and the Irish in turn from the Spaniards, and the Scots are so named after the woman Scota, ... 50

CHAP. X.—Of the Origin of the Picts, their Name and Customs, . 54

CHAP. XI.—In what manner the Scots first gained a settlement in Britain, ... 55

CHAP. XII.—Concerning the arrival of the Romans in Britain, and their achievements in that island, ... 57

CHAP. XIII.—How the Emperor Claudius came to Britain, . 58

CHAP. XIV.—Concerning the events which thereafter happened in Britain, the building of the wall, the passion of Ursula with her companions at Cologne, the reception of the Catholic Faith, and the rest, ... 59

CHAP. XV.—Concerning the Strife between the Picts and Scots, . 61

BOOK II.

CHAP. I.—Follows here the second book of British history. Of the return of the Scots into Britain, and their league with the Picts, and the wars that were soon thereafter carried on by them, and the building of a wall, ... 64

CHAP. II.—Of the sending of Bishops to Scotland, and the consecration of several of them in that country, likewise of their holy lives, and the marvels that they wrought, . . 65

CHAP. III.—Concerning the affairs of the Britons, . . 67

CHAP. IV.—Of Merlin the Prophet, ... 72

CHAP. V.—Of Aurelius Ambrosius and his reign, . . . 78

CHAP. VI.—Of King Arthur, ... 81

CHAP. VII.—Concerning Eochodius, Aidan, and Eugenius, kings of Scotland, and men of noted sanctity that were born in their reigns, ... 85

CHAP. VIII.—Concerning the arrival of Gormund, first in Ireland, then in Britain, and his cruel dealings with both lands ; also of the rule of the Saxons in Britain under Gormund, . . 89

CHAP. IX.—Of the outward form and appearance of the English, and how they differ in appearance and stature from the rest of

Book II—*(continued.)*

PAGE

nations ; likewise of the mission of Augustine for their conver-sion, and of his preaching,　.　　.　　.　　. 89

Chap. X.—Of the conversion of Oswald, likewise of the too great austerity of the bishop who was sent to him, of the wisdom of bishop Aidan, and of the conversion of the Britons to the faith, 91

Chap. XI.—Of the Life of Oswald and Aidan,　.　　.　　. 94

Chap. XII.—Concerning the death of Malduin, the reigns of Eu-genius the Fourth and Eugenius the Fifth, Saint Cuthbert, the Venerable Bede, and the Monastery of Melrose,　.　　. 98

Chap. XIII.—Concerning the reign of Achaius, and the eminent valour and piety of his brother William ; likewise of the per-petual peace between the French and the Scots, and of the founders of the University of Paris,　　　　.　　. 100

Chap. XIV.—Of the death of Congall, the reign of Dungal, the contention between the Picts and Scots ; likewise of the war against Alphin, whom in the end they slew, and of the deeds of others,　.　　.　　.　　.　　.　　. 102

BOOK III.

Chap. I.—Of the incontinence of Osbert, king of Northum-berland, and his death ; of the slaying of Ella and the other cruelties practised by the Danes ; likewise of many kings of England,　.　　.　　.　　.　　.　　.　. 109

Chap. II.—Of the reign of Donald the Scot, and the expulsion of the remnant of the Picts ; of the deeds of Constantine Eth, or Aetius, of Gregory, Donald, Constantine, and Eugenius, kings of Scotland,　.　　.　　.　　.　　.　　. 112

Chap. III.—Of the children of Knoth, king of England. Of the character of Edward, the miracles that he did, and his chastity ; likewise of the overthrow of Harold, king of England, by the Norman,　.　　.　　.　　.　　.　　.　. 115

Chap. IV.—Of the Kings of Scotland and their deeds,　.　　. 117

Chap. V.—Concerning Malcolm Canmore and Machabeda, kings of Scotland ; likewise of the death of Saint Edward, king of England, the flight of Edgar with all his children and house-hold into Scotland, and of the marriage of Saint Margaret, his daughter, and the children that she bore,　.　　.　　. 121

Chap. VI.—Of the deeds of the English ; first of the invasion of England by William of Normandy the Bastard, and his slaying of king Harold. Of the independence of the Scots; of William's issue and his death, .　　.　　.　　.　　. 127

CONTENTS

Book III—(*continued.*)

PAGE

CHAP. VII.—Of the reign in England of William Rufus, how he was an overbearing and irreligious man, and met with a condign end,   129

CHAP. VIII.—Of the rest of the acts of Malcolm, king of the Scots, and how the holy life of his wife brought him too to the practice of piety, ...   130

CHAP. IX.—Concerning Donald, Duncan, and Edgar, kings of the Scots, their children, and their deeds, .   .   131

CHAP. X.—Of Alexander the Fierce, king of the Scots,   .   . 132

CHAP. XI.—Of David, that most excellent king of the Scots, in whom are found wonderful examples of all the virtues ; likewise of Henry, his son, and of his grandchildren, the issue of this Henry ; and of Richard of Saint Victor, .   .   . 133

CHAP. XII.—Of Henry Beauclerk, king of the English, and of the affairs of Normandy in his time,   .   .   . 143

CHAP. XIII.—Of Stephen, king of the English, his reign and death,   144

CHAP. XIV.—Of Henry earl of Anjou and king of England,   . 146

CHAP. XV.—Of the martyrdom of the Blessed Thomas, and the sin of the king, ...   150

BOOK IV.

CHAP. I.—Of the war between the foresaid Henry, king of the English, and his son, and the peace that was made between them ; of the defection of the Irish to the English ; and of the penitence of Henry, and the extent of his dominions at the time of his death, ...   153

CHAP. II.—Of Richard, the emperor's son, king of the English, who went as a warrior to the Holy Land, but on his return was, by the duke of Austria, wickedly taken prisoner, and by his own people nobly ransomed ; here too is treated of the reason of an abundance and of a scarcity of children ; something likewise about robbers, ... 154

CHAP. III.—Of John, that far from worthy king of the English ; of the interdict which was laid upon England, and of the assignment of the tribute to the Roman pontiff ; the poisoning of the king, and its censure, ... 157

CHAP. IV.—Of Malcolm, grandson of David, king of the Scots, and all that he did, and how he never entered the married state,   162

CHAP. V.—Of William, king of the Scots, his captivity and his ransom ; of the lavish building of monasteries, and other matters that came to pass in his time, .   .   . 163

CONTENTS

Book IV.—*(continued).*

PAGE

CHAP. VI.—Of William the Scot and Alexander, William's son, and of a miracle done by William; of the war with John of England, and the peace that was made with the same, and the treaty by the swearing of the oath of fealty, . . . 167

CHAP. VII.—Of Alexander, son of William, and his wars with John of England. Of the interdict on Scotland, and when such a thing is to be feared, ... 170

CHAP. VIII.—Of Henry, king of the English, and his son, and of the prophecy of Merlin about them, ... 173

CHAP. IX.—Of Edward, son of Henry the Englishman, his war with the Welsh and his victory over them; likewise of the expulsion of the Jews, ... 175

CHAP. X.—Of the monasteries that were founded by the Earl of Fife, and something by the way about the seclusion of nuns and their rule of life; of the marriage of King Alexander the Second, his life and praiseworthy death, and of the destruction by fire of men and towns in Scotland, ... 177

CHAP. XI.—Of Alexander the Third, king of Scotland, and the dispute that took place in the matter of his coronation; of Egyptian days; of free will; and of the genealogy of the Scottish kings, ... 182

CHAP. XII.—Of the translation of the remains of Saint Margaret of England and Malcolm, king of the Scots; of the marriage of Alexander and the dispensation that was granted him thereanent. Of the punishment inflicted upon vagabonds and Jews, and other events of his reign, ... 185

CHAP. XIII.—Of what took place in Britain at this time, according to the narrative of Caxton the English chronicler in the first place—with the refutation of the statements made by him; follows, in the second place, another narrative, as we find it in the Scots chroniclers, ... 191

CHAP. XIV.—A truer version of the deeds of William Wallace or Wallax, ... 195

CHAP. XV.—Of John Cumming, regent of Scotland; of the rest of the feats of Wallace, and of his miserable ending, but his happy change from this life, ... 202

CHAP. XVI.—Of those famous theologians Richard Middleton and John Duns: likewise of the contest for the Scottish throne, and of the feats of the new kings of that country, . . 206

CHAP. XVII.—Containing many reasons in support of the claim of Robert Bruce; and, in preface to these, the whole issue of Malcolm down to the present king is given in full, . . 209

CONTENTS

BOOK IV—*(continued.)*

PAGE

CHAP. XVIII.—Of the objections that may be urged against this conclusion, and their solution, ... 215

CHAP. XIX.—Of the acts of Robert Bruce, king of Scotland, and the calamities which befell him, ... 220

CHAP. XX.—Of Edward the Second, king of the English ; and of the manner of waging war among the Britons, . . . 225

CHAP. XXI.—Of the war which the Scots waged against Edward the Second and its happy result ; likewise of the learned men who at that time flourished in Britain, ... 227

BOOK V.

CHAP. I.—Of the rest of the warlike deeds of Robert Bruce and his brother done against the English ; and of the unwise treaty that was made at Stirling, ... 231

CHAP. II.—Of the immense army that the English king brought against the Scot ; of the prelude to the battle, and the valour that was shown therein by Randolph and a few among the Scots ; of Douglas's loyalty and kindness towards Randolph, and the speech that was made by both kings to their soldiers, . 233

CHAP. III.—Of the drawing up of the two armies in order of battle, ... 238

CHAP. IV.—Of the establishment of Robert Bruce in the kingdom ; of the skirmishing raids made by the English ; and of the death in Ireland of Edward Bruce, ... 242

CHAP. V.—How the kings ravaged each the other's country. Of the policy of delay adopted by Robert, and how he then carried the attack into England ; his address to his soldiers ; Edward's exhortation to the English. Of the battle and the victory won by the Scots, ... 245

CHAP. VI.—Of what took place in England in the time of Robert Bruce ; chiefly of the factions and quarrels of the nobles of the kingdom which arose through the arrogance of Hugh Spenser, 250

CHAP. VII.—Concerning Isabella, sister of the king of the French, how she was sent to France by her husband, the English king, and of her banishment there along with her son. Of the captivity of Edward, and the prophecies of Merlin ; further, of the passage of the Scots into England, and of their return from England, ... 253

CHAP. VIII.—Of the complaint made by Edward the father, and how he was carried to another prison, where he was put to death with terrible tortures, ... 262

CONTENTS xi

BOOK V—(*continued.*)

PAGE

CHAP. IX.—Of the deeds of Robert Bruce, king of the Scots, and Edward the Third, king of the English; likewise of the peace that was brought about through the marriage of their children; and of the death of Robert, ... 263

CHAP. X.—Of the wise regency of Scotland at the hands of Thomas Randolph, and his end through the treachery of a monk, 266

CHAP. XI.—Of the brave deeds of James Douglas and his death; and of the succession of Edward Baliol in Scotland, his victory, his coronation, and, finally, his flight, ... 269

CHAP. XII.—Of the attack made upon the Scots by Edward of England and Edward Baliol; of the siege of Berwick, and how it was in the end taken by storm after a battle in which very many of the Scots lost their lives, ... 271

CHAP. XIII.—Of the tyranny of Baliol in Scotland; of his oppression of David, and the accession of Robert Stuart to the side of David, ... 274

CHAP. XIV.—Of the return of earl Randolph to Scotland; of the choice of guardians, the captivity of one, and the brave deeds of the other; of cities that were set on fire and their restoration, and various events of war, ... 276

CHAP. XV.—The siege of the castle of Dunbar, and its courageous defence by a woman; how the siege was raised by reason of the invasion of England by the French; of divers losses upon both sides; and of tournaments, and how far they are lawful, . 279

CHAP. XVI.—Of the siege of Perth and Stirling; of the recovery of Edinburgh; the renown in war of Alexander Ramsay; of the welcome given to king David, and the fealty sworn to him by the Scots, ... 282

CHAP. XVII.—Of the tutors who were placed over Edward the Third, king of the English, in the time of his youth. Of the treaty that was made between the Scots and the English. Of the pre-eminent virtue of Robert Bruce, and the independence of Scotland, as against Caxton. Of the strife that ensued concerning the right of that prince to bear rule, with a repetition of some things relating to the death of his father, . . 286

CHAP. XVIII.—Of the dangers that beset the favourites of kings, and of the factions that arose in Scotland under David Bruce, . 290

CHAP. XIX.—Of the siege of Calais, and the unfortunate expedition of David Bruce in England, and his captivity there. Of Edward's deeds of violence in Scotland, and the election of a governor of Scotland; and how some famous men came by their death, ... 292

CONTENTS

Book V.—(*continued.*)

PAGE

CHAP. XX.—How Eugene, the Frenchman, was sent into Scotland, and of all that was wrought by the Scots along with him against the English. Of the honourable return of the Frenchman. Of the violent attack made by the English upon Scotland, and their rueful return to England, and of what the Scots did thereafter, ... 294

CHAP. XXI.—Of the return to England from Scotland of king David without compassing his end. Of the captivity of John, king of the French, and the adroit escape of Archibald Douglas. Of the ransom at last of David, and the death of the queen, with her eulogy, ... 298

CHAP. XXII.—Of the death of Edward the Third and his son. Of the reign of Richard the Second, and of those whom he ennobled, and of his wives, ... 301

CHAP. XXIII.—Of the rest of the deeds of King David ; how he succeeded in getting the church tithes, and gave his counsel as to the choice of an Englishman to be king of Scotland, and, when his counsel was despised, took to wife a young girl ; how he sought a divorce from her when he found her barren ; his death, ... 303

CHAP. XXIV.—Concerning Richard of England, how he took his uncle prisoner, and was himself made prisoner by his subjects and slain. Of the creation and banishment of dukes. Of Henry the Fourth and Henry the Fifth of England ; and of Robert Stewart, the Scottish king, ... 307

BOOK VI.

CHAP. I.—Of the killing of a servant of Dunbar and the truce which was thereby violated ; and of the cruel revenge that was taken and the stratagem which was conceived by certain lords ; also of divers revolts and their issues, ... 310

CHAP. II.—Of the expeditions of John of Gaunt, Archibald Douglas, the English, the French, and Richard, king of England. Of the Scots invasion of England, and of the charter that was found, ... 312

CHAP. III.—Of the battle that was fought at Otterburn, and of other conflicts between the English and the Scots ; and chiefly between Henry Percy or Persy, and James Douglas, . . 315

CHAP. IV.—Of the rest of this said battle, and its renewal by the bishop of Durham ; and of the capture of Lindesay and his release, ... 324

BOOK VI—*(continued.)*

PAGE

CHAP. V.—Of the choice of the younger Robert as Regent of Scotland, which this writer can no way approve ; and of the expedition against England on the part of Robert, which had indeed a prosperous issue, but was none the less far from praiseworthy,   329

CHAP. VI.—Of the death of Robert the Scot, the second of the name, and of his issue. Of the coronation of Robert the Third, who was formerly called John, and of his character ; further, concerning the rising under Alexander Buchan, and the duel fought by thirty Wild Scots against other thirty,   .   .   331

CHAP. VII.—Of the creation of new dukes ; and of the conspiracy and rebellion of the earl of March against the king and realm on account of the wrongful retention of his daughter's dower when she had been repudiated. Of the death and valour of Archibald the Terrible. Of the invasion of Scotland by Henry the Fourth of England, and the vengeance that the earl of March took upon the Scots, likewise of the destruction and captivity of the Scots, ...   335

CHAP. VIII.—Of Henry the Fourth of England, who escaped plots that were laid for him, and tamed rebellious men ; and of the death of Robert the Third of Scotland in sorrow at the captivity of his son, ...   340

CHAP. IX.—Of the achievements of Henry the Fifth, king of the English, and of James the First, king of the Scots ; and of the good faith kept by the Scots with the French ; of the various fortune in war of both, and of the death of Henry the Fifth and his eulogy, ...   342

CHAP. X.—Of the restoration to his earldom of George earl of March ; of the destruction of the castle of Jedburgh ; and of the dispute that arose as to the legality of the imposition of new taxes. Of the battle at Harlaw, and the men who there lost their lives. Of the foundation of the University of Saint Andrew ; of the death of Robert duke of Albany, and an estimate of his achievements, ...   346

CHAP. XI.—Of the return of James the First, the Scot, into his kingdom by way of the marriage that he contracted ; the author's opinion concerning the ransoming of kings ; and of the sins of the kings against the state, ...   350

CHAP. XII.—Of the marriage of Lewis the Eleventh, king of the French, and Margaret of Scotland. Of the crime committed by James Stewart, and his banishment, and how he, with his fellow-conspirators, was punished. Of trial by jury or assise of the nobles of Scotland. Of the rebellion of Alexander of the Isles, and his petition for mercy, ...   353

CONTENTS

Book VI.—*(continued)*.

PAGE

Chap. XIII.—Of the twin sons that were born to the king, and of the fresh institution in their case of the order of knights, after the custom of Britain. Of the making of a cannon, and in defence of engines of war generally. Of the rising of the nobles. Of the conflict between the Wild Scots. Of the vain attempt that was made to seduce the Scots from the French alliance; and of the disheriting of the duke of March; of the death of Alexander Stewart, and of his heir, . . . 360

Chap. XIV.—Of the murder of James the First, and the treason of the earl of Athole. Of the outward aspect and the moral characteristics of this same James the First; the good faith that he kept towards the French, and other his praises, . 364

Chap. XV.—Of the fearful but well-deserved punishment that was inflicted upon the parricides of James the First, and of the marriage of the queen his wife with a man of obscure condition, and the banishment of her new husband, . . . 368

Chap. XVI.—Of the deeds of Henry the Sixth of England, and the death at Orleans of Thomas Montacute. Of the French maid; Philip of Burgundy; the ignoble marriage of the queen of England; the unhappy marriage of Henry with the Lotharingian. Of various rebellions of the English nobles against the king, ... 371

Chap. XVII.—Of the birth of Edward of England and the rebellion of the duke of York. Of the various fortune of King Henry. Of York's ambition of the crown; and of the various chances of the war, and attempts of the nobles, . . . 377

Chap. XVIII.—Of the marriage of James the Scot, the Second, who was called Red Face; of the struggle for power with the Douglases; and, in connection therewith, of the danger to the state which comes from the exaltation of powerful lords. Of the reign of this same James the Second, his issue, his death, and his praise, ... 381

Chap. XIX.—Of the coronation of James the Third; of Henry the Sixth and the things done by him in Scotland and England. Of the death of the queen of Scotland and her incontinence. Of the capture and the restoration of the duke of Albany. The death of bishop Kennedy and his encomium, . . . 387

Chap. XX.—Of the character and the death of the duke of Clarence and the earl of Warwick. Of the deeds of Edward, Richard, and the Henrys, kings of England, and various occurrences. Of the wickedness of Richard and his miserable death, and of the marriage of Henry the Eighth and of his sisters, . 389

ADDITIONAL NOTES.

PAGE
I. POPULATION OF MEDIEVAL CITIES,   .   .   .   395
II. PASSAGE ON 'NOBILITY,'   397

APPENDICES.

Compiled by THOMAS GRAVES LAW.

I. BIBLIOGRAPHY OF JOHN MAJOR AND HIS DISCIPLES—

JOHN MAJOR—

    Logic and Philosophy, ...   403
    Scripture, ...   410
    History, ...   411
    Chronological Index, ...   411
    DAVID CRANSTOUN, ...   412
    GEORGE LOKERT, ...   414
    WILLIAM MANDERSTON, ...   415
    ROBERT CAUBRAITH, ...   417

II. PREFACES TO JOHN MAJOR'S WORKS, .   .   .   418

INDEX, ...   451

Illustrations

Reduced facsimile of the title-page of Major's Commentary on
    Matthew, Edition 1518, ...   at page 403

Reduced facsimile of an old engraving of the 'Assembly of the
    Saints,' printed by Major in the Commentary on Matthew,
                                                        at page 450

EDITOR'S PREFACE

b

EDITOR'S PREFACE

To the Volume which is now placed in the hands of the members of the Scottish History Society it falls to me to add a few words of preface at once as editor and translator.

On the first suggestion of the book by the Council, Mr. Æneas Mackay kindly offered to contribute towards it a Biography, already written indeed for another purpose, but which as revised for this work has been so much enlarged as to become not only by far the most complete account of the Life of Major which we have, but also an estimate of his place in philosophical and theological literature such as is nowhere else to be found.

To Mr. Law we owe the Bibliographical Appendix, which has grown from the meagre and often erroneous catalogue in Freebairn's edition of the History into the ample though even now probably not exhaustive list to be found at the end of this volume. That Appendix has been supplemented by a Bibliography of Major's disciples, and to the same hand is due the collection, in the second Appendix, of those Prefaces and Dedications to Major's works, which from their subject-matter, from copious personal references to himself, to the objects of his address, and to others of his friends and pupils, will be recognised by the student of scholastic philosophy as possessing a real historical value. These Appendices in fact go far to render the present volume not merely a contribution to Scottish History, but an illustration of Scholastic method and teaching as these were exhibited in a great Scottish schoolman, now almost forgotten, but in his own day a man of outstanding influence. This collection of Prefaces may also serve to show the rich harvest which awaits the explorer of that field in literature; for the publication of the Prefaces alone in the works of one who was the centre of a movement, and in the works of his pupils, can hardly fail to throw light upon many other parts of history.

So much I have thought it right to say in regard to the structure and framework of this volume; but before I venture to say something from the translator's point of view, I should like to put on record, even though I may be unable to repay, my debt to one whose help and service have been unfailingly placed at my disposal in the progress of my work. It was Mr. Law who first suggested to me that I should undertake this translation, and to my eyes the traces of his judgment and suggestion are so plainly visible on every page that I seem to usurp a place to which I have no claim when I write as if I were the editor of the work.

To the external history of Major's life—as that has now been written by Mr. Mackay, with as much completeness as we may ever expect to have it presented to us—I have nothing to add. Nor have I any contribution to make, unless indirectly and by the way, to an estimate of his relation to the thought of his time. But just as in the intimate intercourse of daily life certain features in the character of a friend come to impress themselves insensibly upon one, so, in the peculiar relation which a translator of some years' standing comes to hold towards his original, do certain characters and even mannerisms gain an aspect and a prominence which no ordinary study can afford. I think that it will not be out of place if I should here try to indicate some of those features in this History which have impressed me in this fashion.

It will be seen that in the first sentence of his History Major declares that he writes this work in the manner almost of the theologians ('theologico ferme stylo'), and in its dedication to king James the Fifth, where he deals with the objection which might possibly be urged against him—a 'theologian'—that he writes a history, he says that he utterly dissents from the view of those who hold that it is not becoming to a theologian to write history. 'For if', he says, 'it belongs to a theologian most of all to lay down definite statements in regard to matters of faith, and religion, and morals, I shall not consider that I transgress my province if I relate not events only, or how and by whose instigation such events came to pass, but also if I say definitely whether such and such things were rightly done or wrongly; and throughout my work, yet most of all in matters that are ambiguous, I have made this, first of all, my aim, that you [i.e. the king] may learn from the reading of this present history, not only what has taken place, but also how that particular matter ought to have been dealt with, and that you may thus discern, at the expense of a little reading, what the experience of centuries, if it were granted you to live so long, could hardly teach you.' This passage is a key to the manner of Major's history. He has not indeed, in the modern sense, any notion of a philosophy of history; but he separates himself once for all from the chronicler and the annalist. To him history is important from the practical value of the lessons that it contains; one might almost say that the writing of his history possesses for the writer its chief interest in the opportunity that it affords for a full and free discussion; and there cannot be a doubt that in Major's case that discussion is made vivid to us from the action of an eminently independent judgment. Examples of this discussion are strewn too thickly in his pages to make it necessary to refer to them; but I think that the reader will recognise that it is there that Major warms to his task, and not seldom, in the midst of practical lessons which to men of the present day may suffer sometimes from being obsolete and sometimes from being over-obvious, throws incidentally a side-light upon the thought of his own times that has a real historical importance. From his 'In Quartum' I will quote two passages which illustrate his conception of a theologian's duty. The first runs thus: 'Now the manner of the scholastics, and a laudable manner it is, is this: that every man shall say freely what he thinks—with all observance, as matter of course, of the forms of courtesy, whether with those that are older than himself, or with his contemporaries. Aught else is unbecoming to a theologian.'[1] The second passage bears specially upon the value of discussion or debate. 'To forbid discussion is to entangle men in the error of Mahomet, who prohibited discussion in regard to his law, fearing that by discussion the falsehood of his erroneous and execrable sect might be discovered; for it is by comparison and discussion, and by no other way according to the light of nature, that an intricate matter can be cleared up.'[2]

The theological or scholastic manner pervades the History; and Major as a true scholastic gives evidence throughout of that intellectual subordination to Aristotle which for several centuries marked the course of European thought. Some acquaintance with his

---

[1] Modus autem scholasticus est et laudabilis ut quilibet libere dicat quod sentit: honore tamen semper servato tam apud maiores quam apud equales. Alioquin theologum dedecet.—*In Quartum* : Dist. xviii. Qu. 2. fol. cxxxviii. ed. 1521.

[2] Prohibere enim disputationes est homines in errorem Mahumeti involvere: qui de sua lege disputationem vetuit, ne falsitas suae erroneae et execrandae sectae disputando deprehenderetur. Collatione namque et disputatione materia intricata, et non aliter, naturaliter invenitur.—*Ib.* Dist. xxiv. Qu. 13, fol. clxx.

history—what indeed Major would himself have called 'tantilla lectio'—will impress that fact upon the reader unforgetably. Facts or inferences drawn from the writings of Aristotle go further than anything else to solve the vexed question of the birth of Merlin, and to explain the failure on the part of the Scots to take the castle of Berwick in 1355; but it is naturally in the great questions of the government of states and of how a man shall lead a life conform to the dictates of reason that the commanding and universal presence of 'the Philosopher' is chiefly felt. There is a passage in the fifth chapter of the first book of the History in which Major enumerates the illustrious philosophers and theologians who have gone forth from the University of Oxford. When I showed that passage to a friend to whom I am under more obligations than to any other in the matter of this translation, and who supplied me with notes in elucidation of the life of those men, he added in regard to one of them, that 'of course he wrote upon the Sentences. Major does not seem to consider any one worthy of notice who did not'. It was an agreeable pleasantry; it was also strictly true. But however strongly marked may be the traces of Aristotle in the History, it is again to his purely scholastic work, as that is seen in the 'In Quartum,' that we must go for the most striking illustrations of reverence, in this independent thinker, for the universal philosopher. In discussing questions connected with drinking—such as drinking for a wager (invitations 'ad potus equales')—he says that in this matter as much importance should be attached to the opinion of Origen and Augustine as to that of Aristotle[1]. In another passage he describes the famine of the year in which he was writing, 'in ligua Hoccitana in urbe Lemouicensi'[2] and pictures a certain Sortes (a favourite name in his arguments) on whose face the calamitous condition is plainly written. 'Yet I may believe', Major goes on, 'that Sortes will probably survive until the new harvest is collected in his barn, though in great penury; and even now he suffers hunger, and a morsel of garden stuff, or barley bread, or a few beans would be sweeter to him than a partridge to the mouth of an abbot. The question is this: Am I bound, under pain of otherwise committing a sin, to succour him? It is answered affirmatively. This is proved by the words of Christ, in the twenty-

---

[1] Origeni presbytero et Augustino in hac materia non est minor fides habenda quam Aristoteli.—*In Quartum*, Dist. xxvii. Qu. 8, fol. cxxxvi.

[2] *i.e.* Limoges.

fifth chapter of Matthew : " I was hungry and ye gave me no meat,
I was thirsty and ye gave me no drink, I was a stranger and ye
received me not, naked and ye clothed me not, in pain and in
prison and ye visited me not." And afterward the conclusion
follows : " Go ye into eternal fire." Wherefore the rich glutton
who refused the crumbs of his bread to Lazarus was buried in hell,
Luke xvi. Come hither, as my third witness, thou blessed John
Evangelist ; say too what thou dost think as to these two cases.
The blessed John makes answer : " Why question me ? Hast thou
not read in the third chapter of the first Canonical Epistle : ' He
that is rich in this world's goods and seeth his brother in need, and
closeth his bowels against him, how doth the love of God abide in
him ? ' " As much as to say : " To me it seems incredible that the
love of God abideth in him." I do not believe that Aristotle
would have spoken otherwise.' [1] In another place he marshals the
arguments by which he would have endeavoured to lead Aristotle
to embrace Christianity : ' If Aristotle, or any other intelligent
heathen, were half-doubtful which creed [Christianity or Mahomet-
anism] he should embrace, knowing that he must give his assent
to one, but ignorant to which it should be given, I would use, with
Aristotle, this argument—" That law censures all vices even more
severely than you yourself in your Ethics censure them, and exalts
all virtues to the stars [2] ".' I add one more example of the place
occupied by Aristotle. To the justification and sanctions of marriage this is added : ' Besides, Aristotle, the patriarchs, and other
men who have deserved heaven, entered the married state.' [3]

I should like now to say something about the singular fairness,
the anxious impartiality, of Major's judgment of the English
nation, the cordiality of his appreciation of English customs.
There may indeed be some injustice in characterising this mental
attitude of his as ' anxious ', for it seems to belong to the very
nature of the man and to have been no more than confirmed by
his training and by his conception of the functions of the theo-

---

[1] . . . Non credo Aristotelem aliter fuisse dicturum.—*Ib*. Dist. xv. Qu. 7,
fol. lxx.

[2] Si Aristoteles staret subdubius vel alius gentilis ingeniosus ad quem ritum se
converteret, sciens quod uni teneretur assentire nesciens tamen cui · · · quae
quidem lex vitia omnia rigidius quam tu ipse in Ethicis damnat, et virtutes ad
astra effert.—*Ib*. *In Prologum*, Qu. 3, fol. v.

[3] Praeterea Aristoteles, patriarchae, et viri celo digni matrimonium contraxe-
runt. — *Ib*. Dist. xxvi. Qu. 3, fol. clxxxviii.

logian. Attention has been directed by Mr. Mackay to his views
of the advantage to both nations of a union of the crowns.   In our
own country, and at the time of his writing, there was probably no
one who shared his views, and even fifty years later, we find in
our great humanist, George Buchanan, whom the world has recognised as upon that side of life the true exponent of the modern
spirit, a resolute opponent of union.   Yet it is not only
because in this matter John Major showed the insight of a philo-
sophic statesman that his position is unique among Scottish
writers.   He lost indeed no one of those opportunities which the
nature of his narrative so abundantly afforded to strike home the
lesson that, with two neighbouring nations of such spirit as the
Scots and English, there could be no chance of a permanent peace
save in union of the crowns by way of intermarriage.   But he went
much further.   As if he were an apostle with a message to his
race, his History bears the mark, in one aspect of it, of a homily in
which his hearers are adjured to cast away all 'nasty expressions'
—that habit 'illote loqui'—about the men of a neighbouring
country.   Mr. Mackay points out (p. xxxiii.) that though Major was
a Cambridge man, he frankly acknowledged the superiority of
Oxford in numbers and reputation.   This simple recognition of the
truth is characteristic of him.   That he was to his heart's core a
Scotsman is written in every chapter of his History; yet he did
not on that account refrain from pointing out that the ecclesiastical polity of Scotland is not worthy of comparison with that of
England (p. 30); that in the art of music the English take precedence alike of Frenchmen and of Scots (p. 27); that the Scots are
prone to call themselves of noble birth (p. 45); that many Britons
(who in the case in point were Scots) were inclined to be ashamed
of things no way to be ashamed of (p. 7); that the Scottish gentry
of his time educated their children neither in letters nor in morals
(p. 48); that—hating Caxton as he did—still if that were true
which Caxton affirms, that the Scots, in the ravaging of Northumberland, slew young men, and women too, with every circumstance
of cruelty, then in that case he must condemn them and abhor
them for such wickedness (p. 226); that the English 'in civil
polity are at least not less wise than we—and to my thinking they
are wiser' (p. 347); that the English showed their affection for
their king (Richard Cœur de Lion), and acted rightly in selling
for his ransom every second gold or silver vessel which was used in
the service of God (p. 155); while in such a judgment as that which

he passes on Edward the First (p. 223), expressed with all severity of censure in regard to his political action, yet admitting the possibility that even here the plea might be urged that he had acted on an 'ignorance that was invincible', we have a remarkable combination of national fairness and theological justice. It gives him pleasure too to call attention to that notable example of English courtesy which restored to the shrine of Saint Duthach at Tain the tutelary shirt which was found on the dead body of the earl of Ross after the battle of Halidon Hill (p. 273).

I do not know whether before Major's day we had as a nation reached a more candid estimate of England than that which found this quaint expression in Wyntoun :—

> 'Set we haiff nane affectioune
> Off caus till Ynglis natioune,
> Yeit it ware baith syn and schame
> Mair than thai serve, thaim to defame.'[1]

It was something to have got so far. But I like to think that Major has proved his right to a place among notable Scotsmen as an example perhaps more eminent than any other of a man who has shown the possibility of combining the strongest attachment to his own country and the frankest appreciation of the virtues of another.

To the fairness of his appreciation of Englishmen one exception has to be made. The name of Caxton is familiar to all Britons— both 'English Britons and Scottish Britons', to speak with Major,— and we have, not without reason, accustomed ourselves to look upon the first English printer as a national benefactor. It seems strange, therefore, and almost incredible, to have him presented to us as a man who wrought nothing but evil. That Major says nothing of Caxton as a printer, and nothing of the invention of printing, is not so strange ; for recognition of the importance of the art is not frequent within the hundred years that followed its invention. There is a reason, however, for Major's abhorrence of Caxton ; for it seems plain from Major's calling him 'Anglus Chronographus', 'historicus Anglus', and from the general character of his many quotations from the 'Chronicle', that Caxton was believed by him to be the original writer of that work, and not merely the printer, and perhaps the editor, of Trevisa's translation of the old *Chronicle of Brut.* And not only was Caxton, on that showing, a foolishly

---

[1] *Cron.* Bk. IX. ch. 20, Laing's ed. vol. iii. p. 72.

credulous person; he was the mouth-piece also of many of those sayings, on the English side, the use of which, upon one side as well as the other, Major so heartily abhorred. Nothing in Caxton made for national amity, and that was Major's ideal for both kingdoms. It must be admitted too that when Caxton said that 'the king of Scotland became his [king Edward's] man, and had all his lands of him'; that the Scots 'chose unto their king William Wallace, a ribald and a harlot, comen up of nought'; that Pope John the Twenty-second 'was wonders sorry that Christendom was so destroyed through the Scots'; that Edward Balliol lived at Dunpier (in France) on his own lands, 'as well he might, till that the Scots would amend them of theyr misdeeds . . . so he forsook his realme of Scotland, and set thereof but little price', his language was well fitted to exasperate a sensitive nation. Yet Major is ready to make 'allowance in a measure—if not altogether—for an unlettered man: he followed simply the fashion of speech that was common amongst the English about their enemies the Scots' (p. 287).[1]

In the last book of his History Major quotes the French historian Robert Gaguin several times, and with a minuteness which shows that Gaguin's *Compendium super Francorum Gestis* was well known to him. Gaguin was born about 1425, and died in 1502. His *Compendium* was first published in 1497, and received the high commendation of Erasmus and Cornelius Girard, 'Hieronymianae vallis canonicus regularis'[2]. Erasmus praises the honesty and the erudition of Gaguin, and then proceeds:—'The man who has exalted his native land, and enriched her, and adorned her by

---

[1] I may note here that as a mere handbook Caxton's Chronicle must have been of great service to Major. The references to Caxton—apart from the frequent mention of him—might have been largely increased had I always had the 'Chronicle' by me for consultation. It was probably, for instance, from Caxton that Major took the observation that king Harold delighted to travel on foot rather than on horseback—given in Caxton (fol. lxii.) thus :—'Of Kynge Harold that had leuer go on fote than ryde on hors backe.' The constant references to Caxton and quotations from him, throughout the History, led to the belief—which would have been very startling to Major—that he had made a translation of Caxton's Chronicle :—'Caxtonum Latine reddidit',—Wodrow's *Catalogue of Scottish Writers*, p. 2. Edin. 1833. He is credited with such a translation also in Crabb's *Universal Historical Dictionary* (1833), and probably in many other books of reference.

[2] The commendations of Erasmus and Girard are to be found at the end of the *Compendium*, ed. 1511.

worthy writing, has assuredly done work equal to that of him who has bedizened her with spoils and trophies and statues, and that sort of monument.   For neither brazen tablet, nor inscription, nor medal, nor pyramids can either declare more truly or more safely guard the renown of kings than these will be declared and guarded by the writings of an eloquent man.   From this day forth the renown of France, which hitherto has lain hid in narrow space, shall shine forth like a thunderbolt, and from a Frenchman's mouth, but, as is more fitting, in the trumpet tones of Rome, shall reach the ears of all nations[1].'   Cornelius Girard praises the French historian for his impartiality.   'You spare', he says, 'neither your own countrymen nor your country's enemies; . . . neither hatred of the foreigner nor affection for your own people can make you swerve from the path of justice.'   Gaguin was a 'theologian' of the university of Paris—he had written a treatise *De Puritate conceptionis Virginis*; in his old age he had written a history of his own country, the first, as it would appear, in which the writer had placed before him as his constant aim the duty of telling what he believed to be the truth, without respect of nation.   It is evident that Major knew Gaguin's work well. We have seen that while he was himself strongly convinced that the theologian who wrote a history needed no excuse for so doing, he still thought it well to justify this course in the eyes of his king and country.   We know that a union between Scotland and England had the first place in his aspirations, and that in the mutual asperities of the national tempers and the foolish habit of recrimination he saw as serious an obstacle to this con- summation as in the jealousies of kings and statesmen.   If it must be considered fanciful to suggest that a study of Gaguin's History gave the impulse to the writing of his own, it will be admitted that the historical and contemporary parallel is not without interest.

There are but two editions of Major's *Historia :* the original, which was printed in Paris in 1521, in the lifetime of the author, but while he was in Scotland; and that which was printed in Edinburgh by Robert Freebairn in 1740.   In both editions the running headline is ' De Gestis Scotorum'.   The edition of 1521

---

[1] Mr. Hume Brown has pointed out to me another laudatory mention of Gaguin by Erasmus : ' Robertus Gaguinus, quo uno litterarum parente, antistite, principe, Francia non injuria gloriatur.'—Erasm. *Opera*, iii. 1782.

swarms with errors in the printing of proper names—errors of such
a nature that the discovery of the true reading, in the great
majority of cases in the edition of 1740 does credit to the care
and ingenuity of Freebairn and his editor.   Except in this matter
of proper names, and the extending of the contractions of the
original text, the edition of 1740 neither shows, nor needed to
show, many changes from the original.   The one unfortunate
change made in Freebairn's edition is in the reading of the clan
names (p. 334), on which the footnote *in loco* may be consulted.
In the ordinary course of translation, and for convenience of reference, I have used Freebairn's edition, but I have in some cases
preferred the punctuation, or the freedom afforded by no punctuation, of the original; and in those cases, not very many, where the
text seems to be corrupt, I have drawn attention to the fact in
a footnote.   Freebairn's edition is nothing but a reprint of the
original, with correction of its errors of names of places and
persons.   In the footnotes I have referred to Freebairn's edition
as ' F.', and to the original as ' Orig.'

The many footnotes to this book bring to my remembrance the
help which has been most willingly rendered to me, in answer to
my inquiries, by friends almost innumerable, and by many men of
learning and position to whom I was quite unknown.   Let me
have the pleasure of here gratefully recording my obligations to
Mr. Æneas Mackay, who was good enough to read with me a large
part of the manuscript, and to suggest many notes connected with
Scottish history and in other directions; Mr. P. Hume Brown;
Professor Herbert Strong; Mr. David Patrick; the Reverend Dr.
Jessopp; the Marquis of Bute; Professor Copeland, Astronomer
Royal for Scotland; Dr. Dickson, of H.M. General Register House;
Count Ugo Balzani; Mr. James Gairdner; M. Delisle of the Biblio-
thèque Nationale in Paris; Mr. John Taylor Brown; Mr. J. R.
Findlay; M. Beljame of Paris; Sir Arthur Mitchell, K.C.B.;
Captain G. D. Clayhills Henderson of Invergowrie; Mr. Robert
Bruce Armstrong; Mr. Gordon Duff; Mr. Francis Hindes Groome;
Mr. David MacRitchie; the Reverend J. C. Atkinson, D.C.L.; the
Reverend John Owen of Dulverton, perhaps the chief authority in
Britain on the Scholastics; Professor Kuno Meyer; my cousin, Mr.
Archibald Constable; Mr. W. B. Blaikie; and Mr. Ian Mackay,
whose kindly service to me during a temporary residence at Rouen
I like here to remember in connection with the large service
rendered to Scottish history by his grandfather, the late Mr. Cosmo

Innes. To Mr. David Douglas I am indebted for the loan of his copy of that not very common book, the *Compendium* of Robert Gaguin ; to Emeritus Professor Blackie, to Dr. Joseph Anderson of the Society of Antiquaries, and to Mr. George Neilson, I am under obligations for the loan of other books. To many Librarians, both in England and in Scotland, and especially to the Keepers of the Advocates' Library and the Edinburgh University Library, I am indebted for bibliographical information and help, and to the latter library for the loan of the copy of Major's Commentary on St. Matthew, from which the characteristic illustrations, which are bound up in the Appendix, were taken. My demands upon the forbearance of Mr. Main, Mr. Mill, and Mr. Whamond of the Signet Library are only rendered tolerable in the remembrance of them by the ready helpfulness with which these demands have been met at all times.

A. C.

December 1891.

LIFE OF THE AUTHOR

LIFE OF THE AUTHOR

JOHN MAJOR or MAIR was born in 1469-70, the eleventh year of the reign of James III., at Gleghornie, now a farm-house, perhaps then a hamlet, in the parish of North Berwick, about two miles inland from Tantallon[1], the castle of the Douglases, and three miles from Hailes[2], the castle of the Hepburns, to both of which families, though himself of humble origin, his talents introduced him. Crawford, the historiographer, in the Life prefixed to Freebairn's edition of Major's History, dates his birth as early as 1446, and Dr. Mackenzie, in his *Lives of Scots Writers*, as late as 1478; but he corrects this in the preface to his second volume from information he had received from Paris, and assigns 1469 as the true date. A passage in one of Major's works proves that he was really born in 1469-70, for he states in the preface to a new edition, published in 1519, that he had then reached the confines of his forty-ninth year; and this is confirmed by the fact that he graduated as Doctor in Theology at Paris in 1505, a degree which could not be taken under the age of thirty-five[3]. Major was alive in 1549, when he was excused from attending

Major's birth, 1469-70.

---

[1] Appendix II., p. 437.   [2] Appendix II., p. 425.

[3] I am indebted to Mr. Archibald Constable for directing my attention to this passage : ' Licet enim Martinus Magister [*i.e.* Martin le Maistre] quæstione penultima de temperantia dicat seniores junioribus in re scholastica invidere; non sum de numero juniorum ; *nam hoc libro absoluto quadragesimi noni anni fimbrias aggredior.*'—Johannis Majoris in exordio prælectionis lib. quarti sententiarum ad auditores propositio. See Appendix II., p. 437. This Preface is not printed in the earlier editions of 1509 and 1516. Mr. Hume Brown has supplied me with the further corroboration of this date that a degree in theology could not be then taken at Paris before the age of 35. It is due, however, to Dr. Mackenzie, a writer some-what unfairly disparaged, to mention that he arrived at the true date of Major's birth in the correction made in the Preface to the second volume of his *Lives of Scots Writers.*

a Provincial Council at Edinburgh on account of his age, and
died in that or the following year, when his successor as
Provost of the College of St. Salvator at St. Andrews was
appointed. His long life of seventy-nine years was thus passed
in the century which preceded the Scottish Reformation, a
memorable period in the history of Scotland and of Europe.

At Gleghornie,
near North
Berwick.

He refers to Gleghornie as his birthplace in the History [1], and
styles himself 'Glegornensis' in the titles of several of his other
works. In his quaint manner, when he mentions any event
which occurred near North Berwick, he notes the precise distance, a token that he retained an affectionate recollection of
his early home. The oatcakes baked on the girdle over the
ashes, the mode of grinding meal and brewing beer, the way
of catching crabs and lobsters at North Berwick, the habits of
the Solan Geese of the Bass, the popular superstitions still
current in the most civilised part of Scotland [2], even the exact
time at North Berwick, are described with the close observation of a frequent eye-witness, and leave little doubt that he
was born in one of the thatched cottages whose fragile character he deplores [3], and was the son of one of the labourers, or
perhaps one of the small farmers, probably of some church
lands in the neighbourhood. It is possible his father was the
tacksman of Gleghornie itself, whom he uses as an illustration
in a passage of his Commentary on the Fourth Book of the Sentences of Peter Lombard [4]. But of his parents or descent nothing
is certainly known. A boy of parts in that age, however
humble his parentage, had opportunities of distinguishing himself if he chose Learning or the Church as his profession. A

---

[1] *History*, I. vi. pp. 33-4.

[2] Dubitatur adhuc : Isti Fauni et vocati *brobne* [*brownies*] apud nos domi qui non
nocent, ad quod propositum talia faciunt. Respondetur : multa referuntur de
talibus : ut proterere tantum tritici in una nocte vel sicut xx. viri terere possunt.
Projiciunt lapillos inter sedentes prope ignem ruri, ridere videntur, et similia
facere. Insuper dubitatur : an possunt futura predicere ; et movetur dubitatio.
Sunt aliqui apud nostrates Britannos qui more prophetico futura predicunt utpote
de morte et homicidio aliquorum.—*Expos. in Matt.*, ed. 1518, fol. xlviii.

[3] *History*, I. v. p. 30.   [4] Dist. xv. Quæst. 45.

pious reference to the custom of his childhood amongst the country-folk of Scotland, that when the children went to bed they asked their parents' blessing with outstretched hands, and the father gave it with God's blessing added, shows one part of his education had begun at home [1].

His name is a common one in Scotland ; indeed in the Latin form of Major it is known in England and on the Continent. It may have been derived from the office of Maor (*Scotice* Mair) or serjeant, the executive official of the Celtic thane, who remained attached to the court of the sheriff; or, more probably, in Lothian it meant no more than 'elder', when, surnames coming into use, it was necessary to distinguish between two persons of the same Christian name.   It is noticeable that in several of the entries in the Registers of Paris, Glasgow, and St. Andrews, he is described as 'Johannes (*i.e.* filius) Major*is* '[2], as if his father had first assumed the surname.   Whether he owed it to his parents, or to the monks who detected his aptness for learning, Major received the rudiments of a good education in his own neighbourhood, almost certainly at the school of Haddington, already noted amongst the schools of Scotland, where a little later John Knox was a scholar.   In remembrance of this, in some of his works he describes himself as 'Hadingtonanus', and in the dedication of his treatise on the Fourth Book of the Sentences to Gavin Douglas, Bishop of Dunkeld, and Robert Cockburn, Bishop of Ross, he makes the following grateful reference to his connection with Haddington and its school :—'These reasons have led me to dedicate this work to you, for not only is each of you like myself a Scottish Briton [*Scotus Britannus*], but also my nearest neighbour in my native land.   The Dialogue in the Preface to my treatise on the First Book explains the distance from the birthplace of one of you

His name.

At school at Haddington.

---

[1] *Ibid.* Dist. xxiii. Quæst. 2.

[2] So Prantl in his *Geschichte der Logik*, iv. 217, throughout calls Major Johannes Majoris.   But I incline to think, on a view of the whole evidence, that this is merely from his name usually appearing on the title-pages of his works in the genitive case.

[Gavin Douglas, who was born at Tantallon] is not more than a Sabbath-day's journey. Haddington has a still fuller right to rejoice in the origin of the other [Robert Cockburn], the town which fostered the beginnings of my own studies, and in whose kindly embraces I was nourished as a novice with the sweetest milk of the art of grammar, and carried on in my education to a pretty advanced age [*longiuscula ætas*], and it is not more than five miles from Gleghornie where I was born. So that many persons call me not wrongly a Haddington man. Besides, I have enjoyed the friendly and familiar society of you both, at home as well as at Paris, and have been honoured by your public commendation, of which I cannot speak fully in few words. Therefore, as Sallust says of Carthage, " I prefer to be silent rather than say too little ". For these causes I have determined to dedicate this work to you, which I pray you to review not with severe and harsh eyebrows, but with the benignant and modest countenances habitual to you. Farewell. Paris, in the College of Montague, the Kalends of December 1516.'

That he was one of the youths of humble origin his country has often produced, eager to learn, patient in study, fond of argument, and of comparison, with what is called an inquisitive intellect, is proved by his subsequent career.

Before 1493 in north of England or the Borders.

A curious but tantalising reference in his History as to his personal experience informs us that Major spent seven years in the north, or more probably the borders[1], of England. When defending his country from the charge of poverty, on the ground that oatmeal was a common diet (for long before Dr. Johnson this was a vulgar scoff), he remarks: 'It is the food of almost all the natives of Wales and of the northern English, as I know from my own seven years' experience of that people [*ut a septennio expertus sum*[2]], as well as of the Scottish peasantry, and yet the main strength of the Scottish

---

[1] A somewhat minute knowledge of the Borders between England and Scotland is shown in his *History*, I. v. p. 19.

[2] Perhaps the meaning is ' as I have known by experience for seven years ',

and English armies is in the peasantry—a proof that oat bread
is not a thing to be laughed at.'

But as he positively states in the Dedication of his edition
of Aristotle's Ethics to Wolsey [1] that he first crossed the Borders
when he went through England to Paris in 1493, it would seem
that he considered Gleghornie on the Borders,—a flexible term
at this period of internecine raids, and his acquaintance with
the habits of the English may have been derived from the
Northumberland moss-troopers.

He chose the vocation of a travelling scholar, an excellent
combination of the Middle Ages, in many respects preferable
to the more sedentary training of modern times.   His name
does not appear as a student at either of the Scottish universities then founded, in both of which he was afterwards
a teacher, but before 1493, when already a man of twenty-
three, he found his way to Cambridge.   That university, though
somewhat inferior to Oxford in numbers and reputation, as
he notes with a candour creditable to a Cambridge man, and in
spite of the attractions of Baliol College, possibly because of the
dislike of North-countrymen which was a tradition of mediæval
Oxford, was then a favourite school for Scottish students.
George Wishart, the first of the Scottish Reformers, was not
long after a student at Corpus Christi, in the same university.

He studied for a year, but attended lectures apparently
only for three months [2], at God's House, the earlier foundation
converted into Christ's College in 1505.   He selected it for a
reason strange to us, but at that time natural, because it
was situated in the parish of St. Andrew [3], the patron saint of
Scotland, and of the diocese to which Major himself belonged.
The church dedicated to that saint still stands opposite the
College gate over which, as at St. John's, the other foundation
of the Lady Margaret, the mother of Henry VII. and grand-

(margin note: 1493, at God's House, Cambridge.)

---

but this scarcely removes the puzzle of the passage, as Major had been in England
long before 1518, the date when his History was written.
    [1] See Appendix II., p. 448.   [2] *History*, I. v. p. 25.   [3] *Ibid.*

mother of Margaret, wife of James IV., the Tudor arms are boldly sculptured. It may have been a consequence of this portion of his education that he became through life a strenuous advocate of the union of Scotland with England. The higher culture and refinement of English life certainly made an impression on the country-bred Scot.

' While I was a student at Cambridge,' he says in one of the sidenotes which relieve the dry style of his History, ' during the great festivals I spent half the night awake listening to the bells. The university is on a river, so from the undulation of the water their sound is sweeter.' With the freedom from prejudice which was one of his characteristics, he remarks that the bells of St. Oseney, the cradle of Oxford, ' are the best in England, and that as in music the English excel all nations, so they excel in the sweet and artistic modulation of their bells ' [1].

'No village of forty houses is without fine bells. In every town of any size you hear the sweetest chimes from terce to terce.' He enlarges, and, as his manner is, generalizes from his observations, the minuteness of which is noteworthy: ' although you may find a few as finished musicians in Scotland as in England, there are not nearly so many of them [2].'

These remarks, intended for the ear of his own countrymen, to prompt them to the study and practice of music, have been long in bearing fruit. To a Scottish student returning from the English universities, the bells of his native town are not yet such as he would willingly lie awake to hear, and still too often recal by contrast the chimes of the churches and college

---

[1] *History*, III. i. p. 110.

[2] *Ibid.* I. iv. p. 27, with which compare I. v. p. 30, where he laments that the Scottish priests were ignorant of the Gregorian Chant, and his statement (VI. xiv. p. 366) that James I. learned music in England. ' Bells were not universal in parish churches in Scotland even at the end of last century. It often happened that there was nowhere to hang them: a theologian of 1679 inveighs against " that pitiful spectacle, bells hanging upon trees for want of bell houses.' "—Joseph Robertson, *Scottish Abbeys and Cathedrals*, p. 102.

chapels on the banks of the Isis or the Cam, the sweet changes rung in the towers of St. Mary in both universities, or of Christ Church, where the bells of Oseney Priory are said to have found a home in the Gatehouse tower.

From Cambridge Major passed in 1493 to Paris, probably his original destination. Paris was then, especially for theologians, the most famous university in Europe. Its colleges were crowded with students from almost all countries, even the distant extremities of Europe—Scandinavia, Spain, Scotland—as yet without complete universities of their own. There were as many as 10,000 at the lowest estimate. But national jealousy and the growth of Oxford and Cambridge had recently withdrawn the English students, and the Scotch who continued to frequent it were now enrolled in the *Natio Alemanica* (or German) which had been substituted for the older name of the *Natio Anglicana*. Before he crossed the Channel Major had probably visited Oxford as well as Cambridge, and his brief notes on the universities[1] and a few of the principal towns in England, which bear marks of personal observation, deserve notice, as there are few diaries of intelligent travellers in the end of the fifteenth century now extant[2]. 'Londinum', he says, 'which was called by the Britons London, is situated on the Thames, a river thrice the size of the Seine at Paris. It is visited by the ships of all nations, and has a very fine bridge and church. One mile to the west lies Westminster, where there is a royal palace, the monuments of the kings, and the seat of justice. Three miles to the East is Greenwich the royal port, where you may see in abundance barges passing up to London and down to the sea with sails or the tide. London elects a wealthy and senior tradesman yearly as Mayor, before whom a

Description of the English Towns and Universities.

---

[1] He more than once refers to Oseney Priory. The long list of the famous men who had studied at Oxford and the comparison between the colleges at the two Universities indicate a knowledge of both.

[2] *History*, I. v. p. 21.

sword is carried as an emblem of justice, whose duty it is if
corn is dear to import it to lower the price. It exceeds Rouen,
the second city of France, in population, but is far before it in
wealth. It is enriched by being the seat of justice, the almost
constant residence of the king, and by the affluence of its
merchants. Some Englishmen, with whom I agree, count the
population of Paris three times that of London, but it is not
three times as wealthy. In the Thames there are three or four
thousand tame swans; but ', he adds with characteristic caution,
' I merely repeat what was told me, for, though I have seen,
I have never counted them.   York is the second city of
England, the see of an archbishop, distant fifty leagues from
Scotland, a town of large extent, but not rich or populous,
through the want of the three advantages London has. The
third city is Norwich, an Episcopal See, in which that kind of
cloth called Ostade is manufactured, both single and double.
There are other considerable cities,—as Bristol ; Coventry, a
good town without a river, which is remarkable ; Lincoln,
formerly famous, and many more [1]. England has two famous
universities : Oxford, celebrated abroad, which has produced
eminent philosophers and theologians, as Alexander Hales,
Richard Middleton,.John Duns the Doctor Subtilis, Ockham,
Adam the Irishman, Strode, Bradwardine, and others [2].' Of its
colleges he names Magdalen and New as the foremost, each
with a hundred bursaries—some in divinity and others in arts.
' The other university is Cambridge, a little inferior to Oxford
in number of students and reputation for letters.' Of its
colleges he mentions King's, which may be compared with New
College, Oxford ; Queens' ; a Royal Hall—inferior to Queens'

---

[1] The somewhat eccentric list of English towns mentioned by Major is probably accounted for by the fact that in each of them there was a Franciscan
monastery.

[2] See note *Hist.* I. v. p. 23, as to the philosophers named by Major, fourteen
in all, of whom it is noticeable that at least eight were Franciscans.

College—the future Trinity, not yet risen to the dignity of a College; Christ's College, where he studied himself, and Jesus, formerly a convent for women, reformed by Doctor Stubbs[1], the nuns having been ejected. 'I approve', he adds, 'of this ejection, for if convents become houses of ill fame, good institutions must be put in their place.'

'The course of study in the English universities is seven or eight years before graduating as master in arts. They do not pay much attention to grammar. The government of the university is in the hands of a Chancellor, like the Rector of Paris elected yearly, and two Proctors who have jurisdiction over laymen as well as students. The number of students is 4000 or 5000, and though that of laymen [*i.e.* townsmen] is greater, they don't venture to rise against the students, who would soon put them down. The students are all adults, and carry swords and bows, being for the most part of good birth.'

He concludes this fragmentary but interesting sketch by praising the morality of the English in comparison with the Scottish ecclesiastics, and making one of the semi-ironical observations of which studious men are fond: 'For courage, prudence, and other virtues the English don't think they are the least nation in the world, and if they meet a foreigner who has parts or bravery, it is much to be regretted, they say, that he was not an Englishman.'

While the dates of Major's studies at Cambridge and visit to Oxford are not quite certain, the commencement of his curriculum at Paris is fixed by an entry in the Register of Matriculation in the University under the year 1493: 'Johannes Mair Glegornensis, Diocesis S. Andreæ.' He commenced his course of Arts at the College of St. Barbe, of which Etienne

Paris, 1493. Studies Arts at College of St. Barbe.

---

[1] Stubbs is unknown to the historians of Cambridge, and the real reformer and founder of Jesus College was John Alcock, Bishop of Ely (Mullinger, p. 321), to whom Major refers in his Biblical Commentary.

Bonet [1], a philosopher and physician, was then principal, under John Boulac or Bouillache, curate of St. Jacques La Boucherie, afterwards Principal of the College of Navarre, and graduated as Licentiate in 1494 and as Master in 1496. His countryman, John Harvey [2], of the Scots College, was then Rector of the University, and Major held under him the honourable office of Procurator of the German Nation, and became its Quæstor or Treasurer in 1501. From the College of St. Barbe Major

Migrates to Montaigu. migrated at the suggestion of Natalis or Noel Beda [3], afterwards a celebrated leader of the Sorbonne, to the College of Montaigu, then under the government of a Fleming, John Standonk, who reformed it; and Standonk having been banished by Louis XII., Major, by the advice of Boulac, was affiliated to

Elected a Fellow of Navarre. the College of Navarre [4], though he continued to teach philosophy as Regent in Arts in that of Montaigu at least down to and probably after the year 1505, when he graduated as Doctor of Theology. Remaining in Paris for twelve or thirteen years after his graduation he became one of its most famous Professors of Theology, as he had been formerly of Logic and Philosophy. It is probable, indeed, that he lectured simultaneously, as he certainly published his lectures in both Faculties during the same period (1509-1518).

The period of Major's residence in Paris was a marked epoch in the history of France and the University. It was the zenith of the Renaissance. The Revival of Learning, begun in Italy in the fourteenth and fifteenth centuries, had in the sixteenth crossed the Alps, and under the leadership of Erasmus taken root in France, England, Germany, and the Low Countries. It was the France of the last five years of Charles VIII. (1483-

---

[1] As to the Principalship of Etienne Bonet, see Quicherat, *St. Barbe*, pp. 54-64. He was elected 1483, and died 1497.

[2] Of John Harvey I find no mention except in Mackenzie's *Lives of Scots Writers*, 2 Pref. p. 121.

[3] As to Noel Beda, see Hume Brown's *Memoir of Buchanan*, p. 69.

[4] Launoi: *Regiæ Navarræ Hist.* Op. iv. p. 396.

1498), of the reign of Louis XII. (1498-1515), and the first
three years of Francis I. (1515-47), during which Major passed
his life as Student, Regent in Arts, and Doctor in Theology
in its capital.   During these years the consolidation of the French history
during Major's
kingdom and the formation of modern France by the absorp- residence in
France.
tion of the great feudal houses was completed.   Charles VIII. by
marrying Anne, heiress of Brittany, united the French Wales
to the Crown, and Louis XII. retained it, divorcing his wife
Jane of France and marrying the widow of Charles.   He
added himself the large domains of the House of Orleans.
Encouraged by the growth of their kingdom and the divisions
of Italy, the French monarchs made the fatal attempt to annex
parts of the peninsula where so many Frenchmen found their
tombs.   The survivors brought back the learning, arts, and
manners of the more civilised but more luxurious south.
History repeated with altered names the lines of Horace:—

> ' Græcia capta ferum victorem cepit et artes
> Intulit agresti Latio.'

Italy, unlike Greece, was overrun, not subdued.   In 1494
Charles VIII. marched through Rome to Naples; but his
campaign was a triumph not a conquest.   Louis XII. renewed
the war, claiming Milan as well as Naples, for whose partition
he entered into a league with Ferdinand of Aragon.   That
astute monarch succeeded in gaining the whole, and became
in 1504 king of the Two Sicilies.

In 1508 along with Pope Julius II. the two ambitious kings
joined in the League of Cambrai to crush the Republic of
Venice, but the Pope suddenly deserted his French allies and
made a new league, which he called the Holy League, to drive
the French barbarians from Italy.   Though Louis defeated the
Spaniards at Ravenna the aid of the Swiss enabled the Pope to
accomplish his purpose.   The French quitted Italy before the
death of Louis in 1515.   His successor, Francis I., a young
and hazardous monarch, engaged in a contest for the Imperial

Crown and the primacy of Europe with Charles v., who on the death of his grandfather Maximilian became emperor. Francis recovered Milan, but was taken prisoner at Pavia in 1525, and though he broke the treaty of Madrid and resumed the war in Relations of
England and
Scotland. 1529 he was forced to relinquish Italy. While these events were occupying the politicians and armies of Europe, Scotland, which had been at peace with England during the reign of Henry vii., through the marriage of his daughter to James iv., quarrelled with Henry viii., and lost her king by the fatal defeat of Flodden in 1513. Henry viii. was too busy with his relations to the Continent to press his advantage. His aim as regards Scotland was to prevent the French alliance and maintain an ascendancy at the court of his sister's infant son. The failure of this aim was due largely to his sister, the mother of the king, and to Albany, a Frenchman in all but his name, who threw their influence into the scale in favour of France. The Regency of Albany led in 1523 to the renewal by the Scots of the Border War and the siege of Werk, the failure of which destroyed the prestige of the Regent.

During the period the history of which has been sketched in outline, France was both on political and educational grounds the natural resort of the Scottish student ambitious of carrying his studies to the highest point and sure of a hospitable reception from a nation which had never forgotten the ancient bonds that united Scotland and France. France as it then was is described in the beautiful verses of the great contemporary Scottish scholar, the pupil of Major, George Buchanan :

> ' At tu beata Gallia
> Salve ! bonarum blanda nutrix artium,
> Orbem receptans hospitem atque orbi tuas
> Opes vicissim non avara impertiens,
> Sermone comis, patria gentium omnium
> Communis.'

Its Capital has been painted in a brilliant passage of a great French author of our day, who combined the knowledge of an antiquary and the imagination of a poet, with which we may enliven the prose of a biographic sketch.

In the fifteenth century, writes Victor Hugo[1], 'Paris was Paris in the 15th century. divided into three totally distinct and separate cities, each with its own physiognomy, individuality, manners, customs, privileges, and history: the *City*, the *University*, and the *Ville*. The *City*, which occupied the island, was the mother of the two others, like (forgive the comparison) a little old woman between two handsome strapping daughters. The *University* crowned the left bank of the Seine. . . . The *Ville*, the most extensive of the three divisions, stretched along the right bank. The *City*, properly so called, abounded in churches, the *Ville* contained the palaces, the *University* the colleges. The island was under the Bishop, the right bank under the Provost of Merchants, the left under the Rector of the University, the whole under the Provost of Paris, a royal not a municipal office.' Omitting details, let us fix our attention on the University, the part of Paris of which Major was a citizen, for foreign students acquired the rights, indeed more than the rights, of citizens, and the Scotch at this time those of nationality.

'The University brought the eye to a full stop. From the The University. one end to the other it was a homogeneous compact whole. Three thousand roofs, whose angular outlines, adhering together, almost all composed of the same geometrical elements, seen from above, presented the appearance of a crystallisation. The forty-two colleges were distributed among them in a sufficiently equal manner. The curious and varied

---

[1] This bird's-eye view of Paris should be compared with the old plans and maps of the sixteenth century. Zeiller's views were taken in the middle of the seventeenth century, but two show Paris as it was in 1620, and are probably accurate representations of Paris as it was in Major's time. M. Adolphe Berty's 'Plan du Collège de St. Barbe et de ses environs vers 1480' is given in Quicherat's *St. Barbe*. The clever reconstruction by Mr. H. W. Brewer in Rose's *Life of Loyola* unfortunately places Montaigu College inaccurately. The description by Victor Hugo in the text has necessarily, but unfortunately, required to be condensed.

summits of these beautiful buildings were the productions of
the same art as the simple roofs they overtopped ; in fact they
were but a multiplication by the square or cube of the same
geometrical figures.   Some superb mansions made here and
there magnificent inroads among the picturesque garrets of the
left bank, the *Logis de Nevers* and *de Rouen*, which have been
swept away ; the *Hôtel of Cluny*, which still exists for the
consolation of the artist.   The Rouen palace had beautiful
circular arches.   Near Cluny were the baths of Julian.   There
were, too, many abbeys : the *Bernardines*, with their three
belfries ; *St. Genevieve*, the square tower of which, still
extant, excites regret for the loss of the whole ; the *Sorbonne*,
half college, half monastery, an admirable nave of which
still survives : the quadrangular cloister of the *Mathurins* ;
its neighbour, the cloister of *St. Benedict* ; the *Cordeliers*, with
their three enormous gables side by side ; and the *Augustines'*
graceful steeple.   The *Colleges*, an intermediate link between
the cloister and the world, formed the mean in the series of
buildings between the mansions and the abbeys, with an
austerity full of elegance, a sculpture less gaudy than that of
the palaces, less serious than that of the convents.   Unfortunately scarcely any vestiges are left of edifices in which Gothic
art steered with such precision a middle course between
luxury and learning.   The churches, both numerous and
splendid, of every age of architecture, from the circular arch
of *St. Julian* to the pointed ones of *St. Severin*, overtopped
all, and, like an additional harmony in this mass of harmonies,
shot up above the slashed gables, the open-work pinnacles and
belfries, the airy spires, whose line was a magnificent exaggeration of the acute angle of the roofs.   The site of the University
was hilly.   To the south-east the hill of *St. Genevieve* formed
an enormous wen, and it was a curious sight to see the
multitude of narrow winding streets now called *Le Pays Latin*,
those clusters of houses, which, scattered in all directions from

the summit of that eminence, confusedly covered its sides down
to the water's edge, seeming, some of them to be falling down,
others to be climbing up again, and all to be holding fast by
one another.' The more minute geography of the *Pays Latin*
has been learnedly described by M. Quicherat, from whom we
learn that the College of Montaigu[1] stood at the angle between Site of
the Rue St. Etienne des Prés and the Rue des Sept Voies, Montaigu.
having opposite to it on the other side of the latter street the
small College de Portet, the Hotel de Marly, the Cemetery of
the Poor Students, and the Great Gate of the Abbey of St.
Genevieve[2]. At the back of the buildings of Montaigu ran a
narrow lane appropriately called ' La Rue des Chiens', on the
opposite side of which Montaigu possessed two small gardens
bordering on the property of its rival, the College of St. Barbe,
and the cause of frequent quarrels[3].

The Scottish student whose course we are attempting to
follow, poring day and night over ponderous folios we now
scarcely touch with the tips of our fingers, the commentators
on Aristotle and the expounders of the Master of the Sentences, had little time to mark the minute features of the
scene. Still, he breathed its air, and can scarcely have failed
to receive some of the spirit which filled with pride most
scholars, from whatever country they came. A few remembered
with opposite feelings the hardships of the student. Erasmus
was one of these. Buchanan too wrote a poem describing the
miserable condition of the teachers of *Literae Humaniores* in
Paris when without a post. But, returning seven years after
from Portugal, his pen, which could flatter as well as satirise,
celebrated the charms of Paris as those of a beloved mistress,
and his return to happy France, the nurse of all good arts. One

[1] The site of Montaigu, of which some fragments still remained in 1861, is
now occupied by the Bibliothèque de St. Geneviève.
[2] Quicherat's *Histoire de St. Barbe*, p. 17.
[3] *Ibid.* 25.

of its attractions with which Hugo closes his description cannot
have escaped Major's musical ear :—' Behold at a signal proceeding from heaven, for the sun gives it, those thousand churches
trembling all at once. You hear solitary tinkles pass from
church to church ; then see (for at times the ear too seems
endowed with the power of sight) all of a sudden, at the same
moment, how there rises from each steeple, as it were a column
of sound, a cloud of harmony. At first the vibration of each
bell rises straight, pure, separate; then, swelling by degrees,
they blend, melt, and amalgamate into a magnificent concert.
Say if you know anything in the world more rich, more dazzling,
more gladdening, than this tumult of bells, this furnace of music,
these ten thousand brazen tones breathed all at once from flutes
of stone three hundred feet high, than that city which is
but one orchestra, this symphony as loud as a tempest.'

Contrast of
Paris and
Edinburgh.

How different must this have been from the capital of Major's
own country, the gray metropolis of the North, whose silence
was broken not by harmony but by brawls, with one narrow
street from the Castle to the Abbey, the backbone of a
skeleton ribbed on either side with vennels, wynds, and closes,
which ran on the north to the North Loch and its marshes,
on the south to the lower level of the Cowgate, here and there
varied by a small church, monastery, or hospital, but only
with a collegiate church, St. Giles, for a Cathedral, the plain
Tolbooth for a Palace of Justice, and Holyrood, recently
built in imitation of a minor French Palace, for its Royal
residence, as yet without a college, without mansions, and
without walls, and numbering only some four or five thousand [1]
houses, chiefly of wood. Yet, one who viewed the surrounding
country from the low but noble hill, named after Arthur,
guarding Edinburgh on the east, and let his eye follow the

---

[1] *History*, II. vi. p. 82. So the earlier editions of Froissart ; but Buchon
says the correct text is 400 or 500. The truth probably lies between these
figures. But see footnote [1], p. 28.

curves of the Forth, with the Law of North Berwick and the Bass as its outlying forts, the sea-ports of Fife studding its northern margin; on the west the Castle Rock, rising sheer from the North Loch, the woods of the Dean or Den, Drumsheugh, and Corstorphine Hill; and on the south the slopes of the Braids succeeded by the Pentland Hills, with Highland mountain tops beyond the Forth closing the horizon, might claim for Edinburgh a natural site not inferior to Paris, fitting it to be the capital of the small country whose scenery it reproduced in miniature—the Loch, the River, and the Sea, the Moor, the Forest, and the Mountain. Greater than any external difference was the contrast between the intellectual barrenness of Edinburgh and Paris, the venerable museum of learning, the busy hive from which old and new ideas were swarming, to settle in all lands. The Scottish student in Paris passed from the schoolroom to the world, from solitary study to the society of colleges, whose number, Major notes, sharpens wits. The poorest became, as if by natural magic, a free citizen of the university, the mother of knowledge and eloquence, of the arts and sciences: the arts which so long had ruled the past; the sciences, yet unconscious of their young strength, which were to divide the empire of the future.

Three of these Colleges demand our special attention: Montaigu, where Major first taught in arts; Navarre, where, as well as at Montaigu, he lectured on the scholastic philosophy; and the Sorbonne, where he lectured on the scholastic divinity[1].

Montaigu College.

---

[1] 'The epithet of "last of the Schoolmen" is commonly given to Gabriel Biel, the summarizer of Ockham, who taught in Tübingen, and died in 1491. His title to it is not actually correct, and it might be more fitly borne by Francis Suarez, who died in 1617. But after the beginning of the fifteenth century scholasticism was divorced from the spirit of the times.'—Article SCHOLASTI-CISM, *Encyclop. Britannica*, 9th ed. The truth is, no one scholastic can be called the last. The method or form of philosophy so called died at different dates in different countries. A critic who has done me the favour to read this Introduction maintains it is not dead yet, but still taught in Romanist seminaries. It is sufficient for the present purpose to say that no English or Scottish Schoolman later than Major has a place in any of the leading histories of philosophy.

d

He was destined to be among the last of the schoolmen, the teachers of the old learning by the rigid scholastic discipline and methods. The new light of the revival of classical literature had already dawned. The Renaissance, or new birth, from which on the mother's side the Reformation or new form of creed and of morals was to spring, could not but affect the thoughts and opinions of those who were passing through manhood under its influence. To observe how this influence acted upon Major and his pupils gives the uneventful career of scholars a singular and unexpected interest.

The College of Montaigu, an old college of the beginning of the fourteenth century, founded by Ascelin, the Seigneur of that name, had fallen so low towards the end of the fifteenth, that it had only eleven shillings of rent for endowment, its buildings in ruins, and, as might be expected, scarcely any students. John Standonk, a native of Mechlin in Brabant, a man of humble origin, saw in its poverty an object for zeal, and an opportunity for a much-needed reform in the University. This remarkable man, whom Erasmus, no partial judge, describes as one 'whose temper you could not dislike, and whose qualifications you must covet, who, while he was very poor, was very charitable', after taking his degrees in arts and theology with distinction, though poverty forced him to read by moonlight in the belfry to save oil, was placed in this college by the Chapter of Notre Dame, its superior, in 1480, became its principal in 1483, and Rector of the University in 1485. He sought out the titles of its property which had been lost sight of, and secured new endowments, especially from Louis Malet, Sieur de Granville, Admiral of France. The constitution he introduced was based on rules of economy and asceticism resembling those of a monastery. He had seen with regret, continues Crévier, the historian of the University, whose narrative we abridge, ' that the bursaries founded for the poor had often been swallowed up by the rich, and determined to

Standonk's reforms.

found a College for the true poor, amongst whom, he remarked, were often to be found elevated spirits and happy natural parts, reduced by misery to a state unworthy of their genius, but who, if cultivated, might become great men and pillars of the Church. With this view, and to preserve the College from the invasion of the rich, he subjected his students to a hard life.' At first his scholars were sent to the Convent of the Chartreuse to receive, in common with beggars, the bread distributed at its gates. 'All the world knows', he proceeds, 'the frugal nourishment of these youths—bread, beans, eggs, herring, all in small quantity, and no meat. Besides, they had to keep all the Fasts,—that of Lent was kept also in Advent,—and on every Friday, as well as on special occasions. Nothing could be poorer than their dress and beds. They rose at cock-crow, constantly chanted the service of the Church, worked in the kitchen and refectory and cleaned the halls, the chapel, the dormitory, and the stairs. Their superior was called minister or servant of the poor, not by the too proud titles of master or principal. He received in this world only the cost of his living, dress, and of taking his degrees, exclusive of the *Doctorate*, but a celestial reward in eternity.' Richer students had separate rooms, refectory, and chapel. Their fees were devoted to the maintenance of the poor. Remembering his native as well as his adopted country, Standonk instituted similar colleges at Cambrai, Louvain, Mechlin, and Valenciennes, so that the College of Montaigu became the chief of an order. The peculiar dress of its students was a small cape or hood, from which they were called Capetians, a symbol of their poverty, and, like the garb of Charterhouse boys, exposing them to the gibes of wealthier scholars.

The noble aim of Standonk, like that of the religious orders, broke down through being carried to an extreme. Erasmus, a contemporary of Major at Montaigu, has left

Erasmus' satire on Montaigu.

a biting satire on it in his colloquy—of *Ichthyophagia*— between a Salt-fishmonger and a Butcher, who complains of want of custom from a college which ate no meat.

'About thirty years ago', says the Fishmonger, 'I lived at the college called Vinegar College [i.e. *Mons Acetus*],' a pun on Mons Acutus, or Montaigu.——*The Butcher.* 'That's indeed a name of wisdom. Did a Salt-fishmonger live in that sour college? No wonder he is so acute a student in divinity, for I hear the very walls speak divinity.'—*The Fishmonger..* 'Yes, but as for me I brought nothing out of it, but my body infected with the worst diseases, and the largest quantity of the smallest animals. . . . What with lying hard, bad diet, late and hard studies, within one year, of many young men of a good genius some were killed, others driven mad, others became lepers, some of whom I knew very well, and, in short, not one but was in danger of his life. Was not this cruelty against our neighbours? Neither was this enough, but, adding a cowl and hood, he took away the eating of flesh.' More follows to the same purpose. It is easy to see the exaggeration, but Erasmus, too wise to rest in exaggeration, closes with the remark: 'Nor do I mention these

Ascetic discipline.

things because I have any ill will to the college, but I thought it worth while to give this warning lest human severity should mar inexperienced and tender youth under the pretence of religion. If I could but see that those that put on a cowl put off naughtiness I should exhort everybody to wear one. Besides, the spirit of vigorous youths is not to be cowed to this sort of life, but the mind is rather to be educated to piety.' Not less sensible are the remarks of Crévier, who condemned Erasmus for want of moderation in his censures. 'The health of young men requires to be attended to, and it is to attack it by two batteries to fatigue the spirit by study and the body by a too severe regimen. The discipline of Standonk has not been able to maintain itself. Besides mitigations

.introduced by usage, it had to be softened by express rules.'
Yet it was still described by a German artist, who visited Paris
in 1654, as 'a stately college in which ill-bred boys [*ungerathene
Kinder*] are treated as if in a House of Correction. We were
not allowed to visit it with our sword, supposing it might be
used to set them free'[1].

Erasmus had the bodily infirmity which, as in a great chief
of our literature lately lost, too often accompanies intellectual
power. He said of himself he had a Protestant stomach, but
a Catholic soul. A Protestant who has rarely dined in his life
without meat can scarcely realise what a bad fish and vegetable
diet, broken only by frequent total fasts, must have been.
Major, who probably heard the taunts of Erasmus before they
found a place in in his *Colloquies*, takes frequent occasion to
refer to Montaigu College in a different spirit, calling it 'an
illustrious museum', 'a frugal, but not ignoble house', 'the
nurse of his studies, never to be named without reverence'.
Yet he seems himself to have suffered from the hard life,
for he mentions, in the dedication of the *Parva Logicalia*, a
fever which had nearly cost him his life. He had doubtless
seen many of his contemporaries and pupils, besides David
Cranstoun, carried to the Graveyard of Poor Students, which
lay opposite the College gate.

To the Scottish father in the end of the fifteenth century,
inquiring to what college shall I send my son, or to the youth
left to shift for himself with scanty purse, these hardships
were too distant to be thought of. The College of Montaigu
offered the double attraction of economy and fame. Hither,
besides many forgotten names, came, during the time of Major's
connection with it, George Dundas from Lothian, a learned
Greek and Latin scholar, afterwards Preceptor of the Knights
of St. John in Scotland ; Hector Boece, the historian, from
Dundee, who praises Standonk as an exemplar of all the virtues ;

Major's encomium on Montaigu.

Scottish students at Montaigu.

---

[1] *Topographia Galliæ*, by Martin Zeiller ; Frankfort, 1655.

and three other Angus men : Patrick Panther, who became secretary to James IV., writer of most of the Epistolæ Regum Scotorum in James IV.'s and part of James V.'s reign ; Walter Ogilvy, celebrated for his eloquent style, and William Hay, schoolfellow of Boece at Dundee, afterwards his colleague and successor in the King's College of Aberdeen [1]. Here too were four countrymen of Major from East Lothian : George Hepburu[2], of the house of Hailes, Abbot of Arbroath, afterwards Bishop of the Isles, who fell at Flodden ; Robert Walterson[3], a co-regent ; David Cranstoun[4] and Ninian Hume, his pupils. Cranstoun dying young, but already distinguished, left his property to the College ; the other was one of Major's favourite students. In Paris, possibly at Montaigu, as we learn for the first time from one of Major's prefaces, at the same period studied Gavin Douglas, Bishop of Dunkeld, whose chequered ecclesiastical and brilliant literary career gained him a prominent place in the history as well as the literature of Scotland ; and Robert Cockburn, a Haddington man, afterwards Bishop of Ross[5], and Gavin Dunbar[6], afterwards Archbishop of Glasgow, whose studies in philosophy at Paris, and in the civil and canon law at Angers, overlooked by his biographers, are commemorated in Major's dedication of his Commentary on St. Luke.

The number of Scottish students at Paris during the time of Major's residence must have been very considerable, though it is impossible to give an exact estimate. The German Nation, the name substituted for the English Nation in 1378, after the withdrawal of the English, had been originally divided into three tribes : Germania Superior, Germania

---

[1] Hector Boece : *Aberdonensium Episcoporum Vitae*, p. 60.

[2] Uncle of first Earl of Bothwell. See Keith : *Scottish Bishops*, p. 174.

[3] Provost of Bothanis and Rector of Petcokkis, grants a charter of lands in Haddington to support a chaplain at the church of the Holy Trinity at Haddington.—*Great Seal Reg.*, 8th April 1539, No. 1902.

[4] Michel : *Les Ecossais en France*, ii. p. 324. See Appendix I. p. 412 : Bibliography of D. Cranstoun.

[5] Bishop 1508-21.—Keith, p. 42.   [6] Archbishop 1524-47.—Keith, p. 521.

Inferior, and Scotia, which included the Irish and the few English who remained, continued to be the name of the third till 1528, when the tribes were reduced to two: the *Continentales* and the *Insulani*, perhaps a concession to the dislike of the English to be classed under Scotia when the relations between England and France had somewhat improved.

Besides the more celebrated of his countrymen already mentioned, we find references in Major's prefaces to Hugo Spens, his predecessor as Principal of St. Salvator's; Gavin Logy, Rector of St. Leonard's; John Forman, Precentor of Glasgow[1], a kinsman of the archbishop of that name; Peter Chaplain[2], Rector of Dunino, and Peter Sandilands[3], Rector of Calder; Robert Caubraith[4], George Turnbull[5], friends of Ninian Hume,—so, probably, like him, Lothian men; George Lockhart[6] from Ayrshire; Robert Bannerman, Thomas Ramsay[7], William Guynd, and John Annand. The list might be much enlarged from the Accounts of the German Nation from 1494 to 1530, fortunately preserved in the archives of the University, and still extant in the library of the Sorbonne[8]. In the year 1494, when Major

Other Scotsmen in Paris.

---

[1] Protocol Book of Cuthbert Simon, *Grampian Club*, pp. 285, 478, 480, 484, 485, 486.

[2] Canon of St. Salvator and Rector of Dunino.—*Great Seal Reg.* 1513-46, Index, p. 803; *ibidem*, Nos. 354, 2168, 2605.

[3] Hector Boece in *Aberdonensium Episcoporum Vitae*, p. 58, mentions amongst the Professors at St. Andrews, Wilhelmum Guyndum, Johannem Annandiae, ' viros spectatae doctrinae qui tametsi hactenus magisterii in theologio renuerunt fastigium de se modestius sentientes doctoribus tamen eos nemo dixerit eruditione inferiores.' Annand was the first Professor in Arts (in re literaria) of St. Leonard's, *ib.* p. 59.

[4] Robert Caubraith, a pupil of Major, and author of several works on Logic, described by Prantl, iv. p. 257, may perhaps be Robert Galbraith, Rector of Spot in 1534.—*Great Seal Reg.*, No. 1332.

[5] George Turnbull may perhaps be the Rector of Largo of that name.—*Great Seal Reg.* 1517, No. 1355.

[6] George Lockhart, a pupil of Major, wrote several works on Logic, described in the Bibliographical Appendix, *infra*, p. 414.

[7] Canon of St. Salvator, and Rector of Kemback 1517.—*Great Seal Reg.*, No. 175.

[8] Charles Jourdain's *Excursions Historiques à travers le Moyen Age*, 1888: ' Un Compte de la Nation d'Allemagne au xvᵉ siècle.'

passed as licentiate, of twenty-nine fellow-graduates eleven were Scotchmen, besides eight bachelors. His election as Quaestor or Receiver of this Nation in 1501 is proof that he possessed the confidence of his fellow-students, and the passages from the Prefaces to his works printed in the Appendix show that many of them, not only his own compatriots, but Frenchmen, Belgians, and Spaniards, were his warm admirers and personal friends. Seldom has the contemporary fame of a Professor risen higher or spread wider.

The value of oatmeal diet.

Of his favourite and most distinguished pupil David Cranstoun Major tells a significant anecdote[1]. When in his first course of theology, two fellow-students, Jacobus Almain of Sens[2] and Peter of Brussels[3], of the order of Friar Preachers, twitted him in the court of the Sorbonne, on the day of the divinity lecture, before his comrades, that the commons in Scotland eat oatmeal, as they had heard from a friar who had travelled there. They wished, says Major, to try a man whose quick temper they knew, by this jest which was really honourable to his country; but he attempted to deny it as a discredit. We understand, indeed, he adds, 'that a Frenchman coming from Britain brought home with him some of these cakes [panes] as curiosities [monstra]'. He then describes with singular accuracy and evident pride the mode of making them, and recals Froissart's[4] statement that the Scotch, both nobles and commons, used them in their campaigns, as if to say (for he leaves deductions to his readers),—'Let Frenchmen and

---

[1] *Hist.* I. ii. p. 10.

[2] Almain's works on Logic, described by Prantl, iv. p. 238, appear to be lost, but his Theological Dissertation against Cardinal Caietan, and in favour of the authority of Councils as superior to that of the Pope, is preserved, p. lviii.

[3] Peter of Brussels wrote *Quaestiones* on the Organon of Aristotle, a *Commentary* on Peter the Spaniard, and *Quodlibeta.*—Prantl, iv. p. 275. He died 1511. On the title-page of his *Quaestiones*, published after his death in 1514, he is described as 'a most strenuous defender and interpreter of Thomas Aquinas'. He was regarded as a lost sheep recovered for the fold of the Thomists.

[4] Froissart, ii. 19.

Englishmen laugh, my countrymen have won battles on this
fare'. Froissart might almost have been the Frenchman who
brought home the oatcakes, so keenly doés he seem to have been
struck by the poverty of the Scots. 'When the barownes and
knightes of Fraunce, who were wonte to fynde fayre hostelryes,
halles hanged, and goodly castelles, and softe beddes to reste
in, sawe themselfes in that necessite, they began to smyle, and
said to the admyrall, Sir, what pleasure hath brought vs
hyder? we neuer knewe what pouertie ment tyll nowe: we
fynde nowe the old sayinge of our fathers and mothers true,
whane they wolde saye, Go your waye, and ye lyue long, ye
shall fynde harde and poore beddes, whiche nowe we fynde;
therfore lette vs go oure voyage that we be come for; lette vs
ryde into Englāde; the longe leivyenge here in Scotlande is to
vs nother honourable nor profytable.'

To the youth of such a country the food of the College of
Montaigu would not seem so poor as to Erasmus, a native of
wealthy Rotterdam.

In 1499 Standonk, the second founder of Montaigu, was
banished from Paris. He had quarrelled with Louis XII. as to
the privileges of the students of the university, of which he was
so strenuous an advocate that he advised a cessation of all
studies, and even of the services in the churches, if they were
infringed. He had touched the king in a still more delicate
point, the divorce of Louis from Jane of France, the daughter
of Louis XI., and his marriage to Anne of Brittany, widow of
Charles VIII., his half-brother. It was very likely in consequence of this banishment of Standonk, and the royal displeasure with the College of Montaigu, that Major became
affiliated to the College of Navarre, from which he got the
income of a fellowship[1] and the post of theological professor,
but he continued to act as regent in Montaigu, where he had
taken his degree in arts, which entitled him to teach, and did

Major lectures at Navarre College.

[1] Launoi: *Historia*, p. 598.

not avail himself of his right to migrate to Navarre. The
substance of his lectures on Logic, printed before in separate
parts, was collected in 1508 in one volume, printed at Lyons,
His Spanish and dedicated to his pupil Ninian Hume. In the dedication
students. he mentions that he had been urged by Louis Coronel, his
brother Antony[1], and Gaspar Lax[2], three Spanish students, to
print his commentaries on the *Summulae* of their countryman,
Peter the Spaniard. They pleaded that as he had given some
of his lectures on logic to his countryman David Cranstoun,
James Almain of Sens, Peter Crockaert of Brussels, and Robert
Senalis of Paris[3], they had equal reason to ask for a similar
favour. But he urges reasons on the other side (for even the
preface of a schoolman must be argumentative): his own inertia,
the severe criticism of works of living authors, and his change
of vocation to that of the study of the Sentences of Peter
Lombard. He had always been willing to lecture slowly, that
whoever wished might commit his lectures to writing. ' It is
natural, however', he continues, ' that I should publish at
large and distinctly what they wrote down from memory after
dinner and supper. If I had imagined my lectures would have
circulated so widely, I would have bestowed greater pains on
them. But I did not know how to recall them, and since they
were much sought after at the booksellers', I should at least
have ploughed my own ground so far as my poor abilities
allowed. It is easy', he concludes, ' to get angry. Unlearned
as well as learned write poems everywhere. I dedicate these
lectures to you both on account of your noble birth and your
diligence in the knotty points of dialectic—knowing you
will accept this little book, though unworthy of you, out of
regard for the good-will of the author. Robert Walterson of

---

[1] The author of many Logical Treatises.—Prantl, iv. p. 53.

[2] Gaspar Lax, of Aragon, also a writer on Logic.—Prantl, iv. p. 255.

[3] The *Exponibilia*, his first printed work in Paris, 1503 (Bibliography, No. 1),
the Commentaries on Peter the Spaniard at Lyons in 1505 (No. 2); other
Logical Tracts at Paris in 1506 (No. 5).

Haddington, a co-regent with me in Montaigu, and our friend
John Zacharias, beg to be remembered to you.   Farewell.'

A letter from Louis Coronel[1] to his brother Antony is
annexed, written in the enthusiastic vein of a young disciple
overflowing with praise of the learning of Paris, ' whose
streams flow to the remotest nations, and whose purest water
springs from Mons Acutus, " the Hill of God", a rich mountain
in which it pleaseth him to dwell, for the words of the Psalmist
may without absurdity be applied to it—whose founder was
Standonk, whom God has taken to himself[2], and where our
master, John Major, lectured, whose learning will commend
him not only to posterity but to eternity'.   His small part
has been, he modestly says, to revise the press and add a table
of contents, which he dedicates to his brother in studies as
in kin.   In similar, even more high-flown, language Robert
Senalis compared Montaign to Parnassus, the Mons Sacer of
Ovid, ' changing Sacer into Acer, in spite of the false quantity,
to correspond to the French name of Montaigu ', the philosophy
taught there to the fountain of Hippocrene—

> ' Fons nitet in medio vitreis argenteus undis
> Gregorius celeri quem pede ferit equus—

and Major himself to ' the Gregorian horse Pegasus ', for ' its
Pegasus ', he says, ' is that incomparable master in Arts and
Philosophy, my Professor, whom I cannot praise as much as he
deserves, John Major, who flies on his own wings higher than
the clouds would carry him, till he passes above all spirits in
sublimity '.[3]

The treatise or lectures of Major on Logic are in the style
which might be almost called stereotyped of mediæval scholas-

Louis Coronel's encomium on Major.

Major's Lectures on Logic.

---

[1] Louis Coronel of Segovia was less famous than his brother Antony, who
wrote several works on Logic in which he followed Major.—Prantl, iv. 252.
Both brothers were pupils of Major.   Antony edited and concluded Major's
Libri Consequentiarum ; see p. lvi.

[2] Standonk died 1501.

[3] ' Roberti Senalis Oratio ' : Paris, 1510.

tics. He commences with the special proposition or thesis
' Whether complex terms should be used ' [1], as a sort of prelude
or introduction, and then comments in short almost shorthand
tracts on various points of Logic. This is followed by two
books on Terms and a tractate on the Liber Summularum of
Petrus Hispanus[2], which forms the chief part of the book.
Discussions are appended on the Predicables with the tree of
Porphyry ; on the Predicaments ; on Syllogisms ; on Places [de
Locis] ; on Fallacies ; on matters which can be explained and
those which are insoluble ; a small tract entitled, after the
example of Aristotle, Libri Posteriores ; and another, Libri Consequentiarum, begun by Major but concluded by Antony Coronel.
In the same volume is continued a treatise on Parva Logicalia,
probably a separate course of lectures, with a fresh dedication
to Ninian Hume. The whole is concluded with a discussion
of a proposition or thesis ' On the Infinite ', and one of the
Dialogues of which Major, like other Schoolmen, was so fond,
entitled ' Trilogus inter duos logicos et magistrum '.

College of
Navarre.

The College of Navarre which hospitably adopted the celebrated Scottish Regent was in all respects a contrast to
Montaigu. A Royal College founded in 1305 by Jeanne of
Navarre, the wife of Philip the Fair, it had continued to
receive endowments from sovereigns and nobles, and was the
richest, perhaps the only very rich, college in a university where
poverty, although not the extreme poverty of Montaigu, was
the rule. It had twenty bursars in grammar, thirty in logic, and
twenty in divinity, and secured the ablest teachers. Its church
was used by the French Nation and for university sermons, which
gave it a certain precedence. It had the custody of the university archives and a splendid library. A reform of the fifteenth

---

[1] *De complexo significabili.* A fuller list of the contents of Major's Logical
Lectures is given in the Bibliography, and an explanation of some of the terms
used, in Appendix to Life, II. p. cxxii.

[2] Peter the Spaniard, who became Pope John XXI., and whose *Summulæ* were
the text-book of Logic as the *Sentences* of Peter the Lombard, Bishop of Paris,
were of Divinity.

century made it a college ' de plein exercice', with a full curriculum in Arts, in which Logic as well as Grammar and Rhetoric
were taught. It had even retained two courses in Theology, which
the Sorbonne tried to absorb to the exclusion of other colleges.
But its chief fame was due to an illustrious succession of students
and doctors. Launoi, himself a fellow in the seventeenth century,
wrote an elaborate and admirable history of Navarre, which Famous Scholars of
includes lives of ' its host of celebrated men '.   Room is still Navarre.
found in the Annals of Learning in the fourteenth century for
Nicholas Oresme, one of its masters, a political economist, a
Greek scholar, and a mathematician, and Nicholas Clemangis,
the theologian ; in the fifteenth, for Peter D'Ailly, bishop of
Cambray, and John Gerson, ' the most Christian Doctor', and
in the sixteenth, for Budaeus, the friend and rival of Erasmus
in the revival of the study of the classical languages.   To
Launoi's work we owe the most authentic record of Major's
career in Paris, for Major also was deemed one of the chief
luminaries of Navarre.   D'Ailly and Gerson, successively Chan-
cellors of the University as well as Principals of Navarre, led the
famous movement for reform within the church which asserted
itself in the beginning of the fifteenth century, at the Councils of
Pisa (1409) and Constance (1414-18). They were the principal
authors or authorities in favour of the supremacy of General
Councils over the Pope, the early champions of the Gallican
Liberties, who after so many gallant struggles were only
finally defeated by the Ultramontane doctrine of Papal Infallibility established as *de fide* by the Vatican Council of the
present century.   Colleges like nations have traditions, and
the connection of Major with Navarre, where Gerson's name still
exercised great influence, favoured his adoption of the Gallican
position that the Pope was not the ultimate authority when
opposed by a General Council. His views on this point,
carried to lengths from which Major himself would have
shrunk, by his pupils Knox and Buchanan, form a link in the
chain of opinion which produced the Reformation.

A special opportunity arose during Major's residence in Paris of reasserting Gallican doctrines.

The policy which led Charles VIII. and Louis XII. to claim parts of Italy, and to assert their claim by the sword, brought the latter monarch into conflict with Julius II., the strenuous maintainer of the temporal rights and spiritual supremacy of the Papacy. In the course of this conflict Louis tried the bold stroke of calling a Council to overrule the Pope. The Council of Pisa met in 1511, was adjourned to Milan and finally to Lyons, but owing to the failure of Louis's Italian campaign accomplished nothing. During its sittings Cardinal Thomas Cajetan published a book on the papal side, impugn-ing its authority, and Louis applied to the University of Paris to answer it. The task was intrusted to James Almain, a young Master of Arts and member of the College of Navarre, one of Major's pupils. This *Liber de Auctoritate Ecclesiæ et Conciliorum adversum Thomam Caietanum* has been sometimes credited to Major as joint author, but Launoi, our best authority, ignores this. Almain probably sought his advice, and Major we may be certain was present in the crowded auditory of approving theologians when it was publicly read at Paris. The treatise of Almain supported views quite in accordance with the teaching of his master. In the later edition of the works of Gerson[1] there is inserted an appendix 'Doctoris Majoris Doctoris Parisiensis Disputa-tiones de Statu ac Potestate Ecclesiæ excerptæ ad verbum ex ejusdem Commentariis in Librum Quartum Sententiarum'. This appendix contains arguments proving (1) That the polity of the church is monarchical or constitutional (as we now say) as distinguished from absolute; (2) *That Bishops and Parish Priests were both directly instituted by Christ* (a step in the direction of Presbyterian equality); and (3) That the Pope has not the power of the sword over Christian Kings and

Navarre sup-
ports Gallican
doctrines.

---

[1] *Opera Gersoni*; Antw. ed. 1760, vol. ii. pp. 1121, 1131, 1145.

Princes; also Disputations on the Authority of the Council over the Pope and of the Power of the Pope in Temporal Affairs. These latter disputations consist of extracts from Major's later work, 'A Commentary on Matthew', and show that he gave a wide scope to the idea of a commentary in order to introduce opinions he desired to promulgate.

In 1505-6 Major graduated as Doctor in Theology, and as 1505-6 Major by a rule of the College of Navarre Professors in Arts were a Doctor of Theology. obliged to leave off lecturing in that Faculty after attaining this degree, then or soon after he transferred his services to the Theological Faculty, and, still living in Montaigu, commenced to lecture in the Sorbonne on the Sentences of Peter Lombard, the recognised text-book of the theological school.

The Sorbonne had different traditions from Navarre, and The Sorbonne. was the head and centre of Roman orthodoxy. It is perhaps not altogether fanciful to see in the balancing character of his mind some traces of the influence of schools which represented opposite tendencies—Reform and Conservatism, Independence and Authority. A more ancient foundation of the middle of the thirteenth century, the Sorbonne had been instituted and organised by Robert de Sorbonne, chaplain of St. Louis, as a college for secular priests and the cultivation of theology. Its endowments and its numbers were small. It had only thirty fellows (*socii*) and commoners (*hospites*), the former always in orders and bachelors and doctors in theology, the latter, bachelors of the same faculty. But the small numbers and the strictness of the rules as to election of fellows gave the Doctors of the Sorbonne a distinction, and in process of time—especially at epochs when doctrinal questions became prominent—an authority, which led to their being recognised as a necessary constituent part of the divinity faculty, and to the gradual suppression of theological teaching in other colleges. The influence of

the Sorbonne, which became as it were a Divinity Hall, was
exercised against the new light shed upon theology by the
study of the Scriptures in the original languages and affords a
warning to those who would exile theology from the Universities. Before Major became one of the Doctors they had
condemned the study of Greek and Hebrew as adverse to
theology. Shortly after he returned to Scotland they set the
example (immediately followed by Oxford and Cambridge) of
burning the works of Luther. This act was the occasion of a
violent tract by the mild Melanchthon,—' A Defence of Martin
Luther against the furious decree of the Parisian Theolo-
gasters', in which Major came in for a share of the invective.
' I have seen ', he says, ' the commentaries on Peter Lombard
by John Major, a man, I am told, now the prince of the Paris
Masters. What waggon-loads of trifles ! What pages he
fills with dispute whether horsemanship requires a horse,
whether the sea was salt when God made it, not to speak of
the many lies he has written about the freedom of the will,
not only in the teeth of the Scriptures, but of all the schoolmen. If he is a specimen of the Paris Doctors, no wonder
they are little favourable to Luther.'[1]

Sorbonnic
style.

To the Sorbonne, besides graver defects of the scholastic
theology, Major is said to have owed his singularly cramped
Latin. A Sorbonnic style was a nickname for the style
opposed to the easier and better form of composition which
the study of the ancient classics and the use of the vulgar
tongues introduced. Yet Latin at best was now an old-fashioned
garb, worn with grace by scholars like Erasmus, Buchanan,
Scaliger, but to inferior genius or the ordinary man a rigid
uniform which constrained the free play of the mind. Every
one must regret that Major's like Buchanan's history was not
written, as Bellenden's translation of Boece was, in the dialect
of their native country, which both knew so well. They might

---

[1] Melanchthonii *Opera*, i. p. 398.

possibly have preserved for a time Scottish prose, as Dunbar
and Douglas preserved Scottish poetry, to the enrichment of
the future language and literature of Britain.

Four years after his theological degree an attempt was made
by his friend Gavin Douglas to recall Major to Scotland [1].   In
1509 a precept passed the Privy Seal at the instance of
Douglas for his presentation to the office of Treasurer of the
Chapel Royal, then vacant.   But for some reason, probably
Major's unwillingness to quit the duties of a teacher, which he
preferred to those of ecclesiastical office, the project fell
through.   It would appear, however, from a passage in his
Commentary on the Fourth Book of the Sentences, that Major
did revisit Scotland in 1515.   The passage referred to first Major visits
appears in the edition of 1519 [2], and in it he states that when Scotland, 1515.
he had been at home four years before and visited the Monastery
of Melrose, he was told of a frequent custom of the Abbots to
let their rich pastures with the sheep to tenants on condition
that they should be liable for loss of the stock—in other words,
under the contract known in Scottish law as a Bowing Contract [3].   He adds that in answer to repeated inquiries he was
told this custom had led to the pauperisation of the tenants or
sheep-masters, who had formerly lived like wealthy patriarchs.
It is enough, he concludes, to show the iniquity of such contracts.   The passage is curious as evidence how keenly the
Doctor of Theology still watched the rural pursuits in which
he had probably spent his boyhood.   It is a warning also, in
the meagreness of our information as to the details of his life,
against the assumption that he may not have more than once
returned to Scotland during his Paris residence.   It was but
a short voyage of about a week, with favourable weather, from

---

[1] *Memoir of Gavin Douglas*, by John Small, Librarian of the University of
Edinburgh, prefixed to edition of his works.

[2] Dist. xv., Qu. 46, fol. clxiii.

[3] See Hunter, *Landlord and Tenant*, i. 344.   This anomalous form of Lease is
now confined to dairy farms, and as to its local limits.—Rankine, *Leases*, p. 255.

Calais or Dieppe to the English or Scottish east coast ports, yet
had it not been for this solitary and casual reference, we should
not have known that Major ever came back to Scotland till his
return in 1518, the occasion of which will be noticed presently.

Theological   His first published work on theology was his *Commentary on*
Studies. Peter
Lombard.   *the 4th Book of Peter the Lombard's Sentences,* issued in 1509.
This was followed by his Commentary on the First and Second
Books in 1510, and on the Third in 1517. The popularity of
these Commentaries was shown by new editions of the Fourth
Book in 1512, 1516, 1519, and 1521, of the First in 1519 and
1530, of the Second in 1519 and 1528, and of the Third in 1528.

Nor was the scholastic and philosophical activity of Major
confined to the publication of his own works. He edited in
1505, along with a Spaniard, Magister Ortiz[1], the Medulla, or
Essence of Logic, by Jerome Pardus[2]; in 1510 a short tract of
Buridan[3]; in 1512 the epitome, by Adam Godham[4], of the four
Books of the Sentences, as abridged by Henry Van Oyta[5], a
Viennese doctor of the end of the 14th century; and in 1517
he suggested to two of his pupils and superintended the first
issue of the *Reportata Parisiensia* of his famous countryman[6]
John Duns Scotus. Ockham was the pupil of Duns Scotus.
Buridan and Godham were pupils of Ockham[7]. Three cer-

---

[1] Ortiz, at first an opponent in Paris, afterwards a patron in Spain, of Ignatius
Loyola, was one of Charles v.'s agents in Rome in the case of Queeen Katharine.
The biographer of Ignatius states that when Ortiz broke down under the strain
of the spiritual exercises at Monte Cassino, St. Ignatius, to cheer his friend,
danced for him the old national dance of the Basques. It cheered him so that
he was roused from his stupor and finished his exercises.—Stewart Rose, *Ignatius
Loyola,* p. 123. Many of his despatches from Rome, with reference to the
Divorce, are in the Calendars of State Papers, Rolls Series. He is called by
Mr. Froude ' a bitter Catholic theologian, with the qualities of his profession.'—
The Divorce, p. 159.

[2] The contents of the *Medulla* are described by Prantl, iv. p. 246.

[3] John Buridan (*ob. c.* 1358), a voluminous writer on Logic and Metaphysics,
whose works are described by Prantl, iv. p. 14.

[4] See his Life in *Dict. of Nat. Biography.*

[5] A Viennese writer on Theology as well as Logic (*ob.* 1397).—Prantl, iv. p. 103.

[6] *History,* IV. xvi. p. 207.   [7] *History,* IV. xxi. p. 230.

tainly, perhaps all, of these writers were Franciscans. Duns
Scotus was the founder of the school which, taking his name,
separated itself from the hitherto orthodox scholastic doctrine
of Thomas Aquinas[1]. Ockham was the founder of the still Major inclines
to Nominalism.
more radical revolt of the Nominalists against the Realists[2]—
and in this Godham[3] and Buridan[4] followed him. It eventually
led, according to Hauréau, to the dissolution of the Scholastic
Philosophy[5]. While Major is careful not to identify his own
opinions with any of these authors, it is impossible to overlook
the fact that he chose their writings for republication.

In the singular conclusion of his life of Adam Godham,
now for the first time reprinted[6], Major assigns the first place
amongst the learned men of Britain to the Venerable Bede,
the second to Alexander Hales, but he adds Ockham and
Godham would have contended for it were not Hales so much
their senior. These two he pronounces equal, and contrasts
them in a passage which is a sample of his style and criticism

---

[1] Thomas Aquinas and Duns Scotus were both Realists. But Duns set the
first great example of a breach in the unity of scholastic doctrine, so that
Schwegler (*History of Philosophy*, Hutchison Stirling's translation, p. 145), even
says : 'The whole foundation of scholastic metaphysics was abandoned the
moment Duns Scotus transferred the problem of Theology to the practical sphere.
With the separation of theory and practice, and still more with the separation in
Nominalism of thought and thing, philosophy became divided from theology,
reason from faith.'

[2] He is classed by the writer who has most exhaustively examined his writings
as one of the Moderns, or of the school of Scotist Terminists. See Appendix to
the Life, No. 11.

[3] Godham, a somewhat obscure schoolman, whose name was sometimes spelt
Woodham, is rated higher by Major than by the veterans of philosophy. He
attended Ockham's lectures at Oxford, and died, 1358, at Norwich, where he was
a member of the Franciscan Convent, or at Bubwell, near Bury.—*Dict. of Nat.
Biography*, s.v. GODDAM ; Prantl, ii. p. 6.

[4] John Buridan, who died shortly after Goddam, was a much more decided
follower of their common master Ockham, and expressly declared the distinction
between Metaphysics and Theology to be that the former recognised only what
could be proved by reason, while the latter proceeded from certain dogmatic
principles which it accepted without evidence, and reasoned from them —Prantl,
iv. p. 15. Buridan is perhaps now chiefly remembered by the fallacy of the
Asinus Buridani, though the Ass is not to be found in his writings.

[5] *Philosophie Scholastique.*   [6] Appendix II. p. 431.

at their best. 'Ockham and Godham are equals in logic and in either kind of philosophy (Ethics and Metaphysics?). Ockham in commenting on the Sentences is wordy and diffuse. Godham is concise and firm ; if Ockham's dialectic (dialogus) did not stand in the way, the younger writer would carry off the palm. Ockham's intellect was sublime and daring, Godham's noble and solid. The one with knitted brow, lowered eyebrows, and flashing eyes, as a warrior from youth, disputes with gravity. The other, with calm brow and raised eyebrows, laughingly pleases every one, and resolves everything (*diluit omnia*), so that I prefer neither.'

This balancing, hesitating, and inconclusive judgment is very characteristic of Major's intellect. Though he is positive enough in his opinions on individual points, and in resting finally on orthodox conclusions, many of his arguments were, it would be wrong to say sceptical[1], but as little dogmatic as was possible in a schoolman. It is also deserving of note that he praises 'the Dialogus of Ockham', for that work is described in his History as 'treating of many things concerning the Pope, and the Emperor, laying down nothing definitely, but leaving everything to the judgment of his audience'. This too was Major's method when he came to deal with ticklish points as to the Pope's authority. But if Major supposed he really left the question of the Pope's authority where he found it, he deceived himself. The tendency of his thoughts could not be concealed, and his doubts and questions were solved and answered by the younger generation's acts.

Major attempts·
to reconcile
Nominalism
and Realism
on Nominalist
Principles.

The exact position of Major amongst the scholastic philosophers is a subject which would require and repay a separate monograph. It is beyond the power of the present writer to

---

[1] Mr. Owen, in his *Evenings with the Skeptics*, Longmans, 1881, does not hesitate to class even the earlier schoolmen, Erigena, Abelard, Aquinas, as semi-Sceptics, but the tendency became more distinctly marked in William of Ockham and the Nominalists.

furnish it, and would exceed the limits of this sketch, as well
as probably exhaust the patience of most of its readers[1]. Yet
to leave it altogether untouched—to present any however
imperfect a portrait of the last of the Scottish Schoolmen without some notice of his philosophical standpoint
would be the play of Hamlet without Hamlet. Fortunately
Major has himself, in a short passage of the Preface to the
standard edition of his Commentary on the Fourth Book of the
Sentences, published in 1519, given a clue to the aim of his
philosophy. 'I have yet seen,' he writes, 'none of the
Nominalists who has carried his work on the Fourth Book of
the Sentences to the core and the close (*ad umbilicum et calcem*),
and this others retort on them as an opprobrium, saying that
the Nominalists are so occupied with Logic and Philosophy
that they neglect Theology. And yet there are various subjects of Theology which presuppose Metaphysics. I will
attempt therefore to apply the principles of the Nominalists
to the several Distinctions of the Fourth Book of the Sentences,
and to write one or more questions which the Realists too, if
they pay attention, can easily understand. Either way,
Theology, about which I shall specially treat, will be common
ground.' Here again we find Major taking in the great controversy which divided the schools since the time of Ockham,
and some have thought from a much earlier date, the position
of a mediator, and endeavouring for the sake of Theology to
reconcile Realism and Nominalism.

In 1518, having completed his work as lecturer on the
Master of the Sentences, Major at last accepted the call his own
country made on him to take part in its higher education.
It is possible that his friend Gavin Douglas, now Bishop of
Dunkeld, who revisited France in 1517 to negotiate the Treaty
of Rouen, had renewed his entreaties with success. On 25th

---

[1] See further on Major's position as a Logician and Philosopher, Appendix to
the Life, No. II. p. cxxii.

June 1518 Major was incorporated [1], before Adam Colquhoun, the Rector, as Principal Regent of the College and Paeda-gogium of Glasgow, and is described as Canon of the Chapel Royal at Stirling and Vicar of Dunlop, endowments no doubt bestowed on him to induce him to leave Paris, and which prove that he must have taken orders, though he devoted himself entirely to the educational side of the ministerial office.

In several passages of his writings he defends evidently with a personal reference the ecclesiastics who devoted themselves to philosophy and education in preference to pastoral duties. In one of these he says: ' Nor is there a reasonable ground for frequenting universities, except in so far as a man learns by attending lectures, so that he may return to his flock with greater learning. But if he is sufficiently instructed to be able to draw doctrine from books only, he can do that both in the flock committed to him and on Mount Caucasus, or the Rock of Parmenides. He too who continues to read theology in the university is equivalent to a preacher ; nay more, he creates preachers, which is a greater work than to preach. He is most certainly excused if he has no cure of souls, and if he has simply received the order of the ministry. . . . If such a one, too, residing in a university, has a cure in the neighbourhood, it is not necessary that he should live in his parish, but it is sufficient if he have a good vicar to administer the Sacraments, provided he gives the food of life on festival days to his flock, and hears confessions and doubtful cases. For it is hard to say to a learned man, accustomed to live and converse with learned men, that he ought always to live in a country village. Truly it seems sufficient for him to dwell in the nearest town or city, and frequently to visit his parishioners, taking care that he is not absent on festival days unless for a reasonable cause '.[2]

---

[1] Register of Glasgow College.
[2] *In Quartum*, Dist. xxiv. Qu. 2, fol. clxvii.

In 1522 he is again named in the Glasgow Records as Professor of Theology and Treasurer of the Chapel Royal, as well
as Vicar of Dunlop, and in 1523 he represented one of the
Nations as elector (*intrans*) of the new Rector. On 9th June
of the same year he migrated to St. Andrews, where he was _{Regent in St.}
incorporated under the titles of Theological Doctor of ^{Andrews 1522.}
Paris and Treasurer of the Chapel Royal on the same day as
Patrick Hamilton, the future martyr, who had studied under
him in Glasgow.

Little record remains of Major's Glasgow period. He
doubtless continued, perhaps repeated, his Paris lectures on
Logic and Theology, and we find his name occurring in connection with the election of Rector and other College business.
He was present at a congregation in 1522, when the Rector,
James Stewart, protested against a tax being imposed on the
University[1]. He is styled throughout the entries of the University Records, where his name occurs, 'Principalis Regens
Collegii et Paedagogii', but the principal Regent in the old
constitution of Glasgow was only the senior Professor, and the
office of Principal in the modern sense did not then exist.

The whole of his residence in Glasgow was less than five John Knox one
of his pupils at
years, but it would be memorable, if for no other reason, for Glasgow.
one of his pupils. John Knox, a Haddington boy, had a
link with Major, whose strong local feeling we have seen, and
Major may have been the cause that, instead of going to St.
Andrews, Knox matriculated at Glasgow in 1522. Unfortunately the Glasgow period of Knox's education is the barest
in material of any part of his life. The future Reformer
appears to have quitted the University without a degree, and
his practical intellect led to his commencing life neither as a
philosopher nor a theologian, but as a church notary[2]. His
mind was of the quality which matures late, but often pro-

---

[1] Munimenta Universitatis Glasguensis, p. 143.
[2] Memoir of John Knox, *Dictionary of National Biography*.

duces the strongest fruit. The only reference he makes to
Major belongs to a later period, when they were both at St.
Andrews, in a passage in which he describes his old master as
'a man whose word was reckoned an oracle in matters of
religion', proving that Major retained his previous reputation.

Glasgow was at the time Major lived in it a small but
beautiful city, situated on a fine river, not yet deepened by
art so as to be a channel of commerce. It was chiefly known
as the See of the great bishopric founded by Kentigern,
restored by David I. when Prince of Cumberland, and recently
raised to the dignity of an archbishopric, which embraced the
south-west and parts of the south of Scotland. The University
founded in the middle of the previous century had been poorly
endowed, and did not become celebrated till its reform by
Andrew Melville after the Reformation.

The Archbishop during Major's residence was James Beaton,
uncle of the more famous Cardinal; and the translation of
James to the See of St. Andrews in 1523 synchronises so well
with Major's removal to the elder and then more distinguished
University, that we can scarcely err in supposing that the one
promotion led to the other.

If Edinburgh or Glasgow was a contrast to Paris, much
more was St. Andrews. By nature, the site now so venerable
between the sands at the mouth of the Eden and the rock-
bound coast at one of the extremities of the little realm of
Scotland, seemed destined for a fishing village or haven for
small craft which already in considerable numbers dared the
stormy sea and brought their native land in contact with the
civilisation of Europe. But towns did not rank then by size or
even by wealth. St. Andrews had a threefold dignity in the
eyes of the pious Catholic and the ecclesiastical scholar. It
held the relics of the patron Saint of Scotland. It was the
primatial See. It was the first, and still, notwithstanding
the foundation of Glasgow and Aberdeen, the principal Uni-

versity. The Bulls for its foundation had been obtained by
Bishop Wardlaw in 1411, tutor and friend of James I., who
confirmed the privileges granted to it in 1432. Bishop
Kennedy had founded the first College of St. Salvator in 1456,
and ten years before Major's incorporation St. Leonard's,
or the New College, had been endowed by Archbishop Stewart,
the bastard of James IV., and Prior John Hepburn. St. Salvator was instituted as a College for Theology and the Arts,
for divine worship combined with scholastic exercises. Its
members were a Provost, who was to be a Master or Doctor
in Theology, a Licentiate and a Bachelor of the same Faculty,
four Masters of Arts, and six poor Clerks.

St. Leonard's was modelled after the college for poor scholars
at Louvain, itself a copy of Montaigu College. Its foundation
consisted of a Principal and four Chaplains, two of them
Regents, and twenty Poor Scholars, instructed in the Gregorian
chant, and six of them Students of Theology. Its statutes,
drawn by Prior Hepburn, were of the strictest kind as regards
discipline, and the richer students, not on the foundation,
were to be obliged to conform to them. The scholars were to
be admitted on examination: not older than twenty-one, poor,
virtuous, versed in the first and second parts of grammar, good
writers, and good singers. The subjects prescribed for lectures
were grammar, poetry, and rhetoric, logic, physics, philosophy,
metaphysics, and one of the books of Solomon. It does not
appear that Major, when he came to St. Andrews, was at
first specially attached to either College, and as lectures continued in the Paedagogium, which Beaton converted into the
College of St. Mary in 1527, it is not possible to say where his
lectures were delivered; but he continued to teach according to
the same methods the same subjects as in Paris and Glasgow
—Logic and Theology.

In 1523, 1524, and 1525, he was elected one of the Dean's Offices held by
Major at St.
Assessors in the Faculty of Arts. In 1523 and 1525 he Andrews.

was one of the deputies appointed to visit St. Salvator. In
1524 he was one of the Auditors of the Quæstor's accounts,
and also one of the Rector's Assessors. The last date at which
his name appears at this period was on 22d January 1525. It
re-appears after an interval of nearly six years on 6th November
1531, when he was again elected one of the Deans, probably of
the Faculty of Theology.

During his residence at Glasgow and St. Andrews it appears
probable that Major paid special attention to the philosophical,
and in particular the logical studies he had relinquished for
a time in Paris, but now resumed for the sake of his own
countrymen in the smaller universities of Scotland, which were,
as they have always been, undermanned, and could not afford
in that age separate professors even for philosophy and
divinity. This would account for his Introduction to the
Dialectic and whole Logic of Aristotle, a new and recent
edition of his earlier work, digested in twelve books, which was
issued by Badius Ascensius in Paris, while he was still absent
in 1521, and the 'Eight Books of Physics with Natural Philosophy and Metaphysics,' published in 1526, shortly after his
return, by Giles Gourmont, famous as a printer of Greek, and
soon followed by his Logical Questions, issued from the same
press in 1528. He finished his Aristotelian studies by the
issue of a Treatise on the Ethics, published by Badius in 1530.
He had thus, with a rare completeness, embraced in his
Lectures and Works almost the whole range of the Aristotelian
Philosophy. When we remember that an edition of a single
work of Aristotle, or a single classic author, has been deemed
sufficient for the labours and the fame of a modern university
professor, we appreciate the indefatigable industry of Major,
and we learn how little the nineteenth century can afford to
despise the sixteenth in the matter of philosophical erudition.

Nor were these treatises of Major mere editions or commentaries on Aristotle. He reproduced and reduced in them

Completion of
his study of
Aristotle.

the substance of the thoughts of the great master to the scholastic method. So they were the effort and the fruit of independent thought. The scholastic method was then becoming antiquated, and was alien to the modern spirit. While it addressed itself to the highest problems which the human mind can attempt to solve or pronounce insoluble—the nature of God, the origin of man and the universe, the being and working of the mind itself—it descended also to the most trivial details, and put the most casuistical questions, which the sarcasm of Melanchthon, the satire of Rabelais, and the epigram of Buchanan could hardly exaggerate.

Still Major's work, always acutely critical and argumentative, was at least an educational discipline. It awakened and stimulated thought, perhaps the greatest service any teacher can render to his pupils. It is not surprising that one class of them learnt to swear by their master as an oracle, and another to criticise his method and despise its results.

In 1525 he returned to Paris and the College of Montaigu, probably to escape the troubles of the times. The earl of Angus was then at the head of affairs, and Major's patron, Beaton, had to hide himself in the disguise of a shepherd. Major probably also was glad of the opportunity his return afforded to superintend the publication of his Exposition of the Four Evangelists, which was issued from the press of Jodocus Badius Ascensius in 1529. His absence saved him from being a spectator of, probably an actor in, the trial of Patrick Hamilton, one of his Glasgow pupils, who was condemned for heresy by an Assembly of Bishops and Theologians at St. Andrews, and burnt before the gate of St. Salvator on 29th January 1528; but it was only to see a similar scene in the streets of Paris—the martyrdom of Berquin; for the decree of the Sorbonne in 1521 that 'flames rather than reasoning should be employed against the heresies of Luther' was applied to the Lutherans as well as their works. Amongst

(margin note) Returns to Paris, 1525.

(margin note) His Biblical Commentaries.

the doctrines for which Hamilton died were the assertions
that it was lawful for all men to read the Word of God;
that image-worship, and the Invocation of Saints and the
Virgin, were unlawful; that masses for the dead were vain;
that there was no such place as purgatory; that sin could be
purged only by repentance and faith in the blood of Christ
Jesus. There is no reason to suppose that Major would have
dissented from the sentence any more than his master Gerson
had from that against Huss. The Doctors of Louvain, who
were in close sympathy with the Sorbonne, congratulated
Beaton on having performed a commendable act, and Major's
dedication of his *Commentary on St. Matthew* refers to the
news recently received that Beaton had, 'not without the ill-
will of many, manfully removed a person of noble birth, but an
unhappy follower of the Lutheran heresy'. The allusion is
an euphemistic reference to the martyrdom of Hamilton.

Major con-
demns
Lutheran
heresy.

To St. Andrews during Major's residence came a Highland
youth, attracted by his fame, destined by nature for learning,
already with some of the experience of a man. George[1], the
son of Thomas Buchanan of the Moss, in Lennox, early lost his
father, and was sent when fourteen, at the cost of his maternal
uncle, James Heriot of Traprain, in East Lothian, to Paris;
but after two years' study of the Latin classics the poverty of
his mother brought him home, and he served with the French
troops of Albany at the siege of Werk. The hardship of a
winter camp led to an illness, and, after recruiting his health
at home, he entered the Paedagogium at St. Andrews in 1524.
On 3d October 1525 he took his degree of Bachelor of Arts.
Major having gone to Paris in that year, Buchanan either
accompanied or followed him, but entered, not as might have
been expected the College of Montaigu, but the Scots College
de Grisy, in which he was admitted *ad eundem* as Bachelor on

---

[1] A more favourable view of the character and conduct of George Buchanan
will be found in Mr. P. Hume Brown's *Memoir*, 1890.

10th October 1527. There is no proof that Major was, as has been alleged, at the expense of his maintenance, but probably he befriended a young man connected with East Lothian as well as St. Andrews, whose talents foretold his future eminence. In 1529 Buchanan was elected Procurator of the German Nation, the highest honour then open to the Scottish student, having lost a prior election only through the superior claim of his blind countryman, Robert Wauchope, afterwards Bishop of Armagh. Buchanan has left two remarks on Major, in themselves not unfair, but very unjust if taken as a summary of his whole teaching. 'John Major at that time taught Dialectic, George or rather Sophistic', he says, 'in extreme old age at St. Buchanan. Andrews'; and in the well-known epigram which associates their names, the pupil again expresses his repugnance for the scholastic triflings the younger generation found in works their elders deemed the glory of the University of Paris :—

> Cum scateat nugis solo cognomine Major,
>   Nec sit in immenso pagina sana libro,
> Non mirum titulis quod se veracibus ornat ;
>   Nec semper mendax fingere Creta solet.

> When he proclaims himself thus clearly
> As 'Major' by cognomen merely,
> Since trifles through the book abound,
> And scarce a page of sense is found,
> Full credit sure the word acquires,
> For Cretans are not always liars !

The sting of the epigram is the last, not the first, line, which was taken from Major's description of himself on the title-page of more than one of his books[1]. Neither reverence nor gratitude were qualities of Buchanan, but the difference of age to a large extent accounts for his estimate of Major.

It would be difficult to imagine a greater contrast than the Contrast between Major doctor of the Sorbonne trained at the feet of its masters, himself and Buchanan. recognised as one of them, without poetic imagination, and

---

[1] See Appendices I. and II., pp. 430, 434, 435, 439.

with little experience of practical life except as seen from the cloister and the chair, and his young pupil already versed in the Latin Classics and the thoughts not of Thomas Aquinas and Duns Scotus, Peter the Spaniard and Peter the Lombard, but of Virgil, Horace, Catullus, and Martial, and who had seen not Paris merely but the Camp. A supercilious and unmeasured contempt for old-fashioned learning in a youth of genius has had examples before and since Buchanan. In truth Buchanan learnt more than he was conscious of from Major. The study of the sacred texts, the independent view of the sources of political authority, and the inclination towards exact historical inquiry, were notable points in Major's mental attitude, and can scarcely have failed to influence his students. The common opinion that the seeds of the De Jure Regni, and what are sometimes called the republican, but more accurately the constitutional, views of Buchanan's History were derived in part from Major's teaching, seems well founded. His position marks a stage through which the European mind had to pass before it abandoned scholasticism for humanism, the Roman for the Reformed doctrines, Absolute for Constitutional Government. The same Tendency has indeed been marked in earlier schoolmen by the historians of philosophy. What was special to the case of Major was that this Tendency was during his life coeval with the Renaissance Movement north of the Alps, and that while the Master resisted, his younger and active-minded disciples combined the necessary results of the union of the Tendency with the Movement.

Major's History, a copy of which, printed by Badius Ascensius in 1521, must have been in the St. Andrews Library, probably was known to the omnivorous student whose elaborate work, more than fifty years later[1], was to eclipse its fame.

The form of this History is unique. It is written in a scholastic style, and every now and then breaks out into logical

---

[1] The first edition of Buchanan's History was published by Alexander Arbuthnot at Edinburgh, 1582.

arguments. But what has been called in the nineteenth century the critical spirit, in the mode in which it manifested itself in the sixteenth century, is to be traced from the first page to the last. A renewed zeal for historical study was one of the features of the time. The age of the Monkish Chronicles and the Mediæval Annals was past. It was no longer possible to write history in the style of Matthew Paris and John of Fordun, or of Sir John Froissart, or even of Philip de Commines. With the advent of the new learning the historical instinct led all nations to desire a more exact account of their origin, and a more philosophical narrative of their progress, not merely stating events in the order of their occurrence, but tracing them to their causes. A series of historical works issued from the press of Badius about this period, in some of which there was more, in others less, of this instinct. The history of the kings of Britain by Geoffrey of Monmouth was published in 1508, the History of Scotland by Hector Boece in 1526, and that of Paulus Jovius, *De Rebus Gestis Francorum et Regum Franciae* in 1536,[1] besides some of the best old Chronicles, Saxo Grammaticus and Gregory of Tours. It was probably in contrast to Geoffrey of Monmouth's title to his History ' *Britanniæ Utriusque* regum et principum Origo et Gesta ', that Major adopted the title of ' Historia *Majoris Britanniæ* '.

The lively and inquisitive Italian, Polydore Vergil, who had been sent in 1504 to collect Peter's Pence in England, was specially attracted to the early annals of Britain, and wrote in 1509 to James IV. for information as to the succession of the Scottish kings, but the information does not seem to have been supplied. Shortly before the death of Gavin Douglas in 1523 he met that prelate in London, and resumed his inquiries. Their conversation is typical of the contest going on in many minds between the old traditional and the new critical view of

Margin notes: Scholastic form and critical spirit of his History.

Polydore Vergil and Gavin Douglas.

---

[1] The *Compendium super Francorum Gestis*, by Robert Gaguin, published in 1497, appears to have been well known to Major, and is written more in his spirit than any of the other Histories of his time.

history. It is interesting too as showing that the Bishop's
education in history had not advanced so far as that of his
old friend Major the theologian, although there is some reason
to believe that in theology the opposite was the case, and that
Douglas leant more than Major towards the doctrines of the
Reformation. This is a not uncommon phenomenon. The
critical part of the intellect applies or confines itself to different
departments in different minds. Douglas, according to Vergil,
asked him 'not to follow the account recently published by a
certain Scot which treats as a fable the descent of the Scottish
kings from Gathelus, the son of an Athenian king, and Scota,
the daughter of Pharaoh', and furnished him with the usual
fictitious pedigree to prove it. The Scot was beyond doubt
Major, whose History had been published two years before.
Polydore was, like Major, incredulous. 'When I read the notes
of Douglas', he says, 'according to the fable I seemed to see
the bear bring forth her young. Afterwards when we met,
as we were accustomed, this Gavin asked my opinion', and
Polydore then argued, from the silence of the Roman historians,
that there could have been no Picts or Scots in Britain prior to
the Roman conquest, and, he adds: 'This Gavin, no doubt a
sincere man, did the less dissent from this sentence, in that it
plainly appeared to him that reason and truth herein well
agreed, so easily is truth discovered from feigned phrases'.
The death of Douglas by the plague prevented Polydore from
further enjoying the benefit of his conversation.

The History of Major was entitled *Historia Majoris Britan-
niae tam Angliae quam Scotiae per Johannem Majorem natione
quidem Scotum professione autem theologum.*

Title of Major's
History.

'Major Britain' was no doubt, in its first intention, meant
to distinguish Britain from Brittany, the lesser land of the
Britons, just as Scotland, 'Scotia Minor', in mediæval Latin,
prior to the eleventh century, was distinguished from Ireland,
the 'Scotia Major' of the Scottish race. But it signified the

author's presage of the greatness of the small island whose annals he relates. There is possibly too a play on his own name. It was Major's History of Major Britain. It was also an early essay to find a name that, without offence to the pride of either nation, should comprise Scotland as well as England, for which James I. afterwards hit upon the happy name of Great Britain, leaving to the nineteenth century to give Greater Britain a more fit application to the dependencies and colonies which the natives of the little island have conquered or acquired beyond the Atlantic or in the islands of the Antipodes.

Major dedicated his work in a short preface to his young Major's dedication to James v. sovereign James v., whom he describes as celebrated for his noble disposition and high birth, derived from both kingdoms, alluding to his descent as grandson of Henry VII. as well as heir of James IV. The preface is a defence against the charges of a possible critic that he had deviated from the practice of historians in dedicating his history; that a theologian should not venture to write history; and that he has used the style of a theologian rather than an historian. To the first he answers that he has read no dedication by Sallust or Livy, either because they wrote none, or because their dedications are lost. Sallust, indeed, had no reason for a dedication, as he wrote before the Romans had kings (emperors). Livy, perhaps, had no wish to dedicate, deeming it more glorious to offer the fruits of his labours to the Gods and posterity rather than to any mortal. But nearly all the poets, even when they wrote history, dedicated their works. Valerius Maximus invoked Caesar when about to describe the annals not only of his own but of other nations. St. Jerome, St. Augustine, our own Venerable Bede, as well as other ecclesiastical writers, used dedications. He has followed their example, but, to avoid suspicion of flattery, has left the history of recent times to others. The charge that a theologian should not write history he denies. It is the province of a theologian to define matters of faith, religion, and morals, so he cannot be deemed to depart from it when he not only states acts and their authors, but also determines whether they had been rightly or wrongly done. Besides, it would be his aim that the reader of his History should learn not only what had been done, but also how men ought to act, from the experience of so many centuries. For his style, it might have been more polished, but he doubted if more suitable to his subject. If the names of Scottish places and persons were expressed in Latin words the natives would scarcely recognise them. We see from this curious observation how narrowly Major missed writing in the vernacular. Perhaps, could he have printed his book at home, he might have done so. But, no doubt, he also desired to be read by the learned throughout Europe.

It has always been the aim of our kings, he concludes, to act greatly rather than speak elegantly, so it should be the aim of all students to think rightly and understand the matter in hand sharply rather than to write elegantly or rhetorically. Of this the two Scots, John Scotus Erigena [1] and Duns Scotus, Bede, Alcuin, and many others are examples. It is his hope that the king may read happily the history of his race dedicated to his felicity and live to the age of Nestor.

Scheme of the History.

The history which follows narrates in six books in a succinct style the annals of England and Scotland from the earliest times to the marriages of Henry vii.'s daughters, Margaret to James iv. of Scotland, and Mary to Louis xii. of France, and after his death to the Duke of Suffolk. The part relating to Scotland is naturally fuller, but the combination of the two histories was done of set purpose to aid the view which Major insists on that the two crowns should be united by marriage. With the same object, Major treats the English more favourably

---

[1] Although the epithet 'Erigena' is now admitted to be of later date, the current and better opinion seems to be that John Scotus was an Irishman, but Duns Scotus was almost certainly, as Major thought, a Scotchman.—R. Lane Poole, *History of Mediæval Thought*, p. 55 *n* 2.

than our earlier historians. He is the first Scottish advocate
for the Union. ' I state this proposition,' he says : ' The Scots
ought to prefer no king to the English in the marriage of a
female heir, and I am of the same opinion as to the English
in a similar case. By this way only two hostile kingdoms
flourishing in the same island, of which neither can subdue the
other, would be united under one king, and if it is said the
Scots would lose their name and kingdom, so would the
English, for the king of both would be called king of Britain.
Nor would the Scots have any reason to fear the taxes of an
English king. I venture to answer for the English king that
he would allow them their liberties as the king of Castile
allows the people of Aragon. Besides, in case it is for the
well-being of the republic, it is proper that taxes should be paid
to the king according to the necessity of the occasion. The
Scottish nobles, as I think, are unwilling to have one king with
power over the whole island, and the English nobles are of like
mind, because the nobility would not dare to go against such
a king. Yet a single monarch would be useful even to the
nobles. They would flourish by justice ; no one would dare
use force against another. Their homes and families would
be more permanent. No foreign king would invade their
country, and if they were injured, they would be able without
fear to attack others.'

Such opinions were in advance of his age. It is singular
how a Scotsman bred in France should have adopted them.
Experience must have convinced him that the prosperity of
his country pointed to an English union rather than to a
French alliance.

Another point on which the opinions of Major are un-
expectedly liberal, at least to those who have not followed
with minute attention the course of medieval thought, is as to
the relation between Church and State. In this connection
he repeats the sentiments to which he had given utterance in

commenting on the Gospel of Matthew, and which he may
have learned from the writings of Ockham, D'Ailly, and
Gerson. Referring to the excommunication of Alexander II.
of Scotland by the Papal Legate on the ground that Alexander
had sided with the English barons against King John, he
says: 'Perhaps fearing more than was reasonable ecclesiastical censures, he restored Carlisle to the English king. If
he had a just title to Carlisle, he had no reason to fear the
papal excommunication. Various of his predecessors had held
it, nor do I see how he had lost the right, and whatever might
be the fact as to that, he could have appealed from the legate
to his superior. But perhaps you will object that even the
unjust sentence of a pastor (*i.e.* an ecclesiastic in charge of a
flock and with power to excommunicate) is to be feared. To
which we will easily answer. If it is unjust, it is as if null, and
there is no reason to fear it. For an unjust excommunication
is no more an excommunication than a dead man is a man.
Not only in Britain, but in many other places, men too lightly
entangle themselves with ecclesiastical censures. No one,
unless he commits mortal sin, ought to be excommunicated
either by law or man, and for contumacy alone excommunication is to be pronounced by man. If he will not hear the
church, saith the Scripture (*veritas*), let him be as a heathen
and publican. Therefore by the opposite argument, if he will
hear the church, why should he be ejected from the company
of believers? It follows that we think many persons excommunicated are in grace.' This is bold language for an ecclesiastic of the Roman Church, but by allowing excommunication
for contumacy, Major leaves a loophole through which his
conscience crept when he approved the burning of Patrick
Hamilton. This explains too how he and men of like views [1]

---

[1] Jourdain has an interesting and instructive Essay on this subject, dealing
with writers of an earlier date (*Excursions Historiques*, 1888, p. 524) : ' Mémoire
sur La Royauté Française et le Droit Populaire d'après les Ecrivains du Moyen
Age '.

were tolerated by the Roman Church, which has always
allowed considerable latitude to men of learning and ability
who have conceded to the Church the final sentence—the last
word, whether of temporal or eternal condemnation.

When he deals with John's abdication and payment of the
ransom for his crown to the Pope, Major raises the difficulty
whether a king can give the right of his kingdom or fixed pay-
ments out of it to any other person. If he gave the right of
the kingdom to the Turk or any other not the true heir, the
gift would be plainly null. The proof is: 'The king has the
right of the kingdom from a free people, nor can he grant that
right to any one contrary to the will of the people'.

A king cannot be said to act rightly who, without the
counsel of his nobles, declares that his revenues are to be
given away to any one. The proof is: 'Such a tax, without
express or tacit consent, burdens the people, and such a tax the
people are not bound to pay. Further, the contest between
the king and the Church of England was as to goods taken
from that particular church, and specially from the Cistercians.
It is clear, restitution ought to have been made to the particular church. It was idle in John to suppose that because
he gave a quota to Rome, he was absolved from restitution to
the Church from which he had taken the property.' Here the
doctrine of restitution, a favourite and sound doctrine of the
manuals of the Confessional, is very skilfully turned against both
John and the Pope. It is, after all, robbing Paul although you
pay Peter[1]. He concludes with allowing that if John and the
English people agreed to give an annual payment to the Pope
it would be otherwise, for it does not concern the king's purse,
but is given by the people itself. These are almost the constitutional principles embodied by the barons in the charters
of the Liberties of England, but which Buchanan generally

---

[1] The proverb is more often cited in the reverse form, but is known in both
forms.

Constitutional
Doctrines.

gets the credit of introducing into Scotland. He may have
derived them in part at least from his old master. When we
read Barbour's *Bruce* or Blind Harry's *Wallace*, we trace their
parentage to a still earlier date. They were the fruit of the
War of Independence. Perhaps they may be traced to a more
distant epoch, to the resistance which Galgacus and our remote
Celtic forefathers made to the Roman legions. Major tells an
anecdote which shows they existed before the War of Independence in the breast of the patriot leader. Wallace, he says,
always had in his mouth lines his tutor had taught him :—

> 'Dico tibi verum, Libertas optima rerum ;
> Nunquam servili sub nexu vivite, fili.'

With equal distinctness Major, in treating of the succession
of Bruce, states he does not place Bruce's right on the ground
of priority of descent, but because Baliol, by surrendering the
crown to Edward, forfeited his right. 'A free people gives the
strength to the first king whose power depends on the whole
people. Fergus the first had no other right. I say the same
of the kings of Judea ordained by God.' He further argues
that the people can depose for his demerits a king and his
successors, founding on the precedents of the Roman kingship
which was abolished, and the Carlovingian dynasty which was
founded when Pepin by the will of the people deposed the
Merovingian line.

Government
founded on the
will of the
people.

The proof from the establishment of the Roman republic
shows another source from which views in favour of the
foundation of government on the will of the people were
drawn by scholars in the time of Major. The Greek and
Roman classics, above all Livy, recently translated into French,
and soon after into Scotch by Bellenden, presented the noble
spectacle of a free republic. It is noticeable that Major
frequently reflects on the tyranny and want of patriotism of
the nobles. Wallace is his hero rather than Bruce, and in a
fine passage which reminds us of the poem of Dante in the

Convito [1], he argues that 'there is no true nobility but virtue
and its acts. Vulgar nobility is nothing but a windy mode of
talk.' He laughs at his countrymen, who think themselves all
cousins of the king, and says he used to argue with them jocularly in this way : 'They would grant no one was noble unless
both his parents were noble. If so, was Adam noble or not?
If he was not, they denied the premiss. If he was, then so
were all his children. So it follows either that all men are
noble or none.' It is evident that we are listening to a representative of the Commons, to a forerunner of Robert Burns in
the strangely different garb of a medieval philosopher. A
similar or cognate argument was expressed in the popular
rhyme of the English peasants—

> 'When Adam delved, and Eve span,
> Who was then the gentleman?'

Like all clear-sighted men at this period, Major saw the
urgency of reform in the Church. He approves the saying
of James I., that David I. had injured the Crown by lavish
grants to Bishops and Monks. He expresses his regret at the
poverty of parishes and parish churches in Scotland in comparison with England, at the gross abuses of pluralities and
non-residence, and his surprise that the Scottish prelates had
not earlier applied some part of their great revenues to founding Universities. He especially condemns the wealthy abbots
who live in the court more than in the cloister, who think they
do well when they enrich their convent by oppressing the poor
labourers of the ground. The true end of religion is to subdue
the lusts of the flesh, and wealth is adverse to this end. When

Abuses in the Church condemned.

---

[1] ' It follows then from this,
    That all are high or base,
    Or that in time there never was
    Beginning to our race.'

  .   .   .   .
    Where virtue is there is
    A nobleman, although
    Not where there is a nobleman
    Must virtue be also.'
The Convito, Fourth Book (Miss E. Price Sayers' translation).

he describes Bishop Kennedy's character he blames him for
holding the Priory of Pittenweem *in commendam* along with so
great a See as St. Andrews, and for the cost of his sumptuous
tomb; and he raises the question whether a bishop has more
than a qualified right of property in the revénue he derives
from the church.   In the passages of his History in which
he attacks the oppression of the nobles and the corruption
of the ecclesiastical dignitaries we recall the language of the
Satires of Henryson, Dunbar, and Lindsay[1].   Against the
abuses of ill-regulated monasteries Major more than once
inveighs[2], and though he maintains the binding nature of
vows, he admits the difficulty of the question.   On the
critical point of the privilege of ecclesiastics to be exempt
from the judgment of lay courts, while he takes, as might be
expected, the side of the Church in discussing the struggle
between Henry II. and Becket, he allows this was not by
divine right, and might be otherwise in special circumstances.
He even goes so far as to condemn the multiplication of
miracles, and remarks (though earlier as well as later examples
of the same train of reasoning may be found) that miracles
do not prove holiness, for John the Baptist, the holiest child
born of woman, wrought none, and that a vow of chastity
might be a vow of the foolish virgins if it hurt the state.

   With regard to the facts of his History Major shows a won-
derfully sound historical instinct, distinguishing truth from the
fables with which the Scottish annals were then encrusted.
His work is a sketch, and much is omitted; but the student
who reads it will have little to unlearn.   In this respect he is
far superior to his contemporary Boece, and even to Buchanan,
who copied Boece in the earlier part of Scottish history.

---

   [1] With these passages in the History may be compared his denunciation in his
Commentary on St. Matthew of ' the grasping abbots who make things hard for
the husbandmen ', fol. lxxiv. verso 2.
   [2] Compare Commentary on St. Matthew, fol. lxxiii. verso 2: ' If I were as rich
as Midas, I would rather throw my money into the Seine than found a religious
house where men and women take their meals together.'

He discards at once the foundation fable of the Scottish kings being descended from Scota the daughter of Pharaoh, and takes the firm ground of Bede as to their Irish origin, and inclines to the further opinion, which may be true though not proved, that they came from Spain to Ireland. The Picts, following Bede and their own traditions, he states, came also by way of Ireland from Scythia, and he ascribes probably rightly their name to the practice of painting their bodies. Although he did not succeed in detecting the insertion of forty kings between Fergus I. Mac Fercha and Fergus II. Mac Erc, he shows his distrust of it by reckoning only fifteen where Fordun and Wyntoun had made forty. Buchanan, who ought to have known better, has compiled a list still longer and less intelligible, which corrupted Scottish History at the fountainhead till the sources were purified first by Father Innes, and more completely in our day by Mr. Skene. It is significant of how far Major was in advance not merely of his own but of a later age that Dr. Mackenzie, writing in 1708 his memoir of Major, supposes the reduction of the number of the kings to be a misprint.

He argues from the life of Ninian as well as Bede that the Picts and Britons had occupied Scotland before the Scots migrated from Ireland. Bede's authority and his own knowledge as a Lothian man of the dedication of the Church at Whittingham to St. Oswald, enable him to assert the fact of the whole of Lothian having been in the time of Bede under the Northumbrian kings. He refers to the Commentaries of Bede and to Alcuin as proof of the learning of the Northumbrian ecclesiastics of the eighth century, though he says they were not well versed in the knotty questions of the Schoolmen and the Sorbonne. He says boldly that the Church of St. Columba had priests and monks but not bishops, in which he is in substance right, even though it be held proved that there was an order of bishops whose only known function of preeminence was the ordination of priests. For how different was such a bishop from the lordly diocesan prelates of Major's own time! He gives correctly the date of the union of the Picts and Scots in the middle of the ninth century under Kenneth Macalpine, and leaves as a doubtful point what is still doubtful—how long Abernethy had been the chief seat of the Pictish Church before its transfer to St. Andrews. He remarks that the Picts held St. Andrew in great honour, from which he jumps to the possibly sound conclusion that the Picts held the richer and level parts of the country, while the Scots occupied the mountains. The Anglo-Saxon period of English history and the contemporary history of Scotland from Kenneth Macalpine to Malcolm Canmore is very rapidly sketched, and there are many errors in the attempt to synchronise the kings.

Independent view of the later history. After Canmore the history is more clear and accurate, and though the reigns of the English kings are slurred, a distinct portrait of each of the Scottish monarchs is presented : Alexander the Bold ('audax'), who imitated his father in bravery and zeal for justice ; the good king David ; Malcolm, who followed the piety of his ancestors ; the long reign of William the Lion ; Alexander the Second, who fought with John on the side of the English barons, and lost nothing his ancestors had gained, observing justice during his whole life ; the third Alexander, who rivalled his father in the goodness of his reign. The War of Independence is told as might be expected by a Scottish patriot, and the true characters of Wallace and Bruce are defended against the attacks of Caxton's Chronicle ; but he rejects as fabulous the visit of Wallace to France, which subsequent research has confirmed, on the ground that this visit is not mentioned by the French or the Latin Chronicles of Scotland. David II. he characterises, though brave, as a weak king, and he blames the want of patriotism which led him to name an English prince as his successor. The second and third Robert are less distinctly drawn. James I.

is the finest portrait.   It has been copied in all subsequent
histories.   ' In person short, but stout and robust, of the
finest intellect but somewhat passionate.   Skilled in games,
he threw the stone and hammer further than any one, and was
a swift runner.   He was a trained musician, and second to none
in the modulation of his voice.   In harp playing he surpassed,
like another Orpheus, the Irish and Highland Scots, the masters
of that instrument.   All these arts he learned in France and
England during his long captivity.   In Scottish poetry he
was very skilful, and very many of his works and songs are
still held by the Scotch in memory as the best of their kind.
. . . He was not inferior to, perhaps was greater than, Thomas
Randolph in administering justice.   He excelled his father,
grandfather, and great-grandfather in virtue, nor do I prefer,'
he concludes, ' any of the Stewarts and their predecessors,
without counting the present boy (James v.), to James I.'

Of James II. he says, many gave him the palm amongst .
active kings because he applied all his zeal to war and showed
himself equal to any knight.   ' I place,' however, ' his father
before him both in intellect and courage, but in temper he
much resembled his father.'   Of James III. he speaks with less
praise, giving only the negative encomium, of which his
countrymen are fond, that there have been many worse
kings both abroad and at home.   James IV. was not inferior
to James II., as appears from his deeds.   ' Many of the Scots,
he remarks, ' secretly compare the Stewarts to the horses
of Mar, which are good in youth but bad in old age ; but I do
not share this view.   The Stewarts have preserved the Scots in
good peace, and have held in hand the kingdom left by the
Bruces undiminished.'   There is a boldness in judging and
distributing praise and blame to the kings very characteristic
of Major and his countrymen.   His judgment is not that of a
partisan, but of a contemplative historian.   Not less interesting, pointed, clear, and fair are the brief remarks which he

makes on the character of his countrymen than on those of the
kings.   His foreign residence helped him to gauge their insular
vanity and intense family pride.   But it had not diminished
his patriotism.   Love of his country and desire for its true
welfare is everywhere conspicuous in his writings.   'Our
native soil attracts us with a secret and inexpressible sweetness
and does not permit us to forget it', he wrote to Alexander
Stewart, the archbishop of St. Andrews, while he was still
living in Paris, in the dedication of the edition of his Commentary on the Fourth Book of the Sentences[1].

It was during Major's second residence in Paris that Francis I.
—who, like James V., had at first hesitated to prosecute the
Reformers, and even leant towards them, partly from policy,
as a means of attacking the Emperor through the German
Lutherans, and partly from scholarly tastes, which made him
a patron of the Renaissance—went over to the side of the Old
Church.   He had tried to persuade Erasmus to return to
France and preside over the new Royal College, in which the
three ancient classical languages, Hebrew, Greek, and Latin,
were to be taught; but Erasmus was too prudent.   Francis
had twice saved from the stake Berquin, the translator of
Erasmus, a man, like Hamilton, of good family, but on a third
declaration of heretical opinions abandoned him to his fate.

The Sorbonne
condemns
Erasmus.

The Doctors of the Sorbonne were bitter enemies of Erasmus,
and, led by Major's old patron, Noel Beda, now their Syndic,
they induced the University to condemn his principal works.
His 'Colloquies' had been so popular, that a Paris printer
issued 24,000 copies of one edition; they were even used as a
text-book in some of the University classes.   The Theological
Faculty had already taken the alarm in 1526, and petitioned
Parliament to suppress the work, but nothing was done.   Two
years later Beda, in the name of the Theological Faculty,
applied to the University.   The Faculties of Canon Law and

---

[1] Appendix II., p. 420.

Medicine, and the French Nation, sided with the Faculty of
Theology in condemnation of a book dangerous to youth.
The German Nation was willing to interdict its use in the
classes.   The Nations of Picardy and Normandy desired to
write to the author, asking him to correct his errors.   The
Rector embraced the more severe view, which had the balance
of authority in its favour, and the book was absolutely
condemned.

Beda was at this time so powerful in the University, and Changes in
even with the mob of Paris, aptly styled by Michelet the Francis I.'s attitude.
false democracy, that he was called the King of Paris.   The
influence of his mother Ann, a fervent Catholic, drew Francis
in the direction of Rome.   The excess of Lutheranism began
to show itself in the Anabaptists.   The monarchs of Europe
began to fear that their authority might be impugned as well
as that of the Pope.   A comparatively trifling incident is said
to have finally decided Francis.   Some one—no one knew
who—broke an image of the Virgin and Child on the Sunday
before Easter 1525, in the Rue des Rosiers in Paris.   It was
at once attributed to the Reformers.

The University, led by Beda, went in solemn procession,
preceded by 500 youths with candles, to the place of the
sacrilege, deposited their candles, and returned for a solemn
expiatory service at the Church of St. Catherine.   Two days
later the King headed a still larger procession, in which the
Princes of the Blood Royal, the Ambassadors, the High
Officials of the Court, the Church, and the University, took
part, and replaced the broken image with one in silver, amidst
the acclamations of the people.

A condemnation of the translation of the New Testament,
prepared by the Faculty of Theology in 1527, was at last
issued in 1531.   Encouraged by this success, and the martyrdom of several less conspicuous Lutherans which followed that
of Berquin in 1529, Beda ventured on the condemnation of

Le Miroir de l'âme pécheresse, a mystical and devotional work
by the king's sister Margaret, Queen of Navarre, and he
attacked the Royal Professors, who were now beginning to
carry out a pet project of Francis—the institution of the new
College for free instruction in Latin, Greek, and Hebrew.
His zeal had carried him a step too far. For these offences
he was compelled to make a public apology, was imprisoned
during the King's pleasure, and the uncrowned king, one of
the many victims to the ' vaulting ambition which o'erleaps
itself', died a captive at Mont St. Michel. Francis I., like
Henry VIII., was not a religious but a despotic monarch, who
would brook no rival in Church or State.

The Sorbonne
and Henry
VIII.'s Divorce.

It is not certain whether Major joined the Doctors of the
Sorbonne in their sanction given in January 1530 to the divorce
of Henry VIII., contrary to the wishes of the fanatical but
orthodox Beda. The records of the period have been destroyed; but as the opinion was issued during his residence, it
is probable he concurred in it. While we condemn this act,
it must be remembered that it was in one aspect a declaration of the independence of the temporal power against the
Pope, which would find favour with the Gallican Doctors.
Francis I., in an angry letter to the Parliament of Paris,
expressly condemned Beda's proposal to refer the matter to
the Pope, as trenching on ' the liberties of the Gallican Church
and the independence of the Theological Council, for there
is no privilege belonging to the realm on which we are more
firmly determined to insist'.

Loyola, Calvin,
Rabelais.

Michelet notes that during these years three men, different
in every respect except in the greatness of their fame, came to
Paris to complete their education—Ignatius Loyola, who commenced his education in grammar at Montaigu in 1528, John
Calvin, who entered the College of Ste. Barbe in 1523, and
Francis Rabelais. Rabelais's college has not been discovered,
but probably he was in Paris from 1524 to 1530. With none

of them can Major have had much sympathy; but it marks the pregnant character of the time and place that they produced such contrasts as the ascetic militant founder of the Society of Jesus, whose rule was to surpass even Papal absolutism; the Protestant theologian whose discipline, almost as strict as that of the Jesuits, and founded on principles as plausible, once its premisses are admitted, was to succeed the Lutheran as the latest form of the reformed Church; and the satirist whose coarse and giant laughter, a revulsion from the rules alike of the old orders and of the new sects, was to shake the foundations of the Church in France and become the parent of the best and worst in modern French literature. The irony of Erasmus, and the satire of Rabelais, were almost the only weapons which could be used by reformers who wished to escape the fate of Berquin. Major himself came in for a chance stroke of the lash of Rabelais, who places amongst the books in the library of St. Victor, ' Majoris de Modo faciendi boudinos '—' Major on the Art of making Puddings.'

Before finally leaving Paris for Scotland Major completed his labours in Logic by issuing a new edition of the Intro- duction to Aristotle's Logic in 1527, and a new treatise, Quaestiones Logicales, in 1528, and his labours in Philosophy by an edition of the Ethics of Aristotle in 1530, and his labours in Theology by new editions of his Commentaries on the First, Second, and Third Books of the Sentences in 1528-1530. But the chief employment of this portion of his life was an elaborate Commentary and Harmony of the Four Gospels, which he had projected in 1518, when he published his Exposition of St. Matthew, and now in 1529 published as a complete work. Each Gospel has a separate dedicatory letter. St. Matthew is dedicated to his chief Scottish patron, James Beaton, Arch- bishop of St. Andrews; St. Mark to his old college friend, John Bouillache, Curate of St. James in Paris; St. Luke to James Dunbar, Archbishop of Glasgow; and St. John to his

[margin note: Major's final published works.]

[margin note: His Biblical Commentaries.]

old pupil, Robert Senalis, now Bishop of Vence. The Doubts
and Difficulties he had inserted in the earlier edition of the
Commentary on St. Matthew were not reprinted, but the
complete work had an appendix of four questions :—
(1) Whether the Law of Grace is the only true Law ; (2)
What are the degrees of Catholic Truth ; (3) On the number
of the Evangelists ; (4) On the site of the Promised Land.

Dedication to
James Beaton.   The letter to Beaton explains the object which Major had
in view in this work. It was to show the Harmony of the
Gospels with each other and of each in itself, and to preserve
the tradition of the doctrine of the Roman Church. In carrying out this intention he has refuted the errors of Theophylact [1],
the Bulgarian Bishop, and of the Wycliffite, Hussite, and
Lutheran sects. The errors of others he has noted without
naming them, 'for Christians have been taught not to call a
brother Racha.'

He has dedicated it to James Beaton, because he owed to
him a good part of his studies, alluding doubtless to the offices
he had held at Glasgow and St. Andrews, and who became a
teacher on this subject, was suitable to Beaton's name, profession, race, education, and conduct (*mores*). 'His name
"Jacob" means a supplanter, as he had been of heresy,
and "Beaton" signifies a noble herb, an antidote to poison,
as he had shown himself of the vigorous poison of the
Lutherans. His profession and office made it his duty to study
and preach the Gospels, and his race, as that of every illustrious family, to protect the Church. Finally, his conduct in
removing, not without the envy of many, a noble but unhappy
follower of the Lutheran heresy.' The work which follows
His orthodoxy
united with a
reforming spirit. answers to the design. It is a rigidly orthodox commentary,
in which Major allows himself much less freedom than in his

---

[1] Theophylact, Archbishop of Bulgaria (d. 1112) achieved a lasting reputation
by his Commentaries on the Gospels, the Acts the Epistles of St. Paul, and
the minor Prophets.—Hardwicke's *Church History of the Middle Ages*, p. 273.

writings on the Books of the Sentences, or in his History, or even in the Doubts which he had inserted in the earlier edition of the Commentary on St. Matthew. If he spares others who have held erroneous views, he never hesitates to condemn in the strongest language the heretics who had denied the doctrine of transubstantiation,—Berengarius, who had been condemned by the Council of Vercellae, Wyclif by that of Constance, and the Germans of his own time who had revived the same heresy, and of whom he did not know whether Oeco-lampadius, Zwingle, or Luther was the worst. Transubstantia-tion, he vehemently reiterates, is the doctrine of Scripture, of the Church, and of the Fathers of the Church. It is also the doctrine 'of our Theological Faculty of Paris[1]. Whoever denies it is a foolish heretic.' He defends the monastic life and the celibacy of the clergy against the Lutherans[2], but admits that there were monasteries and nunneries which required reform, and again, as in his History, he mentions with approval the case of the English nunnery which, when he was pursuing his studies at Cambridge, he had seen transformed into a college by the Bishop of Ely[3]. So too he strongly con-demns the bestowal of livings on unworthy priests, or even the preference of a less worthy candidate and the pluralities which were so common in the Church in his day. 'Those deceive themselves,' he says, 'who think that the approval even of the Supreme Pontiff can reconcile such things to the dictates of Conscience[4].' He insists on the duty of preaching, especially by the prelates of the Church. In a curious passage[5] which seems to have a personal reference, in commenting on the fact that some of Christ's kinsmen did not acknowledge Him, he adds 'just as our relations treat us as mad because we spend

---

[1] In Joann. caput vi., fol. cclxxxviii.   [2] In Matth. fol. lxxii.
[3] John Alcock, Bishop of Ely, was the Reformer of the Nunnery of St. Radegunde, which he converted into Jesus College, Cambridge.—Mullinger, p. 321.
[4] In Matth. fol. lxxx.   [5] In Marc. fol. cxvi.

g

our whole activity in philosophy and theology. They wish us
rather to apply ourselves to the law to gain honour and
wealth, and take offence at all knowledge which is not lucra-
tive. According to their false estimation we exist for them
and not for our own salvation and the glory of God. For
they say, What profit does he bring to us? Let his library,
with its books, be burnt. And they think the more sublimely
any one philosophises, and thereby magnifies the power of
God, that he is so much the greater fool[1].'

· Such have been the recriminations of those who pursue knowledge for its own sake, and of those who follow it for gain, in
all ages; but probably at no time was the contrast sharper than
between the monastic student of the middle ages, who had
taken the vow of poverty, and the practical man his relative
or neighbour, who devoted his life to the acquisition of
wealth. While strenuously maintaining the worship of the
Saints against the Lutherans and other heretics, he admits
that there was a possibility of abuse which must be corrected
by the proper ecclesiastical authorities[2]. The use of Images
in Churches he altogether approves, and condemns the revival
by Wyclif and Luther of the heresy of the Greek Church in
the time of Leo the Iconoclast with regard to them[3]. These
examples may suffice to indicate the spirit of the teaching of
Major as a biblical Commentator. He stands firm in the
old paths of the Roman and Catholic Church, and treats all
deviations from its doctrine as pestilent and poisonous heresy.
But like the best Romanists of his age, he favours reforms
within the Church and by the Church itself.

The last of Major's published works was a return to his
earliest master. The Ethics of Aristotle, with Commentaries
by himself, were printed at the press of Badius Ascensius in
1530,[4] shortly before his return to Scotland.

---

[1] In Marc. fol. cxvii.
[2] In Joann. fol. cccxxii.
[3] In Joann. fol. cccxiii.
[4] Appendix I., p. 407.

More interesting even than the subject of the work is the Dedication of
Major's Com-
Preface which preserves the memory of the relations between mentary on
the Ethics of
Major and the great minister of Henry VIII.   As it contains Aristotle to
Wolsey.
several references to his own life, and is one of the best of
his numerous dedications, we give a translation of what were
probably his last published words, for the twenty years he still
survived were spent in other pursuits than authorship[1].

On the Kalends of June 1530 he wrote to Wolsey the following dedicatory letter :—

> ' To the most Reverend Father and Lord in Christ, Lord
> Thomas Wolsey, Cardinal Presbyter of the Holy Roman
> Church by the title of St. Cecilia, Archbishop of York,
> Primate of England, and Legate *a Latere* of the Apostolic
> See, John Major of Haddington, with all observance, greeting.

> ' I have often and long determined with myself, and conceived
> in my mind, most bountiful of Prelates, to dedicate to some English
> prince the first fruits of my poor thoughts, such as they are, and
> that for good reasons as I think.   The first of them, not to be
> diffuse, is the love of our common country, which is innate in all
> living creatures; for we, separated only by a small space, are
> enclosed together in one Britain, the most celebrated island in all
> Europe, as in a ship upon a great ocean.   My second reason is
> our community of religion and of studies.   My third and, not to
> multiply words, my last and strongest reason is the desire to avoid
> ingratitude, the least note of which was deemed even by the
> Persians the most odious stain.   For I have been received and
> honoured by Englishmen with such frequent hospitality, such
> humane and genial converse, such friendly intercourse, that I
> cannot be longer silent without showing a forgetful mind.   Forty[2]
> years ago, if I reckon rightly, when I first left my father's house
> and went through England to Paris, I was received and retained
> with so great courtesy by the English, that during a whole year I
> learned the first rudiments of a good education in arts in the very
> celebrated College of Cambridge, now illustrious by the name of
> Christ.   Afterwards, so far as I was permitted by the never-changing

---

[1] For the original, see Appendix II., p. 448.

[2] It was really thirty-six or thirty-seven, for Major went to Paris in 1493, after,
as this Preface informs us, a year's residence in England.

sea (*per mare perpetuum*), I always made my journeys to and from France through England. Besides, what I hold and will always hold in fresh and constant memory so long as there is breath in my body, it is now the fourth year since your Grace, Most Reverend Legate, most bountiful and chief of the ecclesiastical dignitaries of England, entertained with the old hospitality of Christians one of my humble condition when I was again making my journey to France, and invited me to the College of Letters, then recently founded by your magnificent beneficence at Oxford[1], to do the best I could to enlighten it by my presence and teaching, and made me the offer of most splendid remuneration. But so great a love possessed me for the University of Paris, my mother, and for my fellows in study, besides the desire to complete the books which I had already begun, that I could not accept the post so freely offered and so honourable. Now therefore, that I may not seem altogether forgetful of such great benefits, and that I may produce what during so many years I have laboured with, I inscribe and dedicate to you, who are both so great a Prince in ecclesiastical rank and the Maecenas not only of all theologians but of all men of letters, that most celebrated work on Ethics, written by Aristotle, the Prince of philosophers in the judgment of many, and explained by my own commentaries, of however little value these may be. As in the rest of his writings he has surpassed others, in this work he seems to have surpassed himself, that is the power of human nature. For in almost all his opinions he agrees with the Catholic and truest Christian faith in all its integrity. He constantly asserts the Free Will of man. He declares with gravity that suicide, to avoid the sad things of life, is the mark not of a truly brave but of a timid spirit. He separates honest pleasures which good men may seek after from the foul allurements the Turks propose for themselves. He places the happiness which man may attain to in the exercise of the heroic virtues. And he pursues with admirable judgment the examination of the two kinds of life, I mean the active and the contemplative, which were figured in the Old Testament by the sisters Rachel and Leah, and to us by Martha and Magdalene[2].

---

[1] Christ Church was begun by Wolsey in 1525, but never completed on his plan. The Cardinal's College, as it came to be called, was forfeited by Henry VIII., and finished on an inferior scale by the king.—Brewer's *Henry* VIII.

[2] Mary, the sister of Martha, supposed by mediæval commentators to be Mary Magdalene.

For he applies the one to the life of the gods, the other to the life of mortals.

In fine, in so great and manifold a work, if it be read as we explain it, you meet scarcely a single opinion unworthy of a Christian man. Wherefore, Most Magnificent Father, as you lately received me with such humanity and benevolence, we beg you now to accept this new birth, which, even if it were, as I wish, much better than it is, was long ago your due, and is now at last dedicated from my heart to your Eminence.'

Do the Latin superlatives and high-flown style strike us as antiquated and exaggerated? Let us recognise qualities which are better than any style, however perfect in taste and proportion—the ardent patriotism, the Academic spirit, the recognition of the nobility of the morals of the heathen philosopher, and the warm gratitude for Wolsey's kind offices. Let us remember too that when Wolsey had offered to place Major in the College which he was endowing with more than royal munificence, he was at the summit of his power; but when this dedication was written he had fallen so low that in England there was scarcely any one 'so poor to do him reverence.' In October of the previous year he had been prosecuted under the Statute of Provisors for accepting the Legatine office, which entailed the penalties of Praemunire and placed all he possessed at the king's mercy. On the 17th of that month he had been compelled to surrender the Great Seal; an inventory of all his goods had been taken, and two days later he had confessed the charge and submitted himself to the king's pleasure. Though pardoned in February 1530, and restored to the Archbishopric, he had been finally deprived of his other great benefices, Winchester and St. Albans. He had retired to his diocese in failing health and fallen spirits, and at the time when Major was writing this dedication he was travelling by slow stages from Grantham to Newark, and from Newark to Southwell, where he spent Whitsuntide.[1]

Time and tone of Preface honourable to Major.

---

[1] Brewer's *Reign of Henry* VIII., ii. 413.

He lived till 29th November 1530, and wrote many piteous and unavailing letters to the king to be restored to some portion of the property of which he had been stripped, and, above all, that the Colleges of Ipswich and Christ Church might be spared. They were the darling objects of his beneficence, and intended to perpetuate his name. 'By Wolsey himself,' writes Mr. Brewer, 'the loss of power, the forfeiture of his estate, and even his exile to York were regarded with indifference compared with the ruin of his colleges. For recovery of the former he made little or no effort. For the preservation of his colleges he bestirred himself with ceaseless and untiring energy, employing all the little influence he possessed, or believed he possessed, with men in power to rescue them from the hands of the spoiler.'

It may also be noted to the credit both of Wolsey and Major that Wolsey was a pronounced Thomist, and had even acquired the epithet of *Thomisticus*. Yet this had not hindered the Cardinal from offering the post of teacher in his college to one who like Major inclined to the position of the Scotist philosophy, and did not prevent Major, while insisting on the Freedom of the Will, the key-note of Duns Scotus' separation from the doctrine of Aquinas, from expressing his gratitude and dedicating his work to Wolsey.

To both the great Minister and the great Schoolman the Renaissance had imparted some of its reconciling influences. When we consider Major's work as a whole we are sensible that he was more in place in the Sorbonne than he would have been at Christ Church, in a college which retained the old subjects and methods of teaching rather than in one which aimed at adopting the new learning. Still his connection with the college ennobled by the name of Christ at Cambridge, when a student, and his narrow escape from becoming a Professor in the college which received the same name at Oxford, and favoured a reform in education, was something more than an accident in his life. It shows how near he stood, and was deemed by some of his contemporaries to stand, to the parting of the ways between the Mediæval and the Modern plans of University education. But when he was summoned to his own country as a director of public instruction, it was the Mediæval Scholasticism and not the Modern Humanism that he followed both at Glasgow and St. Andrews. He was a Modern only in Logic, and in the restricted and technical sense in which that word was used to denote the school which made the doctrine of ' Terms ' the cardinal part of Logic. He was a keen reformer of ecclesiastical abuses, but was not prepared for reform either in dogmatic theology [1] or educational methods.

The Bibliography of Major's works compiled by the learned zeal of Mr. T. Graves Law, Librarian of the Library of the Writers to the Signet, and the kind aid of the keepers of the principal Libraries where his works are still to be found, is a valuable key to the biography of Major, and an interesting chapter in the history of the early French press. For it was in France that all his works were printed. The art of printing, like the other fine arts which were the offspring of the Revival of Letters, was a late comer to Northern Britain. Chepman and Millar's press, in the Southgait of Edinburgh, issued its first sheets, the *primitiae* of Scottish printing, in 1508, and its last, so far as known, in June 1510. A single sheet of eight small leaves which contains the *Compassio beatae Mariae* is the solitary record of the names of John Story the printer and Carolus Stute the publisher. A copy of *The Buke of the Howlat*, discovered by Mr. David Laing, in the binding of some early Protocol Books, completes the brief sum of Scottish printing between 1510 and 1520, one of the most active periods of the early press of France and Germany. The first work of Thomas Davidson, the next Scottish printer, did not appear till 1542, when Major had for twelve years

Bibliography of his works illustrates his Biography.

---

[1] This is strikingly shown by his dedication in 1530 of a new edition of his Commentary on the First Book of the *Sentences* to John Mayr (or Major), the Suabian called Eck, from his birthplace, the most celebrated champion of the Church against Luther. Appendix II., p. 449.

ceased publishing. Necessity as well as choice, due to his long
residence in France, made him select Lyons and Paris as the
birthplace of his literary children. There was no press in his
native country which could have issued his voluminous works,
and few buyers had there been such a press. How different
was the case in France, whose famous printers vied with each
other in producing them, and the demand was sufficient to
produce editions of the same work by different publishers, and
frequent revised editions of some by Major himself. A rapid
survey of these will illustrate at once the activity of the French
press and the popularity of Major. Major seems to have commenced by printing at Paris in 1503 his first Logical Lectures
on *Exponibilia*, at the press of John Lambert, and two years
later he issued his Commentaries on the logical *Summulae* of
Peter the Spaniard from the press of Francis Fradin in Lyons.
In 1508 John De Vingle, another Lyons printer, father of the
more famous Peter, the Calvinist printer of Geneva, published
his whole lectures on Logic as a Regent in Arts, which were
sold in the same town by Stephen Queygnard, and of which
there was a new edition in 1516. He had also in 1505 issued,
along with Magister Ortiz, in Paris, the *Medulla Dialectices* of
Jerome Pardus. In 1508 his Commentary on the Fourth Book
of the Sentences was printed by Philip Pigouchet, and sold by
Ponset le Preux, and it was republished by Badius Ascensius
in 1516; and in 1516 his lectures in Arts were reprinted in
Paris by John Grandjon, and sold by Dyonysius Roce.

Why several of these earlier works were published at Lyons
has not been clearly ascertained. It may be conjectured that
as Lyons was as early as Paris[1] a centre of printing[2], and
already possessed forty printers in the fifteenth century,
although Paris had more than double that number, some
chance introduction may have led Major to resort to them.

---

[1] Monteil: *Histoire des Français*, iii. p. 305.
[2] Brunet, *Supplément par un Bibliophile*, s.v. LYONS, notes that it was then
the chief market for books, as Frankfort afterwards, and now Leipzig.

The Lyons printers and publishers employed by Major were His numerous
Francis Fradin (1505), Stephen Queygnard (1508), John De printers and publishers.
Vingle (1508), Martin Boillon (1516). An edition of the
Summulae of Peter the Spaniard was published in Venice by
Lazarus de Soardis in 1506, and another at Caen in 1520.
With these exceptions, and after 1516, Paris became his sole
place of publication, and his principal publishers were John
Grandjon and Badius Ascensius. But besides these we find
frequently the following Parisian printers and publishers:
John Parvus (Petit), who appears to have been a partner of
Badius: Constantine Lepus, James le Messier, J. Borlier, John
Lambert, Dyonysius Roce, William Anabat, Giles Gourmont,
the partner of Petit after the death of Badius, Durand Gerlier,
and Johannes Frillon.

Several of the last-named printers, with the exception of
Petit and Gourmont, were probably pirates, who then as now
preyed upon the works of celebrated and fashionable authors,
and may be left in the obscurity they merit. Grandjon and
Badius deserve a brief record. Of Grandjon little is known John Grandjon.
except that he was one of the most voluminous publishers or
bibliopoles of the University of Paris, and that his shop was in
the world-famed Clos Bruneau, with whose name the Parisian
students startled the ears of the watch by their cry, ' Allez au
Clos Bruneau, vous trouverez à qui parler'. His sign, which
hung over his shop, and was engraved as a device on his books,
was a group of great rushes (magni junci) in a marsh, a pun on
his name of Grand or Grant Jon.

Jodocus Badius was a still more celebrated printer, and Jodocus
deserves recognition by Scottish historical students, for to Badius.
his press we owe the two first printed histories of Scotland,
that of Hector Boece, as well as that of John Major. Born
at Asc, near Brussels (whence his name Ascensius), about
1462, after finishing his education at Ghent and Brussels, and
visiting Italy, he settled in Lyons as a lecturer on Latin, but
derived probably a larger income as corrector of the press for

Jean Treschel, one of the earliest Lyons printers. Marrying
the daughter of Treschel, he migrated to Paris about 1498,
and there began to print on his own account. His press, of
which a facsimile is given on the title-page of his books,
was established in the Aedes Ascensianae, and, till his death
about 1536, was the most prolific in Paris. No less than 400
volumes, the greater part folios and quartos, issued from it.
They included the most important Latin classics, on several
of which he wrote a Commentary, a translation by his own
hand of Sebastian Brand's *Ship of Fools*, and many historical,
philosophical, and theological works. He was employed not
only by French but also by English and Scottish authors, who
were doubtless attracted to a printer who was also a scholar.
He began to print for Major in 1516, and continued to do so
down to 1530. His eldest daughter, the wife of Robert
Stephen or Etienne, became the ancestress of a famous race
of printers. The second was the wife of Jean Roygny, who
carried on his father-in-law's press, and the youngest of
Michael Vascosanus, also a well-known Parisian printer. His
son Conrad became a Protestant, and retired with his brother-
in-law Robert Stephen to Geneva. If the epigram of his
grandson Henry Stephen could be trusted, Badius must have
had several other children, though his books were his most
numerous progeny. A sentence which he inscribed on several
of his volumes may be commended to publishers :—' Aere
Meret Badius Laudem Auctorum Arte Legentium,' which may
be freely translated :—

> ' His authors praised his grateful heart,
> His readers praised his graceful art.'

In one of Major's volumes Badius celebrates the author in
Latin verse[1], and Major frequently records his gratitude for

---

[1] IODOCUS BADIUS LECTORI.
Quartum Maioris, Lector studiose, suprema
  Iam tersum lima, perlege, disce, cole.
Quem si cum reliquis trutina perpenderis eque :
  Pridem alijs maior, se modo maior erit. [From the *In Quartum*, ed. 1521.]

the care of the press of Badius. One of these passages will appeal to the feelings both of the reader and the writer for the press. ' I had no human aid', he writes, ' except that of the printer, who has laboured with the greatest vigilance that commas, periods, and other stops should not be left out, although the copy was written by various hands ; for my amanuensis was sometimes prevented by the lectures which he had to attend, and my own handwriting was difficult for others to read'.[1]

Another point of contact between Major and the early Parisian press deserves mention. Uldericus Guerinck or Ulric Gering, the French Caxton, or first Parisian printer, was closely associated with the College of Montaigu. During his life he was a constant benefactor of its poor students, and by his will he left it the half of his goods and the third of the debts due to him. With the proceeds of this legacy the College bought the farm of Daunet, near the Marne, and the Hotel de Vézelay, which was situated between Montaigu and the College of St. Michel. On the latter site were built rooms for the classes of Grammar and Arts soon after 1510, the year when Gering died, and in the Chapel of the College a portrait of its benefactor was hung with an inscription describing him as ' Proto-Typographus Parisius 1469 ', and recording his benefaction. In these class-rooms Major may have lectured, and in that chapel he must have frequently worshipped [2].

Ulric Gering, the first Parisian printer, a benefactor of Montaigr.

In 1531 Major returned from Paris to St. Andrews, and resumed his lectures on Theology. Three years after, the death of Hugh Spens [3] caused a vacancy in the office of Provost of St. Salvator, and Major was appointed. The first entry of his name in that office after his return is on 4th November 1535, when he was again elected an Assessor of the Dean of Faculty of Arts. He was annually re-elected, at least till 1538. He was

Major at St. Andrews. Provost of St. Salvator.

---

[1] Exordium Libri Quarti Sententiarum. Appendix-II., p. 439.

[2] *Annals of Parisian Typography*, by Rev. W. Parr Gresswell, 1815, the frontispiece of which is the portrait of Gering.

[3] His tomb bears the inscription, ' Obiit anno domini 1534, et 21 die Julii.'

also one of the Rector's Assessors from 1532 to 1544, with
which was generally joined the office of Rector's Deputy: the
Assessor was one of the Council of the Rector, and the Deputy
his representative when absent. In 1539 he founded, along
with William Manderston, a chaplaincy or bursary in St.
Salvator's, and endowed it with the rents of certain houses in
South Street, St. Andrews. The holder was to celebrate
masses for the souls of the founders and their relations, and
of James v., Mary of Guise, and Cardinal Beaton. In 1545
Peter, the Chaplain of St. Salvator, is mentioned as his
coadjutor, and Major ceased, from the increasing infirmity of
age, to hold any of the annual offices of the University, but
retained the Provostship till his death in 1549 or 1550, when
he was succeeded by William Cranstoun.

Buchanan spoke of him as already in extreme old age in
1524. This appears to us somewhat of an exaggeration, as he
was only fifty-four. Perhaps, as has been suggested, the ordinary limits of human life were counted shorter in that age than
in ours. The date of his birth, now precisely ascertained,
proves that before his death he exceeded by ten years the
term of life allotted by the Psalmist.

Another reason may be suggested for the censorious tone
of all Buchanan's notices of Major. If we could implicitly
credit the gossiping and malicious Doctor of the Sorbonne,
James Laing, Major had actually taken part in the condemnation of Buchanan for heresy in 1539, because he
recommended James v., as it was absurdly put, to eat the
Paschal Lamb in Lent, or, as the fact may have been, to
break the fast which the Roman Church enforced during
that season. 'The king', says Laing, 'summoned the Doctors
of Theology at St. Andrews, amongst whom was John Major,
a man of the greatest piety and learning in Philosophy as
well as Theology . . . and when the question was proposed to
him he answered: "He who says, Most Christian king, that

James Laing's
story of Major
and Buchanan.

you ought to eat the Paschal Lamb wishes you to become a Jew, and to live according to the customs of the Jews, who deny that Christ has yet come or was born of the Virgin. For the Paschal Lamb is an institution of the ceremonial law, and every ceremonial law is dead once Christ has suffered, as the apostle clearly says in the fifth chapter of the Galatians."[1]

Though this story bears the marks of being largely apocryphal, Cardinal Beaton appears certainly to have been the instigator of Buchanan's imprisonment, from which he escaped, as he tells us in his own Life, while the guards were asleep[2]. When he was again arrested in Portugal, one of the charges against him was that he had eaten flesh in Lent[3], and there is nothing improbable in this having formed part of the earlier accusation in Scotland, or that Major may have been consulted by James v. on the point. If so, Buchanan's dislike of Major had another ground besides his contempt for the logical and sophistical teaching of the Professor.

That the closing years of Major's life were those of enfeebled age is shown by the appointment of a coadjutor, and by the fact that he was excused from attending the Provincial Council of Edinburgh in July 1549, in whose records he is described as Dean of the Faculty of Theology of St. Andrews, on the ground that he was 'annosus, grandaevus, debilis'.[4] Although Buchanan exaggerated, Major's productive life ended with his second residence in Paris. No later work proceeded from his ready pen, and we have scanty notices of what he did in St. Andrews as head of St. Salvator. Perhaps the absence of a press in Scotland capable of producing such works as his, and the occupations of the principal of a College, precluded him from further literary labours. But there were other and deeper causes. The state of Scotland was not favourable to the calm

---

[1] Jacobus Langaeus *De Vita, Moribus atque Gestis Haereticorum nostri temporis*. Paris, 1581.   [2] *G. Buchanani Vita Sua.*   [3] *Ibid.*
[4] Joseph Robertson : *Ecclesiae Scoticanae Concilia*, p. 82.

production or revision of philosophical or theological commentaries. The time for contemplation had passed, the time
for action had come. Major was not a man of action. To
one who had finally chosen to abide by the old church and
yet had fostered some liberal ideas, which he hoped the
Church would itself realise, the progress of the Reformation
and the means adopted to stifle it must have produced thoughts
best buried in silence. It was too late to change his opinions.
However liberal in other matters, the Holy Roman Church was
still to the venerable Doctor of the Sorbonne the exponent of
sound faith in religion. It is seldom that a man of serious
thought alters his views after middle age. Had he been
twenty years younger it might have been different.

Knox and
Major. Two glimpses of Major in his old age are given in the
History of the Reformation by John Knox, which show that
although he adhered to the old church he was willing to hear
its abuses condemned in the strongest language. In 1534 a
Friar William Airth preached at Dundee against the abuses
of cursing and of miracles, and the licentious lives of the
bishops. John Hepburn, Bishop of Brechin, having called him
a heretic for uttering such opinions, 'the Friar, impatient
of the injury received, passed to St. Andrews and did communicate the heads of his sermon with Master John Mair,
whose word then was holden as an oracle in matters of religion, and being assured of him that such doctrine might well
be defended, and that he would defend it, for it contained no
heresy, there was a day appointed for the said Friar to make
repetition of the sermon '. Airth accordingly re-delivered it in
the parish church, and amongst his hearers were Major and
the other heads of the University. The sermon was on the
text, 'Truth is the strongest of all things'. Knox gives its
substance, which was certainly bold enough, but as it touched
chiefly morals and not doctrine it might escape the charge of
heresy. 'One matter', says Knox, 'was judged harder, for he

alleged the common law, "That the Civil Magistrate might correct Churchmen and deprive them of their benefices for open vices ".'

It shows the critical moment the Reformation had reached in Britain that the same Friar, according to Knox, having escaped to England, was cast into prison by Henry VIII. for defence of the Pope. But Henry, as Buchanan tells us, was then intent on his own ends rather than purity of religion, ' burning men of opposite opinions at the same stake '.

Major at Knox's first Public Sermons.

Major was again present at a still more memorable occasion thirteen years later, in 1547, when Knox first preached in public at the earnest request of John Rough, Minister of St. Andrews, Sir David Lindsay, the poet, and Balnaves, a lawyer, one of the first Judges of the Court of Session. His text was from the seventh chapter of Daniel, 'And another King shall rise after them, and he shall be unlike unto the first, and he shall subdue three kings, and shall speak great words against the Most High, and shall consume the saints of the Most High, and think that he may change times and laws, and they shall be given into his hands until a time and times and dividing of times'.

After explaining the prophecy of the fall of the four empires—the Babylonian, Persian, Grecian, and Roman, he declared that on its destruction rose up that last beast, which he declared to be the Roman Church ; but before he began to open its corruptions he defined the true kirk as that which heard the voice of its own Pastor Christ, and would not listen to strangers. Then, grappling more closely than any preacher had yet done with the corruptions of Rome, ' he deciphered the lives of the Popes and of all shavelings for the most part, and proved their doctrine and laws to be contrary to those of God the Father and of Christ '. The reigning Pontiff, we should remember, was Alexander VI., ' that monster', to quote the just condemnation of Villari, whose enormities made even the

vices of Sixtus IV. to be forgotten. Knox's crucial instance of
false doctrine was the same as Luther's—'Justification by
works, pilgrimages, pardons, and other sic baggage, instead
of by faith through the blood of Christ which purgeth from
all sin.' Treating of the ecclesiastical law he condemned the
observance of days and abstinence from meats and marriage,
both of which Christ made free. He reached his climax by
quoting the claims alleged on behalf of the Pope, as 'That he
cannot err, can make wrong of right and right of wrong, and
can of nothing make somewhat'. Finally, he said, turning
from the congregation to the seats of honour, 'If any here
(and there were present Master John Mair, the Provost of the
University, the Sub-prior, and many Canons with some Priors
of both orders), will say that I have alleged Scripture doctrine
or history otherwise than it is written, let them come to me
with sufficient witness, and I, by conference, shall let them see
not only the original where my testimonies are written, but
prove that the writers meant as I have spoken.' Even this
daring language would apparently have passed unchallenged
had not Hamilton, the Archbishop-elect, written to Winram,
the Sub-prior, rebuking him for suffering it. A conference was
accordingly held, in which Winram disputed with Knox, but
left the brunt of the argument to a Friar Arbuckle, for
Winram himself already inclined to the reformed doctrines,
which he ultimately adopted.

Major and
the Scottish
Reformation.

To understand the position of Major, the representative of
a former generation brought face to face with the ideas and
events of the new era, when, in Scotland at least, Reform came
so quickly as almost to outstrip the Revival of Learning, we
must recal briefly the course of Scottish affairs from his return
to St. Andrews till his death.

St. Andrews was then, more than at any other time, a
political and religious centre; and, though himself inactive,
Major came constantly in contact with the chief actors

in the tragedies of which Scotland, not yet finally committed to the Roman or the Reformed Church, became the scene.

The young king, James v., whose tutor and playfellow had James v. been David Lyndsay of the Mount, whose father had chosen Erasmus as preceptor for his bastard half-brother, the Archbishop of St. Andrews, whose confessor, Seton, had imbibed some Reformed doctrines, whose uncle, Henry viii., had plied him with flattery and promises, wavered, like Francis i., between Rome and the Reformation. He gave signs that he might accept the latter. He set on foot a reform of the Cistercians, the richest and most corrupt of the older orders of Monks. He employed Buchanan to describe the hypocrisy which made even more odious the Franciscans, whose poverty and asceticism had sometimes become the cloak of a still more dangerous licence, threatening the family, and not merely the cloister, with corruption. He had at last succeeded in obtaining a portion of the exorbitant revenues of the Bishops for the foundation of a College of Justice, one of the most urgently needed reforms; for the Baronial and Ecclesiastical Courts rivalled each other in the delay, the cost, and often the denial of justice.

But other influences operating on the unstable mind of James prevailed. In 1534 Henry viii.'s divorce received the sanction of Parliament. Whoever, knowing the facts, judged it by any but a purely English standard must have begun to doubt whether good morals and justice were always on the side of the Reformers. One of its consequences was to put an end to the project of James's marriage to Mary Tudor, now disinherited. In 1535 he refused to meet his uncle on the English side of the Border, and in March of the following year a treaty of marriage was made between him and Mary de Bourbon, daughter of the Duke of Vendome. In winter he went to France, and, displeased with his proposed bride, pre-

h

ferred the delicate beauty of Madeleine, the daughter of Francis I.
The Scotch King was received by the French Court with the
honours usually paid only to the Dauphin, and the citizens
of Paris thronged to see him, and receive his largesse as he
passed through the streets of their beautiful capital. Madeleine
having died in midsummer 1537, an embassy, with David
Beaton, Bishop of Mirepoix, at its head, soon negotiated
another French alliance. The choice fell on Mary, daughter
of the Duke of Guise, widow of the Duke of Longueville. This
marriage, celebrated at St. Andrews in June 1538, finally decided the King in favour of the Roman Church. The family
of Guise was devoted to it. The uncle and brother of the
new Queen were Cardinals, and David Beaton secured the

Cardinal
Beaton.

same coveted dignity by promoting the match as Wolsey had
done by a similar service. Roman ecclesiastics of the worldly
type have always been promoters of politic marriages in the
interests of the Church. In 1539, soon after christening the
young prince, the first short-lived fruit of the marriage, in his
cathedral, James Beaton died. He had not been a favourite
with the King, who had even written to the Pope, complaining
of the aggrandizement of this obscure family, but he succeeded
in transferring or leaving his wide benefices to his kinsmen.
His nephew, David, already Abbot of Arbroath, became Archbishop; Dury, a cousin, Abbot of Dunfermline; and Hamilton,
another of his kin, Abbot of Kilwinning. David Beaton now
acquired complete ascendancy in the councils of the King.
He persuaded the clergy to the politic step of making James a
larger grant out of their revenues. As Archbishop he convened an assembly of nobles, prelates, and doctors of theology,
of whom Major was one, at St. Andrews, and pronounced an
oration against the danger to the Church from heretics who
professed their opinions openly even in the Court, where they
had found (he said) too great countenance. Sir George Borthwick, captain of Linlithgow, was condemned in absence for

denying the authority of the Pope and accepting the heresies of England, and his image was burnt in the Market Place of St. Andrews [1]. Henry VIII. made a last attempt to have a personal interview with his nephew, but Beaton's influence prevented it. A war ensued, in which the defeat of the Scotch under Oliver Sinclair at Solway Moss proved fatal to James, who sank under the blow, and died at Falkland on 14th December 1542, seven days after the birth of Mary Stuart. In spite of a will produced, it was alleged forged by Beaton, appointing him Regent, the Estates chose Arran as next heir to the Crown. Beaton was for a short time put in ward, but made terms with Arran, and became Chancellor in 1543. The failure of Henry's negotiations for the marriage of the infant Queen to his son Edward was followed by Hertford's ruthless raid, which revived the old hatred of the English throughout Scotland. On 1st March 1546 George Wishart was burnt before the gate of the Archbishop's castle at St. Andrews. Four other victims of humble birth had shortly before been executed at Perth. In less than three months, on 28th May, the Cardinal was murdered in his own castle by Norman Lesley and a small band of young men of good family from Fife, some of whom had private wrongs to revenge, but chiefly in retaliation for Wishart's death. Shutting themselves up in the castle, where they received supplies from England, and were joined by persons of like mind, amongst whom was John Knox, they were closely besieged by the Regent's forces, and compelled to agree to terms by which, on receipt of absolution from Rome, they were to surrender the castle. In the meantime the siege was raised, and the son of Arran given them as a hostage. It was during this critical interval that Knox preached the daring sermon at which Major was present. In the summer of 1547 the absolution arrived, but its terms were equivocal, and the besieged refused to accept it. In June, Strozzi, the French Admiral,

Murder of the Cardinal.

---

[1] May 1540.

arriving with a fleet, the siege was renewed. ' Cannons were
planted, some on the steeple of the Parish Church, some on
the tower of St. Salvator's, and some in the street that leads
to the, castle.' On 29th July a breach in the south wall
forced a capitulation. The besieged saved their lives, but
were sent to France as prisoners in the French galleys. The
death of Henry VIII. had prevented the coming of an English
fleet for their relief. Another raid by Hertford, now the Protector Somerset, followed, and the loss by the Scots of the
battle of Pinkie led to the infant Queen being sent to France
for safety. Supported by French troops the Scotch were able
to make head against the English, and recover the castles
which had been lost, and Scotland was made a party to the
French peace with England in April 1550. It was probably
shortly before its conclusion that Major died.

Death of
Major 1550.

Who can wonder that amid such scenes an old man who had
survived his generation held his peace. The flames kindled by
the Inquisition were being revenged by the dagger of the
assassin. Almost the last news he heard was that the Lamp
of the Lothians, the fine Church of Haddington, at whose
altars he had worshipped, had been burnt; almost the last
sight he saw was the flash of cannons on the Castle from the
tower of St. Salvator. On the one side stood the Church in
which he had been born and bred, the Queen Dowager, his
patrons the bishops, and most of his older friends both in
France and Scotland; on the other, his ablest pupils and an
increasing number of the Scottish people, both gentry and
burghers. For the one cause fought the French Monarch and
Court, whose brilliant corruption he must well have known;
for the other, the English king was defying the laws of his
own realm to carry out his will, while his generals were harrying, burning, bombarding the Scottish towns in a manner
which recalled the havoc of the wars of Edward I.

The Council of Trent just assembled evinced a desire to

reform the Church from within, and several Scottish bishops, notably Hamilton, the Prelate who succeeded Beaton, were ready to minimise the Roman doctrine and to remedy the most flagrant abuses.   To one who could brook a question upon the matter,—who did not see, as the Reformers did, in the Pope Antichrist, in Rome Babylon, in its doctrine idolatry, in its casuistry a root of moral corruption,—still more to one whose inveterate habit it was to argue everything from both sides, there might well seem room for hesitation, for delay, for choosing the older as the safer path.   Behind the external tumult, to one who was a theologian and philosopher, living in the world of thought more than of action, there were arrayed on the side of Rome, once its premisses were accepted, the forces of Logic and Casuistry, for which he had the affection the adept feels for the weapons of his own craft.

There was also the terror of the stake ; for, after all, most men are human.   Martyrs are amongst the smallest of minorities in the human race.   During the preceding centuries persecution had all but extinguished the doctrines of Wycliffe and of Huss.   Even after the revival of learning had borne its natural fruit in the decay of superstition, it arrested the Reformation in Italy and Spain and the greater part of France. *Character of Major.*

The life whose course from such materials as exist we have followed was not that of a hero or a martyr.   But if the character and conduct of Major have been rightly interpreted they have value of their own not to be overlooked.   They bring vividly before us the Scottish man of learning as he was in this perilous age, when new ideas and a new faith were clashing with the old not merely in the field of argument but by fire and sword.

Major the lifelong student, and devoted professor, who preferred, as he himself says, 'to teach rather than to preach'; fond of his books ; fond of music as the relaxation, and of argument as the business, of his life, but fond also of his pupils *Major and Knox compared.*

and his country, did what lay within his capacity to improve his pupils and inform his countrymen.   But it was beyond his power to reform his age by the potent words, and unflinching courage, which in spite of grave errors make most of his countrymen reverence, and impartial judges of other nations respect, the name of John Knox.   The deeper, stronger work of the Reformer has, as it deserved, lasted longer than the work of his master the Schoolman.   Even when that part of it which is dogmatic has been superseded, that part of it which is moral will continue, for it rests near the foundations of social and religious life, while that part of it which is national will always remain an integral and crucial chapter in Scottish History.   The philosophy and the theology of Major served for his generation only, quickened the thoughts of some of his students by attraction, and of others by repulsion, and then quietly sank into oblivion.   Only a stray passage here and there has been brought to light in modern times by the diligent investigator of the progress of European thought or as an aid to the understanding of his character.

Character o
Major's
History.

'Habent sua fata libelli.'   The short history which he probably valued least of all his works has had a longer life. It was reprinted in the last century by Freebairn, and has always been favourably known to students of Scottish History. In the hope that it may reach a still wider circle, the History is now for the first time translated by Mr. Constable, a task rendered difficult from its terse and occasionally abrupt style, but accomplished through familiarity with Major's thoughts, acquired by a prolonged and patient study of his writings and character.   An estimate of its chief characteristics has already been given in this sketch of the life of the author.   It is not a history to read for new information.   History is a progressive branch of knowledge.   Much more is known now than Major knew of our ancient annals.   But his work will always be interesting as the first History of Scotland written in a critical and judicial spirit, and as presenting the view of that history in its past course and future tendency taken by a scholar of the sixteenth century, who, though he halted in the old theology, was so far as history is concerned singularly far-sighted and fair. Such qualities are not even yet so common amongst historians that we can afford to neglect an early example of their exercise. Æ. M.

APPENDIX TO THE LIFE.

I.—NOTICES OF JOHN MAJOR IN FRENCH AND SCOTTISH RECORDS.

Note.—I am indebted to Monsieur Chatelain of the Sorbonne for an exact copy of the references to Major in the ' Liber Receptoris Nationis Alamanie,' which has been preserved for the years 1494 to 1501. Mr. J. Maitland Anderson, the Librarian of the University of St. Andrews, has done a similar service by making a careful excerpt of all entries relating to Major in the Records of that University. The references to the offices he held in the University of Glasgow have been taken from the printed volume of its Munimenta.

Æ. M.

(1.) *University of Paris.*

Archives de l'Université de Paris. Registre 85.
' Liber Receptoris Nationis Alamanie.'

(Anno 1494).—Sequuntur nomina licentiatorum huius anni.

Johannes Maior dyoc. sanct. Andree, bursa valet 4 sol. 1 lib.

(Anno 1495).—Inter nomina incipientium huius anni :

Dns Johannes Mair dioc. sce Andree cujus bursa valet 4^{or} sol. i. lib. pro jocundo adventu et cappa rectoris. . . . ii. lib.

(At the end of the year 1498, following upon the accounts of the Receiver, *i.e.* ' Robertus Valterson, dioc. S. Andree,' may be seen the signature of the *procureur*, who thus vouched for the Receiver's statement of accounts :—)

Ita est,
Johannes H. Maior.

Anno dominice incarnationis 1501 coadunata fuit Germanorum natio apud edem divi Mathurini ad decem klas octobres super novi *receptoris* electione, ubi pacatissime ut putatur, deo inspirante, delectus fuit magister *Johannes Mair gleguocensis diocesis sanct. Andre.* Qui et receptas et impensas ea serie qua sequitur ut cumque executus est.

The Receiver who succeeded Major, ' Mag. Christianus Hermanni,' was elected in 1502 ' in vigilia Sanct. Mathei.'

A° 1506. Lic. (in theol.) Johannes Major, Scotus, de collegio Montano. Ordo Lic. 55 (Bibl. Nat. MS. No. 15440).

[v. Budinsky : Die Universität Paris, 1876, p. 91.]

(2.) *University of Glasgow.*

COPY of a letter of Exemption from Taxation granted by James v. to the University of Glasgow, confirming prior exemption. 20 May 1522.

This letter is said to have been obtained at their own expense 'per venerabilem virum Magistrum Jacobum Steward prepositum ecclesie collegiate de Dunbertane ac Rectorem Johannem Majorem theologie professorem thesaurarium capelle regie Striuilingensis vicariumque de Dunlop ac principalem regentem Pedagogij Glasguensis.' *Munimenta Alme Universitatis Glasguensis,* I. p. 47.

GENERAL Congregation of the University, 3d November 1518.

Amongst others incorporated by the Rector, Adam Colquhoun, Canon of Glasgow, was 'Egregius vir Magister Johannes Major, doctor Parisiensis ac principalis regens collegii et pedagogii dicte universitatis canonicusque capelle regie ac vicarius de Dunlop.' *Ibid.* II. p. 133.

GENERAL Congregation of the University of Glasgow on 24th May 1522, under the presidency of James Stewart, Provost of the Collegiate Church of Dumbarton, and Rector of the University, and John Major being present, who is described as Professor of Theology, Treasurer of the Chapel Royal of Stirling, Vicar of Dunlop and Principal Regent.

The Rector explained the privileges of the University with reference to exemption from taxation. On the same day Major was appointed one of the auditors of the Accounts of the Foundation of David de Caidyow for a chaplaincy at the altar of the Virgin in the Cathedral. *Ibid.* II. pp. 134, 144. *Ibid.* p. 143.

AT a General Congregation of the University at the Feast of Saints Crispin and Crispinian, 1522, for the election of a new Rector.

John Major was one of the three 'intrantes' who continued James Steward in the office. *Ibid.* II. 147.

PRESENTATION by James v. of Treasurership of Chapel Royal, dated 1st June 1520, in favour of Mr. Andrew Durie in view of the resignation of John Mair, Professor of Theology and last Treasurer. Register of the Privy Seal, lib. v. fol. 144. *See* History of the Chapel Royal—Grampian Club, p. liv. 57-98.

(3.) *University of St. Andrews.*

[*Maioris—Mayr—Maior—Major* used interchangeably. Usually declined according to the context, *Maioris, Maiorem, Maiore.*]

[ACTA RECTORUM.]

1523, June 9.   Incorporated. [Entry as in Irving's Buchanan.]

1523, Jan. 17.   Elected one of the deputies to visit St. Salvator's College. [Entry as in Irving's Buchanan.]

1524, Nov. 7.   One of the Auditors of the Accounts of the Quaestor of the Faculty of Arts for the year 1523-24.

1524, Feb. last.   Elected one of the Rector's Assessors and Deputies.

1525, Jan. 22.   Elected one of the Deputies to visit St. Salvator's College.

1532, Feb. last.   Elected one of the Rector's Assessors and Deputies.

1533, Jan. 15.   Elected one of the Deputies to visit St. Salvator's College.

1534, Feb. penult.   Elected one of the Rector's Assessors and Deputies.

He was further elected to the same posts on the last day of February 1536 ; April 30, 1539 ; March 2, 1539 ; March 1, 1540.

Elected one of the Rector's Assessors on the last day of February 1541, 1542 ; one of the Rector's Assessors and Deputies on the last day of February 1543 ; and (?) 1544.

1545.   There was elected as one of the Assessors, ' Petrum Capellanj Domus Saluatoris Prefectj Coadiutorem.'

The *Assessors* were appointed ' ad assistendum eidem domino rectorj et eidem consiliendum.'
The *Deputies* were appointed ' ad exercendum rectoris officium in eius absencia.'

[ACTA FACULTATIS ARTIUM UNIV. ST. AND.].

1523, Nov. 3.   Elected one of the Dean's Assessors [I.M. *Canonicum* capelle regie Stirlingensis].

Mar. 19.   Elected one of the Dean's Assessors [I.M. *Thesaurarius* capelle regie Stirlingensis].

1524, Nov. 3.   Elected one of the Dean's Assessors [I.M. *Thesaurarius* capelle regie Stirlingensis].

1525, Mar. 4.   Named as one of the Dean's Assessors [I.M. *Thesaurarius* capelle regie Stirlingensis].

Elected one of the Dean's Assessors [I.M. *Thesaurarius* capelle regie
Stirlingensis].   Apr. 8.
Elected one of the Dean's Assessors [I.M. *Thesaurarius* capelle regie
Stirlingensis].   Nov. 3.
Elected one of the Dean's Assessors [I.M. only].   1531, Nov. 3.
Elected one of the Dean's Assessors [I.M. vicarius dunloppij successor
prefecti collegij Sancti Saluatoris].   1533, Nov. 4.

Elected one of the Dean's Assessors [I.M. prefecti Coll. Sti. Salu.].				1534, Nov. 3.
Elected	do.	do.	do.	1535, Nov. 3.
Elected	do.	do.	do.	1537, Nov. 3.
Named as	do.	do.	do.	Nov. 10,
Elected	‾ do.	do.	do.	1538, Feb. 1.

REGISTER OF DOCUMENTS CONNECTED WITH ST. SALVATOR'S COLLEGE.

'Maister Jhon Mayr' is first mentioned as 'Prowest of the College,' 1536, May 3.
on February 1536, and other references to him as ' Prepositus Coll.
Eccles. S. Salvatoris' occur on the following dates: 1540, Feb. 25 ;
1539, Jan. 9 ; 1542, May 31 ; 1544, Aug. 3, Apr. 29, Apr. 30, May 1,
May 2 ; 1543, Apr. 13, Apr. 18 ; 1535, Feb. 15. None of these entries
throw any light on Major's personal history, with the exception of that
under Jan. 9, 1539. This is a charter granted by Major in conjunction
with William Manderston, founding a chaplaincy or bursary (Capel-
lania seu Bursa) in S. Sal. College (with power to the Rector and his
Assessors to transfer it to St. Mary's College)—the holder to celebrate
Masses for the souls of the founders and their relations, James v. and
Mary his Queen, Cardinal Beaton, etc. The endowment consisted mainly
of annual rents of tenements in South Street, St. Andrews.

EXTRACTS FROM THE ACTA RECTORUM UNIV. ST. ANDREÆ.

CURIA tenta per venerabilem et egregium virum magistrum alex- 1540, June 15.
andrum balfowr rectorem de Longcardy vicarium de Kilmany
almeque vniuersitatis sancti Andree rectorem In capella beate
Marie uirginis infra claustrum collegij sancti saluatoris situata
martis decimoquinto Iunij In anno domini Jaj vᶜ. xlmo.

In causa exactionum recusatoriorum fore declinatoriarum implice
duplice et triplice venerabilis et egregij virj magistri nostri magistri
Johannis maioris prepositj collegij sancti saluatoris et domini Johannis

II.

NOTE ON THE SCHOOL OF THE TERMINISTS TO
WHICH JOHN MAJOR BELONGED. CHIEFLY FROM
Dr. CARL PRANTL, *Geschichte der Logik*, Band IV. Leipzig, 1870.

THE series of Terminist Scotists commenced with Nicholas Tinctor[1],
who was followed by Pardus[2] and Bricot[3]. A pupil of Pardus and
of Bricot, John Major taught at Paris in the college of Montaigu,
was an extremely fertile writer, collected numerous scholars round
him and excited them to literary activity. While we must refrain
from referring to his Commentaries on Peter Lombard and the
physical and ethical writings of Aristotle, we find a number of
smaller or greater works by him on Logic in which he frequently
treated the same subject in new editions. He edited an edition
of the Commentary of John Dorp[4] on Buridan[5], to which it is

---

[1] Prantl, iv. p. 198, 199. Tinctor published a Commentary on the *Summulæ*
of Petrus Hispanus, which is expressly designed on the title-page as '*Secundum
Subtilissimi doctoris Johannis Scoti viam compilatum*,' and a later work, in which
he is described as a follower of Thomas Aquinas, is only according to Prantl (note
117) 'a bookseller's puff or advertisement'.

[2] Hieronymus or Jerome Pardus, a lecturer on Logic of the school called by
Prantl 'Terminist Scotists.' His *Medulla dyalectices*, 1505, edited by Major
and Jacobus Ortiz, is his only known work.—Prantl, iv. p. 246.

[3] Thomas Bricot, who published alone or in collaboration with George of
Brussels several logical tracts between 1492-1505.—Prantl, iv. p. 199.

[4] John Dorp's Commentary was first published at Venice 1499, and twice by
Major, Paris 1504, folio, and Lyons 1510, quarto. At the close of the latter
edition Dorp is called 'verus nominalium opinionum recitator'.—Prantl, iv.
p. 237, note 357.

[5] John Buridan, who died not before 1358, was one of the earliest Nominalists,
and following Ockham declares Theological Dogma and Philosophy to be incom-
mensurable. 'Metaphysics differs from Theology in this, that while both treat
of God and Divine Things Metaphysics does not consider God and Divine Things
except in so far as they can be proved and concluded or induced by demonstrative reasons. Theology, on the other hand, holds certain articles of belief as
principles without evidence, and considers further what can be deduced from
such articles.'—Prantl, iv. p. 15, note 58.

unnecessary further to refer, as he added to Dorp only some short marginal notes. But in addition he composed several treatises which were collected and printed more or less completely, some of them as Commentaries on Petrus Hispanus, and others Lectures he gave in the Faculty of Arts (Libri quos in artibus emisit). At a later date he collected the Logic of Aristotle and the Summulæ of Petrus Hispanus in an *Introductorium,* and finally he added *Questiones* with reference to the old Logic (*Vetus Ars*).

If we first confine ourselves to the order of the collective edition, we find it commences with a treatise *De complexo significabili,* in which he gives, like his master Pardus in his *Medulla,* an affirmative answer to the question as to the existence of complex terms. Then follow two *Libri Terminorum,* in the first of which, after fixing the logical meaning of the word Term, almost all possible divisions of the Term are discussed by means of doubts and their solutions, and in the second book the same subject is treated in somewhat altered order, after which he places *Abbreviationes Parvorum Logicalium*[1]. Next follow the *Summulæ,* that is, a commentary on Petrus Hispanus, where we find in the introduction a reference to Gerson's utterances on the use of logic, and also a ridiculous play of letters with the word *Summulæ.* The contents of this part are a commentary on the first four tracts of Petrus Hispanus, where at the close of the doctrine of Judgment (following Bricot)[2] there is a special explanation of the term *Contingent,* and of the question current since Buridan wrote as to the variation of the middle term[3]. Besides, the subject of the divisions of the Term is again examined, with reference to the views of Marsilius[4], and at the close of the Categories a Tree of the Predicaments is added. In treating of the Syllogism Major repudiates the Fourth Figure as an unnecessary multiplication more sharply than earlier writers. He adduces, like his teacher Pardus, sophistical examples for each Mood. The Topics and the refutation of Fallacies he treats summarily, because especially in the first there is much unnecessary matter.

---

[1] The *Parva Logicalia* were topics which were not treated specially by Aristotle, but deduced by minor authors from passages in his works.—Prantl, iv. p. 204, note 153.

[2] Prantl, iv. p. 203.   [3] Prantl, iv. p. 34.

[4] Not Marsilius of Padua but of Inghen (d. 1396), a leading Professor of Logic at Heidelberg, whose writings are very voluminous, and in general follow Ockham, Buridan, and other Nominalists though with some variations.—Prantl, iv. pp. 94-102.

A second division of the work begins with the *Exponibilia* [1] in which there is nothing new, for he follows Paulus Venetus [2] and Petrus Mantuanus [3]. Then follow the *Insolubilia*, with reference to which the statement of the principles of others affords the chief interest, for in this part also he follows the explanations of Paulus Venetus. The Commentary added to the second Analytic appears in an improper place and calls for no special remark. We have this portion of the work not from the hand of Major but of his pupil Coronel. The *Parva Logicalia* follow in six tracts, from which we learn that they were reckoned a part of the *Vetus Logica* [4] while the *Consequentia* and *Exponibilia* were deemed to belong to the *Nova Logica*.

The contents of this part consists of a controversial exposition of Petrus Hispanus with frequent use of Peter of Mantua and George of Brussels. Finally there is inserted a concise exposition of the *Obligatoria* [5] and *Argumenta Sophistica*, in which we notice a disposition to contest every proposition sophistically, and in addition a monograph on *the Infinite* in which all possible sophisms which belong to this subject are examined. After what has been said it is not necessary to examine in detail the two last-named writings of Major on Logic, for in the *Introductorium* he merely repeats what he had written before, and the *Quæstiones* are only a commentary of the usual kind on the *Vetus Ars* in the sense of the Terminists.

Among the scholars of Major may be named first *David Cranston* of Glasgow, who taught in Paris, and wrote a treatise on *Insolubilia* and *Obligatoria*. As to the first of these, he proceeds

---

[1] The *Exponibilia* were certain words of frequent occurrence in propositions which required to be expounded to avoid ambiguity and sophisms.

[2] Paulus Venetus (d. 1428) is treated at length by Prantl (iv. pp. 118, 140), who considers his writings as marking the most extreme growth of the Scholastic Logic. He commented on the Physics, Ethics, as well as on the Logic of Aristotle.

[3] Petrus . Mantuanus, a Logician of the Terminist School, published *circa* 1483.—Prantl, iv. p. 176.

[4] The Vetus Logica or Ars was not the older logic in point of time but that which treated of the remoter or less immediate parts of logic, while the Nova Logica treated of the Syllogisms and its parts and forms.—Prantl, iv. p. 176, note 9.

[5] The Obligatoria was the division of Logic which dealt with disputation. The disputant was obliged either to maintain (sustinere) or reject (desustinere) or to doubt (dubitare) the proposition advanced. Hence the doctrine of Obligations was divided into ' Positio' ' Depositio' and ' Dubitatio.'—Prantl, iv. p. 41.

from a statement of the various opinions of others to his own attempt to treat the *Insolubilia*[1] in accordance with the generally accepted rules of Logic. . . . With the *Obligatoria* he adopts, in comparison with Major, a somewhat modified division of the *Term*, where, for the first time, we meet with an express application of the different sorts of opposition to the doctrine of Concepts. From the same school came *Antony Coronel of Segovia*, a very fertile writer, who wrote a Commentary on the Categories, an Exposition of the doctrine of Judgments and the properties of Terms, under the title of *Rosarium*, an Explanation of the Posterior Analytics of Aristotle, and a monograph on *Exponibilia* and *Fallaciae*. He also revised and completed a tract of his master, Major, on *Consequentia*. . . . A second Spaniard bred in the school of Major was *Caspar Lax*. Of his three works, namely *Termini, Obligationes*, and *Insolubilia*, the first is merely a repetition of what Major had taught on this subject. The high self-esteem which the Terminists of the school of Major had reached is shown in a letter of a friend of Lax, Antony Alcaris, which is printed in the treatise of *Obligationes*. In this the 'clear, perspicuous, useful, sweet, and splendid' dissertations of the Modern are contrasted with the 'languid, arid, jejune, obscure, and little pleasing' works of the Ancient Philosophers. . . . Another scholar of Major was *Johannes Dullart* from Ghent, who wrote *Quæstiones* on the Categories and a treatise on the *De Interpretatione* of Aristotle, in which he shows extensive reading, and his decided partisanship with the Terminists. . . . A fellow-scholar of the last-mentioned writer was the Scotchman, *Robert Caubraith. William Manderston*, also a Scotchman, and several other Spaniards of minor note, are described as belonging to the same school.

The reader who desires to follow the intricacies of the mediæval logic must refer for further details to Prantl's exhaustive and learned work.[2] But for the sake of those who may wish to form a general idea of the distinction between the *Antiqui* or *Reales* and the *Moderni* or *Nominales*, and of the position of the Terminists,

---

[1] The Insolubilia were divided into three modes—(1) Those which could not be solved in any way ; (2) those which could not be solved because of some impediment ; and (3) those which were difficult to solve. As example of the first was given an invisible sound, of the second a stone hidden in the earth, and of the third an invisible sun.—Prantl, iv. p. 40, note 158.

[2] Prantl, iv. p. 174, points out that at the close of the fifteenth century the Terminists were the majority, though denounced by the orthodox Thomists.

as the school of which Major was a leader was called, we borrow from the same writer the following passages :—

'We first notice a continuation of the earlier tendencies in Logic until the year 1472, when we find the definition of the Party differences followed by a development through the Terminist Scotism, which was opposed by a preponderating conservative Thomism. From about the period 1480-1520 (*i.e.* practically Major's period) a long series of the now reigning school of the Terminists appears.' . . .[1] If we direct our attention to Paris, it is easily to be understood that in the Sorbonne only the elder views were permitted. On the other hand, the University had actively participated in the gradual development of the various new opinions, and had even accepted the views of the Terminists. But in 1473, in consequence of the intrigues of John Boucard, assisted by a former Sorbonnist, Johannes A Lapide, the Moderns had been placed under a bann, and their works in the Library had even been chained, so that they could not be read. The doctors called *Nominales* were those who on principle attached extreme importance to the properties of Terms, including the doctrines of *Insolubilia, Obligationes, Consequentia*, while the Realists applied themselves to things and despised the doctrine of Terms [2]. The dispute was therefore, in the first place, one as to the method of Logic, and only in the second place concerned with the metaphysical question as to Universals, with reference to which the Terminists claimed for themselves the praise of strict orthodoxy. In the year 1481 the Royal Edict against the Nominalists was rescinded, and their books were again allowed to be read.

At the time therefore that Major came to the University the Nominalist doctrine had resumed its popularity all the more because of the persecution which it had suffered, and Major's own masters in Logic, Thomas Bricot[3] and Jerome Pardus[4], both belonged to it. The subtleties and sophistries which the new Nominal logic of the Terminists in the hands of Major and his followers ultimately led to, as exemplified in Prantl's extracts from their works, largely justified the contempt which Buchanan and other disciples of the Renaissance bestowed on it. But none

---

[1] Prantl, iv. p. 186.

[2] It was with reference to this distinction, perhaps, that Erasmus stated his apophthegm which appears to contain the truth of the matter : ' Cognitio verborum prior est, cognitio rerum potior est,' though that apophthegm has a wider application than the merely logical controversy of the Schools.

[3] Prantl, iv. p. 199.   [4] *Ibid.* p. 246.

the less was this stage in logical doctrine an attempt to clear the meaning of words from dubiety in the same line which William of Ockham formerly, and Hobbes and Locke subsequently, followed. It was also, as has been generally recognised by historians of philosophy, both through its merits and demerits, one of the causes which led to the dissolution of the Scholastic Philosophy. That Major belonged to this school in Logic (for though he made an attempt to reconcile the Realists and Nominalists, it was, as we have seen, by assuming the principles of the latter) reacted on his philosophical position, and made him incline to the views of Ockham, the works of two of whose followers he edited. But in Theology he claimed to be and was strictly orthodox, and ends several of his theological treatises with the usual formula, that he submitted all he taught to the Church and the Theological Faculty of Paris.

It is proper to keep in view that he was also a Scotist, and promoted the publication of the *Reportata*, an abridgment of the Parisian Lectures of the Doctor Subtilis. Both the followers of Thomas Aquinas and Duns Scotus claimed to be orthodox, and that their philosophy kept within the limits which the Church allowed to the Schools. Perhaps the Scotists were even more vehement than the Nominalists in the assertion of the soundness of their Theological Doctrine, in order to allay suspicions. But the Roman Church, as if by natural instinct, and the historians of philosophy who have regarded the subject from an external standpoint, concur in regarding Aquinas and not Duns as its true champion among philosophers. Scotism is now almost dead, and the present Pope is doing his best to revive the study of Aquinas. But important as Thomas Aquinas is in the history of philosophy, the attempt to restore his old authority as the Master of Philosophy in the nineteenth century is a hopeless attempt. Scholasticism in any form is now impossible.

The Terminists, as the School to which Major belonged was styled, in some respects occupied an intermediate position between the Scotists and Thomists, the Nominalists and the Realists, but with a decided leaning to the former; and Major is frequently claimed by historians of philosophy, as by Tennemann[1] and

---

[1] Bohn's Translation of Tennemann's History of Philosophy, p. 241. Ueberweg does not mention Major by name, but reckons amongst the Nominalists who followed Ockham in the fourteenth and fifteenth century several of his masters: ' John Buridan, Rector of the University of Paris, of importance because of his

Prantl[1], as a Scotist and Nominalist. It was natural that Major should adopt this school. He claimed Duns Scotus as his country-man, for he had no more doubt of Duns's Scottish than Wadding in the following century had of his Irish origin. His chief masters were Franciscans, who believed in Duns Scotus as a member of their own order. And he came to Paris at a time when the Nominalist development of Scotism was the reigning philosophy in the university.

Similar causes led him to adopt (following Ockham, Gerson, and D'Ailly) the anti-papal position of the Gallican Church.

The Franciscans, speaking generally, for there were exceptions, opposed the absolute claims of the Ultramontane Italian Popes. Their doctrine of Evangelical Poverty cut at the roots, as has been well pointed out by Mr. Owen[2], both of the temporal power of the Pope and the excessive wealth of the prelates and some of the ecclesiastical orders. No one accepted more completely than Major this doctrine. Indeed most, though not all, of his opinions which appear to us bold and anti-papal may be traced to this source. In his writings we constantly come across passages which appear to be copied almost word for word from the works of Ockham or of Gerson. It is because of this that he may be considered, as Ockham has also been, an unconscious precursor of the Reformation in spite of his resting finally in all questions of Faith in rigidly orthodox conclusions.

Nor can we overlook the fact that, like so many other Schoolmen, the method he adopted of arguing all questions on two sides, the Yes and No method as it has been styled,—the doubts which he raised and by no means always solved, and the habit of leaving

---

examination of the Freedom of the Will and his Logical works; Marsilius of Inghen; Peter D'Ailly, who while defending the Church Doctrine yet gave the preference to the Bible above Tradition, and the Council above the Pope; and John Gerson, D'Ailly's scholar and friend, who combined Mysticism with Scholas-ticism.'—*Geschichte der Philosophie*, ii. p. 215. In an instructive passage, too long to quote, he compares Duns Scotus with Kant, and shows how the critical tendency begun by Duns was carried further by Ockham and the Nominalists, ii. p. 204.

[1] Prantl treats Major throughout (iv. p. 247 *et seq.*) as belonging to the Scotist Terminist or Terminist Scotist School.

[2] Dr. Karl Werner, who writes from the Roman point of view, coincides with Mr. Owen on this point, and remarks that Ockham's opposition to the Papacy turned on the dispute raised by the Franciscan zealots as to the vow of purity.— *Die nachscotistische Skolastik*, Wien 1883, p. 17.

many points to the judgment of his readers, had, what Mr. Owen has called, with reference to the greater names amongst the Scholastics, a skeptical tendency. It is possible to exaggerate this tendency, but it is impossible to deny its existence. He followed Duns Scotus too in submitting all authority, even the authority of the Church in philosophical matters, and especially in the practical and moral department of conduct, to the test of reason and justice. This it is which has caused the 'Subtle Doctor' to be looked upon with suspicion by the Church, and to be regarded by historians of philosophy as the first great dissolvent of the older orthodox scholasticism. Major and the Terminists were less bold in philosophising than Duns, less bold in action than Ockham, but not the less did their writings and the opinions they introduced tend in the same direction. It was no accident which led Major to direct the republication of the Lectures of Duns at Paris and the logical treatises of the disciples of Ockham.

Prantl, to whom we are indebted for the substance of most of this note, but who must not be held responsible for the view taken in it, remarks in the Preface to his fourth volume, after having made a thorough examination of every known work of the logicians of the later period of scholastic logic, that to describe even useless works is not in itself useless if it saves others from a like labour. But this is a too modest under-estimate of his own valuable labours and of the writings of the Schoolmen.

Their method and philosophy were not a mere marking of time, or a retrogression. It is true they were not great original thinkers like the chief masters of Greek or Modern Philosophy. But they conducted a progressive process—a disputation, to use a word which would have been more familiar to them—between Dogmatic Theology, Ancient Philosophy, and Mediæval Thought, which was necessary to the mental development of Europe. 'Mens agitat molem et inter se corpora miscet.' In this development Major took a minor but a distinct part, as will be acknowledged the more his writings are studied with the attention directed, neither to their form, which is thoroughly scholastic, nor to their explicit conclusions, which are completely dogmatic and orthodox, but to their 'obiter dicta' and ultimate tendency.

It was even, we may venture to say, this tendency, which had more free play when he came to write history, that gave its critical, practical, and independent character to his historical work ; for the thoughts of such a man in the ages of Scholasticism were not disconnected, but pervaded by the same method to whatever subject he turned them. This consideration may also justify the length of the present note in a work primarily concerned only with Major as a historian and not as a philosopher.

.Æ. M.

HISTORIA MAIORIS BRITANNIÆ
TAM ANGLIÆ QUAM SCOTIÆ, PER
IOANNEM MAIOREM, NOMINE QUIDEM
SCOTUM, PROFESSIONE AUTEM THEO-
LOGUM, E VETERUM MONUMENTIS
CONCINNATA

PREFACE

To him who is illustrious at once for his most admirable
natural endowment and for his most lofty descent in
the line of both kingdoms of Greater Britain, to James
the Fifth, King of Scots,

John, Major by name, Scot by nation, theologian of the
university of Paris by profession, with prayers for his
prosperity, offers the homage that is due to his King.

In commencement of this narration of the glorious deeds of
your ancestors, of those men who have been our kings and
princes from the cradle of history even to this present,
and in the dedication of that work to your name of most
fortunate omen, Fifth James, King of Scots, of happiest birth,
from whom too we all of us hope the best and greatest things,
I have thought right to undertake the clearing of three points
and their defence from misrepresentation. This the first, that,
as almost all men say, contrary to the habitude of the old
historians, I seek a patron for this my small lucubration ;
secondly, that I, a theologian by profession, should write a
history ; and thirdly, that I use a style more congruous to a
theologian than to a historian.

For removal accordingly of the first objection, and for my
justification in the eyes of those who pretend that it is not
fitting to dedicate a historical work to any person, seeing that
he who seeks for a patron must put on the mask of a
flatterer rather than that of a historian, whose first law it is
to write the truth ; all that these objectors urge in support
of their contention is this : that neither Sallust, nor Livy,
nor any one of the ancients made dedication of his works. I
frankly confess that I have never read any dedication made by
them, whether because they observed no such use, or because

these have come to be lost in lapse of time, as has befallen so many other things. Sallust, indeed, had no occasion to dedicate his work, since in his day the Romans were as yet without kings; and Livy perchance had no wish to take this course, thinking it more glorious to accomplish for the gods and for posterity all that mighty work of his than to inscribe the same to any mortal man. But the poets almost all of them, although themselves too have written histories, dedicated their poems to princes; and Valerius Maximus, when he was about to narrate the memorable achievements not only of his own race but of foreign nations likewise, makes his address to Caesar. Our own Jerome likewise, when he was setting himself to translate both profane and sacred histories, was not silent as to the person to whom he would dedicate his work. Augustine did the same, and that writer, whom, though he be one of ourselves, I yet reckon to be no way contemptible, but venerable rather—I mean Bede[1],—and almost all the rest of the ecclesiastical historians. For which reason, seeing that to your Highness and to your ancestors we owe all that we have, I think it right and proper to dedicate this work now undertaken to the same. Yet lest my work should contain any suspicion of flattery, I have left untouched, to be dealt with by other hands, matters of most recent date.

From that second objection, that it is not becoming in a theologian to write history, I utterly dissent. For if it is the special province of a theologian to lay down definitions in regard to faith, and religion, and morals, I will not believe that I transgress when I narrate not only what has come to pass, or by whose counsel such and such matters were carried, but if I also make distinct definition whether these matters were carried rightly or wrongly. And, indeed, I have given my utmost endeavour to follow this course in all cases, and most of all where the question was ambiguous, to the end that from the reading of this history you may learn not only the thing that was done, but also how it ought to

---

[1] Orig. 'et licet nostras non contemnendus auctor, immo venerabilis, Beda';
F. 'et licet nostras non contemnendus auctor, immo Venerabilis Beda'. The punctuation of the original seems to give a more graceful sense.

have been done, and that you may by this means and at the cost of little reading come to know what the experience of centuries, if it were granted to you to live so long, could scarcely teach.

I proceed to the consideration of the third objection. I confess that I might have used a more cultivated style; I question if that style would have been more convenient. For if one should give what would be almost a Latin turn to the names of our own people and places, scarcely should we that were born in Scotland understand what was meant. And inasmuch as our princes have ever aimed rather to act nobly than to speak elegantly, so with those who have given themselves to the pursuit of knowledge it is of more moment to understand aright, and clearly to lay down the truth of any matter, than to use elegant and highly-coloured language. I call to witness two most famous Scots—who bore each of them the name of John[1]—and Bede, and Alcuin[2], and a hundred more[3], who, when they first learned Greek and Latin, chose rather so to write that they needed not an interpreter than with a curious research of language.

This then, most gracious King, is what I held it right to say in behalf of the work which I have undertaken. Accept the same, I pray, with favour. May you read to good purpose this history of your ancestors now dedicated to your felicity, and may you live happy to the years of Nestor!

From the worthy and no way ignoble college of Montaigu at Paris.

---

[1] *i.e.* John Scotus Erigena and John Duns Scotus. See *infra*, pp. 101, 113, 206, 228-230.

[2] See *infra*, p. 102.

[3] 'et sexcenti alii'. 'Sexaginta' was used by the Romans for any large number, and 'sexcenti' was often used to express an immense and indefinite number. A contemporary use of the phrase will be found in Erasmus, *Paraclesis* (ed. 1520, p. 192—of the 'regula' of Christ as compared with the 'regula Francis-cana'): Denique qua (ut sexcentas etiam addas) nulla possit esse sanctior?' An instructive series of examples in which the vague use by our early historians of 60,000 led to long-lasting misconceptions will be found in an article by Mr. J. H. Round on 'The Introduction of Knight Service into England' in *The English Historical Review* for October 1891.

A HISTORY
OF GREATER BRITAIN

BOOK I.

CHAP. I.—*A short Preface by John Major, theologian of Paris, and Scotsman by birth, to his work concerning the rise and gests of the Britons. Likewise concerning the name and the first inhabitants of Greater Britain*[1].

IN few words, and in the manner almost of the theologians, I am about to write an account of Britain, by far the most famous of islands, and one which, in the opinion of illustrious writers, may be reckoned even by itself as a second world. I shall treat first of the reason of its name, then in general terms of the kingdoms of which it is composed, and last of all I shall deal at length with those kingdoms and their special history. Our ancestors called Britain by the name of Albion. Of the origin of this name Caxton, the English chronicler, gives the following visionary[2] account: There was a certain king of Syria, by name Diocletian, to whom his wife, Labana, bore three-and-thirty daughters. Of these the eldest was called Albine. The king gave his daughters in marriage to three-and-thirty princes of his kingdom; but they despised their husbands, and in one night slew them every one. The

Britain called Albion.

---

[1] 'Greater Britain'. The phrase 'Britannia Major' is not common; but it was used, a little later, in the title of Bale's *Illustrium Maioris Britanniæ Scriptorum, hoc est, Angliæ, Cambriæ, ac Scotiæ Summarium*, Ipswich 1548. In the edition of 1557-1559, printed at Basel, the title is *Scriptorum Illustrium Majoris Britanniæ, quam nunc Angliam et Scotiam vocant, Catalogus*. On the other hand, the editor of Ptolemy's Geography (Strassburg, 1522) applies the words to England alone: 'Britania maior cui nomen est Anglia'. Geoffrey of Monmouth's History, printed in 1508 by Badius Ascensius, the printer of Major's History, has the title *Britanniæ utriusque Regum et Principum origo et gesta*. 'Britannia minor' and 'parva Britannia' are in frequent use to designate Aremorica or Armorica—which we now call Brittany.

[2] 'somniculosam'. Camden, *Brit*. ed. 1600, p. 88, uses the words 'somniata filiola' of Scota, the daughter of Pharaoh.

king thereupon banished his daughters from his kingdom, but
gave them a ship and a full provision of food. At the end of
their long wanderings by sea they came to an island (which is
called Britain), and after Albine—for she was, as it were, their
leader and queen—they called the island Albion. A short time
thereafter the women had intercourse with demons and brought
forth giants, who practised in that country cruelty and robbery,
until a certain Brutus slew them, and, taking possession of the
island, called it, after his own name, Britain.[1]

   This narrative of Caxton's seems to me partly fabulous—
he found a handle for his fiction in the story of the children
of Aegyptus and Danae—partly ridiculous, and partly to have
some connection with historical fact. For where shall you
find three-and-thirty daughters born of one woman? How
shall you believe that these slew every one her husband; and
that, set adrift, without so much as an oar, on a boundless
ocean, they did not utterly perish? I hold it further for altogether improbable that a demon, whether succubus or incubus,
should have been able to convey from foreign shores any seed

---

[1] 'The Chronicles of England', known as 'Caxton's Chronicle', was a repro-
duction by him of the popular 'Chronicle of Brut'. The account taken from
Wynkyn de Worde's edition (1528) is as follows:—
   'It befell thus that this Dioclesian spoused a gentyll damoysel that was wonders
fayre, that was his vncles doughter Labana, and she loued him as reason wolde,
so that he gate on her xxxiij doughters, of the whiche the eldest was called
Albyne, and these damoyselles whan they came vnto age became so fayre that it
was wonder . . . And it befell thus that Dyoclesyan thought to mary his
doughters amonge all those kynges that were at the solempnite. . . . And it
befell thus afterward that this dame Albine became so stoute and so sterne that
she tolde lytel pryce of her lorde and of hym had scorne and despite, and wold
not do his wyll. . . . Wherfore the kyng that had wedded Albyne wrote the
tatches and condicyons of his wyfe Albyne, and the lettre sent to Dyoclesyan
her fader. . . . And than said Albyne: Well I wote, fayre systers, that our
husbondes haue complayned vnto our fader vpon us . . . wherfore systers my
counseyle is that this night whan our husbondes ben a bedde, all we with one
assent to kytte theyr throtes, and than we may be in peas of them. . . . And
anone all the ladyes consented and graunted to this counseyle. And whan nyght
was comen, the lordes and ladyes went to bedde. And anone as theyr lordes
were aslepe, they kytte all theyr husbondes throtes. . . . Whan Dioclesian theyr
fader herde of this thynge, he became wroth ryght furyously agaynst his
doughters, and anone he wold them all haue brent. But all the barons and
lordes of Sirrye counseyled not so for to do suche straytnes to his own doughters,
but shold voyde the lond of them for euermore, so that they never sholde come
agayne, and so he dyd. . . . Than went out of the shyppe all the systers and

that should still retain its potency, when the ocean lay between.[1] More truly may we conclude, with other writers, that
it was from its white headlands that this island was named
Albion, for the rocks upon its eastern coast are of a snowy
whiteness. What Caxton says of Brutus, on the other hand,
has a historical foundation; for it is the opinion of most
writers that Britain takes its name from Brutus. Geoffrey of
Monmouth, a British monk, and also Caxton, relate that Brutus
of Troy made prayer to Jupiter, Diana, and Mercury, that
they would grant him somewhere a fit place of habitation.

And as to this Geoffrey quotes the following verses:—

> Goddess of shades, and huntress, who at will
> Walk'st on the rolling spheres, and through the deep;
> On thy third reign, the earth, look now, and tell
> What land, what seat of rest, thou bidd'st me seek,
> What certain seat, where I may worship thee
> For aye, with temples vow'd and virgin quires.

And when he had done his prayer, the goddess answered
Brutus thus:—

> Brutus, far to the west, in the ocean wide,
> Beyond the realm of Gaul, a land there lies,
> Seagirt it lies, where giants dwelt of old;
> Now void, it fits thy people: Thither bend
> Thy course, there shalt thou find a lasting seat;
> There to thy sons another Troy shall rise,
> And kings be born of thee, whose dreadful might
> Shall awe the world and conquer nations bold.[2]

---

toke the londe Albion as theyr syster called it, and there they went vp and downe,
and founde neyther man ne woman ne chylde, but wylde beestes of dyuers
kyndes. And whan theyr vitayles were dispended and fayled, they fedde them
with herbes and fruytes in season of the yere, and so they lyued as they best
myght, and after that they toke flesshe of dyuers beestes and became wonders
fatte, and so they desyred mannes company, and mannes kynde them fayled.
And for hete they wexed wonders couragyous of kynde, so that they desyred
more mannes company than ony other solace or myrth. When the deuyll that
perceyued went by dyuers countrees and toke a body of the ayre, and lyking
natures shad of men, and came in to the londe of Albion, and lay by those
women and shad tho natures vpon them, and they conceyued and brought forth
gyantes.'

[1] Cf. Bk. II. ch. iv.

[2] Geoffrey of Monmouth (fl.? 1100-1154) was archdeacon of Monmouth and
afterwards bishop of St. Asaph. The verse translation is Milton's. Caxton's

Now there is no one so ignorant as not to know that this is
a falsehood.   For we nowhere read that the oracles made use
of verses of this nature or of such language ; and further, the
Stygian Diana knows, with definiteness, nothing concerning
the future.   Nor again were demons found inside of images.[1]
To know the future belongs to God alone.

In the Ecclesiastical History of the English people by the
Venerable Bede, a man of very wide reading[2], we find it
written[3] that the name of Britain was given to the island by an
Aremoric tribe of the Gauls, which first of all inhabited the
southern part of the island ; for which reason the island was
called Britain by that Gallic tribe, and not contrariwise.   But
whencesoever the name, the island has now for many centuries
been known as Britain.   And about this Britain of ours, you
will not wonder if many curious notions as to its origin have
from time to time been hatched[4].   For it stands not otherwise with the first beginnings of the Romans, the Gauls, and
many other peoples ; of these too there are varying opinions.
Let this then suffice as to the name of the island.   I follow
the opinion of the Venerable Bede, among British historians
chief.

---

version, which is not an exact rendering of the verses as quoted by Major, is as
follows :—' Brute wente vnto the ymage and said : Diane, noble goddesse that
all thynge hast in thy myght, wyndes, waters, woodes, feldes, and all thynges
of the worlde, and all maner of beestes that ben therin, vnto you I make
my prayer, that ye counseyle me and tell, where and in what place I shall
haue a conuenyent place to dwell in with my folke.   And there I shall make in
the honour of the a fayre temple and a noble, wherin ye shall alwaye be
honoured.   When he had done his prayer, Diane answered in this maner.
Brute, sayd she, go euen forth thy way over the see in to fraunce to warde the
west, there ye shal fynde an yle that is called Albion, and that yle is becom-
passed all with the see, and no man may come therein but it be by shyppes,
and in that londe were wont to dwell gyauntes, but now it is not so, but all
wylderness, and that londe is destenyed and ordeyned for you and for your people.'
—*Hist. Reg. Brit.* lib. i. § 11.

[1] A good example of Major's independent judgment.   Compare Minucius
Felix, *Octavius* ch. 27 : ' Isti igitur impuri spiritus, daemones, ut ostensum
a magis, a philosophis et a Platone, sub statuis et imaginibus consecratis de-
litescunt.'   Elmenhorst, as quoted by Ouzel in his edition of the *Octavius*, refers
further to Lactantius ii. 15, 16 ; Tertull. *Apol.* cap. 22 ; Chrysost. *in Psalm.*
113, 134 ; Gregorius P.P. in *Epist. ad Saxones*, t. 2. Concil. fol. 132.

[2] lectorem latissimum.

[3] *Hist. Eccl.* i. 1.   [4] Pullulaverint.

CHAP. II.—*Of the description of Britain and its extent : that is, its breadth, length, and circumference ; also of its fruitfulness, alike in things material and in famous men.*

In the preceding chapter we have spoken of the origin of the names of Albion and Britain as applied to our island. We have now to speak of the island itself. Britain is a many- Britain. angled island of the ocean, separated by the sea from the whole continent—as Virgil has it in his verse :

Et penitus toto divisos orbe Britannos[1].

To the east lie Gaul, Belgium, and Germany. Between Calais or Isius[2] and Dover is a great strait of thirty miles[3], which a ship under a fair wind may cross in two hours. In other parts it is separated by a greater breadth of ocean from every land. To the south-west lies Hesperia, to the west Ireland, Hesperia. which is likewise an island, to the north the islands of the Orkneys. From south to north its length is eight hundred miles. The point of departure you may take in this way :— from Penwichstreit[4], fifteen miles beyond Michaelstow in Cornwall, to the furthest point of Caithness. We may put the matter more clearly thus :—the length extends from the furthest harbour of Wales in England to the end of Caithness in Scotland, which we now call Wick of Caithness. Whatever former writers have said of the breadth of the island, this I would have you know : that it presents a great diversity. In some places, as from St. Davids[5], the extreme point of

---

[1] *Ecl.* i. 67.

[2] Isius ; more commonly Itius. Some writers identify it with Wissent or Witsand, near Calais.—Danville, 'Mémoire sur le port Icius', *Mémoires de l'Académie des Inscriptions*, xxviii. p. 397. Lewin, *The Invasion of Britain by Julius Caesar*, 1859, identifies it with Boulogne, and Professor Airy with some place at the mouth of the Somme. Major calls Somerset—Captain of Calais— 'Itiorum ductor', Bk. VI. ch. xvii.

[3] 'Triginta millia passuum'. The Roman 'mille passuum'= 1618 English yards—about one-tenth shorter than the English mile. Whether these are taken as Roman or as English miles, Major's estimate of the distance is inaccurate, for the Straits of Dover are only 21 miles wide at that part. Taken with what he says of the time in which the Straits may be crossed, one might suspect a mis-print for 'viginti'.

[4] 'a Penwichstreit hoc est a Penuici strata', *i.e.* Landsend.

[5] Orig. prints 'Meuenia', and F., copying the mistake, prints 'Mevenia'; but Camden (ed. 1600) has 'Meneuia, quam . . . Angli hodie *S. Dauid* vocant.'

Wales, to Yarmouth in Norfolk, we find a breadth of two hundred miles; in most places, however, the breadth is less— say eighty, seventy, or sixty leagues[1]. We must, therefore, reduce this variety of breadth to a mean measure, as the philosophers would say. I conceive the whole island to have a mean breadth of seventy leagues. I mean that it is equal in size to another country four hundred leagues in length and seventy leagues in breadth. Ptolemy, in his Geography, gives it after Ceylon[2] the first place among islands, and Solinus calls it another world[3], and its renown is evident from the records of Greek and Latin writers. And though Cicero, in a letter to Trebatius[4], calls Britain barren, and affirms that it yields no grain of gold, or of silver, or of brass, while it is wanting too in every liberal art, some allowance must be made for a man whose attention was engaged by other matters, and who had not, like the second Pliny, and Ptolemy, and other writers of their kind, made an exhaustive study of cosmography and of the fertility or barrenness of various countries. For more than most does Britain abound in minerals, such as gold in Crawford Moor in Scotland[5], while silver, brass, and iron are found almost everywhere. It yields, too, a sulphurous and bituminous kind of earth, whose fire is hotter and more active than a fire obtained from wood. This is no matter for wonder, since in denser matter there is more of form than there is in rarer. Now as, according to the philosophers, vigour of action proceeds from form, there must of necessity be greater vigour

The excellence of Britain.

---

[1] The 'leuca'=one and a half Roman miles.   [2] Taprobana.

[3] '. . . nisi Britannia insula non qualibet amplitudine nomen pene orbis alterius mereretur.'—Iul. Solini *Polyhistor.* The *Polyhistor* was an abridgment of geography taken almost entirely from Pliny. It was very popular in the Middle Ages, and was one of the first books printed.

[4] *Epist. ad Fam.* vii. 7. *Ib.* vii. 10.

[5] Cf. the Second Report of the Royal Commission on Mining Royalties, issued in May of the current year, and in particular the evidence of Mr. Cochran-Patrick, who, when asked whether any great quantity of gold was formerly produced in Scotland, answered: 'A very large quantity. Indeed, nearly the whole of the gold coinages of Scotland were minted out of the native metal, and the records . . . of the Mint show that a very large amount of gold was brought into the Mint from Crawford Moor and the Leadhills, and other parts of Lanarkshire and Dumfries-shire. I remember in one case that one miner brought in 8 lbs. weight (Scots) of gold in one week, and was paid for it at the mint rate.'

of action where there is more form.   Now earth is denser than wood, for which reason this substance, rather than wood, is used by smelters of iron.   It produces, however, more smoke than is the case with wood, but of the latter fuel there is no scarcity[1].   The island has, further, a sufficiency for its own needs of soil fitted for the culture of wheat, winter wheat[2], pease, oats; an abundance too of pleasant rivers, well-watered meadows, rich pastures for its herds of cattle; nowhere shall you find softer or finer wool.   The woods are well stocked with stags, hinds, and wild boars; and nowhere, it is thought, do rabbits swarm as they do here.

The inhabitants of all Britain are of a proud temper and given to fighting, and though many may come by their death within the island in civil war, they are still in force sufficient not only to resist a foreign invader, but even to carry the struggle into his country.   This matter has been fully treated by foreign historians, and with them I leave it.

Wheat will not grow in every part of the island; and for this reason the common people use barley and oaten bread. And as many Britons are inclined to be ashamed of things nowise to be ashamed of, I will here insist a little.   And first I say this: that though the soil of all Britain were barren, no Briton need blush for that—if we approve the answer made to a certain Greek by Anacharsis the Scythian[3].   For when this Greek was taunting Anacharsis with the barrenness of Scythia, well did Anacharsis answer: 'Thou indeed art a disgrace to thy country, but my country it is that disgraces me.'   And I

---

[1] It is rather difficult to reconcile this assertion—'eis ligna pro igne non desunt'—with the words in chapter vii. of this book: 'In partibus Scotiae meridionalibus pauca sunt nemora.'   The latter statement is in accordance with the generally-received opinion that 'the southern division of Scotland was not a well-wooded country'.   Cf. Mr. Cosmo Innes's *Sketches of Early Scotch History*, p. 101, and the Acts of the Parliaments of Scotland, under TIMBER, FOREST, VERT.

[2] 'siligo'.   Cf. Pliny xviii. 10: 'To returne to our winter white wheat called Siligo, it never ripeneth kindly and all togither, as other corne doth: and for that it is so tender and ticklish, as that no corne will less abide delay' etc.— Philemon Holland's translation, 1601.   The whole passage is worth consulting in connection with what Major afterwards says about the proportions of grain and flour in the making of bread.

[3] Diog. Laert. *de vitis philosophorum* lib. i.

go further : I say that he should not have said ' my country disgraces me ', unless in the opinion of the unthinking. In both Hesperiae [1], in several provinces of both Gauls [2], nay further, in the Promised Land in the fourth zone, bread made from barley is in common use. Just such bread were Christ and his apostles wont to eat, as may be seen from the fourteenth chapter of Matthew and the sixth chapter of John. Pliny, too, makes mention in his thirtieth book [3] of meal made from oats, and there is in Normandy, near to Argentolium, a village called Pain d'Aveine [4]. But you may object that it is so called in derision, and because such meal is an uncommon thing among the Gauls. I say, for my part, that I would rather eat that British oaten bread than bread made of barley or of wheat. I nowhere remember to have seen on the other side of the water such good oats as in Britain, and the people make their bread in the most ingenious fashion. For those who may be

How oats are prepared for bread.

driven to use it, I will explain their method. The oats having been grown in a soil of a middling richness, they roast the grain thus : a house is built in the manner of a dove-cot, and in the centre thereof, crosswise from the wall, they fix beams twelve feet in height. Upon these beams they lay straw, and upon the straw the oats. A fire is then kindled in the lower part of the building, care being taken that the straw, and all else in the house, be not burnt up [5]. Thus the oats are dried,

---

[1] Major in chapter ii. means Spain by ' Hesperia '. By ' both Hesperiae ' he means Spain and Italy, which was anciently known as Hesperia.

[2] *i.e.* G. cisalpina and G. transalpina.

[3] Pliny (iv. 13 in Holland's translation) : 'Three days sailing from the Scythian coast there is the Iland Baltia, of exceeding greatnes. . . . There be also named the Iles Oonæ, wherein the inhabitants live of birds egges and otes.' Cf. Pomponius Mela, *de Situ Orbis* iii. 6 : ' In his esse Oaeonas, qui ovis avium palustrium et avenis tantum alantur.' Is it possible that the ' Iles Oonæ ' were Scottish islands ?

[4] ' Aveine, avoine, avena [oats], d'où le suffixe d'Isigny-pain-d'aveine.'—*Hist. et Gloss. du Norm.*, by E. Le Héricher, vol. ii. p. 180. Isigny, if this is the place referred to by Major, is on the sea-coast of Normandy, but not near Argentan.

[5] For a like method in Ireland, compare ' In the remote places of Ireland, in the stead of Threashing their Oats, they vse to burne them out of the straw, and then winnowing them in the wind, from their burnt ashes, they make them into meale.'—*A New Irish Prognostication*, or *Popish Callender*, 4to, Lond. 1624, p. 40. For the continuance of the practice in Scotland, see Johnson's

and thereafter carried to the mill, where, by a slight elevation of the upper millstone the outer husk gets shaken out. The flour alone then remains, dried, and in good condition, more excellent by far than the flour that is used by confectioners[1] in any part of the world. From this dried grain, which from its resemblance to lentil flour they call by that name, after it has been ground small in the manner of meal, the oaten bread is made. As the common people use it both leavened and unleavened, oats are very largely grown. Just eat this bread once, and you shall find it far from bad. It is the food of almost all the inhabitants of Wales, of the northern English (as I learned some seven years back), and of the Scottish peasantry; and yet the main strength of the Scottish and English armies is in men who have been tillers of the soil—a proof that oaten bread is not a thing to be laughed at. But that you may know how to get good oats, observe this rule. If from a fixed quantity of oats, even with the outer husk, you get an equal or greater quantity of flour, your oats are good and full-bodied; but if the quantity of flour be less, then the oats are not good. In Britain the quantity of flour thus obtained is often greater than that of its oats. From a smaller quantity of compact and firm meal, you shall get, because of its rarity, a larger quantity of flour; and from equal quantities of meal you shall often get unequal quantities of flour. Bakers often find this to be the case with corn; and a purchaser will pay a different price for the same quantity of wheat in two villages not far distant from one another.

The testing of oats.

This is a slight digression, and not an irrelevant one, as the

---

Journey to the Western Islands :—' Their method of clearing their oats from the husk is by parching them in the straw. Thus, with the genuine improvidence of savages, they destroy that fodder for want of which their cattle may perish.' Cf. also the Rev. J. L. Buchanan's *Travels in the Western Hebrides*, 1782-1790, p. 103 :—' They burn the straw of the sheaf to make the oats dry for meal.'

[1] 'Aromatarius'. From Major's *In Quartum*, 45th question of the 15th distinction, we gather that the 'aromatarius' was the 'restaurateur' or 'confectioner' who hired out silver-plate for students' breakfasts ('in doctoratu vel in alio prandio'). About that time, however, glass was beginning to take the place of silver, and Major approved the change, since 'glass was quite as clean and decent', and the newly-made doctor could get the use of an excellent service for four or five 'solidi'.

following story will show. When my fellow-countryman, David
Cranston[1], was taking his first course of theology[2], he had as
fellow-students and bosom-friends James Almain of Sens[3],
and Peter of Brussels[4], one of the order of Preachers, who
along with him attended the arts class under me. These men
one day, in the course of a discussion on Founder's Day[5] at
in the courtyard of the Sorbonne, brought this accusation
(based on the report of a certain religious) against the common people in Scotland, that they were in the habit of using
oaten bread. This they did, knowing the said Cranston to
be a man quick of temper, and to the end that they might
tease him with a kindly joke ; but he strove to repel the
charge as one that brought a disgrace on his native land. We
hear besides of a certain Frenchman, who brought this bread

---

[1] David Cranston was the author of a small work in quarto entitled *Positiones
phisicales magistri*, a copy of which is in the University Library, Edinburgh.
He also wrote additions to the *Moralia* of J. Almain (1518), to the *Questiones
Morales* of Martinus de Magistris (1510), and to the *Parva logicalia* of Ramirez
de Villascusa (1520?), copies of which are in the British Museum. There are
ascribed to him also *Orationes*, *Votum ad D. Kentigernum* and *Epistolae*.
In conjunction with Gavin Douglas he compiled the tabula for Major's commentary on the fourth book of the *Sentences*. He bequeathed the whole of his
property to the college of Montacute. The *Dictionary of National Biography*
gives us the dates of Cranston's activity ' (fl. 1509-1526)', and says that he became bachelor of theology in 1519 and afterwards doctor. From the letter,
however, by Robertus Senalis, dated ' xiiij. Calendos Decembres Anni MDXVI.',
which is addressed to Major and is prefixed to the 1521 edition of his *In Quartum*, it appears that Cranston had died before that date : ' Consules partim
tuorum auditorum insignium sed defunctorum memorie inter quos precipui fuerunt
Iacobus Almain Senonen : Dauid Craston [*sic*] tuus conterraneus : et Petrus
Bruxellensis, etc.'

[2] ' de prima Theologiae licentia foret ' probably means that at that time he
was studying his first course in theology, after passing in arts.

[3] James Almain, French theologian, born at Sens about the middle of the
fifteenth century. He was in 1512 professor at the college of Navarre. He
wrote many works on logic, physics, and theology, the most important of which
was *De autoritate ecclesiæ, seu sacrorum conciliorum eam repræsentantium*, etc.,
contra Th. de Vio, Paris, 1512, in which he opposes the Ultramontane doctrines
of De Vio, afterwards better known as Cardinal Cajetan. Almain died in
1515.

[4] Peter of Brussels ; *i.e.* Pierre Crockaert, a Dominican friar and scholastic
philosopher, professor at Paris and licentiate of the Sorbonne : born at Brussels ; died in 1514.—Franklin, *Dict. des noms latins.*

[5] ' Dies Sorbonicus '. Mr. P. Hume Brown tells us that this answers to our
Founder's Day.'

with him to his own country on his return from Britain, and showed it about as a monstrosity.[1]

The bread is baked upon a thin circular iron plate, of about an ell in diameter. The plate is supported on three feet, each of them in two parts, and thus so far raised above the flame that the bread, covering the whole surface of it, may be perfectly baked. These are the iron utensils of which Froissart in his Life of English Edward, the third of that name, makes mention; how the king came upon Thomas Randolph, earl of Moray, and the lord Douglas, in a stronghold, and did not dare to attack them, and how the Scots were driven on a sudden to make bread of meal and water, the which the nobles as well as the commoner people (since necessity knows no law) began to eat.[2]

Yet another way of preparing their bread is practised at a pinch: a flour-paste is spread out and placed near the fire, until it is rightly baked. Townsfolk laugh at country-folk for this; nevertheless Sacred History makes frequent mention of just such bread, under the name of hearth-cakes[3],

---

[1] Cf. Æneas Sylvius, *Commentarii Rerum Memorabilium*, p. 5. (Frankfort, 1614.)

[2] Cf. Froissart: 'They [the Scots] are ever sure to find plenty of beasts in the country that they will pass through. Therefore they carry with them none other purveyance but on their horse : between the saddle and the pannel they truss a broad plate of metal, out behind the saddle they will have a little sack of oat-meal, to the intent that when they have eaten of the sodden flesh, then they lay this plate on the fire, and temper a little of the oatmeal, and when the plate is hot, they cast off the thin paste thereon, and so make a little cake in the manner of a cracknel or biscuit, and that they eat, to comfort withal their stomachs.'— *Chronicles*, etc., Bk. I. ch. xix. John Bourchier, Lord Berners's translation, ed. 1812; but with modernised spelling. I have failed to find in Froissart the reference in the text to Randolph and Douglas; perhaps because I have been able to consult only one recension of the *Chronicles*. The different recensions vary a good deal in their contents.

[3] 'Panis subcineritius'. Cf. the Vulgate version of Gen. xviii. 6; Exod. xii. 39; and passim. The word is in frequent use in the Vulgate, but it has no place either in dictionaries of classical Latin or in Ducange. From the *Itala und Vulgata* of Rönsch we find, however, that it was not the invention of St. Jerome, but had a place in the Old-Latin and in the Ante-Nicene Latin Fathers. 'Hearth-cake' is the rendering of the Douay version in the cases mentioned above. The English version takes no heed of the special meaning of the word— but translates 'cake baken on the coals' (I Kings xix. 6), 'a cake not turned' (Hosea vii. 8).

that is, bread baked under or near the embers. Our countrymen call it Bannoka—(to Latinise the word of the vulgar).
Following the Sacred Scriptures we shall call it hearth-cake.

CHAP. III.—*Concerning things that are lacking in Britain, and
what the country possesses in their stead ; and concerning the length
of the day in that land.*

I HAVE spoken in the last chapter, though not doing more
than to skim the surface, of those things which Britain
possesses in abundance. I purpose now to say something of
what the island lacks. The vine you will nowhere find, nor
any trace of it [1]; though I have read in Bede [2] that it was known
to grow in some parts of the island. Perhaps he is thinking
of a sourish wine, called by the people verjuice [3], which is
produced in the southern parts of the island ; or perhaps in
his day the grape-vine really did grow there. God has endowed the Britons with many good gifts that other kingdoms
lack ; but the converse of this is likewise true. On no one
kingdom has He bestowed every bounty—but to different kingdoms has granted differing blessings, in such wise that, no one
finding in himself a full sufficiency, but needing ever another's
aid, men might learn to be helpers one of another—after
the apostolic precept, ' Bear ye one another's burdens' [4]. The
worth of wine God has thus bestowed on the Britons, in
giving them other merchandise, in exchange for which foreign
nations carry thither their wine [5]. In the most barren parts of

---

[1] Cf. Aeneas Sylvius, as quoted in Mr. P. Hume Brown's *Early Travels in
Scotland*, p. 28.

[2] *Hist. Eccl.* i. 1.

[3] ' Veriutum '=omphax et omphacium (Migne) ; oil or juice of unripe olives
or grapes. ($\delta\mu\phi\alpha\xi$=an unripe grape ; ' verjuice '=vert jus).

[4] Gal. vi. 2.

[5] A favourite reflection with Major. In his *In Secundum* (1528) chap.
v. of the 17th distinction, after discussing the comparative salubrity of different countries, he proceeds : ' There is no one who will not call his native
land the Land of Promise. . . . If a country lack some things—well, it abounds
in others. If the Britons must fetch their wines from France, they make repay-
ment by tin, and wool, and fish, and hides. And this is the good providence of
God, that no country abounds in all things, to the end that all may mutually be
helpful.'

the country is a wealth of sheep and oxen, whose hides and
wool may be exchanged for wine; but the grape vine in its
natural kind He did not give, to the end that mortal men
should confess the omnipotence of God, who needs the help of
no man: but let men learn that they need the help, as we have
said, of their brethren—according to that saying of Virgil:—

'Here corn, there grapes come more prosperously; yonder
the tree drops her seedlings, and unbidden grasses kindle into
green. Seest thou not how Tmolus sends scent of saffron, India
ivory, the soft Sabaeans their spice, but the naked Chalybes steel,
and Pontus the castor drug, Epirus mares for Elean palms?'[1]

The Britons further brew from barley a most excellent ale. The making
They would refuse to drink such ale as is brewed at Paris, of ale.
but to the making of their own they bring no small ingenuity. First of all, they put the barley for two or three days
in water, and, when it has swollen, they remove it, and lay it out
flat indoors, that it may become moderately dry. Thereafter
the barley is trodden underfoot by active youths whom they
summon for the purpose of dancing upon it. Often enough
the grain is swept together and piled to the height of a foot
upon the bare ground; upon this heap too the dancing goes
on till the inner grain is extruded or shows signs of sprouting.
The next step is to gather all the grain into a large heap,
which emits on all sides a powerful odour. It is then dried in
the manner of oats, being subjected to nine changes of tempera-
ture, and again swept together. In this condition it is no
longer barley, but what they call 'braxy'[2]; whether the change
operated in it is one of accident or of essence matters not. The
braxy is then ground in a mill. Many persons in Britain grow
rich by this means, though they may possess no special skill
or mechanical contrivance—may have nothing in fact but the
money to buy a quantity of barley, which they sell to certain
women[3], who in turn make the braxy into liquor in the follow-

[1] *Georg.* i. 54-59 (Mr. Mackail's translation; Lond. 1889).

[2] 'Braxium'. Low Lat. 'brassare'; Gael. 'bracha', 'braich'; Fr. 'brasser';
Eng. 'brew'. Cf. 'braxy' mutton; when it begins to ferment.

[3] Called 'brewsters' (braciatrices). 'Braseum ordei', 'braseum avenae',
occur frequently in the Exchequer Rolls. In 1509, *e.g.* a quantity of barley was
delivered to certain women of Edinburgh for ale to be used in the king's household, vol. xiii. p. 146. See also *ib.* p. 540.

ing way. Using only pure water, either that which is taken from
a running stream, or rain-water collected in a cistern, they boil
it, and in a boiling state pour it into a large vessel.   Into this
they pour the braxy, mix the whole together, and lay cloths
over the vessel that the contents may boil for five or six hours.
Next, from a small hole in the bottom a long piece of wood,
by which the vessel is closed, is slightly raised, so that the
liquid, not the grain, is distilled.   The liquor is then received
into a large vessel, where in Scotland it is once more subjected to boiling heat.   But, for the production of an excellent
drink, the second boiling—as I know from experience—is of
the greatest moment.   This twice-boiled liquor is then kept
for thirty hours in other vessels, whence it is gently drawn,
all care being taken that the lees be left behind.   The scum is
then added to the liquor in those fresh vessels; for the scum
is the lees of the old ale, and there is much of it left at the
bottom.   In place of the scum some persons take a branch
of a young hazel[1], and throw it into the liquor, and this
serves the same purpose as the scum.   The ale then rarefies
in its own vessels, in the manner of must, and bursts through
the sides; but after two days it is a wholesome drink, and
according to the abundance of barley and the paucity of the
water the drink is strong or, contrariwise, weak.   The purity
of the water is in a large measure ensured by its being boiled,
as may be seen in the case of ptisane and other distilled waters.
No one who is accustomed to this beverage will prefer a northern wine: it keeps the bowels open, it is nourishing, and it
quenches thirst.

From what I have now said of wine and ale, it is plain
that wine has not the merit of producing a stronger race of
men.   Taking the whole of Christendom, the drinkers of wine
are not more numerous than the drinkers of ale.   Wine is used
in a small part only of Normandy or Picardy.   In Lower
Germany, in Flanders, in Poland, Ruthenia, Livonia, Prussia,
Pomerania, in the three divisions of Scandinavia, the western,
eastern, and southern, the vine does not flourish; nor yet in
the neighbouring islands of Britain, Ireland, the Orkneys, and

---

[1] ' circulum coryli tenellae'. The wood of the hazel was used for the divining
rod. Major, however, does not suggest a magical intention here.

others still more northern (of which I shall speak further)—
which, taken together, make up a half of Christendom. The
vine in fact is found in barely one-half of the world. The same
is true of that part of the equator beyond Sarmatia, Tartary,
and such regions as these ; and of the neighbourhood likewise of
the antarctic circle and antarctic pole. From all this 'tis plain
enough that Britain cannot claim the vine ; but she has another
wholesome drink brewed of barley, oats, and wheat ; and, thus
furnished, it follows of necessity that though the vine be
wanting, she has flute-players and whistlers, to quote the
Philosopher upon the Scythians in his Posteriora[1]. Being
destitute of the vine, it follows *a fortiori* that the Britons
have not the orange, the olive, the fig, and the rest of fruits
like these—without all which we can make a good shift to
live. And, to say the truth, we could dispense with wine too,
but for the consecration of the Holy Blood of Christ, for which
but little wine is enough.

Treating of the division of the seasons in Britain, some The seasons
writers have made the longest working day to have eighteen in Britain.
hours, and the shortest winter's day but six ; but there is not
much weight in this observation, since the island, as we have
already said, is of a considerable length, and a small part
of the land towards the north will show greater variation of
time and season than an equal part near the Equator. In
Maidens' Castle,[2] or Edinburgh, the longest working day is of

---

[1] ' . . . et per consequens, licet non sint vites, stat esse sibilatores seu tibicines.'
The reference is to Book I. ch. xiii. § II of the *Analytica Posteriora*, where
Aristotle is treating of demonstrative proof, and quotes, as τὸ τοῦ 'Αναχάρσιδος,
this example of a far-fetched reason : ' Similar to this are far-fetched reasons,
as that of Anacharsis, who said there were no flute-players in Scythia because
there were no vines.' Aristotle says nothing about ' sibilatores ', which makes it
probable that Major quoted from memory—and indeed he varies the form of the
argument. Aristotle says the Scythians had no flute-players because they had
no vines ; Major says we have no vines, and therefore we have flute-players.

[2] Castrum Puellarum '. The ' Edin ' in the Gaelic Dún-Edin (Welsh Caer-
Eiddin) ' defies ', so I am assured by Professor Kuno Meyer, ' all explanation
from Celtic ', and it is commonly said that it is really the Anglo-Saxon name
Eadwine. ' Eadwinesburh ', however, would have given ' Edinsburgh ' ; ' for
the genitive *s* is never lost in such derivations '. If Edinburgh, then, is con-
nected with Eadwine, it must be ' as a comparatively late translation of the
Gaelic Dún-Edin '. Whatever may be the derivation of ' Edinburgh ', ' Castrum
Puellarum ' is certainly a false translation of some form of the original name.

eighteen hours, and in winter this is reduced to one of six hours only. But further north you shall find the longest day to have nineteen hours, the shortest but five. There indeed, or in the neighbouring islands, that saying of Juvenal's is made good : *Et minima contentos nocte Britannos*[1]. In summer the nights of the north have more light, since the sun declines but a small way below the horizon. Two of the islands are called Sky and Luys—that is, Twilight and Light—because the nights of summer are there but a kind of twilight. I am not forgetting that in some parts of the world one half of the year is night, the other half, day. But that is not the case with Scotland. Nor would I have you believe Aeneas Sylvius (though I name him with respect) where he makes the winter day of Scotland to be but two or three hours in length, and therefore[2] finds it to be greatly shorter than at Rome. That he said merely in strong hyperbole[3]. At York the days of winter are longer

---

The ' Maidens'' may have had its origin, as the late Dr. Robert Chambers thought, in a ' Mai Dun ', which would represent a Celtic ' Maghdún '=' dún [or fort] of the plain '. The Marquis of Bute, in a letter to the *Times* of February 25, 1891, conjectures that in the course of time the belief arose that the ' Edin ' was derived from the Irish saint Edana, a nun, who in the Arthurian legend is stated to have established churches and schools in some of the principal fortresses, of which Edinburgh was one, lying in the track of King Arthur. The Irish, he remarks, had the habit of prefixing ' Mo '=' my ' to the names of their saints, in sign of affectionate respect ; hence Edana became *Modana* (in Cornish *Modwenna*); and her churches in Galloway, *Maidenkirks*. Medanburgh, on English tongues, easily slipped into the more intelligible Maidenburgh, which then became Latinized into ' Castrum Puellarum '. Dr. Skene, on the other hand, in his *Four Ancient Books of Wales*, vol. i. pp. 85, 86, calls this nun of the Arthurian legend ' Saint Monenna '. For Major's own derivation of ' Edinburgh ', from ' Heth,' king of the Picts, cf. ch. xiii. of this Book. The form ' edenesburg ', it may be added, is found in a charter of David I. printed in the *Registrum de Dunfermelyn*, p. 15. Dalrymple in his version (1596) of Leslie's *History* writes ' Madne Castle '. Cf. Father Cody's note *in loco*, p. 361.

[1] Juv. ii. 161.

[2] ' Sed tamen ', which does not seem to make sense. I therefore venture to translate ' therefore '.

[3] Cf. what Major says about Aeneas Sylvius (afterwards Pope Pius the Second —he is the only Pope who ever visited Scotland), in his *In Secundum* chap. v. of the 17th distinction (1528): ' Aeneas Sylvius says that when he was in Scotland the winter day was but three hours long ; but, saving his reverence, he says what is not true [facit commenticium]—(I speak not against the supreme pontiff, but against Aeneas Sylvius before his elevation to the pontificate) . . . but perhaps a man may be pardoned because he finds a variation of three hours between Rome and the promontory of Berwick.' See Aeneas Sylvius, *Com. Rer. M.*, p. 5.

than in Edinburgh ; in London they are longer than at York, and in the southern part of Hampshire again they are longer than in London. So that in the matter of length of day in Britain there is no small variety.

CHAP. IV.—*Of those who have possessed Britain, how the peoples of Wales are Aremoric Britons, and the Scots are Irish Britons, and of the threefold language of the Britons.*

I FIND in Britain first of all one kingdom, that namely of The Aremoric the Britons, and already of old that people had occupation of people. Wales, and they speak the primitive tongue, and the Britons of Aremorica in Gaul understand this tongue. This is a proof that the Britons had their origin from the Aremoricans; so much must be admitted, or the converse of it. Following the Britons, the Picts invaded the island, and made of it two kingdoms— of the Picts, namely, and the Britons. Following the Pictish invasion came that of the Irish Scots ; and so it came about that in the island there were three kingdoms and three kings. Now the Picts and Scots began to vex the original Britons with frequent invasion ; and when these could no longer bear up against them, they besought the Romans to help them ; and when at last the Romans grew weary and refused to give further help, the Britons betook them to the Saxons ; and when Hengist the Saxon answered their prayer, seven kings, as will be shortly seen, landed in the island with intent to found kingdoms there. So that there came to be altogether ten kingdoms in the island,—and that too in the days of Bede,— of which two, those of the Picts and Scots, were, as one may say, large, and seven, those of the English, I am inclined to think, were small, both in extent and in resources. The third kingdom was Wales. At the present day, however, there are, and for a long time have been, to speak accurately, two kingdoms in the island: the Scottish kingdom namely, and the English. For those seven kingdoms, before the conquest of Wales, were united into one kingdom of England, and thereafter Wales was made sub- ject to the English. So that the whole part of the island which is held by the king of the southern island is called the kingdom of England, and the rest is the kingdom of Scotland. Yet all the inhabitants are Britons—a fact that I think is established by what has been said. I will try, however, in a few words, to make good my contention. Either the original inhabitants of the island alone are Britons, and therefore the

That the Scots are Britons.

dwellers in Wales at this present will be the only Britons, against all common use of language ; or the English, who are descended from the Saxons, and others of foreign origin, but are natives of the island, are Britons ; and in this way it will behove us to speak of the Scots born in the island as Britons also, and by like reasoning we will say that the Picts too are Britons in respect that they were born in the island ; just as we ought to [1] call those men Gauls that were born in Gaul. I say, therefore, that all men born in Britain are Britons, seeing that on any other reasoning Britons could not be distinguished from other races ; since it is possible to pass from England to Wales, and from Scotland by way of England to Wales, dryshod, there would otherwise be no distinction of races. This notwithstanding, and though I reckon both Scots and Picts to be alike Britons, yet to make some distinction between them, when I come to speak of the wars that they have waged with the Britons, I shall call them Picts and Scots and not Britons ; for in this matter I approve the opinion, based upon the speech of the common people, of the philosopher in his second book *De Caelo*, where he says : ' Our speech should be that of the multitude, but our thought the thought of the few ' [2].

The speech of the Britons.

You must know further, that there are in the island three different tongues, and the speaker of no one of these understands another. The first of these, in the southern parts, is the Welsh tongue ; this is in use by the Britons who speak the British language [3]. The second is more widely spread throughout the island, and is in use by the Wild Scots and the island Scots ; and this is the Irish tongue, though it may be called broken Irish. The third tongue of this island, and the chief, is the English, which is spoken by the English and by the civilised Scots.

---

[1] F. ' oportebat ' ; Orig. better, ' oportebit '.
[2] Cf. Bk. II. ch. iv.
[3] ' Britones britonisantes ' ; cf. the French ' Breton bretonnant '.

CHAP. V.—*Of the situation of Britain, that is, of England and Scotland, and of their rivers, and, in special, of the wealth of London.*

INTO two kingdoms then, and under two kings, all Britain is now divided. The English king possesses the southern part. On all sides save the north the ocean is its boundary. The Isle of Wight, fifteen leagues in length, in the ocean, is part Wight. of this domain; likewise two islands of small importance, Guernsey and Jersey,[1] some four or five leagues in length, situated between England and Normandy. The southern boundary of Scotland adjoins the northern boundary of England, or indeed coincides with it. Six leagues to the east the river known in the vulgar tongue as the Tweed severs England Tweed. from Scotland, so that, from one of its banks, Englishmen can fish, from the other Scots. After a course of six leagues, the Tweed enters Scotland; not that[2] it flows from England into Scotland, but contrariwise. By the monastery of Kelso it receives the tributary Teviot, whence comes the name of Teviotdale. Scotland extends southwards three miles beyond the monastery of Kelso. Its western boundary is the river Solway, where the sands are full of peril. The Solway falls into the Western Ocean, and for a long space separates Scotland from England. Beyond this boundary the Scots possess Red Kirk[3], and beyond Red Kirk is a debateable land scarcely one Debateable league in breadth. This land is without inhabitants, inasmuch as the Scots aver that it pertains to them, and the English, on their part, say the same. Three leagues beyond the Solway the English have the small fortified city of Carlisle. The boundaries have a breadth of some five or six leagues; but that region is indifferently cultivated, by reason of Scottish and

---

[1] Orig. 'Darsi & Iarsi'.

[2] F. has 'quia', and 'quia' is constantly used for 'quod' in ecclesiastical Latin, *e.g.* St. Augustine; but Orig. reads 'quod'.

[3] 'rubrum templum'. There is a 'Red Kirk' to the west of the Kirtle (as I am told by Mr. R. B. Armstrong) in a very correct MS. map (1590) in the British Museum—'A Platt of the opposite Border of Scotland to the West Marches of England'. Red Kirk was in the possession of George Grame, a younger son of Richard of Netherby and grandson of William Grame, *alias* Long Will, chief of the clan.

English robbers and inveterate thieves.   On the eastern Scottish marches by the shore, and in Teviotdale where it adjoins that region, and in the part to the west by the river Solway, the boundary line is of the clearest; but between Teviotdale and the Solway it remains doubtful, and is matter for contention between the Scots and the Englishmen.

The rivers of England.

In England there are, further, three chief rivers, the first of which, the Severn, or, by its British name, Habern, is in mid Wales.   This river has its source to the east, making towards Shrewsbury; afterwards, flowing southwards, by Bridgenorth, Worcester, and Gloucester, it turns westward by Bristol, and in some parts is the boundary between England from Wales.

The second river is the Humber, which winds its way towards the southern part of Yorkshire; into it flow Trent and Ouse, making of the Humber a mighty stream, who then carries them with him into the Northern Ocean.

The third river is the Thames, which takes part of its name from an Oxfordshire streamlet, and flows by London.   'Tis a river of no great size, save when it is increased by the flowing tide.   In Britain you need not look for a large river—and the reason is this : that its streams flow across the island—following not its length, but its breadth, which is not great. The sea on one side or other is at hand, and soon swallows them.   For in their course rivers tend to join one with another, and lose their old names as they receive tributary streams.   Not otherwise does the Metro increase—not otherwise the king of European rivers, the Danube himself[1]; for in his long course the Danube receives the waters of sixty large streams.   In Britain, however, you shall find rivers equal to the Marne, or the Seine before its union with the Marne; only, as there is in parts but small depth of water, they are not well fitted for navigation. Full of fish they are, and fair to see, since they flow for the most part over pebbles and sand.   The Thames at London is three times as large as the Seine at Paris, because further up

---

[1] The Metro (Metaurus), a river in Umbria, has a course of no more than 40 or 50 miles, and is famous only for the battle between Hasdrubal and C. Cl. Nero B.C. 207.   Major takes the Metaurus as a type of small and unimportant rivers, the Danube as a type of the greatest.   Silius Italicus (viii. 450) describes the Metaurus as a mountain torrent rather than a river.

even than London Bridge the ocean rushes, under agitation
of the moon ; and so it happens that the largest vessels in
Europe can make their way to London Bridge.   Londinum is London.
called by the Britons London, and is the capital of England,
and of all the cities of Britain the largest and the fairest in its
situation.   There shall you find merchant vessels from every
part of Europe.   The city is adorned with a right noble
bridge, on which are houses richly built, and likewise a
church.   One mile beyond the city westward you reach Westminster, that is, the Western Monastery.   The king's palace
is there, likewise monuments of kings, and the supreme courts
of justice in constant session.   Between the monastery and
the city, on the banks of the river, are the palaces of the
bishops and nobles ; while near them are the dwellings of
the handicraftsmen—and so the whole city in all its length
lies along the river.   Three miles eastward, likewise on the
Thames, is Greenwich, the common dockyard of the kings
of England.   There you shall find ships (which they call
' barges ') in great numbers, ascending the river to London,
and descending to its seaport—not drawn, as in the Seine, by
horses, but either answering to the action of the wind, or
simply to the flow and ebb of the tide without wind[1].   Every
year is chosen one of a craft, opulent and up in years, as
prefect.   Him they call mayor of the city, and before him is
borne a sword, in symbol of justice.   Of the royal preroga- The Mayor of
tives it is the king's Justice that falls to his share.   If there the City, who
is the chief
shall chance a scarcity of provisions in the city, it falls to him magistrate of
to send to foreign countries and find a remedy for such scarcity. the people.
In point of population I place London before Rouen, the
second city of both Gauls.   In wealth it surpasses Rouen by
much, for three things go chiefly to the enriching of this city :
the supreme courts of justice ; the almost constant presence of
the king, who at his own expense provides for a great household and supplies to them all their food ; and—what is the
strongest element of all—a great concurrence of merchants.   Yet,

---

[1] Cf. Dunbar's description in his ' London, thou art, etc. ' :—
    ' Where many a swanne doth swymme with wyngis fare ;
    Where many a barge doth saile, and row with are.'
                            —Ed. *Scot. Text Soc.*, p. 227.

in the judgment of some Englishmen—and this is my own judgment too—Paris has a population three times greater than that of London ; but I do not reckon the wealth of Paris to be three times greater than the wealth of London [1]. There are to be found on the Thames three or four thousand tame

Of swans. swans ; but though I have seen many swans there, I did not count them ; I merely report what I heard. The second city

York. is York, the seat of an archbishop, and fifty leagues distant from Scotland. In circuit it is great, but not in population or in wealth ; in respect of these matters it falls much behind London. It has no duke apart from the king, nor a resident archbishop, by

Norwich. whose favour the city might be enriched [2]. The third city is Norwich, an episcopal see, in which is made that kind of cloth which is called 'ostade'[3], both double and single. Other cities there are and wealthy, such as Bristol ; Coventry—it has no river, and that is worth noting, but 'tis a goodly city ; Lincoln, of renown in old days, and many other cities and villages [1].

Universities of England : Oxford. There are, further, in England, two illustrious universities : of which one—I mean Oxford—is famous even among foreigners. Into it, as I have heard, the kings of England dare not set foot, lest they should meet with insult, on account of insolence which was offered to a certain holy virgin by one of the kings of the English [4]. In ancient times this university has pro-

---

[1] See APPENDIX, on the Population of Medieval Cities.

[2] The archbishop's palace, demolished during the civil war of the 17th century, was at Cawood, ten miles south of York. The last duke of York was Henry Tudor (1491-1509), afterwards Henry VIII., when the dukedom merged in the crown. The Plantagenet dukedom of York (1385-1461) also merged in the crown. From 1461 to 1491 there was no duke of York.

[3] From Worstead, a village—once a manufacturing and market town—twelve miles north-east of Norwich. Some say that the Flemings first established here the manufacture of woollen twists and stuffs, but the foreign immigration is doubted by Rye (*Popular History of Norfolk*). The trade moved to Norwich in the reign of Richard II., and the town of Worstead declined.—*National Gazetteer.* A magnificent Church was raised at Worstead 'by the liberality of the merchants who founded here the "worsted" trade'.—Rye's *Popular History of Norfolk.* 'Ostada panni species ex lana subtiliore contexti, non unius usus, idem quod nostris *Estame*; unde Anglis Voosted stockings, tibialia sic contexta, Gall. bas d'estame. Haud infrequens nostratibus vox Ostade.'—Ducange ; who quotes a book as 'bound in ostada '.

[4] Miss Norgate, in her *England under the Angevin Kings*, vol. i. p. 43, tells the story, and gives a reference to William of Malmesbury, *Gesta Pontif.* lib. iv. § 178. In the fifth chapter of Mr. James Parker's *The Early History of Oxford*,

duced philosophers and theologians of renown—such as Alexander Hales, Richard Middleton, John Duns, that subtle doctor, Ockam, Adam of Ireland, Robert Holkot, Bokinham, Eliphat, Climito Langley, John Roditon, an English monk, Suiset, a most ingenious mathematician, Hentisbery, a very skilful dialectician, Strode, Bravardinus, and many more [1]. Famous colleges there are too in that university, founded by kings, queens, bishops, and princes, and from their revenues provision is made for the education of many scholars, whom at Paris

---

772-1100, printed for the Oxford Historical Society, 1885, there is an account of St. Frideswide's Nunnery, with a full discussion of the various legends that surround the memory of its founder. I quote Mr. Parker's translation of William of Malmesbury's narrative : '[Frideswide], the daughter of a king, despised marriage with a king, consecrating her virginity to the Lord Christ. But he, when he had set his mind on marrying the virgin, and found all his entreaties and blandishments of no avail, determined to make use of forcible means. When Frideswide discovered this, she determined upon taking flight into the woods. But neither could her hiding-place be kept secret from her lover, nor was there want of courage to hinder his following the fugitive. The virgin therefore found her way . . . into Oxford. When in the morning her anxious lover hastened thither, the maiden, now despairing of safety by flight, and also, by reason of her weariness, being unable to proceed further, invoked the aid of God for herself, and punishment upon her persecutor. And now, as he with his companions approached the gates of the city, he suddenly became blind, struck by the hand of Heaven. And when he had admitted the fault of his obstinacy, and Frideswide was besought by his messengers, he received back his sight as suddenly as he had lost it. Hence there has arisen a dread amongst all the kings of England which has caused them to beware of entering and abiding in that city, since it is said to be fraught with destruction, every one of the kings declining to test the truth for himself by incurring the danger.' Miss Norgate adds, as to this 'dread amongst the kings of England': 'It must be supposed that the councils held at Oxford under Æthelred and Cnut met outside the walls : we cannot tell whether any countenance was given to the legend by the circumstances of Harold Harefoot's death ; but from that time forth [1040] we hear of no more royal visits to Oxford till 1133.'

[1] Alexander Hales, surnamed 'doctor irrefragabilis', entered the order of St. Francis, was a voluminous author, and in theology the master of Duns Scotus. He died in 1245.

Richard Middleton or de Media Villa, also a Franciscan, taught theology at Oxford and Paris. He died in 1300. Some of his works, including a commentary on the Master of the Sentences, were printed at Venice in 1509.

John Duns, or Scotus, 'doctor subtilis', was the founder of the Scotist school of theology adopted by the Franciscans. There has been much controversy regarding the birthplace and native country of Duns, the year of his birth (1265 or 1274), and the college at Oxford to which he belonged. As to his birthplace, however, compare Major (Bk. IV. ch. xvi.), where he speaks of Duns

we call 'bursars'. Some colleges are of a reputation beyond the others, the new college of the blessed Magdalene, and a college founded by a bishop of Winchester (who was once a

---

as 'born at Duns, a village eight miles distant from England, and separated from my own home by seven or eight leagues only'. His principal theological work was the *Quaestiones in libros Sententiarum*, known as the *Opus Oxoniense*. The traditional date of his death is 1308. His complete works were published by Wadding in 12 vols. fol., Lyons 1639.

William Ockham, 'doctor invincibilis' or 'singularis', a Franciscan, condemned for nominalism and excommunicated. He wrote commentaries on the Sentences, printed at Lyons in 1495, also a treatise on the power of the emperor and the pope, in which the former is exalted at the expense of the latter. He died unabsolved from his excommunication, it is said in 1347.

Adam of Ireland, a Franciscan, wrote *Quaestiones quodlibetales* and a commentary on the four books of the Sentences. His date is about 1320. Cf. *Bibliotheca Britannica Hibernica* and J. A. Fabricius's *Bibliotheca Latina*, under ADAMUS.

Robert Holkot, of the order of St. Dominic, a follower of William Ockham, a doctor of Oxford, and a liberal interpreter of Scripture. He wrote many works on Scripture (*De Studio Scripturae*) and the several books thereof. In philosophy he was a rigid Peripatetic. He died of the plague in 1349.

John Bokingham, a doctor of theology, who expounded the Master of the Sentences in the schools at Oxford. He was the author of *Opus acutissimum in iv. libros Sententiarum* (printed at Paris in 1505), a copy of which is in the Bodleian. By Pits, under date 1399, he is identified, doubtfully, with the bishop of Lincoln of that name.

Robert Eliphat, a Franciscan or Augustinian, studied at Oxford, and obtained his doctorate at Paris. Pits says 'he never made an end of writing on the Sentences'. He flourished during the reign of Edward III.

Climiton Langley was skilful in astronomy, as well as in theology, and wrote on both these subjects. He flourished about 1350.

John Rodington, a Lincolnshire man, became a Franciscan, and was provincial of his order in England. Pits quotes Major as his authority for the statement that Rodington taught philosophy and theology at Oxford before going to Paris. He wrote numerous works on the Sentences, was a strenuous opponent of the Immaculate Conception, and died at Bedford in 1348.

Roger Suiset, according to Pits, who quotes this passage from Major, was commonly called the 'Calculator'. Mr. Brewer (*Monumenta Franciscana*, 1858, p. xliv) says that Suiset's profound mathematical researches 'commanded the praises of Leibniz'. He was a Cistercian. His *Insolubilia* was printed at Oxford about 1483. He wrote also on the Sentences. His date was about 1350.

William Hentisbery or Heytesbury was, says Pits, a man of acute intellect but contentious mind, and had no taste for anything but logical subtleties, in the discussion of which he spent his life. He wrote a treatise on 'De Sensu Composito'. Major is quoted as the authority for Hentisbery having taken his master's degree at Oxford. He lived in the reign of Richard II.

Ralph Strode, a native of Caermarthen, a famous musician and poet, a scholar, and a wit. He wrote on logic and theology, was famous for his controversy with

fellow of New college[1]). Each of these colleges has a hundred
bursars, of whom some give themselves to the study of divinity
and the hearing of lectures, and others continuously to letters.

There is yet another university, that of Cambridge, somewhat Cambridge.
inferior to Oxford, both in the number of its scholars and in
reputation for letters. It too possesses very fair foundations
of kings and queens. One of these, and indeed the chief, is
King's college[2], worthy to be placed along with New college in
Oxford. There is too the Queen's college[2] (that is, founded
by a queen), a very fair building, and the King's hall[3], in
revenues and in bursars not inferior to Queen's college. Another college is Christ's[4] (in which I formerly heard lectures for
three months—for this reason, that I found it to be situated
within the parish of Saint Andrew). A certain convent for

Wicliffe, and was probably author of an Itinerary to the Holy Land. He·was a
a friend of Chaucer, who dedicated to him and to Gower his ' Troilus and
Creseide ':

> ' O moral Gower, this book I direct   *
> To thee and to the philosophical Strode.'

There is a valuable contribution to our knowledge of Strode in the Introduction
to the edition of the fourteenth century poem *Pearl* recently issued by the Rev.
Israel Gollancz. London : 1891. Mr. Gollancz thinks it possible that Strode
may yet be proved to be the author of that poem. He flourished about 1370.

Bravardinus. Thomas Bradwardine, ' doctor profundus ', commentator on the
Sentences, c. 1350, of whom Chaucer writes :

> ' As can the holy doctour S. Austin
> Or Boece or the bishop Bradwirdyn.'

[1] The foundation stone of Magdalen college was laid in 1473. It was
founded by William Waynflete, bishop of Winchester. Waynflete was educated
at Winchester college, and probably at New college, Oxford, but his name is
not among the fellows.

[2] King's college was founded in 1441 by Henry VI. Queens' college was
founded in 1446 by Margaret of Anjou, queen of Henry VI., and ' re-founded '
in 1465 by Elizabeth Woodville, queen of Edward IV. The name of the college
is therefore generally printed ' Queens'' (not ' Queen's ') college.

[3] King's hall was the nucleus of Trinity college. Cf. Willis and Clark's
Architectural History, etc., vol. i. p. lxxv.

[4] Christ's college, an extension of God's House (first founded in 1439), which
had been transferred to its new site in St. Andrew's Street by King Henry VI.
It had its name changed in 1505, on its re-endowment by the countess of Richmond and Derby, mother of Henry VII.—Willis and Clark's *Architectural
History, etc.*, vol. i. pp. lvi., lxx. As Major calls it Christ's college, it is clear
that his history was written after 1505; but his residence there was certainly
before he went to Paris in 1493. Cf. Introduction to this volume.

women[1] was changed into Jesus college, by the counsel of a
most learned and worthy man, Stubbs[2], a doctor in theology.
Those women refused to keep their enclosure, and added to
their own a society of students of the other sex; and this
was a scandal to men of serious mind.   Wherefore, when
these had been turned out, and other foundations for the
common life had been prepared, there were admitted in their
place poor students, who should give themselves to letters
and the practice of virtue, and bear fruit in their season.
This expulsion of women I approve.   For if, from being
nurseries of religion, these houses become nurseries of prosti-
tution[3], honest foundations must be put into their place.   There
are besides many other colleges in which lectures are given
daily.   The course of study in the arts is in these universities of seven or eight years before the taking of the Master's
degree.   A Chancellor (whom in Paris they call a Rector)—a
man always of grave repute—is every year elected from the
highest faculty[4].   The Chancellor of Oxford was Thomas
Bradwardine.   Two Proctors are chosen yearly; in their hands
are all the functions of justice—for their authority extends over
every layman in the city.   And though in number the laymen
be equal to or more than the scholars, as a matter of fact they
dare not rise against them; for they would be crushed forthwith by the scholars.   In either university you shall find four
thousand or five thousand scholars; they are all of them no

---

[1] The nunnery of St. Rhadegund.   In 1497, and through the exertion of John
Alcock, bishop of Ely, the nunnery was suppressed by royal patent, in consequence of the conduct of the nuns, which 'brought grave scandal on their profession, and in the reign of Henry VII. not more than two remained on the
foundation'.   Cf. Mr. J. B. Mullinger's *University of Cambridge from the
Earliest Times, etc.*, pp. 320, 321 ; Cambridge, 1873.

[2] Stubbs has not been clearly identified.   There was an Edmund Stubbs, D.D.,
master of Gonville hall in 1503, who died in 1514.   Cf. Cooper's *Athen. Cantab.*
vol. i. p. 16.   From Bliss's ed. of Wood's *Athenæ Oxon.* vol. ii. col. 694, *s. v.*
JOHN MORGAN, we learn that in 1506 Mr. Lawrence Stubbys S.T.B. was presented by the abbot and convent of Oseney to the vicarage of Cudlington on the
death of John Morgan.   Stubbs's connection with Oseney, and Major's intimate
knowledge of that House, make it possible, if we admit that kind of intercourse
between the universities, that this Stubbs is the 'learned and worthy man' of
the text.

[3] Cf. what Major says, Bk. IV. ch. x. of the disorders in the nunnery of North
Berwick.

[4] 'the highest faculty,' *i.e.* theology.

longer boys; they carry swords and bows, and in large part are of gentle birth. In the colleges however they do not give themselves to the study of grammar.

In England every village, be it only of twelve or. thirteen houses, has a parish church[1]; their places of worship are most richly adorned, and in the art of music they stand, in my opinion, first in all Europe. For though in France or in Scotland you may meet with some musicians of such absolute accomplishment as in England, yet 'tis not in such numbers[2]. Their churchmen are of an honest walk and conversation, and should they be taken in adultery or fornication, yea, though they were beneficed priests, from their place they are compelled to go. In courage, in prudence, in all virtues of this nature, Englishmen do not think themselves the lowest of mankind; and if, in a foreign land, they happen upon a man of parts and spirit, "'tis pity,' they say, 'he's not an Englishman'.

English musicians.

CHAP. VI.—*Of the boundaries of Scotland, its cities, towns and villages; of its customs in war, and in the church; of its abundance of fish, its harbours, woods, islands, etc.*

In the old days the Scots and Picts had as their southern boundary that Thirlwall wall which Severus[3] built at the

---

[1] Cf. Bk. III. ch. vi., where Major says that every village, 'etiamsi duntaxat xx. sit ignium ', has its parish church.

[2] Cf. Erasmus, *Praise of Folly*, pp. 101, 102, ed. Basil. 1676 :—' It seems as if nature, just as she has implanted in every mortal his own peculiar share of self-esteem, has done the same by each nation, and almost by every city. And thus it comes that Britons claim for their peculium beauty of person, music, and good feeding. The Scots plume themselves on their noble descent, on kindred with their royal house, and, I must add, upon their power of splitting a hair in argument. The French assume the monopoly of fine manners; the Parisians in particular think that none may even approach them in a mastery of theological science. The Italians assert a special supremacy in polite letters and eloquence. And thus has every nation the happiness to apply this flattering unction, that it alone is not a barbarian.' As to the condition of musical culture in Britain at the present day as compared with the rank of our country in that respect in the sixteenth century, it is worth noting that Mr. Rubinstein has just expressed his opinion that while in Germany 50 per cent. of the population know good music, and in France as many as 16 per cent., in England the percentage is not more than two.

[3] Thirlwall is on the line of Hadrian's Wall. It is said that the wall was here ' thirled ', *i.e.* bored through, by the Caledonians. Cf. Dr. Bruce's *Handbook*, p. 188 (ed. 1885) ; and see footnote on p. 60 of this volume.

river Tyne; but at the present day the southern boundary of
Scotland coincides with the northern boundary of England.
The chief city in Scotland is Edinburgh. It has no river
flowing through it, but the Water of Leith, half a league
distant, might at great expense be diverted for the purpose of
cleansing the city; but, after all, the city itself is distant from
the ocean scarce a mile. Froissart compares Edinburgh to
Tournay or Valenciennes; for a hundred years, however, the
kings of the Scots have had their residence almost constantly
in that city[1]. Near to Edinburgh—at the distance of a mile—
is Leith, the most populous seaport of Scotland. On the descent
thither is a small village, very prosperous, inhabited by weavers
of wool—which gives its name to the best cloths in Scotland[2].
Then there is Saint Andrews—where is a university, to which
no one has as yet made any magnificent gift, except James
Kennedy, who founded one college, small indeed, but fair to
look at and of good endowment. Another university is in the
north, that of Aberdeen, in which is a noble college founded
by a bishop, Elphinston by name, who was also the founder of
the university. There is, besides, the city of Glasgow, the seat
of an archbishop, and of a university poorly endowed, and not
rich in scholars[3]. This notwithstanding, the church possesses
prebends many and fat; but in Scotland such revenues are
enjoyed *in absentia* just as they would be *in praesentia*,—a
custom which I hold to be destitute at once of justice and

The cities of Scotland: Edinburgh. (margin)

A University. (margin)

Another University. (margin)

A third. (margin)

---

[1] 'For Edinburgh, though the king kept there his chief residence, and that it
is Paris in Scotland, yet it is not like Tournay or Valenciennes, for in all the
town there is not four thousand [but read for this, in the best editions of
Froissart, FOUR HUNDRED] houses; therefore it behoved these lords to be
lodged about in villages, as at Dunfermline, Queensferry [Quineffery], Kelso
[Cassuelle], Dunbar, Dalkeith'.—Bk. II. ch. ccxxviii, Buchon's ed. vol. ii.
p. 314; Bourchier's ed. vol. ii. p. 7.

[2] The words 'admodum opulenta' would apply to Broughton—but hardly so
the description, as compared with other villages, of 'angusta'. Besides, though
there was a cloth known as 'bartane' or 'bertane' (cf. *Accounts of the Lord
High Treasurer of Scotland*, 1473-1498, pp. 188, 119, 231, 400), that was a
linen cloth which took its name from Bretagne (see Littré, *s.v.* BRETAGNE).
The village in question may have been on the site of Picardy Place or Greenside,
a resort of French weavers 170 years later—but it remains unidentified. On the
history of Broughton there is much to be learned from the *History of the Barony
of Broughton*, by John Mackay, Edin. 1867.

[3] The dates of foundation of the universities of St. Andrews, Glasgow, and
Aberdeen are, respectively, 1411, 1450, 1494.

common sense.   I look with no favour on this multitude of universities; for just as iron sharpeneth iron, so a large number of students together will sharpen one another's wits[1].   Yet in consideration of the physical features of the country, this number of universities is not to be condemned.   Saint Andrews, the seat of the primate of Scotland, possesses the first university; Aberdeen is serviceable to the northern inhabitants, and Glasgow to those of the west and the south.

There is, in addition, the town of Perth, commonly called Saint John or Saint John's town[2], the only walled town in Scotland. Now if towns in general had even low walls, I should approve of it, as a means of restraining the robbers and thieves of the realm[3].   The Scots do not hold themselves to need walled cities; and the reason of this may be, that they thus get them face to face with the enemy with no delay, and build their cities, as it were, of men.   If a force twenty thousand strong were to invade Scotland at dawn, a working day of twelve hours would scarcely pass before her people were in conflict with the enemy. For the nearest chief gathers the neighbouring folk together, and at the first word of the presence of the foe, each man before mid-day is in arms, for he keeps his weapons about him, mounts his horse, makes for the enemy's position, and, whether in order of battle or not in order of battle, rushes on the foe, not seldom bringing destruction on himself as well as on the invader,—but it is enough for them if they compel him to retreat.   And should

The promptitude of the Scots in driving back a foe.

---

[1] Cf. what Major says in his 'Propositio ad Auditores' in his *In Quartum Sententiarum*: 'For truth is discovered through disputation and the exercise of men's wits, and doubts are resolved by the meeting of various minds, when otherwise the formation of opinion can be naught but a journey through dark waters and mist.'   In the same connection he quotes with approval the line, 'Laudamus veteres, sed nostris utimur annis.'

[2] Cf. Hector Boethius, *Murthlac. et Aberdonen. Episc. Vitae*, p. 29 (Bannatyne Club ed.): 'Perthi (nunc Sancti Johannis oppidum vocant).'

[3] Major agrees with Aristotle (though in this case he does not name him) as to the importance of walls for a city.   Cf. *Pol.* vii. 11.   It should be noted that he does not reckon the fortification of Edinburgh, which took place in 1450, after the battle of Sark; and his absence from Edinburgh, while the fortification of the city was going on after Flodden, may account for his taking no note of this addition to the number of Scottish fortified towns.   Pedro de Ayala says (*Early Travels in Scotland*, p. 47) that Scotland had only one fortified town. Cf. Leslie's *History*, Cody's edition, pp. 8, 103; and on the general question Buchanan's famous lines :—

Nec fossa et muris patriam sed Marte tueri,
Et spreta incolumem vita defendere famam.

the enemy chance to come off victor, then the next chief gathers
another force, always at the cost of the people themselves who
take part, and goes out to further combat.   There are in Scotland for the most part two strongholds to every league, intended both as a defence against a foreign foe, and to meet
the first outbreak of a civil war; of these some are not strong;
but others, belonging to the richer men, are strong enough.
The Scots do not fortify their strongholds[1] and cities by en-
trenchments, because, were these to be held at any time by the
enemy, they would simply serve him for a shelter; and thus it
would no way profit the Scots, especially within the marches of
the enemy, to possess fortified cities or even strongholds.

Ecclesiastical polity of Scotland.

The ecclesiastical polity of Scotland is not worthy of comparison with that of England[2]; · the bishops admit to the
priesthood men who are quite unskilled in music, and they
ought at least to understand the Gregorian chant[3].   It
happens sometimes that thirty villages, far distant one from
another, have but one and the same parish church; so that a
village may be separated from its parish church by four or five,
sometimes by ten miles.   In the neighbouring chapels of the
lords, however, they may have a chance to hear divine service,
because even the meanest lord keeps one household chaplain,
and more, if his wealth and other provision allow it.   In war
these men are not inferior to others that are laymen; mass they
celebrate before midday.   From what has now been said it
follows that in Scotland the cures are few, but wealthy; and
their wealth disinclines the curates to serve their charges in
person.   It would however be better to multiply the cures, and
lessen the revenues, and the bishops should have an eye to this.

Villages and houses of the labourers.

Further, in Scotland the houses of the country people are
small, as it were cottages, and the reason is this: they have
no permanent holdings, but hired only, or in lease for

---

[1] The words are 'artificiose invadunt'.   The reading 'invallant' has been
suggested, but the word seems to want authority.   'muniunt' is another proposed
reading, and a further suggestion is to read 'praeterea' ('besides') for 'propterea'
('because').

[2] For Major's preference for the ecclesiastical polity of England, cf. Bk. III.
ch. vi.

[3] Before bursars were admitted to St. Leonard's college, St. Andrews, they
were tested in the Gregorian chant.   At Winchester college, in our own day, the
one question asked of the young candidates for admission was—'Can you sing?'

four or five years, at the pleasure of the lord of the soil;
therefore do they not dare to build good houses, though stone
abound; neither do they plant trees or hedges for their
orchards, nor do they dung the land; and this is no small
loss and damage to the whole realm. If the landlords would
let their lands in perpetuity, they might have double and treble
of the profit that now comes to them—and for this reason: the
country folk would then cultivate their land beyond all comparison better, would grow richer, and would build fair
dwellings that should be an ornament to the country; nor
would those murders take place which follow the eviction of
a holder [1]. If a landlord have let to another the holding of a
quarrelsome fellow [2], him will the evicted man murder as if he
were the landlord's bosom friend. Nor would the landlords
have to fear that their vassals would not rise with them against
the enemy—that is an irrational fear. Far better for the king
and the commonweal that the vassal should not so rise at the
mere nod of his superior; but that with justice and in tran-
quillity all cases should be duly treated. Laws, too, can be
made under which, on pain of losing his holding, a vassal must
take part in his lord's quarrel. This readiness on the part of
subjects to make the quarrel of their chief their own quarrel
ends often, of a truth, in making an exile of the chief himself [3].

England excels Scotland, by a little, in fertility, for the
former country is not removed so far from the path of the
sun; but in fish Scotland far more abounds [4]: that is, that very
nearness to the sun of the other country God has made up
to us in another way. <You will tell me, perchance: 'The
northern sea is deeper than the southern, on account of the
air that has been turned into water'; and that is plain
enough from this sign, since the ocean flows from the north

Abundance of fish in the Scottish seas.

---

[1] Feu-ferm, or permanent holding by money-payment, although not unknown
at a much earlier period, became more common after the statute 1457, c. 71.
The progress of feu-ferm is traced in *Exchequer Rolls*, vol. xiii. pp. cxii-cxxv.
Sir David Lyndsay took a different view of this tenure in consequence of its re-
sulting in enhanced rents. Cf. *Satire of the Three Estates*, vol. ii. p. 224, Laing's ed.

[2] 'unius animosi terras'. The same use of 'unus'=French 'un', is found on
p. 38, 'unus Scotus sylvester', and *infra*, Bk. III. ch. v. 'Makduffum de Fyfa
Thanum, unum praecipuum regni'. Cf. also 'unas mittit literas', Bk. IV. ch. xx.

[3] Cf. Bk. VI. ch. xvii.　　　　　　　　　　[4] Pedro de Ayala says (*Early
Travels in Scotland*, p. 44) that 'piscinata Scotia' was a proverbial expression.

southwards>[1].   But whose ordination, if not that of the Divine
Wisdom, was this—that the northern people, far from the
sun, should be blessed with deep waters, and, in consequence,
with waters that abound more in fish ; since wherever, in sea or
river, there is greater depth, there, other things being equal,
is greater store of fish.   To the people of the North God gave
less intelligence[2] than to those of the South, but greater
strength of body, a more courageous spirit[3], greater comeli-
ness.   Every year an English fleet sails for Iceland beyond the
arctic circle in quest of fish ; and from us they buy both
salmon and other kinds of fish.   In most parts of Scotland
you may buy a large fresh salmon for two duodenae, in other
parts, however, for a sou ; and for a liard you may carry away
a hundred fresh herring[4].

---

[1] ' Forte dices : mare apud Septentrionem est profundius quam apud meridiem
propter aerem in aquam conversum ; et istud a signo patet, cum a Septentrione
Oceanus decurrat.'   The whole statement is to us not so much staggering as
meaningless ; but it was a commonplace in the school-books of the time.   In
one of these—the *Margarita Philosophica Nova*, of which several editions were
published in the first quarter of the sixteenth century, an encyclopædia of the
arts and science is rendered accessible—all by way of dialogue between master and
scholar—to the young student ; and in every division of the book the commanding
influence of Aristotle is felt.   In the fourth chapter of the ninth book we have the
' discipulus ' begging to be instructed in the ' qualities of the elements and their
transmutations'.   The ' magister ' is satisfied with the general intelligence of his
pupil in saying that fire and air are related in respect of *heat* ; fire and earth in
respect of *dryness* ; air and water in respect of *moisture* ; water and earth in
respect of *cold* ; while fire and water on the one hand, and air and earth on the
other, are *not* related ; he is not so well pleased that the ' discipulus ' should
express a difficulty in seeing how air can ever be moister than water.   The
magister accordingly explains that air has intrinsically greater moistening power
(*magis humectat*) than water, by reason of its penetrability, while water has
extrinsically more moistening power than air by reason of its density.   But their
united virtues are of course stronger than either by itself.   If we do not yet
understand how the air was turned into water because ' the ocean flows from the
north southward ' (but cf. Arist. *De Coelo*, ii. 4), we at least see how it is that
water, with this large infusion of the moister element of air, should produce more
fish—which was what had to be shown.

[2] It was a constant wonder with Continental scholars that Buchanan should
have been born in Scotland.   On one of his portraits we have the inscription :—
          Scotia si vatem hunc gelidam produxit ad arcton,
          Credo equidem gelidi percaluere poli.

[3] Cf. Bk. I. ch. vii. (where Major quotes Aristotle to this effect), ch. viii.,
and Bk. v. ch. xiv.

[4] The ' escu ' (Lat. *scutum*), Mod. French ' écu.'   Major's ' scutum solare '=
two francs.   The ' sol ' or ' sou ' (Lat. *solidum*)=the French shilling (' whereof

Scotland can show rivers, too, excellently furnished with fish, such as the Forth, which flows into an arm of the sea likewise called Forth, four leagues in breadth. Near Leith it has the name of the Scottish Sea, since it separated the southern Picts and Britons from the Scots. Between Saint John and Dundee fflows the Tay; the Spey, the Don, the Dee are famous rivers of Aberdeenshire[1]. Besides these there are the Clyde, the Tweed, and many other rivers, all abounding in salmon, trout, turbot, and pike; and, near the sea is great plenty of oysters, as well as crabs, and polypods[2] of marvellous size. One crab or polypod is larger than thirty crabs such as are found in the Seine. The shells of the jointed polypods that you shall see in Paris clinging to the ropes of the pile-driving engines[3] are a sufficient proof of this. In Lent and in summer, at the winter and the summer solstice, people go in early morning from my

---

ten make one of ours'—Cotgrave's *Dict.* : London, 1650). This is to be understood of the 'sol Tournois', which, translated as 'a piece of Tours', is frequently used by Major. The coinage of Tours was less valuable by one-fifth that of Paris. A livre of Tours, *e.g.* = 20 sous, a livre of Paris = 25 sous ; a sou of Tours = 12 deniers, a sou of Paris = 15 deniers. The liard was a coin = three deniers, or the fourth part of a sou. The 'duodena' = a piece of twelve deniers. ' The words *libra, solidus, denarius*, from which are derived our £ *s. d.*, represented in the West of Europe the same proportions from the time of Charlemagne. The pound or livre = twenty shillings or sous ; the shilling or sou = twelve pence or deniers. But the value of the livre or pound depended on the extent to which in a given country and at a given time the currency had been depreciated. This . . . process was carried much further in France than in England ; hence the French livre is now a franc (about $\frac{1}{25}$ of our pound). The French sou (or 5-centime piece) is not quite a halfpenny in value, and the denier, if it were still a coin, would be worth $\frac{6}{12}$ of a centime '.—From Mr. A. H. Gosset's edition of *L'Avare*, 1887, p. 97.

[1] No part of the Spey flows through Aberdeenshire.

[2] Major's 'polypes' or 'polypus', which he distinguishes from the 'cancer,' is without doubt our lobster, whose shape closely resembles that of the crayfish.

[3] 'Polypedum articulorum testae in Campanellarum funibus Parisii pendentes.' I wish very particularly to thank M. Auguste Beljame of Paris for his explanation of this difficult passage: 'Campanella = *cloche, sonnette*, i.e. a bell. But *sonnette* means also a pile-driving machine, so called from the action of the men who pull the ropes being the same as that of bell-ringers.' Major's Paris 'polypedes' were without doubt crayfishes, which were found on the ropes of the pile-drivers when these had been for some time in the water of the Seine. In our own day (see Professor Huxley's *The Crayfish*, p. 10) 'Paris alone, with its two millions of inhabitants, consumes annually from five to six millions of crayfishes, and pays about £16,000 for them '.

own Gleghornie and the neighbouring parts to the shore, drag out the polypods and crabs with hooks, and return at noon with well-filled sacks. At these seasons the tide is at its lowest, and the polypods and crabs take shelter under the rocks by the sea. A hook is fastened to the end of a stick, and when the fish becomes aware of the wood or iron, it catches the same with one of its joints, thus connecting itself with the stick, which the fisherman then at once draws up. But not only is there abundance of fish in Scotland, but also of salt, which is sold in equal measure with even the poorest oats. Iceland, which is destitute of wheat, is the most fertile of all lands in fish.

Abundance of salt.

Iceland has no bread.

Near to Gleghornie, in the ocean, at a distance of two leagues, is the Bass Rock, wherein is an impregnable stronghold. Round about it is seen a marvellous multitude of great ducks (which they call Sollendae) that live on fish. These fowl are not of the very same species with the common wild duck or with the domestic duck; but inasmuch as they very nearly resemble them in colour and in shape, they share with them the common name, but for the sake of distinction are called solans. These ducks then, or these geese, in the spring of every year return from the south to the rock of the Bass in flocks, and for two or three days, during which the dwellers on the rock are careful to make no disturbing noise, the birds fly round the rock. They then begin to build their nests, stay there throughout the summer, living upon fish, while the inhabitants of the Rock eat the fish that are caught by them, for the men climb to the nests of the birds, and there get fish to their desire. Marvellous is the skill of this bird in the catching of fish. At the bottom of the sea with lynx-like eye he spies the fish, precipitates himself upon it, as the sparrow-hawk upon the heron [1], and then with beak and claw drags him to the surface ; and if at some distance from the rock he sees another fish, better than the first that has caught his eye, he lets the first escape until he has made sure of the one that was last seen ; and thus on the rock throughout the summer the freshest fish are always to be had. The ducklings, or goslings, are sold in the neighbouring country. If you will eat of them twice or thrice you shall find them very savoury ; for these birds are extremely fat, and the fat skilfully extracted is very service-

Solan geese.

---

[1] Cf. Virg. *Georg.* i. 405, *Ciris* 488.

able in the preparation of drugs; and the lean part of the flesh they sell. In the end of autumn the birds fly round about the Rock for the space of three days, and afterward, as in flocks, they take flight to southern parts for the whole winter, that there they may live, as it were, in summer;—because, when it is winter with us it is summer with the people of the south. These birds are very long-lived—a fact which the inhabitants have proved by marks placed upon certain of them. The produce of these birds supports upon the Rock thirty or forty men of the garrison; and some rent is paid by them to the lord of the Rock[1].

Scotland possesses a great many harbours, of which Cromarty, at the mouth of the northern river[2], is held to be the safest— and by reason of its good anchorage it is called by sailors

The harbours of Scotland.

---

[1] Part of Boece's account of the Bass (1526) may be given in Bellenden's translation (1536): ' Thocht thay have ane fische in thair mouth abone the seis, quhair thay fle, yit gif thay se ane uthir bettir, thay lat the first fal, and doukis, with ane fellon stoure, in the see, and bringis haistelie up the fische that thay last saw; and thoucht this fische be reft fra hir be the keparis of the castell, scho takkis litill indingnation, bot fleis incontinent for ane uthir. Thir keparis, of the castell forsaid, takis the young geis fra thaim with litill impediment; thus cumis gret proffet yeirlie to the lord of the said castell. Within the bowellis of thir geis is ane fatnes of singulare medicine; for it helis mony infirmiteis, speciallie sik as cumis be gut and cater disceding in the hanches of men and wemen.'—Vol. i. p. xxxvii.

Lesley (1578), in Dalrymple's translation, writes as follows: ' Mairatouer, thay are sa greidie that gif thay sie ony fishe mair diligate neir the crag, the pray, quhilke perauentur thay brocht far aff, with speid thay wap out of thair mouth, and violentlie wil now that pray invade, and quhen thay haue takne it will bring it to thair birdes . . . finalie of thir cumis yeirlie to the capitane of the castell na smal bot ane verie large rent; for nocht only baith to him selfe and to vtheris obteines he sticks, fische, ye, and the fowlis selfes, quhilkes, be cause thay haue a diligate taste, in gret number ar sent to the nerrest tounes to be salde, bot lykwyse of thair fethiris, and fatt quhilkes gyue a gret price, he gathiris mekle money; of thame this is the commone opinione, that by vthiris vses thay serue to, they ar a present remeid against the gutt, and vthiris dolouris of the bodie.'—Scot. Text. Soc. ed. pp. 25, 26.

These extracts show something of the place in our early Scottish histories that was accorded to the solans of the Bass. Major, writing in Latin, cannot be to us so picturesque as Bellenden and Dalrymple, but it should be remembered that while his successors may have seen what they describe, he was familiar with the Bass from his boyhood. As to the support of the garrison at a later date, we find Sir John Dalrymple writing to George, Lord Melville, June 23, 1689: ' It [the Bass] can hold out, for the sollen gies and other fowls is mor than sufficient to sustean the garrison.'—_The Melvilles_, edited by Sir W. Fraser, vol. ii. p. 113.

[2] Flumen Boreale—the Moray Firth.

Sykkersand [1], that is, 'safe sand'. Every seaboard town has
a sufficient harbour.   Now Scotland is so cut up by arms
of the sea, that in the whole land there is no house distant
from the salt water by more than twenty leagues.   In
many parts Scotland is mountainous, but it is on the mountains that the best pasture is to be found.   Many men hold
as many as ten thousand sheep [2] and one thousand cattle, and
thus draw corn and wine from sheep and kine.   Near to Aber-

The Alps of
Scotland.

deen are the Alps of Scotland, vulgarly called the Mounth
of Scotland [3], which formerly separated the Scots from the Picts.
These mountains are impassable by horsemen.   Round about
the foot of the mountains are great woods.   There, I incline

The Caledonian
Forest.

to think, was the Caledonian Forest, of which Ptolemy and the
Roman writers make mention, and in these woods is found an
incredible number of stags and hinds.   At that time Aberdeen

Aberdonian
Scotland.

was the seat of the Scottish monarchy [4], though the kings of the
Scots were crowned at Scone.

Outside Britain the king of the Scots possesses several

Islands that are
subject to Scot-
land.

islands, such as, to the north, the Orkneys, which the Greeks
and Latins ever spoke of with a sort of horror.   More than
twenty of them are now inhabited, and some are twelve leagues
in length.   Shetland is the most easterly, and is fifty miles in

---

[1] In Mercator's map of Scotland (1597), Cromarty is called ' Portus Salutis'.

[2] From the context one must suppose that Major is speaking of the Highlands.
Mr. Cosmo Innes in his *Lectures on Scotch Legal Antiquities*, pp. 263-4, says
'there were at that time [1600] no cattle or sheep reared in large flocks and herds
in our Highlands . . . there was nothing but the petty flock of sheep or herd of
a few milk-cows grazed close round the farm-house, and folded nightly for fear of
the wolf or more cunning depredators'. This statement, if we may credit Major,
needs some qualification. Cf. also what Major says *infra*, at the end of chapter viii.
about the wealth of cattle, sheep, and horses among one part of the Wild Scots ;
and so early as 1296 Edward the First ordered 700 sheep to be brought from the
county of Athol and delivered to the nunnery of Coldstream, in indemnity for the
damage done to that House by the English army.—*Documents illustrative of the
History of Scotland*, ed. by the Rev. Joseph Stevenson, Edin. 1870, vol. ii. p. 34.
As to the number of sheep 'apud Britannos', Major writes further in the *In
Quartum* (46th question of the 15th distinction) that you may find there a man
who owns more than the 7000 sheep of Job—sometimes even 10,000, and this
happens mostly where the country is mountainous.

[3] 'Scotiae montes vulgariter dicti'. Cf. Skene's *Celtic Scotland*, vol. i.
pp. 10-14, ed. 1876. 'Beyond the Munth', *i.e.* from Aberdeen northwards, is
a phrase quoted by Mr. Innes (p. 114 of *Lectures on Legal Antiquities*) in connection with a combination of burghs.

[4] This is a noteworthy statement.

length. They produce in plenty oats and barley, but not wheat, and in pasture and cattle they abound. Orkney butter, seasoned with salt, is sold very cheap in Scotland.

Between Scotland and Ireland are many more islands, and larger ones than the Orkneys, which likewise obey the Scottish king. The most southerly is Man, fifteen leagues in length, which we have ourselves caught sight of at Saint Ninian [1]. In it is the episcopal see of Sodor, at the present day in the hands of the English. There is also the island of Argadia [2], belonging to the earl of Argadia, which we call Argyle, thirty leagues in length. There the people swear by the hand of Callum More, just as in old times the Egyptians used to swear by the health of Pharaoh. The greater Cumbrae is another island, rich and large. Another is the island of Arran, which gives the title of earl to the lord Hamilton. <Then there is the island Awyna, in which is the cell of Saint Aidan. In it were formerly most excellent religious, and Bede says that it ought to belong to the Britons, but the Picts made grant thereof to Scottish religious. This island lies further to the north than Bute, and is but six miles from the coast of Ireland>[3]. There is further the island called Isola, or in the common tongue Yla, an exceeding beautiful island. Therein is wont to dwell the Lord Alexander of the Isles, whom men used to call the earl of the Isles. In this island he had two fair strongholds of large extent, and thirty or forty thousand men were at his beck. This Yla I take to be the Thyle, or Thule, which was in such evil odour with the Greek and Roman writers, of which Virgil has that *Tibi serviet ultima Thule* [4]. For, or Shetland, or Yla, or Iceland, Thule must needs have been. Now Iceland, which is beyond the arctic circle, the Romans never reached. There is further the island of Bute or

Margin notes:
The hand of Callum.
The earl of Arran.
The cell of Saint Aidan.
Isola or Isla.
Thule.
Bute.

---

[1] Whithorn.

[2] In Mercator's map the name Argadia is applied to the district between Loch Fyne and Loch Long.

[3] 'Est insula Awyna . . . Ipsa autem est Butha borealior sex mille passibus ab Hibernia solum distans.' There is some confusion here. By 'Awyna', 'quae videlicet insula ad ius quidem Brittaniae pertinet' (Bede, *H.E.* iii. 3), Major must mean Iona, but his geographical description applies rather to the island of Sanda, called by the Danes 'Havin' or 'Avona', and 'still [1854] called "Avon" by the highlanders.'—*Orig. Par. Scot.*, vol. ii. pt. 1, p. 9. It is distant about four miles from the south coast of Kintyre, and about eighteen miles from the coast of Ireland.   [4] *Georg.* i. 3.

Rothesay, and the island of Lismore, which gives a title to the episcopal see of Argyle[1]. Far to the north is the island of Skye, fifteen leagues in length. The island of Lewis has a length of thirty leagues. Besides these are many other islands, of which the least is greater than the largest of the Orkneys. In that region are great lakes, wherein are islands, as Loch-

Lakes that
contain islands.

lomond, the island of Saint Colmoc, in which is a Priory of Canons Regular, Lochard, three leagues in length, Lochban-quhar[2], Loch Tay, Loch Awe, with a length of twelve. Other islands there are too in the sea as well as in the fresh water.

The speech of
the Islanders.

All these islands speak the Irish tongue, but the Orkneys speak Gothic. That great-souled Robert Bruce in his last testament gave this counsel to those who should come after him, that the kings of the Scots should never part themselves from these islands, inasmuch as they could thence have cattle in plenty, and stout warriors, while in the hands of others they would not readily yield allegiance to the king, whereas with the slender title of the Isles the king can hold them to the great advantage of the realm, and most of all if he should make recompence to others of a peaceful territory.

British flesh-
foods.

The mutton of the Britons is inferior to the same meat in France, and less savoury; the opposite is the case with beef;—and, as I think, the reason is this: a poor herbage makes a savoury mutton, and a rich herbage an unsavoury. I used to marvel when in the neighbourhood of Paris I saw the sheep being driven to poor pasture, and when I asked the reason, I was told that otherwise the meat would not be good. In Britain the sheep are horned, and are not gelded. Their

Horned sheep.

horns are almost as the horns of stags. Near Paris the sheep are hornless. This points to the possession of a moister climate by Britain, and the islands are more moist than the other parts. For a solar écu, that is, for two francs, a large ox may be bought in the northern parts of Scotland; for five or six sous of Tours[3] a ram; for six or seven pieces of Tours[4] a fat capon or a goose. In the southern parts of Scotland everything is a little dearer; in the north the best of fish may be had for next to nothing.

Scottish
Horses.

Horses they have in plenty, and these show a great endur-

---

[1] Ecclesia Lesmorensis alias Ergadiensis, A.D. 1420. —Vatican MS. in Brady.
[2] Vennachar.   [3] solidis Turonensibus.   [4] Turonis.

ance both of work and cold.   At Saint John and Dundee
a Highland Scot[1] will bring down two hundred or three
hundred horses, unbroken, that have never been mounted.
For two francs, or fifty duodenae, you shall have one ready
broken.   They are brought up alongside of their dams in the
forests and the cold, and are thus fitted to stand all severity of
weather.   They are of no great size, and are thus not fitted to
carry a man in heavy armour to the wars, but a light-armed
man may ride them at any speed where he will.   More hardy
horses of so small a size you shall nowhere find.   In Scotland
for the most part the horses are gelded, because their summer
pasturing is in the open country, and this is attended by small
expense; yet such a horse will travel further in a day, and for
a longer time, than a horse that has not been gelded.   He will
do his ten or twelve leagues without food.   Afterwards, while
his master is eating his own victual, he puts his horse to
pasture, and by the time he has had a sufficient meal he will
find his horse fit to carry him further.   On the sea-coast,
where pasture is not so plentiful, such horses cannot be
reared.   Some stallions are kept by great men in stables,
because these are of a higher spirit than other horses, but
in the matter of riding they are neither swifter nor more
willing.

In the southern parts of Scotland forests are few[2], for which
reason coal is burned, and stone peat or turf, and not wood,
as we have said above; stone-peat is less hard than coal>[3].
Aeneas Sylvius says that the Scots use black stones for fuel in
an iron cradle, meaning coal or sulphureous earth by ' black
stones'.   Heather or bog-myrtle grows in the moors in greatest
abundance, and for fuel is but little less serviceable than juniper.

---

[1] Cf. *ante*, p. 31.   [2] Cf. *ante*, p. 7.

[3] 'Quia pro igne habendo carbonibus, et petris seu peltis, et non lignis
(ut superius diximus) utuntur: carbone petra est minus dura.' [F., like Orig.,
prints 'peltis,' but in his Errata changes the word to 'petis'.]   Two kinds
of peat were recognised in Scotland, as was also the case in Ireland: one, the
common peat or turf; the other, so hard that Major calls it ' petra ',—less
hard than coal.   'Cum petariis et turbariis' is a common phrase in charter
Latin.   For Ireland cf. Carve's *Lyra*, p. 43 : 'Habet et Hibernia duplicis
generis cespites, alios graciles, alios duros, et crassos, lapides quoque carbonibus
sua virtute consimiles, qui pro maximo fabrorum ferrariorum commodo variis in
locis effodiuntur.'

I have here to coin a Latin word[1] from the vulgar tongue, because I do not fancy that the plant was to be found in Italy ; but you may meet with it in the wood of Notre Dame near to Paris, though it does not there grow to such a height as in Britain. Some of our countrymen suppose the land on which this plant is found to be worthless and barren ; but I on the other hand look upon it as eminently valuable and fruitful ground. The plant when dried after the manner of juniper makes excellent fuel, and I much prefer it to coal; but just because they have the thing abundantly, they hold it cheap. Under this plant and in its neighbourhood the pasture for cattle is such that you shall find none better.

CHAP. VII.—*Concerning the Manners and Customs of the Scots.*

Mutual recriminations of the English and the Scots. HITHERTO we have had under review the soil of Scotland, its rivers and its animals, with the islands that are situated beyond the bounds of Britain. We will now speak for a little of the manners and customs of the Scots. I have read in histories written by Englishmen that the Scots are the worst of traitors, and that this stain is with them inborn. Not otherwise, if we are to believe those writers, did the Scots overthrow the kingdom and the warlike nation of the Picts. The Scots, on the other hand, call the English the chief of traitors[2], and, denying that their weapon is a brave man's sword, affirm that all their victories are won by guile and craft. I, however, am not wont to credit the common Scot in his vituperation of the English, nor yet the Englishman in his vituperation of the Scot[3]. 'Tis the part of a sensible man to use his own eyes, to put far from him at once all inordinate love of his own countrymen and hatred of his enemies, and thereafter to pass judgment, well weighed, in equal scales ; he must keep the temper of his mind founded upon right reason, and regulate his opinion accordingly. Aristotle observes in the sixth book of his *Politics*[4] that southern peoples excel the northerners in

---

[1] 'haddera'. It is curious that Major should have coined this word, when 'erica' is in common use in Pliny for heath and broom.

[2] 'traditionum' Orig. and F. : an evident misprint for 'traditorum'.

[3] *Cf.* Bk. IV. ch. xix., where the death of Edward the First is used as an occasion to express the same feeling.

[4] *Pol.* vii. 7 : 'Those who live in a cold climate and in [northern] Europe

intelligence, and that, on the contrary, northerners have the advantage in warlike virtue. In northern nations, therefore, we need not expect to find craftiness in war, or guile. But in the matter of prejudices that have their root in hatred, bear this in mind: that two neighbouring kingdoms, striving for the mastery, never cherish a sincere desire for peace. Let pass before your eye in silent review all Europe, Africa, and Asia, the three principal parts of the world, and I am much mistaken if you do not find this to be the case. Now between England and Scotland a man may pass dry-shod, and both nations labour incessantly for the extension of their boundaries. And though in the number of its inhabitants, in the fertility of its soil, England has the advantage over Scotland, the Scots, truly or untruly, strongly suspect that they can make head against the English—yea, even should these bring in their train a hundred thousand foreign fighting men. And this is no empty assumption on their part. For though the English became masters of Aquitaine, Anjou, Normandy, Ireland and Wales, they have up to this date made no way in Scotland, unless by the help of our own dissensions; and for eighteen hundred and fifty years the Scots have kept foot in Britain, and at this present day are no less strong, no less given to war, than they ever were, ready to risk life itself for their country's independence, and counting death for their country an honourable thing. And if the Alps, the Pyrenees, the Rhine, the sea itself, hardly suffice to make war impossible among nations of a more peaceful temper than the Britons, it is no matter for astonishment if the maintenance of peace is in very truth no easy matter among various kingdoms in one and the same island, each of them the eager rival of its neighbour in the extension of its marches.

Those wars are just which are waged in behalf of peace; and to God, the Ruler of all, I pray, that He may grant such a peace to the Britons, that one of its kings in a union of marriage may by just title gain both kingdoms—for any other way of reaching an assured peace I hardly see. I dare to say that Englishman and Scot alike have small regard for

He clears away what is objected to the Scots.

Peace, by way of intermarriage.

---

are full of spirit but wanting in intelligence and skill; and therefore they keep their freedom, but have no political organisation, and are incapable of ruling over others.' Cf. Major, Bk. I. ch. vi. (p. 32), and Bk. V. ch. xiv.

their monarchs if they do not continually aim at intermarriages, that so one kingdom of Britain may be formed out of the two that now exist[1]. Such a peaceful union finds continual hindrance in each man of hostile temper, and in all men who are bent upon their private advantage to the neglect of the common weal. Yet to this a Scottish or an English sophist may make answer : 'Intermarriages there have been many times, yet peace came not that way.' To whom I make answer, that an unexceptionable title has never been in that way made good,

The children of Margaret. whatever our historians may fable about the blessed Margaret, who was an Englishwoman. That the Scots never had more excellent kings than those born of Englishwomen is clear from the example of the children of the blessed Margaret, kings that never knew defeat, and were in every way the best. A like example you shall find in the second James, whose mother was an Englishwoman, while to prophesy about the fifth of that name, the seven-year-old grandson of an Englishman, would indeed be to pretend to see clearly into a future charged with clouds[2] : but my prayer to God at least is this : that in uprightness of life and character he may imitate those Jameses, his father, his

The Scots : their temper haughty. great-grandfather, and great-great-grandfather.

Sabellicus[3], who was no mean historian, charges the Scots

---

[1] There is no more remarkable feature in this History than the repeated expression of the author's desire for a union between the countries. This is the first utterance of that sort, but compare further Bk. IV. ch. xii. on the marriage of Alexander the Third with a daughter of Henry the Third, and on the marriage of Margaret, daughter of Alexander the Third, with the king of Norway. For the fullest statement of Major's opinion see Bk. IV. ch. xviii., and cf. also Bk. V. ch. xvii., on the marriage of David the Second with the sister of Edward the Third.

[2] 'de Jacobo . . . adhuc indicare tenebrosa est aqua in nubibus aeris.' This is a favourite metaphor with Major. We find the same words in Bk. II. ch. v. and Bk. V. ch. vii, about the prophecies of Merlin, and the same with scarce a variation in the 'Propositio ad Auditores' (quoted above, p. 29).

[3] *i.e.* Marcantonio Coccio, born in 1436 in the ancient territory of the Sabines. His master, Pomponius, therefore named Coccio 'Sabellicus'. He became professor of Eloquence, and is the author of a history of Venice, *Rhapsodiæ Historiarum Enneades*, etc. He died in 1536 'gallica tabe ex vaga venere quaesita non obscura comsumptus'. The following are the more relevant passages in the History of Sabellicus :—' The English people are blue-eyed, of fair complexion and goodly appearance ; tall of stature, fearless in war, the best of bowmen. Their women are of an outstanding beauty ; the common people ignoble, untutored, and inhospitable ; the nobility have gentler manners, and are more conscious of the duties of a civil behaviour. With head

with being of a jealous temper ; and it must be admitted that
there is some colour for this charge to be gathered elsewhere.
The French have a proverb about the Scots to this effect : ' Ill
est fier comme ung Escossoys', that is, ' The man is as proud
as a Scot'. And this receives some confirmation from that
habit of the French when they call the western Spaniards birds
of a fine feather; and Dionysius, in his *De Situ Orbis*, speaking of the Spaniards, gives them this character, ' that they
are of all men the haughtiest'. Now the Scots trace their The Spaniards
descent, as we shall show further on, from the Spaniards, and a proud race.
grandchildren mostly follow the habits of their ancestors—
witness the Philosopher, in the first book of his *Politics*,
where he says, ' The boastful man takes readily to jealousy'.
A man that is puffed up strives for some singular pre-eminence
above his fellows, and when he sees that other men are equal
to him or but little his inferiors, he is filled with rage and
breaks out into jealousy. I do not deny that some of the
Scots may be boastful and puffed up, but whether they suffer
more than their neighbours from suchlike faults, I have not
quite made up my mind. Many a trifling thing is said that will
not bear examination. I merely remember that Sabellicus
thus expressed himself. Perchance he had seen a few Scots

---

uncovered, and bending on one knee, they greet a guest ; should it be a
woman, they offer a kiss. They take her to a tavern and drink together.
And that is a thing truly disgraceful. Let all that is lustful remain far from
us . . . There are many towns in the land, the chief among them Lundonia,
the royal seat, by corruption of language now called Londres. Scotland
is the furthest part of England to the north. . . . Not far distant lies Hibernia,
which the common people call 'Hirland'. The dress of these islanders is the same;
there is indeed scarce any point of difference betwixt them—the same tongue,
the same customs. Their intelligence is quick ; they are prone to revenge ; in
war they are of a notable fierceness; they are sober, most patient of hunger.
They are of an elegant stature, but careless of civilised ways. The Scots are so
called from their painted bodies, as some hold ; it was of old the common custom
to burn patterns into the breast and arms; to-day that custom has fallen from use
in most cases, and those that observe it are the Wild Scots. They are by nature
jealous, and hold the rest of mortals in scorn ; too readily do they make a boast
of their noble descent, and, though in the depths of poverty, will claim kinship
with the royal stock ; they delight in lying, and keep not the peace ; in other
respects they are as the English.' [Then follows the story of Aeneas Sylvius
and the coal, and of the Barnacle Geese.]—*Enneadis decimae liber quintus* (vol.
i. fol. cli.) ; Venice, vol. i. 1498 ; vol. ii. 1504.

at Rome engaged in litigation connected with their benefices, and these men no doubt, as is customary with rivals, were full of mutual jealousy. The French speeches that I have quoted date from the time of Charles, the seventh of that name. At that time Charles had Scots in his service in his war with the English ; and as Charles had at first but a scanty treasury, his soldiers were forced to seize what provision they could from the common people. With those poor people they dealt harshly, and the Scottish nobles (just as they use to do in their own country) despised them as being ignobly born ; so that, first among the common people of France, and afterwards with the nation at large, they came to have this reputation of haughtiness. There sprang up at that time among the French yet another saying about the Scots. 'The Scot', they said, ' brings in a small horse first, and afterwards a big one ',—a saying that had its origin in this wise : the Scots soldiers had the habit, when in the field, to march in troops, just as most of the French do at this day, and that they might the more easily find quarters in the dwellings of the country people, they sent their amblers and sorry nags in front with a small body of men ; and when these had once got admission, they were soon followed by the men of rank with their chargers, and the main body of the troop. That all Britons are of a temper proud enough, I take to be established by the argument from universals—not the logical universal, but the moral, since it admits of some exceptions ; but that they are prouder than the Germans, the Spaniards[1], or the French, I do not grant.

We will now proceed to another charge that is brought against our countrymen. It is said that the Scots were in the habit of eating human flesh, and those who bring this charge shelter themselves under Jerome, where he writes : ' What shall I say of other nations—how when I was in Gaul as a youth, I saw the Scots, a *British* race, eating human flesh, and how, when these men came in the forests upon herds of swine and sheep and cattle, they would cut off the buttocks of the shepherds and the paps of the women, and hold these for their greatest delicacy ? ' You cannot say that he means the

The Scots in the habit of eating human flesh.

---

[1] For the Spaniards who attended Major's class in Paris, see the Introduction to this volume.

Goths or the Irish Scots, because of the word *British*. Well, to this from Jerome I make answer: Even if all the Scots did so, 'twould bring no stain on their posterity : the faithful in Europe are descended from the Gentile and the infidel ; the guilt of an ancestor is no disgrace to his children when these have learned to live conformably with reason. Besides, though a few Scots of whom St. Jerome thus writes, did as he reports, in their own island even the Scots did not generally live in such fashion —a conclusion that I take to be proved thus : Bede, writing three hundred years after Jerome, where he treats of the first emergence of the Scots in history, and he was their neighbour, says not a word of this. Strabo seemed to attribute the custom to the Irish, and to certain savage Scots.

I further note that the English Bartholomew, in his *De Proprietatibus*[1], says of the Scots 'that among the Scots 'tis held to be a base man's part to die in his bed, but death in battle they think a noble thing'. To him I make answer that this is no way to be imputed as a fault, that death in arms and in a just quarrel is a fair end for a man.

Most writers note yet another fault in the Scots, and Sabellicus touches this point : That the Scots are prone to call themselves of noble birth ; and this I can support by a saying about the Scots that is common among the French, for they will say of such an one : 'That man's a cousin of the king of Scots'[2]. To speak truly, I am not able to acquit the Scots of this fault[3], for both at home and abroad they take inordinate pleasure in noble birth, and (though of ignoble origin themselves) delight in hearing themselves spoken of as come of noble blood. I sometimes use humorously the following argument in dealing with such of my fellow-countrymen as make themselves out to be of noble birth. One thing must be granted me : that no man, namely, is noble, unless one of his parents be noble ; and that it is absurd to call any one ignoble whose parents are noble. This granted me, I pro-

The Scots boast of their kinship to the king.

---

[1] The first Encyclopædia of English origin, *De Proprietatibus Rerum*, was written by Bartholomeus de Glanville about 1360, and translated about 1398 by the Cornishman, John de Trevisa.

[2] Is regis Scotorum cognatus germanus est.

[3] Leslie says (P. 96 of his History, ed. Cody) : 'quhen sum writeris in thame noted sik vices they spak no altogither raschlie'.

ceed to ask, whether Adam were of noble birth, or no. If the
first—it contradicts one part of the premiss. If the second—
all his children were ·of noble birth. And so you must grant
all men noble, or all ignoble. Besides, concerning the first
nobleman, I change the question, and ask, ' How came he by
his nobility ?' Not from his parents—so much is known ; and
if, first of all, you call him a nobleman who is the son of one
who is not noble, you contradict the premiss. Poor noblemen
marry into mean but wealthy families. In this way some of the
Scots ennoble their whole country. Such unions are recognised
in Scotland as well as in England. But to such Scots I am
wont to say, that then, their blood being mixed with ignoble
blood, there is no pure nobility. I say, therefore—There is
absolutely no true nobility but virtue and the evidence of
virtue. That which is commonly called nobility is naught but
a windy thing of human devising. Those men are termed
nobles who draw a livelihood from what they possess—and by
whatever means they came by their possessions—without pursuit
of any handicraft, most of all if they can also claim an ancient
descent, whether they won their wealth by just or by unjust
means, and if it remain for generations in their family : these
in the eyes of the world are noble. Hence it follows that
kings drew their origin from shepherds, and shepherds again
their ·origin from kings. The first part of the corollary is
plain, and up to this point is declared. If a shepherd buy
lands with his much wealth, his issue acquires somewhat, if but
little, of nobility. His grandson, grown wealthier still, ad-
vances a step in nobility ; but with the lapse of time riches are
added to riches : the owner now becomes a mighty chief, and
takes to wife the daughter of a king—who just in the same
way had climbed to his present eminence. I shall now state
the second part of the corollary, where one monarch drives
another from his throne. The exile is forced to take service
as a soldier or to accept some other place of inferiority, and
from his proud estate must sound the lowest depth. Therefore—. Sabellicus asserts that the Scots delight in lying ; but
to me it is not so clear that lies like these flourish with more
vigour among the Scots than among other people[1].

The nobles in
Scotland.

---

[1] See APPENDIX for a translation of the 14th question of the 24th distinction
in the *In Quartum*, where the question of nobility is treated at greater length.

CHAP. VIII.—*Something further concerning the manners and customs of the Scots, that is, of the peasantry, as well as of the nobles, and of the Wild Scots, as well as the civilised part.*

HAVING said something of the manner of life and character of the Scots, it remains to continue the same subject in respect of their civilised nobles, as many before me have done. The British nobles are not less civilised than their peers on the continent of Europe. They form a certain community apart from the common people. Of outward elegance I find more in the cities of France and their inhabitants than among the Britons; but in the country, and among the peasantry, there is more of elegance in Britain. In Britain no man goes unarmed to church or market, nor indeed outside the village in which he dwells. In their style of dress, and in their arms, they try to rival the lesser nobles, and if one of these should strike them they return the blow upon the spot. In both of the British kingdoms the warlike strength of the nation resides in its common people and its peasantry. The farmers rent their land from the lords, but cultivate it by means of their servants, and not with their own hands. They keep a horse and weapons of war, and are ready to take part in his quarrel, be it just or unjust, with any powerful lord, if they only have a liking for him, and with him, if need be, to fight to the death. The farmers have further this fault: that they do not bring up their sons to any handicraft. Shoemakers, tailors, and all such craftsmen they reckon as contemptible and unfit for war; and they therefore bring up their children to take service with the great nobles, or with a view to their living in the country in the manner of their fathers. Even dwellers in towns they hold as unfit for war; and in truth they are much before the towns-folk in the art of war, and prove themselves far stouter soldiers. Townsfolk are accustomed to luxurious eating and drinking, and a quiet fashion of life, and have not the habit of bearing arms; they give in therefore at once when brought face to face with the hard life of a soldier. The farmers, on the other hand, brought up in all temperance of drink, and continuous bodily exercise, are of a harder fibre. Though they do not till their land themselves, they keep a diligent eye upon their

Marginal notes:
The British nobility are a civilised nobility.

Dislike of the farmers to till the soil themselves.

servants and household, and in great part ride out with the neighbouring nobles.

Among the nobles I note two faults. The first is this: If two nobles of equal rank happen to be very near neighbours, quarrels and even shedding of blood are a common thing between them; and their very retainers cannot meet without strife. Just in this way, when Abraham and Lot increased in wealth, did their shepherds not keep the peace. From the beginning of time families at strife with one another make bequest of hatred to their children; and thus do they cultivate hatred in the place of the love of God.

The second fault I note is this: The gentry educate their children neither in letters nor in morals[1]—no small calamity to the state. They ought to search out men learned in history, upright in character, and to them intrust the education of their children, so that even in tender age these may begin to form right habits, and act when they are mature in years like men endowed with reason. Justice, courage, and all those forms of temperance which may be put to daily use they should pursue, and have in abhorrence the corresponding vices as things low and mean. The sons of neighbouring nobles would not then find it a hard thing to live together in peace; they would no more be stirrers up of sedition in the state, and in war would approve themselves no less brave—as may be seen from the example of the Romans, whose most illustrious generals were men well skilled in polite learning; and the same thing we read of the Greeks, the Carthaginians, and the Persians.

Further, just as among the Scots we find two distinct tongues, so we likewise find two different ways of life and conduct. For some are born in the forests and mountains of the north, and these we call men of the Highland, but the others men of the Lowland. By foreigners the former are called Wild Scots, the latter householding Scots. The Irish tongue is in use among the former, the English tongue among the latter.

---

[1] It was in 1496, when Major was abroad, that the remarkable Act was passed which ordained that all barons and freeholders should send their sons to grammar schools at eight or nine years of age, and keep them there till they have 'perfect Latin', and thereafter to the schools of 'art and jure' for three years.

One-half of Scotland speaks Irish, and all these as well as the
Islanders we reckon to belong to the Wild Scots. In dress,
in the manner of their outward life, and in good morals, for
example, these come behind the householding Scots—yet they
are not less, but rather much more, prompt to fight ; and this,
both because they dwell more towards the north [1], and because,
born as they are in the mountains, and dwellers in forests, their
very nature is more combative. It is, however, with the householding Scots that the government and direction of the kingdom
is to be found, inasmuch as they understand better, or at least
less ill than the others, the nature of a civil polity. One part of The Wild Scots.
the Wild Scots have a wealth of cattle, sheep, and horses, and
these, with a thought for the possible loss of their possessions,
yield more willing obedience to the courts of law and the king.
The other part of these people delight in the chase and a life
of indolence ; their chiefs eagerly follow bad men if only they
may not have the need to labour ; taking no pains to earn
their own livelihood, they live upon others, and follow their
own worthless and savage chief in all evil courses sooner than
they will pursue an honest industry. They are full of mutual
dissensions, and war rather than peace is their normal condition.
The Scottish kings have with difficulty been able to withstand
the inroads of these men. From the mid-leg to the foot they
go uncovered ; their dress is, for an over garment, a loose plaid,
and a shirt saffron-dyed. They are armed with bow and
arrows, a broadsword, and a small halbert. They always carry
in their belt a stout dagger, single-edged [2], but of the sharpest.
In time of war they cover the whole body with a coat of mail,
made of iron rings, and in it they fight. The common
folk among the Wild Scots go out to battle with the whole
body clad in a linen garment sewed together in patchwork,
well daubed with wax or with pitch, and with an over-coat of
deerskin [3]. But the common people among our domestic Scots

---

[1] Cf. Bk. I. ch. v. (P. 32).

[2] Cf. Bk. v. ch. iii. for a rather different description of the arms of the
Wild Scots at Bannockburn. May the description here be that of the Wild
Scots' accoutrements as Major knew them, and that in Bk. v. be based upon
an older chronicler ?

[3] The old notices as to the Highland dress are collected in *Transactions of
the Iona Club*, vol. i. p. 25 *seq.* (1834).

and the English fight in a woollen garment.   For musical
instruments and vocal music the Wild Scots use the harp, whose
strings are of brass, and not of animal gut ; and on this
they make most pleasing melody.   Our householding Scots, or
quiet and civil-living people—that is, all who lead a decent
and reasonable life—these men hate, on account of their differing speech, as much as they do the English.

CHAP. IX.—*Concerning the various origin of the Scots, and the
reason of the name.   For the Scots are sprung from the Irish, and the
Irish in turn from the Spaniards, and the Scots are so named after the
woman Scota.*

UP to this point we have been telling of the origin of the
Britons, and of the customs of the Scottish Britons.   It remains
to say something of the origin of the Scots.   Some of the
English chroniclers affirm that the descent of the Scots as well
as of the Welsh may be traced to Brutus.   Brutus, they say,
had three sons, the name of the first, Locrinus, to whom he
gave England for his kingdom.   The name of the second son
was Albanac ; to him he gave the northern part of the island,
and after him it was called Alban.   On the third son, Camber,
he bestowed the western part of the island, and it after him
was called Cambria, and, at a later date, Wales.   This fable
about Brutus we did not, in an earlier part of our work, accept ;
and whatever (if indeed there were any such person) may be
the fact about his sons, it is attested by a multiplicity of proof
that we trace our descent from the Irish.   This we learn from
the English Bede[1], who had no desire to attenuate the lineage
of his kingdom.   Their speech is another proof of this : at the
present day almost the half of Scotland speaks the Irish tongue,
and not so long ago it was spoken by the majority of us, and
yet between Britain and Ireland flows such a breadth of water
as we find between France and England.   They brought their
speech from Ireland into Britain ; and this is clear from the
testimony of our own chroniclers, whose writers were not negli-
gent in this respect.   I say then, from whomsoever the Irish
traced their descent, from the same source come the Scots

The sons of
Brutus.

The Scots
descended from
the Irish.

The Irish
descended from
the Spaniards
and the Scots
from the Irish.

_____
[1] *Hist. Eccl.* i. i.

though at one remove, as with son and grandfather. But the
Irish had their origin from the Spaniards, a fact that I take to
be admitted by the chroniclers. Starting from Braganza, a city
of Portugal, and from the Ebro which receives most of the
rivers of Spain, many of the inhabitants joining together went in
quest of a new settlement and put out on the wide sea, just as
they do at this present. In the space of three days they made
a certain island, moderately peopled, and inasmuch as the
inhabitants could offer no resistance, there they settled themselves, and gave the name of Hibernia to this island, either
because the greater part of the Spaniards came from the river
Ebro [Hiberus] in Spain, or after a certain soldier of Spain named
Hiberus, as some will have it, whose mother's name was Scota.
So that by some the island was called Hibernia, after Hiberus;
by others Scotia, after Scota. In the time of our ancestors it was
more commonly called Scotia, but, in process of time, to mark
its distinction from the Scots of Britain, it came to be known as
Hibernia, not as Scotia. In some of our chroniclers we read
that a certain king of the Greeks, by name Nealus, had a son
called Gathelus, whom for his evil deeds he banished, and that
this Gathelus set out for Egypt, and there got to wife a
daughter of Pharaoh, by name Scota; but when Pharaoh in
his pursuit of the Hebrews was drowned in the Red Sea,
Gathelus and Scota with their children were driven from
Egypt, and, taking ship in search of a new country where they
might dwell, in course of time came to the Spains [1]. They
settled themselves in Lusitania, which is now called Portugal
and is a part of Spain, and there built and fortified the city of
Braganza. Others of their following, however, penetrating
further into Spain, reached the river Hiberus; and after dwelling there, they and their descendants, for two hundred years,
began to seek a new place of habitation, and came to the island
which is now called Hibernia. And if this story be true, the
Irish Scots are descended from the Spaniards.

As to this original departure of theirs out of Greece and Egypt,
I count it a fable, and for this reason: their English enemies had
learned to boast of an origin from the Trojans, so the Scots

---

[1] *i.e.* the Roman provinces of Hispania citerior and Hispania ulterior, which
together made up the peninsula.

claimed an original descent from the Greeks who had subdued the Trojans, and then bettered it with this about the illustrious kingdom of Egypt. But seeing that all history and the similarity of language went to prove that the Irish sprang from people of Spain, they added yet this : that the Greeks and the Egyptians, from whom they claimed a still further and indeed original descent, spent two hundred years in western Hesperia. From all this it seems that some true statements are mixed up with statements that are doubtful. For it is certain that the Irish are descended from the Spaniards and the Scottish Britons from the Irish—all the rest I dismiss as doubtful, and to me, indeed, unprofitable. Our chroniclers relate yet another absurd story: to wit, that Simon Brek and the men of Spain who landed in Ireland both made a new language and put to death the whole population of the island. But, first, it would be both an inhuman thing, and one that served no purpose, to clear the island of slaves, women, and children. Antoninus [1] and Vincentius [2] tell us that the Spaniards landed in Ireland with a large fleet and took possession of it as they saw good, whether with the sword or by peaceful means. What advantage could they reap by this destruction of an unwarlike race? Secondly, as to this making of a language—'tis a thing contrary to all reason. If two races that speak different languages mix one with another, a language is produced which holds of both, so far as speaking is concerned, but which has more resemblance to that language of the two which is the more civilised and the pleasanter to hear. This is clear from a consideration of the English tongue, which has much in common with the Saxon. But owing to Danish and British influences it is much changed from the Saxon. And we southern Scots differ in our speech from the language of England on account of our neighbourhood to the Wild Scots. The same thing may be seen with the

---

[1] Antoninus was archbishop of Florence; ob. 1459. He wrote a chronological history, which he called a ' Summa Historialis'.

[2] Vincentius Bellovacensis [*i.e.* of Beauvais] a Dominican, fl. in the 13th century. He wrote a ' Speculum Doctrinale' which embraced all the sciences. Among the books in the small library of the monastery of Kinloss there were found, before 1535, ' quatuor Vincentii volumina, tria Chronicorum Antonini, and two of the works of John Major upon the Sentences.—*Records*, etc., ed. by Dr. John Stuart, 1872.

people of Picardy, in their use of the French language, on account of their proximity to the people of Flanders. Everywhere the same fact may be noticed. The Irish language is very near the Spanish. The Spaniard in his morning greeting says 'Bona dies', the Irishman, 'Vennoka die'. The Spaniards, like the Gascons—as we observed when we were in Paris—put *b* for *v*, unless they have changed their speech[1]. The Irish too, use the same funeral dirges as the Spaniards, and their customs are the same in many ways.

Ireland is an island about half the size of Britain, not so far to the north, and situated to the west of Britain, on all sides encompassed by the sea, and by as much distant from Britain as Britain is from Gaul. No serpents are to be found there, and if you so much as place near a serpent in any other country a bit of Irish earth, that serpent dies. The island produces a kind of horses, which the natives call *Haubini*[2], whose pace is of the gentlest. They were called *Asturcones*[3] in old times because

The situation of Ireland.

Irish soil kills serpents.

---

[1] 'Vennoka die' is evidently meant for 'beannacht Dé' (pronounced 'beanaχt dyē', 'blessing of God', a very common Irish greeting. 'beannacht' is borrowed from the Latin 'benedictio', and 'Dé' (the genitive of 'Dia') has nothing to do with 'dies'; but Major is so far correct about *b* and *v* that in certain cases *b* in Irish becomes *v*.

[2] Cf. Littré *s.v.* HOBIN : 'nom d'une race de chevaux d'Ecosse, qui vont naturellement le pas qu'on appelle l'amble'. Ital. *ubino*, Dan. *hoppe*=a mare, Fris. *hoppa*, our *hobby*. Howell (*Lexic. Tetrag.*) has 'HOBBIE, cheval irlandois'. Cf. 'Sunt etiam in hac insula [Ireland] praestantissimi equi, adeo ut Munsterus l. 2. Cosmograph. in descript. Hibern. asserat, "gignit Hibernia multos equos, gnaviter incedunt, studentque velut data opera mollem facere gressum, ne insidenti molestiam ullam inferant". Et Jovius, "equi tota Hibernia incorrupta sobole gignunt, mollissimo incessu Hobinos Angli vocant, et ob id a delicatis expetuntur, ac in Gallia, Italiaque nobilioribus foeminis dono dantur. Ex hoc genere duodecim candoris eximii purpura et argenteis habenis exornatos in Pompam summorum Pontificum sessore vacuos duci vidimus".'—Carve : *Lyra* ed. 1666, p. 43. For the number of 'equi discooperti [as distinguished from 'equi cooperti '] qui dicuntur hobelarii', among the Irish troops serving in Scotland in 1296, cf. *Documents illustrative of the History of Scotland*, ed. by the Rev. Joseph Stevenson, 1870, vol. ii. p. 125.

[3] Cf. Pliny : *Nat. Hist.* viii. 42. 'Out of the same Spaine, from the parts called Gallicia and Asturia, certaine ambling jennets or nags are bred, which wee call Thieldones : and others of lesse stature and proportion every way, named Asturcones. These horses have a pleasant pace by themselves differing from others. For albeit they bee put to their full pace, a man shall see them set one foot before another so deftly and roundly in order by turnes [mollis

they came from Asturia in Spain, and indeed the Spanish
colonists brought those horses along with them. The French call
these same horses English Haubini or Hobini, because they get
them by way of England. This island, further, is no less fertile
than Britain, and abounds in fair rivers well stocked with fish, in
meadowland and woodland. The more southern part, which
also is the more civilised, obeys the English king. The more
northern part is under no king, but remains subject to chiefs
of its own. In all that has now been told—of the horses, of the
serpents, and of a soil that is fatal to all poisonous animals—
we find a proof of the quiescence of its sky. For these
Whence this   are not the result in the first instance of the soil itself, nor yet
peculiar virtue of the moveable sky, for part of Ireland is situated under the
in the soil?   same parallel with Britain or with a part of Britain. Wherefore it is from the influence of that sky which can suffer no
disturbance that the soil of Ireland draws this virtue [1].

CHAP. X.—*Of the Origin of the Picts, their Name and Customs.*

LET us now leave the Irish Scots, settled in the island of
Ireland, and speak for a little of the Picts who were the
second, after the Britons, and, according to true history, before
the Scots, to found a kingdom in Britain. As the Venerable
Bede says in the first book, and the first chapter, of his Ecclesiastical History of the English nation, the Picts (by their own
report) put out to sea from Scythia with a few ships of war,
and, driven by a storm beyond the bounds of Britain, came to
Ireland, where they found the nation of the Scots in possession, and sought from them a settlement for themselves in these
parts, but obtained none. But to the Picts the Scots spoke
thus : ' We can give you good counsel as to what you may be

---

alterno crurum explicatu glomeratio], that it would doe one good to see it.'—
Holland's trans., 1601.

[1] Cf. Aristot. *de Coelo*, Bk. II., and Bacon's comment :—' Aristotle's temerity
and cavilling has begotten for us a fantastic heaven, composed of a fifth essence,
free from change, and free likewise from heat.'—*Descriptio Globi Intellectualis*,
ch. 7, Ellis and Spedding's ed. vol. vi. p. 525. As to the virtues of the climate
of Ireland cf. Giraldus Cambrensis, who attributes the singular salubrity of his
birthplace, Manorbeer in Pembrokeshire, to its nearness to Ireland.—*Itin.
Kambriae*, lib. i. cap. 12.

able to do.   Another island we know, not far from our own, towards the rising sun, which, in a clear day, may in the far distance be discerned.   If you have a mind to make for that island, you will be able to dwell there.   For though the inhabitants should resist your landing, yet, with us to help you, all will turn out to your furthest wish '—the Scots, in this counsel of theirs, acting on that common proverb: He who A common will not receive you as a guest in his own house praises the proverb. entertainment that you will meet with from his neighbour, that he may be rid of you.   The Picts then made for Britain, and began to dwell in the northern parts of the island towards the east; for the Britons were in occupation of the southern portion.   And since the Picts were wifeless, they sought wives of the Scots, who on this condition only would grant the request, that, when any doubt arose in the matter of succession, they should choose their king rather from the female line than The queens of from the male line, a practice which, it is well known, prevails the Picts. with the Picts to the present day.   They got the name of The origin of Picts either because they excelled in beauty of person and their name. bodily strength, or because their dress was mostly of many colours, as if painted.

CHAP. XI.—*In what manner the Scots first gained a settlement in Britain.*

To the Picts (as we have said) the Irish Scots gave their daughters in marriage, and, moved by a desire to see their children, they made no infrequent visits to the Picts, now settled in Britain.   There they took note of certain parts, in every way most fit for the pasturing of cattle, which the Picts had not yet occupied, and likewise of many small islands between Ireland and Britain.   Other islands too they saw, in their many voyages, on the western shore of Britain, more northerly than Ireland.   All this they reported to their own people; and when the Irish Scots had considered the matter, they led into Britain yet a third nation, for it was with Reuda Chief Reuda. as their leader that the Scots set out from Ireland, and whether by friendly consent or by the sword gained a settlement in Britain by the side of the Picts.   From this leader it is, according to Bede [1], that they are to this day called *Dahal-reudini*. For in their tongue *Dahal* means a 'part'. Our own

Fergus.

chronicles, however, bear that Fergus, son of Ferchard, set foot in Britain before Reuda, and that he showed in his armour a red lion, and was the first of the Scots who bore the sceptre in Britain, as witness the verses well known among our people: 'In Albion's realm first king of Scottish seed, Fergus the son of Ferchard bore mid his troops the ensign of a red lion, roaring in a tawny field.'

Concerning the date when this same Fergus set foot in Britain, take the following verses: 'Fergus, who first gave laws and kingly rule to the Britons, lived before Christ three hundred years and thirty.'

Fergus brought with him from Ireland the marble chair in which the kings of Scots are crowned at Scone [2]. It is said that Symon Brek, when he set out from Spain for Ireland, found

The marble
stone.

this marble stone, fashioned like a chair. This he regarded as an omen of the kingdom that was to be. But this story about Fergus in no way conflicts with the statement of the Venerable Bede. For it was but a feeble foundation of the kingdom that Fergus laid, and it was the son of his great-grandson,

Rether.

Rether, as our chroniclers call him, or Reuda—to speak with Bede—who confirmed that first foundation, and added to his kingdom both what he won from the Picts and somewhat too from the Britons. He invaded that part of the country of the Britons to which he gave a name made famous by his fall in battle, *Retherdale* to wit; that is, the valley, or part, of Rether, in English *Rethisdaile*, and to this day it is called *Ryddisdaile* [3], inasmuch as it was there that Rether, king of the Scots, lost his life. Very like this is to what we read of the mighty empire of the Assyrians, whose beginnings some writers trace to Bel, but others to Ninus Nembrothides. For the first foundation of that empire, small in outward measure, but great in promise, was laid by Bel, and afterwards received a mighty increase by Ninus Nembrothides. So much then let it suffice to have said concerning the first coming of the Scots and Picts into Britain.

---

[1] *Hist. Eccl.* i. 1.

[2] For the legends connected with this stone see Mr. Skene's *Coronation Stone*.

[3] Redesdale, in Northumberland.

CHAP. XII.—*Concerning the arrival of the Romans in Britain, and their achievements in that island.*

BY the Romans, at that time the masters of the world, Britain Julius Caesar. had never been reached, and was indeed unknown; but Julius Caesar, in the six hundred and ninety-third year from the foundation of the city, in the sixtieth year before the Incarnation of the Word, when he had subdued Gaul, hastened into Britain, and there his reception was of the fiercest. He lost a large number of foot-soldiers, of his horse the whole, and in a storm a great part of his ships. For not only did the Britons make stand against him; the youth of the Scots and Picts were also there, as Caxton, the English historian, makes mention. For they were in fear lest, should the Romans break their fast with the Britons, they would sup with the Scots and Picts, as the proverb goes: ' 'Tis become your own concern when your neighbour's house takes fire.'

Wherefore, though the three British kings—to wit, the Briton, the Scot, and the Pict—were at war among themselves, against Caesar and their most powerful foe, the Romans, they went out to battle of one mind, ready to fight in one solid mass; and, that I may say much in few words, when they had slain some of the Romans and routed the rest, they forced Caesar to show his back. He then returned to both Caesar's flight. Gauls, and when he had recovered himself, collected again a mighty fleet (six hundred vessels, as they say), and hastened a second time against the Britons, by whom he was nobly met, and his horsemen were routed utterly. The tribune Labienus, Death of a Roman of renown, was there slain; but Caesar gathered once Labienus. more with care the wandering and scattered Romans. He again attacked the Britons, and now successful, now suffering defeat, at last came out the conqueror. After this victory he Caesar's brought a large part of the Britons under Roman rule, and victory. forced Cassibellaunus, king of the Britons, to surrender. This king bound himself to pay yearly to Caesar, as representing the Roman people, three thousand pounds of silver. Caesar then journeyed through the northern parts of the island, and came to the Scottish Sea that is called Forth, and sent letters both to the Scots and to the Picts, in which he showed how that he

had subdued the Gauls, the Germans, and the Britons, and
counselled them to submit to ' the Romans, the masters of the
world, and the toga'ed race'; and when the Scots and Picts
made small account of these letters, he sent them others of a
threatening sort.   An answer then they made forthwith, that
they were moved neither by the fair words of the Romans nor
yet by their threats, that with the help of the gods and with
their own right arm they trusted to defend their remote and
difficult recesses; but were it otherwise, they would spend
their life for their country's freedom, and not without fearful
bloodshed should the Romans establish their rule among them.
Meanwhile, and when Caesar was awaiting the answer of the
northern kings, he received sudden tidings of the Gauls, that
these were rebelling against the Romans.   When he heard
this, he determined to make all speed to both Gauls, choosing
rather to bring to terms a people once subdued, now in rebellion,
than during such rebellion to attack another foe—lest he might
thus lose the whole result of his laborious toil.   But before

A memorial
in stone.

his departure he ordered that a building of stone should be
raised near the water of Caron [Carron][1], as a memorial of his
victory—herein imitating Hercules, who in the western part
of Spain left two pillars in everlasting monument.

CHAP. XIII.—*How the Emperor Claudius came to Britain.*

Claudius
Caesar.

IN the seven hundred and ninety-ninth year of the city,
Claudius, fourth emperor after Augustus Caesar, came to
Britain, and, without any battle or shedding of blood, within
a very few days reduced to submission the largest part of the
island, which was still in a measure rebellious.   To the Roman
empire he added the islands of the Orkneys which lie to the
north of Britain, of which we have above made mention.   But
in the sixth month from his setting out from Rome he

Britannicus.

returned thither, bestowing upon his son the name of Britannicus.   This journey to Britain he accomplished in the fourth
year of his reign, which year answers to the forty-sixth from
the Incarnation of the Word.   And here it is to be noted

---

[1] The monument known as ' Arthur's O'on ', ' Julius Hoff ' ; figured in Camden's *Brit.*, p. 1223, ed. 1722, and in Gordon's *Itin. Septent.*, p. 24, ed. 1726.

as a wonderful thing how he left untouched the Scots and the Picts, for to the Orkney islands he went by sea; but his was not the daring spirit of Caesar, and for this reason he passed by each of the two kings who had withstood Caesar with success.

From Bede and discourse of history it is made clear that afterwards the Scots and Picts made a sudden attack upon the Britons along with the Romans—unless it were argued that those kings promised to obey the Roman rule, and then at once on the departure of the Romans rose in revolt— a thing which I find nowhere recorded. In the time of the emperor Claudius, a mighty war began between the confederated Scots and Picts on the one hand, and the Britons on the other—a war which lasted without a break for one hundred and fifty-four years. According to our chroniclers, the Romans were aiming, with the help of the Britons, at making the Scots and Picts tributaries to them; which when these peoples came to understand, they made a fierce attack upon the Romans and the Britons, sparing neither sex, and levelling with the ground some fair cities of the Britons— Agned for one, which, when it had been rebuilt by Heth, the king of the Picts, came to be called Hethburg, and to-day is known to all men as Edinburgh, the royal seat in Scotland; Carlisle, too, and Alinclud or Alclid, which I take it, is the city now known as Dunbarton. Afterwards, in the year one hundred and fifty-six of the Incarnate Word, when Antoninus Verus, fourteenth from Augustus, began to reign along with his brother, Aurelius Commodus—in whose time the holy man Eleutherius was pope at Rome—Lucius, the British king, wrote a letter to the pope, praying for baptism, and to his prayer the pontiff religiously assented; and thus, the faith once received, the Britons kept it intact and unassailed even to the days of Diocletian.

Hethburg. Edinburgh.

Pope Eleutherius. Lucius, the first Christian king of the Britons.

CHAP. XIV.—*Concerning the events which thereafter happened in Britain, the building of the wall, the passion of Ursula with her companions at Cologne, the reception of the Catholic Faith, and the rest.*

IN the hundred and eighty-ninth year from the Incarnation of our Lord, Severus set foot in Britain, to the end he might help the Britons against the Scots and Picts, and he saw that there was much need to build some kind of wall between them.

A wall built. He made a wall accordingly, of stones and turf, as is told by Bede in the fifth chapter of the first book of his history of the church among the English nation [1]. This wall extended between the rivers Tyne and Esk. A proof this is that the Scots and Picts did not acknowledge Roman rule. And further, in the year of our Lord two hundred twenty and five,

Ursula. Ursula, and along with her eleven thousand virgins, were to have journeyed to Aremorica, that they might there find husbands, because at that time the Aremoricans refused to take Frankish women to wife. These maidens took ship on the river Thames, but when a storm of wind arose they were tossed towards the Rhine, and so reached Cologne. With them Govan, the king of that country, and Elga his brother, together with his vassals, desired to have carnal dealing, which thing the maidens resisted with all their force, and then the tyrants slew them. This Saint Ursula was the daughter of Dionoth, the ruler of Britain, and granddaughter, by a sister, of the king of the Scots. Thereafter, Govan and his brother Elga gather a large army, desiring to bring ruin on the country of those maidens; and when they had set foot in Britain, they began to destroy its cities, strongholds, and above all (for they were infidels) its churches, and the Christians they everywhere put to the sword.

Alban. Saint Alban suffered at that time. At length a certain Roman,
Gratian. by name Gratian, comes to Britain, puts Govan to flight, and claims for himself the crown of the Britons. He in turn was slain by the Britons for his misdeeds. After his death Govan returned yet once more to Britain, and wrought evil more than ever. The Britons thereupon approached the king of the

---

[1] Bede led Major and all subsequent Scottish historians (except Buchanan) into error on this point. In recent years it has been proved that this wall was built by Hadrian, though it is possible that Severus repaired it before commencing his Caledonian campaign [A.D. 208]. See Dr. Collingwood Bruce's *Handbook*, p. 82, third ed. 1885, and Mr. Scarth's *Roman Britain*, p. 59. Buchanan shows (*Rer. Scotic. Hist.*, p. 5) that he saw Bede's error, and distinguishes between the wall of Antonine between the Forth and the Clyde, which was repaired by Severus (cf. Mr. Rhys's *Celtic Britain*, p. 91), and that of Hadrian between the Tyne and the Solway. It is noteworthy that Major seems strangely ignorant of the classical accounts of Britain.

Aremoricans (that is, of Little Britain), by name Aldrey, be- Aldrey.
seeching him to come to their help.   He sends his own brother
Constantius into Britain, who kills Govan, and puts all the
infidels to the sword.   This done, Constantius became king of
the Britons, that is, of that tract of land in the island which
the Britons were the first to take possession of.   Here once
more the Britons began openly to worship Christ.   The Scots,
too, in the seventh year of the emperor Severus, in the time of
Victor, first received the Catholic faith.   Some verses well
known among the Scots declare this date, and thus they run :—

> Two hundred years and three after Christ had finished His Work
> Scotland began to follow the Catholic Faith.

This Victor was the successor of Eleutherius.

CHAP. XV.—*Concerning the Strife between the Picts and Scots.*

In the two hundred and eighty-eighth year of the redemp- A war that had
tion of the world there arose a quarrel between the Scots and its origin on ac-
Picts by reason of a certain Molossian hound of wonderful swift- count of a dog.
ness, which certain Picts had taken secretly from the Scots, and
which they refused to restore.   It was at first a war of words,
but grew too soon to a strife of arms among those neighbouring
peoples.   Behold from how small a spark a great pile may be
kindled![1]   Meanwhile a certain Carausius is set over the Britons Carausius.
by the Romans,—a man who troubled the whole country by his
insatiable greed.   The Roman emperor therefore sent an order
to the Britons, to the effect that this Carausius should secretly
be put out of the way.   But when Carausius got wind of this,
he went forthwith to the Scots and the Picts, brought these to a
peaceable mind by large gifts, and the promise of still greater
things if they would but stand by him in driving the Romans
from the land.   To this they give their assent willingly.   Trusting then to such help as this, he drives the Romans out of the
country, and claims the crown of the Britons for himself.   But
when the Romans heard how matters went in Britain, they
sent a certain Bassianus, one of their generals, with a great army Bassianus.

---

[1] ' Ecce quomodo ex scintilla ignis ingens rogus coaluit.'   In the Vulgate (St.
James iii. 5) 'Ecce quantus ignis quam magnam sylvam [Gr. ὕλην, Eng. *matter*]
incendit ! '

into Britain. This Bassianus came to an understanding with
the Picts, and with their help managed to subdue the Britons
who were on the side of Carausius. He promised to bring
further help to the Picts, and to keep in check the Scots,
against whom he knew the Picts to cherish a lively hatred on
account of the wars that had been going on between them.
Albeit, Bassianus was conquered and slain by Carausius and

Bassianus slain. the Scots, the help of the Picts notwithstanding. Carausius
then frees the Britons, who had been tributary to the
Romans from the days of Julius Caesar, from such servitude
and tribute; but he was at last stabbed by one of his own

Maximus. soldiers. After his death, Maximus, who then had the command in Britain, thought the time had come when he might
gain possession of the whole island, yet saw no hope of bringing things so far while the Picts and Scots made common
cause against him. He turned his mind first, therefore, to the
Picts, as thinking them the stronger, and made with them a
treaty of peace, by which they were to attack the Scots, thinking, when once the Scots were expelled, that he should have no
hard task in driving out the Picts, and so at length gain the

The Picts
against the
Scots. sovereignty over the whole island. The Picts then wage war
against the Scots, give every village to the flames, and at the
point of the sword bring universal ruin on the country.

Death of
Eugenius. Eugenius, the king of the Scots, they slay along with his son.
Following whereupon, one Ethach by name, the brother of
Eugenius, is forced to leave his native island, with his son Erth
or Eric, and to repeat that word of Virgil, where he says—

Nos patriae fines et dulcia linquimus arva[1].

The remnant of Scots, whom the sword had spared, made
their way to Norway, Ireland, and the circumjacent islands.
The Scots, then, driven from the kingdom, and the Picts
wasted in their wars with the Scots, Maximus marches upon
the Picts with a great army, and reduces them to a tributary
condition. Now, had Maximus only been able to follow up
the victory he had won, he might have made himself sole ruler
in Britain; but here was verified once more that saying of a
Carthaginian noble about Hannibal, that Hannibal indeed

---

[1] *Ecl.* i. 3.

could win a victory, but knew not how to use it. The same thing has happened with Pompey and Caesar, and most other generals.

At this same time a certain abbot, by name Regulus, under admonition of an angel, brought into Britain relics of the Blessed Andrew, the head namely, an arm, and three fingers of the right hand, and he arrived by divine guidance in the country of the Picts. At that time Hurgust, son of Fergus, was king over that people, and he built for the Blessed Regulus and the brethren of his company a church every way noble, and granted them possessions whence they might gain their living. Thereafter, too, Hungus, king of the Picts, by reason of the special devotion in which he had the Blessed Andrew, bestowed upon that saint, on account of a miraculous victory won over the Britons, the tenth part of his lands. Further, in the year three hundred and ninety-four after the Virgin had become a mother, Pelagius the Briton, by his denial of the grace of God, sowed in the Church a pestilent poison. This is understood by most men as the question of a special auxilium. It is more agreeable to the teaching of the saints that no mortal, without the prevenient grace of God, without special auxilium, can elicit an act morally good: according to that saying of the Wise Man, ' I could not preserve myself continent except God gave it '[1],—that is, by a special gift. It is not the general co-operation of God that is here discussed. For that is necessary to every act, good as well as evil. The same is true of an act of faith, following that which the Truth speaks in the Gospel: ' No man cometh unto me, unless my Father draw him.' The Father draws him on whom he bestows a special grace of faith. Let this then suffice to have said in our fifteenth chapter, and of the expulsion of the Scots from Britain. And herewith we make an end of the first book.

Abbot Regulus.

Gifts made to Andrew the Apostle.

The necessary grace of God.

---

[1] *Book of Wisdom*, viii. 21.

BOOK II.

CHAP. I.—*Follows here the second book of British history. Of the return of the Scots into Britain, and their league with the Picts, and the wars that were soon thereafter carried on by them, and the building of a wall.*

IN the year three hundred and ninety-six from the redemption of the world, in the time of the emperors Honorius and Arcadius, the scattered Scots returned to Britain, after an exile of three-and-forty years; and this they did partly at the prayer of the Picts, who had been wasted by the tribute exacted from them by the Britons. The Scots then, in large part by the help of the Picts, received their own lands again, and, burying the memory of ancient strife, they made a new treaty of amity, remembering that word of Sallust, where he writes: 'By concord little things grow great; by discord things the greatest fall to naught'[1].

Return of the Scots to Britain.

Further, in the year of our Lord four hundred and three, Fergus son of Erth,—who was son to Echadius[2], who was brother to Eugenius, the king who had been defeated by Maximus in war,—a youth of spirit, with his two brothers, Lorn and Angus, gained possession of the whole kingdom of Scotland up to the Scottish Sea[4]. Between this Fergus, son of Erth, and the first Fergus, son of Ferchard, we reckon fifteen kings of the Scots, whose reigns cover a space of seven hundred years, as you can gather from history. That same Fergus then, son of Erth, and the Picts together, attack their ancient enemy the Britons; and when these saw no way to make face against the double enemy, they sent for succour to the Romans, who answered indeed their prayer, and when they

Fergus the Second,

---

[1] *Jugurtha*, ch. x.

[2] Perhaps 'Eochodius'; cf. Bk. II. ch. vii.

[3] Orig. 'Barno et Tenago'; F. corr. 'Loarno et Tenego', for which read 'Loarno et Angusio'.

[4] The Firth of Forth, sometimes called the Scotswater.

had set foot in the island, gave themselves to the building of a
wall, much more to the north than was the first wall built by
the Romans. The second wall was even eighty miles further The Second
to the north than was the first wall. The country that was thus Wall.
bounded Maximus, the British general, added to his kingdom. Maximus.
This wall began at Abercorn, and tended across the country to
Alcluyd, passing by the city of Glasgow and Kirkpatrick[1].
By the inhabitants it is called Gramysdyk[2]. But not content-
ing them with such works as these, the Romans and the
Britons wage open war against the Picts and Scots, and in a
certain great battle slew Fergus, king of the Scots, with a Fergus slain.
multitude of the Picts. We now have seen the slaying of three
kings of the Scots. The first was he who was killed by the
Britons, from whom Riddisdal is named[3] ; the second, Eugenius
by name, lost his life at the hands of the Britons and the Picts,
and now we read of Fergus, son of Erth, slain by the Romans
and Britons. After this war the Scots and Picts were driven
to retreat beyond the Scottish Sea. But straightway after the
departure of the Romans, Eugenius, son of Fergus, along with Eugenius.
the Picts, attacks the Britons, and inflicts upon them a defeat
so great that they were forced to implore the Romans to come
to their help. About the Britons I marvel, for this reason :
they were three to one, and under the same king ; and the
Scots and Picts, if we do not count the circumjacent islands,
held a mere corner of the country, scarce a third part of the
island. The Romans once more sent an armed force, and with
their help the Britons regained their ancient boundary in the
Scottish Sea.

CHAP. II.—*Of the sending of Bishops to Scotland, and the conse-*
cration of several of them in that country, likewise of their holy lives,
and the marvels that they wrought.

IN the year of our Lord four hundred and twenty-nine, pope Palladius is sent
Celestine consecrates as bishop Saint Palladius, and sends him into Scotland.
to Scotland. For the Scots were at that time instructed in
the faith by priests and monks without bishops. Palladius

---

[1] *i.e.* Kilpatrick.   [2] Graham's Dyke, *i.e.* Grim's Dyke or 'Devil's Dyke'.
[3] Cf. p. 56.

E

Servanus is
consecrated by
the hands of.
one bishop
only.
ordains as bishop Servanus, and sent him to the islands of the
Orkneys that he might preach the gospel to those who dwelt
there.   Hence it is plain that a bishop, where need is, can be
consecrated by one bishop, and it is not of the essence of a
bishop that he be ordained by three.   Those persons err nevertheless who ordain otherwise, where a trinity of bishops may be
had[1].   James the Less was appointed overseer[2] of Jerusalem by
Peter, John, and James the son of Zebedee; following which
example overseers are appointed by three presidents[3].   Servanus
Kentigern. baptized the Blessed Kentigern.   Further: five years after the
sending of Palladius to British Scotland, the same Celestine
Patrick. consecrates Saint Patrick, a Briton by race, as overseer, and
sends him to the people of Ireland, and he, by the holiness of
his life and the wonderful works that he did, converted the
whole of Ireland to the Christian faith.   Forty years he ruled
the church in Ireland, and then, full of days and in the odour
of sanctity, fell asleep in the Lord.   At this time Saint Ninian
Ninian.. visited the Blessed Martin at Tours, concerning whom Bede, in
the third book, at the fourth chaper of the same, speaks thus:
' The Blessed Ninian, bishop of the race of the Britons, a most
reverend and holy man, who had been instructed in all things
at Rome, founded Candida Casa, that is, a church built of
stone, in a manner not in use among the Britons; wherefore it
Candida Casa. came to be called Candida Casa.   He built there a church in
honour of the Blessed Martin, where this same Ninian and
other holy men now rest.'   The Britons were then in occupation of the place, because it belonged to the province of the
Bernicii—the kingdom of the Northumbrians is thus divided
because the more northern portion thereof is called Bernicia.
At this time, and even to the days of Bede, Candida Casa
belonged to the Northumbrians.   Bede wrote, having regard

---

[1] The consecration of a bishop by the present discipline of the Roman church
must be performed ex necessitate praecepti by not less than three bishops, except
by a papal dispensation which may allow two assistant priests to take the place
of two bishops.   Some few theologians have, however, maintained that three
episcopal consecrators are required ex necessitate sacramenti, and that a consecration by a single bishop, without at least a papal dispensation, would be invalid.—Ferraris: *Prompta Bibliotheca*, s.v. EPISCOPUS.

[2] antistitem.

[3] a tribus praesulibus antistites instituuntur.

to his own day, and not to what might be in the future.
You will then understand how the Blessed Ninian came to
preach the Word of God to the southern Picts and Britons,
and the same you may gather from his collect, in which these
words are found : ' God, who didst teach the peoples of the
Picts and Britons by the instruction of Holy Ninian, bishop
and confessor ',—in which is no mention of the Scots[1].   But
now, and for many years, since the overthrow of the Pictish
kingdom, the Scots hold both the place and the remains of the
saint.   The Picts had many times possession of Lothian and The superiority
those parts beyond the Scottish firth, and the better and more of the Picts.
fruitful portions that lay still further to the north ; and this
came to pass, both because they had the advantage of the Scots
in being the first to land in the island, and because, as I incline
to think, they were somewhat superior to the Scots in numbers
and in bodily strength.   A proof of this I see herein, that
though they were leagued with the Scots, it was they who
occupied what parts of the country were reconquered from the
Britons—a fact that argues greater sagacity in them, or
superiority of some sort.

CHAP. III.—*Concerning the affairs of the Britons.*

WE have already made mention of Constantius, the brother
of the king of the Aremoricans.   This Constantius had three
sons born to him : Constantius namely, Aurelius Ambrosius,
and Uther.   A certain Pict made away with Constantius ; and The treacherous
thus it happened : the Pict, hating Constantius, gave out murder of
that he had a secret which must be disclosed to Constantius Constantius.
alone, and thus he took the king unawares.   Hence let kings
learn not to give audience, unless in the presence of their own
people, to men of whose good faith they have not assurance[2]
—a caution which may be fortified by that example from
the Book of Kings, where we read that Aioth took Eglon

---

[1] Cf. the *Breviarium Aberdonense* for the 16th of September.
[2] This warning is repeated in Bk. III. ch. viii., on the occasion of the death
of Malcolm Canmore.

unawares and made away with him [1]. Constantius, the eldest

born of the sons of Constantius, had become a monk of Winchester; but Vortiger, the earl of Wessex, withdrew him from
the coenobitic state that he might be set over the kingdom,
for his brothers were of an age too tender to hold the sceptre.
Herein Vortiger acted wickedly—stripping of his habit a
monk without whom the civil government might have been
carried wisely enough. That way of the wise men I approve
rather, which holds that, in the case of a monk at least who
is not in sacred orders, it is open to the supreme pontiff to
grant him dispensation, so that he may return to the world for
the conduct of weighty matters which can be settled in no
other way; but that there was in this case such a call I cannot
see. Constantius, then, once withdrawn from the coenobitic
state, all things were at the nod and beck of Vortiger. He
brought together one hundred Picts whom he used as his body-
guard, treated them courteously, enriched them with many
gifts, and gave them to understand [2] that if he were to gain
the height of power in the kingdom, he would raise them to
places of authority. These Picts, therefore, that they might
do Vortiger a pleasure, by a deed of daring rashness murdered

king Constantius. Vortiger thereupon orders his hundred
Picts to be seized, and sends them to London, where, under the
sword of the avenger, they paid the penalty of their crime.
This he did that, under a cloak of deceit, he might hide his
own guilt [3]. Now when the guardians of the brothers of
Constantius learned what had happened, and chief among them,
one Joscelin, bishop of London, they send their charges to the
king of Little Britain, who receives them kindly. When the
Picts heard of the slaughter of their own soldiers, they were
filled with indignation at a crime so foul, so dyed with
treachery, and, with the Scots, their confederates, they make

---

[1] Judges iii. 20-22. The spelling 'Aioth' is curious. Heb. has אֵהוּד (Ehud),
LXX. 'Αώδ, and Vulg. 'Aod'.

[2] 'eis dans intelligere'; 'giving them to understand' has a strangely modern
sound; but this instance proves that the phrase must have been in use in Major's
day, and such colloquial expressions are not uncommon in consequence of Latin
being then used as the language of conversation.

[3] 'ut suam innocentiam sub dolo malo occultaret'. There is some confusion
here; but the sense is plain.

for the northern part of the Britons' country, which they laid
waste, nothing sparing.   In their rage they threw down the
wall built by the Romans for the purpose of warding off hostile
attacks upon the Britons.

At that time it began to be bruited that Aurelius
Ambrosius and Uther, the brothers of murdered Constantius,
were on their way with an armed force to attack Vortiger.
<To the Saxons, who were then heathens, Vortiger now The Saxons
sends for a large body of soldiers, and they, with a great are called into
army, make a descent upon Britain>[1], under the leading Britain.
of Hengist and his brother, Horsa by name, and drove back
the enemy from his borders.   This done, Hengist makes
Vortiger king, on the understanding that he should have a
place given him wherein to build a castle, and land for his men
—a condition that was readily granted.   Meanwhile Hengist
sends to the Saxons for a large force and for women.   Among
these, one Ronovem, a beautiful maiden, the daughter of Ronovem.
Hengist, came to land in Britain.   In all, they freighted a
hundred vessels with soldiers and women.   Some time thereafter, Hengist invited Vortiger to come to see his castle, and
when the time came for the king to retire to rest, Ronovem,
Hengist's daughter, entered his chamber, and drank to the
king's health from a golden cup or bowl filled with wine, saying, 'Wassaile', or 'Wachtheil'.   Now the king understood
not the tongue in which she spoke, and from his interpreter he
learned that the maiden in drinking thus wished him good
health.   In the end, falling in love with his heathen girl, he
asked her in marriage ; and Hengist consented thereto on the

---

[1] Orig. : 'Ad Saxones tunc paganos pro multo milite mittit, quod cum copioso
exercitu . . . in Britanniam . . .'   This use of 'pro', which is common with Major
(cf. *infra*, 'pro multo milite et mulieribus'; Bk. III. ch. iii., 'pro Edwardo . . .
Angliae primores mittunt'; and Bk. III. ch. xv. : 'ita quod Reges pro regni
primoribus et eorum conjugibus mittunt') might be illustrated by a number of
instances from medieval Latin.   In a monograph upon Talbot's Tomb, in the
parish church of Whitchurch, Salop, by the Rev. W. H. Egerton, Rector of
Whitchurch (Oswestry, 1885, p. 5), the inscription on Talbot's sword is given as
'SUM TALBOTI PRO VINCERE INIMICOS MEOS'.   Though this use of 'pro' is not
classical, one seems to see it in the act of growth (as has been pointed out to
me by Professor Herbert Strong) in such a sentence as 'misimus qui pro vectura
solveret'—Cic. *ad Att*. i. 3.   The use of 'quod' as above is also curious.   I
have treated it as a misprint for 'qui'.

condition that the king should grant him the whole of Kent
for his people; and this the king secretly yielded.   But this
thoughtless marriage of his with a heathen damsel, whose
character was all unknown to him, and the loss to his kingdom
of large possessions, which accompanied the union, were his
destruction.   It was this conduct that stirred up some men of
rank in the kingdom, who soon stripped Vortiger of the
sovereign power, and placed the crown on the head of his son
Vortimer, born of a Christian woman.   This Vortimer, so soon

Vortimer.

as he became king, made peace secretly with the Christian
Scots and Picts.   With their help he drove the Saxons and
Hengist out of the kingdom, and not long thereafter, Ronovem,
Hengist's daughter, Vortimer's stepmother, makes away with
Vortimer by poison.   A well-known custom this is of step-
mothers—by treachery to make away with their husbands'
children.   Let sons then, and especially wealthy sons, beware
of a stepmother as they would of Cerberus.   The Britons soon

Vortiger.

thereafter restore this same Vortiger, who before had been
despoiled of his kingdom, but made with him this condition:
that he should on no account receive Engist into the country.
This notwithstanding, Ronovem declared to Engist, her father,
how she had made away with Vortimer by poison, and how
Vortiger was once more king, and therefore beseeches her
father to descend upon Britain with an armed force.   Engist
invaded Britain then with fifteen thousand fighting men, and
when Vortiger with the Britons would have made stand against
him, he refused the combat, saying that he had come because
of that Kent which before had been granted to him, and not
to fight with the Britons; that he was ready rather to bring

Engist's
treachery.

them succour against the enemy.   He besought the Britons
therefore to appoint a day when he might meet them, saying
that he should take with him no more than of mounted men
four hundred, while the king should have in his train the like
number of trusty Britons.   The meeting took place accordingly
near Sarum, that is, Salisbury, on a certain hill.   Engist had
ordered his men to carry each of them a dagger concealed in
his boots, and when he gave the word—'The time is come to
speak of peace and friendship'—they were to make a sudden
rush upon the Britons thus caught unarmed and unawares.   To

Engist then they gave heed, and there fell through Saxon treachery upon that hill ten hundred and sixty noble men among the Britons. Vortiger, the king, was taken, and that he might escape with his life, he handed over to the Saxons his strong places, cities, and all munition of war, and with the Britons fled into Wales,—where to this day may be found the true Britons and the British tongue.

This done, the pagan Engist destroys and tramples in the dust clergy, churches, all that pertained to divine worship, and commands, under the severest penalty, that thenceforth no man shall call the country 'Britain', but only 'Engist's land'. On seven of the chief men among the Saxons he bestowed seven kingdoms. In Kent he himself continued to abide as over-king. The kingdom of Kent has one boundary in the eastern sea, and extends along the river Thames. The second king was Suuthsaxon; this is the kingdom of the southern Saxons. It was bounded in the east by the kingdom of Kent, in the south by the ocean[1] and the Isle of Wight, in the west by Hampshire, in the north by Surrey. The third kingdom was formerly that of the eastern Saxons, bounded in the east by the sea, in the west by London, in the south by the Thames, in the north by Suffolk. The fourth kingdom was that of the eastern English. Norfolk and Suffolk are contained therein, and for its boundaries it has, on the east, the sea; on the north, Cantibrigia or Cambridgeshire, in which the chief town is Cambridge; on the west, the fosse of Saint Edmund and Hertfordshire; and on the south, Essex. The fifth kingdom was that of the western Saxons, which has on its eastern limit the southern Saxons; to the north, the Thames; to the west and south, the ocean. The sixth kingdom, that of the Mercians, was the largest of all; the river Dee, near Chester, and the Severn near Shrewsbury, and as far as Bristol, formed its western boundary; the eastern boundary was the eastern sea; on the south it touched the Thames at London; its northern limit was the river Humber. In some parts to the west you have the river Mersey as far as the angle Verhal[2];

The kingdom of Kent. Seven kingdoms in England.

The river Humber.

---

[1] mare Oceanum.
[2] *i.e.* Wirral, the point of land between the Mersey and the Dee.

the Humber, on the other side, falls into the eastern sea[1].
It is from the river Mersey that the kingdom takes the name of
Mercian. This Mercian kingdom is divided into three parts—
that is, West Mercia, East Mercia, and Middle Mercia. The
seventh kingdom was that of the Northumbrians, touching on
its eastern side the kingdom of the Mercians, having for its
northern limit the Forth, that is, the Scottish firth, as its name

The Wall.
at this day bears witness, and as is plain also from the wall
which begins at that sea and extends to Kirkpatrick[2], Glasgow,
and Dumbarton. Some assert that this wall was built by
Bilenus, a king of Britain, who thought he should thus, once
for all, put to rest the question of the boundary between his
own land and that of the Scots and Picts. Meanwhile this
kingdom was divided, and the northern part was called the
kingdom of the Bernicians.

CHAP. IV.—*Of Merlin the Prophet.*

WE have seen how Engist plundered the Britons of a large
part of the kingdom and handed it over to the Saxons, from
whose birthland it came to be called Anglia. In their own
tongue it had the name of <'Engist land', that is, 'the land of
Engist'>[3]. Afterwards, for brevity's sake, and from much inter-

England.
course with the Britons, it was called 'England', and rightly
the word should be spoken as if spelled with an 'e' and not
with an 'i'. The Latins called the country 'Anglia'. Now,
had they at the beginning followed the vernacular speech, they
should have called it 'Engist's land', but inasmuch as they did
not use this term, but called the country itself 'Anglia', that
word now stands for the country. For, to speak with Horace,
'an arbitrary thing indeed is all the rule and law of language'[4];
and, to quote the philosopher in his books *De Caelo*, 'we have
to speak as the many speak, but we should think with the few'[5];

---

[1] Orig. and F. 'mare occidentale'; an evident mistake.   [2] *i.e.* Kilpatrick.
[3] 'Engist Land, hoc est terra Engisti.'   [4] *Ars Poet.* 72.
[5] Major's second quotation of these words; cf. Bk. I. ch. iv. I have not
found the very words in the *De Caelo*, but in Bk. II. ch. ii. of that work Aristotle
deals with our use of such expressions as 'above and below', 'right and left',

that is, our language must be that of the common people and
the multitude, but our thoughts should be the thoughts of the
few—that is, of the wise; for, comparatively, the wise are few.
We feel therefore that the word 'Anglia' stands for the 'land Anglia.
of Engist'.

Now since the Saxons had apportioned among themselves
the richer part of the kingdom, Vortiger, with the Britons,
made for that part, of difficult approach, which is called
Wales; and there, on Mount Breigh [1], began to build a fortress,
the strongest he could, for defence against the Saxons;
but this work he could no way complete, for, build what he
might by day, at night it crumbled to ruin. And seeing this,
Vortiger marvelled not a little, and gathered to him the wise
men among the Britons, demanding of them the cause of this
instability. And they, when they had taken counsel together,
make answer that there was need of the blood of one born of a
woman who had never known a man, that he must place this
blood in the fortress, and that so he should be able to build it
securely [2]. It may be that they were unable to tell him the

---

in respect of things in nature which are not thus conditioned, and justifies such
use. In the 45th question of the 15th distinction of the *In Quartum* Major says
that a man who affects singularity of speech should not attempt to converse with
his fellows; he should rather betake himself to the caves of the desert.

[1] Cf. Geoffrey of Monmouth, Bk. vi. §§ 17, 18, 19; Hearne's Robert of Gloucester, p. 127; and Drayton's *Poly-Olbion*, as quoted in Mr. Stuart Glennie's
Arthurian Localities, p. xxiv.—

　　'And from the top of Brith, so high and wondrous steep,
　　Where Dinas Emris stood . . .'

[2] An example of a kind of superstition widely spread, and active in some
countries even at this day. The *Times* of January 26, 1891 quotes an
account, by Mr. Spring, chief engineer of the Kistna bridge, 'of an affray
between the Punjabee workmen and the Telinga inhabitants of the vicinity,
which . . . seems to have arisen from one of those extraordinary superstitious
panics . . . to the effect that the Government, when commencing a great public
work, instructs the employés to collect children's heads for the purpose of offering a propitiatory sacrifice to the deity'. From the *Pioneer Mail* (Allahabad)
of Feb. 26, 1891, we learn that a rumour 'is current amongst the population of
villages adjacent to the northern section of the Eastern Bengal State Railway, to
the effect that Government is in want of a large number of human heads for the
purpose of laying a secure foundation for a mythical bridge near Rajmahut'.
The building of the Gorai viaduct and of the Hughli railway bridge gave rise to
like panics; and in the *Pioneer Mail* of May 27, 1891, Mr. A. Ross Wilson,
C.E., in connection with the Benares Riots, in February of that year, gives

reason of the instability, and therefore proposed to him a thing that they held to be impossible, lest they should otherwise discover their ignorance.   However that may be, when the king got their answer, he sent messengers through all Wales to make search for one born after this sort; and when these had come to a town named Carmadyne [1], the same which afterwards was called Carmalin, tired with their journeying they dismounted near the gate of the city, willing to have some rest and refreshment.   Close at hand were some young fellows at play, and at the end of their game, no uncommon thing, one of the youths said angrily to Merlin, ' Begone, thou fatherless loon !'   Which when Vortiger's messengers heard, they ask who then was father to this Merlin ; and the rest are ready with their answer, that indeed they know not his father, but his mother they know, for she lived in St. Peter's Church in that same town among the nuns.   Learning this, the messengers approach the mayor of the town, declaring to him the commands of the king.   By order of the mayor they carry the mother with Merlin her offspring to the king, and he, with the judges of the matter, questions her in private concerning Merlin's father.   And she makes answer that she had indeed no kind of knowledge who he was.   For, she went on to say, there came in to her once, when every door was closed, a well-favoured man (such at least she thought him), and he had many times had to do with her.

The birth of Merlin.

---

evidence that ' in beginning the works towards the filtering beds, there was an excitement in consequence of rumours that children were required.   They had to be killed, it was said, for advancing the work.'   I owe these references to my cousin, Mr. Archibald Constable, formerly of the Oude and Rohilkund Railway Company.   I am also indebted to him for pointing out the following sources of information on the subject : *Notes and Queries*, 7th Series, vol. vi. pp. 265, 349 ; *ibid.* vol. vii. p. 13; an article in the *Cornhill Magazine* for Feb. 1887 on ' Kirk-Grins.'

[1] Caermarthen.   ' There were two Merlines ', says Giraldus Cambrensis in his *Itinerary* (Rolls Series ed., vol. vi. p. 133), ' the one named also Ambrose (for he had two names), begotten of a spirit, and found in the town of Caermarthen, which took the name of him [Caervyrdhin] . . . who prophesied under king Vortigern ; the other born in Albany or Scotland . . . This Merlin was in the time of king Arthur, and prophesied fuller and plainer than the other.'   ' Kermerdynn ', ' Kermarden ', ' Kayrmerdyn ' are other spellings.   Cf. Dineley's account of the Duke of Beaufort's Progress through Wales in 1684 ; Lond. 1888.

This matter may be explained in three ways; and, firstly, The threefold view of the paternity of Merlin.
thus: The woman was ashamed to declare the father of
Ambrosius Merlinus—perchance he was a religious, or within
the forbidden degrees, or a man of mean condition—and,
as women will do, she fell to lying about it. A second
explanation is this: a succubus demon may have had a
fruitful seed from some man, and either have secretly opened
the closed chamber, or entered with the seed by chink or window, and then, assuming the body of a man[1], have had
knowledge of the woman, thrown into her the fruitful seed;
and thus she might conceive, but not without the seed of
man. I come now to the third fancy: a demon can open
a door without a key; for if he can move a horse or a
body, how much more easily may he take from the lock the
small iron bolt which keeps it closed, and in secret let in a
woman's lover. There is a gloss[2] upon that of the sixth
chapter of Genesis, where we read ' the sons of God knew the
daughters of men', which might be urged in support of the
second explanation. But against it this is to be objected:
those whose member is long (an observation made by Aristotle
in his *Problemata*[3]) emit not a fruitful seed; and for this
reason : that in the distance to be traversed, and the length of
time before the seed may be taken into the womb, it loses its

---

[1] For Spirits, when they please,
Can either sex assume.—*Paradise Lost*, i. 422.

[2] There were two brief commentaries on the Vulgate known in the middle ages
by the name of Glosses. The first and more famous was the *Glossa Ordinaria*,
compiled from the writings of the Fathers, and especially from those of his own
master, Rabanus Maurus, by Walafridus Strabo, a Benedictine of Fulda, born in
806. This Glossa, which was referred to as 'the tongue of the Holy Scripture',
was quoted as a high authority by Aquinas, and was as familiar to the biblical
student as the Master of the Sentences was to the scholastic. The second and
shorter Gloss, the *Glossa Interlinearis*, so called because it was written between
the lines of the text, was compiled by Anselm, who taught theology at Paris, and
was afterwards dean of Laon (died 1117). To these was sometimes added in the
same volume the *Postilla* of Nicholas de Lyra, a converted Jew, and afterwards
a Franciscan friar, *circa* 1291. The *Glossa Ordinaria* was written on the top
and margins of the page, the *Interlinearis* between the lines, and the *Postilla* at
the foot. A complete edition of these Glosses was printed in seven vols. folio at
Venice in 1588, under the title: *Biblia sacra cum glossis interlineari et ordinaria, Nic. Lyrani postillis et moralitatibus, Burgensis additionibus et Thuringi
replicis et indice alphabetico.*   [3] *Problem.* iv. 21.

Arguments
against incubi
as fathers.
potency; therefore, and all the more, will this be true of the
demon incubus and succubus. And a second objection is this:
that on this view a virgin might conceive *in sensu composito*[1],
a thing that belongs only to the Virgin Mother of Christ.

Perhaps the first explanation is one to be well pondered, but
in regard to it I will now say nothing, unless that a demon
might be able to preserve the potency and warmth of seed.
The second is not conclusive. I deny that a woman who con-
ceives in such fashion can be called a virgin, since, whether
consenting or resisting, she has received the seed of a man,
whether she were called virgin or not; but the Virgin Mary
conceived without the seed of man. The woman in question,
however, was not without a seed of man; nor does the gloss on
the sixth chapter of Genesis demonstrate the proposition, since
by the sons of God are meant the sons of Seth, and by the
daughters of men the daughters of Cain. I accept the first,
therefore, or the third view as the more probable, dismissing
the second as in itself suspicious, and also as failing to prove
the birth of Merlin without a father. For whosoever was that
seed, received by the incubus or the succubus demon (if such
was indeed the manner of it), that man was Merlin's father;
and I deny therefore that Merlin had no father. I speak not
of the absolute power of God; for God can supply the potency
A maxim in
theology.
of a father's seed. By a maxim in theology, whatever God can
do by means of a secondary cause, that He can do by Himself

---

[1] A proposition is to be understood *in sensu composito* when the attribute can
only be predicated in respect of its subject as affected by some special property,
or accepted under a certain hypothesis: a proposition is to be understood *in
sensu diviso* when that property or hypothetical condition has to be removed
before the proposition may be a true one. Thus, 'a blind man is unable to see',
'what God foresees necessarily comes to pass', are true *in sensu composito*,
false *in sensu diviso*. On the other hand, 'a blind man is able to see', 'what
God has foreseen may not come to pass', are true *in sensu diviso*, false *in sensu
composito*.—Cf. Signoriello: *Lexicon Peripateticum*, p. 66 (Neapoli, 1881). For
example: theologians commonly remark that when Isaiah said 'a virgin shall
conceive', he did not mean a virgin *in sensu diviso* (*i.e.* one who was a virgin up
to that point), but he meant a virgin *in sensu composito*, a virgin after or including the idea of conception. Again, when the Thomist theologians are pressed
with the objection that their 'physical premotion' destroys the freedom of the
will, they reply that the will is free to resist such grace *in sensu diviso* though
not *in sensu composito*. See on this subject Renan's *Studies in Religious History*
—'Congregation de auxiliis', p. 381.

alone. For, granting the opposite, God when He worked with a secondary cause would be more mighty than when He worked by Himself alone—which to say is impious.

Merlin then denounced the wise men of Wales (and in this matter I count them as fools, that they did not declare at once their ignorance—for to every mortal man far more things must be unknown than known), and shows to the king the true cause of the instability of his building ; for he commands the workmen of the king to dig deeper into the earth below the fortress. This doing, they find underground a large lake. He then demanded of the wise men what would be found at the bottom of the lake, and when they said that indeed they knew not, he causes the water to be drawn off and carried away by channels ; for Merlin affirmed that there were at the bottom two caverns, and in these two dragons—which afterward were found there sleeping, as Merlin had said,—and the one was white, and the other red, and once disturbed they fell to fierce combat one with another ; and the white dragon drove the red dragon to the far end of the lake, and then the red dragon turned upon the white one, and forced him in like manner to fly. Now, while they were thus in mutual combat, the king inquired of Merlin what these dragons portended, and Merlin made answer that the white dragon meant the Saxons, and the red dragon the Britons, who with great bloodshed should be driven from their country ; and, as to things that concerned the king, he said that before fifteen days had passed the brothers of Constantius would arrive, with intent to kill the king ; wherefore let him leave the building of his fortress.

Many things of this sort the demon was able to reveal to Merlin—such as that of the fighting dragons and the lake ; but as to things future and contingent,—for example, that the Saxons should conquer the Britons, or that the brothers of Constantius would slay king Vortiger,—the demon had not the power to foretell with certainty. He can indeed read the signs of the times and forecast the future more clearly than is possible to man ; but the purely contingent he cannot with certainty foretell.

[marginal note: Dragons found at the bottom.]

[marginal note: Merlin's gift of prophecy—whence he had it.]

CHAP. V.—*Of Aurelius Ambrosius and his reign.*

Aurelius
Ambrosius.

MEANWHILE, and not many days thereafter, Aurelius Ambrosius and his brother Uther land at Totnes[1] with a large army. The Britons go eagerly to meet them with an auxiliary force, that they may make Ambrosius their king. Without resistance on the way he made for London, and there received the sceptre of sovereignty. Vortiger, when he learned this, fled to a certain stronghold of Wales, by name Gerneth[2]; Aurelius Ambrosius set fire thereto, and the devouring flames made an end of Vortiger and his men. This done, Aurelius Ambrosius sends an embassy to Constantius, king of the Scots, and to the Picts, to the end they should help him in driving Engist and the heathen out of the island. The Picts made answer that they were under a treaty with the Saxons, and therefore refuse their help; but Constantius the Scot sends an auxiliary force, under a certain general of renown, to the aid

Death of
Constantius.
Congal.

of Aurelius. While the war was going on, Constantius died without issue, and to him succeeded his nephew Congal, son to his brother Dungard, who ratified the treaty of peace with the Britons which had been begun by Constantius, and thus a continuous war went on among the four peoples. For the Britons and the Scots on one side fought against the Saxons and the Picts on the other. Whence this of Bede: Between the Saxons and the Picts, whom one and the same necessity had drawn to make a common stand, the war is carried on with their joint forces against the Britons and the Scots[3].

Gabrian.

In the sixteenth year of the reign of this Congal, Saint Gabrian[4],

---

[1] Cf. Geoffrey of Monmouth, Bk. viii. § 1.

[2] Called in a footnote to Hearne's Robert of Gloucester, p. 135, 'Genor castel in Yrchne'. Cf. the *Merlin* of the Early English Text Society, and specially the Introduction by Mr. W. D. Nash, on ' Merlin the Enchanter and Merlin the Bard'.

[3] Bede: *H. E.* i. 20.

[4] Gabrianus, or rather Gibrianus, is claimed as a Scottish saint by Boece, Leslie, Camerarius, and Dempster, who calls him Gibirinus. But Flodoard, the historian of the church of Rheims (Bk. IV. ch. ix.; ed. Guizot, p. 525), says expressly that he came from Ireland, or, as an ancient breviary of Rheims explains, 'insulam Hiberniam in qua est Scotia'. Saint Gibrian, who was a priest, took with him into France six brothers and three sisters, who established

a Scot, with a following of brethren and sisters, is found leading
a life of austerity near to Rheims in Gaul, and there he and
they now rest. Engist was defeated by Aurelius Ambrosius The defeat of Engist.
and the Scots, and therefore he gathered a small army and
hastened to the Picts, that he might thus increase its numbers;
but he was intercepted by the Britons and the Scots, and with
almost his whole following was put to the sword. Engist's
son Ochta, however, fled to York; but when he could no Ochta or Otho.
longer defend that city, he asked for mercy. Mercy he
obtained, and likewise the land of Galloway, which was
bestowed on him and his people—that land in which the
Blessed Ninian was buried. In the end Aurelius Ambrosius Death of Aurelius.
perished by poison; perchance it was a certain heathen Saxon
that did the deed, disguised as a monk, that he might the
better take the king unawares. He was buried in the
monastery of Stonehenge, which Aurelius himself had built
in honour of the Britons that had been slain by Engist.

At his death there was seen a star of singular brightness, which A comet seen —what this may portend.
they call a comet; the same portends the death of princes, as
Aristotle says in his book concerning Meteors[1]. But, what-

---

themselves on the river Marne. He died and was buried in the country, in the
diocese of Chalons, but the renown of the miracles wrought through his intercession caused his body to be exhumed and translated to Rheims. His feast was
kept on the 8th of May, the day of his translation.

[1] Cf. *Meteorologicorum lib.* I. cc. vi. vii. for Aristotle's opinion about comets.
Professor Copeland, Astronomer-Royal for Scotland, has been kind enough to
supply me with the following references to the supposed influence of comets:—
In Pingré's *Cométographie*, tom. I. (Paris, 1783), pp. 313 and 314, will be
found about all that is known concerning the comet which appeared at the death
of Aurelius Ambrosius. Sigebert's *Chronographia*, as stated at the head of p.
237 (*u. c.*), appeared in 1513, and was doubtless well known to Major. In the
classics there are many allusions to the supposed effects of comets: particularly
in Aratus; Claudian, whose line (*de bello Getico*, 243) 'in coelo nunquam spectatum
impune cometam' was being constantly quoted in the middle ages; Juvenal,
vi. 407, 'Instantem regi Armenio Parthoque cometen Prima videt'; Manilius
(*Astron.* i. 890); Virgil (*Georg.* i. 488; *Aen.* x. 272); Lucan; Silius Italicus;
Tibullus (ii. 5, 71); Valerius Flaccus; and Statius (*Theb.* i. 707-9), 'quis letifer
annus Bella quibus populus, mutent quae sceptra cometae'. Almost the only
printed work on comets extant in 1520 was Thurecensis phisiti *Tractatus de
Cometis* (*s.a.* circa 1474), in which there is a good deal about their supposed
evil effects. But in Lubienictz, *Theatrum Cometarum* (Amstel. 1667), vol.
ii. will be found the fullest particulars of all the misfortunes that have accompanied the appearance of Hairy Stars.

ever the philosophers may say, I can see no cause in nature
why such a portent should rather occur in the case of the
death of kings than of their subjects; and yet such things we
read, and in our own day we have seen comets at the death of
many kings, discerned even over the countries of kings at the
point of death. The meaning therefore of comets I leave to
the divine pleasure and free will. Yet by means of comets
does God very often reveal to princes their approaching death,
that, abandoning their sins, they may quickly betake them to
repentance. Of certain comets, however, the causes are purely
natural; yet even so there is no absurdity in opening up some
meaning that they may contain for us. For from eternity
God has seen with clearness the whole future contingent, and
has given signs of certain effects, and the natural causes of
these signs productive of such effects, as we can see in the case
of the rainbow, treated in the book concerning Meteors [1], and

A dragon seen
near the comet.
in the book of Genesis [2]. Near to this comet was a dragon,
which sent forth rays eastward. Uther, Merlin, and many
more, saw this comet, and Merlin declared to Uther its hidden
signification. Through this comet he knew Aurelius Ambrosius,
though the two were far distant from one another, to be dead.
By the ray to the east, he declared that Uther should have a
son, who should gain possession of both Gauls and many kingdoms in the east, and who should far excel in. renown all the
Britons.

After the death of Aurelius Ambrosius, therefore, Uther
begins to reign, and in memory of the portent he ordered
that two dragons should be painted, the one of which he ever
carried before him in battle, while the other he left behind him
in Winchester, and for this reason he was called by the Britons

Gouran.
Uther Pendragon. With Gouran the Scot, son of Dongard,
after the manner of his ancestors, he made a treaty of peace.

The deeds of
Uther Pen-
dragon.
But this Gouran fell by the treachery of his nephew, the son
of his brother. Ochta and Ossa, the sons of Engist, soon
rebelled against Uther Pendragon, and in a pitched battle he
defeated them, and had them imprisoned at London. Uther
thereafter, being enraged against the Earl of Cornwall, laid

---

[1] Arist. *Meteorologicorum lib.* III. c. iv.   [2] Gen. ix. 13.

siege to his castle, and as he lusted to lie with the wife of the earl, he changed himself by means of Merlin's incantations into the outward seeming of her husband, and so, the woman all ignorant of the crime, he had to do with her, and by her he Birth of Arthur. begat Arthur, afterwards king.   Herein Merlin sinned, in co- Merlin's crime. operating with the king, so that he should have carnal dealing with the wife of another, nor can he by any means be cleared of blame in the matter.

Many rhymes are current as to all that Merlin foretold His prophecies. in the presence of king Vortiger as about to happen ; but they are ambiguous, being of this nature : that till the event his prophecies are not recognised as such.   Wherefore, to augur anything from his prophecies is as if one had to find one's way through the mists of a clouded sky [1].   I should have placed more faith in the prophecies of this man had he foretold with certainty the purely contingent. That method of proceeding is but darkness.   Quite other- wise does it stand with John the Evangelist in the Apoca- lypse, a book which the Church has received as divinely inspired, and in such a matter the Church cannot err. Merlin it merely permits to be read [2].   I shall say but little of these prophecies, but where now and again the English chroniclers make mention of them, I shall use the opportunity for a mere word of remark [3].

CHAP. VI.—*Of King Arthur.*

Concerning the life of king Arthur, I find a great variety of statement.   For he died in the year of our Lord five hundred

---

[1] Quocirca est tenebrosa aqua in nubibus aeris de illius prophetiis augurari. Cf. *ante*, Bk. I. ch. vii. p. 42.

[2] Alain de Lille (Alanus ab insulis), a Cistercian monk, and one of the greatest of the earlier scholastics, ' doctor universalis ',—born 1114, died 1202,— wrote, about 1170, a commentary on Merlin, which was printed at Frankfort, in 1603, under the title *Commentarii in divinationes propheticas Merlini Cale-donii cum hujus vaticiniis.*   Merlin's Prophecies had previously been published in Spanish (Burgos, 1498 ; Seville, 1500), and in French, at Paris, by Robert de Borron, 1498 ; in Italian (Venice, 1480 ; Florence, 1495).   The first English edition seems to have been that of London, 1529.

[3] Cf. Bk. IV. ch. viii., on the prophecy about Henry the Second and his son ; Bk. IV. ch. xix., about Edward the First ; Bk. V. ch. vii., on the death of Edward the Second.

F

The death of
Arthur, and his
assumption of
the kingdom.

and forty-two—but inasmuch as he was a bastard, his origin is a more doubtful matter, and it is a question how he came to his kingdom. For Anna, the sister of Aurelius, bore in lawful marriage these children, namely Valvanus, a man illustrious in arms and of bright renown among the Britons, and Modred the elder: both of these she bore to Loth, the lord of the Lothians, who also was the father of Thenew[1], the mother of Saint Kentigern, whence by right of succession the kingdom of the Britons should have fallen to Modred. But here the Britons say that Modred and Valvanus were under age, and as the need was urgent, and a hostile invasion was imminent, they were held to be unfit to guide the affairs of the Britons. Wherefore into the hands of Arthur, albeit he was a bastard, they gave the reins of government. Now I am not prepared to deny that, in

How the trans-
ference of kingly
power may
legitimately be
made.

case of necessity, it is within the rights of the people to transfer from one race to another the kingly power; but let that be always done after weighing carefully all the circumstances and with deliberation. And they should rather have said that to Modred, inasmuch as he was under age, a coadjutor should have been given. However this matter should have been undertaken, what is certain is this: that Arthur, youth as he was, was declared king of the Britons. But his natural endowment

The natural
endowment
of Arthur.

was of the noblest; he was fair and beautiful to look on, of a most chivalrous spirit, and none was more ambitious of warlike renown. The Saxons he drove from the island, the Scots and the Picts likewise (if we are to credit British chroniclers) he brought under subjection, and compelled to obedience. At Edinburgh, in Scotland, was Arthur's kingly seat, and to this day that spot near Edinburgh bears his name[2]. He is said to have tarried some time in the castle of Stirling; but the Scots were not then in possession of that region. The king of the Scots (as they relate) went out to war with Arthur, and so became subject to him, or was joined in a league of friendship

He determines
to destroy the
Scots.

or by necessity. He set before him to destroy all the Scots once for all, and would have done this had they not come to

---

[1] Orig. and F. 'Thameten . . . genuit'. Thenew is still honoured in Glasgow as Saint Enoch.

[2] This mention of Arthur's Seat, and that of Dunbar in 'The Flyting'—part I. p. 22, S.T. Soc. ed.—are about the earliest in our literature.

him as suppliants. Such is the relation of Geoffrey of Monmouth [1]. And not only did he subdue the whole of Britain,
but also Ireland, Norway, the islands, the whole cluster of isles
that are scattered about the western coasts of Britain—and yet
not these alone, but the Gauls and the neighbouring Germans
he brought under his rule, and bestowed great territories on his
own illustrious warriors. To his cousin Loth he gave the
kingdom of Norway and all Lothian (of which part I am a
native). For this reason, in the Gests of Arthur, Loth is The achieve-
commonly [2] styled 'of Lothian'. From every quarter there came ments of Arthur.
to him illustrious men, ambitious of renown in war. All of native place of
them he received with gracious liberality, and bestowed on them Major.
munificent marks of favour. In Cornwall he held his Round The Round
Table, at which sat his chief men in such wise that no strife or Table.
struggle of priority might arise among them. In time of war
his harness was of the noblest, for his breastplate was worthy of His armour.
so great a king, and on his head he bore a golden helmet
adorned with the image of a dragon; on his shoulders too a
mighty shield he bore, on which was painted the form of the
Holy Virgin. At his girdle hung Calibur, the best of swords,
and he bore a long lance whose name was Ron.

The Britons reckon Arthur among the Nine Just Men. The Nine Just
That you may understand what I have now said, know that Men.
certain peoples, and among these in a special manner the
Britons, count nine just men, whom by universal consent they
hold (albeit erroneously) to have title to this distinction:
three of them heathen; three, of the Hebrew race; and the
like number, worshippers of Christ. Among heathens they
count Hector of Troy, Alexander of Macedon, and Julius
Caesar; among Hebrews, David, Joshua, and Judas Macca-
baeus; among Christians, Arthur, Charles the Great, and
Godfrey of Boulogne. Now, though certain of these have
gained renown among men in the matter of war, yet others
have been more eminent soldiers than many of these. And

---

[1] Bk. ix. § 6.
[2] Orig. and F. 'comiter'; F. in Errata 'communiter'. Orig. prints the
word as a contraction 'cōiter'; and two lines lower prints 'comiter et liberaliter'
without contraction, which is probably the reason for reading 'communiter' in
this case.

what title to the name of 'just' shall we find in Caesar, considering this, that he overthrew an aristocratic republic, the most famous since the beginning of the world, and by the exercise of tyranny assumed the sole power to himself? And though Hannibal of Carthage, himself a soldier of splendid valour, granted the first place to Alexander of Macedon, I at least am not able to assent to such an attribution, seeing that through mere lust of rule he aimed at gaining for himself the kingdoms of others, that no way pertained to him. This triple trinity of just men others, and more wisely, are slow to admit; but, however that may be, Arthur was renowned in war. I

Anguischel.

have read, in the histories of the Britons, that Anguischel, king of the Scots, when he was about to lead a great force beyond sea to fight along with Arthur, marched against the emperor of the Romans, with Arthur returned to Britain, and was slain in his first conflict along with Gawain against Modred; and Arthur caused his body to be carried with all honour into Scotland. While Arthur was at war with the Romans, news was brought to him that Modred was unlawfully intimate with his queen Gaunora, and had proclaimed himself king of Britain. Considering this, he returned to Britain, and Modred met him with a great army; for Modred had with him various among the Britons, Saxons, Picts, and Scots, and those who were ill-affected towards Arthur. For albeit the king of the Scots loved Arthur on account of his uprightness, among the Scots themselves he was hated, perchance because they desired to serve under Modred for the pay that he would give them. In the end there were fought three battles between Arthur and Modred, and both Arthur and Modred thus came by their end. But Arthur, when he knew his wound was mortal, said that he was setting out for a certain island that he might there be cured, and that he would thereafter return to reign again. Wherefore the Britons had the expectation that

The proverb concerning the return of Arthur.

Arthur after a long time would return. So that this came to be a proverb when one who shall never come back was yet looked for—'You are waiting for such an one, as the Britons for their Arthur'. This is but the blind affection of a people

The return of Charles of Burgundy and James the Scot.

for their king, whom, all dead though he be, their unreason leads them to think of as still among the living. Just the same has been said of Charles of Burgundy; and of our own James, the fourth of the name, a like invention has found favour[1]. Hence you can understand the readiness with which the common people believed the Stygian Jupiter, Hercules, and such men as that sort of people is prone to marvel at, to be immortal; and how the wiser sort, who knew the groundlessness of this belief, were yet unwilling to go contrary to it, lest the ignorant in their indignation should destroy them.   But, however this may be, Arthur was buried in Glastonbury, and at his burying was sung a verse in no way differing from the opinion of the vulgar, which verse runs thus:

' Here lies Arthur, great king was he, and king will be.'   The Epitaph of Arthur.

The extravagant laudation of Arthur by the Britons leads to a partial doubt of the facts of his life.   The prayers that were made to him from a bed of sickness, and many other things that are related concerning Arthur and Valvanus, in respect to events that are said to have come to pass in Britain at that time —all these I count as fiction, unless indeed they were brought about by craft of demons.   And for this reason certain writers, like him of Bergamo in the Supplement to his Chronicles[2], hold Arthur himself to have been a magician.   But to this belief, about a king of such renown, I cannot give assent.

CHAP. VII.—*Concerning Eochodius, Aidan, and Eugenius, kings of Scotland, and men of noted sanctity that were born in their reigns.*

EUGENIUS, or Eochodius[3], on the death of his father's brother,   Eochodius. succeeded to the kingdom of the Scots, and he reigned three-

---

[1] Bishop Leslie says in his History, as to the fate of James the Fourth after Flodden, that 'many have this opinion, that our king yet lives; and now in pilgrimage with far nations, in special Jerusalem, where the Sepulchre of our Saviour, and other holy places he visits, and in dule and dolour devoutly drives over the rest of his days'.—Father Cody's edition of Father Dalrymple's translation of Leslie (with modernised spelling), part III. p. 146. Cf. his note upon the passage.

[2] Jacques-Philippe de Foresta, called Bergamensis after the town of Lombardy where he was born.   He wrote a chronicle from the creation of the world till the year 1505, to which he made a Supplement.   He was also the author of a work *De Selectis et Claris Mulieribus*, and of another under the title *Confessionale* or *Interrogatorium*.   He died in 1515.—[Moreri.]

[3] Orig. and F. 'Archadius'; F. in Errata 'Eochodius'.

and-twenty years.   In his days came Saint Columba from
Ireland, and gave to Brude, king of the Picts, full instruction
in the faith, and built in Scotland many monasteries.   A contemporary of Columba, and his very dear friend, was the
Blessed Kentigern, who was renowned for many miracles.   He
rests in Glasgow.   In honour of him was founded the church
of Glasgow, second to no church in Scotland for its beauty, the
multitude of its canons, and the wealth of its endowments.
Not long time thereafter the chapter of Glasgow had gained
so great a fame for wise and weighty counsel that men of
renown among the Westerns were ready in a doubtful suit to
place the whole decision of the same in its hands.   About this
time lived Saint Baldred.   It is related of him that his body
was laid entire in three churches not far distant one from the
other: Aldhame, namely, Tyninghame[1], and Preston; of which
the two first named are villages distant from Gleghornie about
one thousand paces; the third, one league.   In these three
places Saint Baldred taught the people by word and example,
and on his death all three fall to arms in strife for the possession of his body.   The same body was found numerically[2]
in different parts of the house, and thus each of these
villages rejoices at this day in the possession of Saint Baldred's
body.   I know that there are not wanting theologians who
deny that such a thing as this is possible to God, namely, that
the same body can be placed *circumscriptive*[3] in different places;

Columba.
Kentigern.
Glasgow
church.

Baldred buried
in three places.

Whether a body
can be in diffe-
rent places.

---

[1] Tynigamen.

[2] 'numero'.   Cf. Signoriello : *Lexicon peripateticum*, pp. 150, 151, *s.v.* GE-
NERICE—SPECIFICE—NUMERICE : 'A specific difference is *formal*, since it takes
place in respect of the *form*; a numerical difference is called *material*, because
matter is the principle whence proceed several individuals of the same species.'

[3] 'Circumspective' is opposed to 'definitive' and 'reflective'.   Cf. Signoriello
u.s. pp. 64, 65 : 'That thing is said to be "circumscriptive" or "commensura-
ative" in a place, which occupies that place by contact of dimensive quantity; in
in such fashion, indeed, that each of its parts corresponds to the single parts of
the place, and so that the whole is included in the whole place.   "Definitive" is
said of that which is in a certain place, but which does not occupy space *per con-
tactum virtutis*, but by operation, as is the case with angels, or *per informationem*,
like as the soul is within the body.   "Reflective" is said of that which knows no
determination of place, but is whole in every place and whole in every part of a
place; and that belongs to God alone.   It is fitting that the body and an
Angel and God should be occupants of place in differing fashions.'

but their proof of this I cannot allow, as I have shown at more length elsewhere in my commentary upon the fourth book of the Sentences[1].

Aidan, king of the Scots, took so much to heart the death of Saint Columba that he survived him but a short time. Him Eugenius succeeded in the kingdom. In his days Saint Dronstan[2], an uncle on the mother's side of the king, led the life of a monk, and was renowned for the miracles that he did. Saint Gillenus[3], too, a Scot, gained fame in Gaul by his miracles, and

Aidan.

Eugenius.
Dronstanus.

Gillenus.

---

[1] The late Bishop Forbes, in the article BALDRED in Smith's *Dictionary of Christian Biography*, quotes a similar legend, as to the triplication of his body, in the case of the Welsh saint Theliaus (see Capgrave's *Leg. Aur.* fol. cclxxxi. verso), and refers to this passage of Major's *In Quartum*, question 4th of the 10th distinction, where, in treating of the Holy Eucharist, Major 'seeks to prove, by the example of the body of St. Baldred, that the same body can be in diverse places *simul et semel*'. Major there writes that 'God can place the same body *circumscriptive* in two, three, and so on without end, totally diverse places. The proof of this conclusion: in the Life of Saint Martin we read that the Blessed Ambrose while celebrating at Milan was present at the burial of Saint Martin at Tours. The same appears in regard to the body of the Blessed Baldred, which is said to be at Aldhame, Preston, and Tyninghame, near to Gleghornie and those parts. This is a trite story, and an opponent will deny it, and I confess that he may do so without incurring the charge of contamination of the faith, since many doubtful things are put down in some Lives of Saints. The fact is proved by the appearance of Christ to Peter as Peter was flying from Rome—for the place is known well enough, namely, Domine, Quo Vadis?' Major goes on to suggest an instance where the body of Sortes (a favourite figure in his arguments) may be found in two places—say Seville and Edinburgh. He gives a number of reasons for the possibility of such an occurrence, and concludes: 'For these reasons I hold by the affirmative side of the title of this question— say, that God is able to place the body *circumscriptive* in several places, just so many as pleases Him.' It is in the course of the same 'question' that Major says that God may have made the whole body of Eve by placing the rib in many places, and dismisses the objections to this theory that had been raised by Gregory of Ariminum—'sed de hoc suo loco'.

[2] The founder of the monastery of Deer in Aberdeenshire. Cf. Dr. John Stuart's Preface to *The Book of Deer*, published by the Spalding Club in 1869. Dronstan's name assumes the forms of Drostan, Dunstan, Dustan, Throstan, and the honorific form of Modrustus.

[3] Gillenus has no place in the *Dictionary of National Biography*. His name occurs in Smith and Wace's *Dictionary of Christian Biography*, as that of a person 'spoken of by the Scotch annalists, Fordun, John Major, Camerarius, and Dempster, as a Scot who lived in Gaul, and was a disciple or contemporary of St. Columbanus'. Perhaps the name 'Gillenus' is one of the many forms of 'Kilian'. The Bollandist biographer at least says of Saint Kilian's name: 'S. Kiliani nomen molliri et receptiori modo efformavimus, tametsi non ignoremus varias ejusdem expressiones, Kyllena, Killena, Killinus, Killenus, Quillianus,

Columbanus.

Fiacre.

The ways to
Heaven.

the sanctity of his life. In that same France our own Saint Columbanus[1] was held in veneration for his miracles. And Saint Fiacre[2], of royal birth, led the austere life of a hermit in the diocese of Meaux. For he knew that to the land of promise no road lay but by the Red Sea, the desert, or the crossing of Jordan. By the Red Sea the martyrs of the new-born church entered the Jerusalem which is above, and by the washing of regeneration, that is, the passing of Jordan, little children belong to the land of the second promise. And when the Blessed Fiacre was now well stricken in years, the way to paradise by way of Jordan did not suffice him, nor did tyrants now call for the blood of martyrs; wherefore he chose for himself the third way, that is, the desert, for severer penance, that he might thus most surely gain the heavenly paradise. By reason of the many miracles that he did, and the sanctity of his life, which was known of all men, that place is visited yearly from all parts of France.

Chillianus, Chilianus, Cilianus, Caelianus et alias apud Serarium et alibi.' The Gillenus of the text, however, was not, in all probability, the Saint Kilian who was the apostle of Franconia (martyred A.D. 689), but rather the Kilian mentioned by Dr. Lanigan in his *Ecclesiastical History of Ireland*, vol. ii. p. 443 (*fl. circa* A.D. 650), who was buried at Montreuil in Picardy, 'where his relics are held in veneration'.

[1] Saint Columbanus, the apostle of the Burgundians of the Vosges district of Alsace, and founder of the monasteries of Luxeuil (A.D. 590) and Bobbio (A.D. 613), was born in Leinster about A.D. 543.

[2] According to Dr. Lanigan it was after A.D. 628 that Saint Fiacre withdrew, from Ireland, to France, where he erected at Breuil a monastery in honour of the Virgin Mary. He was the first cultivator of the forest between Meaux and Jouarre, and became the patron saint of gardeners.

The name of this saint is now best known in its transference to the hackney carriage of Paris, which got its name from the fact that the proprietor of the Hotel de St. Fiacre, in the Rue St. Martin, in 1640 kept carriages on hire. Over his doorway was an image of the saint. This meaning of ' fiacre ' had not become so common in 1650 as to find a place in the French and English dictionary of Cotgrave, who describes ' fiacre' as the ' Mal S. Fiacre, a kind of scab, or great wart, in the fundament '—for the removal of which the help of the saint was invoked. There is a legend that after Henry the Fifth of England had been defeated at Baugy by Charles the Sixth of France and his Scottish troops, the Englishman destroyed in his rage the monastery of St. Fiacre—' parce que ce Saint était un Prince d'Ecosse '—and was forthwith attacked by this malady. Unless a reference to Saint Fiacre in one of John Major's own works—*In Quartum* (ed. 1521), 45th question of the 15th distinction—must be regarded in the light only of a singular coincidence, there would seem to have been a much earlier connection in Paris between Saint Fiacre and the hiring of horses;

CHAP. VIII.—*Concerning the arrival of Gormund, first in Ireland, then in Britain, and his cruel dealings with both lands ; also of the rule of the Saxons in Britain under Gormund.*

ABOUT this time a man of Africa named Gormund, famous in war, a heathen too, but aiming at new territories, made his descent into Ireland with a large army, and brought into subjection a great part of that island.   And when the Saxons in Britain came to hear of this, being inferior to the Britons, they sent an embassy to Gormund the African, praying him to come to Britain, and promising to confer on him the supreme power.   Whereupon he lands in Britain, and, with help of the Saxons, wrought indignity on the churches and on all that pertained to the Christian religion, and so restored the heathen way and infidel worship among the Britons.   But Gormund tarried no long time in Britain, but led all his African train into Gaul, that by land he might return to his own; and to the Saxons who had been at his bidding in the war against the Britons he made over their territory, and so the heathen came to hold that part of Britain which the Saxons call England. One may believe, however, that with them some Britons were mingled.   Hence it is plain that among the Britons the Christian religion flourished in Britain, and oftentimes was overthrown by the unbelievers.

The cruelty of Gormund.

The perfidy of the Saxons.

The establishment of heathenism.

The Saxon rule.

CHAP. IX.—*Of the outward form and appearance of the English, and how they differ in appearance and stature from the rest of nations ; likewise of the mission of Augustine for their conversion, and of his preaching.*

WHEN Gregory the First happened once upon certain English children at Rome, and asked who these might be, and was then told that they were English and heathen, he answered: 'Angels indeed they are in outward seeming, for so their countenances bear witness; endeavour must be made that they become angels too in their mind and faith.'   For we observe that near the Equator, near the path of the sun,

The English are like angels to look at.

---

for in that work, where Major is dealing with the relations of buyer and seller, he uses this illustration among many others : 'Suppose that I hire out my horse to you for the purpose of going to and returning from Saint Fiacre, and you pay me fourpence a day for the use of it . . .'

those whom we call Ethiops and Indians are born black, inasmuch as heat, the mother of swarthiness, is found in moist

Differences of
bodily appear-
ance.

bodies.   At a greater distance from the path of the sun, διὰ
Meroes and διὰ Syenes[1], and διὰ Alexandrias, men are born
blackish, and these we call white Moors.   Consequently as we
approach more nearly to the Arctic pole, the tendency is ever
to a less degree of blackness; and thus, as inhabiting ever a
colder region the one than the other, the Gauls are seen to be
the most of them[2] whiter than the Spaniards, the Britons than
the Gauls, the Germans than the Britons, the Goths than the
Germans.   If you take the complexion of individuals only, it
is true that you shall find certain northerners nowise fair or
beautiful.   Beyond the Arctic circle, and close by the Arctic
pole, they say that some are foul of aspect, but this comes
from skiey influence[3] and not from the cold.   In some parts of
Africa they relate that men are born with the head of a dog.
This too is a matter of skiey influence[3], and carries with it no
other inference.   The same rule as to white and black men
holds good from the Equator to the Antarctic pole; and if
certain among the northern peoples have got a changed complexion in old age from an intemperate way of life, this proceeds from their evil habits and not from the aspect of their
sky.   Now the English are both a northern people, and their
young men use no wine, so that it is no marvel if their bodily
form is of graceful beauty, and most of all in the time of youth.

To the English then, in the five hundred and eighty-fifth
year after the Virgin bore a son, Gregory sends that most

The monk
Augustine sent
to England.

excellent man—the monk Augustine.   When this same Augustine had made his landing in Kent, he seeks audience of the
king of Kent, of the race of Engist, by name Adelbert, and
sought from him allowance to preach the Gospel in his king-

---

[1] Cf. Herod. ii. 30.   Syene is the modern Assouan.   'The latitude of Syene—
24° 5′ 23″—was an object of great interest to the ancient geographers.   They
believed that it was seated immediately under the tropic, and that on the day of
the summer solstice a vertical staff cast no shadow, and the sun's disc was
reflected in a well at noonday.   The statement is indeed incorrect ; the ancients
were not acquainted with the true tropic : yet at the summer solstice the length
of the shadow, or $\frac{1}{400}$th of the staff, could scarcely be discovered, and the
northern limb of the sun's disc would be nearly vertical.'—(Smith's *Dict. of Geog.*)
[2] Orig. 'plurimi'; F. 'plurimum'.   [3] Cf. p. 54, note [1].

dom. Now Adelbert was a man easily bent towards what was
good, and so granted to Augustine his desire, ministering also
to him and his following in what was needful. Augustine
laboured so strenuously that in a short space of time he
brought to the faith the king himself and almost the whole
people of Kent. Passing on to Rochester, he began there too
to preach the word of God ; but the common people derided
him, and threw fish-tails at the man of God ; wherefore
Augustine made his prayer to God that for a punishment of
this sin their infants should be born with tails, to the end they
might be warned not to contemn the teachers of divine things.
And for this reason, as the English chroniclers relate, the Some born
infants were born with tails. This tailed condition is by no with tails,
means to be attributed to skiey influences ; nor, at that period, and why.
do I deem that men were indeed born with tails ; but for a
time only, and to the end that an unbelieving race might give
credence to their teacher, was this punishment inflicted. I
cannot give my assent to the Scots and the Gauls, who assert
the opposite. Of his companions, who had come with him
from Rome, Augustine consecrated two as bishops : Justin, Bishops.
to wit, whom he placed over the see of Rochester, and Mellitus
as bishop of London. In the matter of the celebration of
Easter these two bishops wrote to the Scots.

CHAP. X.—*Of the conversion of Oswald, likewise of the too great
austerity of the bishop who was sent to him, of the wisdom of bishop
Aidan, and of the conversion of the Britons to the faith.*

WHEN it came to the knowledge of Oswald, king of the Oswald.
Bernicians, that the southern Englishmen had piously received
the word of God, he sends to the elders of the Scots, praying
that on him they would bestow some grave man, well-fur-
nished in the Christian faith, as bishop, for he believed that,
seeing the life and doctrine of such an one, the people that
was subject to him might be imbued with the Christian
religion ; for this same Oswald had been for no short time an
exile from his own kingdom with the Scots. With them he
had had long experience of the walk and conversation of the

faithful, and the Catholic faith approved itself to him. His messenger received from the Scots the warmest welcome, as was right; wherefore they sent to him a bishop. But this bishop used at the first too great austerity, and so did little good with the English. And, returning to his own, he said that the English were a race no way inclinable to what was good. Now when he was speaking thus in an assembly of

The wisdom of Aidan.

most religious fathers, one of them, Aidan by name, a most honourable man, and withal of utmost perspicacity in judgment, makes objection in these words: 'Perchance thou hast not followed the teaching of Paul, and given, first of all, milk, and afterwards the stronger food. For thy part it was to lead the people by degrees to the faith and to right conduct,—to make easy the foundation, and afterward to build upon it a lofty pile. For 'tis an old proverb: "Feeble beginning shall be followed by happier fortune"[1].' And since Aidan spoke so shrewdly, and since he was known to be a man of holy life— albeit not by all men, for it had been hid under a bushel—they make him bishop, and send him with a following of religious

Aidan is made bishop.

monks to the English. Upon this matter I prefer to quote English Bede rather than our own chroniclers. For the Venerable Bede, in the third chapter of the third book of his History of the Church of the English people, writes as follows: '[They sent to him] Aidan, a man of a singular mildness of disposition and piety and moderation, full of zeal to God, although not altogether according to knowledge; for he was wont to keep Easter Sunday after the custom of his own people from the fourteenth to the twentieth moon, since in this manner too the northern province of the Scots and the whole nation of the Picts were in use to celebrate Easter, believing that they followed therein the written precept of the holy and praiseworthy father Anatolius[2], the truth of which almost every one can easily determine[3]. On the arrival of the bishop the king granted him, according to his desire, his

---

[1] Debile principium melior fortuna sequetur.

[2] Bishop of Laodicea; the inventor in A.D. 276 of the Paschal computation.

[3] 'Quod quidem an verum sit, penitus quisque facillime agnoscet.' In Holder's edition of Bede, the reading is 'quod an uerum sit, peritus quisque facillime cognoscit'.

episcopal see in the island of Lindisfarne. And then it was truly often a right fair sight, inasmuch as the bishop had not perfect mastery of the English tongue, to see the king himself interpreting to his chiefs and councillors the heavenly word; for during the long time of his banishment he had perfectly learned the language of the Scots. From that time there came daily many from the country of the Scots to Britain, and from those provinces of the English over which Oswald held rule, and with great devotion preached the word of God, while those among them who had received priestly consecration administered the grace of baptism to all that believed. Churches were built here and there; a joyful people flocked to hear the word of God; lands and estates were granted by the royal bounty for the building of monasteries. The children of the English, as well as those of riper years, were instructed by Scottish teachers in the study and observance of the discipline known among the regulars; since for the most part these preachers were monks. Bishop Aidan was himself a monk, having his appointment from the island called Hy[1], whose monastery had for a long time the pre-eminence among all the monasteries of the northern Scots, all those of the Picts, and had the direction of their peoples. That island belongs indeed by right to Britain, for it is separated from that country by a small firth only; but it had been long since given by the Picts, who inhabit that district of Britain, to the Scottish monks, through whose preaching they had come to the faith of Christ.'

So far Bede, to the letter of his words; and from his narrative it is plain that Oswald was filled with zeal towards God. One church I know founded in his honour in Lothian: Whit- Lothian. tingham, to wit, distant two leagues from Gleghornie. In the time of Bede all Lothian was subject to Oswald. And so much is clear, because he says that the island of Hii, to the north of Arran[1], ought to belong to the Britons. This is clear, that in the time of Bede, or at least in the time of Oswald, few among the Scots were able to speak English. But you will say: Aidan was an islander; therefore your conclusion

---

[1] *i.e.* Iona.

[2] On this indication of geographical position compare note to Book I. p. 37, on the island of Sanda as 'more northerly than Bute'.

does not follow. Though it be not a full and logical conclusion, I must hold it to be a true one [1].

I RELATE the lives of men who were famed for their piety at
greater length than those of warriors, to the end that the
reader may feel his heart grow warm within him and strengthen
himself with this spiritual marrow. For, to quote from Bede,
in the fifth chapter of his third book: 'Not otherwise was the
life of Aidan than his doctrine. He had no care or love for
the things of this world. All that was given to him by the
kings and rich men of his age he delighted to bestow upon the
poor when they met him with an entreaty for alms. His habit
was to travel on foot, and not on horseback—unless by the
urgency of a greater necessity—from place to place, in town or
country. Wherever his eye lighted upon any men, were they
rich or poor, thither upon the spot he turned aside, beseeching
them, if they were unbelievers, to take the oath of allegiance
to the faith, and, if they were of the faithful, establishing them
with words of comfort, and exhorting them by word and deed
to almsgiving and the practice of good works. Such was his
daily work.' In the sixth chapter of the same book Bede tells
how king Oswald once received a prayer for alms from certain
poor persons as he sat at meat, and how the king broke in
pieces the silver dish set before him on the table, and gave the
fragments thereof to the poor. Seeing which, and moved to
admiration at the pious act, bishop Aidan, for he was present,
seized the king by the right hand, and said, 'Never may this
hand grow old!'—and the event was according to the prayer
of his benediction. After king Oswald had fallen in battle with
the heathen, his arm and his right hand in the time of Bede
did not know decay. Bede tells in his third book of many
miracles done by the king and bishop Aidan—and in point of
time he was not far removed from them. In the end of the
fifteenth chapter, after telling of the miracles of Aidan, he has,

The life of
Aidan.

The life of
Oswald.

The hand
of Oswald.

---

[1] The punctuation of Orig. and F. makes different sense here. Orig. is
evidently right.

further, this : 'The manner of this miracle I have from no
doubtful source, for it was told to me word for word by that
most trustworthy presbyter of our church, Cynimond, and he had
it from the very presbyter Utha, on whom and through whom
the same was wrought.' And his conclusion of the seventeenth
chapter is in these words :—so far as
I learned from those who knew him, he was careful to neglect
none of those things which are appointed to be done in the
evangelical, apostolical, or prophetical Scriptures, but laboured
with all his strength to perform them all. These things I
much love and admire in the aforenamed bishop, because I
doubt not that they were well-pleasing to God. But that he
did not observe Easter at its proper date, either from ignorance of the canonical time, or, if not ignorant of this, yet
yielding to the antiquated authority of his own people, I no
way praise nor approve. Yet this I approve in him, that in
his celebration of Easter he had nothing else at heart, he
revered and he preached nothing else, but what we too hold
firm, the redemption of mankind by the passion, resurrection,
and ascension into heaven of Jesus Christ, the Mediator
between God and man.' So far Bede, word for word. And to
what he has written I add certain propositions : Aidan had no
blame, but did well, in celebrating as he celebrated. The
proof of this : For a morally good act it is not essential that
the act be directed by true knowledge ; but it is enough that
it be directed by invincible error[1] ; and such was the case with
that father. The pontifical human law was against him ; but
this he was not bound to know ; and he ruled his conduct
herein by sacred Scripture and pious feeling, and in this too
walked in the footsteps of those who had gone before him.
In human positive laws every man has a wide latitude of his
own.

For seven years Aidan held his bishopric in England. To
him succeeded Finan, a Scot, a monk from the same district
with Aidan, and both in matter of the faith and integrity of
life he kept fresh the footsteps of his predecessor. Ten years
only he survived in the exercise of the episcopate. To him

A wrong observance of Easter.

Aidan without sin in celebrating Easter at a different time.

Finanus.

---

[1] Cf. Bk. III. ch. xi., on the conditions of a morally good action.

succeeded Colman, of the same region and place in the island of Hy [1]. In his day arose in England among the princes and the clergy the great question as to the observance of Easter. Colman claimed to have on his side Aidan, Finan, Saint Columba, and Anatolius. On the other side was the greater part of the clergy, and chief among them was one Ronan [2], a Scot by nation, but educated, according to Bede, in Gaul or Italy. This was a question merely of observing a law of human ordinance, and Colman ought to have yielded to the popular feeling, and to the use and wont, if such there were, among the Britons; for the use and wont of a place is to be followed, according to the proverb, 'If you are at Rome do as the Romans do', and the rest. And this has application to a law of human imposition, of which I am now speaking. Custom is the interpreter of human law, and may restrict and even sometimes repeal such law. Not otherwise we find that the Gauls eat animal food on the Saturdays [3] between the feasts of the Nativity and of the Purification, and do not fast on the nine vigils of the Apostles, and in many parts of Spain it is the custom to eat the extremities and the inwards of animals on all Saturdays whatsoever, with the exception of Lent; and yet in such points as these in other kingdoms the common human law is just the opposite. Hence is plain that the Venerable Bede should not have laid such weight on a point like this, when the contention was as to the customary human law in a particular locality; and inasmuch as Aidan and his successor had already introduced the Scottish mode into the northern parts of England, Colman had no right to insist upon the contrary mode, albeit it was the custom of the Romans, and of the majority, as in a similar case we have declared concerning the Gauls and the Spaniards [4]. However this may be,

---

[1] *i.e.* Iona.

[2] ' Romanus ' Orig. and F. Cf, Bede: *H.E.* iii. 25. Dempster calls him ' Romanus ' or ' Romianus ' ; but ' Ronan ' is plainly the right form.

[3] In diebus Sabbatinis.

[4] The reference is to Major's *In Quartum*, 5th question of the 15th distinction. As to the customs of the different countries in the matter of fasting, he writes : ' The Gauls are not obliged to fast as often as the Britons ; for the Britons fast upon all the principal festivals of Our Lady, though the law enjoins fasting only upon the eve [*profestum*] of the Assumption. On the other hand,

Colman had no mind to make a long stay among the English, but besought them that they would grant him to carry away the bones of Saint Aidan as relics. Some part of the bones they gave him in answer to his petition, but the remnant they kept in the bishopric over which he had held rule in England.

To Colman succeeded Tuda, a Briton. He had been educated Tuda. among the southern Scots, and, as the manner of the Scots was, he wore a tonsure[1]. Religious men, both English and Scots, followed Colman into Scotland[2], and he carried them with him to a certain island of Scotland[2], by name Inisboufinde[3], that is, 'the island of the white calf'; and inasmuch as the habits of

---

the Britons make a heavier meal in Lent than do the Gauls, and custom is the interpreter of the manner in which the lenten fast shall be observed, on the supposition that it is of human ordinance. Do you not see how in France the Gauls eat flesh on the Saturdays between the festival of the Birth of Christ and the Purification? . . . It is elsewhere plain that the Catalonians eat some flesh meats on all Saturdays except in Lent—not so the Britons and the Gauls— and custom suffices to excuse the Catalonians.' Major further writes of those ' non comedentibus carnes in quarta feria in Scotia Britanna, quia passim illic abstinent ab esu carnium '. Cf. also *Life of George Buchanan*, p. 367, by Mr. Hume Brown, who quotes from Buchanan's Life written by himself: 'Crimini dabatur [*i.e.* to Buchanan] carnium esus in Quadragesima, a qua nemo in tota Hispania est qui abstineat.' In the *Book of Merlin* (E. E. T. Soc., p. 11) the penance enjoined upon Merlin's mother by her confessor is 'that alle the Saterdayes while thou lyvest, that thow ete mete but ones on the day'. As to the custom in England at a later date, we find that a Jesuit father, Jasper Heywood, who came into England in 1581, taking the place of Parsons, 'to the trouble of our church and to the sorrow of cardinal Allen and of all good men presumed to abrogate the ancient national fasts of Friday and certain vigils of the B. Virgin, which had been religiously observed from the very cradle of the English Church.'—John Mush in his *Declaratio Motuum, etc.*, as quoted in *A Historical Sketch of the Conflicts between Jesuits and Seculars in the Reign of Queen Elizabeth*, by T. G. Law, Lond. 1889 ; Introd. p. xxii.

[1] ' corona '. ' Corona was the exclusive name of the Roman tonsure, whereas in the semi-circular form, such as practised by the northern Irish, there was no corona.'—Lanigan's *Eccl. Hist.*, vol. iii. p. 78.

[2] *i.e.* Ireland. It is to be noted that Bede, whose narrative Major follows, calls Ireland by its old name of ' Scotia ' ; Major makes the mistake of supposing it to be our Scotland. To quote the first sentence of Mr. Skene's *Celtic Scotland* : 'The name of Scotia or Scotland, whether in its Latin or its Saxon form, was not applied to any part of the territory forming the modern kingdom of Scotland till towards the end of the tenth century. . . . Ireland was emphatically Scotia, the ' patria', or mother-country, of the Scots.'

[3] Cf. Reeves's *Chronicon Hyense* and Lanigan's *Eccl. Hist. of Ireland*, vol. iii. p. 79—the island, off the coast of Mayo, now known as Innisboffin.

the Scots[1] and the English differed in many points, he went
over to Ireland, and obtained for the English religious a certain
place.   And they, when they had received from him instruction
in our holy religion, raised that place, which was once of no
account, to a singular pre-eminence, and in the time of Bede
reception was granted there to Englishmen only[2].   Such,
according to Bede, was the estimation of the religious at that
time, that no man would pass a man of religion on the road
without he received his blessing in spoken word, or at least by
a motion of the hand.

CHAP. XII.—*Concerning the death of Malduin, the reigns of
Eugenius the Fourth and Eugenius the Fifth, Saint Cuthbert, the Venerable Bede, and the Monastery of Melrose.*

ABOUT this time died Malduin, king of the Scots, and
Eugenius the Fourth, his grandson, succeeded him.   In his
days Saint Cuthbert, son of the king of Ireland, who, first
under Saint Columba and afterward in Melrose, had been a
monk, and who had been a disciple of Saint Boisil the abbot,
was ordained bishop in England after Saint Colman.   Into the
monasteries of Saint Cuthbert's foundation no woman dares to
set foot; and for this Bede assigns the following reason: that
five monks, namely, of the monastery of Coldinghame[3], though
living apart from the nuns of the same foundation, yet fell into
fleshly sin with these; for which cause the whole monastery
was destroyed by fire.   To this day the same rule is observed
in the monastery of Melrose, which, since the time of Bede,
has increased in a marvellous manner.   The situation indeed of
that monastery on the river Tweed is most fit for the exercise
of a devout life, for it stands in a wood remote from any habitation of men.   Its rule is that of Saint Bernard.   A wonderful
sound is heard, so they say, in the church or in the cloister,
which portends the death of any of the religious[4]; whereupon

Marginal notes: Cuthbert. / The monastery of Melrose. / A wonderful sound.

---

[1] *i.e.* the Irish Scots.

[2] Bede, *H.E.* iv. 4, and Lanigan, vol. iii. pp. 166, 168, 169.   The foundation for English monks was at Mayo, that for Irish monks at Innisboffin.

[3] Bede: *H.E.* iv. 25.

[4] Peter Swave, a Dane, who visited Scotland in 1535, refers to this tradition
regarding Melrose.   Cf. Mr. Hume Brown's *Early Travels in Scotland*, p. 57.

they all, hearing the sound, prepare for confession.   I tell this as the common opinion of the people, not as a matter of· faith.

After this, Eugenius the Fifth reigns in Scotland, and, fol- Eugenius the
Fifth. lowing him, Amberkeleth, who met his death by an arrow, Amberkeleth. as he was fighting against the Picts.

About this time Bede flourished.   <He was born in the Bede. northern parts of England.   Though some have it that his body rests at Genoa, I have read in the English chronicles>[1] that he never passed beyond this island, and was buried at Durham, near the place of his birth.   Whether from some malady, or from old age, he lost his eye-sight ere he died, yet even so was in use to preach to all who came to hear him, and in the end to bestow his blessing upon the assembled multitude.   Now he had a wicked serving-man, in whom this much preaching had wrought weariness, and once upon a time he led the man of God to a place full of stones that he might preach there, telling him that a goodly congregation was before him.   And when at the end, as his custom was, he was bestowing his blessing, there was heard a voice saying, 'Amen, Venerable Bede'.   With divine and human learning he was excellently furnished, and withal was a man of zeal, which I approve yet more.   And therefore he is reckoned in the list of the Saints.   In the year of our Lord seven hundred and thirty-four, and of his life the seventy-second, he fell asleep in the Lord.   In the end of his book concerning the church of the English nation he writes thus : that in the seven hundred and thirty-first year of the Incarnation, the Picts and Scots, content with their boundaries, do not invade the English[2], which year was the two hundred and eighty-fifth from the arrival of the English in Britain.

---

[1] Orig. and F.: ' de parte Boreali Angliae natus, licet corpus ejus aliqui apud Genuam [' F. Genoam'] referant.   Apud Anglorum annales legi, etc.'   The punctuation of this seems to be faulty, and I have in the translation divided the sentences differently.   Bede died at Jarrow A.D. 735.   The legend of his burial at Genoa probably had its origin in a confusion with him of a monk of the same name who died at Genoa about A.D. 883.

[2] *H. E.* v. 23 : ' Scotti qui Britanniam incolunt, suis contenti finibus, nil contra gentem Anglorum insidiarum moliuntur aut fraudium.'

CHAP. XIII.—*Concerning the reign of Achaius, and the eminent valour and piety of his brother William; likewise of the perpetual peace between the French and the Scots, and of the founders of the University of Paris.*

Achaius,
William the
Scot.

ABOUT this time Achaius is king over the Scots.   His brother William bore arms in all wars under Charles the Grèat, and was that one of his twelve famous soldiers who was commonly known among our own people as Scotisgilmor[1].   This hero, intent always on warlike things, was never married.   He founded in Germany fifteen monasteries of the order of Saint Benedict, and at his own cost endowed the same, enjoining that over them Scots should at all times be placed[2].   Of these monasteries two are at Cologne, and the rest in other parts of Germany.

---

[1] Lists of the 'douze pairs' (sometimes sixteen in number) or 'duke-peers' are given in *The English Charlemagne Romances*, E. E. T. Soc., vol. ii. p. 193, but I have not identified this 'tall Scots knight.'

[2] Like 'Sanctus Gillenus Scotus' and 'noster sanctus Columbanus' and ' Fiacrius', see *ante*, pp. 87, 88, the ' Scots' for whose behoof these fifteen monasteries in Germany were founded were Irish-Scots; but the Scots of modern geography, just as they 'ousted their Irish progenitors from the name itself', ' by virtue of the equivocation' ousted them also 'from pecuniary foundations abroad which were restricted to Scotsmen'.   The late Rev. A. W. Haddan, in an article on 'Scots on the Continent in the Early Middle Ages' contributed to No. cxvi. of *The Christian Remembrancer*, says that ' the great movement organised by S. Columbanus numbers scarcely one Briton among the armies of its Irish promoters', while ' the case was widely different with the Scots', *i.e.* the Irish.   In their ranks we have Saint Gall, the apostle of north-eastern Switzerland, and Virgilius, the apostle of Carinthia.   ' Colman, the "patron of Austria", canonised at Melch on the Danube in 1025 ; John the Scot, bishop of Mecklenburgh, martyred by heathen Sclavonians in 1055 ; a cluster of Scottish monasteries dependent on S. James of Ratisbon, the foundation of Conor-o. Bryan, king of Munster, and pushing eastward as far as Vienna, during the twelfth century, carry us onward to the ever-receding frontiers of heathendom, at the later as at the earlier period.'   The Bollandist biographer of Saint Kilian has an interesting passage on the nationality of the 'Scottish' missionaries : ' Scotia, quae et Hibernia dicitur, insula est maris Oceani, foecunda quidem glebis, sed sanctissimis clarior viris ; ex quibus Columbano gaudet Italia, Gallo ditatur Alemannia, Kiliano Teutonica nobilitatur Francia. . . . Dixi, et iterum repeto, me inter Scotos et Hibernos arbitrum sedere prorsus non velle ; lites ipsas suas dirimant ; Tros Rutilusve fuat S. Kilianus, nullo discrimine habebo.[2]

For a more particular account of the Irish monasteries in Germany see Dr. Wattenbach's *Die Kongregation der Schotten-Klöster in Deutschland*, translated

It was about this time that there was made between
the French and the Scots that league of peace which thenceforward has endured unchanged and inviolate[1]; and indeed
you shall scarce find among any two kingdoms in Europe a
peace more solid and sincere. To this king of the Scots Charles
the Great made petition that he would send to him learned
men. And for answer there are sent to France John the Scot[2],

The peace
between the
French and
the Scots.

Learned men
sent from Scot-
land to Paris.

by Dr. Reeves in the *Ulster Journal of Archæology*, July and August 1859. We
find there a record of the foundation of an Irish monastery in 1076 at Regensburg
[Ratisbon], shortly after at Kiev, in 1140 at Nürnberg, in 1142 at Constance,
in 1183 at Eichstadt (whose church was 'transferred to abbot Gregory and the
Scotic nation'), a little later at Kellheim, at Oels in Silesia ; while twelve
monasteries seem to have been specially recognised as standing in some connection with St. James's at Ratisbon. Schmeller (*Bairisches Worterbuch*, vol. iii.
p. 416) is quoted as speaking of fifteen houses—' by a mere oversight ' says Dr.
Reeves ; but the coincidence with Major's text should be noted. Of the twelve,
or fifteen, we have so far become acquainted with the following nine : St. James's,
Weyh St. Peter, Würzburg, Nürnberg, Constance, Vienna, Memmingen, Eichstadt, Erfurt. 'At the end of the fifteenth century', to quote Dr. Wattenbach,
' no Scotic monk had arrived within the memory of man, and their very name
was so completely forgotten that the Dukes of Münsterberg, in the document in
which they propose to incorporate the Abbey of Oels with some other foundation,
speak of it as having formerly belonged to the *Wendish* brethren. The Wends
had disappeared from the inhabitants of the country, so likewise the Scots from
among the monks—all that remained was the memory that they belonged to a
foreign race.' At Nürnberg, in the fifteenth century, wine came to be sold in the
monastery as in a tavern, and that a missing wife ought to be looked for in the
Scots monastery became a proverb. 'At St. James's the Scotch of Scotland
turned the tide of affairs to their own profit, and went so far as to say that
the Irish had thrust themselves in, and for that very reason had brought about
the decline of the colonies. Pope Leo x., on July 31, 1515, did actually make
over the monastery of St. James to the Scotch, and appointed, as superior, one
John Thomson, who drove out the Irish, and introduced Scottish monks from
Dunfermline.

[1] This legendary alliance of Achaius and Charles the Great, as has been
pointed out to me by Mr. Hume Brown, is as strongly insisted on by French as
by Scottish historians. The league is specially mentioned in the marriage-con-
tract of Queen Mary and the Dauphin. Buchanan (*Rer. Scotic. Hist.*, p. 89,
ed. Ruddiman) gives the following reason for the alliance : ' Ab Achaio primum
inter Scotos et Francos inita est amicitia maxima de causa, quod non modo
Saxones Germaniae cultores, sed qui in Britannia ceperant sedes, Gallias piraticis
incursionibus infestabant.'

[2] John Scotus Erigena, an Irish Scot, as his name implies, was born in
the early part of the ninth century. He died in 883 or 884. All the Scottish
historians relate that to their countryman belongs the honour of being the first
teacher of the University of Paris. Modern research has shown that that

Clement, Alcuin [1]; and these men when they landed on the
French coasts declared that their merchandise was the knowledge that they professed.   At first sight it must seem passing
strange that in a small corner of the world men should be
found better furnished with learning than in all other parts
of the same; yet, if we will rightly weigh the matter, the
wonder is no way so great.   Very many, as Bede relates,
who never left the boundaries of Britain, spoke Greek and
Latin [2].   A great company of the religious, as is fitting indeed
for the truly religious, had found refuge in solitude from the
storms of this present world, and given themselves to study and
to prayer; and though their strength might not lie in the
unravelling of scholastic and Sorbonic puzzles, yet in the expo-
sitiou of the Sacred Scriptures their learning was with the best.
It was this knowledge of Scripture that they professed, and
commentaries upon Scripture by no means to be slighted were
written by Bede and Alcuin; and Aidan and Colman could have
done the same, but that they had the oversight of a great
bishopric, and so gave themselves up to that life of action to
which they were called.

CHAP. XIV.—*Of the death of Congall, the reign of Dungal, the
contention between the Picts and Scots; likewise of the war against
Alphin, whom in the end they slew, and of the deeds of others.*

IN the eight hundred and second year from the redemption
of the world Congall, king of the Scots, passed from life to

---

university did not come into existence till, at earliest, the close of the eleventh
century, and that Abelard is the teacher to whom most of the credit must belong
in forming the nucleus of the university.   See Thurot, *Thèse sur l'université de
Paris.*

   .1. Clement was also an Irish Scot.   The chief authority for his life is the
anonymous monk of St. Gall, who tells the story of the two Scots of Ireland,
named Clement and Albinus (not 'Alcuinus'), who on the coasts of France
called out to the crowds flocking to purchase, 'If any man desireth wisdom, let
him come to us, for we have it to sell'.   On this further question of disputed
nationality, and whether Albinus is another name for Alcuin or not, see
Buchanan's *Rer. Scotic.* lib. v. Rex 65, and Dr. Lanigan's comment, *Eccl. Hist.*
vol. iii. pp. 208-211.

   [2] Bede: *H. E.* v. 20, 22.

death, and was succeeded by Dungal, in the days of the Dungal.
emperor Lewis.   Of seven years only was his reign; and in
the course of the same, after a fifty years' peace with the Picts,
new seeds of war sprang up, and on this wise: When the
Picts first gained footing in Britain, wives were given them
of the Irish Scots, from whom the British Scots have their
descent, upon this understanding—that in case of doubt the
kingdom should fall to the woman and not to the man.
Founding their contention upon this agreement, the Scots
said the time was now come when the kingly power of the The contention
Picts fell by right to them, that is, to the Scots.   But as to the Scots.
this right the Picts began to shuffle; and whether the result
came from consideration of the law of the case, or from the
urgent actual fact, the seeds were sown of a war that was full
of danger in the future.   After Dungal, Alphin bears rule Alphin.
among the Scots, and the war against the Picts that was begun
by his predecessor he waged with such persistence that he
never, as it were, in the course of it stopped to draw breath.
In the third year of his reign, and on Easter Day, a great
battle was fought between him and the Picts.   Very many
famous men among the Scots there met their death, yet victory
remained with the Scots.   Thereafter, in the twelfth year of
his reign, on the kalends of August, Alphin attacks the Picts
in a fierce-fought battle, where most of the Scots perished, and
Alphin himself was taken by the Picts, and without ruth The beheading
beheaded.   Alphin then being slain, the sovereignty of the of Alphin.
Scots fell to his son Kenneth.

   This Kenneth had gained no small skill in matters of war Kenneth.
along with his father, and possessed not only a fearless courage
and strength of body, but also that discretion without which
bravery in the field of battle profits not.   He called into
council the chief men of his kingdom, and because he knew his
own people to be slow to rouse against the Picts, by reason of
the various disasters they had suffered at the hands of that
people, he aimed to move them by a set speech, for he was
mighty in words.   And thus he is said to have begun : ' Were Kenneth's
it not that I know you, ye Scots, to be at all times inclined to speech.
war, my speech with you this day might be more studied and
filled with matter.   It escapes you not, my chiefs, that the

reason is fivefold for the justice of our cause: first, on account of
the theft and the detention of that Molossian hound ; secondly,
that by pact and treaty of our ancestors the kingdom of the
Picts is rightfully ours ; thirdly, in that the enemy in our
despite have leagued them with the Saxons ; fourthly, that in
old times they drove our fathers from this island ;—nor is it
easy to believe that two neighbour kingdoms can live in mutual
amity on one and the same part of a country with naked earth
for boundary betwixt them ; wherefore it behoves us either
to drive them out of the island or some day ourselves to suffer
exile ;—and fifthly, in that they cruelly slew my dearest father,
a man worthy to rule, a man the most deserving of your
remembrance, and in the slaying of him violated all laws
human and divine, seeing that they beheaded him when captive in their hands.   Of his death the infamy (unless it be
yours to avenge it with the sword) will redound throughout
the ages upon you, who are his members like as he was your
head.   If ye are men worthy of your ancestors, worthy of
your sires, this horrible wickedness of theirs shall not go
unavenged.   And there is no reason why you should dread a
conflict with the Picts.   Granted that they were victors in the
last battle, their victory was no bloodless one, they gained it
with great slaughter to themselves.   That kingdom of the
Picts which is in our hands (provided you quit you like men)
I will divide among you after your deserts, reserving for
myself the right only of superior and the glory of the
strife.   Brave men's part is this : to live with honour or to
die nobly.   But yours will be no noble life if you shall leave
unpunished the murder of him who was my dear father and
your king.'

And so with few words he made an end, exhorting them by
the spirits of their fathers, by the love and reverence they
bore to himself, by the gods above, that they should go forth
with him to battle against their mortal enemy the Picts.   Yet
with all his urgent suasion he implanted no desire of battle in
these inexorable chiefs.   Forasmuch as they had before now
made trial of the strength of the Picts, and had been more
often worsted in fight than they had gained the day, they
chose for a time to hold their breath rather than rashly venture

on a struggle whose event they had reason to fear; for they were unwilling to risk the loss of children, wives, life, and country. But the king was wroth, and, with a mind exasperated against the Picts, he cunningly contrived a trap wherein to catch his chiefs, and so bend their minds to war. He bade them all, namely, to a supper, after which they should spend the night with him. And when the great men of the kingdom were asleep upon their beds, he calls to him a certain kinsman and familiar friend, and clothes him in a suit of fishes' scales— lustrous these are by night—and gives him further a reed, through which he was to speak, and to command the chiefs in the name of God that they should obey their king in the matter of this war with the Picts, promising them too the victory, though not a bloodless one, and for a reward the country of the Picts. At early dawn then, on the following day, the chiefs are found talking of the angel who had appeared during the night. The story reached the ears of the king; he feigned himself from the first incredulous, the better to divert them from his stratagem, and at length, but some time thereafter, when he saw them to be of one mind intent on war, brought together a great army of the Scots, and laid waste far and wide the Pictish territory, sparing nothing to fire or sword, and firmly bent either to bring destruction on the kingdom of the Scots, or once for all to drive the Pictish people from the face of the earth.

Kenneth's stratagem.

When Drusco, the king of the Picts, understood thus much, filled with rage against the Scots, he got together a large army of the Picts, and as he was drawing near the line of the Scots, and took up a fair position, the better to encourage his men to struggle to the utmost, he is said to have exhorted them as follows :—

Drusco, king of the Picts.

'It is no secret to you, my strong-hearted Picts, how that fellow, Kenneth the Scot, has the firm determination utterly to over- turn our country and our kingdom, a thing that I have learned from some whom he holds to be among his faithful followers. It is a commonplace with prudent and sagacious kings that they must search out the secret intentions of the enemy. Now Kenneth's chief men follow him unwillingly, and in the hour of need they will desert him. He indeed is inflamed with rage

Drusco's speech.

and has a stormy soul because of the slaying of his father; but, as ye well know, " Anger clogs the mind of a man, so that he shall not be able to see things as they are ".   Therefore, all in disorder, and with no proper equipment, he invades our land, and knows not the difficult places of it.   We, on the other hand, have all our wits about us, we know every inch of our territory, we are going to fight for our country, nor will Kenneth be any way hard to conquer, if only you quit you like men.   Our ancestors, no way better men than ourselves, once drove his ancestors from the island; we once took captive his father, a man of fiercer temper than himself, and as a captive slew him.   We have the English on our side; they hate this race with its constant plotting of wars.   High-couraged Picts, it rests with your right hands, this very day, to deal destruction irretrievable on the Scots; and he who shall take alive this foolhardy youth, that he may suffer a penalty harder than his father's, shall receive a rich reward; and we will lesson this fickle race, ever prone to war and not to peace, that henceforward its best part will be to make for peace and not for war.'

A fierce battle.   This said, and the signal given on both sides, they incontinent engage in battle, and here the eager trumpet, there the clarion, urges the warrior to the horrid onset; the contest was fierce, its issue long time doubtful.   Now the Scots are victors, anon they seem to yield before the enemy's attack; in the end, when the dust of battle cleared away, the victory was to

Drusco is taken. the Scots.   Drusco, the Pictish king, is taken, and with a goodly escort Kenneth sends him to the Scots; nor does he even then grow slack, mindful of that proverb, 'Many understand to conquer who know not to use the victory'.   He lays waste the villages of the Picts, he spares nor age nor sex nor religion, but smites all alike.   Now, when the Pictish chiefs saw the unbridled rage of Kenneth, as one man they made stand against him, and he who should have been successor to Drusco

A second speech of the Pict. spoke in few words thus to his men : ' Ye see, high-couraged Picts, the inhumanity, yea the brutal cruelty of those Scots, how their aim is our destruction, even the extinction of the race of Picts and all memory of it among men.   Now, many things may well serve to quicken us in this call to war; but, above all, the remembrance that we are sprung from the Scythians. For at all times the Scythians have been an unconquerable race; let us fight then for our country, for hearth and home, for our churches, freedom, for life and honour, and with God to guard us and your own valour, my hope is this, brave men, that we shall be avenged on the insults of those Scots.' This said, he gave the signal to rush upon A second battle. the foe, and again the battle raged fierce and hot. In that conflict many Scots were slain, but of the Picts a far greater number, while the remnant was put to rout. Yet a third time the remaining phalanx of the Picts makes a desperate assault A third battle. upon the Scots, and its leader with these words encouraged his men : ' Not to hope for safety is the only safety of the conquered [1]. Should we now turn our backs the Scots will take advantage of our fear, will follow us up and put us to the sword. Let us then show a bold front, and thus, my men, let us conquer—or die the death of the brave.' This said, again they attack the Scots, but are overcome by Kenneth, of all men the bravest. Nor did Kenneth return to Scotland till he had either put to fire or sword all the Picts, or driven them as A sevenfold exiles from their country. I find it somewhere written that he fight in one day. was attacked by the Picts, now rendered desperate, seven times in one day, and that as often he routed them, standing to his ground by day and night. Afterward, returning to Scone, he beheads Drusco, the Pictish king ; and thus was the kingdom Drusco of the Picts, which had endured for more than eight hundred beheaded. years in Britain, brought to naught by Kenneth and added to tion of the Picts. his own. Utterly do I abhor the inhumanity shown by this man towards the servants of God, and women, and children ; for such wild rage as this against persons unfit for war is not found even among civilised heathens. And so Kenneth first began to rule in northern Britain one hundred and four [1] years after the death of Bede.

Kenneth reigned, after the expulsion of the Picts, sixteen years, and [died ?] about the year of our Lord eight hundred

---

[1] ' Una salus victis nullam sperare salutem ' : *Aen.* ii. 354. Compare Corneille in *Horace*, Act ii. sc. 7 : ' Ce n'est qu'au désespoir qu'il nous faut recourir.'

[1] Orig. and F. ' 50 ' ; F. in Errata, ' 104 '.

and thirty-nine, in the time of the emperor Lewis. About him we have these verses of the Scots:

> 'Tis said that Kenneth first bore sway among the men of Alban,
> Alphin's son he was, and many wars he waged,
> Twice eight years he reigned from the expulsion of the Picts.

In the conduct of war Kenneth cast into the shade all who had gone before him. After his day we find scarce any mention of the kingdom of the Picts, and, whether justly or unjustly the Scots took their lands, justly in the end they held them. For what is no man's property admittedly belongs to the occupier. Among our annals I find a catalogue of Pictish kings, but it would serve no end to insert it here; therefore I let it be. Somewhat about these I may, however, be allowed to put down, to the end that there be a right understanding of **The date of the arrival of Columba.** the boundaries of the Scots. Bede writes thus:[1] Saint Columba came to Britain in the reign of that most mighty king of the Picts named Brude. To Brude succeeded Garnard, son of Dompnach, who built the collegiate church of Abernethy after that the Blessed Patrick had brought thither Saint **Bridget's endowment.** Bridget. This king bestowed upon the Blessed Virgin, and the Blessed Bridget, along with nine virgins who had attended her, those endowments which are now held by the provost and canons. At that time Abernethy was the bishop's see and also **The capital of the Picts in Scotland.** the capital of the Pictish kingdom. Some place the building of this collegiate church twenty-six years and nine months before the foundation of the church of Dunkeld; others allow to it a priority of two hundred and forty-four years. That I may not offer as certain what is uncertain, I will express myself in this matter doubtfully. The Picts held the more fertile part of the island, the plains, and the sea-coast places; the Scots, on the other hand, possessed the mountainous and more barren regions. The Picts held Saint Andrew in great honour, and most of all when Hungus[2] the Pict put to flight Athelstan of England near to Athelstanford. There it was that the cross of St. Andrew appeared to Hungus, when in **The apparition of the Cross of Saint Andrew.** time of need he had been made king of the Picts. The place is one league distant from Haddington.

---

[1] *H.E.* ii. 4.

[2] ? 'Hinguar', to which 'Hungus' of the next chapter is corrected in Errata of F.'

BOOK III.

CHAP. I.—*Of the incontinence of Osbert, king of Northumberland, and his death ; of the slaying of Ella and the other cruelties practised by the Danes ; likewise of many kings of England.*

Not long time before the expulsion of the Picts, the king of Northumberland was one Osbricht, a man of unbridled lust ; Osbert. he had unlawful dealings with the wife of one of his nobles, named Guerne, against her will. Loathing the foulness of this thing, she declared the whole matter to her husband; and he betook him to the Danes, of whose blood he too came, that with their aid he might not let this wickedness go unavenged. To him the king of the Danes sends two brothers, Hinguar and Hubba, with a great army, into Northumberland, and Osbert killed by the Danes. they slew Osbricht, the king of the Northumbrians. Thereafter they take York, a city strongly fortified, by assault. Against them king Ella led an army, and laid siege to the town. When the Danes were become aware of this, they left the town, and, on a certain piece of level ground near the city, they joined battle with Ella, and slew him. Whence the place Death of Ella. had its name, for in English it is called Ellis-Croft[1].

On the death of Ella they occupy all Northumberland, and afterwards Nottingham, and then made for Nichol and Lindesen and Holland[2]; and so with fire and sword they open a way to Tethford[3]. There they found Edmund, king of Norfolk and Suffolk, a man worthy of a heavenly crown, and when Hubba and Hinguar vainly tried to turn him from the faith, they slew Saint Edmund.

---

[1] The author of the Chronicle (*circa* 1350) known as Brompton's (Twysden's *Scriptores Decem*, 1652, col. 803) has the words : 'Locus ubi bellum fuit vocatur modo Ellescroft.' Drake (*Eboracum*, 1736, p. 78) quotes Brompton, and adds 'There is no place in or near the city that I can fix this name upon'. Thomas Gent (*Hist. of York*, 1730, p. 199), quoting Brompton, calls the place Ell-Croft.

[2] 'Nichol', called by Major, Bk. III. ch. xiii. 'Nicol sive Nicolai', is, according to Camden, the 'Norman' name of Lincoln. Lindesen is Lindsey (the 'Lindissi' of Bede, *H.E.* ii. 16), the south-eastern division of Lincolnshire, the others being Holland, the south-western division, and Kesteven.

[3] *i.e.* Thetford.

him. This Saint Edmund we have as a patron of our nation
of Almain, because, not so long since, the same was in use to
be called the English nation. This is clear from the legend
upon a seal at the time when I myself belonged to that nation ;
but the two nations were afterward made one, and were called
the nation of the Germans; and not unreasonably, for, compared with the Germans, very few of the English at Paris
graduate in arts[1]. He is buried in Suffolk at St. Edmundsbury ;
that is, the town is called the tomb of Saint Edmund[2]. It is
said to possess the largest bell in all England. There is in
England a great plenty of bells of the finest quality ; because
in the material for making bells England abounds. And just
as in music its people are said to surpass the rest of men[3], so
too do they make with their bells the sweetest and skilfullest
melody. You shall find no village of forty houses without its
peal of five sweet-sounding bells, and in what town you please,
of whatever size, every three hours the sweetest chime will
break upon your ears. When I was a student at Cambridge,
I would lie awake most part of the night, at the season of
the great festivals, that I might hear this melody of the bells.
The university is situated on a river, and the sound is the
sweeter that it comes to you over the water. No bells in
England are reckoned better than those of the convent at
Oseney[4]. When a special sweetness of tone is desired, silver is
plentifully mixed with the ordinary material of which they are

The German nation at Paris.

Bells in England.

---

[1] The punctuation of this passage is wrong in F. ('quia pauci admodum
Anglorum, Parisii respectu, Germanorum etc.'). As early as 1245, in a Bull of
Innocent the Fourth, the four Nations of France, Normandy, Picardy, and
England are distinctly recognised. The English Nation was composed of three
tribes—Germany, Scandinavia, and the British islands, and had for its patron
saints Charles the Great and Saint Edmund. During the Hundred Years' War,
the name 'English Nation' became an offence to French ears, and in 1378
the emperor Charles the Fourth, then on a visit to Paris, expressed his wish that
the name should be changed. It was not, however, till 1436 that the designation
'German Nation' displaced the other in the university registers.—Jourdain :
Excursions Historiques et Philosophiques à travers le Moyen Age, p. 366. Cf.
Mr. Hume Brown's *George Buchanan*, pp. 76, 77.

[2] Orig. 'in sanct Edmunds Burri' [F. 'in Sanct Edmundusburri] sepelitur ;
hoc est, villa sepulcrum sancti Edmundi appellatur.'

[3] Cf. *ante*, Bk. I. ch. v. p. 27.

[4] The origin of Christ Church College.

made. The people of Valenciennes and of Flanders are said to
follow the same method in the system of sweet chimes as the
English.

But a little while thereafter many of the Danes, and among
them Hinguar and Hubba, were slain by Alured, king of
Suffolk. While these things were happening, the Danes who
had accompanied Gormund the African into Gaul return to
England, and, joining themselves to those of their nation in The Danes
Northumberland, the Danish force was much increased. They grow stronger.
carry on the war against Edward, son to Alured. This Edward
was succeeded by his son Adelston, who destroyed most of the
Danes, and many too he drove out of the island. I do not
think I am wrong in holding that it was this same Adelston Adelston.
that Hinguar, king of the Picts, of whom I spoke in the preceding chapter, slew at Elstonenfurd in Lothian. The place
ought to be called Adelstanfurd [1], after the king of England
who there lost his life.

Thereafter—for here I pass by in silence some obscure
kings of England—reigned Saint Edward, son of Edgar. Edward.
He was treacherously murdered by his stepmother, the
queen of England, in order that her son Eldred might so Eldred.
come to the throne, and in the year of Christ nine hundred
and eighty, which was the twelfth year of his reign, he
was buried in Glastonbury with many of his predecessors.
After Eldred, king of England, Sweyn of Denmark bore rule Sweyn.
in England. This same Sweyn—his name signifies in English
'sow' and 'hog' [2]—had a peaceful reign of fifteen years in
England, and was buried at York. After Sweyn, Knoth, or Canute.
Canute, the Dane, reigns in England. Along with him Edmund Edmund.
Ironside [3], son to Eldred, bore rule in part of the kingdom.
This Edmund was treacherously made away with by Edrich de
Straton. This traitor invited the king to breakfast. He had

---

[1] The popular pronunciation in our own day is ' Elshenfuird ', not 'Athelstaneford ' or even ' Alshenford '. It appears that this was the case also at the beginning of the sixteenth century, and even earlier, for the spelling ' Elstanford ' is
found in the *Registrum de Dunfermelyn* (p. 204).

[2] This is a mistake. Swinburne (*i.e.* Svendbjörn) is not ' son of a pig ', but
' son of Svend', *i.e.* Swain=a young man.

[3] Orig. ' Irensidus '; ch. iv. of this Bk. ' Irnsyd '.

made a picture of a bow full bent, with an arrow, and as the
king, that he might view this thing the better, drew nearer, an
arrow was shot at the king by a man in hiding, and thus he
was killed.   Behold then, how in a thousand far-sought ways
kings and princes meet their end, from envy of their wealth
and power [1].

CHAP. II.—*Of the reign of Donald the Scot, and the expulsion of
the remnant of the Picts ; of the deeds of Constantine Eth, or Aetius, of
Gregory, Donald, Constantine, and Eugenius, kings of Scotland.*

ON the death of that Kenneth who had almost annihilated
the Picts, his brother Donald began to reign ; and in his days
the small remnant of Picts, with the aid of the English,
brought a force against him ; but he destroyed them all.   It
was not the custom at that time in Scotland for the youthful
sons of the kings to succeed to the throne, but rather for the
kings' brothers, if these were more powerful than their children,
and more fit to bear rule.   To Donald succeeded Constantine,
or Constans.   In his day the residue of the Picts, with the help
of the Danes, invaded Scotland yet again ; and against them
Constantine led with him to war some Picts who had remained
subject to the Scots.   By the treachery of these men
Constantine met with his end, in a place which is called 'the
battle of the black cave' [2].   After Constantine reigns Ethus,
son of the great Kenneth, and he was swifter of foot than
Asahel [3] or the Oilean Ajax.   In agility of body he was far the
first of all those who were contemporary with him.   Against
Ethus rose in rebellion Gregory, son of Dongal, giving forth
that he had a right to the kingdom, and in a pitched battle at
Strath [4], Ethus perished.   About these men I find among our
old chroniclers the following verses :

' Wing-footed Ethus, brother of Constans, had reigned,
    When he fell mortally wounded by the sword of Gregory, son of
    Dongal.'

Donald.

How paternal
uncles used to
succeed to the
throne in Scot-
land.

Constantine.

Ethus.

Gregory.

---

[1] Cf. the story in ch. iv. of this Book, where the countess of Angus kills
Kenneth the Second in much the same way.
[2] *i.e.* Inverdovat.   Cf. *Celtic Scotland*, vol. i. pp. 327-28.
[3] Orig. ' Asahele ' ; F. wrongly ' Ahasale '.
[4] Cf. *Celtic Scotland*, vol. iii. p. 123.

After the death then of Ethus, Gregory was solemnly Gregory.
crowned at Scone in the year of our Lord eight hundred and
seventy-five. He granted again to the Church, and in larger
measure, those privileges which before his day had been curtailed.
He appeased too the frequent strifes and enmities among the
chief men of his kingdom. He then invaded Ireland, which he The subjection
claimed for his own by right of succession, and in no long time of Ireland.
he subdued that island, and also, partly by his clemency
and wisdom, partly by force, the northern part of England[1].
And then he came to a peaceful end, and was buried in the
island of Iona. All that Kenneth had been able to accomplish
against the Picts by his sagacity and force of arms Gregory
was able to bring to pass by a happy chance. And though in
war I could not equal him with Kenneth, yet in humanity I give Comparison
him the pre-eminence, because, as indeed becomes a king, he Kenneth and
showed a noble clemency in his dealings with the poor and Gregory.
those who were unfit for arms. In his reign, according to
Helinand[2], flourished John the Scot[3], a man renowned for his John the Scot.
learning, of keen intelligence too, and most ready of speech,
who by desire of Charles the Bald turned the *Hierarchia* of
Dionysius the Areopagite from Greek into Latin[4]. He
afterwards went over to England, and in the monastery of
Malmesbury the boys whom he there instructed stabbed him,

---

[1] This is taken, according to Mr. Skene (*Celtic Scotland*, vol. i. p. 331), from
a copy of the Chronicle of St. Andrews which states that Gregory subdued
'Hiberniam totam et fere Angliam'. It has been copied by later chroniclers,
but Mr. Skene prefers the reading 'totam Berniciam et fere Angliam' (cf. *Chron.
Picts and Scots*, p. 288), and remarks that there is no trace of any conquest
of Ireland, and that 'Hibernia' seems to have been substituted for 'Bernicia'.

[2] Helinand—otherwise Elinand, Elimand—was a religious of the abbey of
Froimont of Citeaux towards the end of the twelfth century. He wrote a
Chronicle in forty-eight books, and a Supplement to the same ; also 'De laude
vitae claustralis'. Before he became a monk he had been a favourite at the
court of Philip Augustus. According to the 'Roman d'Alexandre', as quoted by
Moreri :—

> 'Quand le Rois ot mangié, s'appela Helinand,
> Pour li esbanoyer, commanda qu'il chant.'

[3] *See* note, p. 102.

[4] Printed at Cologne in 1502, with a Commentary of Hugh of St. Victor, and
again at the same place, with a Commentary of Dionysius the Carthusian, in
1536.

H

so it is related [1], and tortured him to death with their writing-
styles.   His tomb, at the left side of the high altar, bears this
inscription :—

> In this tomb lies the wise and holy John
> Who, living, was endowed with marvellous learning [2].

A like story is told of Saint Felix : that he was stabbed to
death, by cobblers' awls.

Donald.

After Gregory, Donald, grandson to Kenneth the Great, and
son to king Constantine, bears rule among the Scots.   He was
one who reckoned no labour too severe, if so he might safeguard
the lands that Gregory had won ; for 'not less of valour does
it take to guard than gain'.   Now it is Ireland [3] that he visits,
now the English territory lately made his own, and imposes
laws upon his subjects.   The Danes made earnest entreaty with
this Donald that he should join them in a war against the
English ; but to this he would no way consent, for he reckoned
it a shameful thing to be beholden to heathen men in the disturbance of faithful worshippers of Christ, even though these
had no rightful title to their lands.   And for this I commend
the man, and consider him worthy of praise only a little after
Gregory himself.

Alfred the Saxon.

In the tenth year of the reign of Donald dies Alfred, king
of the West Saxons, and is succeeded by his son Edward.

Constantine the Scot.

After Donald, Constantine, son of Ethus, begins to reign, in
the year of our Lord nine hundred and three.   This Constantine waged many wars against Edward the Englishman and his
bastard son Edelstan.   To Eugenius, the son of Donald, he
gave the domain of Cumbria.   This same Constantine thereafter invades England with a large army ; but, suffering defeat
in battle, he basely lost those lands of Cumbria [3] which the
Scots had held from the days of Gregory four-and-fifty years.
So he returned to Scotland, for four years more held the

---

[1] This is the story told by Matthew of Westminster, but it had its origin in a
confusion of John Scotus Erigena with John of Saxony, whom Alfred called
about 884 from France into England.   Cf. *Histoire Littéraire de la France,*
tom. v. p. 418.

[2]   Clauditur hoc tumulo Sanctus Sapiensque Joannes,
          Qui didatus erat jam vivens dogmate miro.

[3] Cf. the footnote in the supposed conquest of Ireland on the preceding page.

[4] Cf. the statement at the beginning of chapter iv. of this Book.

kingly sceptre, at length became a religious at St. Andrews, and in that condition for five years more stayed there till his death.

CHAP. III.—*Of the children of Knoth, king of England. Of the character of Edward, the miracles that he did, and his chastity ; likewise of the overthrow of Harold, king of England, by the Norman.*

WHILE Knoth, or Canute, reigned over the English, there were born to him two sons: Harold, to wit, and Hardicanute. Hardicanute was of great bodily activity, and therefore delighted to travel on foot rather than on horseback.   Harold Harold. as a king, followed rather his own arbitrary will than the dictates of reason.   His reign accordingly was without benefit to his people, and it lasted for two years only.   To him succeeded Hardicanute, his brother ; and at the very beginning of his reign he caused to be disinterred the body of his dead brother, Harold, and cast it into the Thames, the river which flows past London.   There certain fishermen found it by night, and buried it in the church of Saint Clement[1].   This Hardicanute did, because king Harold had banished his mother and his uncle, and he then recalled them from their exile.

After the death of Hardicanute the princes of England decreed that they would have none of Danish race to rule over them ; for they found themselves now fit to make head against the Danes, inasmuch as Hardicanute had left behind him no male issue, but a daughter only.   The chief men of England send then for Edward who was at that time in exile among the Edward. Normans ; and he, after he had assumed the kingly crown, persevered in that integrity and sincerity of life which had marked him as a boy.   This Edward was a man of the highest natural endowment, and had been piously and religiously brought up from his earliest youth,—a condition which tends not a little to holiness of life and renown in after years.   Whence we have that of Aristotle in the second book of his *Ethics* : 'It matters not a little, but rather much—nay rather, it matters every- The education thing—whether boys are brought up to one sort of habits, or of children.

---

[1] Hence called 'St. Clement Danes'.

another'[1]. And here he confirms his opinion, too, with the
authority of his teacher Plato, using the analogy of the new-
made earthen jar or pot, according to that saying of Horace :
' A long time will a jar retain the odour of that with which it
was filled when newly made'[2]. Those who in youth are ill
taught, who are allowed to grow up untrained, and are foolishly
humoured, turn out liars and enemies of religion. Not such
upbringing as this had that Edward, of whom we are now
speaking ; for he learned to reverence God, and to fear Him as
a son may fear his father. He had a special devotion for the
Evangelist John, and besought his intercession for himself with
God. When he was one day passing from Westminster to
London, a certain pilgrim besought him, by the love of God
and John the Evangelist, for an alms ; whereupon the king, all
unobserved, threw towards him a golden ring, notable for the

Miracle of the
present of the
golden ring.

precious stone that it bore. This ring then John the Evangelist afterwards gave back to certain English pilgrims, instruct-
ing them how they were to give it to the king, and to declare
to him the hour of his death, just as he then told the same to
them[3]. At the elevation of the body of Christ, in the sacrifice
of the altar, Edward saw once in a vision the king of the
Danes drowned in the sea, when this king had it in his mind
to come to England and bring disturbance upon Edward.

The vision of
the Dane.

Edward declared this vision of the drowning to those who stood
near, and even so it turned out. This Edward had to wife a
daughter of Godwin ; but he never sought to know her in way
of marriage ; and, like Chrysanthus and Daria[4], they observed
a holy virginity all their days.

Edward's
virginity.

Edward was buried in Westminster, in the year of the
world's redemption ten hundred and sixty-five. To him succeeded Harold, son of earl Godwin. This Harold, when he

---

[1] *Nic. Eth.* ii. 1.   [2] *Epp.* i. ii. 69.

[3] Camden tells this story in connection with Havering in Essex, which was
believed to have been called ' Have ring ' in consequence.—*Brit.* p. 385, ed.
1600.

[4] Chrysanthus was the son of a Roman senator in the reign of the emperor
Valerian. When he became a Christian his father forced him to take a wife,
and gave him Daria, the lady philosopher. But Chrysanthus treated her as a
sister, and they took counsel to be virgins till death.—From the Menology of
Basil, as quoted in Smith's *Dict. of Christian Biography*, s.v. CHRYSANTHUS. ·

was once making sail for Flanders, and was driven by contrary winds, fell into the hands of William, duke of the Normans, who took him bound by oath to take to wife the daughter of William, and to hold England for his, that is for William's, advantage; and on that condition Harold was allowed freely to return to England. The wrongful act of the Norman.

CHAP. IV.—*Of the Kings of Scotland and their deeds.*

LET us here leave for a little the affairs of England and take up in order the course of events in Scotland, whose narrative has suffered some interruption.   Malcolm, son of Donald, Malcolm. was king over the Scots in the year of our Lord nine hundred and forty-three.   To him Edmund, king of England, brother to Eldred, had given Cumbria[1]; and for that region he did homage and fealty to the Englishman.   For he judged it better to do this than to live in daily war.   This Malcolm came to his end through the treachery of the Scots of Moray. His successor was Indulphus, son to Constantine, who was Indulphus. slain by the Danes when they were ravaging the country. After him, in the year of our Lord nine hundred and sixty-one, Duffus, son of Malcolm, reigns over the Scots.   He was a man Duffus. given to peace, but in his day the northern parts were infested by robbers, and while he was in pursuit of them to seize them, he was murdered in his bed; his servants, forgetful of their duty, had deserted him.   To Duffus succeeded Culinus, son of Culinus. Indulphus.   A lustful man he was, and, following the example of Sardanapalus, was a dishonourer of virgins.   As he was ravishing once the beautiful daughter of a prince, that illustrious man, by name Richard, slew him; and there were few that grieved much at his death.   Hence let kings learn not to dishonour the daughters or the wives[2] (which is a greater sin) of their nobles, seeing that if these nobles are men of sense and spirit they will not be balked of their vengeance by the head of a king.   To Culinus succeeded Kenneth the Second.   He was treacherously Kenneth the Second.

---

[1] Cf. ch. ii. of this Book.
[2] Cf. the conversation between Macduff and Malcolm Canmore, ch. v. of this Book.

slain by a woman. This woman was countess of Angus. She
invited the king to a breakfast, whereat she showed a statue
which discharged arrows, and by one of these the king was
slain, just as was done in the story related in the first chapter
of this book [1].

Constantine the Bald.

Further, after Kenneth's death, in the year of our Lord nine
hundred and ninety-four, Constantine the Bald, with the help
of confederates, and in despite of a multitude of the nobles,
placed the crown upon his own head. This was the beginning
of a long strife amongst the Scots ; and so it came about that
the realm of Scotland was scarcely at any time brought nearer
to its ruin. One faction followed this Constantine ; Malcolm
and the bastard brother of his father, a mighty man of war,
had the favour of all the rest. It chanced that both leaders met
in battle one day in Lothian, near to the river Almond, six
miles distant from Edinburgh, and both were slain, but they say
that the victory remained with Kenneth. On the death of

Gryme, Malcolm.

Constantine, Gryme, who had followed his fortunes, claims the
sovereignty. Then began the contest with Malcolm, Kenneth's
son, for the kingdom. And when, to put an end to so long a
strife, a duel, as it were, was determined on, with few soldiers
on each side, and Malcolm came off the conqueror, he would
not assume the crown until the nobles should all agree that he
was to be king ; and this they did, as we read, in the year of
our Lord one thousand and four. Malcolm reigned for thirty
years. He had for his heir one only daughter, whom he gave

Cryninus.

in marriage to Cryninus, abthane of Dul [2],—that is, seneschal
of the king in the isles, him who was receiver of the royal
revenues. In the thirteenth year of the reign of this Malcolm,
Edmund Ironside, of whom we made mention a short time
since, was king of England. In the end this Malcolm was
murdered near to Glamis, by certain traitors belonging to the
party of Gryme.

---

[1] ' Sicut superius capite primo hujus libri diximus ' ; referring to the story of
Edmund Ironside and Edrich de Straton.

[2] The Irish Annals call him abbot, but though bearing this designation—
Cronan, ' abbot of Dunkeld '—' he was not an ecclesiastic, but in reality a great
secular chief, occupying a position in power and influence not inferior to that of
any of the native Mormaers '.—*Celtic Scotland*, vol. i. p. 390.

Malcolm was a man of such wasteful prodigality that he had left for himself no piece of land in the kingdom, but had bestowed upon his princes and courtiers the whole of the royal domains.   Herein he greatly erred, and dishonoured indeed, so far as in him lay, his state as king; for though niggard-liness, and most of all in a king, be a vice more foul than prodigality, yet in one no less than in the other, as is observed by Aristotle in the first chapter of the fourth book of his *Ethics*, lies a blot, and most rarely is prodigality found alone, and without avarice to attend it[1].   For when a man bestows upon certain persons more than is fitting, needs must he wring from others that to which he has no claim[2].   To such a pitch of poverty was Malcolm reduced that he was forced to lay his complaint before the chief men of the kingdom.   These, then, and the nobility, came to this agreement with the king: that after their own death the king should maintain their heirs at his own costs, and should receive the revenues of each until he had reached the age of twenty-one, an arrangement which every year brings much profit to the kings of the Scots.   For it may happen that the king draws yearly a thousand or more from one out of twenty nobles, according as his son is younger or older, and his inheritance more or less rich; and hitherto, and last of all, he has had also the marriage of the young man in his control, out of which he can fetch no little profit.   He can also make provision for his own proper household by marrying them to heiresses[3].

In all this king Malcolm acted most honourably.   For he was unwilling that the common people should be weighted

The application of the xe to the state treasury.

---

[1] Orig. : 'Nam licet illiberalitas prodigalitate foedius in rege praesertim sit vitium, ut Aristoteles quarti Ethicorum primo ait : tamen in utroque est labes, et rarissime prodigalitas simplex sine avaritia iuncta invenitur.'   F. : 'Nam licet illiberalitas, prodigalitate foedius, in rege praesertim, sit vitium, ut Aristoteles iv. Ethicorum primo ait, *Tamen in utroque est labes, et rarissime prodigalitas simplex, sine avaritia juncta, invenitur.*'

[2] This sentence is also part of the quotation from Aristotle, who says in effect : 'Most prodigals err more actively on the side of taking.   They take whence they ought not.   They must take in order to keep going, and they concern themselves as little where the money comes from as where it goes.'   Cf. Cicero *de Officiis*, i. 43 : 'Sunt autem multi qui eripiunt aliis quod aliis largiantur '.

[3] See further on this subject Book IV. ch. v.

with taxes, however empty his own purse might be; and therefore did he make this petition to the chief men and nobility of the kingdom, that they would be pleased to make some provision for himself, and for future kings of Scotland, without oppression of the common people. They showed wisdom in consenting to his request, for they held their lands by grant in perpetuity from the king; and they discovered an honourable means whereby, without risk to himself, the king might gather in a large sum of money. This law of the realm is not without its uses; for, when they have once completed their one-and-twentieth year, the young men enter upon the enjoyment of their own property, and, at the same time, for the reckless among them every opening is closed that might lead to the squandering of their substance in their youth [1].

Duncan.

Malcolm, then, being laid to rest with his fathers in the island of Iona, where the greatest part of his forebears had been buried, Duncan, his grandson by his daughter Beatrice, began to reign; and his reign was of six years. It was in the

The Danish kings.

second year of his reign that Knoth, the Danish king of the English, died, and was succeeded by his son Harold. The

The Norman kings.

same year Robert duke of Normandy went the way of all flesh, and in his room was chosen William, called the Bastard, a boy of seven years; he had the support of Henry king of the French, who was guardian to the boy. I make mention of this William and his times, because he had no small dealings

The murder of Duncan.

with the Britons, as shall afterwards be told. This Duncan [2] was secretly put to death by the faction which had been till then in opposition. He was mortally wounded by one Macha-beda [3] at Lochgowane, and was thence carried to Elgin, where he died. He was buried by the side of his fathers in Iona. Now those kings showed a grave want of foresight, in that they found no way of union and friendship with the opposing

---

[1] Cf. Bk. IV. ch. ix. on usury—'haec foenebris pestis'.

[2] Orig. and F. print 'Malcolmus', an evident misprint for 'Duncanus'. Orig.: ' Hic Malcolmus a factione opposita adhuc latenter peremptus est per quendam nomine Machabedam ; apud Lochgowanen etc.'. F. : ' Hic M., a factione opposita adhuc, latenter peremptus est, per quendam nomine Machabedam, apud etc.' I have not been able to make sense of either punctuation, and suspect that the original is corrupt.

[3] Macbeth.

faction: for either they should have banished them from the land of their fathers as disturbers of the common peace and welfare; or, if this opposite faction was carrying on its designs in secret, and was unknown to the king, he should not at least have taken measures against it without a large army at his back: for to gain a kingdom many a wicked act is done— *The kingdoms prepare for war.* following that saying always in the mouth of Cæsar: 'If the law must be violated, let it be violated at least for empire; in all else follow after piety.'   Give them but the chance—and those men are few indeed who will not risk their all for a crown—though their title to it may be far from clear.   This Machabeus, or Machabeda as some speak it, when Duncan[1] *Machabeda.* had been thus betrayed to his end, assumed the sceptre of sovereignty, usurper fashion, to himself, and would have pursued the sons of dead Duncan[1] to their destruction.   For Duncan[1] had two sons: to wit, Malcolm Canmore, that is, Malcolm of the big head, and Donald Bane.   These were borne to him by a sister of Siward earl of Northumberland.   For two years her two brothers stayed in their own country, hoping for victory; and when they could strive no more, Donald took his course to the Isles and Malcolm to Cumbria.

CHAP. V.—*Concerning Malcolm Canmore and Machabeda, kings of Scotland; likewise of the death of Saint Edward, king of England, the flight of Edgar with all his children and household into Scotland[2], and of the marriage of Saint Margaret, his daughter, and the children that she bore.*

This Malcolm Canmore, though he had a just right to the *Malcolm* kingdom of Scotland, remained in England during fourteen *Canmore.* years, till at length his friends alike and his rivals called him back to the paternal home: his rivals, indeed, to the end they might destroy him; and his friends that he might put to the test his chance of sovereignty.   In the first year of the

---

[1] Orig. and F. 'Malcolmus.'

[2] Orig. and F. 'in Scythiam'.   The belief in the Scythian origin (cf. the speech of Drusco, the Pictish king, in Bk. II. ch. xiv.) shows itself even in a misprint.

reign of Macbeth, Harold was succeeded by his brother
Hardicanute, the last king of the Danish line in England.
This Macbeth afflicted with divers punishments those who
favoured Malcolm Canmor: some he despoiled; some he cast
into loathsome dungeons; others again he not only stripped
of all that they had, but drove them exiles from the kingdom,
and there were not wanting some that he beheaded.   Among
the remnant was Macduff, thane of Fife, one of the chief men
of the kingdom.   Now Macbeth mistrusted this man sorely,
and insulted him with these words—saying that he would soon
bring him under the yoke, even as an ox in the plough.   But
Macduff feigned to take this as said in jest, as if he were innocent of what was meant, and so turned aside the rage of
the king; and, withdrawing himself in secret from the court,
took ship for England.   Macbeth thereupon seized upon all his
possessions for the royal treasury, and declared him at the
horn an enemy of the commonweal, banishing him too in perpetuity from the kingdom.   But this action displeased the
rest of the nobles greatly, inasmuch as the king on his own
authority only, without summons of the supreme council, had
proscribed a man of this quality.

Now when Macduff was come to the presence of Malcolm
Canmore, and was urging him to return to the land of his
fathers, promising him that the nobles and the common people
too would welcome his arrival,—he, desiring to put Macduff's
good faith to the test, declared that for three reasons he should
prove himself an unserviceable king: first of all, that he was
by nature voluptuous, and by consequence would deal wantonly
with the daughters and (what is a much greater wrong) the wives
of the nobility; secondly, that he was avaricious, and would
covet all men's goods.   To these two objections Macduff makes
answer: 'In the kingdom of Scotland, all northern and cold
though it be, you shall find a wife, the fairest you will, who
shall alone suffice for your needs.   There is no prince, whether
in England or Scotland, who will not readily give you his
daughter in marriage.   And for avarice, you shall use as your
own the whole possessions of the realm; and there is naught
that the people will deny you if you but ask it in the way of
love and with no desire for strife.'   To all this Malcolm then

made yet a third objection, saying: 'I am a liar, a man of deceit, unstable in all my ways.' And then to him Macduff is said to have made this answer: 'Dregs of the race of man, begone; begone, thou monster among men—fit neither to reign nor live.'[1] Now Malcolm, when he had thus proved the honesty and good faith of Macduff, declared to him the true reason wherefore he had made these objections, and bade him be of good courage,—promising him that if, as he trusted, God should restore the sceptre to his hands, he would make double restitution whereof Macduff had been despoiled. Yet he was unwilling to take his departure from England, where already he had been an exile fifteen years, till he had come to speech of Edward, king of the English, and had received the king's gracious consent that he should depart. And Edward received him with all kindness—for all men were sure of the kindest reception from him—and granted him support both of money and men.

Meanwhile arise mutterings of revolt in Scotland against Macbeth, and on the first arrival of Malcolm and Macduff the princes and people welcomed them gladly, and met their king with tokens of joy; which when Macbeth the usurper came to know, he fled to the northern parts of Scotland. Thither *Flight of* Malcolm pursued him, making no delay, and after a short *Macbeth.* struggle, Macbeth, who was much inferior in his forces, was at Lumphanan slain. Meanwhile, however, when news of his *His death.* death was brought to the followers of Macbeth, they carry to Scone one Lulach[2], his cousin, nicknamed the simpleton, and *Lulach the* there crown him, judging that some part of the nobles and *silly.* the common people would be with them; but when they found he had no following, they fled. When Malcolm came to know what had happened he sends men in search of Lulach, whom they find and put to death at Strathbogie, and the few who *His end.* had still clung to him hid themselves as best they could. On the final overthrow of this evil faction, Malcolm was brought to Scone, and there, in the year of our Lord one thousand and fifty-seven, was solemnly crowned.

---

[1] Shakespeare has embodied this conversation in *Macbeth,* though it was through Hector Boece (Holinshed's translation) that he had it.

[2] Orig. and F. 'Lutach'; but see Mr. Skene's *Celtic Scotland,* vol. i. p. 411.

We are told that now, when the king was once firmly seated on his throne and the country was in full possession of the blessings that flow from a settled peace, Macduff sought of the king three favours in consideration of the good service he had rendered. First of all, that his successors in the thaneship of Fife should place the king at his coronation on the throne; secondly, that when the royal standard was unfurled against the enemy, it should fall to the thane of Fife to lead the vanguard[1], that is, the first line of battle; and thirdly, that all his descendants should have remission where one of them was accidentally the homicide of a noble, on paying a fine of four-and-twenty marks, and in the case of the slaying of a serf for a fine of twelve marks. Homicides were accustomed to claim absolution, by this privilege of law granted to Macduff, on payment of such a sum of money for Kinboc[2]. Now Macduff erred in making such demands as these. The first demand and the second were too well-fitted to secure for him the anger[3] of the other nobles; and the third, when we take into consideration the proneness of the people to homicide, was most unjust; for thus, under cover of an unintended injury, a long-standing feud might find satisfaction and a far too easy shelter. But however this may be, a partial if not a complete excuse may be urged in behalf of the king: the desert of Macduff was great, and the king neither dared, nor indeed desired, to refuse him in anything.

Some time after this the king comes to hear of a certain knight[4], commonly called a 'miles'[5], who had conspired against him along with some men of Belial. Of set purpose then he took this soldier as his body-servant, when he went a-hunting, and while they were once in pursuit of the wild beasts, he contrived to get this man far separated from the rest. Then,

The demands of Macduff.

The argument against them.

A daring and wrongful deed of king Malcolm.

---

[1] Cf. Bk. v. ch. iii. *de acierum instructione.*

[2] 'Kinboc': probably a misprint for 'Kinbote'. Cf. Sir John Skene, *de Verb Signif.* s.v. 'BOTE'=fine for slaughter of a kinsman. Mr. Skene gives an account of these privileges in *Celtic Scotland*, vol. iii. pp. 304, 305. Cf. also Sir John Skene *u.s.*, s.v. CLAN MACDUFF.

[3] Orig. and F. 'Indignationem aliorum principum duo prima facile poterant ei parere'; I have read 'parare'.

[4] eques auratus.   [5] quem vulgo militem vocant.

leaping from his horse, the king commanded the soldier to fight him like a man in single combat, where they were seen of none, and to cease from treachery and underhand attempts upon his life. Whereupon the soldier threw himself at the feet of the king, and, humbly imploring pardon for himself, made a full discovery of his accomplices in crime. The king granted him pardon. So far from approving this action of the king, I condemn and abhor it utterly. It is plain that this soldier showed himself of a timorous nature in declining the single combat; and had he been a bold man, of warm temper, he would not have declined it when it was offered to him, lest he should thus incur the accusation of cowardice. But the issue of such a contest is doubtful. The soldier had little to risk but his life and what small property he might possess. The fall of the king on the other hand would have been fraught with disaster to the state. Further, the king erred herein most of all : for, suppose the soldier had been truly guilty of the king's death, yet the king himself, alike before the beginning of the combat and after its issue, would still have stood guilt-less, had it chanced that he were slain by the soldier; but, as things turned out, he exposed himself, an innocent man, to the risk of death, and, so far as in him lay, afforded to this soldier the opportunity of becoming a homicide. Besides—and this consideration is the weightiest of all—he thus placed the kingdom in great jeopardy of a long-lasting strife, in the course of which, for the most part, much innocent as well as guilty blood is shed. And, to make an end, consider this too : that the king is a public person, and without the consent, express or implicit, of his people, has no right to expose him-self to the chances of war—a consent, I say, that shall be con-sonant with reason.

It was at this time, in the year one thousand and sixty-six, according to our chroniclers, that Edward, king of England, died. The English histories, and for this period they are more trustworthy, place the date one year earlier. This was that Saint Edward the Confessor, of whom I have made mention above. And Edgar Atheling, king of the English, having at heart the misfortunes of his country, took ship with his mother, his sister, and his whole household, desiring to return to the land

Death of Edward.

Edgar.

of his birth. Tossed by contrary winds, he was driven on the
Scottish shores, at a place which, for that reason, is called by
the inhabitants St. Margaret's Bay. But king Malcolm, learning they were English people, went down to the ships ; for he
spoke the English tongue like his own, which at that time was
a rare thing for a Scot. This was no wonder, for he had passed
fourteen years and more of his boyhood as an exile in England,
at which time he had conceived a great fondness for the foreign
tongue. After long converse with her, and the performance
of many kind offices, the daughter of the king of England,
Margaret by name, by reason of her gifts at once of mind and
her outward charm, won such favour with Malcolm that he
took her to wife. She bore to him six sons : to wit, Edward,
Edmund, Etheldred, Edgar, Alexander, and David ; and two
daughters : Matilda, afterwards queen of England, and Mary,
afterwards count, or countess, of Boulogne. In the days of this

Marianus. king lived Marianus Scotus[1], noted as a historian and writer on
chronology, and as a theologian of weight. He wrote a history
of the world from the creation to his own times, one book on
chronology, and one on the harmony of the Evangelists. He
became a monk at Saint Martin's of Cologne, was afterwards
translated to Fulda, and there abode for twelve years. Thereafter, by the order of the abbot of Fulda and the bishop of
Mayence, he lived at Mayence ; then for seventeen years at
Saint Martin's, and there he died, not without renown for his
holy life, in the year of our Lord one thousand and eighty-six,
and of his age the fifty-eighth. Further, in the time of this
king Malcolm, William the Bastard took possession of England.
Leaving Malcolm, then, for a little, let our narrative turn to
this William.

---

[1] Marianus Scotus, an Irish Scot, was born in 1086. Dr. Lanigan (*Eccl.
Hist. of Ireland*, vol. iv. p. 7) says of his Chronicle, which was printed at Basel
in 1559, that ' it exceeds anything of the kind which the middle ages have produced, and would appear still more respectable, were it published entire '.
There are said to be several unpublished works by him in the library of
Ratisbon, and MS. notes on all the epistles of St. Paul in the imperial library
at Vienna.

CHAP. VI.—*Of the deeds of the English; first of the iuvasion of England by William of Normandy the Bastard, and his slaying of king Harold. Of the independence of the Scots; of William's issue and his death.*

In the year of our Lord one thousand and sixty-six William, duke of Normandy invaded England; and Harold king of England goes to oppose him, with but a small following of soldiers, for indeed he was unpopular with the English. I follow here the English chroniclers. William makes of Harold a threefold demand: that he shall have Harold's daughter in marriage; or that he shall hold England of Harold; or that he shall try the fortune of war. Harold made choice of the third, and in that war he fell. Thereafter at the closely following feast of the birth of Christ, William was created at London king of the English. He went in a short while to Normandy, and in the second year of his reign returned with his wife Maud to England, and at the feast of Whitsuntide crowned her as queen. Next he marched against the Scots. But Malcolm the Scot and William made a treaty, as Caxton asserts[1], on these terms: that Malcolm should hold Scotland of the king of England, and William received homage of him therefor. That this statement is untrue is plain from all the British writers who used the Latin tongue. Homage was rendered indeed for the county of Cumberland, which is situated in England, and which the kings of the Scots held of England, and granted always to their eldest sons, who did homage for that county to the kings of the English. Although Malcolm had made this treaty with William, he all the same often laid waste Northumberland beyond the river Tees. Kings observe a treaty of peace only when they will. After a great slaughter at Gateshead, Malcolm got possession of all those parts, but not of the strong places, nor of the munitions of war. William, king of England, had a brother who was bishop of Bayeux. Him he had made earl of Kent, and he now sent him against the Scots with a

William the Norman. Harold.

Malcolm's treaty with William.

---

[1] In his Chronicles, folio lxxvi. ed. 1528—'that the Kyng of Scotlonde became his man, and helde all his londe of hym'.

great force of Englishmen and Normans. These Malcolm put
to the rout, and pursued them even to the river Humber.
Thereafter duke William sent his son Robert against the Scots,
to make war on them. But he never attacked them; nor
indeed did he do aught but build a new castle on the Tyne,
the better to resist an invasion. Now it is a thing unheard of,
and among the Scots simply inconceivable, that a Scot at peace
in his own kingdom ever recognised as his temporal superior
either the English king or any one else. This may be gathered
from the whole past history of the country, for the Scots at all
times resisted the inroads in the island of Romans and Britons,
and more than once invaded them—witness their historian and
fellow-countryman Bede. Now king Malcolm after his accession to the crown at no time had suffered from civil wars in his
kingdom, but was held in great veneration by nobles and
common people. And the case, which I will now propose,
would be altogether parallel: that is, if the French king were to
say that the king or kingdom of the Spains was subject to him,
simply because the earldom of Flanders, which had its origin
in the house of France, was so subject. I grant indeed that
king Malcolm was subject to the English king in respect of
Cumberland; whether this carries with it or does not carry
with it the consequence that therefore Malcolm was uncondi-
tionally subject to the Englishman matters not. Yet the
kingdom of Scotland was never subject to England, nor the
Scot to the Englishman, in respect of the kingdom of Scotland,
just as Charles, count of Flanders, is not subject to the Frenchman in respect of the kingdom of Spain.

This William had by his wife Maud these children: Robert
Curtoys [2], William Rufus [3], Henry Beauclerk, and some fair
daughters. And when he was nearing his end, he devised
Normandy to Robert Curtoys, England to William, and to
Henry gold and much furniture. After a reign in England of
twenty years he met the common fate of all men, and was
buried at Caen in Normandy. I remember to have read in the
chronicles of the Scots that this William made a reckoning of
the parish churches in England, and found the tale of them

The Scots were at no time tax-payers or bene-ficiaries [1] in respect of any one.

William's issue.

His death and place of burial.

---

[1] The 'beneficium' bound the vassal to his superior.
[2] *i.e.* Curthose.   [3] Orig. and F., 'Rous'.

seventeen beyond the five-and-forty thousand [1]. In England, as The parishes of England. we have said above, every village has its parish church, though the village may count perhaps but twenty hearths [2]. In Scotland this is not so; and in this point, as in many others, I reckon the ecclesiastical polity of the English to be preferable to the ecclesiastical polity of the Scots [3].

CHAP. VII.—*Of the reign in England of William Rufus, how he was an overbearing and irreligious man, and met with a condign end.*

On the death of his father, William Rufus or Rous took up William Rufus. the reins of government in England, but handled them without discretion, and not as befitted a king. He made light of holy places and religion [4]; he banished from England the Blessed Anselm, archbishop of Canterbury, a man of most upright character, for no other cause than that he had rebuked the conduct of the king; and Anselm then went to Rome, where in great part he wrote his books, which in my opinion are no way to be despised. Into such an insanity of wickedness did this king fall, that he laid waste many religious houses with their possessions, and on their ruin planted a fair and large forest, wherein he collected an immense multitude of wild animals of every kind. He built from its foundations the great hall in Westminster, in which the highest court of justice is held. Shortly thereafter he went a-hunting in the foresaid forest, and as he was walking there, a certain courtier with a bow shot an arrow at a small bird; but the arrow, glancing from the knotty branch of a tree, struck and killed the king. Whence let kings in days to come learn that they may not scatheless defile for their own will and pleasure the holy places

---

[1] Spelman (*Glossary* ed. 1687, p. 218) states the parish churches at 45,011 at the date of Domesday Survey, but Sir Henry Ellis (*General Introd. to Domesday*, vol. i. p. 286) says that the whole number actually noticed in the survey amounted to a few more than 1700. It would appear that Major and Spelman must have had access to some common authority, and Spelman in fact refers to Sprott's Chronicle (*circa* 1274) :—' Repertum fuit primo de summa ecclesiarum xlv. m^l. xi., summa villarum lxiii., m^l. iii^{xx}., summa feodorum militum lx. m^l. iic. xv., de quibus religiosi xxviii. m^l. xv.'

[2] Cf. Bk. i. ch. v.   [3] Cf. Bk. i. ch. vi.

[4] Orig. and F. ' religiones ' ; ? ' religiosos '.

of religion, inasmuch as whereby a man sins thence too shall
come the penalty of sin.   Of the holy place he made a profane
pleasance ; but a great and public sin must needs be followed
by a condign punishment [1].

CHAP. VIII.—*Of the rest of the acts of Malcolm,. king of the
Scots, and how the holy life of his wife brought him too to the practice
of piety.*

IN the one-and-thirtieth year of the reign of Malcolm
Canmore died William the bastard.   Margaret, the wife of
Malcolm, being herself a most devout woman, made of this
sagacious and high-spirited king a man wholly religious ; this
saintly woman made of him a saintly man.   And it is no
wonder : for, as the royal psalmist sings, ' With the holy thou
wilt be holy '.   This woman was wont to be present daily at
five masses celebrated in succession, and the king at two or
three.   They fed daily three hundred of the needy, and with
their own hands gave them to eat and drink.   On each day in
Advent and in Lent the king was accustomed to wash the feet
of six poor persons, and the queen did the same by a far larger
number.   He built the church of Durham, which the Britons
call Dura ; he was at the time in possession of that part of the
country.   The foundations of the building were laid by Turgot,
the admirable bishop of the see, by the convent, the prior, and
the king [2].   He richly endowed too the church of Dunfermline.
But while Malcolm was besieging the fortalice of Alnwick, a
certain soldier brought to him the keys of the castle on the
point of a spear, and so put the king off his guard, and

---

[1] Major thus attributes the formation of the New Forest to William Rufus,
not to William the Conqueror, and he is here in agreement with Caxton, who
adds, as to the manner of Rufus's death, that ' it was no meruayle, for the daye
that he dyed he had let to ferme the archebysshopryche of Canterbury '.—
Chronicles, fol. lxxvi. ed. 1528.

[2] Turgot was prior (not bishop) from 1087.   The bishop was William of St.
Carilef, who held the see from 1080 to 1099, but was for three years of that time
in exile.   It is supposed that it was during his banishment in Normandy that he
conceived the design of rebuilding Durham Cathedral.   That Malcolm was
present at the ceremony of the foundation seems very probable.   Cf. Simeon
of Durham, in Twysden's *Scriptores Decem*, col. 218.

slew him. Hence let those to come take warning, and never give audience to an enemy but in presence of many soldiers [1].

From what has just been said it is clear that though Malcolm held certain places in Northumberland up to four-and-twenty leagues, the English were nevertheless in possession of various fortified places that lay between the parts held by Malcolm and Scotland. This is clear from the case of the new castle, which is distant two-and-twenty leagues from Alnvicus or Alnwick, and ten from Berwick.

CHAP. IX.—*Concerning Donald, Duncan, and Edgar, kings of the Scots, their children, and their deeds.*

WHEN Malcolm Canmore had thus been taken off his guard and slain, Donald Bane, trusting to the support of the king of Norway, invaded the kingdom of the Scots. But Duncan, a bastard son of Malcolm, rose in rebellion against Donald his paternal uncle, and putting his uncle to the rout, placed the crown upon his own head. Here we see plainly how no nearness of kinship stands in the way of one who will grasp at a kingdom. Malcolm Canmore had left behind him sons of an excellent disposition; and yet here is their father's brother, an aged dotard—and a bastard, and such an one rarely comes to good—disturbing their rightful inheritance. This scoundrel of a bastard reigned for a year and a half. He met his end by the craft of his uncle Donald [2] and the earl of Mearns, by name Malpet, and on his death Donald reigns once more.

Now when Edgar the Englishman, an exile from his native land, the brother of Saint Margaret, saw how matters stood, he sent his nephews, the rightful heirs to the Scottish throne, into England; and there some of them died. We have no certain knowledge of the manner of their death; but three of them survived. The eldest of these was Edgar; and under the guidance of his uncle Edgar, he rose against Donald Bane, and

Donald Bane.

Duncan.

Edgar.

---

[1] Cf. Bk. II. ch. iii., on the murder of Constantius.

[2] 'Patrui sui Donaldi . . . dolo interiit'. There is no nominative, and grammatically the reference is to Donald Bane, but the context shows plainly that Duncan is intended.

wrested from him, his father's brother, the sovereignty.   Inasmuch as Saint Cuthbert had appeared to him at the beginning
of the war and promised him that he should be victorious, he
bestowed upon the church of Durham the lands of Coldinghame

Matilda.
at Berwick[1].   This Edgar gave Matilda[2], whom our writers

Maud.
call Maud, to Henry king of the English in marriage, and
Mary his younger sister to Eustace, count of Boulogne.   Edgar,
when he had reigned in peace for the space of nine years, was
buried in Dunfermline close by his father under the high altar.

CHAP. X.—*Of Alexander the Fierce, king of the Scots.*

ON the death of Edgar, in the year of our Lord eleven

Alexander the
Fierce.
hundred and seven, Alexander, surnamed 'the Fierce', took
up the reins of government.   He was thus called because his
paternal uncle, the earl of Gowry, bestowed upon him at his
baptism the lands of Liff and Invergowry[3].   Certain of his train
belonging to Mearns and Murvia, or Moray, made an attempt
upon his life by night, using stratagem therefor; but his chamber
servant let him out by a privy.   And since, by God's help, he
had made good his escape, he founded at Scone a rich monastery
of canons-regular[4], endowing the same with the domain of Liff
and Invergowry, and without delay pursued his enemies in their
flight to the northern parts.   When he came to that very
rapid river, the Spey, he found that the robber enemy were on
its opposite bank.   The king was counselled not to attempt
the ford.   But, as soon as he set eyes upon the enemy, he
could not contain his rage, gave the standard into the hands of

---

[1] Coldingham was for a long time a cell to the great monastery of Durham.
Cf. the Rev. J. L. Low's *Durham*, in 'Diocesan Histories', p. 27.

[2] The eldest daughter of Malcolm and Margaret was christened 'Editha', but
she changed her name to Matilda in compliment to her husband's mother.   Cf.
Mr. E. W. Robertson's *Scotland under her early Kings*, vol. i. p. 152.

[3] Buchanan says Alexander was called 'the Fierce' from the character of his
exploits.   It is Bower, the interpolator of Fordun, who gives the singular reason
reproduced by Major, of which I find no explanation attempted anywhere.

[4] Alexander the First re-formed the old Culdee foundation of Scone in 1114 or
1115, and established in it a colony of canons-regular of the order of St. Augustine,
whom he brought from the church of St. Oswald, at Nastlay near Pontefract.

his body-servant, and successfully makes the passage of the
ford, he and his man alone out of the whole army. Now, for Alexander's
rashness.
acting thus I hold the king to blame; for it was the part of a
foolhardy man, not of a brave man, thus to expose himself to
such a contest with the enemy. Not so long before had the
commonweal been shattered by the loss of a lawful monarch;
and it behoved the king to bear that in remembrance. Nor
can I praise the soldiery, that they did not by force prevent
the king, but gave up into the hands of a serving-man,
Alexander Caron, that standard which should ever be borne
before the king by a sufficient body-guard. This serving-man,
because he was skilled in single combat, and in a certain duel
had struck off, by one deft stroke, the hand of an Englishman,
was called Skyrmengeoure, that is, the 'gladiator' or 'con-
tender' and that to this day is the name of the constable of
Dundee [1], who is descended from him. Having routed the
enemy, the king returned to the southern parts of the kingdom,
endowed the church of St. Andrew of Kilrimont, bestowed
upon the blessed Andrew the 'cursus apri' [2], added to the
riches of Dunfermline, founded Scone, and built a monastery
for canons-regular in the island of Emonia, near to Inver-
keithing, which is now called St. Columba's isle [3]. Seventeen
years he reigned, and had an honourable burial at Dunfermline
by the side of his father, of whose fortitude of mind and zeal
for justice he was a true and worthy imitator.

CHAP. XI.—*Of David, that most excellent king of the Scots, in
whom are found wonderful examples of all the virtues; likewise of
Henry, his son, and of his grandchildren, the issue of this Henry; and
of Richard of Saint Victor.*

ON the death of Edgar and Alexander without issue, David, David, a king
of renown.
their brother, succeeded to the throne, in the year one thousand

---

[1] William Wallace in 1298 granted a charter of land in Dundee and of the
constabulary of the castle to Alexander 'dictus Skirmischur' for his services as
standard-bearer.

[2] That is, in its modern name, 'Boarhills'. It was the district in the neighbourhood of St. Andrews which, in the Legend of St. Andrew, was given to
the church by Hungus, king of the Picts.

[3] Now 'Inchcolm'.

one hundred and twenty-four. He was a more excellent man
than his two brothers, and reigned for twenty-nine years and
two months. The proud he tamed, beating them down as
with a hammer, but to all that submitted duly to his authority
he showed himself merciful and gracious; giving fulfilment of
that of Virgil, where he says 'parcere subjectis et debellare
superbos'[1]. And here I will make my frank confession that it
transcends my feeble powers accurately to take the measure of
this man; yet within my narrow limits I will try, hurriedly it
must be, to set down this and that concerning him.

Stephen the
Englishman.

With Stephen, king of the English, he fought two great
battles[2], one of them at Alertoun, in which he was victorious. He
laid waste all Northumberland and Cumberland, and regained
possession of these regions as a ransom for prisoners that he had
taken. In the same year he again invaded England, and
another bloody battle was fought between him and the English,
that of the Standard, in which the Scots were beaten; and at

A treaty of
peace.

length a treaty of peace was made between Stephen the
Englishman and David the Scot upon these terms: that
Northumberland should remain in the hands of Stephen and
Cumberland in those of David. But this peace lasted no long
time, for David got ready a fresh army wherewith to invade
England; whereupon Turstan, archbishop of York, went to
meet David at Marchmont castle, that is, at Roxburgh, and got
David to assent to a truce for a time. But when the time
of truce was out, he ravaged Northumberland to the utmost,
so that king Stephen was unwilling to grant that region,
according to his promise, to Henry, son of this same king
David, whom Matilda had borne to him. King Stephen therefore came to Roxburgh with a large army in the year eleven
hu ndred and thirty-eight; but, seized with a panic terror, he
ret urned to his own country without doing any hurt to the
  cots. In the following year king Stephen came to Durham,

---

[1] Virg. *Aen.* vi. 854.

[2] The battle of the Standard was fought August 22, 1138, on Cowton (or
Cutton) Moor, two miles from Northallerton. George Buchanan, like Major,
ollows Fordun and Boece in assigning a victory to David at Northallerton, but
th e battles of Allerton and of the Standard were one and the same. Cf. Mr.
Hume Brown's *George Buchanan*, p. 130.

and tarried there fifteen days, the while David tarried in Newcastle, and there they treated again about a peace.   It was then
that Matilda, queen of England, who was niece to king David
by his sister Mary, came to that king, and entreated her uncle
to consent to a peace.   And peace was made on this wise: that Peace estab-
Henry, son of David, should do homage to the English king lished.
for the earldom of Huntingdon, and should have free possession of the earldom of Northumberland.   For the mother of
this Henry was daughter to Matilda, and heir to Valdeof, earl Matilda.
of Huntingdon, who was son and heir to Siward, earl of
Northumberland.   David then returned and went to Carlisle,
where he built a very strong castle, and raised to a great height
the walls of the town.   Thither did his niece, the empress
Matilda, send to him her son, the future king of England, and
there at the hands of king David did he receive his knighthood.

In this year Alberic the legate, bishop of Ostia, went to Alberic the
visit king David while he dwelt at Carlisle.   For the rest, legate.
Henry, the only son of David, married Ada, daughter of the Ada.
earl of Warren, and by her he had three sons: to wit, Malcolm,
the future king of Scotland; David, afterwards earl of Hun- Henry and
tingdon and Gariach, and William, who also afterwards became his issue.
king of Scotland.   Three daughters too were born to him:
Margaret, whom he gave in marriage to the duke of Brittany,
and Ada, to the count of Holland.   The name of the third
was Matilda.   She died in tender age.   Further, in the year of
our Lord eleven hundred and fifty two, Henry, the only son of
David, heir to his crown and likewise of his holy life, died at Death of
Kelso, and there was buried.   David, his father, had founded Henry.
this monastery, and most richly endowed the same.   In various
places did David found monasteries, of which some are very David's lavish-
wealthy, such as Kelso, Jedburgh, Melrose, Newbattle, Holin- ness to monas-
culstramen[1], Dundrennan, Holyrood at Edinburgh, Cambus- teries.
kenneth, Kinloss, one for nuns at Berwick, for nuns at Carlisle
one; one of Praemonstratensian canons at Newcastle.   There
too he founded a monastery of Benedictines.

The first James, when he visited the tomb of David, is James the First
reported to have spoken thus: 'There abide, king most pious, his taunt.

---

[1] Holmcultram, in the county of Cumberland.

but likewise to Scotland's state and kings most unprofitable';
meaning thereby that on the establishment of some very
wealthy communities he had lavished more than was right of
the royal revenues. And I myself am of the same opinion;
for he made grants to those communities of more than six-
score thousand francs from lands held in perpetuity by the
crown; and upon the building of these religious houses he
must have expended a much larger sum[1].

That these
religious houses
should have
been more
sparingly
endowed.

Hereupon I may be allowed to make some observations. If
he had taken count of those religious houses which had been
founded by his predecessors, and likewise had considered that
the Scots were wont to pay exceeding little in the way of taxes
to their king, and further had foreseen the kind of life which
the religious would come to lead, never would he have enfeebled
the royal revenues for the aggrandisement of religious houses
and their enrichment beyond what was wise. That wealth was
indeed the offspring of a truly pious sentiment, but the wanton
daughter ended by suffocating her mother. But all this
notwithstanding, the king acted herein not wrongly, but, much

What suffices
to constitute a
morally good
action.

rather, piously. For the constitution of an action that shall
be morally good it is not necessary that it flow from a true
understanding; it suffices that it be prompted by invincible
ignorance, or by an error for which the agent is not responsible[2].
Those men were eye-witnesses of piety in its primitive fervour,
and inasmuch as the abbots of those days made a religious use
of their wealth, so did princes imagine that it would be for

He censures
travelling friars.

ever. But now for many years we have seen shepherds whose
only care it is to find pasture for themselves, men neglectful of
the duties of religion, and all because, in the foundation of
those institutions, no heed was taken for their prudent regula-
tion. Behold then here what may happen to religion from the
possession of great wealth! By open flattery do the worthless

---

[1] In this matter Buchanan quotes Major with approval, and more kindly than
in his autobiography. Cf. Mr. Hume Brown's *George Buchanan*, p. 311.

[2] In the 14th question of the 24th distinction of the *In Quartum*, Major gives
a curious example of 'invincible ignorance' in the case of a pope to whom a
'divisus ab orbe Britannus' may have brought commendatory letters from a king,
or, it may be, from other honourable men, extolling the bearer as a man of the
highest worth. If such commendations are not justified, the pope may be
credited with invincible ignorance, since 'papa non est supra jus naturae'.

sons of our nobility get the governance of convents *in com-mendam*[1]—the wealth of these foundations is set before them like a mark before a poor bowman—and they covet these ample revenues, not for the good help that they thence might render to their brethren, but solely for the high position that these places offer, that they may have the direction of them and out of them may have the chance to fill their own pockets. Like bats, by chink or cranny, when the daylight dies, they will enter the holy places to suck the oil from out the lamps[2], and under a wicked head all the members lead an evil life, according to the proverb, ' When the head is sick, the other members are in pain'. An abbot once grown wealthy has to find sustenance for a disorderly court of followers—an evil example to the religious; and not seldom, bidding farewell to the cloister, makes for the court, heedless of that wise saw, ' As a fish out of water cannot live, so neither one of the religious outside the cloister '[3]; and if his body do indeed chance to be in the cloister, yet in the spirit of his mind and the manner of his life he is as one without.   He may have brought ruin on

---

[1] Compare what Major says *In Quartum*, 14th question of the 24th distinction, of the prelate who holds a benefice *in commendam*—that he is rather a bailiff (*procurator*) than a prelate of that church.   In the 13th question he says that when Paul the Second was asked by some one to present him to two bishoprics, on the ground that he was the son of a king, Paul answered that he would not grant him that dispensation were he the son of God.   Major's comment is : ' I say this answer was worthy of God's vicar.'   In the 23d question of the 24th distinction Major tells the same story, but tells it of Pope Benedict the Twelfth, ' a man whom neither the menaces of kings nor the soft words of princes and kins-folk could turn from the narrow path of rectitude. . . . And when his kinsfolk endeavoured to persuade him that it was his duty to provide for those of his own blood, with this most admirable jest, and it was worthy of so great a pontiff, he made answer, saying that the Roman pontiff had no kinsfolk.   O man, I say, worthy of the High-priesthood !   Thou honour of the Cistercians !   Thou rival of St. Bernard, in the path of virtue.   For on the one part of the centre of virtue Bernard dug new cisterns, by means of which, and on methods yet untried, he might attain to the centre of virtue ; but Benedict, sustained by virtue in angelic fashions, does here, as it were, point with his finger to the centre of virtue.'

[2] A similar comparison is made in the 12th question of the 24th distinction in the *In Quartum*—with some violence to natural history : ' Those men, I say, are as owls ; for by night they make their way into the temple to suck the oil ; and when that is gone the lamps give light no more.'

[3] Cf. Chaucer : *Prologue to Canterbury Tales*, ll. 179, 180 :—
    ' Ne that a monk, whan he is cloysterles,
    Is likned to a fissche that is watirles.'

the farmer-tenants of the convent by raising their rents for the benefit of his own purse, and yet think—but therein he greatly errs—that he has acted rightly. The duty and the aim of the religious should be this: to live in the cloister without the society of secular persons; let them not return to that Egypt on which they have turned their backs, nor remember any more the good things of fortune. Let them reckon an abbot who becomes his own land-steward to have taken upon himself a function far removed indeed from the practice of true religion, just as, among the apostles, the office of Judas as keeper of the purse was found to be more full of peril than another. Duties such as these are to be undertaken by men of the most approved integrity only. It behoves them to be frugal and sparing in food and drink, that so they may withstand the assaults of the body. For that is the true end of religion, and that end is promoted rather by the possession of this world's goods in moderation than by their abounding; the wealth of an abbot, therefore, should not permit him to keep more than one or two servants[1].

David was remarkable for the virtues of temperance, fortitude, justice, clemency, and regard for religion. He ate in moderation, was very sparing in drink—all that savoured of luxury was hateful to him. For, when his queen died in

The meaning of 'religious'.

David's upright life.

---

[1] Major's commentary on the Fourth Book of the Sentences furnishes many illustrations of his views as to the manner of life of bishops and abbots. Thus, in the 18th question of the 24th distinction, he says that he considers twelve or fourteen servants to be a sufficient allowance for a bishop, and if the number were fewer it would be better. He points out that in the actual expenditure of money we have not a proper measure of a bishop's extravagance or moderation, since the capon which costs two pennies Scots, 'hoc est parvo albo', in the diocese of Ross will cost six times as much at Paris or Edinburgh. In the 20th question of the 24th distinction he severely censures the beneficed cleric who cares more for his own flesh and blood than for the orphan children of Christ and for his poor, who can hardly get kitchen to their bran loaf, while he himself lives like a swine of Epicurus. In the 22d question of the same distinction he blames the unlettered vulgar, and most of all the inhabitants of both kingdoms of the Britains, who in this matter are the greatest sinners, for their laudation of any prelate who fares sumptuously and splendidly, and feeds his household not only on barn-door fowls but on partridges and pheasants. If such a prelate, he says, has spent the revenues of the church upon his kinsmen and his household, the common people will extol him, saying that he has nobly raised his house above the poverty of its original foundation, and deserved well of his household, while every wise man knows that out of what was dedicated to the service of God he has erected an altar to Baal.

the flower of her youth, he kept inviolate his widowhood for three-and-twenty years.   He was not to be moved to think of marrying again, nor did he outside the bonds of matrimony offend by word or deed in any single point against the law of chastity.   He held in firm check and brought into due subjection the nobles of his kingdom.   Not only did he make a spirited resistance to his powerful enemy of England, who was in possession of many points outside of England, but even recovered these, and so increased his own possessions.   With an equal balance he dealt justice to the poor man as to the rich.   We read in his Life that, when he was one day about to A memorable instance of his go a-hunting, and already had his foot in the leather or the justice. stirrup[1], a certain peasant approached him with a petition for justice; and the king returned to the palace that he might hear and try the cause[2].   And thus he was wont to act in respect of many poor persons who could not easily get their causes tried in the ordinary course of law.   Rich men, for the most part, he dismissed to the judges, but to the suits of peasants he listened seriously and kindly, so that some of them, in rustic fashion, would now and again argue with him on this point or that; but, like the wise man he was, these things moved him not, and as if he were one of themselves he had compassion upon them, and never lost his temper.   He was wont to give of his own means to him who had lost a suit, when he thought the quarrel just.   Hence it came about that people resorted to him ever more and more.   And although his kindness toward the common people made him hail-fellow-well-met with all, and indeed he seemed to know somewhat of every man's craft, yet from his nobles and men in high position he required the observance due to a king, so that by all he was feared and loved ; yet he coveted to be loved rather than to to be feared.   When he once saw some distinguished men in An instance of sorrow for the loss of his own son Henry, he invited them to a his patience ; banquet, and there, feigning a cheerfulness he did not feel, proposed a multitude of arguments that might tend to mitigate their grief.   He was aware of his own impending death a full of his prevision;

---

[1] Scansili seu stapeda.

[2] Dante (*Purgatorio*, canto x. 73-92) tells a similar story of the emperor Trajan ; and Cary, in a note on the passage, says that the original seems to be in Dio Cassius, lib. lxix., where it is told of the emperor Hadrian.

year before it came to pass, whether from the intimations of
nature or, as is rather thought, by divine communication; and
for a whole year before his decease he doubled his accustomed
alms, and imparted the same with his own hands.   Every
Sunday he received the most sacred body of Christ.   When he
felt his end to be drawing near, he caused his grandson Malcolm
to take a journey of inspection of every part of the kingdom,
just as we read that David did with Solomon [1]; and he commended Malcolm to the care of the earl of Fife, whom he
trusted greatly.   Before that time he had carried his grandson
William to Newcastle, and had bestowed upon him all the
lands which he held in Northumberland—a matter this, in
which I cannot think that he showed his usual wisdom; for so,
as time went on, all sense of brotherhood and kinship between
the king and William would suffer extinction.   Rather should
he have bestowed upon his first-born and heir a country of
assured boundary, and on William some territory in the centre
of the kingdom.   And when he felt that he was taken with a
mortal sickness, he demanded that provision which is made for
the last journey, that so he might more readily come to the
end of the same [2]; and inasmuch as he was unwilling to receive
the viaticum in his own house, and yet on foot was unable to
reach the church, he was borne by some of the religious and
some persons of the court to his church; and when he had
heard divine service and devoutly received the eucharist, he
felt that death was knocking at the door, and demanded extreme
unction, and received it, like the Blessed Martin, on the naked
earth.   Now when the religious perceived the devout bearing
of the king, they made all haste with the anointing; and he,
being aware of this, commanded them to do all their business
with due leisure and little by little; and, as he could, he made
the responses at every point.   When all was completed, he
folded his arms in the form of a cross upon his breast, and with
his hands unfolded towards heaven fell asleep in the Lord, not
without due honour for his holy life.

---

[1] I Chron. xxiii. I.

[2] 'ut celebrius de via ad terminum proficisceretur'.   Probably we ought to
read 'celerius', for it was considered an important point that the last agony,
when the evil spirits were in conflict with the good, should not be prolonged.

Miracles are no way needed to attest holiness of life [1]; since, Holiness of life
is not invariably
attested by
in his lifetime, John Baptist (than whom none holier is found
among those born of woman) is not reported to have wrought miracles.
any miracle. Miracles take place on account of the incredulity
of a people, and for various other reasons. In virtue and
renown this David excelled Fergus son of Ferchard, and Fergus David is pre-
ferred b
son of Erth, the first Kenneth, Gregory, his own father and the rest.
brothers. As to the Ferguses there is no manner of doubt, for
I place before them all the others that I have just named.
And though Kenneth was more combative than David, and
under incitement of the insults offered to his father entered the
fierce lists of Mars against the Picts, and manfully conquered
that people and put them to rout, yet in true fortitude I can
no way give him pre-eminence over David, who, in addition,
was crowned with temperance, justice, clemency, and piety.

Finding four bishoprics in his kingdom, he founded nine He founds nine
bishoprics.
more. He caused harbours to be made along the sea-coast.
With the nobles and chief men of the country he showed himself a king; with the poor he was as a father. Observant he
was of religion in the church services and the hearing of mass;
nay,—what is the chief wonder of all,—in his very court you His religious
court.
would have found a cloister of religious persons. He expelled
from his company all who were stained with vice, like as proper
bees drive out the drones from their hive. By word and
example he trained up well-born children in the ways of virtue,
and brought them to be of one mind in the school of conduct.
With a good king you shall find the court good, and with a bad
king you shall find the court bad, all the world over. Nor is
it hard to give a reason for this. The inferior spheres are The king a
pattern to his
courtiers.
regulated in their course according to the motion of the
primum mobile [2]: courtiers make it their study to please their

---

[1] St. Peter Damian (*ob.* 1071) had already said that we must not estimate sanctity
by miraculous power, since nothing is read of miracles done by the B. Virgin or
St. John Baptist. Cf. Addis and Arnold's *Catholic Dictionary*, s.v. MIRACLES.

[2] Cf. *Parad. Lost*, iii. 481-484 :—

> They pass the planets seven, and pass the fixed,
> And that crystalline sphere whose balance weighs
> The trepidation talked, and that first moved ;

with Professor Masson's note *in loco* on the old astronomical system.

king, show themselves apes as it were of his every action, and imitate what they see to be agreeable to him.

About the time of this David lived Richard of Saint Victor, a Scot by birth, a religious of the Augustinian order, and he was second to no one of the theologians of his generation ; for both in that theology of the schools where distinction is gained as wrestler meets wrestler on the battlefield of letters, and in that other where each man lets down his solitary pitcher, he was illustrious[1]. He published a vast number of most meritorious lucubrations. In one sermon of his, concerning the virgin mother of Christ, he was the first to make a distinct declaration that she was born without the stain of original sin. He was buried in the cloister of St. Victor of Paris, and his tomb bears this inscription :—

For virtue, genius, every art renowned,
Here, Richard, thou thy resting-place hast found.
Scotia the land that claims thy happy birth,
Thou sleepest in the lap of Gallic earth.
Though haughty Fate hath snapt thy short-spun thread.
No scathe is thine ; thou livest still though dead.
Memorials of thy ever-during fame,
Thy works securely keep thy honoured name.
With step too slow death seeks the halls of pride,
With step too swift where pious hearts abide[2].

---

[1] Richard of Saint Victor died about 1173. There are several editions of his works, of which the best is that in folio, Rouen, 1650. It is confirmatory of Major's description of him to find that he had constant disputes with the abbot of St. Victor, and had at the same time a strong natural bent towards mysticism.

[2] I have to thank Mr. Hume Brown for supplying me with this excellent rendering, in a medium in which I have no skill. The Latin original is as follows :—

Moribus, ingenio, doctrina clarus, et arte,
    Pulvereo hic tegeris, docte Richarde, situ.
Quem tellus genuit fœlici Scotica partu :
    Te fovet in gremio Gallica terra suo.
Nil tibi Parca ferox nocuit, quæ stamina parvo
    Tempore tracta, gravi rupit acerba manu :
Plurima namque tui superant monumenta laboris,
    Quæ tibi perpetuum sint paritura decus.
Segnior ut lento sceleratas mors petit ædes,
    Sic propero nimis it sub pia tecta gradu.

CHAP. XII.[1]—*Of Henry Beauclerk, king of the English, and of the affairs of Normandy in his time.*

AFTER the death without heirs of William Rous, that is, the Red, his brother Henry Beauclerk succeeded to him in England. Henry took to wife Matilda, commonly called Maud, sister to Edgar and to David. In his day the Blessed Anselm returned to England, and was kindly received by Henry. Meanwhile there sprang up a quarrel between Robert Curtoys[2] duke of Normandy and Henry the Englishman his brother; and Robert made a descent upon England with a large army. But by the counsel of their chief men a peace was arranged between them on this wise: that Henry should pay yearly to Robert a sum of one thousand pounds sterling (this pound is worth three nobles), and that the longer liver of the two should succeed to the other. Robert thereupon returned to Normandy whence he had come; and after a short while came to his brother with a small following, and remitted to him the payment of this slender pension. Henry at length went to Normandy; but Robert had come to be hated by the Normans, and he therefore made Normandy over to his brother Henry, who carried Robert his brother with him to London. After no long time his daughter Matilda, for she rejoiced in her mother's name—the sister of David king of the Scots had borne her to him—came to marriageable years. This daughter English Henry gave in marriage to the emperor Henry[3]. Soon after this William and Richard[4], sons to the king, were drowned, on the Blessed Katherine's day, as they were passing from Normandy into England. On the death of the emperor Henry[3] the empress Matilda returns to England. To her the nobles of England do homage: first of them all, the archbishop of Canterbury, and in the second place, as Caxton will have it[5], David king of the Scots—and

Marginal notes: Henry Beauclerk. Bishop Anselm. Robert the Norman. The gold coinage of England.

---

[1] Orig. misprints 'XIII.' for 'XII.', and misnumbers the rest of the chapters to the end of the book. F. copies the mistake.

[2] *i.e.* Curthose.

[3] *i.e.* the Fifth. He died in 1125.

[4] This is Richard of Chester, an illegitimate son of Henry the First.—See the Rev. J. F. Dimock's preface to the seventh volume of the works of Giraldus Cambrensis, in the Rolls Series, p. 27. The wreck of the White Ship happened in 1120.

[5] Caxton: *Chronicles, u.s.* fol. lxxviii.

after them the rest of the nobles. If he understands this
homage as done for the kingdom of Scotland, I deny the statement, as one that cannot be proved. Amongst the Scots is
but one unbroken opinion : namely, that in matters temporal
their kingdom has never been subject to any. For the territory
that it had in England, I frankly admit that it paid homage
to Matilda, and I make the admission the more readily, in that
Matilda was daughter of a sister-german of David. Among
the Scottish chroniclers I nowhere find it stated that David
ever journeyed to London for the performance of this service.
He did indeed visit the central parts of England, as the
English chroniclers themselves confess, and that with a large
armed force, that he might bring succour to his niece Matilda,
and in all good peace returned from mid England into Scotland. This Matilda was afterwards had to wife by Geoffrey,
earl of Anjou, to whom she bore a son, Henry, commonly
called Henry son of the emperor. A short time thereafter
the king of the English passed from life to death in Normandy[1].
His heart was buried in the chief church of Our Lady at
Rouen, and his body in the monastery of Reading, which himself had built. He reigned for thirty years and four months.

CHAP. XIII.—*Of Stephen, king of the English, his reign and death.*

AFTER the death of Henry, Stephen count of Boulogne [2] was
crowned king of the English. For he was sister's son to this
Henry lately deceased. And William, bishop of Canterbury [3],
who had been the first to swear fealty to Matilda, anointed
Stephen king, and Roger [4], bishop of Salisbury, was likewise of
that party. Now I condemn those priests as altogether fickle and
unjust, seeing that they preferred to the king's own daughter,
to whom too they had sworn fealty, his nephew by a sister,

---

[1] Henry the First died December 1, 1135.

[2] Bolonia :—generally ' Bononia '.

[3] William of Corbeil, archbishop.

[4] This was that bishop Roger who won the favour of Henry the First
because he said mass in a shorter time than any other priest.—Professor S.
R. Gardiner's *A Student's History of England*, vol. i. p. 126.

This they would not have attempted without the hope of some particular advantage to themselves, wherefore they must stand charged as worthless violators of their oath. For it behoved them to take due counsel with the lay nobility as to the true and incontestable heir, and not by ways indirect, for his advantage or their own, to make an unlawful king.

In the first year of his reign Stephen visited the northern parts of England, that he might exact homage from David, king of the Scots, for the lands which the latter held in England (for this Stephen was sister's son to David)—a demand that David, like a righteous man, refused : not only because he had already paid homage to Matilda, but also in that he knew the right to the crown to belong in no way to Stephen.

In the fourth year of king Stephen, Matilda returned to England, and went to a city called Nicol or Nicolai [1], which Stephen forthwith besieged ; but the empress made her escape therefrom without scathe to herself or her following ; and after their departure Stephen takes the town. Ralph· earl of Chester meanwhile, and Robert earl of Gloucester, lord Hugh Bygot, and lord Robert Morlay raised a large army against Stephen, and led him captive to the castle of Bristol. Thereafter they placed the empress Matilda on the throne ; but the people of Kent and William Preth [2], with his followers, favoured the side of Stephen, who was now imprisoned ; and with them, according to Caxton, was the king of the Scots. Thus they brought it so far that they weakened the following of the queen, and took captive the chief men upon her side, to gain whose ransom Stephen was allowed to go free. From Winchester the queen went secretly to Oxford, and there she tarried some time ; but when she learned that the earl of Gloucester had been taken prisoner while he was defending her interest, she left Oxford all unobserved, by water, and went to Wallingford, and there abode. What Caxton says, and says at much length, about David, king of the Scots [3], is mere

Arrival of Matilda in Engla⟨n⟩d.

---

[1] 'The cite of Nicholl' (Caxton, *u.s.* fol. lxxix.), *i.e.* Lincoln. See *ante*, p. 109.

[2] 'Preth'. Caxton, *u.s.* fol. lxxix., writes of 'William of Pree and his retynue'.

[3] Caxton says (*u.s.* fol. lxxix.) that Stephen 'assembled a grete hoost and went towarde Scotland for to haue warred vpon the kyng of Scotland. But he came

raving ; for he favoured the side of the empress, his niece, and took part in the battle in which Stephen was made prisoner. About this time, according to Caxton, the French king repudiated his wife the heiress of Gascony, and Henry earl of Anjou and duke of Normandy took her to wife. And afterward, in the eighteenth year of king Stephen, Henry invaded England with a large army ; but, without coming to the resort of war, they made this agreement: that the one should hold the one half, and the other the other half, of the kingdom. But in the following year Stephen pined away with melancholy. For melancholy shortens life, and the greater the melancholy, the more rapid is the shortening ; wherefore there can be so vast a melancholy that in short space it shall consume the life of a man, according to that saying of the wise man : *A sorrowful spirit drieth up the bones* [1]; wherefore 'tis a prudent man's part to mitigate the force of sorrow.

Henry.

Death of Stephen.

The evils of grief.

CHAP. XIV.—*Of Henry earl of Anjou* [2] *and king of England.*

AFTER the death of Stephen from melancholy,—since to have been happy once, and no longer to be happy, is a great misfortune [3],—Henry succeeded him in the whole of his possessions ; and he was a very powerful king, seeing that, besides all England, he bore sway over Aquitaine, Anjou [4], and Normandy. He it was who, in his youth, was knighted, at Carlisle, by David the Scot. When he had once got the mastery in England, he created Thomas Becket bishop [5] of London, archbishop [6] of Canterbury, and chancellor of England. In the fourth year of his reign, Henry took possession of Wales. There in some

Henry of Anjou : his power.

Thomas Becket.

---

agaynst him in peas and in good maner, and to hym trusted, but he made to hym none homage, for as moche as he had made vnto ye empresse Maud.'

[1] Prov. xvii. 22.　　　　　　　　[2] Andium.

[3] Cf.　　　　　　　　nessun maggior dolore,
　　　　　Che ricordarsi del tempo felice,
　　　　　Nella miseria, e cio sa'l tuo dottore.—Dante, *Inf.* canto v. 121.
It was probably from Boethius, *De consol. philos.* lib. i. pr. 4, and not from Dante that Major borrowed this utterance. Cf. Cary's note on the passage in the *Inferno.*

[4] Andegavia. ·　　　　　[5] praesul.　　　　　[6] archiflamen.

measure the Britons still dwelt, and preserved the independence
of their princes; but the Scots, as Caxton asserts, held Carlisle
city in Cumberland, Bamburgh, New Castle upon Tyne, along
with the county of Lancaster, all in England.

About this time Thomas of Canterbury was banished from
England, because the king desired to subject churchmen to the
judgment of the secular courts, and that man of God, Thomas
of Canterbury, resisted any such sentence, and therefore was
driven into exile.   The question whether the clergy are, under
the divine law, exempt from lay jurisdiction is pretty frequently
discussed among men of learning.   And, though neither side
be without support from men of that sort, I hold the affirmative
answer to be more agreeable to reason.   This appears from that
of Boniface the Eighth in the chapter *Quenquam* concerning
assessments[1], in the section *Cum igitur*[2], where he says, 'Since,
therefore, churches and churchmen, and their possessions, are
by human law and, yet further, by divine law exempt from the
exactions of secular persons', and the rest.   It is not fitting
that the church of the true God and His ministers should be
in a worse condition than the ministers of a false God; and
under Pharaoh priests had an immunity from taxes imposed by
the king.   For, as we read in the forty-seventh chapter of
Genesis[3], Joseph brought under subjection to Pharaoh the
whole land of Egypt, and all its peoples, from one end of the
borders of Egypt to the other,—all but the land of the priests.
And from that time to this day, in all the land of Egypt, a
fifth part is paid to the kings; and this takes place as a legal
enactment except from the priests' land, which was free from
this obligation.   And in the first book of Esdras, at the
seventh chapter, king Artaxerxes wrote to his ministers, 'We
command you also, that ye require no tax, nor tribute, nor
yearly imposition of any of the priests or Levites, or
singers, or porters, or ministers of the temple'[4].   The same
is clear from the ninety-sixth distinction chapter *Duo sunt*,
chapter *Cum ad verum*, and chapter *Imperator*, with the Glosses

Marginal notes:
Banishment of Thomas of Canterbury.

Whether the clergy are by divine law exempt from lay jurisdiction.

---

[1] de censibus.

[2] *Corpus Juris Canonici*, ed. Richter, Lips. 1879: c. un. C. XXXV. qu. 1.

[3] verses 20-22.   [4] I Esd. vii. 24.

thereto[1]. Nor is that objection, urged by others, of weight:
namely, that Paul made his appeal to Caesar, a layman, where
he says, in the twenty-fifth chapter of the Acts, ' I stand at
Caesar's judgment-seat, where I ought to be judged '[2]; and for
this reason : in a case where the ecclesiastical power is wanting,
it is permitted to appeal to a lay court, as appears in the
twenty-third, *q.v.* chapter *Principes seculi* [3], where Isidore says,
' Secular princes sometimes hold within the church the supreme
power, in order that by the exercise of that power they may be
a support to ecclesiastical discipline '. But these powers would
not be necessary within the church, unless only for this cause :
that the thing which priests are unable to compass by the
spoken word of teaching this power may effect from fear of
discipline. For often does the kingdom of heaven profit from
an earthly kingdom on this wise : that when those whose place
is within the church act contrary to her faith and discipline,
they may be brought to naught by the rigour of an earthly
ruler ; and that so the power of the prince may place upon the
proud neck the very yoke which the church with all its claims
cannot impose, and so communicate the virtue of its power as
to be worthy of the reverence to which it makes its claim.

Let princes know, then, that they will have to render an
account to God for the church whose guardians they are
by Christ's appointment. For whether the peace and good
government of the church be increased in the hands of faithful princes, or whether these suffer detriment, He who has
delivered to them the power over His church will exact a
reckoning for the same. The Gloss is here as follows : Laymen
have within the church jurisdiction of many kinds, and that
even when in their persons they are incorrigible, as in the
thirty-sixth distinction *Eos qui*[4]. Just so, when they aim at
subverting the faith, as in the eighth distinction *Quo jure*[5].
Just so, when a cleric has committed forgery ; concerning the
charge of forgery, *Ad falsariorum.*

---

1 *Corp. Jur. Can. u.s.* coll. 339, 340, 341. c. 7. C. XII. qu. 1. ; c. 6. D.
XCVI. ; c. 11. D. XCVI. (Si inperator).

2 verse 10. 3 *Corp. Jur. Can.* c. 20. C. XXIII. qu. 5. col. 936.

4 *Ib.* c. 1. C. XXXVI. qu. 2. col. 1290.

5 *Ib.* c. 1. D. VIII. col. 12.

Now there was no ecclesiastical authority which could have passed sentence upon Paul, both inasmuch as the Mosaic law was no longer in force, and as they would have wrongly condemned an innocent man ; wherefore he appealed to Caesar. And though some instances might be brought to prove that a cleric may not be judged by a layman, yet it does not follow that this has the sanction of divine law. This is plain from a case in point : To keep one's vow is enjoined by the divine law, but in certain cases the obligation does not exist, and so in the case under discussion. And because at the present day this question is being discussed in England [1], I give my opinion in these few words. Let them consider the cause for which the Blessed Thomas lost his life, and in such a matter, or matters of the same sort, let not laymen interfere as against ecclesiastics. Let them likewise consider those customs observed from of old among ecclesiastics, and in respect of these let them make no innovation. I have not heard this matter discussed but in the abstract ; of its special applications I have no knowledge ; I do not therefore insist further.

While the Blessed Thomas was in his seven years' exile from England, and all his friends and familiars had on his account been sent into banishment, the French king brought about a reconciliation between the English king and Thomas, but because the story of this man has been told again and again, and his life is known to many, I shall spend but few words in the relation.

---

[1] This refers to the struggle in 1515 between the secular and ecclesiastical jurisdictions in Standish's case, ' in the course of which Henry the Eighth is said to have expressed himself as determined to endure no division of sovereignty in his realm '. Henry Standish, the Provincial minister of the Franciscans (made bishop of St. Asaph in 1519), had taken, in 1515, the opposite side to the abbot of Winchelcombe in the controversy occasioned by the abbot's sermon against an Act of Parliament, by which the secular courts had been enabled to pass judgment upon all persons in orders, except those in the three holy orders of bishop, priest, and deacon, without the intervention of any ecclesiastical court. See Bishop Stubbs's second lecture on the history of the Canon Law in England in his *Seventeen Lectures on the Study of Medieval and Modern History*, Oxf. 1886, p. 318. Cf. also the Rev. J. H. Blunt's *The Reformation of the Church of England*, 1882, pp. 395-399, and, for Standish's attitude in the matter of the Divorce, Sander's *Rise and Growth of the Anglican Schism* (Lewis's trans. 1877), p. 65.

CHAP. XV.—*Of the martyrdom of the Blessed Thomas, and the sin of the king.*

AFTER his return from a seven years' banishment, Thomas went first of all to Canterbury; and on the fifth day after the celebration of the festival of the birth of Christ—which same day the Church now holds dedicated to his memory—he met

The martyrdom of the Blessed Thomas of Canterbury.

his death. His murder was compassed in this manner. While king Henry was sitting at breakfast on the festival of the birth of Christ, the remembrance of Thomas came into his mind, and he at once burst out with these words: 'Had but the king some men of spirit ready to do his bidding, not long would they leave without result his anger against Thomas.' Soon thereafter, answering thus the outburst of the king, certain men of Belial planned how they might get rid of Thomas.

The parricides of Thomas.

These are their names: William Breton, Hugh Morvil, William Tracy, and Reginald Bersson,—that is, in Latin, ' filius ursi',— knights all. They make for the church of Canterbury, and there, close by the altar of Saint Benedict, they murder the man of God, who in the year of the redemption of the world eleven hundred and seventy-two perished by the swords of

The king's sin.

wicked men. Mightily did this king offend against God. First of all, in that he wished to subject churchmen to the judgment of secular persons; secondly, inasmuch as he banished Thomas when the latter was righteously defending a righteous cause, against which the king was unable to make a just defence; and, yet further, inflicted upon the kin of Thomas a shameful punishment, and on others, who had joined themselves to him in his need, inflicted a like punishment; and, what is worse, he was the means of slaying in the house of God a holy priest; for the king's speech it was which gave the occasion of so fearful a murder. But he who is the occasion of any hurt is reckoned to have done the hurt. Behold, then, how that king was in travail with crime, conceived in grief, and brought forth iniquity. Still greater was the wrong done by the king to the actual murderers; for he was the guilty cause of a murder, according to that word of Christ to Pilate: ' Wherefore he

who delivered me to thee hath the greater sin'[1].   Where
is law? where justice? where the Christian religion? where
the laws of God?—to murder a holy bishop of God in God's
holy temple!   But it was after a splendid feast, and when he
was inflamed with wine, that the king conceived this grievous
thing, and brought forth iniquity following upon the injustice
with which his soul had been in travail.   For, grant one un-
toward accident, and many evils follow; this you shall find in
the first book of the *Physics*.

And thanks to this it is that something may be said
here by the way about those British customs that up to
this present are observed—all unworthy of observance as
they are—at the feast of the Nativity.   On these holy days
it is the wont of the Britons to indulge in much superfluous revelling, in banquets rich with every dainty, and all
sorts of drink.   They begin their Christmas banquet on the
festival of the birth of Christ, and bring the same to an end
after mid-day on the festival of John; the days that follow
this sumptuous banqueting they spend in devilish dances and
lewd songs;—so far do they carry it, that the kings send for the
the nobles of the kingdom and their wives.   These men show
themselves most unwise in thus taking their wives with them
to these orgies of the court, for it would better become the
chaste matron to stay at home.   And if some among the chief
men or the barons do not attend the king, they provide like
feasting in their measure for their own people.   With these
the festival is kept in a tavern, not in a church, in such intemperance of eating and drinking as is the enemy of chastity, in
dances and lewd songs that are equally her foe.   Outside
Britain, in France for instance, in Flanders, and other parts
beyond the sea, these festivals are more fitly celebrated; for
there a moderate meal is taken at mid-day, soon thereafter the
people go to church to hear the gospel of God[2]; and such likewise is the custom observed at Easter, at Pentecost, and the
rest of the solemn festivals.   If this Henry, of whom we are
now speaking, had eaten in moderation, and thereafter had

British customs at the festival of the birth of Christ.

---

[1] St. John xix. 11.

[2] ut verbum Dei evangelizans audiatur.

heard the word of God in church, he would not have
brought forth a murder odious in the sight of God. But
so much is on this point enough [1]. With the martyrdom of
the Blessed Thomas of Canterbury we will make an end of
this Third Book.

---

[1] As curiously illustrating the different attitudes of Erasmus and Major to
Becket, compare Erasmus's dialogue narrating the visit of Colet and himself in
the year 1514, that is only four years before the date of Major's History, to
the shrine of Canterbury :—'Colet asks the guide whether St. Thomas-à-Becket,
when he lived, was not very kind to the poor? The verger assents. "Nor can
he have changed his mind on this point, I should think," continues Colet,
"unless it be for the better." The verger nods a sign of approbation. Whereupon Colet submits the query whether the saint, having been so liberal to the
poor when a poor man himself, would not now rather permit them to help
themselves to some of his vast riches, in relief of their many necessities, than let
them so often be tempted into sin by their need. And the guide still listening
in silence, Colet in his earnest way proceeds boldly to assert his own firm con-
viction, that this most holy man would be even delighted that, now that he is
dead, these riches of his should go to lighten the poor man's load of poverty,
rather than be hoarded up here. At which sacrilegious remark of Colet's, the
verger, contracting his brow and pouting his lips, looks upon his visitors with a
wondering stare out of his gorgon eyes, and doubtless would have made short
work with them, were it not that they have come with letters of introduction
from the archbishop. Erasmus throws in a few pacifying words and pieces of
coin, and the two friends pass on to inspect, under the escort now of the prior
himself, the rest of the riches and relics of the place. All again proceeds smoothly,
till a chest is opened containing the rags on which the saint, when in the flesh,
was accustomed to wipe his nose and the sweat from his brow. The prior,
knowing the position and dignity of Colet, and wishing to do him becoming
honour, graciously offers him, as a present of untold value, one of these rags.
Colet . . . takes up the rag between the tips of his fingers with a somewhat fasti-
dious air, and . . . then lays it down again in evident disgust. The prior, not
choosing to take notice of Colet's profanity, abruptly shuts up the chest, and
politely invites them to partake of some refreshment.' The dialogue—'Pere-
grinatio Religionis ergo'—is quoted at some length in Mr. Seebohm's *Oxford
Reformers* (PP. 287-293), from which work the extract given above is taken.

BOOK IV.

CHAP. I.—*Of the war between the foresaid Henry, king of the English, and his son, and the peace that was made between them; of the defection of the Irish to the English; and of the penitence of Henry, and the extent of his dominions at the time of his death.*

AGAINST Henry the father Henry the son rose in rebellion, and not undeservedly, just as David's sons rebelled against David on account of the murder of Uriah. But at length a peace was made between father and son. Henry the son bore sway in the time of his father, but as he did not survive his father he is not reckoned among the kings. The elder Henry got possession of a great part of Ireland, as our own chroniclers relate; but the manner of our loss of Ireland they do not report[1]; whether we lost it through some negligence of our kings, or because we made demands[2] of the people beyond the rightful tribute, they thought it better to leave Ireland than to keep it. I take it that the English king makes little or nothing out of his possession of Ireland. When king Henry died his sovereign power extended far and wide. He was in peaceful possession of Aquitaine, Anjou, Normandy, and Ireland; all these he had by hereditary right, except Wales and Ireland, which he obtained by conquest. For the murder of the Blessed Thomas, as the chroniclers relate, a deep repentance overtook him. He died in the thirty-sixth year of his reign.

War between father and son.

Ireland is lost by us to the English.

Countries that acknowledged Henry's sway in his old age.

---

[1] See *ante*, p. 113, note [1].

[2] Orig. and F. 'exposuimus'; ? expoposcimus.

CHAP. II.—*Of Richard, the emperor's son*[1]*, king of the English, who went as a warrior to the Holy Land, but on his return was, by the duke of Austria, wickedly taken prisoner, and by his own people nobly ransomed ; here too is treated of the reason of an abundance and of a scarcity of children ; something likewise about robbers.*

INASMUCH as Henry the elder brother survived but a short time, Richard succeeded to Henry the son of the empress. This Richard went to Palestine and the Holy Land, and recovered many of the possessions that had been taken from the Christians, and still more might have been recovered had he and the French king been of one mind. But meanwhile he learned that his brother John, earl of Oxford, had formed designs against England, and thither he returned. On his journey, however, he was taken prisoner by the duke of Austria, and delivered to the emperor, in whose power he remained a fast prisoner, until he might be able to pay to the emperor a ransom of one hundred thousand pounds sterling. To supply such a ransom there was sold every second gold or silver vessel among those which were used for the service of God, while many among the monks, and most of all those of the Cistercian order, sold their books. One thing here I approve ; but the rest I condemn. Wrongful and contrary to the law of nations was the action of the duke of Austria and the emperor in thus taking prisoner a man who had done good service to the Christian commonwealth. Small share had they, I reckon, of the faith or of the Christian religion. It behoves Christian princes to join with one mind in driving beyond their bounds that Mahometan tribe ; but, alas ! they take more care to quarrel among themselves and to increase each one his own territory than to labour for the greater glory of God. Wherefore, if I may use such language, it would seem that God, in weariness and disgust of them, permitted them to harass and fight with one

King Richard.

He is taken prisoner ;

is ransomed.

---

[1] It was Richard's father, Henry the Second, who was Henry 'Fitzempress', his mother Matilda having married the emperor Henry the Fifth. So singular a mistake as that of the text, followed, as it is, by a correct statement in the first sentence of the chapter, makes one suppose that the headings of the chapters may be not Major's work but his printer's.

another. Among the common people there is more of religion,
more soundness in the faith. The other action I approve:
this, to wit, that the English showed their affection for their
king; and they acted rightly in selling every second vessel. For
the patrimony of the Crucified One is with justice to be spent
on pious uses, when the needs of the clergy and holy places
have first been met; and among works of piety this of ransoming the captive, and most of all when he is a good king, *The magnificent clemency*
occupies by no means the lowest place, but rather the highest *of the English*
place of all,—and to all this add the circumstance that he was *in this ransom
of their king.*
one who had the strongest claims upon the whole Christian
commonwealth. But the king lived thereafter for a short time
only. For he was a high-spirited man; yet in this wise, and
with some deep design, he was without cause cast into prison
by his own Christian brethren, who ought to have succoured him
in his extremity—whence it came to pass that sorrow shortened
his days [1]. He reigned exactly nine years, and he left no issue.

But here perchance you will ask why the common people have *The reason of
an abundance*
many children, and why with the nobles this is not so. It is not *and of fewness*
difficult to assign a natural cause for the fact. The nobles are *of children.*
given to rich foods and an over-indulgence in the same, and are
addicted too much to pleasure; their wives grow sluggish in the
ease and quiet of their lives, and, like their husbands, are intemperate in diet. Now such things are unfavourable to fruitfulness. The diet of the common people, on the other hand, is
coarse in kind, and has in it much superfluous strength; in
sexual pleasure they are sparing; their days are spent in continuous bodily exercise, and this conduces more than aught else
to a prolific and fruitful seed. After a moderate supper, or
with none at all, generation is more probable than after a
sumptuous feast; nor can a drunken man have knowledge of
a woman, since from the oppression of the natural forces
he cannot emit a fruitful seed. Sometimes, too, God gives
children; this you can gather from the psalmist in the psalm,
' Blessed are all they that fear the Lord', where it is written,
' For thou shalt eat the labours of thine hands: O well is thee,

---

[1] Richard Cœur-de-Lion died of the wound he received at the siege of Châlus
in 1199.

and happy shalt thou be'[1]. Those men, for the most part, who
have to struggle for their daily bread by working with their own
hands observe more fully than others the commands of God and
of those that are set in authority over them; wherefore it is
here added, ' Thy wife shall be as the fruitful vine upon the
walls of thine house; thy children like the olive-branches round
about thy table. Lo, thus shall the man be blessed that feareth
the Lord'[2]. And, applying this argument *a contrario*, he who does
not fear the Lord shall not be thus blessed. I do not deny that
the possession of children may in some cases be an evil; where,
for instance, the parents are hard and unjust, and where, like
Niobe in the fabling of the poets, they show to their children

To be childless
may be good in
some cases.
an inordinate affection. Wherefore to be childless, even in the
state of marriage, is no effectual sign of the divine displeasure,
since this condition may be common to good and bad alike.
And this is plain in the case of this very Richard, whom we
reckon worthy among kings, and prefer before his father[3]; but,
all intent as he was on the things of war, he had little inclination for a husband's duty. I do not forget that some women
are barren and unfruitful, others fruitful and prolific; but this
condition may co-exist alike where the husband is impotent
and in the reverse case, and the consideration is therefore no
way pertinent.

The English
robbers, Robert
Hood and
Little John.
About this time it was, as I conceive, that there flourished
those most famous robbers Robert Hood, an Englishman, and
Little John, who lay in wait in the woods, but spoiled of their
goods those only that were wealthy. They took the life of no
man, unless either he attacked them or offered resistance in
defence of his property. Robert supported by his plundering
one hundred bowmen, ready fighters every one, with whom four
hundred of the strongest would not dare to engage in combat.
The feats of this Robert are told in song all over Britain. He
would allow no woman to suffer injustice, nor would he spoil

---

[1] Ps. cxxviii. 1, 2.   [2] *Ib.* 3, 4.

[3] Richard's crusade and his Norman wars did not leave him much leisure for
work at home; but modern research has shown him to have been something
more than a great soldier, and the late Mr. J. R. Green (*Stray Studies*, p. 216)
calls attention to his lavish recognition of municipal life. In the first seven
years of his reign he granted charters to Winchester, Northampton, Norwich,
Ipswich, Doncaster, Carlisle, Lincoln, Scarborough, and York.

the poor, but rather enriched them from the plunder taken
from abbots. The robberies of this man I condemn, but of
all robbers he was the humanest and the chief[1].

CHAP. III.—*Of John, that far from worthy king of the English ;
of the interdict which was laid upon England, and of the assignment
of the tribute to the Roman pontiff ; the poisoning of the king, and its
censure.*

On the death of Richard, that most Christian hero, his brother   English John.
John—a fickle man he was and greedy of empire—succeeded
him. He waged a war with France, in which he lost utterly the
duchy of Normandy and the earldom of Anjou. Returning to
England, he begged a tithe of the clergy, to the end he might
recover the territories in France that had been lost. About
that time the convent of Canterbury elected as archbishop
of Canterbury Stephen Langton, a very learned man. At
this the king took offence, and sent into exile the prior of
Canterbury, with the convent, forbidding at the same time
that any pontifical precept should be received in regard to
Stephen Langton. Meanwhile the Roman pontiff besought
the king to restore to their places the prior and convent, and
when the king obstinately refused to obey, the pontiff laid all
England under an interdict, and long-lasting quarrels ensued   England laid
between the pope, on behalf of the clergy, and the king. At   under an
interdict.
length Innocent the Third, who was at that time pope, sent to
the French king, and besought him to invade the kingdom of
England, and take it for himself, on account of the obstinacy
shown by the king of England. When English John came to
hear of this—whether it was that he feared to lose his kingdom,
or that he was moved by true contrition—he resigned the
kingdom of England and of Ireland into the hands of the Roman
pontiff, in the hope that he might thereby soften his heart, and
promised for himself and his successors that they should hence-

---

[1] Camden (*Britannia*, p. 642, ed. 1600) quotes Major as his authority for the
story of Robin Hood. For another early Scottish reference to the story, see
Mr. Æ. J. G. Mackay's *William Dunbar*, Introd. pp. ccliv.-cclvi. Major calls
Robin Hood ' Robertus Hudus '.

forward hold England and Ireland of the Roman pontiff; to
which the cardinal, who was present on behalf of the pontiff,
as the custom is, readily assented.   And at that time Peter's
pence, that is, the pence given to Saint Peter, were first imposed ; for English John obliged himself and his successors to
pay yearly a thousand silver marks, that is, two thousand
nobles, or six thousand francs, to the Roman court.

England made
subject to the
Roman pontiff.

But here a difficulty occurs by the way : Whether, namely,
any king have the power to bestow on any one the rights of
his kingdom, or its fixed revenues ?   The answer may be made
by propositions ; of which—

Whether a
king have the
power to
alienate the
rights of his
kingdom.

The FIRST is this: If the English or the French king were
to part with his rights in respect of his kingdom to the Turk,
or any other not rightful heir of the same, to that other these
rights are worthless.   The proof: The king holds his right
as king of a free people, nor can he grant that right to any
one against the will of that people [1].

SECOND proposition ; That king acts wickedly who, without
ripe counsel held with the nobles of his kingdom, bestows
upon any other the revenues to be granted by the people.
The proof: Such king, without the explicit or interpretative
consent of the people, lays a burden on that people.   But
such a tax as this the people is not held bound to pay.

THIRD proposition : Since the dispute was between the king
and the English church as to the properties that had been
taken from the latter, and most of all from the Cistercian
religious, it behoved the king to make a particular restitution
to the church.   This is clear : For he spoiled them of property
which he did not restore.

FOURTH proposition : That manner of restitution does not
suffice which gives one quota to the Roman church in place of
the many of which another particular church has been de-

---

[1] Cf. the still stronger expressions in the 10th question of the 15th distinction
of Major's *In Quartum*, fol. lxxvi. ed. 1521 : ' Whence it is plain that kings are
instituted for the good of the people, as the chief member of the whole body,
and not conversely. . . . In the second place it follows that the whole people
is above the king [quod totus populus est supra regem] and in some cases can
depose him . . . The king hath not that free power in his kingdom that I have
over my books.' Cf. also ch. xviii. of this Book : ' Rex enim non habet ita
liberum dominium in suo regno, sicut tu in tunica tua.'

spoiled ; and if John sought in this way to find some shield
or shelter to secure him against full retribution, he acted
without due consideration. For, grant the opposite : Then
any tyrant may spoil a church of a hundred thousand pieces
of gold by taking absolution from the Roman pontiff, and yet
all the time possess wherewith to make restitution—to say
which is to talk nonsense.

FIFTH proposition : If John and the English people had
covenanted together as to this yearly tribute to the pontiff, it
was justly paid ; but nothing of it came from the royal purse—
the whole tribute was taken from the people. For the king
collected more than he handed over to the pontiff. Three
hundred marks he gave in respect of Ireland, and seven
hundred in respect of England. I do not believe that he could
raise yearly, in that part of Ireland which alone he held, three
hundred pounds ; but in England alone he collected much
more than the total amount. But however this may be, since
the pontiffs are in possession the money has to be paid to
them ; and it is so paid [1] ; and for this purpose they keep a
collector in England ; and the kings of England, when they
come to the throne, receive investiture of the pontiffs by a
legate [2]. Some time after this, however, occurred a breach
between John and his nobles ; wherefore these send an embassy
to Philip, the French king, praying him to send over to them
his son Lewis, and saying that they would make him king of
the English. He was welcomed by the English.

A short time thereafter a certain monk of the monastery of

---

[1] In the 4th question of the 24th distinction of the *In Quartum*, fol. clviii.
Major writes thus : ' For if it be admitted that the supreme pontiff has dominion
in matters temporal *causaliter*, and can effect much towards the deposition of
kings by persuasion, by counsel, yea, by provoking some to use the sword against
others—when these are the destroyers of the faith and once for all avail nothing
to the Christian commonwealth—this is more lightly to be borne, and no way
contradicts what I have said. If even some kings, in concert with their peoples,
have surrendered to the Roman pontiffs, as is reported of the English—that
touches my contention not at all. For a collector of the Roman pontiff collects
money in England—from every house a penny, as I have understood. But then
it behoves us to consider whether it was the king by himself alone who made this
surrender, or the king and the people. I do not, however, believe that the
English would ever suffer the pontiff to depose their king and put another in his
place.' [2] Orator.

Swynesheid [that is, ' caput porci '] took the life of the king
by poison, in the following way. He gave the king to drink
of a cup of ale that had been poisoned, and the king ordered
the monk to drink of it the first. That is the wretched condition of great men—that they think or fear that every one
wishes to deceive them.   But, at the king's command, the
monk, without a sign of fear, drank half of the contents of
the cup, and the other half the king drank off, fearing no
harm ; and thus did both perish by the same poison [1]. The
monk had been moved to this deed for the relief of his country [2].
The king had been heard to say again and again as he sat at
meat that the loaf which used to be sold for a penny should
soon come to cost twenty shillings. The monk, who felt that
such a thing would be very disastrous to the common weal,
thought it would be a meritorious act to take the life of the
king ; but before he would commit the deed he went to his
abbot, and by the abbot's counsel it was that he administered
the poisoned draught. He sought absolution, however, of the
abbot before the act. For the monk who showed in this
fashion his love for his country five monks every day make
special prayer, nor will they desist thus to pray till the day of
judgment.

In this part of my narration I follow Caxton the English
chronicler to the letter, merely translating the language used
of us Britons into Latin [3].   Here I seem to be brought face to

---

[1] John died at Newark, October 19, 1216—' of a fever inflamed by a glutton-
ous debauch' (Green, ed. 1875, p. 126) ; ' worn out in mind and body ' (Gardiner, vol. i. p. 185) ; ' fell ill at Swineshead abbey, in Lincolnshire, whether
of poison, as some say, or, as others think, of grief and rage at his loss' *i.e.*
' of his baggage and treasure' (York Powell and Mackay, p. 130) ; ' perhaps
poisoned ' (J. Franck Bright, vol. i. p. 140).

[2] Ad hanc provinciam subeundam.

[3] The following is the story, told by Caxton (fol. lxxxvii.), upon which Major
bases his own narrative and his criticisms :—' And so it befell that he [king John]
wolde haue gone to Nicholl, and as he went thyderwarde he came by yᵉ abbey
of Swynestede, and there he abode two dayes.   And as he sate at meet he asked
a monke of the hous how moche a lofe was worth yᵗ was set before hym vpon
the table.   And the monke sayd that the lofe was worth but an halfpeny.   O
said the kyng tho, here is grete chepe of brede.   Now quod the kynge, and
I may lyue, suche a lofe shall be worth .xx. shyllynges or half a yere be gone.
And whan he had sayd these wordes, moche he thought and oft he syghed,
and toke and ete of the breed and sayd, by God yᵉ wordes that I haue spoken

face with a mass of follies.   A great wickedness it was in this monk, at no bidding but his own, to kill a king ; for, grant it that the commonwealth may take some profit by the death of kings, yet on no consideration can it be allowed to a private person, and in signal measure to a monk, to kill them.   Something vulpine too there was in the absolution granted by the abbot before the deed.   And besides, that celebration of masses seems a piece of madness, as if this sinful monk had therein acted the part of a good man.   The probability is that the abbot and the religious approved the action of the monk, and by doing so took away from him the very chance of a true repentance ; and if he died impenitent, he is damned.   Thus then was John, king of the English, after a reign of fourteen years and five months[1], slain by a wicked monk.   I shall now leave Lewis, the son of Philip, dwelling among the English, that I may bring to an end the narrative of the things that meanwhile had come to pass in Scotland.

---

it shall be soth.   The monke that stode before yᵉ kynge was for these wordes full sory in his herte, and thought rather he wolde himselfe suffre deth, and thought how he myght ordeyn therfore some maner remedy.   And the monke anone went to his abbot, and was shryuen of hym, and tolde the abbot all that the kynge had sayd, and prayed his abbot for to assoyle him, for he wold gyue the kynge suche a drynke that all Englonde sholde be glad therof and ioy full.   Than went the monke in to a gardeyn and founde a grete tode therin, and toke her vp and put her in a cuppe, and prycked the tode through with a broche many tymes tyl that the venym came out on euery syde in the cuppe, and then toke the cuppe and fylled it with good ale, and brought it before the kynge and knelynge sayd : Syr, quod he, wassayle, for neuer the dayes of your lyf dranke ye of so good a cuppe.   Begyn monke, quod the kynge.   And the monke dranke a grete draught, and after toke the kynge the cuppe, and the kyng also dranke a grete draught and set downe the cup.   The monke anone ryght went in to the farmery and there dyed anone, on whose soule God haue mercy Amen.   And .v. monkes synge for his soule specyally, and shall whyles the abbey standeth.   The kyng arose up anone full euyl at ease, and commaunded to remeve the table, and asked after the monke.   And men tolde hym that he was deed, and that his wombe was broken in sonder.   Whan the kynge herde this, he commaunded to truss, but it was all for nought, for his bely began to swell of the drynke that he had dronken, and within two dayes he dyed, on yᵉ morowe after saynt Lukes daye.'

[1] Major is mistaken in what he says of the length of King John's reign.   John reigned from 1199 to 1216 ; and Caxton is on this point quite right.

CHAP. IV.—*Of Malcolm, grandson of David, king of the Scots, and all that he did, and how he never entered the married state.*

Malcolm.

ON the death of that David who had, with excellent wisdom, held rule over the Scots, his grandson, Malcolm, in the fourteenth year of his age, was crowned king. In the first year of his reign, Sumerled, chieftain of Argyll, and his grandson rose against the king; but the agents of Henry were able to allay the rebellion of those grandsons. English Henry meanwhile, the son of the empress, and cousin to Malcolm the Scot, showed secretly a strong inclination to friendship with him and his, and recovered at the hand of this youth and his governors that territory of Northumberland which the kings of the Scots had for a long time held [1]; Cumberland and Huntingdon he left to the Scots. But thereby this young Malcolm roused against himself the displeasure of the Scottish nobles; for they said that he was too friendly with the English king, and that he had no right thus to attenuate the land over which he was set to rule, without the consent of its leading men. And thus it came about that in a national council [2] at Perth the earl of Stratherne and five other earls conspired to take possession of the king's person, not with intent to harm him, but for the better preservation of the kingdom during his youth. But the king got news of this design and made his escape.

English Henry.

Northumberland becomes subject to the English king.

It was about this time that Galloway rose against the king; but in one year he so fully quelled this insurrection, that the Galloway chieftain, one Angus, leaving his son as hostage with the king, renounced the world, became a canon in the monastery of the Holy Rood at Edinburgh, and in the rule of Augustine ended his days in peace. But the king led a great army against the men of Moray—they had long been disturbers of the kingdom with their harrying and plundering. He destroyed them to a man, and put in their place others of a peaceful temper. About that time Sumerled, chieftain of

Angus becomes a monk.

---

[1] Cf. *Celtic Scotland*, vol. i. p. 471, and *Scotland under her Early Kings*, vol. i. p. 353.

[2] 'congregatione publica'. Cf. Mr. Innes's *Lectures on Scotch Legal Antiquities*, 1872, p. 99.

Argyll, got together from Ireland and the other islands a large army, to make war against the king, and a battle took place at Renfrew, when the chieftain was slain by a few men on the king's side.

The king had meanwhile reached the years of manhood, and the wise men about him counselled him to take to himself a wife; but to them he would not consent, saying always that he had vowed himself to virginity; and this vow he observed to the end of his days. Now his observance of this vow might well have entitled him to be reckoned among the foolish virgins[1] had it been, for instance, a likely thing that his unmarried state would bring on a civil war or other great disaster for his country; but seeing that he was not without adult brothers to succeed to him, he did right to observe his vow, once he had made it, because no reason for the breaking of the vow appeared. He ended his days at Jedburgh after a reign of twelve years; but his body was carried to Dunfermline, the centre almost of the kingdom, and there honourably buried. There from of old to the present the kings of the Scots have their tombs. Behold how profitable a thing it is to be descended of chaste and pious ancestors! The great-grandsire of this man and the mother of his grandfather were very pious persons, his grandfather was filled with devotion to God, and Henry, his father, held before him the pattern and likeness of his grandfather to follow after it.

The Scot dies unmarried, and is not to blame.

The offspring of chaste persons are like to follow in their steps.

CHAP. V.—Of William, king of the Scots, his captivity and his ransom; of the lavish building of monasteries, and other matters that came to pass in his time.

MALCOLM the Maiden was succeeded by William, who was crowned in the year of our Lord one thousand one hundred and sixty-five. He did homage to Henry of England for the lands which he held in England; and by the advice of the English king, contrary to the wish of the Scots, he passed into France; but Northumberland was restored to him. In the

William succeeds to the throne.

Northumberland is regained.

---

[1] fatuorum virginum.

year of our Lord eleven hundred and seventy-four there sprang
up a quarrel between Henry of England and William the
Scot; for William had inflicted a great defeat upon the
northern English, and had thereafter returned in peace to his
own people.   This action of his I condemn; for when he had
recovered his own property without recourse to arms, he ought
not to have entered upon a war.   And yet, not satisfied even
now, a second time he entered England with a large army, and
gave all to plunder and pillage; but while his army was

William is
taken.

scattered for plunder, the king incautiously remained behind
with a small guard; so that the English surrounded him, took
him captive without the shedding of a drop of blood, and
carried him to king Henry the elder.   It was because the
English king had caused his son to be crowned—and, from the
hatred that he bore to Saint Thomas, by the bishop of York [1]—
the one of them was called the Elder, the other the Younger;
and the elder Henry sent William to Normandy to be safe-
guarded in the castle of Falaise.   But David of Huntingdon,
who had stayed behind in England, then passed into Scotland,
and governed the country in the absence of his brother William.
In the following year, however, the Scots sent an embassy to
Henry of England to treat concerning a ransom for their king;
and this end they gained by promising that the Scots would no
longer engage in war against him, and in security therefor they
make over to him the four strongest fortresses in the kingdom:
Berwick, to wit, Roxburgh, Maidens' Castle[2], and Stirling; and
on these terms William returned to the Scots.

Revolt and
cruelty of
Gilbert.

In the same year the rest of the Scots were attacked by one
Gilbert, son of Fergus of Galloway, who cut out the tongue
and both the eyes of his own brother, when this man refused
to take part in his wicked designs.   Against this Gilbert
William marches with a large body of soldiers; and when
Gilbert saw that he could make no stand, he betook him as a
suppliant to the king, imploring his forgiveness, and obtaining
it.   Further, in the year eleven hundred and seventy-six,

---

[1] Though the papal brief forbidding the coronation had been forced upon the
archbishop on the previous day, Henry the Third was crowned by archbishop
Roger, June 14, 1170.

[2] Cf. p. 15, note [2].

William founded the monastery of Arbroath [1], a community, I Building of monasteries. Arbroath. say, second in wealth to none in Scotland, and indeed I know not if there be one more richly endowed in all Britain; and David of Huntingdon founded the monastery of Lin- Lindores. David of Huntingdon. dores. This is that David of whom mention is made in a book well known among the French, which is entitled ' concerning the sons of three kings '—to wit, of France, England, and Scotland—and a similar book we have in our own vernacular tongue [2]. Countess Ada, king William's mother, founded at Haddington a convent, fair and well-endowed, for nuns of the order of Saint Bernard [3]. There was something marvellous in the eagerness of this family to build monasteries, yet ever with the result of damage to the royal revenues. The lavish expenditure of the royal patrimony upon monasteries is condemned. The revenues of the kings of the Scots are derived chiefly from their own property in land, and thus they have been from the beginning. It is not only becoming, but even necessary, that a king should have sufficient private means, for thus will he not be under the necessity of burdening the common people with tolls and taxes. And inasmuch as they on no account refrain from the imposition of taxes, it is highly imprudent to diminish the royal revenues; and yet men of our own nation, and courtiers most of all, are found to extol to the skies those kings who portion out the royal revenues among their friends. Such men are led astray by a blind and partial affection, to the neglect of the common weal. Here I will dare to say that the three estates of the

---

[1] Dedicated to Becket. The date of the foundation is 1178. See *Registrum de Aberbrothoc*, p. xi.

[2] Orig. ' et non differunt [F. ' differentem '] ab hoc in nostra lingua vernacula librum habemus.' Brunet (ed. 1862, vol. iii. col. 1126, *s.v.* LIVRE) quotes five editions of this work in French, of which the first four were printed at Lyons— in 1501, 1503, 1504, 1508—and the fifth at Paris, undated, but about 1530. The National Library of Paris possesses six MSS. of the work; and a MS. catalogue of MSS. in the same library attributes the work to Charles Aubert, who wrote also a 'Histoire d'Olivier de Castille'. There seems to be no trace of the edition ' in nostra lingua vernacula' except in Major, and it is possibly one of many books now lost that were printed by Walter Chepman in the early years of the sixteenth century.

[3] The Convent of Haddington was founded in 1170. ' The lands commonly called the Nunland, now called Huntington, belonged likewise to the nuns of this place.'—Spotiswood's *Account of the Religious Houses that were in Scotland at the time of the Reformation* (in Keith's *Scottish Bishops*, ed. 1824, p. 462).

A law that
would be profit-
able to the
kingdom in the
future.
realm ought to be called on to give sanction to a law forbidding the king to make a grant in perpetuity of the royal lands to any one, and thus to alienate them from the royal treasury, without the assent of the three estates; and if they should make lavish alienation of those lands, then might the next king recover them with interest. To this law the king ought to give his consent. By this means no one will be able to put it down to avarice that he makes no grant of lands. Servants —for wages paid, for offices conferred, for heiresses (where the right of marriages remains in his hands)—he will have in abundance.

A rebel Wild
Scot is hanged.
About this time, a certain Wild Scot of Ross, named Mac-william, otherwise called Donald Bane, rebelled against the king, and stirred up a large part of the neighbouring country. Against him the king and his brother brought an army; but while the king was making a halt at Inverness, some of his nobles, who had gone on before him with a light-armed troop, found the rebel with a small following in a moor which is called Makardy[1]. They put him to death, with fifty of his fellows, and brought his head to the king, who caused the same to be hung up to public view.

Richard the
Englishman.
Further, after the death of the elder Henry—for the reign of the younger Henry is not worthy to be reckoned—Richard became king of the English. He made restitution to the king of the Scots of those fortalices which he had held in security for the captivity of William, and restored likewise the hostages and the ten thousand pounds for which they had put themselves under obligation to his father. He also made null and void all those obligations by which William, when he was a prisoner, had bound himself; demanding, however, that the kings of the Scots should do him homage, mediate or immediate, for the lands which they possessed in England. All this Richard did in the first year of his reign. In the same year king William gave the earldom of Huntingdon to his brother David in possession.

A rising in
Galloway.
About this time, after the death of that Gilbert, son of

---

[1] 'The Moor of Mamgarvy.'—E. W. Robertson's *Scotland under her Early Kings*, vol. i. p. 393.

Fergus, who had put out the eyes of his brother [1], there rose in his place a man of Galloway, who invaded the rest of the Scots. Against him marched Rotholand [2] on the part of the king, and defeated him, and afterwards slew besides another rebel of Galloway, by name Gelecolne [3]. Rotholand, however, lost his brother in that battle. In reward of the loyal service done him by this Rotholand, king William bestowed upon him in perpetuity Galloway and the land of Carrick. Meanwhile the English king gave to the Scottish king in marriage Emergarda, his own kinswoman, and daughter of the earl of Beaumont; and David of Huntingdon, brother of the king of Scots, took to wife a daughter of the earl of Chester.

Rotholaod.

Emergarda.

CHAP. VI.—*Of William the Scot and Alexander, William's son, and of a miracle done by William ; of the war with John of England, and the peace that was made with the same, and the treaty by the swearing of the oath of fealty.*

AFTER the return of English Richard from his attempt to recover Judaea, and when he was, by reason of his captivity, put into great straits for money, William the Scot gave him in free gift two thousand marks; wherefore the love in which either held the other was no less than that of David and Jonathan ; nor do we read anywhere of a peace more truly maintained between Scots and English than in their day. So true it is that a harmonious movement in the spheres above finds a tranquil and melodious echo in the spheres below. William also swears fealty to John the English king for the lands that he held in England, safeguarding only the honour and liberties of the kingdom of the Scots. In the same year the Scottish nobles took the oath of fidelity to Alexander, son of William, then a child three years of age. At that time the earl of the Orkney Islands [4] put out the eyes of the bishop of Caithness and cut out his tongue. The king pursued the earl with a large force, but the latter fled ever from one place of hiding to

The love and concord between Richard of England and William the Scot.

Wicked act of the tyrant of Orkney.

---

[1] *i.e.* Uchtred. E. W. Robertson (*u.s.*) vol. i. p. 380.

[2] *i.e.* Roland. *Ib.* vol. i. pp. 387, 390, 392.

[3] *i.e.* Gillecolum. *Ib.* vol. i. p. 387.

[4] *i.e.* Harald MacMadach.

another; and it is no wonder: these islands are situated
beyond the Scots boundaries. But at length the king yielded
to the prayers of his nobles, and granted his pardon for this

The remission
of his punish-
ment is con-
demned.
crime on the payment by the earl of a large sum of money. I
consider this penalty to be insufficient for an injury so atro-
cious; for the greater—the more uncommon—the nature of a
crime, so much the deeper should be the branding of it, that
warning may thereby be given to those who come after. Our
chroniclers relate further that in the year of the redemption of

A miracle done
by William.
the world one thousand two hundred and six, William, in the
presence of many persons, cured a youth who was suffering
from a grievous malady. Two years after this, Alan of Galloway, son of Rotholand, took to wife Margaret, daughter to
David, earl of Huntingdon.   During the two years that
followed, the fearful seeds of war were sown broadcast between
the Scots and English. Their kings raised each of them a
large army, determined to commit their cause to the fortune
of war; and when they were drawing always nearer to one
another, some men of sense, both Scots and English, take up
the matter, and try by the counsels of prudence and moderation to mitigate the angry feelings of their kings, and so
arrange the quarrel without bloodshed. For they knew that
the issue of war is ever doubtful, and best of all they knew
that among those who should lose their lives in the inevitable
struggle would be their dearest friends. For does not the
conqueror in battle also suffer loss of men, or it may be of
property ? The commanders of hostile armies, when the first
movement of offence is still to make, when both sides are
unbroken, are wont to listen to reason. Between these enemies
accordingly peace was made, on this settlement : that William
should give in marriage his two daughters, Margaret and Isabella, to Henry and Richard, the two sons of John; but a
short time hereafter a quarrel sprang up between John and his
nobles, of which the result was that these marriages were not

A new law for
the acknow-
ledgment of an
obligation and
the taking of an
oath of fidelity.
concluded. It was further determined that for the future the
kings of the Scots should not in their own person do homage
for the lands that they held in England, inasmuch as the Scots
asserted that it was not fitting for their kings to take the oath
of fidelity to a superior ; but that the eldest sons of the kings

should do so.   Alexander, son of William, accordingly took
the oath of fidelity in London to John the English king, and
was by John invested with the insignia of knighthood, and
honourably sent back to Scotland.

In the selfsame year there happened a heavy flood, when in
Scotland the swelling rivers broke from their customed channels,
and when, notably in Perth, the Tay broke down the great
bridge of Saint John, and carried away many houses ; so great
was the flood that William the king, David his brother, and
Alexander, scarce made good their escape in a boat.   In one What may be
place there may be a larger amount of snow than in another, the cause of
floods.
and likewise a breaking forth of the springs whence rivers
have their source, and thus comes a melting of the snow when
one looks not for it, and a sudden increase of the rivers takes
place.   This may proceed from the stars and planets being at
the time in the moist signs, so that the floodgates may be un-
barred in this region and not in that.

In this year John of England took possession of a large part
of Ireland, and subdued the rebels of Wales.   In the following
year king William sent an army into Ross against Gothred
Makwilliam.   Gothred was at length taken, through the Gothred's
treachery of his own people, and came half-dead into the hands punishment.
of justice ; for, when he was taken, he refused both meat and
drink ; but he was beheaded, and justly ; for he who against
all justice desired to be exalted and to be made a king, or the
equal of a king, deserved that his power should wane and that
he should be brought low.   He who pulls down the powerful
from their seats and exalts the humble brings the haughty
and ambitious man to ruin.   In the year twelve hundred and
fourteen, William king of the Scots was taken with a grievous
sickness, and fell asleep in the Lord in the seventy-fourth year
of his age, and of his reign the forty-ninth.   He was honourably buried in the monastery of Arbroath, which he himself
had built[1].

---

[1] It is curious that Major in his account of William's reign does not refer to
the Council of Northampton (1176) where the archbishop of York claims
Scotland as part of his province.   The Scots appealed to the Pope, who forbade
the archbishop to press his claim.   See *Scotland under her Early Kings*, vol. i.
pp. 378, 379.

CHAP. VII.—*Of Alexander, son of William, and his wars with John of England. Of the interdict on Scotland, and when such a thing is to be feared.*

Alexander the Scot.

John of England.

A mythical story of an incubus.

AFTER the death of William, Alexander the Second was invested with the regal insignia; and not long thereafter the general discontent with John of England, of which mention has before been made, grew stronger. About two years before the death of William, there had appeared a simple fellow who went on asserting that John, king of England, was the incarnate devil. Him the king first of all threw into prison, and thereafter hanged. As to this matter our chroniclers report that, moved thereto by the story told by this simple fellow, men began to examine with more particularity the pedigree of the king of England; when 'twas found that one of his predecessors, Geoffrey, earl of Anjou, when he wished to enter the married state, pursued a fair woman with a view to marriage, and without consideration of the race to which she might belong, when there arrived suddenly upon the scene an unknown stranger, a woman of singular beauty, who refused to hear mass; but the king, inasmuch as he had a goodly offspring by her, for a long time concealed the matter as best he could; but at length he caused her to be held in church by four soldiers, when at the elevation of the body of Christ she vanished from the sight of all in a cloud of smoke and sulphur, and never did she reappear. Of this woman, then, they affirm that the Henry who caused the murder of the Blessed Thomas, and those other kings of England, were born [1]. I look upon this story as the invention, pure and simple, of some Scot who did not like the English; but it commended itself to the Scots, and was no doubt carefully treasured by them. In matters themselves improbable, I am inclined to assent neither to my own countrymen as against the English [2]

---

[1] The author of *The Complaynt of Scotland* (p. 133, ed. Leyden) says that since the days of Hengist and Horsa the English kings have been usurpers:—
'The maist part of thay tirran kings that hes succedit of that false blude hes beene borreaus to their predecessours.'

[2] Miss Norgate (*England under the Angevin Kings*, vol. i. p. 143) names as

nor in similar case to Englishmen as against my own countrymen.

After this, Alexander the Scot, in the third year of his reign, laid siege to Norham, and at a later date he subdued the whole of Northumberland. But I must marvel at the obscurity in which those chroniclers have left this matter, and their careless treatment of it, seeing that they do not tell us how then the Scots came to lose those territories of theirs in England; for, from what has just been said, the chroniclers next in date would seem to say that this strip of land was in the hands of the Scots, since Norham is the boundary to-day, and it is distant scarce a stone's throw from the Tweed [1]. But let us resume the narrative of events. When Alexander was returned to Scotland, John the Englishman invaded that country, gave to the flames Dunbar and Haddington, and, when he learned that Alexander had collected an army, made no delay to withdraw himself. But when John was once off, Alexander invaded

The deeds of Alexander.

---

the authority for this story Giraldus Cambrensis *de Instructione Principum*, dist. iii. c. 27, and suggests that it may have arisen in the popular mind as some explanation of the career of Fulk the Black, son of Geoffrey Greygown. There is some difficulty in following the story as told by Major. He seems to speak of two women. Geoffrey earl of Anjou 'fecit mulierem speciosam pro conjugio venari'. In the very next line we read of the appearance of 'una speciosissima ignota', who was not only in the habit of refusing to hear mass, but who had already borne goodly offspring to the king. Giraldus's story is quite simple : 'There was a certain countess of Anjou of outstanding beauty, but of unknown origin, whom the count had married solely from the attractions of her person. She rarely went to church, and when she did go there, she showed little or nothing of a devout bearing. She would never stay to hear mass, but departed in haste immediately after the gospel. But at length, when this had been for some time observed, not only by the count, but by others, she was one day seized by four soldiers, in accordance with instructions from the count, in the very act of leaving the church at her customary hour. Tearing from their grasp the cloak by which she was being held, and leaving behind her two young sons whom she had been holding under the right fold of her garment, she caught up under her arm her two other little sons, who had been standing under the left fold, and in sight of all vanished through a high window of the church. And so it was that this woman, whose face was better than her faith, never more appeared, neither she nor her two children. King Richard would often quote this story, saying it was no wonder that, sprung from such a parentage as this, fathers and sons should never cease to quarrel one with another, nor yet brothers with brothers, for that he and his, who came from the devil, must needs return to the devil.'

[1] Berwick was taken by the English in 1482.

England, laid siege to Carlisle, a small city, but very strongly
fortified, reduced the same, and then kept it in his own hands.
From this it clearly follows that in the time of Alexander and
John the boundary was the same as at this present. Further:
when one faction of the English desired to have Lewis, son of
Philip of France, for their king, Alexander the Scot goes to
meet him at Dover, that he might there bid him welcome and
help him to a peaceable accession, and, his errand done,
returns without disturbance to his own country.

Scotland placed
under interdict. It was about this time that Gualo, the legate apostolic, discharged against Alexander the last weapon of the church, and
placed the kingdom of the Scots under interdict, until reparation should be made for the losses inflicted on the English,
and Carlisle, so lately wrested from them, restored into their
hands. And Alexander, fearing perhaps more than he need
have done the censures of the church, made restoration of
Carlisle, and paid a vast sum of money to the legate for
Excommunica-
tion—in what
respects to be
feared...
Carl's'l. absolution. If his title to Carlisle had been just, he need not
have feared the stricture of excommunication. Several among his
predecessors had held Carlisle, and I do not see how he had
lost his right to the city; and, however this may be, he ought,
in an unjust or even a doubtful case, to have made his appeal
against this sentence from the legate to his superiors. But
perhaps you will object: that respect must be paid to a sentence passed by a spiritual pastor, even though it be unjust.
The answer is no difficult one: If the sentence is unjust to the
degree of being null, it is in no way to be dreaded; if it is unjust, and yet in such a way that it is real excommunication,
inasmuch as all the essentials of excommunication are to be
found therein, then excommunication, though thus unjust, is to
be dreaded; unjust indeed in that it includes some circumstances by which justice is violated, as, for instance, that the
motive of the sentence is partiality to one side or dislike of the
Excommunica-
tion is not to be
lightly inflicted. other, or something of this sort. In the former case unjust
excommunication is no more excommunication than a corpse is
a man. I may here observe in passing that not only in Britain,
but in most parts of the world, men are disposed to accept
ecclesiastical censures too easily. No man can be liable to
excommunication, whether we regard the matter from the

point of abstract law, or as a sentence inflicted by man, except
for some mortal sin that he has committed ; and for contumacy
only can this sentence be inflicted by man. 'If he will not
hear the church', so speaks the Truth, 'let him be as a heathen
man and a publican.'[1] Wherefore, on the opposite supposition, if he have heard the church, why shall he be cast out,
like a heathen, from the congregation of the faithful? Whence
it comes that we reckon a vast number of excommunicated
persons who are in a state of grace. A sophistical excommunication can harm no man in things spiritual, whether his body
lie in holy ground or in a place unconsecrated; nor is every
truly excommunicated person damned after death, if he have
taken all pains to get absolution.

About this time Preaching Friars first came to Scotland[2].

Preaching
Friars in
Scotland.

CHAP. VIII.—*Of Henry, king of the English, and his son, and of the
prophecy of Merlin about them.*

I now leave Alexander the Scot, and return to the English.
When John had met his death by poison, administered by the
hand of a foolish monk, and Lewis the son of Philip had been
called to the throne by the English, that party among the
English, which had favoured the cause of John, now that he was
deceased hailed Henry, his nine-years-old son, as king. And
about this time Gualo, who had been appointed Roman legate,
excommunicated Lewis and all who held with him ; and by
this means a large number of the English were turned away
from Lewis, and the strength of his following was much
reduced. On this account it began to be mooted whether he
should not return to France ; and at length, with a gift of
money for the charges of his journey amounting to one thousand pounds sterling, peacefully, and attended by a large
company of nobles, he reached the sea. Henry the Third
accordingly reigned in England in peace after the death of
John, and he took to wife Eleanor, daughter of the count of
Provence. Thereafter, in the forty-third year of his reign,

John the Eng-
lish king is
poisoned.

Lewis, son of
Philip, is called
to the throne.

Henry is set up
to oppose him.

---

[1] St. Matt. xviii. 17.

[2] According to Spotiswood, p. 441, their first house was at Edinburgh, founded
in 1230 on the site of what is now Blackfriars Street.

Henry and the chief men of his kingdom passed some law at
Oxford—what this law was I have not discovered [1]— and to the
observance thereof the king as well as the nobles bound themselves by a solemn oath. But the king, at the instance of his
firstborn son Edward, and of Richard his brother, earl of
Cornwall, sent to Rome to obtain a release from the oath by
which he had bound himself. On this account a war began
between the king and his nobles, and in a battle fought at
Lewes in the forty-eighth year of his reign, the king, as well
as the foresaid Edward and Richard, was taken prisoner.

Edward is taken prisoner, but makes his escape.

But Edward, the king's son, broke out of prison and escaped.
Simon de Montfort, earl of Leicester, had him afterwards in
charge at Hertford, and he then made his way to the princes
of the Marches, from whom he had a kind reception. Three
months after this, that is, in August, Edward defeated Simon
de Montfort at Kenilworth, and the partisans of the said
Simon, who in that battle lost his life, were banished from the
kingdom. But, following the counsel of Othobona, the legate,
and the nobles, they were reinstated in their lands from which
they had been expelled; and thus the whole kingdom was
again at peace. Afterward, in the fifty-fifth year of Henry's

Englishmen go to the Holy Land.

reign, some English nobles went to the Holy Land : Edward
to wit, brother [2] of the king, John Vessi, Thomas Clare, Roger
Clifford, Othes Graunston, Robert Bruce, John Verdon. In
that same year died the king—the year of the redemption of
the world twelve hundred and forty-two.

Alexander Hales.

In the days of this king, Alexander Hales, an Englishman
of the Minorite order, the teacher in theology of the Blessed
Bonaventure and Saint Thomas Aquinas, wrote a work, in four
divisions, of great merit ; he was advanced in years, so they say,
before he put on the habit of the Minorites, and of that order
he was the first theological doctor. He was buried in the
convent of the Minorites at Paris, and died in the year of our
Lord one thousand two hundred and fifty [3].

---

[1] 'The Provisions of Oxford', passed in 1258.

[2] For 'brother' read 'son'.

[3] Alexander Hales became a Franciscan in 1228 and died in 1245. See
Monumenta Franciscana (ed. Brewer), pp. 542, 627. St. Francis was afraid of
the introduction of a love of learning into his Order, and on that account—so it
is said—he was not well pleased at the accession of this 'irrefragable' doctor.

Of this Henry Merlin the seer is said to have sung, when he foretold that there would go forth from Winchester, in the year one thousand two hundred and seventy, an English king, who should be a man of truth-speaking lips and sanctity of life, who likewise should be at peace for the greater part of his reign. All which they expound of this Henry, who built at London the monastery of Saint Peter. Simon de Montfort, of whom I have spoken, was born in France. One part of the prediction, however, is interpreted of Edward the son of Henry [1].

CHAP. IX.—*Of Edward, son of Henry the Englishman, his war with the Welsh and his victory over them ; likewise of the expulsion of the Jews.*

EDWARD, who succeeded his father Henry, was a man most   Edward. ambitious of warlike renown. His accession was welcomed with rejoicing by all the English. Edward invaded Wales, and took prisoner the prince of that country, one Llewellyn [2], Llewellyn. whom he kept always near him. He forced this man to swear fealty to himself, and twice each year to attend the parliament at London. But when Llewellyn began to enjoy again the liberty that he for a time had lost, he refused obedience to Edward. Therefore, when a second time he had been conquered by Edward, he came as a suppliant, begged forgiveness, and obtained it, but on this understanding: that if in the time to come he should ever fall away, he should be led to death. Not many days thereafter this very Llewellyn and his The punishment of David brother David, who had shown himself most friendly disposed the Welshman. towards Edward, rebel against Edward and his men ; but in the battle that followed Llewellyn perished. After his death his brother David summons a parliament of Wales at Denbigh ; but Edward takes him prisoner, and slays and quarters him at London. Then, at length, all the Welsh submit to Edward. The subjection of the Welsh. The Welsh, that is, the Britons, had been already conquered by Henry the son of the empress, but not so that they feared to rebel, and indeed they enjoyed some measure of freedom ;

---

[1] Edward the First became king in 1272.
[2] Orig. and F. ' Lewilinum '.

but under Edward they were forced to make an absolute submission.   When he had thus got the Welsh under his hand,
Edward passed over into Gascony, and abode there for a
space of three years.

On his return to England he found that certain men had in
his absence been unfaithful in the administration of justice,
and on them he inflicted punishment according to the desert
of each.   And since a great complaint was raised, and justly
raised, about the Jews, that, through their usurious and fraudu-
lent dealing, they drained poor people of all they possessed, he

The Jews are
driven out.

drove out of the kingdom all Hebrews—who are wont to make
their profit out of Christians, much as mice will do out of a
find of clean wheat—and in gratitude for their deliverance
every one of the common people paid to the king one penny
out of every fifteen.   Hence is plain that kings in their kingdoms, and in each aristocratic polity its leading men, would do
well to drive from their midst those obstinate Hebrews, if they
would escape the necessity of imposing heavy taxes.   This
plague of usury [1] brings in its train all kinds of mischief on
the body politic.   First of all: it gives to the prodigal an
opportunity of prodigality; to one of this sort the greatest
blessing is that he should not be able to lay his hand on
money.   Secondly, by slow degrees and all unobserved these
lenders lay up for themselves a vast amount of money.   Thirdly
—and this is worst of all—God is provoked by their sin of
usury, no less than by their obstinate observance of the ceremonial parts of the Mosaic law, which in these respects is
obsolete.   Now, for any sins that meet not with their due
punishment from the magistrate, and by which the divine
goodness is provoked, God sends His scourge upon a state.
So much is plain from the Second Book of the Kings, where
we read that the people was sorely afflicted for the sins of
David [2].   I praise, therefore, the expulsion from the kingdom

---

[1] Cf. on Major's opinion of usury his *In Quartum*, ed. 1521, fol. cviii.
On the question of usury in the middle ages Jourdain (*Excursions historiques et
philosophiques à travers le moyen âge*—'Mémoire sur les commencements de
l'économie politique dans les écoles du moyen âge') and the Rev. William
Cunningham, in his *Christian Opinion on Usury with special reference to
England*, 1884, may be consulted.   [2] 2 Sam. xxiv. 15-17.

of the Jews, for, by the introduction of the undesirable conditions of which I have spoken, they place a stumbling-block
in the way of many who are weak in the faith; just as the How harlots
chastity of other women must run some risk in the neighbour- bring ruin.
hood of public women of ill renown and a luxurious mode of
life.

CHAP. X.—*Of the monasteries that were founded by the Earl of
Fife, and something by the way about the seclusion of nuns and their
rule of life; of the marriage of King Alexander the Second, his life
and praiseworthy death, and of the destruction by fire of men and towns
in Scotland.*

In the time of that Alexander the Scot who, in obedience to Monasteries
ecclesiastical censures, restored Carlisle to the English king, founded.
Malcolm earl of Fife founded a pair of monasteries[1]: one,
for men, at Culross; the other, for women, at that northern
Berwick[2], in which parish I was born. But as I happen here
upon religious women, it will not be amiss to say one or two
things. Wherever there is a foundation for religious women, Seclusion
these ought to be shut up in the building devoted to their of nuns.
common life, so that they should not have the power of going
beyond its walls, or of association with men. Such is the custom
at Poissi[3], and among religious women who lead a life con-
formable to their calling. For that sex is more thoughtless
than the other—has a greater proclivity to intemperance of
conduct; wherefore, when they have an opportunity of association with men, they easily violate their vow of chastity, and
only rarely and with the greatest difficulty observe it. So that
they ought to be kept apart from men, as it were, by a red-hot

---

[1] 'Bina monasteria'; the expression is used more generally, I think, of the
double monastery, with one part for men and another for women, according to
Celtic custom.

[2] The charters printed in the *Carte de Northberwic*, Bann. Club, 1847, show
that this house was founded at least two generations earlier. The father and
grandfather of earl Malcolm were among its benefactors.

[3] 'Poisiacum'—in Roman times 'Pisciacum'—on the Seine, in the Ile de
France. Poissi was the birthplace of Saint Louis; it was also the scene of the
well-known Conference of 1561. It possessed several religious houses, among
them a Dominican convent of nuns.

M

line. To establish what I assert, I make use of this argument :
When a woman has taken the vow of chastity, she has made
herself liable to every obligation without whose observance
the vow of chastity cannot be kept. But it is a fact that
women who find themselves now and again in the company of
men frequently give way before the temptation to which they
are exposed ; and if there are among them a few who do not
lose their chastity, yet by far the most of them run a risk of
doing so ; and it is always for the safety of the many that
precautions must be taken. Besides : it does no harm to that
small number whose chastity is not in peril from association
with men that they should be kept in restraint, while to much
the greater number it does harm that they should not be so
kept ; therefore, for the safety of their sisters, it behoves the
stronger to make no opposition to a strict seclusion. And if
there are near kindred of the nuns, who are inclined to resist
seclusion on their account, such show themselves friends of the
body but not of the soul. For they know that women kept in
strict seclusion live more religiously than if they are allowed to
go about among men. Although this seclusion may be at
first a hard and indeed a sad experience for women who give
themselves in mature years to a religious life, yet for one
accustomed to good habits of life, for one whose natural tendency is towards what is right, it will not be difficult ; and
young girls on their admission will have no distaste to the
straitness of this rule if they have their virginity at heart ;
and many women would enter these walls devoted to the
common life with a more fervent piety, inasmuch as the female
sex with all due instruction, and separate from men, is wont
to walk the road of a more ardent devotion—that sex of which
the church speaks thus ; ' Make intercession for the devout
female sex ' [1]—in her prayer to the Virgin Mother of God. And
in conclusion I would say that both superiors and women are
bound, at the least by every consideration of what is fitting, to

---

[1] ' Ora pro populo, interveni pro clero, intercede pro devoto femineo sexu '—
from the Antiphon of Vespers and Lauds for Feasts of B.V.M. The clause is
sometimes understood as a prayer for nuns, *i.e.* for women devoted to religion,—
(thus Lord Bute, in his translation of the Breviary, renders it ' make intercession
for all women vowed to God ')—but Major evidently understands devoutness
as a characteristic of the sex. Cf. his expressions in *In Quartum*, 2d qu. of the
33d distinction.

give effectual assent to this ordinance and adopt it as their
own. But whether they should be bound in such fashion that
the breach of the ordinance should be reckoned a sin, and its
observance a thing of absolute obligation—this must wise men
carefully consider ; for the affirmative will perhaps be found
the truer answer, as the argument which I have just made use
of seems indeed to suggest. And certain it is that this is the
safer course.

But perchance you will object, that on their entrance on this An objection.
life they did not intend to bind themselves to this ; and that
no one, unless of his own free will, can be bound to an obligation that concerns himself alone : *Igitur.* The objection is The answer.
a frivolous one, and can be repelled with ease. For under this
rule a vow is made of chastity, obedience, and poverty. Now,
it is not enough to live, so far as mere existence is concerned,
in the house, if all the essentials of its rule are to be infringed ;
as if forsooth the mere entrance to such a house and living
there could be pleaded as an excuse for the stain of sin. Far
better would it be that women and men should marry in the
Lord, than that they became members of a community of evil-
livers, of whose reformation no near hope can be discerned.
To call the Psalmist as my witness ; ' With the froward thou
wilt show thyself froward ' [1]. I have not written what I have
now put down because I think these nuns to be of worse disposition than the rest of women who do not live in seclusion,
for what I say has application to all ; but here I would give
this kindly counsel by the way to the sisters whose lives are
spent in my old neighbourhood [2].

But to return to our historical narrative. Alexander took The wife of
to wife the sister of English Henry in the year twelve hundred Alexander.
and twenty. About two years thereafter the bishop of Caith- A bishop is
ness, when he was making demand of the tithes and church burnt.
dues from his own people, was by them burnt to death in his
own kitchen. And inasmuch as John, earl of Caithness, the
bishop's neighbour, had failed to come to the help of the latter

---

[1] Ps. xviii. 26. In the Vulgate Ps. xvii. 27 : ' Cum perverso perverteris '.

[2] There is no record of any prioress by name between 1477 and 1523. This
renders it not unlikely that there had been some trouble in the community at the
time when Major knew it best ; and his delicacy in avoiding direct reference to
this incident is noteworthy.

when he prayed him to do so, Alexander took from him a large
part of his earldom, and much of his moveable property he
bestowed upon the church ; last of all was this earl too slain
by his own people in the seventh year after the perpetration of
his crime.   In the third year after his marriage, Alexander
was moved by his devotion to Saint Thomas to make a journey
to Canterbury, and when he had tarried some time with English
Henry, and treated with him concerning the peace of their
kingdoms, he returned in safety to his own people.

Gilloschop.   Fourteen years afterward a certain Scot, by name Gilloschop[1],
invaded Moray, and set fire to Inverness ; him the earl of
Buchan, guardian and justiciar of Scotland, put to death, and
with him two of his sons.   Their heads he sent to Alexander.

Balmerino.   Two years after this the convent of Balmerino was founded by
Alexander and his mother, Emergarda, in honour of Saint
Edward ; and in the following year Alexander founded the

Death of Alan   monastery of Pluscardin. In the same year died, at Dundrennan,
of Galloway.   Alan, son of Rotholand of Galloway, who was constable of
Scotland, and for his heirs he had three daughters.   Of these,
the first was married to Roger, earl of Winton ; the second to
John Balliol ; the third to the earl of Albemarle ; and thus
Galloway was divided into three parts, each falling to a woman ;
whereat the men of Galloway were wroth, and chose for their
leader Thomas, the bastard son of Alan, and laid waste the
country on their borders.   But Thomas suffered an utter
defeat at the hands of the king, and as a suppliant begged for
pardon.   The king commanded that he should be taken to
Maidens' Castle [2] at Edinburgh.   In the same year Alexander
gave Marjory in marriage to the earl of Pembroke, marshal
of England.   A short time after this the queen of Scotland,
—she was Henry's sister—made a pilgrimage to Canterbury,
and on her return died at London.   Now, as Alexander

The second   had no issue by this lady, two years afterwards he took a
wife of   second wife, Mary, daughter of Ingelram de Couchi[3], and by
Alexander.   her had a son, Alexander by name.

Some three years after this, when Alexander, with a great

---

[1] Generally 'Gillescop'.   [2] See *ante*, p. 15.
[3] Enguerrand de Couci—whose family motto was—

> Roi ne suis, ne Prince aussi ;
> J^e suis le sieur de Couci.

company of nobles, was at Haddington, Patrick earl of Athole, Patrick is burnt to death.
a young man of happiest promise, was burnt to death in a
house where he was sleeping. The crime was attributed to
the Bissets, who had pursued the earl with deadly hatred. His
heirs, therefore, and his next of kin, fiercely attacked William
Bisset, the head of that family; but by the consent of the
nobles Bisset's lands were confiscated to the king, and the
life of every member of his family was spared, on the condition that they all should leave the kingdom.

In the following year several towns in Scotland—by what Towns are burnt.
means is not known—were burnt to ashes; such as Haddington,
Roxburgh, Lanark, Stirling, Perth, Forfar, Montrose, and, the
largest of them all, Aberdeen. At the first look of the thing,
the origin of these conflagrations seems strange enough. Norwich in England, a very large city, succumbed twice or thrice
to the same fate[1]. It may be that they were sent as a divine
punishment for sin, or that they were the work of evil-disposed
persons bent on mischief. For when we consider that all these
towns are situated by the sea, or in the neighbourhood of rivers,
it is impossible to take refuge in the theory that their destruction was caused by veins of sulphur in the earth.

Further, in the one thousand and two hundred and ninth[2] Death of Alexander.
year from the Virgin's travail, Alexander, in the eight-and-thir-
tieth year of his reign, went that road by which all flesh must
travel, and was buried at Melrose. Sixteen and a half years
was his age when he was anointed king; a man he was worthy
to be a king; piously disposed to churchmen and to the poor;
good men he befriended, bad men he had in abhorrence; with
an equal balance he dealt justice to all; wherefore it admits
of no manner of doubt that at the hand of God, the absolutely
just, he received his great reward. Full of danger is the life
of kings, and when a king has followed after righteousness, his
merit in the eyes of God is great indeed. How difficult are What is meri-torious in princes.
virtue and art you shall see in the second book of the *Ethics*[3],
and what more difficult than to govern aright a great state,
and most of all a northern state, which has been used to no
restraints? Indeed, this man is worthy of all praise. With

---

[1] In 1463 and 1509. The roof of the cathedral was destroyed in the fire of
1509.   [2] This should be 'forty-ninth.'   [3] Arist. *Eth. Nic.* ii. 4.

the English king he had no dealings that were not peaceable. It is the part of wisdom in Scottish kings to cherish peace with their neighbours. Of the possessions bequeathed to him by his immediate ancestors he lost nothing, and his reign was marked from first to last by the observance of a most scrupulous justice toward his subjects. I may compare this man then, using no unfairness to others, with the most illustrious kings.

CHAP. XI.—*Of Alexander the Third, king of Scotland, and the dispute that took place in the matter of his coronation; of Egyptian days; of free will; and of the genealogy of the Scottish kings.*

Alexander the Third.

ON the death of Alexander the Second, his son, the third Alexander, then a boy of eight years, was appointed to be king. But in the matter of his coronation there arose a dispute among the nobility of the kingdom; for some said that it behoved him first of all to be made a knight, or soldier, and thereafter to assume the ensigns of royalty, while others said just the opposite. Yet a third party was found which denied both these contentions, and claimed that on that day nothing ought to be done, because the same was an unlucky and Egyptian day [1]. Now, when the aged Walter Cumming, earl of Menteith, saw how matters stood, he, remembering that of the poet—

Et nocet et nocuit semper differre paratis,

and willing to prevent all risk of dissension among the magnates, used with them this argument towards the maintenance of peace, saying that in a kingly polity the headless body must

---

[1] One explanation of the fact that days of ill omen,—on which it was considered undesirable to begin any undertaking, and even to be bled,—were called 'Egyptian' days may be found in lines 5, 6, of 'Versus de diebus Ægyptiacis' (*Poetae Latini Minores*, ed. Baehrens, vol. v. p. 354), quoted by Mr. Emil Thewrewk de Ponor in the *Journal of the Gypsy Lore Society*, vol. i. p. 372 :—

    Si tenebrae Ægyptus Græco sermone vocantur,
    Inde dies mortis tenebrosos iure vocamus.

But it seems more probable that the appellation had its origin simply in the ascription to the old Egyptians of all mathematical and astrological science, an explanation which has the support of Mommsen, *Corpus Inscr. Lat.*, vol. i. p. 374. The Egyptian days were, according to the Codex Paris. N. 1338, January 1 and 25, February 4 and 26, March 1 and 28, April 10 and 20, May 3 and 25, June 10 and 16, July 13 and 22, August 1 and 30, September 3 and 21, October 3 and 31, November 5 and 28, December 12 and 15. For the literature of the subject Mr. de Ponor's and M. P. Bataillard's notes *in loco* should be consulted.

ever sway to and fro, like an oarless boat upon a stormy sea,
and so got them to consent that the coronation should take
place on the following day.

For his view of the case I will allow myself to state certain Propositions in
propositions. Of these the first is this : A precedent military favour of the
service is nowise essential for the constitution of a true king ; the king.
for these ceremonies of a soldier's service and of the anointing
of a king are of human institution, and imposed as it were
from a feeling of their propriety. Therefore one of them
may be observed without the other. My second proposition
is this : There is no Egyptian day more unlucky for the Of Egyptian
kingly coronation than another. The skiey influences exert days.
no constraining power on a man's free will, which is altogether unmaterial ; and a man who by his own wish and
in the exercise of his reason has been crowned and anointed
upon one day may do as well as if this had happened on
another. In the matter of good luck ask for nothing ; but
ask for a prudent mind, and that every act of your will
may be regulated by wisdom, and then you shall do well.
Though evils may befall a man in the way of punishment,
as it were by chance, I do not for all that deny that the
skiey influences and the changes of the seasons exert a power,
and that a great one, upon seeds, and trees, and animals not
endowed with reason. For it is of much moment to plant
trees and to prune them at full moon and new moon, and to
apply the knife or drugs to the human body as indicated by
the signs of the heavenly system, and at other times [1]. And
though the heavenly influences should incline a man to sensu-
ality, these yet have no binding power upon his choice ; and if
even his wish should take such a direction, it is easy to oppose
the impulse upon reason shown ; and a man has the power so
to accustom himself to resist the sensual impulse, as much in
thought and wish as in the sensual act, that it shall become
more difficult for him to oppose the habit of resistance than

---

[1] ' Et membra corporis in signis prohibitis [? praehibitis] respondentibus ferro
ac medicina, et alio tempore attingere.' Cf. the description of the ' Doctour of
Phisik ' in Chaucer's *Prologue*—ll. 411-413 :

> In al this world was ther non him lyk
> To speke of phisik and of surgerye ;
> For he was groundud in astronomye.

to yield to the sensual impulse.   This is plain in the case
of the brutes, and in those men the evil conditions of whose
birth have been overcome by a virtuous training.   The parental
inheritance of blood, what a man eats, and what he drinks,
have far more bearing upon his impulses than the influence of
the stars [1]. Whence it comes that, albeit we have not the power
to foretell, in human fashion, the course ·of wars among
princes, yet, understanding the secret designs of princes,
and making conjecture as to the sources whence wars may
spring, we may be able to deceive the ignorant vulgar by
telling them that our knowledge has been gained by the
practice of some such art.   But this is the vanity of superstitious and ambitious persons.

Coronation of
Alexander.

King Alexander then, mere boy as he was, seated under a
canopy on the stone chair in the cathedral, and clothed in
costly robes, was anointed by the archbishop of St. Andrews.
And lo! a certain Scot of the mountains, such as they call a
Wild Scot, hoary with age, then appears in presence of the
nobles, and in these words, spoken in his native tongue,
salutes king Alexander: Benach de Re Albin Alexander, mak

---

1 M. Charles Jourdain has pointed out in his essay on Nicolas Oresme and
the astrologers of the Court of Charles the Fifth of France, 1364-1380 (*Excursions Historiques*, p. 562) that the teaching of Aristotle in the twelfth book
of his *Metaphysica* as to the action of ͵the stars (which were supposed to be
intermediaries between God and inferior beings, and for these beings the immediate principle of all life and action) contributed largely in the middle ages
to the acceptance of judicial astrology.   The long struggle of Oresme (d. 1382)
in favour of a rational view was at the time without result ; and even after two
centuries we find a lawyer and historian such as Jean Bodin inclining, in his
' Republic ' (1576), to the belief that in astronomical investigation (if we only
possessed a complete record of the same from the beginning of time) would lie
our only hope of discovering a guiding principle ' to know the changes and ruins
which are to chance unto Commonweals '.   Aquinas indeed rejected the conception that human destiny depended on the stars, and, as is plain from this
expression of Major's opinion, his voice found an echo here and there in the
representatives of Christian orthodoxy.   A singular parallel to Major's view is to
be found in Barbour's *Brus* (xxxvi. 119 *sq.*), written about 150 years earlier.
As to the influence of the stars, Barbour says :

> ' Quhethir sa man inclynit be
> To vertu or to mavite,
> He may richt wele refrenyhe his will
> Outhir throu nurtur or throu skill,
> And to the contrar turn him all.'

Aristotle is then quoted as a well-known example of one whom 'his wit made
virtuous' through his refusal to follow his ' kindly [*i.e.* natural] deeds '.

Alexander, mak William, mak Henry, mak David. And thus he declared the genealogy of the king up to its first beginning, all in the Irish tongue, and not in the English spoken by us southern Scots. Turned into Latin it would run thus :—Salve *The genea-* Rex Albanorum Alexander, fili Alexandri, filii Guillelmi, filii *logical descent* *of the Scots.* Henrici, filii Davidis, filii Malcolmi, filii Duncani, filii Beatricis, filiæ Malcolmi, filii Kenath, filii Alpini, filii Ethachi, filii Ethafind, filii Echdachi, filii Donaldi Brek, filii Occabuid, filii Edaim, filii Gobram, filii Dovengard, filii Fergusii magni, filii Erth, filii Echeach Munremoire, filii Engusafith, filii Fechelmeth Asslingith, filii Enegussa Buchyn, filii Fechelmeth Romaich, filii Senchormach, filii Kruithlind, filii Findachar, filii Akirkirre, filii Ecchach Audoch, filii Fiachrach Catinall, filii Echad Ried, filii Coner, filii Mogolama, filii Lugtagh Etholach, filii Corbre Crumgring, filii Darediomore, filii Corbre Findmor, filii Coneremore, filii Etherskeol, filii Ewan, filii Ellela, filii Jair, filii Dechath, filii Sin, filii Rosin, filii Ther, filii Rether, filii Rowen, filii Dearndil, filii Mane, filii Fergusii primi Scotorum Regis in Albania. Now this Fergus was in truth son of Feredech, though by some, from the mistake of a scribe, he is called son of Ferechar (the words differ but little in sound). Perhaps the difficulty of pronunciation led him to make the change in the name. Then, man by man, without a break, this said Wild Scot recounted the said genealogy, until he arrived at the first Irish Scot who, setting out from the Ebro, a river of the Spains, was the first to set foot in Ireland.

CHAP. XII.—*Of the translation of the remains of Saint Margaret of England and Malcolm, king of the Scots ; of the marriage of Alexander and the dispensation that was granted him thereanent. Of the punishment inflicted upon vagabonds and Jews, and other events of his reign.*

In the following year, Alexander and his mother, with the *Translation of* prelates of the Church, assembled at Dunfermline for the trans- *the remains of* *Saint Margaret.* lation of the remains of queen Margaret ; and when these were once raised, a most sweet fragrance filled the whole church. But while the remains were being carried with all due honour to the monument which marked the resting-place of her husband Malcolm, the bearers found themselves able by no means to

go further, until certain wise men gave them this counsel, to
disinter likewise the bones of Malcolm; and when the saintly
bones were again united either to either, they were carried
without difficulty to the appointed place, where, with due
adornment of gold and precious stones, they remain to this
day[1].

Peace and
union by mar-
riage with Eng-
land renewed. In the following year the chief men of the kingdom sent to
English Henry, to gain from him a renewal of the treaty of
peace, and to ask his daughter in marriage for king Alexander.
Henry granted all their requests, and thus Alexander had to
wife Margaret, daughter of the king of England. The consanguinity that here existed made no stumbling-block, inas-
Dispensation in
respect of near-
ness of kin. much as the Roman pontiff can, for urgent cause, grant a
dispensation in the case of any kinship by blood or marriage
which is not repugnant to the law of nature. No persons,
indeed, are forbidden to intermarry except such as are enumerated in the eighteenth chapter of Leviticus; and there can
be no more urgent cause for dispensation than is afforded by
the establishment of a settled peace between neighbouring and
hostile kingdoms ever ready, like those in question, to rush to
arms[2].

Robbers are
punished. A short time hereafter, from a careless administration of
justice, there arose a grave disturbance, stirred up by evil-
disposed and corrupt counsellors of the king. When this
came to the knowledge of Henry of England, he proceeded
forthwith to Wark, an English castle close to the Scottish
borders, put away from the king those evil advisers, replaced
them with a better sort, and made certain enactments of a
wholesome character for the better conduct of the Scots. And
his action in this matter gained for him no little praise among
the Scots; for he was now an old man, and, disregarding the
infirmities of age, had undertaken a long and toilsome journey.

The Jews are
tortured. In the same year, at Lincoln, once a large city of England,
but now of no great importance[3], Henry punished with death
a number of Jews, because they had crucified a Christian boy,
Hugh by name, and had made an effigy of the mother of

---

[1] Malcolm Canmore, when he had met his death at Alnwick in 1093, was
buried obscurely at Tynemouth. It was twenty years later that his body was
brought to Dunfermline.

[2] Cf. Bk. I. ch. vi. p. 29.   [3] Cf. Bk. I. ch. v. p. 22, note [1].

Christ[1]. But[2] not many days after, Walter Cumming, earl of New robbers. Menteith, and his fellow-conspirators, though often summoned to compear before king Alexander and his tutors, still failed to do so. They feared to face the assize or council of the realm. And not only did Walter, the foresaid earl, and his accomplices, perpetrate this act of disobedience, but, along with Alexander earl of Buchan, William earl of Mar, John Cumming, Hugh Abernethy, and a number of their following, he seized king Alexander at Kinross by night, while he slept, and shamelessly carried him, in negligence of every form of courtesy, to Stirling. These men then went on to maltreat and oppress by all means they could the former ministers of the king. For when the administration of justice is once allowed to grow slack, the stronger aim at the ruin of the weaker, and stop at nothing ; so that then indeed that word of the wise man is verified to the full, — ' Woe to the land whose king breaks bread in the morning'[3] ; for in the childhood of a king the chief men impudently try to carry all at their own will and pleasure. In acting thus they not only commit a sin ; their conduct is at the same time most imprudent ; for often, when the king comes to mature years, he punishes those princes for the crimes they committed in his youth. But, in the same year, the very doer and first contriver of this deed of shame came to his end by poison ; nor did his wife escape the suspicion of having compassed his death. This woman, holding the Scottish nobility in scorn, married an Englishman of low birth, by name John Russel ; and on this account she was, with her husband, ignominiously proscribed. But though this proscription of the clan Cumming was well deserved, it was not then and there carried out, owing to the

---

[1] Chaucer mentions the murder in the end of the Prioress's Tale :—

> O yonge Hugh of Lyncoln ; slayn also
> With cursed Jews (as it is notable,
> For it nys but a litel while ago).

Cf. *Hughes de Lincoln: Recueil de ballades anglo-normandes et écossaises relatives au meurtre de cet enfant.* Publié, avec une introduction et des notes, par Fr. Michel. 1834.

[2] ' Sed non multis, etc.' The ' sed ' probably refers to the ' aliqua statuta salubria pro Scotorum moribus ' of the end of the last paragraph.

[3] Ecclesiastes x. 16 : ' Vae tibi terra, cujus rex puer est, et cujus principes mane comedunt.' The condition of his own country, whose king was at the time a boy six years of age, was no doubt in Major's mind ; and it would seem to be by a misprint that the most relevant part of the verse is omitted.

The noble
family and
faction of the
Cummings.
strength and numbers of that family. The clan Cumming
counted among its members at that time two-and-thirty
knights, without reckoning its nobles. Both kingdoms of
Britain abound in knights. These knights always wear gilded
spurs, and it is ever counted among them the height of
disgrace to fly from the battle-field; the poorest of them
have ten or twelve stout horsemen dependent on them. In
Britain, following herein the French custom, boy-servants are
not in use; their place is ever taken by bearded men fully
armed. The family of Cumming was thus over-powerful with
its nobles and knights—powerful to such a pitch that in my
opinion it has not its like in Britain at the present day. This
condition made rather for the ruin of the family than for its
advantage, for it needs much virtue to bear prosperity.

Birth of
Margaret.
In the year of the Lord twelve hundred and fifty-seven, and
in the thirteenth year [1] of Alexander's reign, there was born to
him a daughter, Margaret by name. And in the same year
Discovery of
a cross.
there was discovered at Peebles a very beautiful and ancient
cross, for which Alexander showed his pious feeling by ordering
that a church should there be built. That year, too, witnessed
The Carmelites
arrive in Scot-
land.
the arrival in Scotland of the friars of Mount Carmel, on whom
Richard bishop of Dunkeld bestowed a chapel near Perth,
at Tullilum [2], and richly endowed the same. There it was that
the Carmelite Order had its first planting. Thereafter, in the
Birth of
Alexander.
twentieth year of his reign, Alexander had a son born to him
at Jedburgh, and the child was named after his father.

In the following year the earl of Carrick died, not in-
gloriously, on an expedition to the Holy Land. He left as his
Martha of
Carriek.
heir an only daughter, whose name was Martha. This Martha,
when she had one day gone forth to take her pleasure in the
chase, chanced to meet a man of noble birth and comely to look
on, in the flower of his age, Robert Bruce. She took him with
her, though he was somewhat loath to go, to her castle of
Turnberry, and there she contracted with him a clandestine
marriage [3]. The thing mightily displeased king Alexander
when he came to hear of it, and he had the design to dis-
inherit the countess; but afterward he changed his mind, and

---

[1] The 13th year was 1262, not 1257.   [2] Founded in 1262.
[3] She was widow of Adam of Kilconquhar. See *Exchequer Rolls*, vol. i. p. lx.

he left her and her husband in peace. This Robert Bruce Robert Bruce. owned the domain of Annandale in Scotland and of Cleveland in England. His father was that Robert Bruce who was surnamed the Noble; and his grandfather was the Robert Bruce who had married Isabella, the second daughter of David earl Huntingdon. In the year of our Lord one thousand two hundred and seventy-four was born Robert Bruce to the said Robert Bruce and Martha, countess of Carrick. In the following year the abbey of Sweetheart was founded by a noble Sweetheart and wealthy woman, Devorguilla, daughter to the one time monastery. Alan of Galloway. A little later the two sons of Alexander died ; so that his surviving child, Margaret, became sole heiress of the kingdom, and she was given in marriage to the king of Norway, whose name was Hangovan [1].

Further, in the year of the Lord twelve hundred and eighty-six, Alexander fell from his horse to the west of Kinghorn, Death of Alexander. broke his neck, and so died ; and his death brought in its train evil consequences for the Scots in no small measure, as will appear from what has still to be told. Here I cannot but greatly marvel why the Scots did not give the heiress of their kingdom in marriage to the English king ; but they preferred to the Englishman a king of Norway, who lived outwith the island. I will state my opinion in few words. The Scots acted, I must hold, most unwisely in the matter of this mar- The unwisdom riage. And I lay down this proposition : There was no king of marrying the whom the Scots ought to have preferred as a husband for the sole heiress of Scotland to the heiress to the king of England. And had the position been king of Nor- reversed—had it been the heiress of England for whom a hus- way. band was being sought—I hold that there could have been found no marriage for her more suitable than with the king of Scotland. For thus, and thus only, could two intensely hostile peoples, inhabitants of the same island, of which neither can conquer the other, have been brought together under one and the same king. And what although the name and kingdom of the Scots had disappeared—so too would the name and kingdom of the English no more have had a place among men—for in the place of both we should have had a king of Britain. Nor

---

[1] *i.e.* Haco. There is confusion here between Margaret, Alexander's daughter, and her child Margaret (the Maid of Norway). See pedigree, pp. 210-11.

would the Scots have aught to fear from taxes imposed by an English king. For the English king I dare to make answer, that he would have respected our ancient liberties, just as the king of Castile[1] at the present day permits to the men of Aragon the full enjoyment of their rights. And, besides, when the commonwealth is to have advantage therefrom, it is right to pay taxes to the king, as they may be called for by any particular exigence. But I take it that the Scottish nobility have an objection to the notion of the rule of a single king throughout the length and breadth of the island; and the same is true perhaps of the English nobility, since the outstanding men among them would not then dare to make face against the king when his power had grown to such a height. And yet the result would have been pregnant with advantage to them. They would have known what it is to have an equal administration of justice; no man would have been able to lay violent hands on his neighbour; their houses and families would have been secured of an undisturbed existence; never would they have known invasion from a foreign king; and if at any time they had to avenge an injury, there would have been no foe within their borders to temper with a sense of insecurity the justice of their quarrel[2].

Our chroniclers of this period tell that Thomas of Ercildoune, called Rhymer, ['hoc est Thomas Rhythmificator'], when he was sitting in the castle of Dunbar, in presence of many Scots and Englishmen, was asked by the earl of March to foretell what should happen on the following day; and that he, heaving a deep sigh, made answer—'Woe to the morrow, a day I say of dule and sorrow, which shall bring upon us before the hour of noon so great a storm that all Scotland shall grow dumb with fear.' The earl of March therefore expected that a strong wind would arise, and made sport of Thomas on their first meeting next day at breakfast; but immediately there arrived a messenger, making all speed, who declared the sudden death of the king. Our writers assure us

The prophecy of Thomas the Rhymer.

---

[1] Ferdinand of Aragon, to whom Major must refer, died in 1516. He is highly praised in the *In Quartum*, ed. 1521, 23d qu. of the 15th dist., as 'that king but lately dead, worthy to be ranked with the greatest kings, who forbade the practice of duels'.

[2] Cf. *ante*, Bk. I. ch. vii. ; Bk. IV. ch. v. ; also Bk. IV. ch. xviii.

that Thomas often foretold this thing and the other, and the common people throughout Britain give no little credence to such stories, which for the most part—and indeed they merit nothing else—I smile at. For that such persons foretold things purely contingent before they came to pass I cannot admit; and if only they use a sufficient obscurity of language, the uninstructed vulgar will twist a meaning out of it somehow in the direction that best pleases them.

This Alexander, in point of goodness, is worthy to be placed alongside his father. Four times a year it was his custom to visit the various districts of his kingdom, when he listened to the suits of the poor and held courts of justice, finding fit redress for every man according to the necessities of his case. The wife of the king of Norway, she who was daughter to the king of Scotland, and heiress of the kingdom, bore a daughter; another Margaret she was—but, along with her mother, she died. And thus there arose no little uncertainty as to the rightful heir to the Scottish throne—a condition fraught with dangers always to a kingdom, as shall be shown in the sequel from the history of the Scots and English. But I will begin with the English chroniclers; and afterward I will pass in review what the Scots chroniclers may have to contribute, and declare what I have come to hold as the truth of the whole matter.

CHAP. XIII.—*Of what took place in Britain at this time, according to the narrative of Caxton the English chronicler in the first place— with a refutation of the statements made by him; follows, in the second place, another narrative, as we find it in the Scots chroniclers.*

As to this present matter, Caxton, an English historian, gives the following account. Alexander, king of Scotland, died after Wales had been completely reduced by Edward. David, earl of Huntingdon, with his issue, ought to have succeeded to the Scottish kingdom, but the most of the nobility were opposed to this. And there was a contention even in the family of David; for he had three daughters, and Baliol had married the eldest of them, Bruce the second, and Hastings the third. These three nobles, on behalf of their wives, laid claim to the throne. When the Scottish nobility perceived the dangers that might flow from this quarrel, they chose Edward of England for their king, and put him in possession of Scotland. Whereupon Baliol, Bruce, and Hastings went to Edward, and asked him which of them was to be king. He, when he had taken counsel with the Scots and considered their chronicles[1], found that John Baliol was the lawful heir, and also that he had to render obedience[2] to the English king as his superior. Baliol then did homage to the king of England. But a short time afterward Edward made a journey to Gascony, which at that time had not been completely conquered ; and for this expedition the clergy came to his help to the amount of the half that they possessed. When John Baliol heard of this, he sent to Rome, praying to be relieved of the oath he had taken to Edward. And not long after Edward gathered a great army wherewith to march against John Baliol, and he took Berwick, the first town you come to in Scotland ; and, after that, he laid siege to the castle of Dunbar, and the Scottish force that came to the relief of the castle was destroyed—even two-and-twenty thousand of them. Amongst the Scots, however, Patrick Graham made a long and stout resistance, but fell at length, fighting to the end, and receiving but scant help from his fellows. The castle of Dunbar thus fell into the hands of the English king, along with three earls, seven barons, and eight-and-thirty knights, that were of its garrison. All these Edward sent to London. John Baliol, and some of the chief among the Scottish nobles, next went to Edward. He sent them to London, and then demanded of them what redress they proposed to make for their former crimes against him. To a man they threw themselves on his mercy, and the only oath that the king exacted from them was that they should thenceforth be faithful to him, and never afterwards bear arms against him or his. Four bishops on the part of the clergy willingly took this oath, as did also John Cumming, the earl of Stratherne, and the earl of Carrick ; and all these Edward sent back to Scotland. But it was not long before

Baliol becomes king.

Scotland, according to Caxton, becomes tributory.

What Edward did in Scotland.

---

[1] 'And kyng Edward, that was full gentyll and true, let enquyre by the cronycles of Scotlonde, whiche of them was of yᵉ eldest blode.'—Caxton, *u.s.* fol. xcii.   [2] *Parere habebat.*

the Scots began to revolt against the English king ; and John
Baliol, when he foresaw the turmoil that would arise, left
Scotland for ever.   But the Scots chose for their king a
certain William Wallace, up to this point a man with nothing William
illustrious in his origin, and he wrought much havoc on the Wallax or
English[1].   The better then to make a stand against Edward
of England, the Scots sent the archbishop of St. Andrews to
France, with the prayer that the king would send his brother
Charles into Scotland, and that so the French and the Scots
might make a joint attack upon the English ; but the French
refused the prayer of the Scots.

It was about this time that Edward sent a strong force
against the Scots under the command of Henry Percy earl of
Warenne, William Latimer[2], and Hugh Cressingham.   With a
small troop of soldiers William Wallax or Wallace met the
English army at Stirling.   At that place a fierce battle was Defeat of the
fought, in which Hugh Cressingham and many of the English English.
lost their lives.   When Edward hears of this disaster, he gets
a large army together, and, entering Scotland on the eve of
the feast of Saint Magdalen's, harries the country as he goes.
He met the Scots on Saint Magdalen's day, and at Falkirk a
battle was fought in which there fell thirty thousand of the
Scots, and of the English as many as eighteen thousand. Great loss on
Among the latter was Frere Bryan Jay[3], a knight and a notable both sides.
warrior too, who had given chase to William Wallace when
he saw the Scot hastening from the field ; but William Wallace
was on the look-out for him, and slew him.   The result of this
battle was that Edward had all Scotland at his will.

Some time after this Edward married the sister of Philip of
France, and again enters Scotland.   This time no single Scot,
with the exception of William Wallace, questions his authority.
But, in the three-and-twentieth year of Edward's reign, this The punish-
perfidious traitor falls into the hands of the English king, ment inflicted
is carried to London, dragged at horses' tails, and in the end

---

[1] 'Wherfore yᵉ Scottes chose vnto theyr kyng Willyam Waleys a rybaud
and an harlot, comen vp of nought, and to englysshmen did moche harme.'—
Caxton, u.s. fol. xciv.
[2] Orig. 'Lawium'; Caxton 'Latomer'.
[3] Orig. 'Frery Bryansay'; F. 'Frery Bryan Jay'; Caxton 'Frere Brian Jay'.

quartered.   Further, his head was mounted upon a spear and
exposed to the view of all men on London bridge.

There then you have English Caxton's story, which we have
turned from English into Latin.   It cannot be said that the
man has spared his anvil, but, with all his forging, the result is
not improbabilities merely, but a mass of incoherencies as well.

For the assertion that the Scots chose, sought, or accepted two
kings, one as superior, the other as subject to him, is wanting
in every element of likelihood.   If the Scots desired that
Edward the First should be their king, to what purpose summon
him as judge among the three claimants of the crown ?   And
further, it is of all things the most improbable that well-born
Scots should choose for their king a man who was a plebeian
and quite unknown ; for sooner than that would they have
chosen one of the three claimants, or one of their own nobles.

Leaving Caxton, then, and his silly fabrications out of the
question, I shall proceed to place the history of the Scots in its
true light.   When Edward had gained possession of the castle
of Dunbar, he marched against John Baliol, who was then at
Forfar.   There John Cumming, lord of Strathbogy, and John
Baliol met him, and the latter surrendered to the English king
every claim that he had to Scotland.   King Edward then sent
John Baliol to London along with his son Edward.   Keeping
Edward in prison, he sends John Baliol into Scotland.   But
the Scots would have none of him, for they knew him not only
to be a man averse from war, but a coward.   Then, when
John Baliol saw that he was despised in his own country,
he went to France, that he might there lead a quiet and private
life [1].   After his departure the Scots choose twelve guardians,
and send into England John Cumming, earl of Buchan, with
instructions to do any harm he could to a nation that his
countrymen had so much reason to hate.   But the English were
in strong force in the western parts of Scotland, as in Ayr and
the district round about, and held various well-fortified castles
with the help of no small following of the Scots.   The Scots
they treated with inhuman cruelty.   This conduct of theirs

---

[1] ' ut quiete vivat et private '; a favourite phrase.   Cf. ch. xiv. ad fin. ' quieti
et vitae privatae me accommodabo '.

stirred the indignation of most of the Scots, and in a signal
manner of Wallace, and whenever they found themselves in a
remoter part in greater numbers than the English they attacked
them.　Our native chroniclers, who have written in the English
tongue, extol this William Wallace to the skies, and relate of William
him that he had never need to strike a second blow.　For so Wallax, or
great was his bodily strength, as well as his courage, that no Wallace.
armour could stand against his sword.　This and much else,
that I confess I reckon among the things that cannot at least
be proved, I will pass over[1].　I will now proceed to examine
the narrative of those historians who have written in Latin, so
far at least as the result of their labours is capable of being
tested.

CHAP. XIV.—*A truer version of the deeds of William Wallace or
Wallax.*

THIS William was sprung from one of the smaller gentle William
families only in the land of Kyle near to Ayr, where, too, his Wallace;
surname is one of the commonest.　He was the second son,—his or'g'n a'd
elder brother was a knight,—and he was robust of body, with courage.
limbs strong and firmly knit, his natural colour somewhat
swarthy, of a complexion partly choleric, partly melancholy; his
temper, therefore, quick and haughty.　Wise and prudent he
was, and marked throughout his life by a loftiness of aim which
gives him a place, in my opinion, second to none in his day and
generation.　If it be said that Robert Bruce was his superior
in military genius, I do not care to range myself on the other
side; but let it be borne in mind that he flourished at a later
date than William.　William had no other instructors in warfare
than experience and his own genius.　When he happened upon
one of the English, who were at that time in great force in
Scotland, and most of all at Ayr, he slew him.　He was attacked

---

[1] In his *In Quartum Sententiarum*, fol. lxxxvi., ed. 1530, Major couples
Wallace with Achilles : ' The poets have fabled that Achilles was brought up on
the muscles of oxen, and not on partridges or pheasants.　And William Wallace,
as our chroniclers have it, used to call for that part of oxen which they call the
nine-plies, and not for partridges or pheasants.'　There is a part of beef called
in Scotland ' the nine holes ' at the present day.

by them many times, but two or even three Englishmen were
scarce able to make stand against him,—such was his bodily
strength, such also the quickness of his understanding, and his
indomitable courage. As time went on, his fame spread ever
the wider, and many of the Scots found with him an asylum
and a sure defence. He set fire by night to the barns of Ayr,
in which were some of the chief men amongst the English, and

those who escaped the flames fell by his sword. This exploit
won for him so much renown that some amongst his country's
nobles, and of higher birth than his own, betook themselves to
him. Among these were two whose names were widely known
—John Graham, knight, and Robert Boyd, both of them men
of tried courage. At length, when he had won important
victories over the enemy, he was hailed as regent by most of the
Scots, with the universal acclamation of the common people.

In the year of the Lord twelve hundred and ninety-seven
he set himself to raze to the ground those castles which the
English held on Scottish soil. There was no extreme of cold or
heat, of hunger or thirst, that he could not bear. Like Hannibal
or Ulysses he understood to draw up an army in order of
battle, while like another Telamonian Ajax he could carry on
the fight in open field ; so that he dreaded not with a handful
of men to scatter and put to open rout the best equipped
battalions of the English. His hatred of the English was as a
spur that allowed him no rest from fighting. The English,
therefore, and along with them the Scottish nobles, pursued
him with a deadly hatred, inasmuch as his conspicuous valour
threw their own deeds into the shade. Yet did some of the
nobles, as well as all the common people, cast in their lot
with him.

When Edward of England heard of all that William
Wallace was doing, he determined to crush him, and sent
a large army against him into Scotland, under Hugh Cas-
singham (whom the English historians call Cressinhame).
When Wallace came to hear of this, he postponed for a time
the siege of the castle of Dundee, which was then his chief
business, that he might bring every obstacle to the English

advance. He attacked them therefore near the bridge over
the Forth at Stirling in a fiercely contested battle. He slew

in fight the English leader, put his troops to the rout, and returned to his besieging of the castle of Dundee, which forthwith surrendered to him. With such a courage did he carry himself, and did his work too in so short space of time, that he soon left not a single Englishman in Scotland, nor yet a Scot who had shown favour to the English. The mass of dead bodies, meanwhile, left upon the field tainted the air, as these will always do, and bred a terrible pestilence, which was followed by a rise in the price of corn. Wallace designed therefore to have his winter quarters in England, and there to keep a large army afoot at English charges. Nor did his conscience herein prick him one whit ; for it was plain abundantly that the Scots had been sore oppressed by the English, that they had suffered great losses at the hands of an enemy from whom they could not, in ordinary course of law, look for restitution—and they gave their minds therefore to meting out some sort of justice to themselves. Wallace sent to the furthest bounds of Scotland to increase as best he might the numbers of his soldiery ; and the Aberdonians, when they showed an inclination to resist his call, he punished with the utmost severity. Others, fearing a like punishment, flocked to him in troops. Then, when he had gathered a large army together, on the feast of All Saints he set out to invade England. One part of his army consisted of disciplined soldiers who had seen much service ; the rest was drawn from the common people, with no attempt at order. It had a firm footing in England on the feast of the Purification of the Virgin Mother of Christ; for though he had been attacked by the English many times both by night and by day, not once—such were his unfailing vigilance and his courage—had he suffered defeat. At length, after three months of such a life as this, he led home his army, rich in the fortunes of war and laden with English spoil. During all that time his army had suffered no disaster. Towards unwarlike persons, such as women and children, towards all who claimed his mercy, he showed himself humane ; the proud and all who offered resistance he knew well to curb.

Soon after this English Edward sent an embassy to Wallace, whose instruction was to tell him that he would not have dared to invade England had England's king been at home. This

Pestilence and famine in Scotland.

filled Wallace with wrath, and he promised the ambassadors
that come next Easter he would invade England, and offer
battle to king Edward in his own kingdom.   He soon got
together an army by the time that he had promised, some
thirty thousand strong.   He offered his men no pay, but each
went to war at his own charges.   King Edward, then, with a
strong army, and Wallace meet face to face at Stanmore [1].
Meanwhile the armies are being arrayed in order of battle,
but Edward, yielding to the advice of his counsellors, refused
the fight.   When the Scottish soldiery became aware of this,
they aimed at taking Edward as he fled ; but the far-seeing
judgment of Wallace prevented this.   He commanded them
to keep their ranks, for he feared that when they were scattered
in pursuit the army of Edward, in its orderly retreat, might
turn and overcome them.   For he said [2] that for him it would
be glory enough to have forced a proud and powerful king to
quit the field in his own kingdom.   Wallace, therefore, withdrew his army, and led it back to Scotland scatheless.   Further,
he deprived of their lands those Scots who had been obstinately
favourable to the English rule, and at his own pleasure conferred the same upon those who had done good service to the
Scottish commonwealth.   And such lands are still enjoyed by
men of our own day, who hold their titles from William
Wallace, then regent.   The Scottish nobles did not relish this
arrangement.   Yet were they powerless to find a remedy.
But just as the renown of William grew from day to day, so
too grew the jealousy of the nobles.   For, ' 'tis the high peaks
that the lightning strikes ' [3].   Under his glory the reputation
of those who had been accustomed to the first place seemed to
dwindle ; without their help he conducted the whole government of the realm, and with few of them was he on a familiar
footing.   Nor is this to be wondered at; for it would have
been no easy matter for Wallace and for them to take common
action on any point.   This Wallace, whom the common people
with some of the nobles followed gladly, had a lofty spirit ; and

---

[1] A barren tract between Westmoreland and Yorkshire.—Hodgson's *Northumberland*, vol. i. p. 71.

[2] Orig. and F. ' dicebant '; read ' dicebat '.

[3] 'feriunt altos fulgura montes'; in Hor. *Od.* II. x. 11, 'feriuntque summos ', etc.

born, as he was, of no illustrious house, he yet proved himself a better ruler, in the simple armour of his integrity, than any of those nobles would have been.   Now there was found in the ranks of the highborn men who hated Wallace the family of the Cummings, which we have spoken of above as one of the most powerful in the country ; but owing to the position of authority that Wallace had gained for himself, and also to his reputation in the field, none of the nobility dared to provoke him openly.   When English Edward comes to hear of the slumbering jealousies amongst the Scots, he invades Scotland with a huge army at once of Englishmen and Scots, to give battle to William Wallace ; and, as seems from every circumstance most probable, it was by the Scottish nobility that he was secretly invited to attack Wallace.   It may be that the nobility looked upon William as aiming at the royal power, and that they preferred English rule to William's.   That is a feature of nobles generally—to prefer the yoke of a superior to that of an inferior.   I fancy, too, that they aimed thereby at weakening the power at once of Edward and of William— which done, the government of the kingdom would revert to them. *Designs of the Scottish nobles.*

The English king landed at Varia Capella[1] ; and Wallace led an army thither against him.   But before the battle began the Scots quarrelled among themselves which should take the command ; and Wallace would yield the place to no single man of them.   Here I cannot approve him ; for it was his country's hour of need, and it behoved him to sink his claims in the expulsion of the common enemy of all.   For a story is told of the lord Stuart, how he likened Wallace to an owl, saying that the owl indeed was at first featherless, and so begged of every other bird a feather, which when it had obtained it swelled in its pride of plumage over the rest of birds ; and not otherwise Wallace, though all his strength was in the support of the nobles, now aimed at having dominion over them.   All this the lord Stuart is reported to have said in William's presence, while the army was arraying for battle. *Wallace's obstinacy censured.*

---

[1] *i.e.* Falkirk—supposed to be the 'kirk on the *Vallum*' or wall of Agricola. Its Gaelic name was Eglais-bhrac = ' spotted church '—latinised into Varia Capella. See Miss Blackie's *Etymological Geography*, 2d ed., p. 97.

But this made no delay in joining battle, and at the first onset
Wallace saw himself deserted by the whole faction of the
Cummings, which had seemed to favour the English king.
Not the less Wallace held his ground with unshaken courage,
and a battle was fought long and fierce. When Robert Bruce,
a Scot of undaunted courage, who aspired to the throne of
Scotland, saw how the fight was stiff and not like to be decided,
he led one division of his army which was under his command so
as to attack Wallace in the rear. For there was a longish hill
behind the Scots army, and when Bruce and his men took note
of this, they fetched a circuit unawares about the hill, and so
fell upon Wallace from behind. Thus attacked—behind, in
front, by overwhelming numbers—he still refused to fly. Two
of the chief nobles fell in that battle—the lord Stuart and
Macduff earl of Fife, likewise John Graham, knight, and a
veteran soldier[1], whom for his strenuous courage Wallace
reckoned without his match among men. In the end, when all
his munitions were spent, Wallace gave the signal for retreat,
and with the surviving remnant of his army took to flight.

There are those still living in our midst who will not suffer the
word 'flight' to be used in reference to Wallace, and will allow
only that he avoided a danger; for 'flight', they say, must ever
bear an ugly meaning. But in this they err. To attack the
attacker by waiting for him; to delay; yea, to fly—these too
are branches of fortitude; for the greatest general that ever
lived not only may fly but in a certain contingency is bound
to fly. For better it is that he should be able to keep himself
and his men in safety against a fitting moment than by
their death bring ruin quick and complete upon his country.
Wherefore Wallace was justified in seeking safety for his men
in flight. He drove his army before him as it had been a
flock of sheep, and himself the shepherd, who in his slow retreat
should keep a watchful eye upon the wolves in pursuit. Yet
one of the English—Frerus Bryangen[2] was his name, and he
was over-anxious for military glory—went ahead of his companions and followed Wallace closely. But Wallace was on
the look-out, and slew him. His death was a lesson to his
brethren to keep their ranks, and not to seek, any one of them,

Marginal notes:

The Cummings desert Wallace.

Stuart is slain.

Wallace sounds a retreat.

When a brave man may rightly fly.

Frere is slain.

---

[1] Militiae pater.   [2] *sic* Orig. and F.   Cf. p. 193, note [3].

to go ahead of his companions. Caxton asserts that the horse
of this highborn and over-combative Englishman stuck in deep
mud, and that it was then that Wallace fell upon him ; but if
he was unable to get out of the mud in the same way that
Wallace got out of it, it does not say much for his soldiering ;
and, besides, he should have been on his guard against a man
of Wallace's strength—against a man too who had Wallace's
just cause of provocation, and who did not fear to ride alone
betwixt two armies.

It is related that after this battle Robert Bruce came to
speak secretly with Wallace, and addressed him in these words : *The speech of Robert Bruce.*
' How comes it, bravest of men, that rashly daring thou dost
wage war with a so mighty king, when this king too has the
support alike of Englishmen and of Scots, and when on all sides
thou hast to fear the ill-will of thy country's nobles ? Dost
thou not see the Cummings, dost thou not see me, and most of
the other chiefs as well, all of us upon the English side ? Few
are the nobles upon thy side ; and though the lowborn people
be with thee, these are more fickle than the wind, and follow
now thy half-ruined fortunes.' I take it that Robert spoke thus,
willing to test the secret bent of Wallace, whether, perhaps,
he were aspiring to the supreme power ; well content, I must
think, however, that William lost the day. To him Wallace
made answer: ' Thy coward sloth is cause of all ; thou didst *Wallace's answer.*
lay claim to the throne, I never ; all that I have done I did
for this reason only : that I am a soldier, and that I love my
country. For I resolved to spare no strain to drive out of this
kingdom every single Englishman ; and had I not been met at
every turn by the opposition of our nobles, 'tis beyond a doubt
that I would have done it ; yea, had those noble persons only
given me to serve under me the men that till their lands, they
might themselves have stayed at home. Consider this: that
whereas I have had under me to-day scarce ten thousand men,
and these of the common people, I should have had, but for the
stumbling-blocks with which our nobles have strewed my path,
one hundred thousand simple tillers of the soil eager for the
fight. But it is to-day that I have felt the full measure in
which I am hated by the nobles ; and let me counsel thee, if
thou hast designs upon the kingdom, beware those all-powerful

Cummings. If they had given a thought to their country's
honour, whatever may have been their prejudice to me-ward,
they ought not to have yielded one step.   And even had they
vowed fidelity to the English king, they were no way bound to
keep it.   When the fulfilment of a promise would bring disgrace, it is well worth while to break it, and to treat that
determination as null and void.   For myself, I am weary of my
life ; I would rather die than live.   By the Holy Ghost I
swear, that for the future I will have naught to do with public
matters, but will devote myself to quiet and the life of a private
person.'[1]   When Bruce heard this speech, though he may not
have regretted Wallace's misfortune, yet it is said that he was
moved to tears, when he considered the strenuous courage of
the man and the grandeur of his words.

CHAP. XV.—*Of John Cumming, regent of Scotland ; of the rest of*
the feats of Wallace, and of his miserable ending, but his happy change
from this life.

John Cumming,
regent of Scot-
land.

AFTER the infliction of this defeat upon Scotland, Edward
thought that everything in that country was peaceably established, and returned to England.   After his departure the
Scots choose for their regent John Cumming and not William
Wallace.   I do not make out that Wallace held any kind of
regency save what he took upon himself; but that regency he
exercised in all uprightness of heart.   Nor was Wallace even
summoned by this regent of the Cumming faction to help him
with his advice in the conduct of the kingdom, though Cumming was fully aware of his pre-eminent worth.   He acted,
perhaps, in this manner, from a feeling that Wallace, who but a
short time before had exercised supreme power, would not readily
have taken a lower place.   But when Edward heard that the
Scots had chosen John Cumming as regent, he got together a
fresh army of thirty thousand men, and intrusted the same to
the command of Rodolph Confrey—an able man he was—with
instruction to make for Scotland.   When Confrey had come as
far as Roslin, he makes a threefold division of his army—to

---

[1] See *ante*, ch. xiii.

each division ten thousand men with its own general. When this came to the knowledge of John Cumming the regent, though he had with him but seven thousand men along with Simon Fraser, he so carried matters that he defeated one division of the English army,—and not that only, for on the self-same day, and with troops exhausted by fatigue, he twice again gave battle, and so put to the rout the whole thirty thousand of the English. When Edward learned this defeat, he collected from among the Gascons, the Irish, the English, even from the Scots who favoured the English rule, a vast army, and, entering Scotland, soon had the whole country at his feet. He spent the winter at Dunfermline, and his son, Edward of Carnarvon, brought from France, by water, a rich provision of food to Perth. Of wine of Gascony there was such plenty that it was sold, you might almost say, for nothing. For three pence, and no more, you might buy a pint of it. Before this, however, there had been a great loss of life on both sides. There was not at that time in Scotland a castle—no, nor a man, with the single exception of William Wallace—that did not own Edward as lord and master. Trusting himself to trackless mountains and inaccessible islands, and the tried affection of his friends, he escaped from the pursuit of the English king and his partisans. Edward himself could not do otherwise than admire the immoveable spirit of the man, and made known to him by a messenger bearing a flag of truce that broad lands in Scotland, and in England too, should be his, if he would but own the English rule. To all this Wallace made but one answer: That never would he yield obedience to the English king. And when Edward got this answer he studied how he might compass his destruction in another way. To any who would take him he promised the richest rewards in lands ; and after many had vainly laboured to take him, Odomar Valancy, at length, and John Menteith, a Scot by birth, and a knight who was held to be one of Wallace's most familiar friends, by a shameful stratagem seize him in the city of Glasgow, and with a great army lead him captive to England, and there, as the English chroniclers have it, they put him to death [1].

Cumming's incredible victory.

Wallace's unshaken spirit.

The betrayers of Wallace.

---

[1] Wallace was executed at Tyburn, August 24, 1305. His sentence ran that his head should be fixed to London Bridge, and his quarters sent to the towns of

Wallace's con-
duct not alto-
gether to be
approved ;
At the first glance I must here condemn Wallace for a want
of foresight, in that he did not for a time use some dissimula-
tion with Edward, even by receiving lands at his hand, that so
he might shelter himself from the designs of his foes. Yet I

yet, on the
whole, it may
be justified.
fancy that he cherished a hope of seizing an opportunity of
attacking the English, and driving them, as he had so often
done already, out of the country. For he may have thought
that a day would come when, wearied of English domination,
the Scots, not unmindful of his ancient fame among them,

An objection,
would once more flock around him. But you will say : He
ought with more prudence to have kept himself out of their

and its answer.
hands ; yet there is an ancient proverb, ' There is no enemy more
deadly than the man of your own household'; and in John
Menteith, to whose two children he had stood godfather, he
had the fullest confidence. Our chroniclers here tell a story

The heaven-
ward flight of
Wallace.
of how an English hermit was witness of several souls taking
their flight from purgatory to heaven, and how one of these
was Wallace ; and as he marvelled much how this could be,
seeing that Wallace had shed man's blood, he got for answer
that it was in a just cause, and when fighting for his country's

What is lawful
in a just war.
freedom, that he had slain others. And indeed I do not forget
that it may be lawful to fight when the cause is just ; but every
war must give occasions of excesses of all kinds and of sins.
Still, a true repentance will sift, as it were, all sins, and make
them as if they had not been. I will not insist on the point
whether in his resistance to Edward he acted aright. They
tell of Wallace that he ever had these lines in his mouth,
which he had learned as a boy from his teacher :—

> 'Tis sooth I say to thee, of all things freedom is the best.
> Never, my son, consent to live a slave.[1]

About this William Wallace our chroniclers in the English
tongue relate that he twice visited France. They tell of his hav-
New feats done
by Wallace.
ing had a sea-fight with Thomas Longueville, a French pirate,
and John Lyn, an Englishman, and of many other notable

Berwick, Newcastle, Stirling, and Perth. Fifteen shillings were paid to John
de Segrave for the carriage of his body 'ad partes Scotiae'. See *Documents
illustrative of the History of Scotland*, 1286-1306, Edin. 1870, vol. ii. p. 485.
[1] Dico tibi verum, libertas optima rerum ;
   Nunquam servili sub nexu vivito, fili.

feats of his they make mention, which I reject as false; and
my rejection of them I base, firstly, hereon, that our Latin
chroniclers relate nothing that he did of any mark after Varia
Capella[1], but give us to understand that he then went into
hiding; and, in the second place, I reject them inasmuch as
the French histories make mention of Scots of far less renown
in war than Wallace, and say scarce one word about him. I
conclude, therefore, that he never visited France. Now, should
any one of the Scots, in spite of these considerations, go on
obstinately to pin his faith to narratives of our own vernacular
speech, and raise this objection—'Either all that the chroniclers *The argument*
relate concerning him is true,—or no single part of it is true, *is refuted.*
—or part is true and part is false; now I cannot admit the
second member of the proposition; nor by parity of reasoning
can I admit the third member of the proposition in all particulars ; therefore I am forced to admit the first'—this argument *Answer to the*
I proceed to refute almost in its own words, thus: 'Either all *refutation.*
that the chroniclers of the English relate about the Scots is
agreeable to truth,—or no part of it,—or some part at least
has a basis of truth.' I imagine that you will grant the third
proposition only, and I give the objection the same turn as
before[2]. Our Latin chroniclers, who wrote not long after the
date of the event, could not be altogether silent as to this double
journey to France, and all the deeds of valour that were done
by Wallace; and the same you may take for true about the
French histories. There was one Henry, blind from his birth,
who, in the time of my childhood, fabricated a whole book
about William Wallace, and therein he wrote down in our
native rhymes—and this was a kind of composition in which he
had much skill—all that passed current among the people in
his day. I however can give but a partial credence to such
writings as these. This Henry used to recite his tales in the
households of the nobles, and thereby got the food and clothing
that he deserved. And again, not even everything that is
written in Latin has a claim to infallibility, but only to a
certain probability; for some of the writings in that language
are known to possess more, and others less, of authority. I am
reluctant nevertheless to deny absolutely, on the ground of

---

[1] *i.e.* Falkirk (see p. 199).   [2] et eundem ramum in objectione do.

such reasons as I have ventured to state, that he ever saw the
shores of France. So much then let it suffice to have briefly
said, in accordance with the demands of this present work, about
the notable deeds of William Wallace; for we have yet to tell
the story of other men not inferior in renown to him, and we
must not spend all our labour in the celebration of one man,
however lofty his distinction.

CHAP. XVI.—*Of those famous theologians Richard Middleton and
John Duns: likewise of the contest for the Scottish throne, and of the
feats of the new kings of that country.*

Richard
Middleton.

It was about this time that Richard Middleton, whom the
French call 'de Media Villa', flourished. He spent much
labour in the writing of four books of no slight merit upon
the Sentences, with Quodlibets[1]. I forget at this moment
whether he studied at Oxford or at Cambridge[2]; but he was
an English Briton. Near to him in date, only later, wrote
John Duns, that subtle doctor, who was a Scottish Briton,
for he was born at Duns, a village eight miles distant from

John Durs
Scotus.

England, and separated from my own home by seven or eight
leagues only[3]. When he was no more than a boy, but had been
already grounded in grammar, he was taken by two Scottish
Minorite friars to Oxford, for at that time there existed no
university in Scotland. By the favour of those friars he lived
in the convent of the Minorites at Oxford, and he made his
profession in the religion of the Blessed Francis. As he was
a man of the loftiest understanding and the keenest powers in
debate, his designation of 'the subtle' was fully justified. At
Oxford he made such progress that he left behind him for the
admiration of after ages a monumental work upon the *Metaphysics* and the four books of the Sentences. These writings

[1] 'Quodlibets' or 'Quotlibets', a name given to questions proposed for free
discussion in the schools of theology. Middleton's 'Quodlibets' were printed
with the commentaries on the Sentences at Venice in 1509. He wrote also on
the Epistles of St. Paul and the four Gospels.

[2] At Oxford; see *ante*, p. 23, note [1].

[3] Major's positive statement as to the birthplace of Duns Scotus may be
admitted to have some value. Scotus is also claimed as a native of Ireland
(Down), and of Northumberland (Dunstane). A monument was erected to
his memory at Cologne in 1513, with the following inscription: SCOTIA ME
GENUIT: ANGLIA ME SUSCEPIT: GALLIA ME DOCUIT: COLONIA ME TENET.

of his are commonly called the English or the Oxford work [1].
When he was afterwards summoned by the Minorites of Paris
to that city, he produced there another set of lectures on the
Sentences, more compendious than the first edition, and at the
same time more useful. These lectures we have but lately
caused to be printed with metal types [2]. In the end he went Death of the
to Cologne, and there died while still a young man. Subtle Doctor.

After the death of Alexander the Third at Kinghorn, there
arose a doubtful and indeed inexplicable question as to the Controversy as
right of succession to the kingdom. John Baliol, Robert to the right of rule in Scotland.
Bruce, and Hastings, each of them set forth his claim in law to
the kingdom of the Scots; but inasmuch as each had a large
following in Scotland, the disentanglement of the legal claim
was no easy matter. They remitted the question to Edward
the First, the same whom men call Edward Longshanks, and Edward Long-
he gave judgment in favour of John Baliol. The story goes shanks declares Baliol king.
that this John promised that he would hold the kingdom of
Scotland as from the English king. For three years then
Baliol held supreme power among the Scots; but as far as in
him lay he permitted the subjection of Scotland to the English
king, and, being otherwise of coward temper, the Scots drove
him from his place, when he passed into France, and there went
the way of all flesh. The story further goes that at the time Death of
when Edward was in Scotland, and was there carrying every Baliol.
thing at his pleasure, Robert Bruce had stirred up John Reid
Cumming—['hoc est rubrum Cumyngum]',—for his complexion
was sanguine—to lay claim to the kingdom; for the Cumming
family was among the most powerful among the Scots. Now
Cumming, inasmuch as he knew that he had no good claim to
urge in his own behalf, was reluctant to follow the counsels and
persuasions of Bruce in this matter. He went further; for he
promised his support to Bruce, who had the clearest right to
the throne, if only he would seize it for himself.

---

[1] opus Anglicanum sive Oxoniense.

[2] 'quam lecturam chalcographis imprimendam hisce diebus dedimus'. Of
this work the following editions are in the Bodleian library : (i) *Questiones
quodlibetales familiarissime reportate per Petrum Thataretum* [more properly
'Tataretum'], fol. Par. 1519 ; (ii) *Lucidissima commentaria sive (ut vocant)
reportata in quatuor libros sententiarum et quodlibeta Io. Duns Scoti*, etc., fol.
Venet. 1607. Petrus Tataretus was a Paris doctor of theology ; and by Major's
'we' (in 'dedimus') we may probably understand the theological faculty of
Paris—or that he himself had a hand in it.

Now here, between our own and the English chroniclers, I find no trifling discrepancy of statement. The English chroniclers give forth that the family of the Cummings was completely loyal to the English rule, and that for this cause it was that John Cumming met his death at the hands of Bruce. Far different is the Scottish version of the story. For our chroniclers aver that by an authentic agreement in writing between Bruce and Cumming they had promised, each the other, to take or wrest by force the kingdom out of Edward's hands, and that this secret agreement was divulged by the Cummings to the English king. Another version of the story is this: that the wife of John Cumming, without her husband's knowledge, declared the secret to the English king; while still others see reason to believe that its betrayal was due to John Cumming himself. But, however this may be, so much is certain, that when English Edward came to hear from the Cumming family of this most secret agreement, he aimed to compass the death of Robert Bruce, and would have succeeded in his endeavour had not Robert made his escape to Scotland. With all the speed he could, Robert bent his steps from London northward; and when he had reached Dumfries, which is a town no long distance from the borders, he happened on John the Red Cumming in a convent of Minorite friars; and there, and before the high altar—such was the fury of his anger—he struck John with his dagger, not thinking otherwise than that he had dealt him a mortal wound. It was about that time that William Wallace was led captive to London.

Robert, when he had thus struck down the Cumming, left the church; and thereupon two among his friends, the lord John Lindsay and the lord Roger Kirkpatrick, perceiving from the pallor of his face that somewhat had deeply moved him, asked him what then it was that he had done; and when he had declared the whole matter to them in its sequence, they asked if the Cumming's wound were mortal. To this he answered that indeed he knew not; whereat they blamed him somewhat harshly, that in a thing of such moment, and where he had to deal with a man of this condition and standing, he had left aught in doubt. Instantly they enter the sacred building, and finding the Cumming on the ground behind the high altar, they ask him whether he

thought he might yet recover. And when he had answered
yes, that indeed he thought he might yet recover from his
wound, if only they would fetch to him a skilful chirurgeon,
these men barbarously slew him. This crime it was that gained
for Robert Bruce the undying enmity of the powerful house of
Cumming. But all the same, his friends remained true to him.
He went to Scone, and there—though his action herein was by
no means without danger to himself, seeing that he had against
him the English king, the Cummings, the Baliols, the house
of Hastings, and all their followers—he assumed the royal Robert Bruce
crown. He lost no time in sending to Rome to crave absolu- is crowned.
tion from the censure of the church that followed the homicide
that had been committed in a church. But before I make the
attempt duly to celebrate the achievements of Robert Bruce, I
will strive to disentangle the intricate questions of law that are
involved in the conflicting claims of himself and his opponents.

CHAP. XVII.—*Containing many reasons in support of the claim of*
Robert Bruce ; and, in preface to these, the whole issue of Malcolm
down to the present king is given in full.

HERE it will be desirable to trace the claim of Robert Bruce Robert Bruce.
from Malcolm Canmore ; for, from what has been said above,
you will remember that there were born to Malcolm Canmore Malcolm Can-
and his wife, English Margaret, six sons and two daughters. more's issue.
Three sons there were, whom I mention only to pass them by ;
for they had no issue, and their lives were not otherwise noteworthy. Three sons in succession held the kingly power :
Edgar, Alexander, and David ; but Edgar and Alexander died
without issue. To David was born one son only, that is,
Henry earl of Huntingdon; and this Henry begot three sons,
to wit, Malcolm, William, and David; but he predeceased his
father. On the death of David, his grandson Malcolm succeeded him, ruled the Scots for twelve years, and died unmarried : to him succeeded his brother William, who was father to
Alexander the Second ; and this Alexander the Second was
father to Alexander the Third by Margaret queen of Scotland,
who was sister to king Edward. To Alexander the Third
were born two sons, but they died both of them without issue.

The third Alexander had likewise one daughter, Margaret by
name, who married the king of Norway ; and to him she bore
an only daughter, Margaret also by name, who died before
she had arrived at marriageable years.   And with this daughter
came to an end the direct succession in the line of actual
monarchs, that is, from Malcolm Canmore and his queen,
Margaret of England.

David of Hunt-
ingdon, of royal
descent, was
never king.

It remains, therefore, to retrace our steps in search of the
nearest rightful heir to the kingdom, and him we find in that
David of Huntingdon who was never king [1].   But to this David

---

[1] The subjoined table of descent will show at a glance what Major's statement is. Isabella, however, who married Robert Bruce was the second daughter
of David earl of Huntingdon, and not, as Major here says, the third daughter.
In ch. xiii. of this Book he rightly says—though without naming her—that the
third daughter of David earl of Huntingdon (*i.e.* Ada) married Hastings.   By

MALCOLM CANMORE = MARGARET OF ENGLAND.

Edgar, King,   Alexander I., King,   David I., King.   Three sons.   Three daughters.
s.p.   *s.p.*

Henry, Earl of Huntingdon
(predeceased his father).
                                         a

Malcolm IV., King.   William [the Lion], King.

Alexander II. = Margaret, sister of
Edward I. of England.

Alexander III.

Two sons,   Margaret, = King of Norway.
s.p.

Margaret,
s.p.

---

this Henry de Hastings she was mother of that Henry de Hastings who was
father to John de Hastings (competitor).   Ada and her descendants, since they
are not here mentioned by Major, are not included in the pedigree now given.

Henry de Hastings claimed that the succession should be divided between the
descendants of the three daughters as co-heiresses.   Edward the First decided
in favour of Baliol on the ground of seniority of descent as against Robert Bruce,
and dismissed the claim of Hastings, because the crown, like other titles or
honours, was indivisible.   For reasons in favour of the view that Marjory was
the daughter and not the sister of Darvargilla, and that Wyntoun's statement,
book viii. line 1264, is an error, see Macpherson's notes, in Laing's *Wyntoun*,
vol. iii. p. 278.

were born three daughters: the eldest of them, Margaret, he
gave in marriage to Alan, earl of Galloway, and to this Alan
she bore three daughters, the eldest of whom, by name Darvargilla, was married to the lord John Baliol. Of this union the
issue was one son, John by name, who afterwards, by arbitral
decree of Edward, was created king of Scotland. This Baliol
king was father to Edward Baliol, who afterwards won the day
at Dupplin, and with Edward Baliol dies away the Baliol name.
The second daughter of Darvargilla was Marjory, whom John
Cumming had in marriage; to him she bore John the Red Cumming, the same whom Robert Bruce slew at Dumfries. To the
same John Cumming, too, Marjory bore an only daughter, whom
David earl of Athole had to wife. By her earl David had
several sons, who have naught to say to our present investigation. David earl of Huntingdon had yet a third daughter,
namely Isabella, who was married to the lord Robert Bruce,
and by her he had one son, also named Robert. This Robert
was father to Robert earl of Carrick; and he in turn was

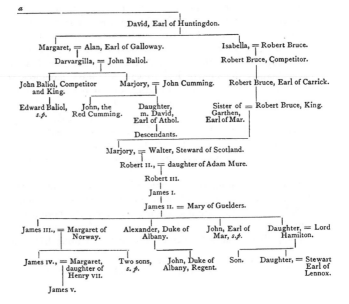

father to king Robert, and had other sons and daughters. But
Robert the king, before he came to the throne, and when he
was earl of Carrick, took to wife the sister of Garthen earl
of Mar, by whom he had an only daughter, named Marjory.
Walter, steward of Scotland, had her to wife, and to him she
bore an only son, who became king Robert the Second. This
second Robert, before he came to the throne [1], had formed an
irregular alliance with one of the daughters of Adam Mure, a
soldier, and afterward, by a dispensation, he made her his
wife, and by her had Robert, the third of the name. This
Robert the Third was father to James the First; and James
the First begot James the Second. James the Second had to
wife Mary, daughter of the duke of Guelders, who bore to him
three sons and two daughters. Of these the eldest son became

The duke of
Albany.

James the Third; the second, Alexander, became duke of
Albany; the third, who died without issue, was John earl of
Mar. The duke of Albany, however, married a wife in France,
from Auvergne, by whom he had John, who at this present is
regent in Scotland.   A sister of James the Third was married
to the lord Hamilton, and she bore to him a son and a daughter,
who are now living.   The daughter became wife to Stewart
earl of Lenox. James the Third had to wife Margaret, daughter
to the king of Norway, by whom he had James the Fourth and
that king's two brothers. These brothers, however, left no

James the
Fourth.

issue.   James the Fourth had to wife Margaret, daughter of
Henry the Seventh, the English king, and by her he had issue,

James the
Fifth.

of whom one only survives, James the Fifth to wit, a boy of
six years [2].   Such then is the genealogy of the Scottish kings.
Whence it follows that John duke of Albany is next heir to
James the Fifth, and next heir to John is that Hamilton whose
grandson is earl Lenox, Stewart by name, and he has brothers
and sisters.

The question of
the succession
resolved.

From this I think it is in part plain to which among the
three claimants the right of succession appertained.   In behalf
of Robert Bruce this argument is adduced : He was born before
John Baliol. But against this we have the following no way
contemptible argument : Either the mother of John Baliol or

---

[1] Iste rex de facto.

[2] This fixes the date of the writing of this part of Major's History as 1518.

the mother of Robert Bruce was heir to the throne of Scotland ; and whichever of these was heir, to her her son succeeds.
And I will take my stand, not only on the mothers of the rival
claimants, but will go further, to the three daughters of David
earl of Huntingdon, and ask which of these was heiress of the
Scottish crown, or would have succeeded to it had she lived,
since the child succeeds to the parent deceased, as it would to
the parent had he lived. But leaving this dispute, which seems
to have given some colour to the judgment of king Edward,
I state my conclusion thus : Robert Bruce alone and his heirs
had and have an indisputable claim to the kingdom of Scotland. This conclusion I do not rest upon the fact that Robert The manifest
had priority to John by way of birth, but upon another argu- Bruce to the
ment, and it is this : John Baliol, born of the elder daughter, kingdom of
departing from his just rights, and relinquishing his whole
claim to Edward of England, showed himself thereby unfit to
reign, and justly was deprived of his right, and of the right
inhering in his children, by those in whom alone the decision
vested. Now this decision vested in the rest of the kingdom.
Secondly, this argument may be used, to the same result : A The consent of
free people confers authority upon its first king, and his power make a new
is dependent upon the whole people[1] ; for no other source of king.
power had Fergus, the first king of Scotland; and thus you
shall find it where you will and when you will from the beginning of the world. I say it was for this cause that the kings
of Judaea were appointed by God. If you tell me that Henry
the Eighth traces his claim to Henry the Seventh, I will mount
up to the first of the English kings, and ask, Whence did he,
then, derive his right to be king? and so would I proceed
throughout the history of the world. And it is impossible to
deny that a king held from his people his right to rule, inasmuch as you can give him none other[2] ; but just so it was that

---

[1] Cf. Bk. IV. ch. iii.

[2] M. Charles Jourdain, in his ' Mémoire sur la royauté française et le droit
populaire d'après les écrivains du moyen âge ' (*Excursions historiques*, Paris,
1888, p. 513) has collected a number of passages from the scholastic theologians
which illustrate Major's doctrine on this subject. Scotus, among others (*in Sent.*
lib. iv. dist. 15. qu. 2), seems to make the consent of the people the source of
all political authority. John of Salisbury (d. 1180), who held kings to be the
representatives of divinity, and as such to be loved, venerated, and obeyed,

the whole people united in their choice of Robert Bruce, as of one who had deserved well of the realm of Scotland. Thirdly it may be argued, only to result in the same conclusion: A people may deprive their king and his posterity of all authority, when the king's worthlessness calls for such a course, just as at first it had the power to appoint him king. This is clear from a consideration of the fact that the kingly rule amongst the Romans had to give way to an aristocracy; and Pepin king of the French was successor to another king who had been deposed. Fourthly it may be argued, in the same direction: In what concerns kings, that is to be done which most conduces to the common weal. An instance in point would be where a country is attacked by a foreign foe, and where the king—we will call him A—cannot defend it, and even consents to its overthrow; and another man—say B—comes to the rescue, snatches his country from the clutch of the invader, and holds it safe with his own right hand. A deserves to be deposed, and B deserves to be in his stead imposed. But just so was it in our own case: *Igitur.* Fifthly it may be argued: John Baliol and the nobles of the realm ought to have been willing that Robert Bruce should bear rule; therefore Robert Bruce ought to have been no less willing to do so. The premiss of this argument is plain. They ought to have wished that that mystical body[1] of which they were parts should endure intact and in good condition; and this result could not have been attained but by the expulsion of John Baliol, and the institution of Robert Bruce to royal power: *Ergo.*

---

nevertheless taught that if a king acted contrary to the law, and oppressed his subjects, he became a tyrant; and he devotes an entire chapter to demonstrate that every tyrant is a public enemy, and that it is not only lawful but just and equitable to put him to death. Gerson, the chancellor of Paris (who would have been a high authority with Major), writes as follows in his *Considerationes principibus et dominis utilissimae, Opp.* t. iv. col. 624: 'It is a further error to hold that kings are emancipated from every obligation towards their subjects; on the contrary, alike by natural and divine law, they owe to their subjects equity and protection. If they fail in this, if they act with injustice in regard to their subjects—above all, if they persevere in their iniquity, the time has come for the application of that law of nature: to meet force with force [vim vi repellere]. Has not Seneca said that there is no victim more acceptable to God than a tyrant?' For a further statement of Major's views see *infra*, pp. 219, 220.

[1] Orig. and F. 'Debebant velle illud quo corpus mysticum . . . maneret incolume'. ? For 'illud quo' to read 'quod illud'.

Sixthly it is argued : It is leisome to a free people in a certain event to depose a king whose mere legal claim admits not of a doubt (this we have already shown), and to appoint as king one who has no such claim as this ; therefore, *a fortiori*, it is leisome in a like case to depose a king whose claim is ambiguous and to place upon the throne another whose claim is likewise ambiguous. Now, just like this is the case which we have now under review : *Igitur*. Seventhly and lastly, this argument may be used : Whose it is to appoint a king, his it likewise is to decide any incident of a doubtful character that may arise concerning that king ; but it is from the people, and most of all from the chief men and the nobility who act for the common people, that kings have their institution ; it belongs therefore to princes, prelates, and nobles to decide as to any ambiguity that may emerge in regard to a king ; and their decision shall remain inviolable. But just thus was it with Robert Bruce, and then most of all when he had driven from the kingdom those who had been active disturbers of the kingdom's peace : *Igitur*. See then by what considerations we have cleared the way for the indubitable claim of Robert Bruce and his successors to the throne of Scotland. And if in addition he had a claim to urge as lineal successor, far be it from me to gainsay that claim ; but the reasons that I have adduced suffice, in my opinion, to demonstrate the conclusion just laid down.

CHAP. XVIII.—*Of the objections that may be urged against this conclusion, and their solution.*

But inasmuch as the solution of doubts is the manifestation of the truth, I will tabulate some arguments which may be advanced against the cogency of the conclusion that I have arrived at ; for that is the chief pillar of a conclusion. First of all, it is argued thus : The kings of England are superior to the kings of the Scots; therefore Robert Bruce acted wrongly in the resistance that he made, and in driving the English out of Scotland. The premiss is doubly plain : first of all, because the kings of the Scots very frequently did homage to the English kings, and went to London ; and, secondly, John Baliol,

[marginal notes:] First Argument. First proof of the antecedent. Its second proof.

who was the lineal descendant of the elder sister, made over
his right : *Igitur.*

First of all, I deny the premiss, and towards the proving
of my point, where you say that the Scots did homage to the
English, I make distinction of the proposition thus : They did
this either in behalf of the counties of Huntingdon, Cumberland, and Northumberland, and in this I am at one with you;
or they did so in behalf of the kingdom of Scotland, and this
I deny. For when your Edward and the Scots, the while the
Scottish throne was vacant, had been for a long time pleading
their respective causes before the Roman pontiffs, and on both
sides had produced what evidence they could muster, the pontiff
gave judgment that in matters temporal the king of Scotland
was subject to no one. So much is plain upon the very face of
the matter; but inasmuch as the Scots, all without a king as
they then were, had no fancy to become Edward's prey, they
took action before the pontiff in behalf of the kings of Scotland
as to those lands which of old they had held in England, to the
end that they should be understood to do homage, mediately,
in respect of those territories only. It is no wise expedient
that kings do such homage as this in their own person.

To the second objection I make twofold answer : this first—
that what John Baliol did he did not of his free will, nor had
he lawful right to the kingdom; this secondly—that, granting
him to have possessed indubitable legal right, and in the full
exercise of his free will to have made over that right to the
English king, such right would have been profitless to that
king. For kings cannot thus, according to their own mere
pleasure, divest themselves of their inherent right to their
kingdom, and confer the same upon another. Whence it
follows, that if the king of the French were to make grant of
the land of France to the Great Turk, such grant would not
hold. As a matter of fact, Charles the Sixth did make a grant
of France to the English king; but, this notwithstanding,
Charles the Seventh and the nobles of France prevented it from
taking effect. For a king has not the same unconditional
possession of his kingdom that you have of your coat[1].

---

[1] Cf. Bk. III. ch. iii., where Major makes use of a similar illustration.

Secondly, it is argued thus: It would have been more The Second
profitable for the Scots to have been under English kings; and Argument,—
therefore Robert Bruce acted wrongly in making the resistance
that he did make.   The premiss is plain: justice and good
government are more firmly stablished in England than in
Scotland; and that advantage the Scots would have had under
English rule [1].

And this argument is supported as follows: The people of its confirmation.
Wales are in a better state under English rule than they would
be under kings of Wales, as has been said above: therefore,
the condition of the Scots would likewise have been better
under English than under Scottish kings.

Of this second argument I deny the conclusion.   For though
it were indeed of more advantage to the common weal that
Sortes[2] should have my house and furniture than that I should The Answer to
have them, it does not therefore follow that I am under obliga- Argument.
tion to make them over to that person.   But I would also wish
to make distinction of the premiss itself, that it would have
more advantage the Scots to have been subject to one king only
than to several kings.   The English king might have held
Scotland by a just title, by marriage, or in some other lawful
way; and then I grant you your proposition;—or he might
have held it by violence and oppression, and such claim as this
is to be denied, nor indeed is it likely to emerge.

From all which I will now be bold enough to make this here- Proposition as
following statement.   There were formerly in Britain nine or of Britain.
ten kingdoms, as is plain from discourse of history.   The
Scots now hold the kingdom of the Picts.   The English hold
Wales, and various of the old kingdoms among the English,
small though these were; and so it comes about that at this
present there are two kingdoms and no more.   It would be of
the utmost advantage to both these kingdoms that they should
be under the rule of one monarch, who should be called king of
Britain, provided only that he were possessed of a just and honest

---

[1] Cf. Bk. IV. ch. xii. p. 190.

[2] 'Sortes' is the name most generally applied throughout Major's *in Quartum
Sententiarum* to the imaginary figure in an illustration.   It is Sortes, for instance,
who lets the farm of Gleghornie to Plato—Plato being the name chosen where
a second figure is required.   For a woman, Berta is the most common name
throughout the *In Quartum*.

title thereto; and to gain this end I see no other means than
by way of marriage[1]; for the kings of each country ought to
give their sons and daughters in marriage one to another, even
though these were within forbidden degrees of kinship, for
which the pontiff could grant a dispensation.   And any man,
be he Englishman or Scot, who will here say the contrary, he, I
say, has no eye to the welfare of his country and the common
good.   For on such a footing only could both peoples live in
peace one with another; and only in time of peace can God,
the Author of peace, be duly worshipped, and only at such a
time can men give themselves to the practice of their religious
duties.

The evils
of war.
Consider for a moment the evils that are brought about by a
state of warfare.   When you find a strip of land whose exact
boundary is uncertain, it is suffered to lie waste; and even when
the boundaries are known, to a distance of eight or nine leagues,
the country is given up to fire and sword.   Many noble men
of both kingdoms meet their end by the sword, so that among
some families of a combative temper you shall not find a single
member who has died in his bed.   Great too is the loss of all
kinds that results when hostile galleys and other vessels meet
upon the sea; great too the expense that is involved in the
maintenance of armies, and the death that lags not far behind.
Would it not then be well worth our while one day to put an
end to all this?   And when by right of marriage any one—be
he Scot or Englishman—came to have a just claim to the
kingdom, the man who should set himself in opposition to
such a consummation would have much to answer for.   And
when it is borne in mind that the two nations are each of
them proud, and confident in valour, I see not how, without
the recognition of some just and undoubted title, such a happy
solution can ever be attained.   I do not forget that there are
crafty men, more bent upon their private advantage than on
the common weal, who will deny what I now affirm, and base
their argument upon this or that sophistical reasoning.   Such,
for instance, are certain powerful Englishmen and Scots, who
themselves aspire to the sovereignty, and therefore are unwill-

---

[1] Cf. *ante*, p. 41.

ing to have over them a king more firmly placed upon his
throne, or who regard foreign kingdoms more with a view to
their own private advantage than to that of the common weal,
and feel that such a union would be to their own loss.   As to   Argument of
the argument that may be drawn from the case of Wales, I   confirmation.
say that Wales and Scotland in this matter are not upon the
same footing.   For the English conquered the Welsh with
ease, but not so the Scots, as the event proved ; inasmuch as
for a long time these have dared to make manful resistance to
the English, and on occasion have even not feared to carry the
attack into the enemy's country.

The third argument is this: If the whole people be above   Arg. 3.
the king, this conclusion follows, that at the will and pleasure
of the people kings might be deposed, which would bring no
little disaster on the state.   The fourth argument is this : Any   Arg. 4.
private owner can sell his lands, or squander his holding, or
make grant of his property to another ; therefore the king may
do the same with his kingdom.   The consequence holds; for when
the opposite of the consequence is given along with the premiss,
this conclusion follows, and 'tis far removed from the truth, inasmuch as the king has not of his kingdom that full and fair
possession which a private owner has of his own estate.

Of the third argument I deny the consequence, for only   Answer to the
with the greatest difficulty could kings be driven from their   third Argu-
kingdom; for were it otherwise, you should have the state   ment.
in continual disturbance from civil war, and 'tis a harder
thing than you think to rob a rightful king and his posterity
of his kingdom.   True it is, nevertheless, that men of old time
have deposed their kings, and rightfully deposed them, for foul
vices of which these showed no mind to be corrected.   But if
kings are any way corrigible they are not to be dismissed, for
what fault you will; but then, and only then, when their
deposition shall make more for the advantage of the state
than their continuance.   And when that happens men may
begin to think of flying ; for unless under a solemn consideration of the matter by the three estates, and ripe judgment
passed wherein no element of passion shall intrude, kings are
not to be deposed.

In answer to the fourth argument let it be said that the   Answer to
the fourth.

conclusion is null. For the king is a public person, and altogether such in this manner, that he presides over his kingdom
for the common weal and the greater advantage of the same.
But when the reins of government are by his very touch defiled,
when he shows himself a squanderer of public treasure, and
brings his country to the verge of ruin, he is no longer worthy
to rule. For he holds of his people no other right within his
kingdom but as its governor. But of his own private property
every man is himself the only manager and judge.

Fifth Argu-
ment. Fifthly it is objected : In a real body the head has the pre-
eminency over all the other members; therefore also in a
mystical body the head is chief over all the rest of the
Answer. members. It is answered : The conclusion is null ; for the
proof from similars fails not, for the most part, to limp on its
fourth foot. Now that we have, as it were, cleared of its
surrounding husk the claim of Robert Bruce to the throne of
Scotland, and made accurate statement of the same, not
omitting the while to clear away those objections that may
here and there be urged against it, it remains to declare his
acts, and tell in what manner he bore himself as a monarch.

CHAP. XIX.—*Of the acts of Robert Bruce, king of Scotland, and
the calamities which befell him.*

THAT man would need the strength of Atlas, or the power,
like Daedalus, to wing a skiey flight, who should rightly tell
the life of Robert Bruce ; but such an one being still to seek,
I propose in a short compass—for indeed the time is wanting,
and the leisure too—to sing this hero's life, tamely enough I fear.

King Robert
Bruce. When Robert Bruce, with the help of his own friends, had
taken his place upon the throne, there marched against him,
in the thirteen hundred and sixth year from the Virgin's
travail, on the nineteenth day of June, Odomar de Valence,
guardian of Scotland, and at Methven met him in battle,
He is defeated. wherein Robert was conquered and put to flight, though with
the loss of few only among those who clave to him. This
defeat the common people chose to look upon as an evil omen
for Robert, and just as if he had been a man fated to bring
ill luck, against whom Fortune had a spite, they utterly

deserted him. He went thereafter to Athole and Argyll, and there lay for certain days in hiding; but on the third day of the ides of August he was once more attacked by English and Scot alike, and chiefly by those of the Cumming family, and again suffered defeat and utter rout. At Dalary, however, he lost but few of his own following. To Saint Duthac[1], which is at the furthest limit of Scotland in one direction, the queen, his wife, made her escape; but she was there taken prisoner by William Cumming, carried by him to the king of England, and by that king kept in strict confinement till the time of the battle of Bannockburn. In the same year did Nigel Bruce, the king's own brother, find a refuge, with a number of the nobles, in the castle of Kildrummie. But that castle by Scottish treachery fell into the hands of the English king, and Nigel Bruce, with many other men of mark, was carried to Berwick, and there paid, he and all his fellows, the last penalty of all. Thomas, too, and Alexander, brothers to the king, were made captive at Lochryan, carried to Carlisle, and there beheaded. Without a brother, without wife, without any of near kin to stand by him, the finger of scorn was on all sides pointed at the Scottish king. Plots were laid against his life by the English, by many among the Scots, and of these most of all by the party of the Baliols and the Cummings—and in such wise that, with the company of one or two faithful followers, he lived from day to day in forest or in thicket, with grass for food, with water for his drink instead of wine. A strange spectacle, surely, this—of a man with manifold kindred in England and in Scotland, the inheritor in both kingdoms of wide domains, destitute utterly of the comforts of existence. Many a time, I take it, must that hero have thought within himself, and said to himself, that he would have better consulted his own safety in leading the life of a private person than in the quest of a kingly throne by the doubtful issue of war. But in a situation so distressful he could not have held his lands securely, nor yet his life. Nothing therefore remained for him but to prosecute and establish his claim to the kingdom; for to Edward of England and to the Cummings he had become so much an object of hatred that from them he could

He is defeated a second time.

His wife is taken prisoner.

His brother Nigel is taken prisoner and slain. Thomas and Alexander, the king's brothers, are taken and slain. Robert Bruce is left desolate.

---

[1] *i.e.* Tain.

hope for no favour. Hunger, therefore, and thirst he bore, and toil and trouble, and sweat of battle, and all contempt and ignominy, with equal mind, or at least with patience, in the trust that Fortune could not remain his enemy for ever. Some men, and such was Priam, have happiness at the outset of life, and, at its close, misery; but others again you shall find whose beginning is in adversity but their end in joy. This man, therefore, labours unweariedly with unconquered spirit to gain a kingdom. Some have affirmed that these hardships at the outset befel him in punishment for his slaying of the Cumming in a church.

But in the following year, when he was in exile among the island Scots, when his spirit revived under the kindly care of a certain noble, he took the determination to regain somewhat of his lands, or lose his life in the attempt. First of all, then, he made for his native soil of Carrick, and there gained possession of one strong fortalice, whose garrison he slew, dividing the spoil among his followers, and summoning his friends, all he could. Thence he sought the northern parts of Scotland. He took by storm the castle of Innyrnes or Invernes, razed it to the ground, and left no single member of its garrison alive; and so he passed through the northern parts. But a little later in the same year John Cumming, earl of Buchan, gathers together a force of Englishmen and Scots, and marches against Robert Bruce. When they perceived, however, that the king showed a fearless front, they make a truce on both sides for a while. About the same time Simon Fraser, Walter Logan, knights both, and many other fighting men, were taken to London, where they suffered the penalty of death. At the hands of the Cummings too, and John Mowbray, a Scot, and the English, Robert Bruce suffered many an insult; but so unwearied was he, and of so stout a heart, in his resistance, that his name and fame grew brighter for the dark days that he had passed through, and his valour stood forth always more shining and conspicuous to all. Edward of England, therefore, brought together a large army, meaning to drive Robert
Death of
Edward. Bruce forth from Scotland; but as he drew near the Scottish borders he fell sick, and so went the way of all flesh.

This Edward Longshanks reigned for five-and-thirty years.

About this matter our chroniclers have several things to say : this, for instance, that a certain gentleman, by name William Banister, saw the soul of king Edward being carried down to hell; and they have many evil things to say of Edward. For myself, I do not place much trust in this sort of fabrication. It is not of yesterday that I have observed how it is the custom of the vulgar Scot to say nasty things about the English [1], and contrariwise. Love and hatred have this in common : that alike they tend to becloud and blind our intelligent judgment of things, and give an erroneous and even perverse interpretation of actions the most excellent, when these are the work of the other side. Now it behoves every man, and most of all a priest, to rid himself of this pestilent habit, and to weigh in equal scales whatever comes before him for judgment. Otherwise such an one is unworthy of confidence ; and in the present instance it will be our duty to pass by what is improbable as if it were untrue. In some things, nevertheless, I do indeed find Edward worthy of censure, inasmuch as, when he had been chosen by the Scots as their neighbour at once and umpire in an abstruse point of law regarding the succession to the throne, he acted wrongly in using this occasion for his own special advantage, in sowing amongst the Scots the seeds of civil war, nay, in giving all care that these same seeds should come to maturity, to the end that when the opposing parties had worn out each of them the strength of the other, or perchance using for himself the support of one of them, he might obtain the kingdom. Now what is truly profitable is ever inseparable from the truly moral. From what had taken place in the past it might have been guessed that some day or other, when hatred of the English rule had reached a certain pitch among the Scots, they would drive the English out of the country, and that one day would thus bear witness to the fruitless sweat of many a hard-won battle. But whatever his wrongful deeds, all might have been cancelled by penitence at the last, had he shown an efficacious intention to make sufficient restitution. But whether he did this, or whether, on the plea of invincible ignorance, he is to be excused for not having done so—seeing that he may

Edward is censured.

---

[1] Cf. Bk. I. ch. vii. p. 40.

have honestly believed his advisers when they told him that he
himself held of John Baliol the right of succession to the Scottish kingdom, and therefore was under no obligation to make
restitution for the injuries wrought upon the Scots—all this I do
not discover to be made out clearly, either one way or the other.

Merlin's prophecy.

Last of all, I note that Caxton makes mention of a prophecy of Merlin's about this same Edward.   For English
Merlin, who was a seer, used to say that one day there should
sit upon the throne a dragon pitiful and brave, who should open
his mouth over Wales, and plant upon Wyk his foot.   All this
they claim to have found fulfilment in Edward ; he conquered
Wales, and by Wyk the English understand Berwick to be signified.   For my part, I grant his courage—to the point of
fierceness ; of his clemency I see but slight indications.   By
Wyk I should rather be inclined to understand Wick in Caithness, the outmost boundary of Scotland.   Merlin says further
that this dragon would place a kingly crown upon the head of a
greyhound, who afterward, from fear of the dragon, should fly
beyond sea.   This they explain of Edward and John Baliol,
though they show no reason for likening Baliol to a greyhound [1].   Merlin's prophecy about this same dragon went
further thus : that the greyhounds should long be bereaved
of father and shepherd, that in those days the sun should be
blood-red ; that the dragon should rear a fox, which should
make war against Edward, and that this war should not reach
an end in Edward's days.   In Edward's days there was a
mighty shedding of blood, and for a long time the Scots
lacked a king.   The fox they interpret to mean Robert Bruce.
But it is a certain fact that Robert Bruce was at the first a
partisan of Edward, though he was born in Scotland, for he held
large domains in both kingdoms of the Britons ; and though at
the first he was a favourer of Edward, yet in the end, and with
just title, he rebelled against him.   It does not therefore appear
how he may be compared to a fox.   But as to these prophecies,
my treatment shall be here, as elsewhere, dry and meagre.

---

[1] We may recall, however, that Baliol, during his captivity in England, found
his chief amusement in hunting.   His establishment then consisted of two
esquires, one huntsman, a barber, a chaplain, a steward, a butler, a washer-
woman, a seamstress, etc.; and he had at least two greyhounds (*leporarii*) and
ten hounds.—See Rev. J. Stevenson's *Documents*, etc., vol. i. p. xlviii.

CHAP. XX.—*Of Edward the Second, king of the English; and of the manner of waging war among the Britons.*

On the death of Edward the First, whom our countrymen commonly call Edward Longshanks, there succeeded him Edward the Second (that is, he was the second Edward after the conquest by the Normans). Him they also name ' of Carnarvon ', seeing that he was born in a certain castle of Wales which is called Carnarvon; and for this reason he is called Edward of Carnarvon. In the thirteen hundred and seventh year from the redemption of the world he received in marriage Isabella, daughter to the French king. He was entirely under the influence of Peter Gavaston, a Gascon; and the demeanour of this Peter therefore reached, and easily reached, such a pitch of haughtiness that he came to hold the chief men of the kingdom in contempt. These men, then, pursued him with their hate, and at London they forced the king to banish him the country. The king sent him, therefore, to the island of Ireland, and granted him full vice-regal power in that part of it which was under English occupation. A little time after he recalls him into England. Whereat those noblemen were enraged not a little, chief amongst them Thomas earl of Lancaster and the earl of Warwick, and they behead Peter. But Caxton says that this Edward gathered together a great army wherewith to invade Scotland, and in the thirteen hundred and fourteenth year of the Lord came to Stirling. Him Robert Bruce met on a certain plain, and there Edward suffered defeat; and many noteworthy Englishmen fell on that day. This battle was fought on the feast of John Baptist. With the remnant of his army Edward made for Berwick, and afterward for London. But in the following Lent the Scots capture Berwick from the English. About this time two cardinals arrived from Rome in Britain, with the hope of establishing a peace between the kings of Britain. When they were near to Durham, these cardinals were robbed of all they carried with them by Gilbert Mitton, an English knight. This man, therefore, was beheaded and quartered, and the four parts of his body sent to the four chief towns of

Edward the Second, also named ' of Carnarvon '.

Peter Gavaston.

Caxton.

Victory of Robert Bruce.

the kingdom. About the same time the Scots ravaged all
Northumberland[1], gave every village to the flames, slew the
men, nay, young men and women too they slew with every
circumstance of cruelty.   In despoiling of churches they
showed themselves brutal and sacrilegious.   Moved thereat,
John the Twenty-second[2], the Roman pontiff, sent the censures
of the church to the archbishops of Canterbury and York, to
the end they should fulminate the same against the Scots.
Scotland they then subjected to an interdict, and one day or
other they excommunicated those three men : Robert Bruce,
Thomas Randolph, and James Douglas, with all their following, until they should make satisfaction for the losses and
calamities that the English had suffered at their hands.   It
followed that many good priests in Scotland, who refused to
celebrate divine service at the bidding of the king, were put
to death.   And these punishments were most of all inflicted
because the Scots did not recognise Edward the Englishman
as their superior.   So far Caxton.

The indepen-
dence of the
Scots.

Some of what this man says is false ; some of it is improbable.   The Scots have at no time recognised the English king
as their superior ; and so much was plainly set forth by John
the Twenty-second.   I cannot lightly grant that the Scots put
to death youths, women, and men unfit for war, for that is to me
improbable, and most of all that such things should have been
done by those illustrious and most magnanimous men ; since
never, in my opinion, for the last five hundred years, has the
other kingdom in our island produced three men more renowned than these.   Though Englishmen and Scots alike
wage war even in the present day in wild and fiery fashion,
such deeds as these are unknown amongst them.   All the
more must they have been foreign to those valiant men.   And
if indeed they acted as Caxton affirms of them, I condemn
them and abhor them for such wickedness.   From such prac-
tices even civilised heathen are wont to abstain.   'Tis the part
of brave and magnanimous men to spare the conquered and
beat down the proud[3].   If one were to assert the same of the

---

[1] 'toke and bore Englysshe mennes goodes as they had been sarasyns or
paynyms.'—Caxton, *u.s.*, fo. lxxxix.

[2] 'he was wonders sory that christendom was so destroyed through the
Scottes.'—*Ib.*   [3] Virgil : *Aen.* vi. 854.

Highland and island Scots, when they had received provocation,
I could not lightly contradict him; but these men are very
rarely taken out in war, for if they find in the southern parts
of the country a man who speaks English, they are but too
ready to seize his goods as their own; nor are they well-
affected toward us on account of our English speech and
customs unlike their own. Hence it comes to pass, that only
in case of necessity, and under the eye of most watchful
generals, are they ever permitted to march against the English,
and all because of the quarrels that arise and the crimes that
they commit, in going and returning. The fact is, that in
actual warfare the southern Scots show themselves no less
humane than the English; for they do not rob women of their
ornaments or their rich apparel, and if any among them should
have been guilty of such an attempt, they are restrained by
the nobles. One thing more I will add : that though, when
the combat is still going on and its issue remains doubtful,
Britons of different kingdoms fight fiercely one with another,
the victor ever shows himself of a singular clemency towards *Clemency o*
the conquered, and this is so even though he have received much *the Britons*
towards a
provocation. But in this devastation of Northumberland, in *conquered foe.*
my opinion, Edward the First inflicted the most severe losses
upon the Scots, and under him many thousands of Scots came
by their death. He robbed them of their kingdom and of all
that they possessed, relying upon the help of wicked men
among the Scots; nor did he make any reparation to the Scots
for the losses that he brought upon them; and the Scots
could not compass justice or other restitution ; therefore was
it leisome that they should win justice for themselves and by
their own hands.

CHAP. XXI.—*Of the war which the Scots waged against Edward
the Second and its happy result; likewise of the learned men who at that
time flourished in Britain.*

On account of the defeat which had been inflicted on his *The deeds of*
nation by the Scots, Edward the Second gathered a huge army, *Edward the*
Second.
and therewith invested Berwick, a boundary town and of the
strongest. When the Scots were ware of this they secretly
invaded England on the western boundary, by the Solway, and

inflicted immense losses on the English; they laid waste all Eng-
York.   land as far as York.   York is distant from the Scottish boundary some fifty leagues or a little more.   Now against those
Scots the English brought together at York a very large army,
to the making of which there went clergy, and common people,
and nobles; and there was fought there, upon the twelfth day
of October, the battle of Myton Upswale[1], in which the English
Slaughter of   were defeated; and of all the Englishmen in that army scarce
the English.   one was found that escaped; for either, seeking safety in the
river, they were drowned, or they fell by the sword of the
Scots.   Thereafter the Scots returned without loss to their
own country; nor did Berwick fall into the hands of Edward.
Caxton.   Think, then, how the English historian whom we are tracking
recounts the story of those times, in a narrative most improbable, which I can do naught but censure and reject.

About that time there flourished in England divers learned
William   men, two of whom—to wit, William Ockham[2] and Walter
Ockham.   Burley[3]—had learned under the Subtle Doctor.   For Ockham

---

[1] Commonly known as the 'Chapter of Mitton', or, according to Caxton,
called by the Scots 'the whyte batayle', from the number of clerics engaged in
it.   Barbour (*The Brus*, cxxix.) writes of

> ' Archaris, burges, and yhemanry,
> Prestis, clerkis, monkis, and freris,
> Husbandis, and men of all misteris,
> Quhill that tha sammyn assemblit war
> Wele tuenty thousand men and mar ;
> Richt gud arming eneuch tha had.
> The archbischop of York tha mad
> Thar capitane.   *   *   *
> Of tha yhet thre hundreth war
> Prestis that deit intill that chas ;
> Tharfor that bargane callit was
> The chaptour of Mytoun, for thar
> Slane sa mony prestis war.'

[2] Cf. *ante*, p. 24 note, and note [3] on p. 229.

[3] Walter Burley, a voluminous commentator on Aristotle, was born about
1275, died 1357.   Nearly twenty separate editions of his philosophical treatises
were published before the end of the fifteenth century.   His writings were
famous throughout Europe.   Of his *Ethics* two editions were printed at Venice
in the fifteenth century, and the same work was one of the first books printed
at Oxford (1517), where it seems to have been used as a text-book at least till
the year 1535.   One of his most popular works was the *De Vita et moribus
philosophorum*, first published in 1467, and frequently reprinted and translated.

was a man of keen intellect; and albeit Altisiodorensis [1] and Bonaventure [2] make mention of the Nominalists, yet before Ockham we read of not one who was profoundly conversant with this way. On the four books of the Sentences he wrote as many books,—on the first book, indeed, he wrote at length. The older writers in this line, and notably the Subtle Doctor, he attacked, yet did he ever hold the latter in high veneration, as appears from what he writes in the second distinction of his first book and in other places. So true is it that these and such like fair debates of the schools have their origin in no unfriendly feeling, but rather, and simply, in the delight of intellectual exercise. In his Dialogues, which contain much that touches the supreme pontiff and the emperor, he lays down no final conclusions, but leaves all to the judgment of his hearers [3]. Ockham came from England with the Subtle Doctor

---

[1] This now almost forgotten theologian, William of Auxerre (died about 1230) was held in the highest estimation by Major, who in his *In Quartum* (Dist. xx. qu. 2) speaks of him as 'gravis et antiquus theologus Guilielmus Altisiodorus', and constantly quotes him as a primary authority by the side of Alexander Hales, Aquinas, Scotus, and Bonaventure. William was born at Auxerre (whence his appellation of Altisiodorensis—Autissiodurum being the Roman name of Auxerre), became archdeacon of Beauvais, and professed theology at Paris. His principal work was the *Summa Aurea in quatuor libros Sententiarum*, a second edition of which was printed at Paris in 1500 and a third in 1518. A fourth edition was apparently published at Venice in 1591. William of Auxerre was the first theologian who drew the distinction between the matter and the form of the sacraments. A characteristic of his theological system (for an account of which see *Hist. Litt. de la France*, vol. xviii. pp. 115-122) was the prominence he gave to Faith as the chief merit of a Christian, maintaining that orthodoxy is a virtue superior to charity, and that salvation is better guaranteed by beliefs than works.

[2] John de Fidenza, better known as Saint Bonaventure, cardinal, bishop, and doctor of the Church, was born in Tuscany in 1241, and died in 1274 while assisting at the Council of Lyons. He wrote commentaries on Scripture and many works of devotion as well as dogmatic theology, the character of which obtained for him the title of 'Doctor Seraphicus'. The best edition of his collected works is that published at Lyons in 1668, in seven volumes.

[3] The Rev. John Owen, author of *Evenings with the Skeptics*, has been good enough to point out to me that Major's language as to Ockham's position— 'nihil definitive ponens, sed omnia auditorum judicio relinquens'—is far from justified. Quoting from Ockham's Dialogue *Super Potestate Summi Pontificis*, as contained in vol. ii. of Goldast's *Monarchia*, Mr. Owen shows that (p. 864) Ockham holds that the Rock, in Matt. xvii. 18, refers not to Peter, but to Christ, and insists that neither the 'Feed my sheep' nor the 'Thou art Peter' sanc-

Burley.

Adam.

to Paris; Germany holds the bones of both[1].   Burley published commentaries upon the books of the *Ethics* which are by no means to be despised.   Of the same date was Adam Godhame, who heard Ockham make his responses at Oxford; a modest man he was, but no way inferior to Ockham in learning or in power of intellect[2].

But lest this fourth book of ours should swell beyond its predecessors, we will reef our sails; and just as our third book came to an end with the narrative of the Blessed Thomas of Canterbury, so will we wind up our fourth with a tribute to these learned Englishmen.   <And just as we ended our first two books with an account of the doings of British Scots, so let these two end with somewhat concerning British English-men[3].

---

tions any authority of place or function in respect of other Apostles.   Further (p. 871), all secular powers are from God, for the terror of the evil and praise of the good; (p. 872) it is expedient that all powers, ecclesiastical as well as secular, should be under secular rule; and (p. 900) the Pope is subject to the Emperor wholly in secular, partly in sacred matters.   He can have no other superiority than Christ and His Apostles had under the Roman Empire.

In his masterly treatise on Ockham's principles (*Evenings with the Skeptics*, vol. ii. pp. 339-420) Mr. Owen remarks that, 'like the free thinkers of the 14th century, Ockham was a thorough-going Erastian'; while M. Hauréau (*Hist. de la Phil. Scol.*) describes the 'Dialogus' as a 'revolutionary pamphlet'.   It is true that Ockham professes not to give conclusions so much as materials for forming them, and reserves his ultimate decision on the papal controversies for a further treatise, which in fact never appeared; but his own judgment is throughout unmistakeable.   Luther, who eagerly studied Ockham, speaks of him as 'undoubtedly the chiefest and most ingenious of scholastic doctors', and in his *Table Talk* (Bell's translation, ed. 1652, p. 354) calls him 'an under-standing and a rich sensible man'.

[1] Scotus died at Cologne (as has been said, p. 206), Ockham at Munich, pro-bably in 1347.

[2] Adam Goddam, Godham, or Woodham, a Franciscan monk (died 1358) resided chiefly at Oxford, Norwich, and London.   Pits calls him 'a man of blameless life, great gravity, acute intellect, and profound judgment'.   His Commentary on the Sentences, or an abridgment of it by Henry Oyta, printed at Paris in 1512, was edited by Major himself, who prefixed to it a brief life of the author.   Major, who had almost as high an opinion of Godham as of Ockham, institutes in his 'De vita Ade' an elaborate and amusing comparison between the two theologians.   See APPENDIX.   There have been attributed to Godham other works in MS., some commentaries on Scripture, treatises on the Sacraments, etc.

[3] 'Et ita ut duos primos libros in Scotis Britannis absolvimus: sic hos duos in Anglis Britannicis claudemus.'

BOOK V.

CHAP. I.—*Of the rest of the warlike deeds of Robert Bruce and his brother done against the English ; and of the unwise treaty that was made at Stirling.*

In the thirteen hundred and eighth year from that of the Virgin's travail, Donald of the Isles marched against Robert Bruce with a large army made up of Englishmen and Wild Scots, and at the river Dee unfurled a hostile standard.   Against him went forth Edward Bruce, brother to Robert Bruce, a man of strenuous energy in war, and Edward fought with him, and conquered him, and took him prisoner when he was in act to fly.   In the following year Robert Bruce conquered the Wild Scots of Argyll and laid siege to their chief, Alexander of Argyll, in the castle of Dunstaffnage.   He was forced to surrender the castle to the king, but he refused to take the oath of fealty.   For himself, however, and his followers he besought a safe-conduct from the king, so that he might thus make his way to England, and there he ended his thenceforth inactive life.   Wretched surely may that man be deemed who chose rather to wait for death in a foreign country than to take and bear what life might bring under his own true king.   In the following year, after he had driven many of the English out of Scotland, the king won over to his own side a large force among the Scots.   In the year thirteen hundred and twelve he besieged and took the town of Perth, and put to the sword the rebels, whether Englishmen or Scots, that he found there.   In the same year was born Edward the Third, called of Windsor.   On Quinquagesima Sunday[1] of the following year James Douglas took the castle of Roxburgh. In the same year Thomas Randolph, earl of Moray, took

Donald of the Isles is taken prisoner.

Alexander of Argyle is conquered.

His death.

Edward the Third is born.

---

[1] 'in carnisprivio'. 'Carnisprivium' or 'carniprivium' was the name given to the Sunday which preceded the Lenten fast ('ante carnes tollendas')—*i.e.* to Quadragesima Sunday before the ninth century, and to Quinquagesima after that date.   Hence the terms 'carnisprivium vetus' and 'carnisprivium novum'. 'Inter duo carnisprivia' was sometimes used to designate the interval between the two Sundays.—De Mas Latrie :· *Trésor de Chronologie.*

Maidens'
Castle.
Maidens' Castle, that is, Edinburgh; and yet again in that
same year Robert Bruce brought the island of Man under his
sway.   And two years thereafter, according to our chroniclers
—three years thereafter if we take the English reckoning,—
The Battle of
Bannockburn.
there followed the great battle of Bannockburn [1].

There is a small stream or large burn that falls into the
noble river Forth.   Upon this burn are situated mills, wherein
are sometimes baked cakes upon embers, which they call
'bannocks'; wherefore that burn has come to be called
Bannockburn.   We have in a former part of our history [2] made
mention of the fact that our common people are so ignorant as
to be ashamed of such a food, though in the sacred scriptures,
and in profane histories as well, we read of it in many connections that are far indeed from being dishonourable.

Stirling Castle.
The source and seed-plot of this fateful war was on this
wise: Edward Bruce, brother to the king, had laid siege to the
strongly fortified castle of Stirling; and he found himself
unable to take it by storm, inasmuch as the castle is situated
on the brow of a hill, and at its very edge, so that the only access
is by a steep slope.   It is distant too a bare two hundred paces
from the Forth, the Scottish firth.   I imagine that this castle
was built by those Britons whose country is now occupied by
the Welsh.   I am of opinion too that the pound sterling had
The pound
sterling.
its first origin and likewise its name from this castle [3].   This
place was held, at the time of which we are speaking, by Philip
Mowbray, a Scot of high repute as a soldier, who had attached
himself to the English side.   With Philip, Edward Bruce made
an agreement on these terms: that if the castle were not
relieved by Edward of Carnarvon before the following year, he
should freely deliver it into the hands of the Scots.   Now when
Robert Bruce came to know of this, he was sore displeased,
and with reason; for he said that the agreement to which his
brother had assented was indeed of the most imprudent, and
he made haste to join his brother.   And there was reason for
his view; for you must consider that English Edward, with the

---

[1] Bannockburn was fought on June 24, 1314.   [2] Cf. Bk. I. ch. ii.
[3] Major's derivation is wrong; but the word 'sterling' is, according to Mr.
Skeat, of English origin—the M. H. G. *sterlinc* being borrowed from it.   A
statute of Edward the First has 'denarius Angliae qui vocatur *Sterlingus.*'

aid of the Scots and the men of Hainault, held Gascony, was married to the daughter of the French king, held Wales too, and a large part of Ireland ; and in Scotland many men of note were still in active enmity to Robert Bruce. So that there can be no doubt that Edward Bruce showed a want of foresight in granting so long a truce to a monarch who had so much within his power.   And in this matter I agree with Robert Bruce ; though God may, accidentally, turn everything into a better course.

CHAP. II.—*Of the immense army that the English king brought against the Scot ; of the prelude to the battle, and the valour that was shown therein by Randolph and a few among the Scots; of Douglas's loyalty and kindness towards Randolph, and the speech that was made by both kings to their soldiers.*

IMMENSE was the army which Edward brought together for the relief of the Stirling castle, and the choicest he could muster out of all the races, whether his subjects or his allies, with which he had to do.   In number of troops and their equipment we read of the like nowhere in Britain.   We are told that Edward had with him three hundred thousand fighting men ; but I find it hard to believe that their tale can have been so great ; not that England by herself alone could not furnish three hundred thousand warriors, for of men in Britain who are in the flower of their life and of warriors the number is the same ; but such a world of men as this their kings either cannot or will not maintain.   When Robert Bruce heard of this formidable advance of the English king, he compelled whence he could all he could, and so had under him five and thirty thousand well-trained soldiers.   He had along with him three men of high renown in the art of war : famous they were throughout Britain for their conspicuous valour ; and these were Edward Bruce his brother, Thomas Randolph, and James Douglas.   He led his army, then, all resplendent in arms, to the burn that is called Bannock, near to Stirling.   [The English king][1], however, when he saw that Robert Bruce had taken his

A huge army of three hundred thousand men.

England's pre-eminence in fighting men.

Three most warlike men.

---

[1] I have supplied these words. There is no nominative in the original ; and 'he' would apply to Bruce.

stand upon a plain every way fitted for a battle indeed, but
right between himself and the castle, could not avoid to marvel,
and very many of his famous warriors marvelled likewise, how,
with so small a force, Robert Bruce stood there, in a direct line
[between two enemies] ready for the combat. Others there
were among the English who were not so much surprised, for
they knew Robert to be a man of most approved skill in battle,
for a long time accustomed to daily fighting, and they judged
that many a high-hearted noble would either conquer there,
or die the death of a brave man. Wherefore their prediction
was that the impending battle would be far from bloodless.

The two opposing armies thus had one another in view at
a distance of a mile, judging, each of them, that to-morrow's
light would bring death along with it for the greater number,
and that a great disaster would surely befal one side or the
other. Edward, however, contrived in some way so to avoid
the Scottish army as to send eighty picked horsemen to Stirling
Castle to Philip Mowbray that so he might observe the day
that had been fixed for its relief. Against these eighty, by the
king's command, Thomas Randolph leads fifty chosen horsemen. In the presence of both kings and of the army they fall

The battle of
the picked men. to arms with eager alacrity. The combat was fierce, and for a
long time it lasted. The lord Douglas meanwhile prays the
king to suffer him to go to the succour of the Scots; but the
king denied him utterly. Douglas, however, when he saw the
combat to be long protracted, began to have his fears for that
most excellent general, Randolph, and with or without the permission that he had craved, he set out to the help of his
comrade. But as he drew near to the scene of the conflict, he
became aware of gaps, as it were, and clefts in the English line,
which came from the enemy falling on all sides. He took up
a position therefore at a distance, for he felt that he should be
acting an ignoble part were he to draw near and in any way
deprive the illustrious leader of the glory that would surely
come to him from the conflict and its issue.

Perhaps you may be inclined to think that the approach of
Douglas struck fear into the enemy. But as there is no doubt
that the enemy was routed already, no one can truthfully aver so
much. The night that followed resembled rather an artificial

day[1]; both armies betook themselves to their tents, but ere
they did so, great bonfires were on all sides kindled in case of
a sudden attack by the enemy in the darkness.   Patrols on
horseback and on foot made their rounds outside the whole of
the camp ; and meanwhile the armies snatch what sleep and rest
they may, so that on the morrow, with their energies refreshed,
they might bring unwearied frames to the combat that lay before them.   But already, in the third hour after midnight, the
drill-masters [2], and the officers who were set over each division,
began to consult as to making an instant attack.

Meanwhile Edward, wearing his royal robes, is said thus to
have addressed his soldiers : 'Were I not face to face with an
indubitable victory, my gallant soldiers, my speech with you
this day would begin in different fashion ; for both in number
and in equipment of our troops we are far superior to those
wretched Scots.   In engines of war, in catapults, in arrows,
and all such machinery of war we abound, while in all these the
Scots are lacking.   Those among them that are of more civility
have no other shirts than what are made from deers' hides, and
the plaids of their wild men are not otherwise ; so that a party
of our bowmen, who are equal to theirs in number, shall slay
those unarmed men before the burden of the fight begins.   And
if you begin to wonder how men like these have sometimes
conquered my subjects, I pray you not so to wonder, since it
was by craft and cunning that they did so, and not by conspicuous valour.   And if perchance they have sometimes
defeated, by their own skill, men who were by no means fit for
combat, or an enemy opposed to them in equal numbers, they
will of a surety make no stand against us, who excel them
vastly in numbers, equipment, and fair training in the field.
The king of Scots has under him an unwarlike race, which
fights too at its own charges, and he has no picked army.   God,
you may believe me, has shut in within this fair field that fox
Bruce, a man who, as a child, owed all his nurture to my dear
father, in order that he may pay the condign penalty of his
wickedness.   At the hands of my father, of brave and happy

Speech of English Edward.

---

[1] Nocte diem artificialem sequente ad tentoria uterque exercitus se contraxit.

[2] 'campiductores'. 'Campidoctor' is recognised as the better form of the word.
Major, however, has ' campiductor' or ' campi ductor' in four other places.

memory, his three brothers lost their lives; for me it remains
to take alive those other two, wicked and crafty men, and bring
them to London, there to expiate their crimes.   I would recall
to you, my nobles, how ye received at the hands of my father
ample domains in the country of these men; make exhibition
then of your strength and valour that ye may redeem the
same from those who now unjustly hold them.   And I promise you, still further, this: that with equitable cord I will
make geometrical apportionment of the whole Scottish kingdom among all well-deserving men, according to the merits
of each; the superiority of the soil only, after the land has
been distributed to my soldiers, will I take care to retain for
myself.   And if, in the coming conflict—which may God
avert!—there shall be some who fall, to the inheritance of the
noble dead their children shall succeed.   If then you desire the
fruition of my promises, betake you with cheerful courage to the
combat, wherein a short two hours—for longer than that the
enemy will not be able to withstand you—shall gain for you
undying glory and fair possessions.'

   Thus Edward.   And on the other side the Bruce, in complete armour all save his head, climbing to the summit of a
certain knoll, and thence plainly visible by all his army (for
he was fair to look upon, handsome of aspect, shapely and
vigorous in body, broad-shouldered, of an agreeable countenance, his hair yellow, as you find it among northern nations,
his eye blue and sparkling, of quick intelligence, and in the
use of his mother tongue as ready as to all who heard him he
was welcome), is said thus to have addressed his soldiers: 'If
ever the Powers above have granted to mortal man a just
cause for which to fight, 'tis to-day, my gallant friends, it is
to us they grant it.   For it is not with us, as with our enemies,
to bring distress within the borders of another country that we
take up arms, but to defend our own—that end which all men
hold it well worth while to win with life itself.   Our strife
to-day is for our worldly goods, for our children, our wives,
for life, for the independence of our native land, for hearth
and home, for all that men hold dear.   The Powers above will
protect the innocent and defend the cause of justice; the
boastful man and the wrongful oppressor they will bring to

Description of
Robert Bruce.

His speech.

the dust. Consider not too carefully that unfortunate beginning of my reign—all these disasters I attribute to my slaying of John Cumming before the altar; that great crime I have wiped out by long repentance and tears; in proof of this I have won over the enemy no mean victories in succession. It behoves not princes whom foul vice has stained to provoke the chances of war, lest God be made angry; and we read, in regard to those who have acted otherwise, that they have brought destruction both upon themselves and upon their soldiers. 'Tis a coward's part to fear the foe for all his motley multitude; for did not Alexander of Macedon overcome Darius when he was surrounded by a greater number; and, what you all know well, did not my brother Edward, Thomas Randolph, and James Douglas, conquer forces greater than their own ?

'It has been told me of that army yonder that it is made up of men who speak six different tongues; the very soldiers are unknown one to another, so that the defection of any one of them from the ranks would not be noticed. It is a slender task that I lay upon you : that each of you slay his man. Ten thousand stout men of war I know, each one of whom will bring death to two of the enemy. Thus shall you have destroyed of their number five-and-forty thousand. And when this is done, as done I hope it will be, you will force the haughty foe to retreat. But if—which thing God forbid !—it happened that we were conquered, the enemy shall celebrate no bloodless victory, and my living body at least ye shall not have among you. We will send so many souls to the shades that for what remains of the enemy the Cummings, or other Scots, shall be able to render an account in a battle that shall cost them little. It belongs to brave men to die nobly or to live nobly. Inglorious our lives will be and full of shame for ever, if they are not knit beyond chance of dissolution with the independence of our country. Our predecessor Kenneth held but a third portion of this kingdom of ours when he subdued the haughty and warlike Pict. Our ancestors, too, made no restitution of territory to the English, but even, and more than once, laid waste their lands in return for attacks that had been rashly made upon themselves. I pray you then, and beseech you, by great Kenneth, by Gregory, by the Alex-

anders, that you quit you like men in the heat of the battle
now before you.   Let us leave to our children as the outcome
of this conflict an example of valour so conspicuous that after
chroniclers must needs leave without an answer the question
whether they must yield the palm to us or we to them.'   And
then, with a smile, and pointing with his right hand toward
the enemy, he added : ' Before the sun set, by God's help, the
English leader shall have parted with his arms, and those arms
shall be yours.   My past experience of this enemy gives me
the certainty that he will not make stand against your onset.'

To such a pitch did the king's speech inflame the hearts of
all who heard it that stretching forth, each man of them, his
armed right hand, they raised an universal shout, ' The day is
ours, or every man of us shall die in battle '.   Thereupon the
king descended from the mound whence he had spoken, and
baring his head embraced each of his chief men ; afterward,
with his eyes fixed upon the army, he waved his right hand,
as it were to each of them, man by man, in sign that they
were all his friends and fellows.

CHAP. III.—*Of the drawing up of the two armies in order of battle.*

The Scots order
of battle.

THE Scot disposed his army in three divisions : the first, that
which the French are accustomed to call the vanguard, he
intrusted to those most trusty captains Thomas Randolph and
James Douglas.   In this line he placed seven thousand of the
Border youth, men who from their earliest years had known
no other occupation than fighting ; along with these he joined
three thousand of the Wild Scots, whose arms consisted of a
two-edged battle-axe, equally sharp on both sides [1] ; men,
these last, who will rush upon the enemy with the fury of a
lioness in fear for her cubs.   Against these the English king
summons eighty thousand warriors.   In the absence of his
immediate followers, king Bruce dared to utter these words :
' Either our men shall slay thirty thousand of the enemy, or
they will gain the day.'   The second army division, ten
thousand strong, he intrusted to that indefatigable warrior
Edward ; but just because he knew his brother's haughty and

---

[1] Note that this is different from the Lochaber axe described on p. 240.

choleric temper to be such that thunder could not stop his course, he joined with him in command several noblemen well up in years, to the end their colder judgment might qualify the youthful ardour of the other. Of the third division, which was fifteen thousand strong, the king himself took command. And now the air resounds with the noise, huge, horrific, of trumpet, clarion, horn, and all such instruments as are used to stir the martial mind. One after the other the king made visitation of the various divisions of his army, carrying where-ever he might go a cheerful countenance along with him ; so that men read, as one might say, victory in his very face, and any man might thank his fortune that under such a king he was soon to enter the lists of battle.

It was at a distance of two arrow-shots that a certain English knight, and a shrewd man too, took note of Robert Bruce as he gave his directions now to this division now to that, and forth-with rode at full gallop against the king, thinking either to bear him to the ground with his lance, or to force him to fly. But the king, rising in his stirrup, thus received the attack. He skilfully evaded the blow from the lance, but at the very moment when his foe was passing him, and in the presence of all, he dealt him, with an iron-studded club, which the while he had been swinging in his hand, so terrible a blow that the knight fell headlong on the ground, a dead man. And when his nobles were for censuring the over-boldness of the king, he took no note of their words ; but with a smile he complained of his luck, seeing that he had broken with that blow as good a club as ever in his life he wielded. The common people, however— as their habit is when the question is of any foolhardy deed— could not find words to praise highly enough this feat of their king. Putting their horses on one side, however, the com-batants prepare to fight on foot. For it is as foot-soldiers and not as cavalry that the Britons have been at all times accus-tomed to fight, placing their hopes of victory, not in the fleet-ness of a horse or the force of its onset, but in their own right arm.

A bold feat of the king.

A battle of foot-soldiers.

Thus then, after the discharge of implements of war, and when in the first onset arrows had been falling like hail, the two hostile forces come breast to breast and close with one another, as two rams will do when they meet in mortal conflict. Wooden lances and darts were launched with utmost swiftness; at a great distance you might have caught the sound of the lances as they snapped. Lances once broken, the fighting is taken up with the double-axes of Leith, the axes of Lochaber, than which is none more strong to cleave, the iron-knobbed staves of Jedburgh, and the two-edged axe and bill-hook. The smiths of Jedburgh fasten a piece of tempered iron four feet long to the end of a stout staff. The double-axe of Leith is very much the same as the French halberd ; yet it is a little longer, and on the whole a more convenient weapon. The smiths put a piece of iron formed hook-wise at the end of a stout staff—this serves as a bill-hook or axe ; this most serviceable weapon is in use among the English yeomen. The Lochaber axe, which is employed by the Wild Scots of the north, is single-edged only [1]. Its course is lined by many a

Great slaughter. corpse, and death's pale face is constant there. Like two blacksmiths, as they deal their blows alternate on the red-hot iron upon the anvil, such is the interchange of blows between the stout warriors on both sides : and long did the result continue doubtful ; for the Englishmen, so superior to the Scots were they in number and equipment, thought shame to fly ; and there were but few who dared to desert, lest in their flight they should be taken prisoners by the Scots.

On the other hand the Scots, mindful of their mutual promise, remained constant therein ; and determined to gain the day, or to make the enemy remember the day only too well, though they themselves could do naught but die a glorious death. The men of the Borders made a fierce onslaught on

The savage courage of the Wild Scots. the enemy ; the Wild Scots rushed upon them in their fury as wild boars will do ; hardly would any weapons make stand against their axes handled as they knew to handle them ; all around them was a very shambles of dead men, and when, stung by wounds, they were yet unable by reason of the long staves of the enemy to come to close quarters, they threw off their plaids and, as their custom was, did not hesitate to offer their naked bellies to the point of the spear. Now in close contact with the

---

[1] Cf. the description of the two-edged axe at the beginning of this chapter, and of the Wild Scots' arms at the end of ch. viii. in Bk. I.

foe, no thought is theirs but of the glorious death that awaited them if only they might at the same time compass his death too. Once entered in the heat of conflict, even as one sheep will follow another, so they, and hold cheap their lives. The whole plain is red with blood ; from the higher parts to the lower blood flows in streams. In blood the heroes fought, yea knee-deep. With marvellous skill did the English bowmen pick out the unarmed Scots ; and when Bruce, whose eyes, as he were another Argus, were in every place, was ware of this, he sent against the bowmen some stout-hearted men, who *The bowmen* forthwith drove them back with great slaughter. Meanwhile, *are driven back.* when the issue of the day was doubtful still, the servants who *The bravery of* *serving-men and* had been left at the tents to guard the horses and baggage of *armour-bearers.* their masters, moved with compassion for the case of their lords, left all and threw themselves upon the foe.

Of the English there fell a much greater number than of the Scots. And at length the English king was counselled by those around him (for his own spirit was too proud), to withdraw from the battle, since otherwise the Scots, careless whether they slew or were slain, would make an end of the king and of his nobles every one. It was urged upon him that he would be acting more wisely for his country if he sought safety in flight, than if he jeoparded the fortunes of England by his own death and the loss of all his nobility.

Edward therefore turns his back. The report goes that the *Flight of the* Scots lost four thousand, and the English fifty thousand in *English king.* that battle ; and besides the slain, count must be made of the prisoners, who consisted of almost the whole English army, with the exception of the king, who made good his escape, attended by a large body of soldiers. Wearied the Scots were with fighting, and for the most part wounded, so that they were not able at once to pursue the English king. Douglas, however, by the king's command, and accompanied by no more than four hundred horsemen, went in pursuit of Edward and his ten thousand mounted troops; and ever as he went other Scots joined themselves to him. But, as the matter *The earl of* turned out, the earl of March, a Scot, granted refuge to the *March grants* *refuge to the* English king in the castle of Dunbar, and sent him by sea to *English king.* England. Otherwise he could not have escaped the hands of

that indefatigable warrior the Douglas, who with an armed
force was lying in wait for the English king near to the
Borders.   But of this hope Douglas was cheated by the
treachery of March.   This was one of the reasons why the
Dunbars lost the earldom of March.   By exchange of an
English captive Bruce recovered his wife, the queen of Scotland.   About this battle a certain religious of Mount Carmel
made a little book, whose beginning runs thus:—

The Scots king
regains his wife.

Verses by a
Carmelite.

> De planctu cudo metrum cum carmine nudo :
> Risum retrudo, dum tali themate ludo.

The verses are rude, and not worthy the attention of the
reader; so I pass them by[1].   In this war the Scots gained
mightily at once in military glory and in material advantage;
and for the losses they had sustained in former times received
a large restitution, won indeed by their own hard fighting,
with the favour of heaven.   Then did the army of Robert
Bruce and his friends extol him to the skies; but the Cummings and the other Scots who had formerly been free with
their threats began to tremble.

CHAP. IV.—*Of the establishment of Robert Bruce in the kingdom ;
of the skirmishing raids made by the English ; and of the death in
Ireland of Edward Bruce.*

AFTER the fortunate issue of the terrible battle at Bannockburn the Scots held at Ayr a great assembly, of the kind which
the Britons call a parliament, whither convened the three
estates representative of the realm, just as a duly constituted
council represents the whole church.   There it was with one
voice determined that Robert Bruce should remain the unques-
tioned king of Scotland ; and, if it should happen that he went

Robert Bruce is
declared king.

---

1 The writer was William Baston, an eye witness of the battle, in which he
was, as he tells us, made prisoner :

> 'Sum Carmelita, Baston cognomine dictus
> Qui doleo vita, in tali strage relictus.'

It will be observed that Major makes no mention of the pits set with caltrops by
which the English horse were lamed.   Baston, however, writes of the

> 'Machina plena malis pedibus formatur equinis,
> Concava cum palis, ne pergant absque ruinis'.

The whole rhyme is printed at the end of Freebairn's edition of Major's History.

the way of all flesh without male issue, that his brother Edward should be his successor; while, if he and his brother should alike die childless, Marjory, daughter to Robert, should be queen.   It pertains to the three estates, in any matter of extreme difficulty, to deal authoritatively with doubtful matters affecting the kingdom, and on occasion to depart, for good and sufficient reasons, from the practice of the common law.   In some other parts of the world, as in the island of Ceylon [1], any one who is up in years, and without children, may be chosen to be king; and if after he becomes king he should have issue, he is deposed.   In some kingdoms, as in Castile and in Britain, a woman succeeds to the throne, and is preferred to the brother of the king; in other kingdoms just the opposite use is in force.   In such positive laws, of human enactment, such diversity may be expected ; but the common law is not lightly to be interfered with, because such change of laws shakes the foundations. *The king of Ceylon.*

Now this matter of the succession to the throne received the most searching investigation at the hand of the three estates. For they saw before them English Edward panting for the kingdom of Scotland, and they knew that in the end, aided by civil war and intestine quarrels, he would be successful, unless a strong man sat upon the throne.   Now the men of Ireland, when they saw the magnanimity of Robert Bruce and his brother, desired to have Edward Bruce for their king, and one party among them sent an embassy into Scotland with that intent.   Robert then sent his brother to Ireland with a middling army, and Edward bore himself there so manfully that in no long time he subdued a large tract of that island. *Edward Bruce subdues Ireland.* In the following year he was there joined by Robert Bruce himself, but on that expedition many men died of famine. *Robert follows him.* When English Edward learned that Robert Bruce had left Scotland, he felt that the proper time had arrived for a new invasion of that country, and sent thither a large army.   The lord Douglas was then guardian of Scotland, and he marched to meet the English force, and routed it.   Three of the English leaders he slew : namely, Edmund Lylaw a Gascon [2], the captain *The English invade Scotland.* *Slaughter of the English.*

---

[1] Major refers to this custom of the Cingalese in his *In Quartum, etc.*, ed. 1521, fol. lxxvi.

[2] The ' Ewmond de Caliou ' of Barbour (*The Brus*, cxviii. 6).

of Berwick, and Robert Nevel; the third, who was a man of rank,
he killed with his own hands.   When English Edward came to
A fleet is sent
against Scot-
land.
hear of this, he sent a fleet of many sails against Scotland (in
vessels of war the English are superior to the Scots) to the end
they should harass and waste the seaboard country.   They
entered the river Forth, and landed at Donibristle; there they
were met by the sheriff of Fife with five hundred men.   But
he did not dare to attack the English, because of their
superiority in number, and abstained from giving battle until
he was joined by William Sinclair, bishop of Dunkeld, with the
members of his court and a few of his dependants.   And the
Second
slaughter of
the English.
bishop rebuked the sheriff of Fife sharply, and over and again
compelled him to give battle to the English.   And there were left
on the field five hundred of the English slain, while many of the
remnant took to flight and were drowned.   It was from this feat
that Robert Bruce called William Sinclair his own bishop.
Birth of Robert
Stuart.
In the same year was born Robert Stuart, son of Walter
Stuart, and by Marjory, daughter of Robert Bruce, he was
grandson of Robert Bruce; and he afterwards became king of
the Scots; and thereafter, in the two following years, the lord
Thomas Randolph, earl of Moray, invaded England and laid
Randolph
brings back
booty from
England.
waste the whole country up to Wetherby, returning home
from this expedition laden with much rich booty and without
loss of men.   In the same year Berwick is recovered from the
Berwick is
retaken.
English.   In the year one thousand three hundred and nineteen, however, English Edward besieged Berwick, but profited
very little in his besieging.   All this is clear from the statements of the English chronicler as quoted above.   Now and
again we repeat by accident a story that we have dealt with
before.   The reason is this: that the English records sometimes deal with a particular incident more at length than do
the Scotch—and sometimes the case is contrariwise.   Further,
on the fourteenth day of October, in the same year, was fought
the battle of Dundalk, in Ireland, and Edward Bruce there
lost his life.   He was unwilling to await the arrival on
the following day of his brother Robert, who was advancing
slowly with assistance, and so it came about that from undue
haste, and a want of that foresight which is necessary in a
soldier, a man otherwise brave and wise came by his end,
amidst the lamentations of all around him.

CHAP. V.—*How the kings ravaged each the other's country. Of the policy of delay adopted by Robert, and how he then carried the attack into England ; his address to his soldiers ; Edward's exhortation to the English. Of the battle and the victory won by the Scots.*

In the thirteen hundred and twentieth year from the Virgin's travail, Robert Bruce summoned a great council of the three estates at Scone. The lord William of Soulis and the countess of Stratherne were there convicted on a charge of treason, and condemned to imprisonment for life, and David, lord of Brechin, who had kept silence regarding a crime committed against the king, was sentenced therefor to death. Now this David was one who had won great renown as a soldier, and for the love of Christ had done mighty deeds against the Hagarenes[1] ; but in the end he sullied his fair life by keeping silence in regard to the abovesaid crime ; wherefore himself and Gilbert of Malerb, and John Logy, knights all, and Richard Brown, a notable warrior, were dragged at horses' tails after the British fashion with traitors, and thereafter beheaded. On which account this parliament came to be called in after times the Black Parliament. Many others there were who were suspected of treason, but because no legal evidence could be produced against them, they were discharged. Upon these traitors lies an everlasting stain, seeing that they dared craftily to plot the death of a king whose life was devoted to the welfare of his country. And in David of Brechin it was a shameful thing that he disgraced his life by this criminal silence. No oath that he had taken to wicked men bound him to silence ; for the seal of [natural] secrecy[2] binds a man by no means so straitly as the seal of confession. For in every case of confession the seal is binding, whether the confession touch the question of some crime as about to be committed, or a crime already committed, such as heresy or treason ; but the seal of secrecy does not in this manner bind a man ; for it behoved him to give warning to the king, that so he might take more careful measures for his own safety, and beware of

Marginal notes:
Assembling of the chief men at Scone.
David, a man of great ability, is beheaded.
The Black Parliament.
The seal of confession. The seal of secrecy to be broken where the life of the prince is at stake.

---

[1] *i.e.* the children of Hagar=the Saracens.
[2] Orig. and F. 'sigilli secretum' ; an evident misprint for 'sigillum secreti'.

his foe; and if this were not sufficient to safeguard the life of the king, he was plainly bound to reveal the traitors by name. So that sentence of death was justly passed upon the aforesaid David. And further, the property of the conspirators was confiscated to the treasury.

Bruce ravages England. In the course of the two following years Robert Bruce invaded England and ravaged and wasted the country up to Stanmor; and when he had returned to Scotland English Edward got together a mighty armament, and by land, and by sea too with his fleet of fast-sailing galleys, penetrated into Scotland, and made his way to Edinburgh. Now when this came to the knowledge of Robert Bruce, he withdrew all supplies along the line of march of the English king; and though he could have brought his people together, he was unwilling to fight with the English a second time on Scottish soil; for he preferred that policy of delay which has the sanction of Fabius the Roman rather than to jeopardise a kingdom, which had been won at such a cost, in a doubtful struggle with the English king. That terrible battle of Bannockburn was still vividly in his memory, and, victor though he was, he could not readily forget the wounds, and horrid consequence of war, at which the day was bought. It was therefore of set purpose that this most

The English king retreats, urged thereto by scarcity of corn, and the Scots policy of delay. perspicacious general refrained from fighting, and rather aimed at compelling the retreat of the English army by contriving a scarcity of corn. This policy of delay, this ability in setting a trap for the enemy, as it were, and playing with him, are things of the first moment in the character of the complete soldier.

In the very same year, however, in the beginning of November, this same Robert the Bruce got together an army of Scots, and therewith made hostile invasion of England; and he reached nearly as far as York. For a distance of fifty leagues he moved from place to place in England and every-

Robert's design. where ravaged the country. Most of all do I admire that conception of Robert's, which led him not to give battle to the English king when he made hostile invasion of Scotland, but rather to carry the war himself into the enemy's country. One of two things must be admitted: either Robert had begun to be ashamed of that policy of delay which he had followed in the past (but in very truth he had no need to blush for it, for his name was in the mouth of every sensible man, for praise and not for blame, in that very matter of delay), or he had come to think it wiser to give battle to the English king in England rather than in Scotland. I believe it was this second consideration that moved him, and that he acted from the ripest judgment of the situation; for, to remove from the Border soldiers any temptation to draw back, he led his army far into England. And when news was brought him by his outposts' that English Edward, with an overwhelming force, was bearing down upon him, he chose for the field of battle a fair plain between Byland and St. Salvator, and in such words as these he warmed his soldiers' hearts for the fight:

'As to the fight that is now imminent, high-hearted Scots, King Bruce— his speech to his soldiers. methinks that there is no need of words from me to you; from the Scottish marches we are distant (as by experience you well know to be the case) good one hundred miles; so that if there should be a few to desert their posts, these must needs fall into the hands of a cruel enemy, and by an angry enemy be slain, or, if they should survive as captives in his hands, such an end will not only be full of disgrace and ignominy for them, but likewise for all their posterity. Ye know, all of you, how disgraceful a thing a low kind of fear has ever been reckoned amongst us Scots, and how fortitude and enterprise are lauded to the skies; now these two qualities for the most part render a man eager for the fight. It remains only that we keep of one mind and bear us in the field as one man, and aim at naught but victory or an honourable death. For, by Heaven I swear it, the Scots shall never have the chance to ransom me, nor shall any Englishmen in their banquetings make sport of the king of Scots. In sacred history we read how Nabuchodonosor, king of the Assyrians, made mock of the last king of Judea in the time of his captivity[1], and jeered at him in his presence; wherefore I would beseech you every one to be of my mind in regard to the battle now before us, and to determine to die the death of the brave or once for all to dash the pride of our foe. And though it may be, indeed, that one or another among you,

---

[1] The reference seems to be to the indignities heaped upon Zedekiah by the Assyrian king. See the last chapter of Jeremiah and parallel passages.

whether from natural disposition, or from starry influences, or
by way of inheritance from his ancestors, may be timorously
inclined, yet 'tis in the power of any man by a strong effort of
the will to subdue this base passion of fear[1]. Before now we
have conquered this same king Edward when we were fewer in
number, and when he had with him a stronger force than now.
Not only did we conquer him, but made him fly before us like
a coward; so that the lesson he has learned is, not conquering,
but flight. But I by long habit am accustomed to the other
way. If there be safety anywhere for our foe and his soldiers,
safest of all is flight before the battle. For we number more
than forty thousand men. Let this therefore admit of no
doubt, that before you have made away with thirty thousand
men, the line of the enemy will be broken. And the victory in
this fight must be won by us unaided, that so we may outdo
the fame of Kenneth, Gregory, David, and the Alexanders.
Wherefore gird you for the fight eagerly, fearlessly, and
approve yourselves brave men, the equals, if not even the
superiors, of your ancestors.'

English
Edward's
speech to his
soldiers.

On the other side the English king is said to have exhorted his
English soldiers with these words: 'Nobles and brave men all,
you have not of a surety forgotten the outrageous conduct of that
most ungrateful Scot, how that in the beginning he espoused
the cause of my most worthy father, and then, urged by his
own ambition of a kingly throne, deserted to the Scots. And
though fortune deserted me at Bannockburn, this is no matter
for wonder; it was the very variety of tongues amongst us, the
very superfluity and superabundance of our soldiery, that
wrought our ruin. When I led my English only with me into
Scotland and sought an occasion of battle, I could no way
bring that coward Bruce to face me. Then, to purge himself
of that foul stain, he came into our boundaries, all unknowing
of the war that should arise; for he thought to himself that,
laden with plunder and captives, he should be allowed to
return in peace to Scotland; but the matter has turned out
otherwise for him, and less fortunately. For we are, in this
place, Englishmen only—face to face with Scots,—in greater

---

[1] Cf. *ante*, Bk. IV. ch. xi. p. 184, and footnote.

number and better equipped. The Scottish kings make payment to no one of their soldiers, but these at their own charges
serve for a few days only, and thereafter make a living by
pilfering from the enemy. You will understand then how such
an army, promiscuously got together from any sort of people,
knows nothing of fighting; to till the field, to work—if you
like—as an artisan—so much any one of its soldiers can do, and
from earliest years has done ; but of war these men know nothing.
Wherefore you need but to fight bravely for a short time, and
you shall put to utter rout that most ungrateful, that most
coward, foe, and all his belongings. If in our own country we
should suffer defeat at the hands of a rabble of men who live
by plunder, the brand of shame may well be legible upon our
brows throughout the world and as long as time shall last.
This stain and vice of fear you must learn to shun as you
would shun Cerberus [1] himself, and like brave men gird you for
the battle with the armour of a lofty courage.'

Thus saying, and when all was in order for the conflict, he
dashed forward against the Scots, calling out continuously,
'Saint George, and Edward of Carnarvon.' The Scots, on the
other hand, entered on the conflict with shouts of 'Saint
Andrew and Robert Bruce, father of victories.' The commanders of both armies made their prayers also to the saints
for victory, and that, supported by their love and favour, it
might be granted them to quit them like brave men. The
battle was contested with fury ; the meadow just now so green
took on a blood-red tint, and in the lower parts deep streams
of blood were formed. But as for every one of the Scots who
fell there fell of the English four, the English turned their
backs, the Scots put king Edward to flight,—and it was the
fleetness of his horses alone that saved his life. Many of the
chief men among the English were slain ; many more were
carried captive into Scotland. The Scots packed together all
the warlike machines and other furnishings of the English
king, and turned their faces homeward, laying waste the while
the country that lay between. And inasmuch as they had
entered England by one road, they quitted it by another, for

The beginning of the battle.

The battle-cry.

The rout of the English.

Escape of Edward.

Victory of the Scots.

---

[1] A common figure. Cf. what Major says *ante*, p. 70, of the stepmother.

in this way they got them a better provision of food; and this
they did, no doubt, because the common Scots, when they go
to war, carry with them but a scanty provender slung in small
sacks across their horses' necks.

CHAP. VI.—*Of what took place in England in the time of Robert
Bruce; chiefly of the factions and quarrels of the nobles of the kingdom
which arose through the arrogance of Hugh Spenser.*

WE will now leave Robert Bruce, in peaceful possession of
the Scottish throne, and narrate what took place in his
day in England.   In doing so we will follow the English
chroniclers, as in such case we always do, since they are better
acquainted with their own affairs.   While Edward was laying
siege to Berwick, which had been recovered a few days before
from the English by the Scots, the Scots invaded England, and
in the battle of Myton[1] routed the English forces.   In con-

Edward has to
give up the
siege of Ber-
wick.

The arrogance
of Hugh
Spenser.

sequence whereof Edward was obliged to raise the siege of
Berwick.   He returned to London, and then began to come
under the absolute influence of his chamberlain, Hugh Spenser.
So strictly did this Hugh keep watch over the king's chamber,
that no one could gain access to the monarch unless by his
will and pleasure, and such an one would always make a gift
to Hugh before he departed.

Now this raised the wrath, and justly raised it, of the
princes and all the nobles of England to such a degree that the
earl of Lancaster and many of his followers marched to the
Welsh border, and there ravaged the territory of Hugh
Spenser and of his son Hugh.   The king, however, sent some
of these indignant nobles into banishment, Mowbray to wit,
and Roger Clefford, and Joslin Davil, and many more.   He
hoped by this means to terrify the earl of Lancaster and his
followers; but so far was he from gaining his end that they
wrought more harm than ever.   The king then sent messengers
to them, commanding them to attend a parliament in London;
and to that parliament came the tribes with great armies.

These are the princes who came with their followings of armed

---

[1] *i.e.* 'The Chapter of Mitton'; see *ante*, p. 228.

men : Humfrey de Bohun earl of Hereford, Roger Clefford, The princes of England who came in armed force to parliament. John Moubraye, Joslin Davil, Roger Mortymer, Henry Trays, John Giffard, Bartholomew Badelessemor [1], Roger Dammory, Hugh Dandale, Gilbert Clare earl of Gloucester.

It was at length determined that Hugh Spenser and his son Exile of Hugh Spenser. should be sentenced to perpetual banishment from England ; yet it was but a short time before the king recalled them into England, and sent into banishment Thomas earl of Lancaster, and his adherents. But the Mortimers, who were members of a numerous and powerful family, managed to gain the king's favour; and they were imprisoned in the Tower of London. Now when the rest of the English nobles came to know of this, they went to Thomas earl of Lancaster, who was then at Pontefract, and told him how the Mortimers had been put into prison. Thomas earl of Lancaster with his followers then laid siege to the castle of Tikhil [2], and against him there king Edward led a large army. With him were joined the Spensers, Aldomar Valance earl of Pembroke, and John earl of Arundel, and they defeated Thomas earl of Lancaster, who first took refuge with his followers at Tetbury castle, and afterwards at Pontefract. In the convent of the preaching friars at Pontefract, Thomas earl of Lancaster, Humfrey de Bohun earl of Hereford, and along with them the barons, met, and there agreed that they should go to Dunstanburgh, which belonged to the earl of Lancaster, until they should be able to arrange a peace with king Edward. But Thomas earl of Lancaster would not agree to this proposal, for he said that he should be called a traitor if he drew near to the Scottish marches, because of the continuing enmity between English Edward and Robert Bruce. But Roger Clefford judged that such removal to Dunstanburgh was a necessity, because of the influence of the king in their present neighbourhood, and, drawing his sword, he told the earl of Lancaster that if he would not accompany himself and the rest to Dunstanburgh, he would slay him, with his own hands, where he stood. Thomas thereupon gave his consent to go along with them, and, with seventy men, made all haste to Dunstanburgh. But when they were come to Boroughbridge, they were met by an army

---

i.e. Badlesmere.   [2] Orig. 'Tilche'.

under Andrew Herkelay, king Edward's lieutenant in the Scottish marches, who put to death the earl of Hereford, Roger Clefford, William Sullage, and Roger Benefeld, and carried captive to Pontefract Thomas earl of Lancaster, who there, in the presence of king Edward and his followers, suffered, along with five other barons, the penalty of death. This Thomas earl of Lancaster is said to have been illustrious for the miracles that he wrought[1].

The passage of the English king into Scotland, and his return.

Thereafter, in the year thirteen hundred and twenty-two, Edward raised an army of a hundred thousand fighting men, and passed into Scotland, desirous to give battle. But the Scots fled from before his face, so that the king was compelled by famine to return. James Douglas and Thomas

The Scots go a-plundering in England.

Randolph, earl of Moray, forthwith march at the head of an army into England, and plunder the country in all directions; Northallerton and many other towns, as far as York, they burned to the ground. Edward gathered a great army against them, and on the fifteenth day after Michaelmas came face to face with the Scots near to the monastery of Beigheland (our

The English are defeated. John the Briton is taken.

people call it Bieland), where the English were defeated. It was in that battle that John the Briton, earl of Richmond[2], the holder at that time of the earldom of Lancaster, was taken prisoner by the Scots, and afterwards ransomed with a great

---

[1] Lancaster had governed, when he was in power, no better than the king; but after his death, in a time of cattle-plague and famine, the people in their despair came to hold him for a martyr and a saint. See York Powell and Mackay's *Hist. of England*, Part i. pp. 213-215. Capgrave (*b.* 1393, *d.* 1464) says in his *Chronicle* (Rolls Series, p. 219) that in the year 1315 'blod ran owt of the toumbe of Thomas duk of Lancastir at Pounfreit'; and, as to the year 1389 (p. 253), that 'this same year was Thomas of Lancastir canonized, for it was seid comounly that he schuld nevir be canonzied onto the time that alle the juges that sat upon him were ded, and al her issew'. Barbour, a still earlier authority—for his *Brus* was written before Capgrave was born—has the following lines about Thomas of Lancaster :—

> ' Men said syn eftir this Thomas
> That on this wis mad martyr was
> Was sanctit and gud mirakillis did,
> Bot invy syn gert tham be hid.
> Bot, quhethir he haly was or nane,
> At Pomfret thusgat was he slane.'—*Brus*, cxxxi. 83 *sq.*

[2] He was no 'earl', but Sir Thomas of Richmond; see *Scala Cronica*, p. 143, as quoted in the Spalding Club ed. of *The Brus*, p. 523.

sum of money. He went over to France and never returned
to England. The annals of the English then go on to tell how
Andrew Herkelay was slain. They say, that is, that he went
out to collect a large body of soldiers, in the king's behalf,
with the view of bringing succour to him against the Scots in
the battle of Bieland, and that he bore himself in that business
slothfully and negligently, inasmuch as he had taken bribes
from James Douglas. The whole story is a dream—it has not
even verisimilitude; for the Scots had no such superabundance
of money as to be in a position to bribe the English; and
James Douglas was the last man to adopt methods of this sort,
a fighter he if ever there was a fighter, to whom the sword,
not gold, was at all times the weapon he would choose to gain
his end. It is besides very improbable that English Edward
would attack the Scots unless supported by a numerous army.
According to the true annals of the English, this Andrew was, *The slaying*
in point of fact, but by no right and legal means, sentenced to *of Andrew Herkelay.*
death by Edward; for the friends of the earl of Lancaster and
the foes of Andrew himself combined to turn the king against
him.

CHAP. VII.—*Concerning Isabella, sister of the king of the French,
how she was sent to France by her husband, the English king, and of
her banishment there along with her son. Of the captivity of Edward,
and the prophecies of Merlin ; further, of the passage of the Scots into
England, and of their return from England.*

ABOUT the same time Edward cruelly ill-treated Isabella, *Isabella, queen*
sister of the French king, and queen of England. At this the *of England, is*
                                                            sent to the
French king was very wroth, and sent heralds to the English *French king,*
king, who were to deliver to him this message: That the king *her brother.*
of England must either do fealty to him for Aquitaine or
suffer loss of that territory. By the advice of Hugh Spenser
the queen was sent into France, in the hope that she might
hinder the war that appeared so like to break out between her
brother and her husband ; but because she tarried too long in
France, Edward the king's son besought his father for permission to go to France and bring back his most pious mother.
To this the king willingly assented, but because they did not

The English king sentences his wife and son to exile. at once obey his order for their return, he banished them from England. Notwithstanding this sentence of exile against Edward, queen Isabella, with her son Edward, John brother of the earl of Hainault, Edward Woodstock, earl of Kent,

They return without leave obtained. returned all of them to England, on the twenty-fourth day of September, in the year of grace one thousand three hundred and twenty-six; and they had with them no more than fifty men in their company. That they dared to land in England with so small a following was a proof of hatred of the king and affection for the queen and her son. Edward of Carnarvon

Edward is taken. was in the end taken, and was lodged in the dungeons of the castle of Kenilworth, there to be in charge of the lord Henry, brother of the earl of Lancaster, who at that time was earl of Leicester. Edward the Third had bestowed upon him the earldom of Lancaster. Inasmuch as the king had caused Thomas earl of Lancaster to be put to death, it was presumed, and rightly presumed, that the strictest care would be exercised by the brother of the man who had thus come by his end. Hugh Spenser, Walter Stapylton, bishop of Exeter, and John Harundel[1], who had all been partisans of the king, were put to death.

Some prophecies of Merlin. About this same Edward of Carnarvon the English histories like to recall certain prophecies of Merlin; for Merlin declared that the waters of the sea would flow over those who had been slain in the time of this Edward—which they interpret of the battle of Bannockburn. Many of the men who fell in that battle, however, were drowned in a deep stream, and far more in the Forth, a most rapid river, where its waters mingle with the salt water of the sea. Merlin said further that in this Edward's days many stones would fall to the earth; and this is interpreted of the Scots, who at that time levelled with the ground castles and cities. They attempt further to disentangle many more of Merlin's knotty sayings; but I confess that I lay no great store by his misty dicta, for they are no more than mist in the clouds of the air[2].

Edward the Third begins to reign in the lifetime of Edward the Second. The English deposed Edward of Carnarvon because he had followed the counsel of wicked men, and anointed as king the third Edward, otherwise called 'of Windsor', in the fifteenth year of his age, that is, in the same year in which he landed in

---

[1] *i.e.* Arundel.   [2] Bk. II. ch. v., note *ad fin.*

England from France. Edward the Second, the father, always
desired to have an interview with his wife, and with Edward
the Third, his son ; but such interview he never attained to.
Perchance the son suspected that his father would seek to have
the crown again for himself—a request which sons are not in
the habit of granting to their fathers—nor yet fathers to their
sons, though fathers have more affection for their sons than
sons have for their fathers. Thereafter, says Caxton, the Scots
gathered a large army, and, invading England, put all to fire
and sword. They made their way as far as Stanhope in Weardale[1], and there they made a stand. Against them the third
Edward now brought a numerous army ; nor, says Caxton once
more, was there ever seen a finer army since Brutus landed in
Britain—for it was made up of one hundred thousand Englishmen and foreigners. I cannot, however, give credence to this
claim, because his father commanded a much larger force than
this at Bannockburn. For fifteen days the Scots kept their
station near a park, for by reason of the English they were
unable to make their way out ; provision of food too began to
fail them. The Scots' position was defended on both sides ; on
the one side was water, on the other the wood or park of Viridalia. Henry earl of Lancaster and John brother to the
earl of Hainault gave their voice in favour of an attack upon
the Scots by water, seeing that the stream was of no great
depth ; but Roger Mortimer, as might have been expected,
was of an opposite way of thinking—for was he not in the pay
of the Scots?—and when he was on patrol duty by night he
allowed the Scots to slip away. But Caxton says last of all,
that on the same night when the Scots made good their flight
James Douglas attacked the army of the king with two hundred lances, that is, with two hundred horsemen (for a lance
and a horseman mean with the Britons one and the same thing),
and arrived as far as the king's tent, and shouted sometimes
Naward, Naward, but at other times A Douglas, A Douglas ;
whereat the king and almost all the rest were affrighted ; but
by God's help the king was neither slain nor yet taken by the
Scots ; and the night when all this took place was one of
clearest moonlight.

An army than which, according to Caxton, there was never a finer.

---

[1] Viridalia.

Caxton is
refuted.

I give you Caxton's very words. Now I do not think you
will easily prove that the Scots bribed the English, nor yet
that they ever came to speech of Roger Mortimer. Unlikely
too it is that the Scots should have slipped away by
bright moonlight, and have escaped detection by at least
a few of the patrols who had not been bribed, and who
would surely have revealed the matter to the third Edward.

Froissart.

We have an account of this war written by Froissart, a historian of Hainault, who dedicated his work to the king of the
English, and who drew his knowledge from John, brother to
the earl of Hainault, and those who were along with him. His
tendency was to magnify rather than to attenuate what made
for the glory of the English ; and for this ¦reason it shall be
my care to follow him to the letter, save for the turning of
the French tongue, for he wrote in French, into Latin ; yet I
will endeavour to reproduce the substance of his views rather
than his words.

The genius of
Edward the
Third, and his
deeds.

Edward the Third was a man of a haughty spirit, and, relying on the counsel of those around him, he studied how he
might inflict some overwhelming defeat upon the Scots. He
sent messengers, therefore, to John of Hainault, with the
prayer that he would come to his support, and for answer
John brought to the help of Edward of England a body of
five hundred horsemen ; from all quarters Edward got together

One hundred
thousand men
in the army of
the English
king.

an army of one hundred thousand men, and therewith made
for the north toward the Scots boundaries. Now when Robert
Bruce was ware of this, and turned in his mind how he was
himself now stricken in years and sick in body, he bade Thomas
Randolph and lord James Douglas to get together a goodly
body of soldiers and invade Northumberland, trusting by a
devastation of that region to withdraw the English army from
the Scots—for Robert was a most far-seeing man. When
Edward heard of the approach of the Scottish army, he sent
his seneschal to see to the strengthening of Newcastle-upon-
Tyne, and to Carlisle he sent the earl of Hereford. The Scots
army was four-and-twenty thousand strong. Our chroniclers

Twenty-four, or
twenty, thou-
sand in the
army of the
Scots.

put the number at twenty thousand, neither more nor less ;
but on this point it may be that credence should be given to
him of Hainault rather than to the Scot ; for though the men

of Hainault had kinship with the English, and had likewise
brought them material support, yet in such a point as this
their estimate may be taken as more likely to be impartial
than that of either Scot or Englishman. Twenty thousand
men then, or twenty-four thousand, the Scots had in their
army—cavalry all of them. The nobles and the wealthy men
among them were mounted on large and powerful horses, the
common people upon small horses ; and they made no use of
chariots, because Northumberland is for the most part a hilly
country. But that race of the Scots, he says, has a most The hardiness
singular endurance of hunger and thirst, and heat and cold. of the Scots in war.
They can live for a long time together, even their men of
good nurture, upon the flesh of wild animals. For the Scots
knew that of flesh they could always have abundance from the Their provision
chase, and they therefore carry on the after-part of their saddle for food.
a double sack of meal, along with a sort of wide iron plate or
griddle, wherewith to make their bread. This griddle they How on an
heat by laying it over a fire, and then upon the griddle they emergency they bake their
spread a very thin paste of flour[1] ; and thus they bake their bread.
bread just as though they had an oven. The whole of Nor- Cruelty of the
thumberland they ravaged ; there was no village that they did Scots.
not burn to ashes, nor indeed was there a single place up to
within five leagues of Durham, where English Edward then
abode, that escaped their universal flames. The English, who Forces of the
were there in force, now became aware of the smoke. Their English.
numbers mounted to eight thousand armed horsemen, thirty
thousand foot-soldiers, four-and-twenty thousand bowmen, and
in addition they had of serving-men a multitude, who carried
provision in plenty. They drew up their army in three lines.
Each line consisted of two wings, and each wing counted five
thousand armed men. In this order they followed up the
Scots by marching in that direction whence the smoke from
the Scottish fires proceeded ; but though they pursued the
search till evening they did not discover the Scots. They
therefore pitched their camp in a glade close by a stream, that
the wearied might find the better refreshment, and that they
might thus await the arrival of their baggage-wagons, which
were not able to travel so fast as themselves. During the

---

[1] Cf. *ante*, p. 11.

whole of that day the Scots were giving to the flames all that
they could lay hands on, and this they did even at no great
distance from the English army ; yet, by reason of the rough-
ness of the road, the English could not reach them. The
dawn of the next day found the English force, drawn up in
line as before, again in vain pursuit of the Scots until the
evening ; and they thus had to pitch their camp again.

The English-
men hold a
council.

Meanwhile the leaders amongst the English consult what had
best be done, for they were daily witnesses of this general con-
flagration by the Scots, and were yet unable by any ordinary
means to reach the offenders. When they had therefore taken
good counsel together, they determined upon this plan : To
retreat in the direction of Scotland as far as the river Tyne,
judging that the Scots would there, under pressure of hunger,
be driven to cross the river, when they should be able to inflict
upon them, in the very act of passage, a crushing defeat. After
midnight, therefore, leaving carriages and baggage behind them,
they make for the Tyne with all speed, and, carrying with them
none but the smallest provision, marched the whole of the
following day without laying down their arms, and did not
break their fast except on the morsel of bread that each had
with him. At sunset only did they allow themselves that
benison of sleep which well-wearied mortals more than all the
rest delight in. On the following day they reached the Tyne,
but the river was in so great a flood that they were unable to
cross it. There for a space of three days, suffering from pri-
vation of every sort, they were compelled to pitch their tents.
When at last these three days of hunger and general misery
were behind them, it was determined by certain amongst the
English, who had not suffered from the attacks of the Scots,
that a march should be made either to Newcastle, which was
distant thirteen leagues, or to Carlisle, which was distant
eleven leagues, for in the neighbouring villages it was known
that the Scots had left no provisions behind them, and the
inhabitants of these villages were scattered far and wide, wandering in bands in search of food. They lost no time, therefore, in sending to those cities for food and drink, and on the
following day they had all they wanted to their heart's desire :
but of the Scots no single scrap of news. On the eighth day

the king ordered it to be proclaimed by public edict that if
any one should bring the king certain intelligence of the Scots
he should be rewarded by the king with a perpetual pension of
one hundred pounds. Which heard, fifteen active and able-
bodied knights took the road, or where there was no road
made one, in full chase, roving here and there and everywhere,
if only they might light upon those Scots. The army meanwhile maintained its position in a well-watered meadow about
two leagues from the Tyne, but the neighbouring villages had
been wasted of all provision, and they remained there for three
days. At the end of that time, one who had gone in quest of
the Scots returned with the news that they were distant at
that moment not more than three leagues from the king and
his army, and with a light heart were waiting the arrival of
the English, in all readiness to come to battle with them.

Forthwith the army was drawn up, as before, in three lines,
and they followed the indications of that explorer towards the
Scots. About mid-day they came in sight of the Scots posted
on a rising ground, and the Scots at the same time caught
sight of them. So soon as the Scots became aware of their
approach they divided their army into three parts, and occupied both sides of the hill and the passage of the river as well,
which they call a ford. When the English now considered
their position, they judged that they could not, without
evident jeopardy, attack them, and they therefore again
pitched their camp. To the Scots the English king soon The demands
sent a messenger, demanding that they should come down of the English
king.
into a proper plain and fight there. But the Scots made The answer of
answer that since the English were in three times greater the Scots.
force than the Scots, and likewise in every way better furnished, they preferred to maintain a more open position, so
that their inferiority in number might be compensated by a
natural environment that was better adapted for defence ; if,
then, the English king desired to fight them, he might try his
fortune as they were, since he was supposed to be ambitious of
military renown. Thus the day came to an end, and as darkness drew on some of the Scots went on night-guard, in case
an attempt should be made by the English to cross the river ;
the remnant kept their place upon the hill. They lighted

great bonfires, but throughout the night might be heard the
sound, deafening, terrific, of their bugles. The English army,
too, had its sentinels posted for the night, and thus, without
coming to the test of arms, the hostile forces spent three full
days, with no incident of war save that two soldiers, for the
trial of their strength, entered the lists of combat, and in
sight of both armies emptied each of them the saddle of his
adversary. But when, on the morning of the fourth day,
Phœbus had risen above the horizon, and the English turned
their eyes to the hill which the Scots had occupied at the first,
no enemy was to be seen, since in the silence of night the Scots
had carried themselves to another hill. The English king
thereupon ordered scouts to go in search of the Scots, and
learned from them how the Scots had planted themselves on
another hill upon the same river. As soon as they had this
news, the English hastened in that direction, and pitched their
camp on a hillock opposite the entrenchment of the Scots.

Douglas, his
doughty deed.   Now it happened that one night James Douglas, with two
hundred picked horsemen, crossed the river, invaded the
English camp, and, making his way to the tent of the king,
cut through two of the ropes which held it, after which, and
when he had slain three hundred of the English, he returned,
with the loss of a few men only, to his own quarters. This
calamity made its own impression upon the English, and
henceforth they were more careful in their choice of sentinels
by night. For eighteen days the two armies maintained their
position without any engagement of importance. But at
length, on the night of the eighteenth day, a Scot was taken
by the English patrol and brought before English Edward,
and he revealed to Edward this fact, that a public order had
gone forth to the effect that all were to hold themselves ready
for battle under the standard of James Douglas, but whither
the generals were aiming to lead them, or what this might
portend, he declared he knew not. The English, therefore,
lost no time in making a threefold division of their army; at
the shallows of the river they placed a most diligent night-
watch, and during all the hours of darkness that followed their
eyes knew no sleep. For the remembrance of the calamity of
the night before was so full of terror that they doubted not

the Scots meditated on that night too a repetition of the attack. Great fires also they kept up the whole night through, that they might more surely detect any movement of the enemy. It was toward dawn that two Scots trumpeters were taken by the English patrols, and these men, when they were brought into the presence of English Edward, declared to him that the Scots had turned their steps homeward, 'and we', The return of they said, 'were commanded to tell you so much as soon as the Scots to their own day began to break, and of intent it is that we were taken country. prisoners, to the end you may follow them if you have a wish to fight'. Thereafter the English king takes counsel with his chief men ; and to this conclusion they came, that it would no way advantage the English king to make haste after the Scots, for there would be risk of no small loss were his army, all weary with its march, to come to battle with the Scots. It was wiser, they judged, to let the Scots army depart with impunity than to expose the whole English army to the hazard of such a conflict. When the English arrived at the camping- The baggage of ground of the Scots, they found the carcases of five hundred the Scots left behind with wild animals, such as deer and the like; for the Scots had killed intent. them lest they should fall, a living booty, into the hands of the English. Besides these, they found three hundred stewing- Stewing-pans pans, made from the hairy hide of animals, in which the Scots made of hide. were used to cook their flesh food. They found too a thousand spits in use for roasting meat, and ten thousand shoes made from undressed leather with the hair on, which the Scots had taken to use when their own shoes had been worn out. Further, they found five naked Englishmen, bound to trees, with their legs broken. These they unbound. Following the counsel of those about him, Edward disbanded his whole army and returned to London. This narrative I have taken to the letter from Froissart [1].

---

[1] Major must have founded this long narrative upon another recension of Froissart than that used by Buchon (Liv. I. ptie. i. chh. 29-44 ; vol. i. pp. 20-32). In that text, *e.g.*, the English find 400—not 300—'chaudières faites de cuir, atout le poil' : and the same text speaks of 'cinq povres prisonniers anglois que les Escots avoient liés tous nuds aux arbres, par dépit, et deux qui avoient les jambes brisées : si les délièrent et laissèrent aller'.

CHAP. VIII.—*Of the complaint made by Edward the father, and how he was carried to another prison, where he was put to death with terrible tortures.*

It happened after this that Edward of Carnarvon was in Berkeley castle under guard of Maurice de Herkelay and John Mactrevers; to these Edward was ever complaining that neither his wife, the queen Isabella, nor yet his son Edward, was permitted to have speech with him. To this his guardians made answer : 'The queen dreads lest you should take her life, and your son has the like fear.' To this he of Carnarvon made the shrewd reply : ' Am I not a prisoner, and altogether in your power, and the king's, and the queen's? How then should I dare, or, daring it, be able to compass, any attempt upon their lives? And God knows that I have never harboured the thought of hurting in any wise either my wife or my son.' A little while hereafter, Edward of Windsor, by advice of Roger Mortimer, placed his father under the custody of Thomas Gournay and John Mactrevers in Corfe Castle : Herkelay he removed from his post of guardian. Now Edward, when he was once deposed, began to conceive for this castle such ungovernable hate, as if it were even a poison[1]. One night, on the prompting of Mortimer, they entered the chamber of Edward of Carnarvon, and, placing a thick plank upon his belly, they pressed the plank down upon him at each corner; thereafter, inserting a kind of tube in his fundament, and keeping themselves some way removed from the same, they ran a spit of copper red-hot through the tube, and so burned and broke his vitals, yet so that the manner of his death should not be apparent. Great God! what treason have we here! what wickedness! a crime indeed that no lapse of time, no punishment can expiate. And this they dared upon the person of their lord and king, and yet more, upon the prisoner for whose safe custody they were to answer. Here then you have the lamentable ending of Edward of Carnarvon, who in this point only sinned, that he followed the counsel of bad men, but was

Marginal notes:
Edward places his father in other custody.

Edward is subjected to fearful torture and slain.

---

[1] 'Quam arcem tanquam toxicum Edwardus exauthoratus odio prosequutus est.' It was at Berkeley Castle, not at Corfe, that Edward the Second was murdered.

otherwise a right-minded man and a brave soldier, clement too Edward is praised.
according to the measure of his own time; therefore he may
have his rightful place by the side of great kings.

CHAP. IX.—*Of the deeds of Robert Bruce, king of the Scots, and
Edward the Third, king of the English; likewise of the peace that was
brought about through the marriage of their children; and of the death
of Robert.*

EDWARD of Carnarvon, then, being dead, and Edward the
Third, called of Windsor, reigning in his stead, I will leave to
speak of English affairs for a little and return to Robert Bruce,
from whom I made this digression. When Robert Bruce had Robert Bruce.
suffered provocation at the hands of the English, he sent his
two chief men, Thomas Randolph and James Douglas, with
fifteen thousand picked soldiers of the Scots, into England,
with the view of humbling the English; and they went so far
as the park in Viridalia, of which we have so lately been speaking. But as I have told the story of this expedition from the
French narrative of the same by Froissart, I will say no more
thereanent, but pass at once to other matters.

In the year one thousand three hundred and twenty-six,
Edward the Third and Isabella, his mother, sent a solemn Edward the Third.
embassy to Scotland; and Robert Bruce granted audience to The English
the same at Edinburgh. It was the business of this embassy to embassy.
propose to give the sister of Edward in marriage to the son of
king Robert, with renunciation every way of that claim of
superiority which had been advanced by the English over the
kingdom of the Scots. Some reparation, however, they did
seek from Robert for the serious losses which he had inflicted
on the English. And so they came to an agreement; and Peace is con-
Robert Bruce counted out thirty thousand marks and gave cluded on the basis of
them to the English, and for his son David, a lad of five years, marriage.
he took the lady Joanna, sister to the English king, to wife.
That notion of an English superiority the Scots at all times
have spurned, for never at any time have they been subject to
any but their own proper king. This notwithstanding, to the
end they might maintain a state of peace and live quietly with

their neighbours, they sought to obtain the seal thereto of the English king and state, and what they sought they obtained.

It was three full years after the settlement of this peace that, at Cardross, in the four-and-twentieth year of his reign, Robert Bruce went the way of all flesh. A king he was worthy to sway the mightiest empire, and as a man one whom, in the matter of a genius for war, I would place even before William Wallace. And though William Wallace was more highly endowed in point of stature and bodily strength than Robert—for in gifts of this sort he surpassed, in my opinion, Alexander of Macedon himself[1]—yet not on that account is he to be reckoned as having superiority in matters of war. But herein William is indeed worthy to be extolled; that, sprung as he was from a mean house, he yet grew to be so great a man, with none to thank therefor but his own right arm and his own genius, and that he drove the English out of Scotland. Yet even here you shall find Robert Bruce not less admirable, though he were born of a noble house and had amongst his kindred by blood or marriage nobles many a one,—for after a beginning of disaster, when he had lost all that he had, when he had not a friend to stand by him, he remained ever of the same unconquered spirit, and drove, in the end, out of Scotland the Scots who favoured English rule and the nobles of England; twice he came to close quarters with the English king in conflicts difficult and formidable, once in Scotland, the second time in England; and as often did he defeat the Englishman. His subjects knew what it was to have just laws administered in their integrity; many changes of policy or government he made worthy of a king, and these remain amongst the Scots to the present day. All this notwithstanding, I do not prefer Robert before Kenneth, Gregory, David, or the Alexanders; nor, on the other hand, do I prefer any one of them before him; they possessed, each of them, their own peculiar excellencies, wherefore I will leave them all in their proper parity of place.

In his last testament Robert is said to have given these injunctions: first, that the king of the Scots should never

The death of Robert Bruce and his eulogy.

An eulogy of William Wallace.

Robert's will and testament.

---

[1] Alexander the Great is generally reckoned among the great men who were of small stature.

renounce possession of the Scots islands, nor make grant of the
same to his nobles[1]; and that provision perchance he made
because it is a matter of utmost difficulty to reach those
islands when there is need to punish transgressors; and for
that reason they rise easily in revolt against their kings.

Secondly: it was provided for in that testament that the
Scots should never grant any long or fixed date to the English
when they were about to engage in war with that nation; and
for this injunction cause may be found in the fact that the
English draw paid forces in plenty from outside their own people,
and these men are skilled in the use of engines of war. The
English too pay heavy taxes to their king for purposes of war,
and he is thus enabled to pass by all that are unfit, and to
choose only the best in arms, while at the same time he can
spend liberally upon the equipment of his army. In a long
continued war he thus depends upon completeness of arrangement and discipline rather than upon the actual strength and
prowess of his soldiers. On the other hand, in time of war the
common people among the Scots contribute absolutely nothing
to the expenses of the king; but rather these go forth with their
king the fit with the unfit alike, so that no discipline is observed;
nor are trained soldiers only chosen, and men unfit to bear
arms rejected; wherefore my wonder is rather that now and
again in a great war the Scots have ever defeated the English.
If those who are not fit to bear arms would but tax themselves
in order that the strong and able-bodied only should be chosen,
the Scots would more often win the day. And in proof of
this I would point out that where the Scots have found themselves in conflict with the English suddenly and hand to hand,
they are wont to be oftener conquerors than conquered.

Thirdly: He made bequest of his heart, that it should be
borne with him by some good soldier setting forth to fight
against the infidel; and this charge he gave to James Douglas,
in whom he most confided;—for before this he had made a
vow that in his own person he would go forth to fight against
the infidel. But though he went not, he was far from committing any sin, since for the good peace of his kingdom,
which only thus could have been secured with any likelihood,

---

[1] Cf. *ante*, p. 38.

This purpose
of the king is
discussed.
he might well have stayed at home. Yet I cannot approve
his purpose, seeing that it carried with it the absence from his
country of such an one as James Douglas ; for the king should
have borne in mind that, the fact of the mutual marriage notwithstanding, the English were still panting for the kingdom of
Scotland, and he knew that the presence of James Douglas was
of the utmost advantage to the kingdom, inasmuch as he
was devoted in no common measure to Thomas Randolph.
But perchance you will urge that, acting thus, Robert showed
the penetration of his judgment, feeling that fortune has no
room for two men where these two are equal, and such I
hold these men to have been ; and thus, taking the fairest
opportunity he could, he sent James Douglas beyond the
kingdom. And if he acted from this motive, he is not to be
censured ; for in the face of a possible civil war his conduct is
not to be called imprudent ; yet, inasmuch as the steadfast
courage of the man was known, and his loyal devotion to the
welfare of the kingdom had been tried so often, I cannot help
thinking that it would have been better had James Douglas
remained at home.

CHAP. X.—*Of the wise regency of Scotland at the hands of Thomas
Randolph, and his end through the treachery of a monk.*

A law made by
Randolph.
AFTER the death of Robert Bruce, Thomas Randolph exercised wise rule in Scotland, and throughout the whole kingdom
administered a perfect justice. He made a law that if any
horseman in dismounting from his horse should have made
fast his bridle to the saddle, and the bridle came thereafter
to be stolen, then the sheriff of that place should be respon-
A proper
example of
justice.
sible for the theft ; likewise in the matter of plough-irons ;
and in the end the sheriff might recover payment from
the king. Now it once came to pass that a certain country
fellow removed his own plough-irons, and made demand of
their value in money from the sheriff, who thereupon instituted the most thorough search for the author of the
crime ; and in the end the very countryman who laid the
complaint was found to be the guilty person ; and when he

confessed to the crime he was hanged.[1] The cause of rich
and poor Randolph weighed in equal scales without favour of
person : homicide he visited not with a fine of money, but
with the extreme penalty, lest otherwise occasion might be
given for the perpetration of homicide. For though by money
the royal purse may grow heavier, yet God is thereby offended,
a way is opened for assassination, justice suffers injury, the
king is contemned, and frequently comes thereby to his end.

And to say in few words what I think of this man's rule, I
can recall no king since Brutus landed in Britain who governed
more wisely than he.   In war he was of all men the bravest ; The eulogy
and though bodily strength be no proof, indeed, of the posses- of Randolph.
sion of that moral fortitude of which I now speak, yet was he
in his outward man eminently well-favoured, and of great
strength ; yet he was far more conspicuous in that fortitude
of soul which constitutes the only true virtue.   Such was the
wide-spread fame of this man amongst the English, that though
they often turned a greedy eye towards the kingdom of Scotland,
by reason of the tender years of its king, yet, thinking of
Thomas Randolph, they judged it best to maintain a state of
peace ; for they felt that during his lifetime it would be a
fruitless task to try to possess themselves of Scotland.

At last it happened that a certain monk of England, who Randolph is
claimed to be a physician, or one skilled in drugs, found his poisoned
way into Scotland, and there contracted a somewhat close through the
intimacy with the regent, and one day indeed gave him, in treachery of
a monk.
place of medicine, poison. The action of the poison was not
immediate and momentary ; rather did it gnaw the vitals step
by step. All this was part of the plan of this perfidious monk,
in order that he might safely return to his own country. Now,
when he was once returned thither, the guardian and regent of
the kingdom began to pine away more and more day by day,
and the report even of his death, albeit a false one, reached

---

[1] This is also the first incident of Randolph's wardenship narrated by Wyntoun (*Cronykil of Scotland*, Bk. VIII. ch. xxiv., vol. ii. p. 377, Laing's ed.) :

'A gredy carle swne efftyr wes
Byrnand in swylk gredynes,
That his plw-yrnys hym-selff stall,
And hyd thame in a pete-pot all.'

the ears of the English king; wherefore he bethought him
that the time was opportune for making an attempt to add
Scotland to his empire, and from all parts he brought together
a huge army, and directed his course toward the marches of
Scotland.   Thomas Randolph, on the other hand, with the
poison working in his body, and borne in a litter, hastened
with a numerous army against the English king.   He, when
he was aware of the approach of the Scots, sent a herald to
make inquiry whether the guardian of Scotland was still in
life ; and when the guardian learned so much, he attired himself magnificently, left his litter, caused himself to be placed
upon a horse, and by the expression of his countenance tried
to dissemble his malady.   He then made known to the English
herald that he and the Scots were full of eagerness to put
Edward's courage to the proof; and thereupon the herald
departed, laden with costly gifts, and declared to Edward that
the guardian of Scotland was indeed in life, and even in the
best of health, and suffering from no disease ; yet was he
interrupted as he spoke by that evil-hearted religious, who
called out, 'Though his belly were of iron he shall not escape
death '.   The English king, however, was counselled that it
would be his wisest course not to break the peace that had
been agreed on, since otherwise he should find himself involved
in a doubtful contest with a warlike people, under the leading
of an illustrious general, in whose good fortune the whole army
had no small confidence, whom every single man loved as a
father, and whom the universal voice proclaimed as the father
of his country.   Edward, therefore assented to this reasoning,
disbanded his army, and went to London, while the finger of
scorn was pointed at that religious as a liar, whose utterances
had proved themselves without foundation.   Yet while the
guardian was being borne in his litter toward Edinburgh, the
pestilence within him gathered strength, and at Musselburgh
he died.   He received honourable burial at Dunfermline by
the side of kings and regents.   This man I cannot count as
inferior to William Wallace; nay, I will not give Robert
Bruce himself a place before him, when I recall the moral
fortitude, the strong sense of justice, the conspicuous virtues
of every sort by which he was distinguished.

*Randolph's
exertions, even
when sick with
poison, for his
country.*

*The death of
Randolph.
His eulogy.*

CHAP. XI.—*Of the brave deeds of James Douglas and his death;
and of the succession of Edward Baliol in Scotland, his victory, his coronation, and, finally, his flight.*

JAMES DOUGLAS, when he went on his journey to western
Hesperia [1] with William St. Clair and Robert Logan, both
knights, for his squires, carried round his neck in a golden
casket the heart of Robert Bruce; and there, bravely fighting against the Agarenes [2], he fell.   It was after this that Death of
Douglas.
Donald earl of Mar was chosen guardian and governor of Donald be-
Scotland; and in his time, that is, in the one thousand three comes regent
of Scotland.
hundred and thirty-second year from the Virgin's travail,
Edward Baliol, a Scot, but at the instigation and with the
support of the English king, made a descent upon Scotland, Baliol's
attempt.
claiming that the succession to the throne lay rightfully with
him. He came to Scotland with no more than six hundred
men for a following, and, relying more upon the help of those
Scots who afterwards were killed in the Black Parliament [3]
than upon his own kindred, he got as far as Dupplin. Against
him marched Patrick Dunbar, earl of March, with thirty
thousand men, and the earl of Mar also with a large number at
his back; and they had scorn of Edward when they saw how
small a troop he had along with him, and so did not place a
proper watch by night. But when Edward was ware of this,
he fell upon them by night when they were heavy with sleep,
and slew them as though they had been so many swine, not a
man of them resisting. Then Baliol, being a man of a high Baliol's happy
augury.
courage, rejoiced greatly at this issue, and taking this happy
beginning of the contest as a good omen, he ventured to fight
with the rest of the nobles in broad daylight. He took his
stand in a position of strong natural defence, and the Scots
rushed upon him, in great numbers indeed, but with a complete
absence of order and discipline. In this battle Edward Baliol
came off victor; the earl of Mar and Alexander Fraser Baliol's victory.
perished, with many of the nobility, and Duncan earl of Fife
was taken prisoner. Edward Baliol next took the fortified
town of Saint John after a slight resistance. Duncan earl of His successes.

[1] *i.e.* Spain.   [2] *i.e.* The children of Hagar = the Saracens.
[3] See *ante,* p. 245.

Fife and William St. Clair, bishop of Dunkeld, then took the oath of fealty to him, and by their help he was invested with His coronation. the kingly crown at Scone. Thereupon David Bruce, a boy of nine years, fled by the direction of his guardians to France, Bruce escapes taking with him his wife, the sister of the English king; and to France. at the hands of the French king he met with an honourable reception. There he found a shelter for eight years and more.

Alas for the shame, the grief of it! Where then was Thomas Randolph, where James Douglas then, to stand by the son of Robert Bruce in the hour of his distress? Surely the warriors were the same as those whom Robert Bruce and Thomas Randolph had never failed to lead to victory; the same indeed,— but it was the leader who was wanting; and so they did but little in the war that is worthy to be told. We read of that army of Alexander the Macedonian, which, while he led it, never knew defeat, that after his death it was conquered with ease. Wherefore you may see that just as the best of generals is a cripple if he have not troops whose delight is in the conflict—in just like case is the best of armies without a proper general. So that Caesar said rightly enough, that he would go in the first place to the western parts of Spain, there to take captive an army that had no leader, and after that a leader who had no army. But in the following year the town of Perth was taken by James and Simon Fraser and Robert Keith. At the storming of that town there were taken prisoner Duncan earl of Fife, guardian under Edward Baliol, and likewise Andrew of Tulibard, who, when he was found guilty of treason against the king, rightly underwent the penalty of death. In that same year John Randolph earl of Moray, Archibald Douglas who was brother to the lord James Douglas, and Simon Fraser lay in wait to seize Edward Baliol, who had got so large a number of Scots nobles to accept his terms of peace; among them he had somehow deflected Alexander Bruce earl of Carrick and the lord of Galloway. But now he began suddenly to be attacked Baliol flies, and on every side, and lost no time in seeking safety in flight, even his friends are on a bridleless horse [1]. Of his supporters there fell on that day slain.

---

[1] Cf. Wyntoun's *Cronykil*, Laing's ed., vol. ii. p. 395 :—

> Bot the Ballyoll his gat is gane,
> On a barme hors with leggys bare ;

i.e. probably, a horse without a saddle. Leslie (Dalrymple's trans. pt. iii. p. 15), says 'the Balie . . . bangs vp on a horsse'.

Henry Baliol, who made most vigorous resistance, and even in his flight put more than one of his pursuers to death, likewise John Mowbray, Walter Cumming, Richard Kirkby, knight. In this battle the earl of Carrick was taken prisoner, and afterwards liberated by the earl of Moray.

CHAP. XII.—*Of the attack made upon the Scots by Edward of England and Edward Baliol; of the siege of Berwick, and how it was in the end taken by storm after a battle in which very many of the Scots lost their lives.*

WHEN Edward of England had knowledge of the divisions and civil war which were then lively among the Scots, he thought that the time was fit for gaining Scotland to himself, and disregarding at once his tie by marriage with that country, the oath that he had sworn, and every obligation of good faith, he collected a huge army of Scots and English; for in this war he had upon his side Edward Baliol and those who ranged themselves with him. In renown, as this world counts renown, Edward was illustrious, but a higher kind of renown would have been his had Robert Bruce or Thomas Randolph been his foe; as things now were, the Scots might have been counted as already vanquished through the dissensions among themselves.

There were two parties, almost equal one with another, who with some show of right claimed the throne, and various homicides were among them mutually committed; both parties were aiming at supreme power. Edward, therefore, judging that a settled peace could never be brought about between them, showed his shrewdness in attaching himself to the party of Edward Bruce, as being the weaker of the two, thinking he should thus best deal destruction on the Scots. Yet Baliol, as is plain from what has been said above, had no shadow of a claim—unless such an one as might be urged in a sophistical fashion; and therefore you shall find all the better men active upon the side of Bruce. The supporters of David Bruce, when they considered the guilefulness and craft of the English king, gave the keeping of the castle of Berwick to the earl of the Marches, and of its town to Alexander Seton. It was at this time that Andrew earl of Moray was taken prisoner by

Scottish factions.

Andrew, earl of
Moray, is taken
prisoner.
Edward Baliol and the English near to the Marches; and
about the same time William Douglas, lord of Liddesdale, who
had been taken by the English, was ransomed. A short time
after the investment of Berwick, on the day before the ides of
Berwick is
invested.
April, the English king arrived on the spot, and made an
attack upon the town both by land and by sea. But the town
was manfully defended by Seton and his men, who burned the
ships and inflicted no small damage upon the besiegers; but in
the storming of the ships a son of lord Seton was taken by the
English. This terrible siege lasted till St. Magdalen's day
without a break.

In the end the Scots made this covenant with the English:
that if within a given time they were unable to succour the
town, they would then make surrender to the English; and
in security for this obligation lord Seton placed his eldest
son in their hands as a hostage. Further, after the capture
of Andrew of Moray, Archibald Douglas, the chief of the
Archibald
Douglas,
governor of
Scotland.
family of Douglas, was chosen guardian of Scotland. He
got together an army of sixty thousand men, supporters of
David Bruce, meaning to make therewith invasion of England,
and thus to raise the siege. But he unwisely listened to the
suasion of the men within the city when they called on him
rather to fight; and when he did not arrive punctually to the
hour, the English leader demanded the surrender of the place,
on the ground of the covenant that had been made between
them. Now when the men within considered the close neighbourhood of a Scottish army, they did not surrender the town.
The hostage
is hanged.
In answer to this the enemy hanged their hostage, Thomas
Seton, on a lofty gallows, in the sight of both his father and
his mother, thinking that his parents, and, most of all, his fond
mother, would be moved, by the death of their son and heir,
The masculine
courage of a
Scottish
matron.
to the surrender of the town. But this brave-hearted woman
preferred the safety of the town and the liberty of her country
to the life of her son; and to her husband, while her son was
ascending the gallows, she spoke these words: 'We are
young—we have other children—let us patiently bear the
death of one.'
Battle of
Halidon.
In defence of the city a battle called of Halidon was fought.
Edward of England and Edward Baliol took up a position

which was every way favourable, for it was upon a height;
while the supporters of David Bruce occupied a hillock,
whence they must go down into the valley and ascend the
other height in face of the enemy when it came to a battle. The
first indeed held the position of strength; and the more cautious
amongst the Scots were opposed to the risk of battle in that
place, and counselled rather an invasion of England, where,
with fire and sword, they might waste the surrounding country,
and thus force the English to withdraw from the blockade. In
the end, however, they followed the counsel of James Douglas,
the guardian, a man in such a case as this rashly daring rather
than brave; but, being guardian, they assented to him. The
battle then is begun; and as the armed men were striving to
climb the flank of the other hill, many of them fell, in the
shower of stones that were rolled down upon them; one of the
enemy indeed sufficed to bar the way to four who were climbing; and so it was that in a bloodless battle the best men who
followed the fortunes of David Bruce lost their lives; and
among them the chief were these: Archibald Douglas, the The illustrious
guardian; James, John, and Alan Stuart, all brothers, and Scots who were
slain.
cousins-german of David Bruce, as well as being cousins-
german of Robert Stuart, afterward king of the Scots; Hugh
earl of Ross, wearing the shirt of Saint Duthac [1] (which, on
the death of the earl, is said to have been restored—an example,
this, of English courtesy—to the town of Tain); Kenneth,
earl of Sutherland; Alexander Bruce, earl of Carrick; Andrew,
James, and Simon Fraser, all brothers, with many other nobles.
After this battle Berwick was surrendered to the English; the Berwick surren-
earl of March and the lord Seton are forced to swear fidelity to dered to the
enemy.
the English king and Edward Baliol; and so it came to pass
that almost all the supporters of David Bruce were destroyed,
or—if they happened to have saved their lives—were compelled
to desert him. Some of our countrymen, on the strength of
an old prophecy—I know not truly what or whence—declare

---

[1] The shirt of Saint Duthac, to which marvellous powers were ascribed, was,
according to the Rev. W. Taylor (*Researches into the History of Tain*, 1882, p.
42), preserved in the Church of St. Duthac, and worn by the earl of Ross when
he went to war. The story, told by the Bollandists (March 8) of the burning
coal carried without injury in his bosom by Saint Duthach as a boy may have
given rise to the attribution of a peculiar virtue to his shirt.

that in the same place there shall some day be fought a battle
lucky for the Scots, fraught with disaster to the English; but
to prophecies of this sort I confess that I attach a very slender
measure of credence.

CHAP. XIII.—*Of the tyranny of Baliol in Scotland ; of his oppression of David, and the accession of Robert Stuart to the side of David.*

Baliol occupies
Scotland.

The English-
man returns
home.

AFTER the battle of Halidon Hill in the neighbourhood of
Berwick, Edward Baliol was put in possession of all the more
strongly fortified places in Scotland, and the English king
returned. In all this the Englishman acted from no virtuous
or kindly motive; we may safely presume that Baliol made
him a secret promise to hold the kingdom from him. For if
the question be put why he should have given his support to
Baliol, who was destitute of any real claim, and utterly passed
by David Bruce to whom he had given his own sister in marriage, I can find and make none other answer than this: that
he saw David Bruce to have the larger and stronger following
amongst the Scots, and had no hope of being able to use him
toward the accomplishing of his own ends in Scotland, while
under cover of Edward Baliol he might, he thought, preserve
some kind of footing there.   But, whatever may have been the

Diminution of
David's follow-
ing.

The strongholds
remaining faith-
ful to David.

truth in the matter, the following of David Bruce had dwindled
to such a degree that in all Scotland there remained no more
than four strongholds which owned his sway, to wit, Dunbarton,
of which Malcolm Fleming was the keeper; Lochleven, which
was held by Alan de Veypont; Kildrummy, in the hands of
Christiana Bruce, and Urquhart, in the hands of Thomas
Lauder. But in the year of the redemption of the world the
thirteen hundred and thirty-fourth, seeds of a fresh quarrel
began to sprout at Perth; for the lord Henry de Beaumont,
David earl of Athole, and Richard Talbot, wished to give
precedence to the daughters of the brother of Alexander
Mowbray over Alexander himself. Edward Baliol took the
part, in this quarrel, of Alexander. Poor Edward had forgotten that of the wise man: 'He who gives judgment between
two of his friends will hardly avoid to offend one of them;
whereas he who gives judgment between enemies will gain a

friend.' The end was that those three persons of importance were highly indignant, and went to their respective homes. Talbot made all haste toward England, but was taken in Lothian; Henry de Beaumont hastened into Buchan in the direction of Dundark, whose fortress he restored, and he came to bear rule in all Buchan. Andrew of Moray laid siege to Henry in Dundark, and forced him to abandon that stronghold and flee into England. The earl of Athole, however, withdrew to Lochindorb, and Edward Baliol betook himself to Berwick. Edward Baliol then, dreading the revolt of these nobles, gave dismissal to Alexander Mowbray, in order that he might gain the alliance of the rest. Upon those earls he bestowed the whole lands of the seneschal of Scotland. Whereupon Alexander Mowbray, when he had parted from Baliol, adhered to Andrew of Moray. Baliol then began to hold all Scotland at his will and pleasure.

The lord Stuart, after David Bruce the rightful heir to Scotland, in his fear of Edward Baliol fled to Dunbarton, and received from Malcolm Fleming a kind and friendly welcome. Further, in the following year, English Edward invaded Scotland with a large army. Edward Baliol had a meeting with him, and these two appointed David earl of Athole to be lieutenant of Scotland, and a short while thereafter English Edward departed into England, taking Edward Baliol with him. From this proceeding I gather that Edward of Windsor aimed at keeping hold of Scotland for himself, since he carried off Edward Baliol into England, even then when this latter seemed to be strongly hated in Scotland. All the lands of the Stuart and of the Cummings of Bute the earl of Athole now fastened upon for himself. Edward of Windsor's aims on the kingdom of Scotland.

At this time there was not a person who in open fashion acknowledged himself a subject of David Bruce, unless you except little lads who in their play would always say that king David Bruce was their king[1]. Robert Stuart began David is looked on as deprived of his kingdom.

---

[1] Cf. Wyntoun's *Cronykil*, Bk. VIII. ch. xxix., vol. ii. p. 413, Laing's ed. :
'Thus wes the kynryk off Scotland
Sa hale in Inglis mennys hand,
That nane durst thaim than wythsay
(At swa gret myscheffe than war thay),

to chafe at this assumption of a claim to his lands which had been made by David earl of Athole, and sent a messenger to the lord of Lochaw, Campbell was his name, beseeching him to send an armed force to his succour. Whereupon Campbell came with four hundred men, and together they laid siege to, and in the end they stormed, the castle of Dunhowm. And when the men of Bute who had been reared under the Stuarts came to hear of this, they flocked to him in crowds, as to their true and rightful lord. And when Alan Lile, the lieutenant, came in turn to know what had happened, he aimed to cut them off, as they marched, with a body of soldiers, and so to destroy them ere they had been furnished with arms. But when those who were called Brandan's servingmen saw this, they made for a heap of stones which they found close by, and with all their might they showered stones, as it were hail, upon the lieutenant; him indeed they stoned to

The slaying of Alan the lieutenant.

death, and those that were with him they put to the rout. For the service that they had rendered they prayed their lord the Stuart that he would hold them free of multure dues[1]; and to this petition the Stuart, as was right, consented. Soon afterward Thomas Bruce earl of Carrick, William Carruther, and many others, joined themselves to the Stuart.

CHAP. XIV.—*Of the return of earl Randolph to Scotland ; of the choice of guardians, the captivity of one, and the brave deeds of the other; of cities that were set on fire and their restoration, and various events of war.*

Return of earl Randolph into Scotland.

IT was at this time that Randolph earl of Moray, leaving David Bruce still sheltering in France, came to Scotland and had a joyful reception from the lord Stuart in Dunbarton; by his aid Clydesdale, Carrick, Kyle, and Cunningham were gained

> Bot chyldyr that na kyndly skyll
> Had to deme betwyx gud and iwyll,
> Na cowth nocht drade thare will to say,
> For thare Kyng wes a child as thai.
> Qwhen men askyt qwhays men thai were,
> Thai rycht apertly wald awnsuere,
> That thai war men to Kyng Dawy :
> Thus said thai all generaly.' ·

[1] The multure dues of the baron's mill—' one of the most grievous oppressions of the peasantry '. Cf. Mr. Innes's *Lectures on Scotch Legal Antiquities,* p. 47.

over to their side, and Robert Stuart and the said earl of
Moray were chosen to be guardians of Scotland. This done,
the earl of Moray marched against the earl of Athole, pursued
him even to Lochaber, and compelled him to swear fealty to
David Bruce. They then called together a council of their
followers at Perth. Those who were present at this council A Council of
were: Andrew of Moray just ransomed from his captivity, the nobles.
Patrick Dunbar earl of March, Lord Stuart, Alexander Mowbray, David earl of Athole, William Douglas of Nithsdale.
But now they learned that Edward of England and Edward
Baliol had arrived in Scotland ; and therefore gave their orders
that the common people should leave defenceless places and
betake themselves to strengths. It was in this year that the
duke of Geller[1], moved as much by English money as by The duke of
English prayers, went forth to fight against the Scots, and Geller.
with a large fleet invaded their country. The guardian, the
earl of March, William Douglas, and Alexander Ramsay met
him in battle at the Borough moor. The fight was a fierce
one, but the Geller men were defeated. On the payment The Geller
of ransom, however, the Geller men were allowed to pass men are
freely into England. Only the duke of Geller, in case he defeated.
should be slain by the Scots under way, was from motives of
humanity attended by the guardian in person ; and the English,
when they came to hear of this, gathered some troops together
all secretly, fell upon the guardian unawares, and took him
prisoner. For though the men of northern nations may indeed The Guardian
excel the southrons in strength and valour, yet in that prudence of Scotland is
which is a first necessity in warfare they are too often found taken.
wanting[2].

After the guardian had been taken prisoner, David earl of David earl of
Athole turned him to Edward of England and Edward Baliol Athole deserts
at Perth, and there gave them his word that, if they would king.
make choice of him for guardian of Scotland, he would in no
long time crush the Bruces, bring them over to the party of

---

[1] Macpherson, in his notes to Wyntoun's *Cronykil* (vol. iii. p. 297, Laing's ed.),
says that the Scottish historians have erroneously called 'the politic ally of
Edward' (whom Major calls '*dux* Gelriæ') 'Earl of Geller instead of Namur,
probably led into the mistake by an Earl of Gueldre (written *Geders*) being at
the same time in the service of England '.

[2] Cf. *ante*, Bk. I. ch. vi. p. 29, ch. vii. p. 44.

Edward, and so keep them settled in that mind; and they for
their part assented to what he said, and departed yet once more
into England.   This David was a fickle man and an ambitious;
though he had succeeded in bringing every Scot to Edward's
side, there is no doubt that he would have ended by turning
against Edward and making a forcible invasion of his kingdom.

His cruelty to innocent people. He was the oppresssor of the innocent and of the poor among
the common people; for all he did he knew no measure but his
own will, heedless of the dictates of reason ; and against guilt-
less men he raged with inhuman cruelty.   He then began to
lay siege to the castle of Kildrummy; whereupon Andrew of
Moray (who, after the capture of his kinsman the earl of Moray,
had been chosen for guardian by the followers of the Bruces)
went forth against him, taking with him two noblemen—strong
men they were and devoted to Bruce—to wit, the earl of March

Andrew earl of Moray is made Guardian. and William Douglas.   There was then fought a fierce battle
in the forest of Kilblene, in the which the earl of Athole,
Walter Cumming, Robert Bred, and many others came by their

A fierce battle. end.   And in the following year the guardian laid siege to the
castle of Lochindorb [1] which was held by the wife of that earl of
Athole who had just been slain.   And she went secretly to the
English king for succour.   A short while thereafter the king
of England came into Moray with a large army, and laid all

The English invade Moray. The burning of Elgin. waste with fire.   Elgin, the chief city of Moray, he gave to the
flames; its church, the seat of the bishop and the dwellings of
the canons, he saved from being burnt.   Thereafter he went to
Aberdeen, and razed that city to the ground.   Thence he
went to Perth, where he commanded that the walls of the city
should be built of fair and noble stones at the expense of six
religious foundations, to wit, of St. Andrews, Dunfermline,
Lindores, Balmerino, Arbroath, and Cupar ; and some strong
places likewise he ordered to be restored, to wit, St. Andrews,
Lochris[2], Stirling, Maidens' Castle[3], and Roxburgh, in the
which he placed his own keepers and lieutenants.   It was at
this time that his brother John arrived, and he wasted with fire
those parts of Scotland which were hostile to Edward, and

[1] Orig. and F. Lochindork.

[2] So F., ? Leuchars. Wyntoun has ' the Pele of Lukrys '.   Orig. ' Lochrien '=
Lochryan.   [3] See *ante*, p. 15.

those of the inhabitants who took refuge in sacred buildings
he burned.   And when Edward rebuked him therefor before John of Eltham
the high altar of Saint John at Perth, and John answered him is slain before the altar.
in stubborn fashion, he was then and therefore put to death by
king Edward.   Consider, then, how God punished the wicked
conduct of John toward sacred places by his death at the hand
of a brother !   For it sometimes happens that God uses a man,
against his will, as an instrument for the avenging of foul
insults offered by another ; just so did he raise up the Syrians
and Assyrians against the Hebrews when they sinned, and these
his unwitting instruments inflicted a punishment of which they
knew not the measure.

After this, leaving Edward Baliol at Perth, Edward the The English
Third went into England ; and Henry de Beaumont, for the king returns home.
avenging of his son-in-law, the earl of Athole, put to the sword
without mercy all upon whom he could lay hands.   In the
same year, in the month of October, Andrew of Moray, who was
called guardian of the Bruces, took by storm the castles of Andrew of
Dunnottar, Kynnef, and Lauriston, which were in the hands of Moray and his notable gests.
the Baliols, and razed them to the ground.   During the whole
of that winter the war went on unceasingly between him upon
the one part and the English with the Baliols on the other,
so that the whole lands of Mearns, Gowry, and Angus were
stripped bare of all provision.   In this year, too, this same
Andrew, with the help of James Douglas, razed to the ground
Falkland, St. Andrews, Lochris[1], and Bothwell.   The castle of
Cupar, however, he was unable to win.   This done, he did not
fear to invade England, and on the northern English he dealt
much damage.   A high-souled man was this Andrew, and ever
eager for the fight, one who took the Bruces for his exemplar.

CHAP. XV.—*The siege of the castle of Dunbar, and its courageous
defence by a woman ; how the siege was raised by reason of the invasion
of England by the French ; of divers losses upon both sides ; and of
tournaments, and how far they are lawful.*

In the following year, and on the ides of February, the castle
of Dunbar was besieged by the lord William Montagu, earl of The siege of Dunbar.

---

[1] Orig. ' Lochbres ' ; ? Leuchars.

Salisbury, and the earl Arundel, Englishmen both, who made
their attack with engines of war marvellous to behold. For
six months the siege went on. But the situation of the castle
is of the most favourable, since it stands over the sea ; and it
was defended by a brave woman, who was commonly known as
Heroic Agnes
of Dunbar. Black Agnes of Dunbar. For she was countess of that place,
and her husband was earl of March, and at that time the most
outstanding man amongst the Scots. She spared no tempting
words to entice the Scots to make stand against the English
king ; and in a time of truce she took her place upon the walls
and began to banter the Englishmen, for of raillery and manly
intellect she had no lack ; wherefore two amongst the English,
earls and leading men they were, prepared to attack the castle.
The fighting
sow. And on a certain day they craftily constructed an engine of
war which is called the sow, beneath which may find shelter a
large number of men, whose aim it is to undermine a fortress.
Agnes's jeers. Now, when Agnes was ware of this, she used this banter with
them, saying that unless the English took good care of their
sow, she would find a way to make her farrow. She then caused
boiling pitch, and burning sulphur, and the like, to be poured
in plenty on the sow, and with heavy logs and stones she made
an end, not of the sow only, but of all her litter.

But the famine of all provisions was heavy within the castle,
and because of two galleys which the English had upon the sea, it
was no easy thing to get victuals by water. Alexander Ramsay,
therefore, was moved to pity for this most heroic woman, and
strove to meet her peril by an effort that was no less perilous ;
for in secret and by night he conveyed food to the castle in
small boats. Agnes thereupon took fresh heart, and on the
following day she exhorted her people to turn the attack upon
the Englishmen at a time when they felt themselves secure.
And her soldiers answered to her call, and slew no small
number of the English. While the siege of Dunbar was still
going on there came to Scotland a fresh body of English
The English
who had lately
invaded Scot-
land are slain. soldiers. Laurence Preston went out to meet them with a
smaller force and gave them a warm reception, for the English
were beaten, and the Scots carried away with them all that
had been taken alive. But in the course of this battle Lau-
Laurence
Preston falls
upon the field. rence Preston had been mortally wounded, and soon thereafter
he died upon the spot where he fell ; whereupon his followers,

in their rage, slew their English prisoners to a man. This The prisoners are killed.
cruelty of the Scots in the slaughter of their prisoners I con- Yet another
demn. Another body of English soldiers invaded Scotland band of English soldiery is slain,
under Richard Talbot, but William Keith of Galleston routed and their leader taken prisoner.
them, and took Richard prisoner.

When the Englishmen saw that they could not [take the
castle of Dunbar by force, they considered how they might
gain their end by guile. Finding Scots to carry their message,
they made promise of valuable gifts to the gatekeeper and the
wardens of the castle if they would betray the same. To this
the wardens consented, but they declared the thing to Agnes.
Some of the Englishmen then made an entrance, and Montagu,
unless in the very act he had been held back by his own men,
would have got within the gates. And Agnes, when she saw
this from an upper tower, made use of this raillery with him,
saying, 'Fare thee well, then, Montagu ; methought thou wert
coming to sup with us, and help defend the castle against
the English king.' Meanwhile the English king had got himself entangled in French wars, and so sent for those who were
besieging the castle of Dunbar, and thus it was that the castle The siege
of Dunbar took no scathe at the hands of its invaders, and was of Dunbar is raised.
saved by Agnes of Dunbar.

In the following year died Andrew the guardian, and in his Death of
place Robert Stuart, though under age, was chosen. He con- Andrew the guardian.
tinued in that office till the arrival of David Bruce. In the Robert Stuart
same year William Douglas of Nithsdale drove the English becomes guardian.
out of Teviotdale, and brought that district under the rule of
David Bruce. This same William fought many times against
the English with a far inferior force, and mostly he came off
conqueror, though his body showed many a wound dealt him
by the foe ; but the more of wounds he got, the better soldier
he became. Now, when Henry of Lancaster, earl of Derby,
heard of the worth and valour of William Douglas and Alexander Ramsay, he was filled with desire to see those men, and
put them to the proof in jousting with the spear. At Ber- Jousting with
wick, therefore, they met one another, properly furnished for the spear.
the contest. It was then that a certain Englishman asked
Patrick Graham whether he were willing to enter the lists
against him. To whom Patrick answered with this humour,
that indeed he would not refuse this challenge, but this counsel

he would give the Englishman : to make certain of a good
breakfast, for he might be assured of this, that he should sup
in paradise ; and, as they met one another in full career, he
slew the Englishman, and, thus it chanced that he spoke truly.

Tournaments
of arms.

For the most part I abhor this dangerous game of jousting
with the spear merely for the sake of making a show ; for anything is hateful which risks the lives of men without necessity.
For this reason I say that those who thus come in conflict in
the course of a war which is just are not to blame ; but if it be
in time of peace, and merely for show, or even for the practising
of themselves in such things, they are sorely to blame. And a

A vulpine
confession.

confession made before such tournaments has in it something
vulpine ; for the intention is immediately thereafter to commit
an unlawful deed. I do not, however, deny the right to joust
with blunted spears, for the sake of exercising the skill of
the combatants, with all precaution taken against a mortal
wound[1].

CHAP. XVI.—*Of the siege of Perth and Stirling ; of the recovery
of Edinburgh ; the renown in war of Alexander Ramsay ; of the welcome given to king David, and the fealty sworn to him by the Scots.*

It was in the thirteen hundred and thirty-ninth year from
the Virgin's travail that Robert Stuart, the guardian, laid siege

Stuart besieges
Perth.

to Perth, a strongly fortified city. In his company were these
nobles : William earl of Ross, Patrick earl of March, Maurice
de Moray[2] lord Clydesdale, William Keith of Galleston, and
many more. The city was at that time in the charge of
Thomas Urthid[3], who had along with him a great multitude
of Scots and Englishmen. The siege was carried on for two
months and two weeks. William Douglas at that time arrived
from France, bringing with him to the help of the Scots five

---

[1] This passage is referred to in Mr. George Neilson's erudite work, *Trial by
Combat*, Glasgow, 1890, p. 289.

[2] In Orig. 'Maubray', F. 'Moubray': a misprint for 'Moravia'. Cf.
Wyntoun's *Cronykil* (Laing's ed.), vol. ii. p. 451 ; *Liber Pluscardensis*, pp. 287,
288. Maurice de Moray was created earl of Strathern in 1343, and three years
later was slain at the battle of Neville's Cross, near Durham. See Fraser's *Red
Book of Menteith*, vol. i. p. 456.

[3] [Uchtrede]—so supplied in brackets, after 'Schyre Thomas', in Laing's ed.
of Wyntoun, vol. ii. p. 454.

ships fully laden with munitions of war, and at his coming the guardian rejoiced greatly. He sent too a messenger to William Bullock, keeper of the castle of Cupar, with the intent to persuade Bullock to swear fealty to David Bruce; and in this he had success, for Bullock joined himself to the guardian, and helped him mightily. William Douglas was wounded in the leg at the siege of Perth, for he was ever exposing himself to risks; and indeed many men both within and without the city were afterward found missing. But in the end, and after two months and two days, the city was taken, though the lives and property of its defenders were spared. By reason of the unceasing slaughter the land had been left untilled, and many perished from hunger. There was a certain country-fellow, by name Crystyclok, who fed, as he were no better than a wolf, on the flesh of women and children [1]. And herein he did wickedly; for though he had to defend his own life in lawful fashion, he had no right to take the lives of others, whatever straits he might have been in for the mere necessities of existence. After the taking of Perth, the guardian laid siege to the castle of Stirling, which, under Thomas Rukby, made surrender with no bloodshed. The custody of this castle the guardian intrusted to Maurice de Moray of Clydesdale.

A Scots country-fellow sinned by eating human flesh.

The siege of Stirling, and its recovery.

The English still had possession of Edinburgh castle, but the Scots recovered it also, and by the following stratagem:—
In the year thirteen hundred and forty-one, William Douglas, William Bullock, and Walter Fraser called to them Walter Currie, who had a ship in the Tay; and he sailed therewith to the Forth, and found a way to the captain of the castle, carrying with him two skins of most excellent wine. And he said to the captain that he would give him two jars of wine, and as much of ale, and thereto a bushel of biscuit, if only he would see to it that he, Walter, took no harm the while he sold the rest, and he promised that he would send the same at dawn the following day. There are not many men who would refuse a present of this sort—with naught to pay for it. Next morning the captain orders the gate to be thrown open, and while

Edinburgh is recovered by a new and cunning stratagem.

---

[1] See Macpherson's note in Laing's Wyntoun, vol. iii. p. 300, upon this Crysty of the Klek—so called from the cleek or hook by which he is said to have taken his prey from the traps which he set for children and women.

he was giving entrance to the horses that carried the jars, there enter eight strong men, cloaked indeed above, but fully armed underneath, and carry with them jars that were filled with water. They kill the warders, and sound an alarm, whereupon William Douglas and his companions, who had been in ambush, appear upon the scene, slay the Englishmen, and take the castle, over which William Douglas placed his bastard brother William Douglas.

Alexander Ramsay's renown as a soldier.

At that time Alexander Ramsay had his dwelling in a cave of Hawthornden, and so great was his fame as a warrior that no nobleman in Scotland was reckoned to be a soldier good and tried unless he had served in Ramsay's band. To his court [1] the lords sent their sons in crowds, to the end they might learn the art of war under so notable a captain. Along with these he many times made inroads into England, carried back rich booty with him, and so maintained a great multitude of followers. And at this very time he had made invasion of England, and was bringing back rich spoils, when the English came upon him in much greater force, so that it looked as every man of them would be either taken prisoner or slain. He gave the order therefore that they should make a feint to fly, when the English, scattered here and there, would doubtless pursue them, and when, on the signal given with the trumpet, they should all of them return in an unbroken body. Which thing they did ; and thus he came off conqueror, for some he slew, some he put to flight, and besides he carried off no small booty.

Whether deceit may be a virtue when used against an enemy.

In a just war it is lawful to make use of a feint and of craftiness. Joshua at the city of Ai [2] did no less, and by the command of the Lord himself. In such a case a man conceals a certain truth which it is not convenient to reveal to an enemy, and by that concealment of the truth the enemy thinks that he is deceived, though there be in truth no intention to deceive.

The return of William Montagu and the things that he did.

At that time William Montagu was taken prisoner in France, but got his liberty from the French king in exchange for the lord John Randolph, earl of Moray, and, coming then into Scotland, found William Bohun, earl of Northampton, in

---

[1] curiam.   [2] Haye.

his own castle of Lochmaben, and lording it far and wide.
This he would not easily brook, and he demanded for himself
the wardenship of the western marches, and he extended these
marches to the lines in which they stand at this day. The
middle marches were in charge of William Douglas, the eastern
marches in charge of Alexander Ramsay, and these two men
extended the marches up to the lands which had been held by
the last Alexander.

In the year of our Lord one thousand three hundred and The welcome
forty-two, when all the English had now been driven furth of given to King
Scotland, and all the Scots likewise who had favoured the David.
English rule, and peace was surely established, the guardian of
Scotland and the three estates sent for David Bruce to come to
them and bear rule over a kingdom at peace within itself. He
therefore, with Joanna, queen of Scotland, who was sister to
Edward of Windsor, landed at Inverbervy, and was hailed
with a universal welcome. This unhappy prince had indeed
suffered all manner of hardship and buffeting of fortune, but
the love for his most excellent father burned still unquenchable The loyalty
in the breasts of all good Scots : and the sons of those fathers of the Scots
who had followed Robert Bruce now turned their backs against king.
such men as English Edward and Edward Baliol, and chose
rather to make hazard of their lands, their lives, and all their
worldly goods than fail in their allegiance to their own true
king. Never indeed was king surrounded by more devoted
chiefs and nobles than this David, who, by reason of his youth,
had in the beginning found a refuge among the French. For
him it was that they had borne the burden and the heat of the
day, and painful watches, and cold, and hunger, and sweat ; for
him, with blood that flowed like water, they had gained a
kingdom, and on him they now bestowed the same in peaceful
possession. We will now then leave David Bruce bearing rule
over the Scots, and take up the history of England where we
made a stay.

CHAP. XVII.—*Of the tutors who were placed over Edward the Third, king of the English, in the time of his youth. Of the treaty that was made between the Scots and the English. Of the pre-eminent virtue of Robert Bruce, and the independence of Scotland, as against Caxton. Of the strife that ensued concerning the right of that prince to bear rule, with a repetition of some things relating to the death of his father.*

The tutors of Edward the Third.

In the year thirteen hundred and twenty-seven Edward the Third was married to the granddaughter of the count of Hainault; and, on account of his youth, there were chosen twelve principal men in England, without whose counsel he should do nothing. These men were every year to give in their account to parliament of what had been done in the time when they had acted in behalf of the king. These were their names: the archbishop of Canterbury, the bishop of York, the bishop of Winchester, the bishop of Hereford; and eight temporal peers—the earl of Lancaster, the earl of Marshal, the earl of Kent, and the earl of Warren; and four knights or barons—Thomas Wake, Henry Percy, Oliver Ingham, and John Rous. Many things, however, were done at the prompting of Isabella, the king's mother, and Roger Mortimer.

The terms of the treaty that was made between the English and Scots in the matter of the marriage of David.

Thereafter, in the second year of his reign, Edward summoned a parliament or great assembly at Northampton, where it was concluded that Edward should give his sister, Joanna of Tours, in marriage to David Bruce, king of the Scots, and renounce his whole claim of superiority over the Scots; and whatever obligations had been acknowledged, or were supposed to have been acknowledged, by the kings of the Scots toward the kings of the English, these he annulled, recalled, and declared to be of no effect, and to all this he

A black cross is restored to the Scots.

authoritatively placed his seal. · Further, he restored a black cross which was held to be a most precious relic, the which his grandfather had carried off from Scone; further, to those lands which had formerly been held by Englishmen in Scotland[1] he renounced all claim in perpetuity; and the Scots were to pay thirty thousand silver pounds to king Edward. The

---

[1] F. 'in Scotiam'; Orig. rightly, 'in Scotia'.

ceremony of marriage was performed at Berwick in presence of
the queen, the mother of Joanna.

In after times Caxton vented his abuse against Robert and
David Bruce, in language that held as many lies as it did words,
for he asserts, forsooth, that from the days of Brutus the Scots
had been vassals, and that Albanactus, the first king of the Scots,
was son to Brutus.   Now in a measure, if not altogether, we may
make allowance for an unlettered man : he followed simply the
fashion of speech that was common amongst the English about
their enemies the Scots.   But let any impartial person, one,
that is, who is neither Englishman nor Scot, and who has
borne no part in the matters at issue between them, let any
such, I say, compare the life of Robert Bruce with that of any   The praise of
one of the English kings, and it may be said that from the days   Robert Bruce.
of Arthur, if that be true which is narrated of him, no more
illustrious king shall be found to have sat upon the throne.
Again, as we have said at the very beginning of our book, it is
not true that the Scots traced their origin to Brutus.   And   The indepen-
disallowing thus their premiss, I deny that the Scots have been   dence of Scot-
subject to the English, or to whom else you will, from the time   land.
that they came first into Britain.   Let Caxton, I say, read and
read again his own Venerable Bede, an Englishman too, and
he will find that not only were the Scots at no time subject to
the Britons, but that many times they boldly attacked the
Britons, even when these had the support of the Romans, and
nowhere in Bede will he find any mention of this superiority
that he claims.   And though John Baliol made submission to
Edward Longshanks, that is, to the first king of that name after
the Normans, this will not help him much : inasmuch as, in the
first place, John had denuded himself of his own lawful claim, if
indeed he ever possessed such a thing ; and secondly, because he
was not in a condition of independence ; and thirdly, because a
free king has no power at his own arbitrary pleasure to make his
people subject to another [1].   And by the same reasoning, the
fact that Edward Baliol made submission to the third Edward,
if such thing were proved, is worthless as an argument.   It was
acting on the advice of his own most prudent counsellors who

---

[1] Cf. *ante*, pp. 158, 216, and footnotes.

were attached to his own side that the third Edward annulled
that theoretical [1] claim of superiority over the Scots.   Nor will
that other argument of this same Caxton much avail, where
he asserts that these counsellors of the king were in this
matter ruled by the mother of the king and by Roger
Mortimer; for that twelve men, the first in authority in the
whole kingdom—four bishops, four earls, of whom some were
uncles to the king, and four venerable barons—that all of these
should be swayed by a single woman and a man of no standing,
this is indeed a thing as little likely as it would have been disgraceful.   Again, to assert that the English had superiority
over the Scots is but to foster amongst Christians causes of
strife and war which are not likely ever to have an end.   It
was in behalf of this claim of superiority that the first Edward
unjustly troubled the Scots and brought destruction upon
many.   And did not William Wallace, Robert Bruce, and
other Scots of those days slay just as many of the English, nor
give themselves any rest till they had brought their boundaries
again to the same point where the last Alexander had left
them?   And did not many lose their lives too under this same
Edward, when he was false to his word? and did he not sin
against his own brother and sister when he espoused the cause
of Edward Baliol?   Now both these Edwards were driven by
the Scottish nobles, with no king to lead them, from the
country, and the English were extirpated; nor did any king
of the English at any time enjoy that superiority they talk
about.   It should be the part of wise and upright historians to
make, where they can, for peace, and not to sow broadcast the
seeds of strife; wherefore I say that these twelve men acted
with a wise and proper judgment when they were chosen to be
the tutors of their king, and when at the Northampton parliament they showed their abhorrence of the shedding of Christian
blood, and put away from their kings as best they could that
great nursery of war, by the annulling of that pretended claim
of superiority (which in very truth was founded only on theory [2]),
seeing that, in behalf of that superiority, in their own day two
hundred thousand of the English and the Scots had lost their

---

[1] mathematicam.   [2] quae in rei veritate mathematica est.

lives ; and the Scots continued not a whit less powerful to resist the English than their fathers had been, and to gain a more settled peace they brought about this marriage. And this, in my judgment, is the course which should ever be followed : that the Scots kings should marry with the daughters of the English kings, and contrariwise ; and thus, some day, shall one of them come to have a lawful right to all Britain ; for without such lawful right I see not how the Scots shall ever master the English, nor yet the English the Scots [1]. This marriage accordingly was accomplished by the advice of prudent men.

After the marriage of Joanna of Tours, the sister of the third Edward, with David Bruce, Isabella, the king's mother, and Roger Mortimer contrived to get both kings under their control. Now Henry earl of Lancaster, Thomas Brotherton, earl of Marshal, and Edmund Woodstock—all uncles of the king—were not the men to brook this condition ; and they desired that Roger Mortimer should leave the court, and that the queen should live on her own means, henceforth not meddling in what pertained to the government of the realm. When the queen came to know of their intention, she persuaded the king her son to get together with no delay a body of men, who should attack Henry earl of Lancaster at Bedford, where he was then dwelling. To this the king consented, and, along with his mother, he rode one night a distance of three-and-twenty miles, with the intent to make the earl of Lancaster their prisoner. But the earl of Marshal and the earl of Kent interceded for the earl of Lancaster, and proposed that he

Contention as to the tutorship of the king.

---

[1] See *ante*, pp. 41, 42, with the references to other passages in this History. Cf. Lord Bacon's *History of King Henry VII.* (Ellis and Spedding's ed., vol. vi. p. 216), as to the marriage of the princess Margaret, daughter of Henry the Seventh, with James the Fourth of Scotland :—' Some of the table, in the freedom of counsellors (the King being present), did put the case,—that if God should take the King's two sons without issue, that then the kingdom of England would fall to the King of Scotland, which might prejudice the monarchy of England. Whereunto the King replied ; That if that should be, Scotland would be but an accession to England, and not England to Scotland ; for that the greater would draw the less : and that it was a safer union for England than that of France.' Henry the Seventh and Major were contemporaries, and this incident may well have been in Major's remembrance when on the last page of his History he describes Henry as ' in omnibus agendis oculatissimus '.

should make payment to the king of eleven thousand pounds,
and should then enjoy the king's peace.   After this a rumour
began to spread in many quarters that Edward of Carnarvon,
the king's father, was still living, and was, indeed, in the
custody of Thomas Gournay, at Corfe castle.   When the king's
brother, Thomas Woodstock, earl of Kent, came to hear of
this, he wrote to Thomas [Gournay], and besought him to do
all he could for the restoring of his brother to his kingdom ;
and it was owing to this interference, and most of all at the
instigation of Mortimer, that he was put to death.   And after
this [1] Mortimer began to swell with pride, for he had the
nobles in contempt, and had no other thought than for his
own private advantage; and, in addition to all this [2], he compassed the murder of Edward of Carnarvon.   At length, in
the year of our Lord thirteen hundred and thirty, he suffered
himself the extreme penalty, and well had he deserved it.   For
a time the sins of men lie hid, but with time, too, they come
to light [3].

Of the slaying of Edward of Carnarvon—as to which see above.

CHAP. XVIII.—*Of the dangers that beset the favourites of kings,
and of the factions that arose in Scotland under David Bruce.*

The dangerous condition of a king's favourite.

HERE let all men reflect how there is nothing more dangerous than to stand in near personal relation to kings.   It is
the habit of men to flatter kings to the uttermost.   When
those flatterers have got themselves enriched with worldly
goods, and their horns begin to sprout with pride, they become
an object of hatred to the nobles of the kingdom ; and if they
act unjustly, and study nothing but their own profit, the
common people detest them.   And so it comes to pass that
most often they fall from their eminence into the lowest place
of all; for such a fate have I seen to overtake some men in my
own day, and the same I have read in history of many more.
Wherefore it is far better to live the life of a private man at
home.   Add this further consideration if you will : that those
who live at the beck and call of kings scarce ever enjoy two
hours on end of peace and quiet.

---

[1] post hunc.   [2] cum hoc.

[3] 'Temporibus peccata latent, et tempore parent'; *sic* Orig. and F., a misprint for 'patent'.

After this[1], as we learn from the chroniclers of our history, John Baliol in France. John Baliol lived as a private person with his son at Dunpier, in France.   He held that estate by favour of the French king, when he had become an exile from his country. After the death of John Baliol, Edward came to France[2]; and he had a promise that the kingdom of Scotland should be his if he would consent to hold the same of the English king; for up to this time it seemed to be believed that he had no small number of adherents in Scotland.   The English historians differ not a little among themselves in what they relate of the affairs of Scotland, nor have they such particular information of all that was done at that time in Scotland as we have now declared the same.   I therefore pass them by when they deal with our matters.   This third Edward, The achievements of Edward of Windsor. sometimes called of Windsor, was a man of a lofty spirit, and ambitious of empire.   He was ever at war with Philip of Valois, with the French king, and with the Scots.   I do not mean to treat at length of the wars that were waged by the Britons, whether Scots or English, outwith the kingdom.

In the same year that David Bruce returned to Scotland, The history of Scottish matters is continued. Alexander Ramsay recovered Roxburgh from the English. David intrusted to him the custody of its castle, and granted to him likewise the sheriffdom of Teviotdale, which had formerly been held by William Douglas.   Now this was most Jealousies amongst the Scots. imprudently done of David, thus to deprive a high-spirited man, who had done eminent service to the state, of an honourable office, even with the intent to confer the same upon a man who was well worthy of it; for what was this but to sow the seeds of jealousy among his own people ?   It was but a few days afterward, indeed, that [William Douglas] cruelly

---

[1] Major writes, 'Post hoc tangunt annales historiæ, etc.'   It is difficult to say what date he refers to; but we do not seem to know the date of John Baliol's death, in France, more definitely than that it was after the beginning of 1315. Cf. the Rev. Joseph Stevenson's *Documents*, etc., vol. i. p. l.   Caxton says that Baliol lived at Dunpier on his own lands ' as wel as he myght tyll y^t the Scottes wold amende them of theyr mysdedes . . . so he forsoke his realme of Scotlonde, and set therof but lytel pryce'.

[2] 'in Galliam venit'.   One would rather have expected 'ivit'.   Major may have written 'venit' instinctively, because he was writing in France; but I rather think that he meant to write 'in *Angliam* venit [? *or* ivit]', for Edward Baliol was already in France with his father.

wounded Alexander Ramsay, who suspected naught of the harm that was meant him, and he further imprisoned Ramsay in Hermitage [1] castle, and there let him perish of hunger. In the days of this Alexander Ramsay many gallant deeds were done in Scotland, and most of all where he himself held command ; and after his death followed every kind of disaster. Be it that David Bruce had reason for his anger against William Douglas, yet it was through Robert Stewart's assurance for his high character that he had found favour with the king; and Douglas was in charge of the castle of Roxburgh, and held too the sheriffdom of Teviotdale. Behold then how David Bruce, by his own imprudence, lost the good service of a most valiant soldier ; and herein he showed himself as far removed as might be from the probity and wisdom of his father.

CHAP. XIX.—*Of the siege of Calais, and the unfortunate expedition of David Bruce in England, and his captivity there. Of Edward's deeds of violence in Scotland, and the election of a governor of Scotland ; and how some famous men came by their death.*

The siege of Calais.

WHILE Edward the Third was laying siege to Calais, Philip of Valois, the French king, sent to David Bruce, and urged him to invade England, in the hope that Edward would then desist from the siege. And David did as the French king desired, and invaded England, laying waste the lands of the church. He would not hearken to the counsel of William Douglas, well-tried as William was in the art of war, but followed the advice rather of younger men. The end was this : that the English attacked David unawares with a large army, and made him prisoner, along with many other men of mark [2].

David's captivity.

It was indeed unlikely that he should meet with success while he was ravaging church lands. It was not the way of his father Robert, fond of fighting as he was, to act in this way.

---

[1] Orig. ' Aruntagis '.

[2] Cf. Wyntoun's judgment, Laing's ed. vol. ii. p. 471 :
Qwhy couth he noucht have in to pes
Haldyn his land, as it then wes,
And hym-selwyn owt of dawngere ?
Qwha standis welle, he suld nocht stere.

It was John Couplant, a Gascon, that made David his prisoner, but not before David had with one blow knocked out two of his teeth. The iron points of two arrows remained fixed in his flesh. One of them, indeed, was removed by a skilful operation; the extraction of the other resisted every attempt that they could make; but when he came to visit the shrine of Saint Ninian in Scotland, the iron came away of its own will by divine intervention. After David had been made prisoner, two strongholds were surrendered to the English : Roxburgh, to wit, to the lord Percy, and Hermitage. At that time the English held March, Teviotdale, Tweeddale, Forestham, the valley of the Annan, and Galloway. Their boundary they placed first at Cockburnspath and Sutra[1], and afterwards at Carlinlyppos[2] and Crossecarne. Edward Baliol was at that time tarrying at Brintel[3], in Galloway, and, along with English Percy, he laid waste Lothian with fire and sword, and passing through the country around Glasgow, he dealt in the same fashion with Cunningham and Nithsdale, and then returned home. This wide-spread plundering and pillaging led to the election as guardian of Scotland of the lord seneschal, who had not fallen into the hands of the English at the same time with David. It was now, too, that William Douglas, son to Archibald, the brother of that lord James who had lost his life among the heathen, returned from France to Scotland. He was the first earl of Douglas. When he came to his own land of Douglasdale, of which the English had lately taken possession, he drove them out, recovered his lands, and likewise gained over to his side the Forest of Ettrick and Teviotdale.

In the thirteen hundred and fifty-third year of the Lord, William Douglas, then prisoner in England, contrived the slaying of David Barclay, a knight, of Aberdeen, in revenge for the death of John Douglas of Dalkeith, at which the said David had been present. For that John of Dalkeith was brother to David[4].

David's feat.

Iron points buried in his body.

A miracle performed by Ninian.

The doings of Edward [Baliol].

The guardian of Scotland.

William Douglas, the first earl.

David Barclay is slain.

---

[1] 'Soltre'. The place is the Soutra of the present parish of Fala and Soutra.

[2] May this be Carlops—which some have derived from *Carlin's Loup?*

[3] 'Brynt-yle' in Wyntoun, Bk. VIII. ch. xl. ; vol. ii. p. 477, Laing's ed.   Sir Herbert Maxwell quotes a 'Bruntland' in his *Studies in the Topography of Galloway*, p. 98. Edin. 1887.

[4] Davidis' ; but ? 'Gulielmi'.

Further, in the thirteen hundred and fifty-third year of the Lord,
William Douglas of Nithsdale was slain by William Douglas,
his godson [1], the lord of Douglas, at Galvort, in Ettrick Forest,
when he was following the chase. Whether his godson were
moved to this crime by the hatred he had conceived to him
[Douglas] for the part he had in the death of Alexander
Ramsay, or simply by a spirit of ambition, I know not : for
they were, both of them, high-spirited men, and their lands
marched one with another. While he lived there was no man
more fond of fighting than this William, whose end I have
just declared, and as between him and Alexander Ramsay, I
know not which excelled the other in a lofty courage and in
good fortune ; but in uprightness and nobility of mind I give
the first place to Alexander Ramsay. For that other was
given overmuch to revenge, and through him it was that not
only many Englishmen lost their lives, but two Scots also of
conspicuous worth. Now we know that bloodthirsty and
deceitful men shall not live out half their days [2] ; wherefore it
is no wonder if he perished by the sword of William Douglas.

William
Douglas is
slain by his
godson.

CHAP. XX.—*How Eugene, the Frenchman, was sent into Scotland,
and of all that was wrought by the Scots along with him against the
English. Of the honourable return of the Frenchman. Of the violent
attack made by the English upon Scotland, and their rueful return to
England, and of what the Scots did thereafter.*

What was done
by Eugene the
Frenchman
when he was
sent into
Scotland.

In the year of the Lord thirteen hundred and fifty-five, the
French king sent a certain noble, Eugene de Garrenter [3], into
Scotland ; and Eugene had in his train but few Frenchmen,
but these were all men skilled in war. They brought with
them into Scotland a sum of money, which should be used for
the levying of an army against the English. Now the guardian
and the outstanding men of Scotland took the money, but
gave naught to the soldiers. This, however, did not hinder
the earl of the Marches and the lord of Douglas from gathering together their own following ; and they invaded the English
borders. William Ramsay of Dalhousie they sent forward

---

[1] filium suum spiritualem.   [2] Ps. lv. 23.   [3] *i.e.* Garancières.

into England with some light-armed troops, with instruction
to harry the country.   And as they well knew that the
English would not delay to bring together an army against
the Scots, they enjoined on Ramsay that he should dissemble,
flying as it were before them, and thus step by step draw the
English after him as far as Nisbet moor ;—all which he did,
and well. . Whereupon the Frenchmen, with the Scots, went *Conflict with the English.*
against that English army, and a fierce battle took place.   In
this conflict fell, on the side of the Scots, that gallant soldier *The Scots that were slain therein.*
John Haliburton, and James Turnbull, both of knightly rank ;
but the Englishmen were worsted.   Thomas Gray, the lieu- *The English are defeated and taken.*
tenant of the English king, with Thomas, his son and heir,
James Dares, and many other good men, were taken prisoners.
For their ransom no small sum had to be paid.   In the same
year Thomas, seneschal, and earl of Angus, and the earl of
March laid siege to Berwick and took the town ; but this was *Siege of Berwick. Berwick is taken.*
done with difficulty.   In the defence of the town Alexander
Ogill, a man of good birth, with many of the English, lost his
life ; and Eugene of Garrenter and his Frenchmen played their *The valour of the Frenchmen, and their return home.*
part like men in this conflict.   Robert the seneschal bestowed
upon them costly presents, and sent them back to France,
seeing they had now accomplished to the full the design of the
king in sending them into Scotland : albeit he did not doubt
but the English king would soon make a fresh attack upon
Scotland, seeing that he had in his keeping the king of Scots,
mindful of that common word amongst the Britons : ' Who
aims at conquering France must needs make a beginning with
the Scots.'   Froissart, when he deals with this matter, *Froissart.*
observes that many of the Scots refused to bear their part with
the Frenchmen when these were storming the ramparts[1] of
Berwick ; and so much I will here allow : that Gascons and *Which nation is the better endowed for the taking of cities by assault.*
southern peoples in general, being more agile, are better
fitted for the besieging of cities and the climbing of walls
than our northern peoples ; and this is plain from what we
know of the Swiss and the Gascons.   Northerners, however,
when once they are arrayed for battle, will do better service
than southrons.   For their temper is warmer, by reason of the

---

[1] Gallis conscendentibus ascendere recusarunt.

antiparistasis [1] of their colder climate, and likewise more hardy. They are, however, much less nimble than the southrons.

When Edward the Third had knowledge of this defeat, he gathered a great army, and, leaving France, took his course against the Scots, and he had with him eighty thousand men in arms. Edward .Baliol, too, joined himself to the king, and brought to his support what men he could. The townsfolk of Berwick surrendered their city without striking a blow; and Edward Baliol, knowing that the Scots would have none of

him, made over his whole claim to the kingdom to the English king. But there are two grounds wherefore this grant was invalid: this first, that in the kingdom of Scotland he possessed no lawful standing whatever; and secondly, that it is no part of a true king to surrender at his own will and pleasure his claim to his kingdom. Both of these contentions we have unfolded in a former part of this book [2].

These two Edwards, however, in their invasion of Scotland, proposed to themselves to take complete possession of the country, and thereafter to return, the one of them to France, while Edward Baliol should be left behind in Scotland. They made their way, then, so far as Haddington; but the Scots had carried off every sort of food and victual, and by sea they lost too a large part of their fleet, which in vast numbers they had brought with them. And, according to the common report, this was the cause of the disaster: The English sailors had disembarked from their vessels, and had demeaned themselves with

---

[1] Though it is difficult to seize Major's point with precision, I think it is plain that he had in his view Aristotle's definition of ἀντιπαρίστασις (or, rather, ἀντιπερίστασις) in the *De Natura*, Bk. VIII. ch. 10, and, more particularly, the passage in the *Problemata*, § xxxiii. 5, in which Aristotle deals with the opposition or counter-action of the surrounding parts, as these express themselves in such pulmonary or gastric affections as sneezing, coughing, panting, and eructation, etc., to which it would seem that northern nations are specially liable. According to Froissart (Bk. I. pt. ii. ch. 16; vol. i. p. 307 ed. Buchon) the Scots were driven back in their assault upon the castle of Berwick; and, says Froissart, 'jamais les Escots ne l'eussent eue, puisqu'ils en étoient maucriés'; *i.e.* 'never would the Scots have taken the town, for they had no sense of discipline' (cf. Godefroi: *Dict. de la langue française du xᵉ au xvᵉ siècle* s.v. *malcrée*=indiscipliné). Major shows that the conduct of the Scots soldiers was without doubt due to no demoralisation, but simply to their national 'antiparistasis'.   [2] Cf. *ante*, pp. 214, 215.

brutal cruelty towards some children of tender age, putting them all to death. They then made for Whitekirk, distant a short mile from the sea. There did certain sons of Belial despoil an image of the Blessed Virgin, richly set with gold, and the leader in this robbery died within the church ; for, as he was passing under the image of the Crucified One, the image, by divine interposition, fell upon his head, even as he was in the act of passing by, and broke that head, on which he was carrying his gold spoils, into small fragments. And a little while thereafter there suddenly arose a sea wind from the north, which burst upon the ships, and many of them were dashed in pieces against the rocks, some indeed were scattered, and so it came about that the English king could get no victualling from his fleet. The English king then, in his wrath, set fire to Haddington, and, along with the town, burnt to the ground that most fair church of the Minorites which is called the lamp of Lothian [1]. Now I for my part do not think it well that the Minorites should possess churches of this sumptuous magnificence ; and it may be that for their sins, and the sins of the town itself, God willed that all should be given to the flames. And then, going further, Edward wasted Lothian with fire, and Edinburgh itself.   This time goes by the name of 'The burnt Candlemas', that is, 'the burnt festival of the Purification', inasmuch as at that time the English king put fire to all, far and wide. Afterward he returned to England by way of the Forest, where, by reason of the Scots lying here and there in ambush, he lost many of his men, and ran no little risk to his own life. And albeit he held the king of Scotland a prisoner in England, yet he did not make way in Scotland more than twenty leagues. In this way, then, the Scots were able greatly to help the French against the English, even though they saw two of their towns in ashes that they might set the Frenchmen free. After the departure of the English king, the lord William Douglas gathered together all who

The English lose their fleet by reason of the cruelty that they had practised.

The miraculous death of a sacrilegious person.

The church of the Minorites is burnt.

The English soldiery slain.

---

[1] 'Laudoniae lampas'. Dr. David Laing, in a note to his edition of Wyntoun's *Cronykil* (vol. iii. p. 247), says that the name *Lucerna Laudoniæ* was given to the choir of the monastery of Gray Friars at Haddington because of its beautiful structure. By some antiquarians, however, the parish church of Haddington is held to be the 'Lamp of Lothian.'

William
Douglas
compels his
own people to
do homage to
the king.
owned allegiance to him, and marched into Galloway, where, in part by the sword in part by persuasion, he gained over all the men of that part to the side of David Bruce. Then Donald Macdowel swore fealty to the king in Cumnock church; and Roger Kirkpatrick brought the whole land of Nithsdale to do the like; the strong places of Dalswinton and Carlaverock he wrested from the hands of the enemy, and then razed them to the ground.

CHAP. XXI.—*Of the return to England from Scotland of king David without compassing his end. Of the captivity of John, king of the French, and the adroit escape of Archibald Douglas. Of the ransom at last of David, and the death of the queen, with her eulogy.*

David returns
into captivity,
his end unac-
complished.
ABOUT this same time king David, leaving hostages in England, returned to Scotland, meaning to treat with his subjects concerning his ransom; but when he was not able to get them to agree to what he sought, he returned once more to England, and set his hostages at liberty. After his departure an inva-
The loyal act
of John Stuart.
sion of England was made by John Stuart, son to the guardian, lord of Kyle, and thereafter earl of Carrick, the same who came at a still later date to be known as Robert the Third, king of the Scots. This John gathered an army, and, marching into Teviotdale, made the inhabitants of that district swear fealty to king David.

John, king of
the French, is
taken, along
with Archibald
Douglas.
In the thirteen hundred and fifty-sixth year of the Lord, John, king of France, was taken prisoner by Edward, prince of Wales; and there was taken with him also Archibald Douglas, son to that right noble James Douglas, who came by his end in battle with the heathen, when he was bearing the heart of Robert Bruce. This Archibald became afterwards lord of
Archibald's
escape.
Galloway and earl of Douglas. But Archibald Douglas made his escape by a most marvellous stratagem. For this Archibald Douglas, as became him, wore armour of great price, and the Englishman, therefore, who had him in charge, treated him with all honour. Now there was a shrewd Scot, William Ramsay of Colluthy, a knight, who perceived this, and feigning furious passion, said to Archibald Douglas, 'How, in the

devil's name, come you to wear this costly armour of your master?' Thereupon the Englishman ordered him to come and clean his leggings and his shoes, and Archibald with all humility obeyed him. And while Archibald was thus busied with the cleaning, Ramsay upbraided him, and accused him of having treacherously slain his master and his own kinsman, William Ramsay, in war, and commanded him to make full search for the body of the dead man, that he might give it honourable burial; and the end was that the Englishman set free his prisoner for a ransom of forty sous, no more, which would amount barely to five francs. Taking lesson from such craft as this, then, men may learn how to escape from the hands of an enemy. No more than five years afterward the lord Borth- *Another astute instance.* wick, a powerful noble, made good his escape by using a like stratagem; for his servant, when evening was come, made his master draw off his boots and then fall to cleaning of them,— and there and then despatched the master into Scotland to fetch back a ransom for them both. I need not say that the master never compeared. But put the case that he who held the prisoners was a cruel man, the servant no doubt jeoparded his own life. Whether such an act be right, or not, I will not speak too confidently.

At this time therefore the English king had in his hands as *Two kings at once in the hands of the English.* prisoners at once the French and the Scottish king; but in the end, though not till David Bruce had spent eleven years amongst the English, the following covenant was made: that David should pay two hundred thousand nobles, spread over a certain number of years, and in security of the payment of that sum should leave sons of the nobles or the nobles themselves in the hands of the English king as hostages. And here I will permit myself to make a few observations. If the *The conditions upon which king David was ransomed by the Scots.* English meant thus to make any claim of suzerainty over Scotland, or meant to force David to an obligation of that claim, or thus demanded of David an intolerable sum of money which could only be paid to the ruin of his realm, then his people ought not to have ransomed him. But my belief is this: that, in acting as they did, neither the nobles nor the people dealt friendly by their king. For though the Scots *The Scots pay no taxes to their king.* were not accustomed to pay taxes either in time of peace or

time of war, yet ought they in such case as this to have made a
concession to their king, and each man of them to have taxed
himself in right proportion and so have paid off the two
hundred thousand nobles in the first year. Whereas, on the
plan of this far-extended payment, I see not how they can be
said to have come to their king's help at all; and their intention was that he should pay the whole out of the royal
revenues, which indeed, from the long-lasting wars, were scanty
enough. The law of nature itself demands the performance of
some services to a king, among them, this: to ransom him,
when he is a prisoner, for a reasonable sum, and most of all if
it seem likely that his liberation shall be advantageous to his
people; for that a king should for long be kept in captivity is
a shame to a nation, and declares that the people are wanting
in proper pity for their rightful head[1]. Far more kindly did
the French deal by John, their king, since to set him at
liberty they were ready to sacrifice a large part of his kingdom.
In yet another way can a people act a wrongful part, when
they refuse to grant a subsidy by way of dower to the
daughters of their king, when these are contracting an alliance
of marriage at once fit and honourable; since no marriage
portion will be paid to him in his own country, seeing that
there no public peace is settled, nor is there a hope of an
honourable alliance.

Strong places
destroyed.   At this time, however, when David recovered his liberty, the
destruction was demanded of some strongholds of the Scots in
Nithsdale which had wrought damage upon the English; and
when he returned to his own country David fulfilled this condition. Dalswinton, Dumfries, Morton, Durrisdeer, he razed
to the ground.

In the year thirteen hundred and fifty-seven the lady Joanna,
queen of Scotland and sister to English Edward, besought her
husband David that she might visit holy men in foreign parts
and her friends in England, and, before she could return, in
The death of
the queen and
her eulogy.   England she died. A good woman and a faithful I declare her
to have been, for she quitted not her husband neither when he
was, in his youth, an exile from his own land in France, nor

---

[1] Cf. Bk. VI. ch. xi. on the ransom of James the First, and the ransom by the
English of Richard the First. Cf. also Bk. IV. ch. ii.

afterward when he was prisoner in England; wherefore, like
Penelope, she is worthy of all praise,—how little soever her life
may have known of worldly felicity, according to that of Ovid,
where he says: 'Had Ulysses the much-enduring never known
misfortune's chance, Penelope might have been a happy woman,
but would have lacked her meed of praise.' And amongst the
wise she has gained an everlasting renown.

CHAP. XXII.—*Of the death of Edward the Third and his son.
Of the reign of Richard the Second, and of those whom he ennobled,
and of his wives.*

LEAVING David Bruce in Scotland, I return to the English.
In the fifty-first year of the reign of Edward the Third died
Edward his first-born, and in the following year Edward himself went the way of all flesh. Every inch was he a man of
war and filled with ambition, and I could find more to praise
in him had he not waged unjust war against his neighbours,
and demeaned himself inhumanly towards the common people,
and poured but his rage upon religious houses. *(margin: Death of both Edwards, father and son.)*

After the death of Edward Windsor—that is, after the
conquest by the Normans, the third Edward—Richard the
Second, son to Edward prince of Wales, reigned in his stead.
He was born at Bordeaux in Gascony, and in the eleventh
year of his age was crowned at London. In the same
year he summoned a national parliament, in which a law
was passed, that every person, male or female, rich or poor,
in England, who had reached the age of fourteen years,
should pay to the king four pennies, that is, an English
groat, equal to three sous of Tours. In the fourth year of
Richard's reign the people were provoked by this grievous
oppression to raise up two men of their own number, Jake
Strawe to wit ['hoc est Jacobum Stramen'], and Walter Tiler,
and these men they followed as their leaders. They went to
London, even to the palace of the king, and broke open the
king's prisons. Many men, and most of all those that were
foreigners, they spoiled of their goods; and they put to death
the king's counsellors. For three days the maddened people
spent their rage in London, breaking open every prison and *(margin: Richard the Second succeeds to the throne.)* *(margin: Revolt of the common people against the king, and their punishment.)*

setting all the prisoners at liberty. They set fire to the house of
the duke of Lancaster, and likewise to Saint John's, a very fair
building in Smithfield. The books of the lawyers and the
advocates they also burned. But on the Monday the mayor of
London and the assembled citizens put James [1] Strawe to death,
and from that time the people began to disperse. But many
among them had been taken, and of that number not one
escaped hanging. Now, this punishment and the bold front
that was shown by the people of London I cannot but approve.
For it is naught but fitting to punish with severity that many-
headed monster, an unbridled populace, when it rises against
its head, to the end that others may see it and take heed.

The king takes to himself a wife, and creates dukes and earls. In the sixth year of his reign Richard took to wife Anna,
daughter of the king of Bohemia ; and in the eighth year he
marched with a large army against the Scots, and when he had
reached the Scottish border, he made a treaty with the Scots,
and, returning to London, creates dukes, marquises, and
earls. In the ninth year of his reign he created Edmund
Langle earl of Cambridge, duke of York ; and Thomas
Woodstock earl of Buckingham he made duke of Gloucester.
These were his paternal uncles. And Lionverius [2] earl of
Oxford he made marquis of Dublin ; and Henry Bolingbroke,
son to the duke of Lancaster, earl of Derby ; and Edward, son
to the duke of York, earl of Rutland ; and John Holonde,
brother to the earl of Kent, earl of Huntingdon ; and Thomas
Moubray, earl of Nottingham ; and Michael de la Pole, earl of
Suffolk and Chancellor of England. In the seventeenth year
of his reign died Anna his queen ; and in the following year he
took to wife Isabella, daughter to the French king—whom,
with her husband, we shall now leave at London, and let our
pen find once more its way to the narrative of the Scots and
their doings.

---

[1] 'Jacobum'. Major translates 'Jake', or 'Jack', by Jacobus. 'Jacques',
the commonest Christian name in France—as indicated by the use of 'Jacques-
bonhomme' and 'la jacquerie',—was rendered 'Jack' in English; but as John
was the commonest Christian name in England, Jack came to attach itself to that
name rather than to James.

[2] *i.e.* Robert de Vere, who was not long afterwards created duke of Ireland.

CHAP. XXIII.—*Of the rest of the deeds of King David ; how he succeeded in getting the church tithes, and gave his counsel as to the choice of an Englishman to be king of Scotland, and, when his counsel was despised, took to wife a young girl ; how he sought a divorce from her when he found her barren ; his death.*

WHEN king David was escaped from the hands of the English, he sent to the pontiff to the end he might get the tithe of the revenues of the Scottish church over a space of three years ; and the pontiff granted him this demand,—which indeed was reasonable. For if church revenues are to be paid in the case of men that are in captivity, they may not be denied in the case of a captive king. David gains possession of the tithes.

In the same year James Lindsay happened to be a guest with Roger of Kirkpatrick, and by night he privily slew Roger, and, aiming to put a great distance between himself and Car-laverock, where he had done this deed, he had scarce covered a distance of three miles or four when he was taken. Whereupon he was carried to David Bruce, and paid the last penalty of his crime. He was among the heirs of those who slew John Cumming at Dumfries, in the church of the Minor friars ; but sometimes the sins of the parents are visited upon their off-spring even to the fourth generation as regards temporal and mundane punishments. The fearful crime of James Lindsay and its punishment.

In the same year there happened in Lothian a marvellous plague of rain, such as had not been seen in Scotland for many hundreds of years. Now this may have had its cause in some watery combination of the stars, just as a special deluge is said to have taken place in the time of Pyrrha and Deucalion. In the thirteen hundred and sixty-first year of the Lord there happened in Scotland as in England a great mortality of men, whether from a contagion of the air, or by infliction of God in the exercise of His righteous judgment for the sins of men ; to the end that if men will not show reverence to God in love they may at least by their fears be driven to dread Him. A marvellous deluge in Scotland. A mighty mortality in both Britains.

Thereafter for the two following years David Bruce gathered a great parliament, wherein he laboured to achieve this end : that they should consent to accept the English king or his

David's counsel as to a choice of a king. heir, or any future heir of the English king, for king of Scotland, seeing that he himself had no issue. What it was that moved him to this counsel was never known; it may be that as a captive in England he had given his secret promise to the English to this effect; or it may be that he thought it profitable for the Scots, and much better for both Englishmen and Scots to live under one king, provided that the Scots might continue to enjoy their independence. But here I will add this one consideration: It would have been of all things the most imprudent to accept as king of Scotland any other than the rightful heir of the English king, since there could have come by this way no union and peaceful settlement of the kingdoms. For if one kingdom shall scarce be able to contain two brothers where one brother is king and the other brother is subject to him in temporalities, and yet continue in peace, what will be the result where you have two brothers bearing rule over two haughty and neighbour kingdoms, each of them confident of superior strength? The three estates used no delay in rejecting the proposition of the king of Scots, declaring that there was not lacking a rightful heir to the kingdom, and one mature in years, after his decease; that this heir had deserved well of his country, and that they would be no party to his disheriting. And thus on every side David found none to follow his counsel; and some men showed therefore such dislike and aversion that they began to plunder the villages and towns of the kingdom, thinking they would thereby strike fear into the heart of the king, and that he would be brought to learn this lesson, that the whole kingdom did not hang and hinge upon the king, but contrariwise. The greater part of the nobles, however, when the king departed from this proposal of his, still stood by him; and then went in pursuit of the others who were disturbers of the peace, and compelled them to return to their allegiance. At the time of the holding of this parliament I have read that queen Joanna was still living; and I take it that in this matter she was the counsellor of her husband, and not very imprudently; for the king loved her dearly, and she was worthy to be loved. For though he had not by this lady the blessing of offspring, those other blessings of religion and the sacrament, which take precedence

The States of the realm do not accept the king's proposal.

The excelling blessings of marriage.

infinite of that first-named blessing, they possessed in all
sincerity.   It was a short time after the holding of this parliament that the queen died.

Now, inasmuch as the Scots had refused to consent to their
king in his proposal of the succession of the English king, he
took to wife one Margaret Logy, a very fair woman, to the *Margaret Logy.*
end he might by her have an heir to the crown.   But when
she bore him no children, he came to scorn her, and publicly
divorced her.   I will use this opportunity to say that the *The practice of*
Scots of the present day find occasion of divorce all too lightly, *divorce should be checked.*
and the most part of the laity hold it sufficient for the salvation
of their souls so long as a divorce be procured in the external
forum [1] on the testimony of false witnesses ; and thus they draw
other women into what is an adulterous connection, believing
them to be their lawful wives.   They ought in this matter to *The case of*
be instructed by the learned, to the end that they may not *those that take another woman*
violate the law of God concerning marriage, which teaches that *to wife in the lifetime of a*
whom God hath joined man may not put asunder.   If a mar- *former wife.*
riage shall once have been contracted ' per verba de praesenti ',
between capable persons, such a tie can for no supervenient
cause be undone by any man, pope or other [2].   But inasmuch

---

[1] 'in foro exteriori '—*i.e.* the courts of law, as opposed to the forum of conscience or tribunal of penance.

[2] In the late Dr. John Stuart's *A Lost Chapter in the History of Mary Queen
of Scots recovered*, a work which had its origin in the discovery by the writer
of the original Dispensation for the marriage of James earl of Bothwell with
Lady Jane Gordon, a full account will be found of the conditions of divorce in
Scotland at that time.   Dr. Stuart points out that ' the result of the canonical
prohibitions absolutely carried out in a small country like Scotland would have
been intolerable, and accordingly its rigour was, from an early period, mitigated
by dispensations from the Holy See '.   From Mr. Riddell's *Peerage and Consis-
torial Law*, vol. i. p. 466, as there quoted, we find that ' if a husband happened
accidentally to learn, no uncommon event in that profligate and dissolute age,
that his consort had carnal intercourse before with a remote relative within the
fourth degree of consanguinity to himself, which made her in the same degree of
affinity to him, or *vice versa*, that was a certain handle to void and annul it at
any time '.   Dr. Stuart also quotes archbishop Hamilton (Sept. 1554) as to the
almost impossibility of finding members of good families who could be united
without finding themselves within the line.   ' From the circumstances of Scotch
society thus described ', he adds, ' it followed that in almost no case could a
marriage between a man and woman of the higher ranks take place without a
dispensation having been previously obtained, and that, in point of fact, a dispensation came in most cases to form part of a marriage settlement.'—Pp. 65-73.

as the precise circumstances of the case as between David Bruce and dame Margaret Logy have escaped my memory, I am unable to express an authoritative opinion on the question whether the divorce was a true divorce or not. Margaret betook herself to the Roman pontiff, who dwelt at that time at Avignon, and in his court on the part of David, as on her own part, much expense was incurred. For acting in this way I censure alike the king and the woman. The woman whom he had once had to wife the king ought not to have driven from him, nor have suffered a woman, once his wife, to pass
outwith the boundaries of his kingdom. That same woman, on the other hand, ought to have stayed at home, and lived religiously, and submitted herself to the royal ordinance, for the king was a kindly man. It becomes not a woman, and least of all a princess, to wander far from home. Nor can I praise either David Bruce or Alexander that they granted leave to their spouses—sisters, both of them, of English kings—to make pilgrimage to Canterbury, or to visit friars in foreign parts[1]. When a king has taken to wife a woman of another kingdom, he should assign to her attendants belonging to his own kingdom, and lead her by the exercise of kindness to change her old skin and put on a new one.

Women should not be suffered to roam abroad.

Death of David. A short while hereafter David died at Edinburgh, in the forty-seventh year of his age and the thirty-ninth year of his reign. He was buried in the monastery of the Holy Rood, in front of the high altar. I can even David with rulers of middling excellence only ; in matters of war he had but small experience ; in the affairs of this world he did not prosper ; but the temper of his mind was not otherwise than one of constant endurance, and fear he knew not. In the end he secured peace within his kingdom. Those Wild Scots whom, by reason of their savage customs, it was not possible to tame, he held at least within check by wise precautions. He took the measure of their customs. He saw them to be covetous of

---

[1] Cf. *In Quartum*, 2d question of the 17th distinction: 'Let not the confessor, as the custom is of many, enjoin pilgrimages, and least of all on women, for whom in my opinion it is a harmful thing to go on pilgrimage without the company of their husbands, and perchance not even in that case. Neither is it becoming in maidens to wander in the fields ; for they can see saints at home.'

independence, of posts of rank, of ownership in land. One he would attract by gifts, another by bestowing on him some high position, and he would instigate them to mutual slaughter. For they were already guilty of death for their crimes, and he himself was, as it were, a public person, and could find no other way to curb those rebellious subjects. In this way, therefore, he brought them to a settled way of living.

CHAP. XXIV.—*Concerning Richard of England, how he took his uncle prisoner, and was himself made prisoner by his subjects and slain. Of the creation and banishment of dukes. Of Henry the Fourth and Henry the Fifth of England ; and of Robert Stewart, the Scottish king.*

I HAVE just told of the death of David the Scot, and will now turn my pen to English Richard, the second of his name.

In the twentieth year of his reign, Richard conceived the evil design to make prisoner his uncle, Thomas Woodstock, English Richard duke of Gloucester, and sent him to Calais, where, by the makes prisoner king's order, he was put to death. Thereafter he sent for the' his uncle. earl of Arundel and the earl of Warwick, whom he kept in his own charge in London. And in the twenty-first year of his reign he gathered a great parliament, in the which the earl of Arundel was condemned to death. This lord was beheaded The sentence on a hill close by the Tower of London, and the earl of War- the earls of wick was sentenced to perpetual imprisonment in the Isle of Arundel and Man.   Thereafter Richard created divers dukes ; he raised The creation the earl of Derby to the dukedom of Hereford, and the earl of of dukes. Nottingham became duke of Norfolk. A short while after- ward, in the same year, there arose a quarrel between the dukes of Hereford and Norfolk, who challenged each the other to single combat ; but when all was prepared for the fight, the king prevented it. The duke of Hereford he condemned to Banishment of ten years' banishment from the kingdom, and the duke of Hereford and Norfolk to banishment for life, and this latter died at Venice. Norfolk. The king further deposed Thomas Arundel, archbishop of Banishment Canterbury, and made him too an exile from England. In of a bishop. the twenty-second year of his reign Richard issued new sealed

letters[1], and thereby got a huge quantity of money, to the
detriment of the common people. And then he went into
Ireland, there to wage war.

The expedition against Ireland.

When Henry Bolingbroke, earl of Derby, whom Richard
had raised to be duke of Norfolk, came to hear of this, he
returned to England, meaning to gain the duchy of Lancaster
for himself. Along with him came Thomas Arundel and the
sons of that earl of Arundel who had been slain. The English
flocked to them in crowds. Richard the king was taken
prisoner, and by the duke of Hereford was committed to the
Tower, where he was closely guarded until the English nobles
should arrive in London. Then all with one voice deposed
king Richard, on the ground of the extortions and unbounded
exactions that he had perpetrated upon the common people,
and of his execution of some of the nobles, and the sentence of
banishment passed upon others, for no sufficing reason. After
the deposing of Richard, they sent him to be kept prisoner at
Pontefract. There he pined away from hunger, and in weariness of soul made change of life for death.

King Richard made prisoner by his subjects and deposed.

He dies of hunger.

Now, if I am to say what I think, certain things in this king
I censure: and, first of all, that unmerited sentence that he
passed upon those noblemen; secondly, the oppression of his
people that he practised for his own enrichment. But the
fickleness that marked the conduct of his nobility and the
common people I can no way approve;—nay rather, I vehemently abhor the same. For so slight a cause to dismiss and
depose a king is nothing else than to make an easy opening for
the horns of rebellion against the state in the case of all kings
yet to come—a thing to be shunned as a plague, and certain
to involve the ruin of any commonwealth. But however this
may be—and whether they had the colour of law upon their
side or no—thus and not otherwise did the English act in this
matter, and they created the duke of Hereford to be king by
the title of Henry the Fourth. And he, when he was placed
upon the throne, created Henry, his son and heir, prince of

Censure of the acts of the king and of the conduct of his subjects.

Henry the Fourth.

---

[1] 'sub novis literis et sigillis'. ' He extorted money without a semblance of
right, and even compelled men to put their seals to blank promises to pay, which
he could fill up with any sum he pleased.'—Gardiner's *A Student's History of
England*, vol. i. p. 283.

Wales, and duke of Cornwall, and earl of Chester. But them Henry the Fifth.
we will now dismiss till we have told of what happened amongst
the Scots during these years.

On the death of David Bruce, in the thirteen hundred and What happened amongst the Scots.
seventieth year[1] from the incarnation of the Word, the three
estates of Scotland convened in Linlithgow to make choice
of a king. The larger and indeed the wiser part agreed
upon Robert Stewart, grandson of king David. Nevertheless Robert Stewart is created king of the Scots.
William Douglas made opposition thereto, asserting on the
part of the Baliols and the Cummings that the succession to
the throne lay with them. But to such a claim as this George
Dunbar, earl of March, and the earl of Moray, his brother,
and the lord Erskine, who amongst them had in keeping
the chief strongholds of the kingdom—Maidens' Castle[2], to
wit, and Stirling, and Dumbarton—manfully opposed themselves; and William Douglas would have exposed his own
foolhardiness, and done nothing more, had he persisted in his
claim. He renounced, therefore, his pretended right, which
in point of fact was none at all; but to James Douglas, his The king's daughter is married to Douglas.
son and heir, was given in marriage the daughter of the king
born in lawful wedlock. Soon afterward they carried Robert
Stewart to Scone, and there crowned him king. In this way
we have the second Robert, king of Scotland, and of the
Stewarts the first king, under which surname the kings of the
Scots are known at this present day. And hence it follows
that seven Stewart kings have now borne rule amongst the
Scots for a term of one hundred and forty-eight years; and
of these kings the present one is a child, in this year fifteen
hundred and eighteen entering upon his seventh year[3]; and
with the first of them we bring this fifth book to a close.

---

[1] That is, as now reckoned, 1371,—the year then running on till the 24th of
March.   [2] See *ante*, p. 15.

[3] This fixes the exact date of the writing of this work.

BOOK VI.

CHAP. I.—*Of the killing of a servant of Dunbar and the truce which was thereby violated ; and of the cruel revenge that was taken and the stratagem which was conceived by certain lords ; also of divers revolts and their issues.*

ABOUT this time, and when a truce was still in force, there went a serving-man of George Dunbar, earl of March, to a fair that was held in the town of Roxburgh, which the English then possessed in Scotland ; and this man was slain by the English in the market-place. Now this man's master, as the custom is, craved punishment of his murderers under the lex talionis ; but to this petition the English turned a deaf ear, and refused all redress. Whereat Dunbar was very wroth ; and at the fair of the following year he gathered his liege men together, with them attacked Roxburgh, and put to death every male person in the place. Of all the goods that had been brought to the market he made distribution among his men, and then laid the town in ashes. Now this deed of his I am far from approving ; rather I abhor it : first, because he thereby dealt a mighty injury to his neighbour ; secondly, because he observed not therein the obligations of a just war ; thirdly, inasmuch as for the death of one man only he slew many innocent persons ; and lastly, because he spoiled them of their possessions. Thus was violated that truce which had endured for fourteen years from the time that David was restored from his captivity, and with its violation all who dwelt about the march and boundaries of these parts gave themselves to fire and slaughter.

A little while thereafter the English entered Scotland with a large army, and invaded the lands of John Gordon, who, along with the earl of March, was one of the chief men ; and him they despoiled of much that he possessed. Whereupon John Gordon was very wroth, and, gathering his friends together, he

Slaying of a
serving-man
of Dunbar.

Dunbar's
wrath.

The English
renew the war.

entered England, and avenged himself by carrying off spoils
twice as many as those that he had lost. Sir John Lilborn
went out to meet him at a place called Carra[1], with a force
twice as great as his own ; and then took place a fierce battle, A fierce battle.
in the which John Gordon was sorely wounded. Nevertheless
he gained the victory, and carried captive into Scotland John The Scots
Lilborn, with his brother and others of the nobles. gain the day.

Henry Percy, earl of Northumberland, when he was ware of
this, gathered a large force, and therewith entered the territory
of the earl of March with intent to lay it utterly waste. When
he was arrived at a wood by Duns, a village which may claim
the glory of having given birth to the Subtle Doctor[2], he
pitched his camp. But by night the Scots, and most of all,
the youth among them, placed small pebbles in skins—much as
you might place pebbles in inflated bladders—and the whole
night long they made with these such a noise that the horses
of the English, breaking rein and bridle, escaped from their
masters. Thus it happened that the army was kept the
whole night from sleep, and the end was, that in much confusion, and without having inflicted any hurt upon their
enemy, they retraced their steps into England.

Thomas Musgrave, captain of Berwick, now went forth to Thomas
carry succour to the earl of Northumberland, but John Gordon Musgrave.
made him prisoner; and on the western marches John Johnston John Gordon.
carried off equal spoils from England. Hence you may behold
how, from the small spark of the slaying of a single serving-
man of the earl of March, there grew a mighty flame, involving
many men in loss of goods and life itself. From all which
I will say this : that the violators of a truce sin grievously, A truce not to
for they have not authority to act from their own kings, and be violated.
they make a plain path for all manner of disaster and sin in
the future. It is often the better course to suffer a trifling
injury than to avenge it, since greater hurt not seldom accrues
to the state from revenge than from toleration.

In the second year of the reign of king Robert, the daughter The daughter
of the earl of Ross was crowned queen. By her the king had of the Earl of
two sons : the one, Walter earl of Athole—who afterward, Ross.

---

[1] Carham. [2] See note, p. 23.

when he was convicted of treason to James the First, was torn
limb from limb—and David earl of Strathern.

Berwick is
retaken.
In the second year of the reign of Robert the Second the
castle of Berwick was taken by seven common men of the Scots.

Birth of
Rothesay.
The revolt
of William
Douglas.
In the same year was born David duke of Rothesay. And in
the tenth year of his reign William, who was the first earl
Douglas, gathered an army of twenty thousand men, and
therewith attacked unawares the village of Penrith [1] at the time
of the fair of that place. He made spoil of all the goods that
were collected for the fair, and carried off many men as his
prisoners, and thus brought down a miraculous pestilence, by
which a third part of all that dwelt in Scotland came by their
end, since God made fast his punishment to the crime that
Douglas had committed.

Rising of
the English.
A little while thereafter the English men of Cumberland
gathered together forty thousand men, and, entering Scotland
by the Solway, put to death many and spoiled them of their
possessions. Now, as these men were on their return to
England, there met them in a narrow pass some five hundred
of the Scots, who, with a mighty noise, rushed upon the
Englishmen, and made great slaughter of them. They spoiled
the English of all they had, and carried away more than three
hundred prisoners. In the eleventh year of his reign the king
sent Walter Wardlaw, cardinal bishop of Glasgow, into France
to the end he might renew the ancient alliance between the
French and the Scots.

CHAP. II.—*Of the expeditions of John of Gaunt* [2], *Archibald
Douglas, the English, the French, and Richard, king of England. Of
the Scots invasion of England, and of the charter that was found.*

John Gant.
In the twelfth year of Robert's reign John Gant, duke of
Lancaster, made his way to the Scottish border and concluded
a truce for a space of three years. It was at this time that
James Straw [3], of whom we have already made mention, made
a violent attack upon London; and when John came to have

---

[1] Orig. and F. ' Penner '.   [2] Joannes Gant.
[3] Orig. ' Stroy ' ; F. ' Strow '. Cf. *ante*, p. 302.

knowledge of this, he took up his quarters at Haddington, awaiting there the end of the rebellion in England.

In the fourteenth year of Robert's reign, Archibald Douglas, lord of Galloway, with the help of the earls of March and Douglas, laid siege to the castle of Lochmaben, and took it. And when the English garrison in the castle of Roxburgh learned what had been done, they sent the baron of Graystock to the castle to be captain there. But George earl of March took him prisoner, and, with him, much gold and silver and a great store of goods, and sent him to the castle of Dunbar. Archibald [Douglas] takes Lochmaben.

In the fifteenth year of Robert's reign English Richard sent the duke of Lancaster with a great army into Scotland, and at the same time a whole fleet of ships of war. But when he reached Edinburgh he wrought no damage on any, did naught in sooth but risk his own men, and so returned home in peace. In the same year the Douglas recovered for the Scots the whole of Teviotdale, where, after the battle of Durham, there had stayed a remnant of the English. And a little while thereafter the Douglas died, in his castle of Douglas, and in the monastery of Melrose received honourable burial. Him James Douglas succeeded in the earldom. At this time it was that the French king sent into Scotland John Guian[1], admiral of France, with a following of two thousand men, who not only stood at their own costs, but brought arms and other sorts of gifts for the Scottish king. This John Guian was of Burgundy, and in all that has regard to war he was a man of renown. He attached himself to the earl of Douglas, who was at that time the best warrior amongst the Scots, and with this same he made many an attack upon England. By help of French skill the Scots got possession of three castles: Furd or Cornubia to wit, Wark, and Cornvalia[2], and razed them to the ground. This done, the admiral of France joined himself A fruitless expedition of the English. Death of William Douglas. John Guian, a Frenchman, and his expeditions along with the Scots.

---

[1] i.e. Jean de Vienne.

[2] 'Werk, Furd and Cornale'—Wyntoun, Bk. IX. ch. vi. 'Werk, Furd et Corwale'—Liber Pluscardensis, lib. x. ch. vii. There is a Cornhill in the parish of Norham (called 'Cornale' passim in the Feodarium Priorat. Dunelm., Surtees Soc. 1872), whose situation relatively to Wark and Furd would make it not unlikely to be the 'Cornvalia' of Major. Why he should have made Cornubia (= Cornwall) a synonym of Furd rather than of Cornvalia is not clear.

to Archibald Douglas, earl of Galloway, the warden of the western marches, and with him entered Cumberland, where he gave all to fire and sword. Last of all, they had the design to lay siege to Carlisle; but when they saw that this might be fraught with some danger to the French, they besieged Roxburgh rather, which castle is more neighbour to the Scots. That castle, albeit, they did not take, and when three months were passed, during which time the Frenchmen took no rest from fighting, they returned, with the full permission of the Scots, to France[1].

English Richard invades Scotland.   At this same time English Richard invaded Scotland. He set fire to the monasteries of Melrose, Dryburgh, Newbottle, and Edinburgh, and without loss of aught returned home. It was after his departure that Robert Stewart, earl of Fife, second son of the king, and with him James earl of Douglas, and Archibald Douglas, earl of Galloway, invaded England with thirty thousand men by way of Solway sands. When they saw the fruitfulness of that country and all its wealth, they carried away much spoil. There was then delivered to Robert, as captain, a very ancient charter, in which it was thus written: 'I King Athelstane Giffis heir to Paulane Odam and Rodam Als gud and als fair als evir tha myn ware; and yairto witnes Mald my Wyff.' And when this same Robert, afterward duke

A very ancient charter of Athelstane.

---

[1] For an account of the expedition of Jean de Vienne see Froissart's *Chronicles*, Bk. II. ch. ccxxviii., ccxxxv., ccxxxvi., ccxxxviii. (Buchon's ed. vol. ii. pp. 314-339). The passages that bear upon the Scots and their unwelcome allies are quoted in Mr. Hume Brown's *Early Travellers in Scotland*, pp. 9-15, and throw light upon Major's statement that it was 'cum Scotorum bona venia' that the French returned home. Robert Gaguin, however (*Compendium R. G. super Francorum gestis*, lib. IX. fol. clxxxii., ed. Paris, 1511), gives an additional reason for the abrupt return of the French force. According to this historian it would seem that on the arrival of the combined French and Scottish forces before Roxburgh [droartum] the French leader, Vienne, desired to storm that strong-hold; but the Scots tried to dissuade him, feeling sure that the place was invin-cible, and the French ended by taking the place by assault while the Scots looked on at their ease ('spectantibus quamsi per ocium Scotis'). Gaguin then goes on to tell how Jean de Vienne 'had been seized with a strong passion for a lady of the royal house, and at length had warning to depart from that Scotland, since the king had begun to hold him in suspicion. Wherefore secretly he got himself on board a ship and betook himself to France.' With a candid appreciation of his own countrymen that reminds one of Major, he adds: 'A very rare thing it is among the French to gain in foreign parts some renown which they do not proceed to tarnish by arrogance or lust.' It is curious that Major, who quotes Gaguin several times, has no reference to this story.

of Albany, and chosen for governor of Scotland, had to give
ear to long charters and letters, he was wont to say that in the
good old days when our ancestors refrained from the prolixity of
his own times there was also to be found among men more good
faith and honest dealing.   And he would prove the same from
Athelstane's letter, which he had by heart and was wont then
to repeat.   The same is in Latin thus: ' Ego Rex Athelstanus do   The translation
Paulanæ dominium de Odam et Rodam, ita libere sicut ego hæc   of the charter.
possedi : et huic dono Matildis mea uxor testimonium dabit[1].'

Archibald Douglas had an illegitimate son, William by   William,
name, a great and famous warrior, who would put to rout   bastard of
Archibald, and
whole troops of the enemy with a handful of his own men.   his excellencies.
The excellencies of this man won for him such high favour
with king Robert that the king bestowed upon him in marriage his daughter Giles[2], with the domain of Nithsdale to
be held in perpetuity by them and by their heirs.

CHAP. III.—*Of the battle that was fought at Otterburn, and of
other conflicts between the English and the Scots ; and chiefly between
Henry Percy, or Persy*[3], *and James Douglas.*

In the one thousand three hundred and eighty-eighth year   The author
from the redemption of the world was fought the battle of   here follows
Froissart.
Otterburn.   And in this part of my history more credence will
be given to Froissart, canon of Thérouenne in Belgium[4], than
to a Scot, inasmuch as we have Froissart's own word that
he held converse with Englishmen and Scots alike, who bore a
part in the battle.   As regards this matter, therefore, I will
follow his statement and opinion ; and that I do so will be
plainly evident to any one who has understanding of the
French tongue, and at the same time has learned to speak
Latin.   I do not mean, nevertheless, to reproduce all that he

---

[1] Rodam = Roddam in Northumberland.   Odam is perhaps the ' villata de
Hoddon' of the *Northumberland Assize Rolls*, Surtees Soc. 1890, p. 314.   Dr.
Dickson of H.M. Register House, has pointed out to me that two vernacular
charters of Athelstane's days are given in Kemble's *Diplomaticus Ævi Saxonici*,
Nos. 359, 360, but I have not been able to identify the charter of the text.

[2] Aegidia.   [3] Percyum seu Perseium.

[4] 'Morinensi canonico seu Tervanensi'.   'Taruenna . . . ville des Morini
dans la Gaule Belgique, auj. *Thérouenne, Thérouanne*, bourg de Fr. (Pas de
Calais).'—Brunet.

has said regarding the matter, but will try rather to give the substance ʾof his narrative of the history, as I have done in similar cases [1].

An expedition of the Scots to which their king was not privy. Froissart, then, tells how the Scottish nobles in assembly at Aberdeen took the determination to invade England, and, gathering an army of thirty thousand men, marched to Jedburgh, declaring nothing all this time to the Scottish king, inasmuch as they judged him to be a man of no experience in war. The chief men among those nobles were James earl Douglas, the earl of March, the earl of Moray, he who bore the name of Dunbar [2], with his brothers, the earl of Fife, the earl of Menteith, Archibald Douglas earl of Galloway, Robert Ekin, the lord Montgomery, William Lindesay and James his brother, Thomas Vaire [3], Alexander Lindesay, John of St. Clair, John Haliburton, Robert Lauder, Alexander Ramsay, the lord Seton, David Fleming, Patrick Hepburn and his son.

The earl of Fife, who was the second son of the king of Scots, invaded England on the western side with a large army ; James Douglas, earl of March, and the earl of Moray, with four thousand chosen horsemen, invaded England on the eastern side, and with all speed, after a march of about thirty leagues, reached Durham, whence returning they laid all waste with fire and sword. They came then to Newcastle, a fortified town upon the river Tyne, where, at that time, two sons of the earl of Northumberland—that is, Henry, commonly called Hotspur, and his brother Ralph—with a great multitude of the nobility, **The bold act of three Scottish nobles.** had taken their stand. Now there were three Scottish earls, men covetous of fame and mighty in war, who had no mind to return to their homes without they had first laid siege to the town ; and they therefore attacked the town, though there were within its walls fighting men—to take no count of the citizens—twice as many as the strength of the besiegers. Outside the gate of the town was a certain rampart made of wood behind which the Scots from without laid their siege ; and soon there came to pass a conflict hand to hand of those two

---

[1] Cf. *ante*, pp. 256, 295.

[2] Orig. 'comes Marchiæ Morauiae Comes Dumbari cognomine etc.'. Froissart says 'le comte de la marche et de Dombar'.

[3] 'Thomas de Percy'—Froissart.

captains of renown, James Douglas to wit, a Scot, and Henry Percy, an Englishman; and James Douglas snatched out of Percy's hands a lance, most beautiful to look on, and, waving the same in the air, called out that he would carry it with him into Scotland. Night put an end to the siege of the town, and on the following day the Scots turned their steps toward Scotland, and laid siege to the strongholds that met them on their march, some of which they took and razed to the ground.

Now Henry Percy desired to pursue the besiegers; but he was dissuaded from his purpose, on the ground that it was no way likely that so small a number would have dared to attack so large a town, which held too so great a garrison, unless it knew itself to have the support within no long distance of a larger army to the which in case of need it might betake itself. But on the following day it came to their knowledge that the main army of the Scots was far distant from this mere handful of men; whereupon Percy and his following not only revived their design to attack the Scots, but carried the same to completion. For, with ten thousand borderers, well trained in all the exercise of war, Henry Percy pursued the Scots, even to the place which bears the name of Otterburn.

The valour of Henry Percy.

Now some of the Scots were at supper, others slept, or were taking rest, for they had that very day been about the besieging of a certain stronghold, and they were weary. The Englishmen did not delay to send out a party to attack them, and three of the Scottish earls, each of them attended by a small number of picked men, went out to give battle against the enemy, calling aloud 'A Douglas, a Douglas', for thus they thought to delay for a time the English onslaught, and gain time for their own men to arm them. I take it that this custom to call aloud the names of leaders in the beginning of a battle has this intent: first, by the renown of a noble name, to strike terror in the enemy, where the fame of some captain has spread far and wide; and secondly, that thereby the leaders themselves may be strengthened and encouraged by the assurance of the love and honour in which they are held. It is to be noted that although, for avoidance of strife, Douglas was chosen to be the captain of this band, the earl of March was either fully equal to him or came but very little short.

The valour of the Scots—how it was shown on a sudden emergency. Whence the custom of calling aloud the names of leaders in battle.

A fierce battle.

Then began a fierce conflict. Percy made the first attack, both because he had the superiority in numbers, and had under him the whole of the young Northumbrian nobility, and also since he was the firstborn son, and of his sons the noblest, of the greatest earl in England; and further, he was very wroth that the Douglas had snatched from his hand at Newcastle that most precious club[1]. On the opposite side you had two earls of Scotland, than whom in all their land none were more notable, or in the things of war more distinguished;—men these were, either of whom felt himself to be a match for the best man in Northumberland. To these was added the earl of Moray, the same who had defeated a man of great renown. These three men, and all their kindred and the nobles that accompanied them, were taking part in the invasion of this part of England with no other end than that of fighting with those terrible sons of Percy, since the father was now stricken in years; and they would sooner have let themselves be torn limb from limb than have fled in coward and disgraceful fashion, or been taken captive. The battle was prolonged till deep into the night; for it was the beginning of August, and the moon gave her light, so that it was possible to distinguish friend from foe[2]. When attacks of this sort are made in an unfamiliar country, the light of the moon is eagerly desired; for otherwise the risk is great, in the darkness, of being struck by friend as well as foe. Just like the mariner, who will not sail unless with light to show his course, lest otherwise the vessel be dashed against a rock.

Now a part of the Scots seemed, even as they were fighting, to have lost ground in a measure, since, though they kept a constant front to the enemy, the English had made way beyond the lines of their first onset. And had not that valiant warrior, Patrick Hepburn, with his son of the same name, borne himself

The struggle for the standard.

like the brave man he was, the standard of the Douglas would have fallen into the hands of Percy's men. For when in course of battle the standard, towards which the combatants ever direct their eye, is once lost, then follows rout to the army.

---

[1] 'clava'; it was a *lance* before, see p. 316. Froissart calls it a 'pennon'.

[2] 'ut hostem ab inimico [lege 'amico'] segregare possent'. The balance of opinion seems to favour the 12th of August as the date of the battle.

For two reasons therefore did Percy's men aim at the capture of the standard: first, that they might thereby and at once put the enemy to rout; secondly, that they might thereby achieve somewhat specially grateful to Henry Percy, if, for the small standard that had been snatched from his hand, they might put into it the chief standard of the Scots.

Patrick Hepburn therefore, with his son, spared nor sweat nor toil to hold the standard, and many were the blows and wounds that he received, nor fewer those that he dealt. When Douglas saw the jeopardy of his standard, and therewith of the battle, his rage was hot within him as he had been a Libyan lion, and alone he raised, or took the same from him who bore it, that club with iron edge, and double edged it was,—a club which two common men might scarce avail to lift,—for he was a goodly man to see, and well-knit, and of mighty strength, and so, before all the line of Scots, he rushed upon the Englishmen. Then did he lay the enemy low with the fury of his blows, so that for a large space about him their dead bodies hid the ground, and with such valour did he ever press forward as he might seem—he one man only—to aim at the destruction of the whole line of the enemy; and thus, looking on one side and the other if he might espy Henry Percy, he went far beyond the line of the first assault, and so was sundered from his own men, since these were busied in attacking others of the enemy or in defence of their own lives. Step by step, however, fired by the bold spirit of their leader, the Scots make their way to the line of the first onset, and the destruction of the English seemed to be at hand. But when the younger Percy was ware of this, he fell upon the Scots, and by them was speedily surrounded. Yet was he not known by them to be one of the leaders, as Douglas was known for such by the English, for they took him to be but a common soldier. He received a heavy wound at the hands of a noble Scot, named John de Makerel,[1] a vassal of the earl of Moray, and he would have been slain, had he not surrendered himself and declared who he was. For an enemy does not readily put to death a leading man in battle; rather, if he can, will he take him prisoner; both for the sake of the

The strength and courage of Douglas.

The younger Percy is wounded and taken prisoner.

---

[1] Froissart has 'Maksuel' = Maxwell.

ransom that he may bring, and from the regard and affection
that a prisoner will afterward show to those who have spared
his life. For the captor will defend his prisoner against his
very father, as being indeed his own property; and if it
happen that a prisoner should come, after he has been taken,
in peril of his life, then will his captor grant him his liberty
and furnish him with arms, and afford him every sort of
succour. This quality of his prisoner, then, this sir John
Makerel—or Marshall, I know not which, for the names
resemble one another, and the French are not noted for correct-
ness in their pronunciation and spelling of British names[1]; and

---

[1] We have Major's own word for it (see Appendix I. 'Bibliography'—' Propositio ad Auditores' *In Quartum* 1519) that his handwriting was bad; and this
may account for most of the curious renderings of British names in the Paris edition
of 1521, which was printed while the author was in Scotland. But his remark is
just on the whole. Froissart's 'Oskesufforch' for Oxford, for instance, and
'Haindebourch' for Edinburgh, probably owe little or nothing to the printer.
It will not be without interest to give some specimens :—

Abercoruie—*Abercorn.*
Abrenefhyns—*of Abernethy.*
Albeuicus, Salcomes—*Abernethy of Sal-
ton.*
Alwemarbre—*Albemarle.*
Balmormoch—*Balmerino.*
Beauchamyc—*Beauchamp.*
Bethwalya ⎱ *Bothwell.*
Bothuilti ⎰
Bolyngok—*Bolingbroke.*
Bombenem—*Bohun.*
Boukgugham—*Buckingham.*
Burrannere—*Burramure.*
Caruicher—*Carruther.*
Cimithrethyn—*Luntrethyn.*
Cochole—*Athole.*
Cokburuspech—*Cockburnspath.*
Corstoryhymus ⎱ *of Corstorphine.*
constorphin ⎰
Comhisbunde — *Inisboufinde* [*Inis-
boffin*].
Dansken—*Dunglas.*
Dasbynton—*Dalswynton.*
Deitonus—*Seton.*
Dodoriald ⎱ *Dundonald.*
dudoualt ⎰
Dunoterkynnef—*Dunottar, Kynnef.*
Duxlin—*Dupplin.*
Errolk—*Errol.*

Galterus Bik, Gartonus Lusueus—
    Walter Bickerton of Lufness.
Golbri—*Gowry.*
Harphordiae ⎱ *Hertford.*
Hetfordiam ⎰
Honic—*Home.*
Hu—*Hii* [*Iona*].
Humpont—*Veypont.*
Inumberbuy—*Inverbervie.*
Kaci—*Tracy.*
Kalymouth—*Kilrimont.*
Kilwoue—*Kilblene.*
Klender—*Callander.*
Lemugstonus—*Livingstone.*
Liler—*Tiler.*
Lanchguhay—*Lochawe.*
Langschaukx—*Longshanks.*
Lawium—*Latimer.*
Lochabin—*Lochleven.*
Mactrevers ⎱ *Maltrevers.*
Martranas ⎰
Makkane—*Maclean.*
Menthechus ⎱
Mentechus ⎰ *Mentetheus.*
Mentehus ⎰
menynghameum— *Cunyngham.*
mucayde gaslz—*Murray de Gask.*
Northanixton—*Northampton.*
Poxis—(? *Popil*) *Peebles.*

then thereafter, through fault of scribes, letters get lost. Some names, however, they write correctly, either because the spelling is easy, or because they are the names of well-known men—in any case, John Makerel declared the quality of his prisoner to the earl of Moray. The earl of Moray said then to him who had made Percy prisoner: 'Thou hast won thy spurs; it remains only to seize the elder brother likewise, and so put an end to all this toil and sweat.' And he commanded his standard-bearer to press forward against the enemy, giving out that he had taken one of the two Percys.

The English, on their side, were now fiercely stirred, and gave themselves manfully to the rescue of their captive chief. Them the Scots withstood, and hotly followed earl Douglas whither-soever he led; and as he went ever further, he was attended at the last by two of his company only, that is, his squire[1], sir Robert Hert, and a priest,—sir William, who came from North Berwick[2], and who was accustomed throughout the whole course of any war to stay by the side of his lord, so that naught could move him from that place. The Britons speak of any men who bear arms, or rather of any good fighting men[3], as little inferior to those that have received knighthood. On that day Douglas desired to confer knighthood upon Hert; but this he refused; because, when men

A hot conflict.

Rondale—*Arundel.*	Togy ⎱ *Logy.*
Schrouwesbern ⎫	Thogy ⎰
Strouesbern ⎬ *Shrewsbury.*	Trennokus—*of Greenock.*
Twrovesthurryum ⎭	Tririarsy—*Gournay.*
Scrauelangum—*Stirling.*	Trystyclok—*Crystyclok.*
Skrenigeorx—*Scrimgeour.*	Tuburi—*Turnburi.*
Spruse—*Pease.*	Turem—*Currie.*
Stanchardum—*Standard.*	Varoye—*Barry.*
Stonsconus—*Johnston.*	Vnghart—*Urquhart.*
Stremlinus—*of Stirling.*	Vodscok—*Woodstock.*
Stropus—*Scrope.*	Voydude—*Boyd.*
Steuhend—*Stonehenge.*	Watre—*Wake.*
Suutsultiae—*of Suffolk.*	Welmin—*de Irvin.*
Tenidalon ⎱ *Tantallon.*	
tintaloya ⎰	

1 armigero.

2 'boreali unico'. I read 'boreali Bervico'; for, says Froissart, 'ce prêtre, je vous le nommerai; on l'appéloit Guillaume de Norbervich'.

3 armigeros seu potius belligeros.

are made belted knights in reward of their valour, lands are
given them in perpetuity, that they may get from these an
honourable livelihood.   Now that presbyter, who, after he
had so skilfully used his halbert, received himself five mortal
wounds, was archdeacon of Aberdeen.   This priest received the
highest praise as a warrior.   You must not marvel that I have
to relate such things of priests; for Britain can show forty
thousand priests who could be matched as fighting men against
a like number of men from any nation.   For every small laird
has one chaplain, who is no despicable soldier, and the great
nobles have as many as five or six who will gird on their sword
and shield and go with their lords to the field.   Yet this is a
fashion that I no way approve.   For inasmuch as their clerical
office is of the Lord, they should spend their time in divine
worship and not in warfare.   Yet I do not deny that for their
country, or to defend their own lives, they may take up arms.

Douglas thereafter received at the hands of the English, and
all at once, three wounds from large and sharp-pointed spears:
the one in the thigh, another in the lower part of the breast,
the third in the leg; and thus they bore him down, and the
mortal wound was given on his bare head.   And this agrees
with the narrative of our own chroniclers, where they tell that
his helmet was loosely fastened.   Some persons, yet with less
of probability, hold that by reason of the so sudden onslaught
of the English he had even forgotten to don his helmet.   The
English, however, did not know him for who he was; and by
good luck, to the end of the combat, his death remained hidden
from the Scots; for the fighting lasted still throughout near
the whole night.   The actual place of conflict was varied from
time to time on account of the numbers of the slain.   While
the battle was at the hottest, sir James Lindesay[2], who was
cousin to the earl, and his brother, came up and asked the earl
how he did, and he answered them saying that he had not an
hour to live; but he added that in this he gloried, seeing that
after the fashion of his ancestors he should meet his end in
battle and not in his bed; and he took them bound before
God to avenge his death, but to reveal naught of what he had

Warrior priests
or religious[1]
in England.

Whether priests
ought to take
part in war.

Death of
Douglas.

---

[1] presbyteri seu sacerdotes bellatores.   [2] Froissart says ' Jean de Saint-Clar '.

said to friend or foe before the end of the battle. For he held
that if his death remained unknown, the very fact that he was
believed to be bearing his part in the attack would bring
victory in the still impending battle; and he bade them raise
aloft his standard, which already seemed in a manner to waver.
And they, like the stout and noble hearts they were, hearkened
to his words, and shouting aloud 'A Douglas! a Douglas!' Percy is taken—
closed around his standard.   the English fly.

Very many were afterward found slain around the anchor of
the English, and Henry Percy was made prisoner by the lord
Montgomery, a brave and noble man. This once known, the
English took to flight. The Scots took captive whom they
would. Among the English prisoners were found two Percys;
sir Robert Ogil; sir Thomas Aberton[1]; sir John Lilborn; sir
William Walsington[2]; the lord of Helcon[3], a baron; likewise
sir John Colpedupe[4], who was seneschal of York, and very
many other noble men. In ending what he has to say concerning this battle, Froissart declares that in the whole book
of his history he has had to tell of no battle so notable by
the valour of its captains, and fought out upon both sides
with such manly courage as this. For not seldom has it
come to pass that one side or the other came off victorious,
it might be from the exercise of this precaution or of that,
or by reason of superiority in the engines of war, or from
cowardice of the enemy; but here, in long and hard struggle
the strife went on, as it might be in a duel, and the victory
seemed to be on one side or the other, not once or twice, but
three times, even four. This writer records the names of many Scots who bore
Scots, of whom the families have now in some cases gone to battle.
the ground, in some cases risen to high rank, while there are
others which have kept the same state which then they had.
This leads me to note the two families of the Hepburns and
the Montgomerys; because in my own day we have seen the
creation of two earls of these families[5]. When the battle, then,

---

[1] Abington.
[2] Walsingham. The original edition of Major reads 'Vahluconus'—a good
example of the French manner of spelling British names.
[3] Helton or Haltoun (or Hetton).
[4] Froissart says 'Colpedich'—really Sir John Copeland.
[5] Patrick lord Hailes was created earl of Bothwell in 1488 (Crawfurd's *Peerage*

was ended, the English took to their horses forthwith and fled,
and the Scottish horsemen went in pursuit of them; because
the very noblest among Scots and Englishmen alike go out to
battle indeed as horsemen, and return from battle in like
fashion, but it is as foot-soldiers that they fight.

CHAP. IV.—*Of the rest of this said battle, and its renewal by the
bishop of Durham ; and of the capture of Lindesay and his release.*

The rising of
the bishop of
Durham.

ON the evening of that day whereon the sons of the earl of
Northumberland had gone forth to fight against the Scots, the
bishop of Durham, with a following of seven thousand men,
arrived at Newcastle. And men began to speak to them in
such words as these : that it was a base thing that they should
stay within the town when the sons of their earl were in the
field, and perchance at that very moment in the thick of the
fight. And when the bishop was inclined to hearken to their
words, he went a-field outside the town, yet to no great distance ; and he took counsel there with his chief men, such as
sir William de Lussy [1], sir Thomas Clifford, and others that
were well-skilled warriors, as to what should be done—whether,
that is, they should make all haste to follow after the Percys,
or remain for the whole of that night near to Newcastle. And
their counsel was that he should not go further.

In the early morning there arrived Englishmen in flight
after the battle, and these declared to him the whole story
of it and its circumstance ; and there fell into the hands of
the bishop sir James Lindesay, as he was in pursuit of the
Englishmen. I will now tell how he chanced to be taken
in this way. When the battle had ended in adverse fashion
for the English, and they began to seek safety by flight,
those of the Scots who had not suffered much hurt, and who
were still eager for the fight, went in pursuit. But amongst

of Scotland, ed. 1716, p. 44); Hugh third lord Montgomerie was created earl of
Eglintoun in the end of 1506 (Fraser's *Memorials of the Montgomeries, Earls of
Eglinton*, 1859, vol. i. p. 28).

[1] Perhaps the ' messire Jean de Say ' of Froissart. M. Buchon (*Chroniques,*
vol. ii. p. 734) says that the Besançon MS. differs much from the text which he
follows in this chapter of Froissart—the hundred and twenty-third of the third
Book—and the one that follows.

the English the only man who escaped was sir Matthew Rademan. For so great was at this point the confusion of the fight that scarce two of those who ffed were able to remain together ; and when sir James Lindesay had marked this Englishman as he fled among the rest, which thing he could do by reason of the fine armour that he wore, he followed him —he alone followed Matthew alone—to a distance of three thousand paces. And when the Englishman saw that the fleetness of his horse would not avail for his escape, he dismounted, and placed his shield, as the custom is, against the back of his left hand, while in his right hand he held his well-sharpened sword. Thereupon sir James Lindesay dismounted likewise, but at some distance ; for he did not dismount when he was close to sir Matthew Rademan, but made fast his horse that it might not break loose, that so as a foot-soldier he might meet another soldier on foot. Thus then the fight began between them. The Scot was armed with a halbert, which seems to have the advantage over sword and shield, and after some fighting he made the Englishman his prisoner, and spoiled him of his sword. The Englishman then besought him to let him depart, and swore a solemn oath that he would thus return to him in Scotland within twenty days, and that the Scot should then deal with him as became a captor with a captive. And to this, without another word, sir James assented, and restored to him his sword and all that he had taken. For with the men of the Borders such is the custom : they wage fiercest war one with another, but the conqueror does not slay his prisoner, but in all clemency spares his life, and grants him for the most part a safe return home, when he pledges his word. But if he do not keep his word, then the conqueror fastens to a horse's tail the effigy of his prisoner, and so carries it across the Borders, whereupon all of his own people acknowledge him for all time to be a perjured and perfidious person, who has brought no small dishonour upon the country that gave him birth. But when sir James Lindesay was leaving sir Matthew Rademan, meaning to return to the Scots, but ignorant of the way, he fell into the hands of the bishop of Durham. For he made the mistake of taking the enemy for Scots, but when he recognised the bishop, he surrendered himself as a prisoner. Then

spake the bishop : ' I have not gone forth to-day to war, and
behold ! I have taken a noble man for a prisoner, and one in
fair armour.' To whom sir James made answer : 'So does
fickle fortune lay her snares for men of war, seeing that I,
who this very night made prisoner of a gentleman, am now
myself led captive away.' He was thus by the bishop of
Durham carried to Newcastle ; and to witness this spectacle a
multitude of Englishmen assemble, and among them came
sir Matthew Rademan, and when he saw sir James Lindesay,
he made confession that he himself was indeed the prisoner of
the prisoner, and thus set him at liberty, and courteously
prayed him that he would be his guest at breakfast. And the
Scot willingly went with him.

Meanwhile had the bishop of Durham got together ten
thousand men, who assembled at Newcastle. And these he
led forth by the Berwick gate, and took a straight road for
Otterburn, meaning to attack the Scots. And when the Scots
by their scouts were ware of this, they deliberated what they
should do with their English prisoners, and likewise whether
they should make a stay where they were, or go on towards
Scotland. The judgment of some amongst them was to put
all the prisoners to death, for they feared lest they might turn
against them in the hour of battle ; but in the end they came
to this determination, that they should take their prisoners
bound by solemn oath to remain their prisoners as before,
whether they suffered defeat at the hands of the English or not,
and likewise that they should give no succour to the English
in the fight. They are said, however, to have bound the
prisoners with cords. And this done, they planted themselves
in the best order for withstanding the onslaught of the
Englishmen. And two brothers were left as fuglemen [1] and
trumpeters, and these they ordered to blow their horns. The
fashion amongst the Scots is this : that every one, when he
goes forth to battle, carries with him, as a man might do when
he goes to the chase, his horn, strung by a cord from his neck,
and at the onset of the battle they stir up their courage with
this sound. The Englishmen then answered to them with a
counterblast ; but when, at the length of two arrow-shots, the

The Scots
almost always
carry horns.

---

[1] Campiductores. See *ante*, p. 235.

Englishmen were close upon the Scots, the Scots sounded a marvellous blast, and remained steadfast in their ranks. Thereupon did George Dunbar, earl of March, a man of keen and fiery temper, and likewise one who had borne no small part in many a warlike fray, stir up by these words the spirit of his men : ' All the burden of battle and its heat has been ours, my noble Scots, throughout this night ; we have put to the rout the flower of Northumbrian youth, with its two leaders ; nothing remains but that we await this priest's attack,— nothing is left for us but that we should each man of us deal two blows, for, believe me, at the third the fugleman will turn his heel, and his flock will follow him. For if the combat should last longer, and we in the end—which God forbid !— should be defeated, we shall basely lose the glory that we have won by the sweat and labour of this night. We shall teach this priest, if we only quit us like men, that it would better become him to apply the birch to schoolboys that will not do their tasks than to enter the lists with bearded men.'

George Dunbar's speech to his men.

Now when the bishop and his men had well considered the bearing of the Scots, they took the determination to retreat, and made no attack upon the Scots ; or, as Froissart imagines, they said amongst themselves that by the Scots they had much to lose and little to gain. When the Scots saw how the English were in retreat, they prepared to refresh themselves with food along with their English prisoners ; and inasmuch as Ralph Percy was sore wounded, he besought the earl of Moray, whose prisoner he was, that he would grant him to go to Newcastle, where he might be cured of his wound ; and he gave his oath that at the word of the earl of Moray he would return to what part of Scotland soever, or pay whatever fine should be fixed by his captor. To this petition the earl of Moray readily gave his consent ; and on the same terms more than six hundred prisoners returned to their homes.

The English retire.

Ralph Percy is released upon oath.

Henry Percy, however, was carried into Scotland, and along with him four hundred other prisoners. Froissart relates how he was told by a certain man of Chastel-Neuf in Béarn, of the household of the count de Foix[1], who had been a prisoner with the Scots, that for his ransom the Scots demanded no more

Henry Percy is carried into Scotland.

---

[1] F. 'quidam de Novo Castro in Berna in domo comitis Foxensis [Orig.

than the English were ready to offer ; and that among the Scots
they met with kindly treatment.   And this statement, too, I
take from Froissart : that from the ransom of all their prisoners
the Scots got no more than two hundred thousand francs ; and
yet in days that were then not long past the duke of Longueville, when he had been taken prisoner among the Flemings[1], was
ransomed to his English captors for a hundred thousand pieces
of gold.   And inasmuch as I no way believe that the duke of
Longueville was a mightier lord in lands and revenues than
was the earl of Northumberland, I take this as a proof that the
northern English and the men of the Scottish borders had more
liberal customs in the matter of ransoms[2].   And for this I

The praise of John Swinton. praise them highly.   Our chroniclers make mention in this
battle of John Swinton with all honour[3].   In it, besides those
that are named by Froissart, there lost their lives John of the
Towers and William Londe, both Scots and knights.   Master
Thomas Barry, who was the first provost of Bothwell, made
many verses about this war—but they were of the rhymed sort,
for thus he begins—

> Let the muse say how great deed
> Shall never want in song its meed.[4]

'Soxensis '].'   Froissart : 'ainsi que me dit au pays de Berne, en l'hôtel du comte
de Foix, Jean de Chastel-Neuf, etc.'

[1] 'apud Morinos', *i.e.* in Belgic Gaul.

[2] Froissart (ed. Buchon, vol. ii. p. 738) says, 'et finèrent les Anglois, et se
rançonnèrent au plustôt qu'ils purent, et retournèrent petit à petit en leurs lieux'.
In a curious passage of the *Chronicles*, Bk. III. ch. cxxiii. (Buchon, vol. ii. p.
731) he contrasts the civil and courteous treatment of Englishman by Scot and
Scot by Englishman with the custom among the Germans : ' Et quand par armes
ils se rendent l'un à l'autre, ils font bonne compagnie sans eux trop travailler de
leur finance, mais sont très courtois l'un à l'autre, ce que Allemands ne sont pas ;
car mieux vaudroit un gentil homme être pris des mécréans, tous payens ou
Sarrasins, que des Allemands. . . . Au voir dire en moult de choses Allemands
sont gens hors de rieulle de raison, et c'est merveille pour quoi nuls conversent
avec eux ni qu'on les souffre à armer avec eux, comme François et Anglois, qui
font courtoisie, ainsi qu'ils ont toujours fait.'

[3] The hero of Sir Walter Scott's *Halidon Hill.* ' I have some thoughts ', Sir
Walter wrote to John Swinton of Broadmeadows, July 10, 1814, 'of completing
a sort of Border sketch of the Battle of Otterburn, in which, God willing, our
old carle shall have his due.'   Homildon was ultimately chosen as the subject of
the poem instead of Otterburn ; 'and from Homildon the scene of action is
transferred to Halidon Hill.'   See *The Swintons of that Ilk*, Edin. 1883, p. 14.

[4] Musa refert fatum fore scriptum carmine vatum.

And so he goes on. But as the verses are of no merit, and indeed are quite unworthy to be quoted, I pass them by.

Archibald Douglas, the earl of Galloway, succeeded to the possessions of James Douglas.

CHAP. V.—*Of the choice of the younger Robert as Regent of Scotland, which this writer can no way approve ; and of the expedition against England on the part of Robert, which had indeed a prosperous issue, but was none the less far from praiseworthy.*

In the thirteen hundred and eighty-ninth year from the redemption of the world, Robert, king of Scotland, was already stricken in years, and no longer equal to the burden of government; and his first-born son, John earl of Carrick, was lame by reason that he had suffered a kick from a horse which belonged to James Douglas of Dalkeith. For which causes the king summoned the three estates to convene at Edinburgh, and there was earl Robert, the second son, chosen for regent of Scotland. Now, whatever our writers may contend, I cannot hold this aged king, I mean this second Robert, to have been a skilful warrior or wise in counsel. That he was unskilled in war was made sufficiently plain in the battle of Otterburn, as the story of that fight is told by Froissart on the authority of Scottish gentlemen. Nor do I see wherefore an aged king, whose long experience might be held to bring wisdom in its train, should be regarded as less fit to bear rule than a young man. And further, if that bodily infirmity which afflicted the first-born son, John, were unaccompanied by any infirmity of mind, it need not have been any hindrance to his exercise of the duties of a king; for he might have ridden on horseback throughout the country. And thus to bestow upon that other the regency was naught else than to run the risk of having two rival kings within the state. For these reasons I am unable to approve this action of the king, and of the three estates, provided that John was a man of sense and worth.

Now inasmuch as Henry Percy was prisoner in the hands of the Scots, the English intrusted to earl Marshal the wardenship of the Marches, and he began to cast it in the teeth of

the Percys and the rest of the English that they had not made
a better fight at Otterburn ; and used big words about what
he would do, he for his part, if he might only come to close
grips with the Scots.   And when the regent of Scotland was
ware of this, he gathered a large army, and, taking along with
him the lord Archibald Douglas, invaded England, harried
the parts where earl Marshal dwelt, and in the end gave over
the desolated country to the flames.   Earl Marshal meanwhile
had been gathering a large army, and with the same he took
up his position on a certain piece of level ground not far
distant from the Scots.   When the Scots saw this, they lost
no time in drawing near with intent to give battle; but
the English leader withdrew his men to a strongly fortified
position neighbouring the plain.   Whereupon the Scots sent
out a flag of truce, and demanded of the English to come
down then into the open and fight with them ; for they had
come to England, they said, for no other reason than to
find out who and what nature of man this English captain [1]
could be, whose bombastic speech was an insult at once to the
English who had been taken prisoners and to their captors.
Whereto the English leader made answer that he dared not
expose to so great risk the warriors of his king ; and when
they heard this the Scots were consumed with laughter, and
flung in his teeth that of Horace, which he borrows from the
fables of Aesop,

'Parturiunt montes, nascetur ridiculus mus.'

On every side of them therefore did the Scots lay waste the
country, and carried home with them no small store of bloodless booty.   The regent's conduct in this matter was blame-
worthy.   For it was not fitting, on the ground of some
unmeasured words uttered by a boastful man, to gather an
army, and carry off the goods of other men.   Robert, stricken
in years as he was, would have given better counsel in the
matter, for he would, without a doubt, have advised his people
to stay at home and keep peace with their neighbours.

Robert the younger, his expedition.

---

[1] Campiductor.   See *ante*, p. 235.

CHAP. VI.—*Of the death of Robert the Scot, the second of the name, and of his issue. Of the coronation of Robert the Third, who was formerly called John, and of his character; further, concerning the rising under Alexander Buchan, and the duel fought by thirty Wild Scots against other thirty.*

In the thirteen hundred and ninetieth year since the Virgin's travail, and in the nineteenth year of his reign, died Robert the Second, in his castle of Dundonald, full of days, for he had passed by near four years the three-score years and ten. He was buried at Scone. And in the same year did Alexander Stewart, earl of Buchan, son to king Robert, give to the flames the cathedral church of Moray of Elgin, which was at that time the glory of the whole country. By Elizabeth, daughter of sir Adam Mure, king Robert had three sons: John, to wit, who was afterward king, and Robert duke of Albany, and that earl of Buchan, Alexander. Thereafter he had by Eufemia, daughter of the earl of Ross, Walter earl of Athole and lord of Brechin, and David earl of Stratherne. For on the death of Elizabeth his queen he made this Eufemia his wife, and for wedlock's sake her children were legitimated. In that year the lord Clifford slew William Douglas of Nithsdale by treachery on the bridge of Dunglas over the Pease[1]. In the same year John eldest born of the foresaid king Robert was crowned as king, and his name of John was changed for that of Robert: and thus he became Robert the Third. For Robert Bruce was the first of the Roberts, not only by the order of his birth, but by his valour and the glory that he won. I take it that the reason for this change of name was that they fancied the Johns to be unlucky kings; only a few days before that time they had seen the French John taken prisoner by the English. Yet I could easily quote illustrious warriors who had borne this name[2]. And, to speak truly, there

Robert the Second dies.

The horrible crime of Alexander Stewart.

What issue Robert had.

A base murder by Clifford.

John son of Robert is crowned under the style of Robert the Third.

---

[1] F. 'super pontem de Danskenum [Orig. Dausken] in Sprusa'. I have to thank Mr. F. H. Groome for this happy solution of a real difficulty.

[2] In his Exposition of St. Matthew, in connection with the naming of the Baptist, Major says that he could quote men famous both in philosophy and war who had borne this name, and instances John Hircanus, John king of Castile, John the voiwode [viuodam], alias huniades (1400-1460), who a few years before had opposed the most powerful and warlike Mohammedans ; it was likewise the name most commonly assigned to a priest about whose name there was a doubt, and the king's clerk [palatinus scriptor] will jocularly be called

inheres in a name naught, whether good or evil. He took to

This marriage
of Robert the
Third not
approved.
wife Annabella daughter of John of Drummond, for he was
moved by her exceeding beauty. It was his duty rather to
take a wife from a foreign kingdom, and not from his own, for
he would thus have made secure a friendly alliance and would
have acted more consonantly to his state in the world ; it is
not right to make men of middling condition grandfathers
and kinsmen of a king, for such conduct tends to bring con-

Robert's just
dealing.
tempt upon the kingly majesty. This Robert wrought no
hurt to his subjects ; he compelled his courtiers to pay for all
they had to the last farthing ; and ever before he took his
departure from any place he made proclamation by sound of
trumpet, four or even six hours in advance of his departure,
that all merchants and others who had sold aught to the
court should receive payment therefor.

The rising of
Alexander
Buchan.
In the year thirteen hundred and ninety-one Duncan Stewart,
son to Alexander earl of Buchan, came with his caterans into
Angus and harried that part. Against him there went forth
Walter Ogilvy with his brother Walter Lichtoun, but they
were overwhelmed by the caterans and with sixty armed men
lost their lives. I find our chroniclers making mention of
many instances of single combat after this time between Scots
and English ; but on these I will not dwell. It is a sin in
kings or men in authority whatsoever to permit, now here now

Conflicts
between two
persons, such as
are called duels,
are condemned.
there, combats of this sort. He who begins the attack is not
free from sin, nor yet the defendant either, if in any other
fashion he can defend his life ; since indeed it has many times
been shown that it was the conquered man whose cause was
just ; for God willeth not to bring to light by such an evil
means as this the integrity of a man when it has been called
in question, but by lawful means the same is to be made plain,
and if by any way whatever the matter of contention still
remains inscrutable, then let them leave it in God's hands ; for
to men it is not given to pass judgment save by allegation and
proof. I add further that the victor gains but small renown,
while the conquered man in the eyes of the vulgar suffers
much disgrace ; he therefore who trusts his life to such a cast
of the dice acts at once imprudently and wickedly. And that

John. John and Robert, he adds, were the names taken by boys when they
formed themselves for their game into two sides.

confession too which is made before the entrance upon a duel is chimerical[1], if he persist in his sin, desiring to take the life of his fellow ; and his own life too, which he is bound to preserve, he exposes to the chance of fortune. Wherefore on no account is such an one to receive priestly absolution, and if in the meanwhile he should die without repentance he will be damned.

Just about this time, however, for the year was thirteen hundred and ninety-six, such a combat took place among sixty men of the Wild Scots. The caterans, that is, the Wild Scots, men of a savage behaviour, were not able to keep the peace among themselves. Two factions, to wit Sceachbeg and his kinsmen, who were called Clan Kay, and Christy Jonson and his followers, who were called Clan Quhele, had come to cherish a fierce hatred one for the other, and they could in no way be got to keep the peace. Seeing this, sir David Lindesay, who afterward became earl of Crawford, and Thomas Dunbar, the earl of Moray, gave this counsel to the chiefs of these factions : that a combat of sixty—that is, of either side thirty —should decide their cause in presence of the king. And to this counsel they willingly consented, and entered on the combat upon the northern island at Saint John. Thirty men, naked but for a doublet[2] that hung from one side, made for the field of battle, armed with bow and double-axe ; and these forthwith met the encounter of a like number, armed in the same fashion, and, like bulls was their onset, headlong unswerving,—so they rushed and struck, thirty upon thirty. Now on the one side, that of the Clan Kay, every man save one was slain ; and of the other side those that survived were eleven. But at the beginning of the combat there happened an incident which must not be omitted. One of the combatants made his escape from the fight, and the nine-and-twenty that were left were unwilling to wage battle against thirty ; nor would those thirty consent to remove one of their own men. And there was not found any man who would take the place of the runaway ; and 'twas no marvel, since to fight for your life, naked but for a plaid, is no trifle[3]. And when

A combat of sixty men.

---

[1] 'Chimaerina.' Cf. *ante*, the 'vulpine' confession.

[2] 'in nudis diploidibus ex una parte.'

[3] 'quia non erat quaestio de lana caprina in diploide ad mortem pugnare'. Mr. George Neilson (*Trial by Combat*, p. 251) points out that the expression

The daring deed of a common man. the king and the nobility had for a long time stood expectant, there appeared in the midst a certain man of the common people, who called out, 'Who will give me a shield to guard my vitals!—and I will bear my part in yonder spectacle ; and if I come forth alive I will go in search of that beaten man my whole life long.' The man who thus bore his part in the combat was not tall in stature, but he was stoutly built, and his limbs well-knit and muscular, and he was one of the eleven that escaped with their lives, and many upon that side might thank his sweat that they were living men at the end of the day. By this means then peace was procured in that region [1].

'de lana caprina' is borrowed from Horace, *Epp.* i. xviii. 15. Cf. however, Major's use of the words about John the Baptist in the Exposition of St. Matthew, fol. xii. ed. 1518 : 'Non habuit zonam coloratam more petulantium scholasticorum pro coloribus certantium, cuius inventio de lana caprina est auctore diabolo'.

[1] The names of the clans which took part in this battle, as given here by Major, and of the clans mentioned in the twelfth chapter of this book as deserting from Alexander lord of the Isles, have occasioned much controversy. In the original edition (Paris, 1521) the names of the here contending clans are given as 'Steachbeus & eius consanguinei Claukay dicti, & Christi Iouson [or, perhaps, 'Iouson'] cum suis qui Clauquhele dicebantur'—rendered in Freebairn's edition (1740) thus : 'Sceachbegus & ejus consanguinei Clankay dicti, & Christi Jonson cum suis qui Clanquhele dicebantur'. In the passage in the twelfth chapter the original edition reads : 'Duae tribus syluestriũ scilicet Claukatã & Claukauel. . . . In festo palmarum sequenti vsque adeo debacchatum est, vt totam progeniem Clanbramerõ tribus Claukatam extinxerit. Tribus hæ sunt consanguinei' etc. The edition of 1740 here reads 'Clankatan & Clancameron [for 'Claukauel']' and 'Clancameronum' for 'Clanbramerõ'. The whole question has undergone a searching examination in Mr. Alexander Mackintosh Shaw's ' *The Clan Battle at Perth in* 1396 : *an episode of Highland History ; with an enquiry into its causes, and an attempt to identify the Clans engaged in it.* Printed for private circulation, 1874'. To that tract the reader must be referred for further information, but I may quote Mr. Shaw's summary as given at pp. 39-40 : 'The most likely solution of the apparent difficulty in this oft-quoted passage of MAJOR's History seems to be this :—The historian follows BOWAR's account of the desertion from the Lord of the Isles in 1429, and of the slaughter of a sept (*progeniem*) of the Clan Cameron in the following year ; but in the mention of the first event he uses a name, *Kauel*, properly belonging only to the chief branch of Clan Cameron—whether to indicate that branch only or the whole confederacy is of little consequence. In the mention of the second event he employs the name *Cameron*, but remembering that he is writing for readers who would have little or no knowledge of Highland family and clan names, and perhaps apprehensive that by using the name *Kauel* he might appear to disagree with BOWAR, he adds by way of explanation the few words 'Tribus hæ sunt consanguineæ ['consanguinei' in Orig.], etc.,' to show that the two names *Kauel* and *Cameron* belong to the same set of people. These words would probably never have led to so much misconception had the

It is a marvel that the king and his nobles were not equal to the taming of these factions. Some explanation is possible when we consider that the king can grant a remission to two men under sentence of death, to the end that in their mutual slaughter the people may have such delectation as arises from such a spectacle ; or, if it is plain that one or other is worthy of death, and each accuse the other, while it does not appear which is the innocent man, then let them put the matter to the test in single combat. But even this method I should be inclined to condemn.

CHAP. VII.—*Of the creation of new dukes ; and of the conspiracy and rebellion of the earl of March against the king and realm on account of the wrongful retention of his daughter's dower when she had been repudiated. Of the death and valour of Archibald the Terrible. Of the invasion of Scotland by Henry the Fourth of England, and the vengeance that the earl of March took upon the Scots ; likewise of the destruction and captivity of the Scots.*

IN the year thirteen hundred and ninety-eight did the third Robert create his eldest born, David Stewart, the earl of Carrick, to be duke of Rothesay, and Robert, his own brother, regent of the kingdom, he created duke of Albany. Before that time they had earls, and not dukes ; in the same year David Lindesay was made earl of Crawford. In the year thirteen hundred and ninety-nine the duke of Rothesay plighted his troth [1], or gave his arles of marriage to Elizabeth, daughter of the earl of March ; and for this cause did the earl her father pay to the king, by way of dower, a large sum of money.   But Archibald earl Douglas promised a yet larger sum, and gave his daughter Marjory in marriage to the said duke ; whereat the earl of March was very wroth, and demanded of the king one of two things : either restitution of the dower, or fulfilment of the contract.   And when the answer of the king no way contented him, he declared to the king with threatening words, for he was a man of influence, that he would have his

Creation of dukes.

Marriage of Rothesay.

Rising of the earl of March.

---

editor of MAJOR's History in 1740 been acquainted with a little of the early history of the Camerons, and allowed the name *Kauel* to stand as MAJOR had put it.' I have to thank Mr. George Neilson for lending me his copy of Mr. Shaw's tract. I would also refer the reader to Mr. Neilson's *Trial by Combat*, chh. 71, 80.

 [1] affidavit seu subarravit.

revenge, and that the kingdom should pay hotly for the insult
done. He therefore made over the custody of the castle of
Dunbar to Robert Maitland [1], his sister's son, and departed out
of Scotland ; and thereafter, under a safe-conduct, he went
into England. But Maitland, by order of the king, made over
the castle of Dunbar to Archibald Douglas, son of earl Archibald. When the earl of March learned what was done he was
stirred to anger, and summoned to him out of Scotland his
sons and his friends, and stirred up the Scottish marches mar-
vellously, for these borderers were his vassals, and men too of
a fiery temper. Along with Henry Percy he came to Peebles [2]
and Lintown ; he laid siege to the castle of Hales ; they had
in mind to stay overnight at Traprain and Merkil [3] ; they had
begun to prepare for supper. But Archibald Douglas came
down upon them with an army ; and when Percy and the earl
of March had knowledge of this they fled the fastest they
could, and left much provision behind them ; and Archibald
Douglas pursued them as far as Berwick.

The writer
condemns the
action of the
king.

Now throughout his conduct of this matter the king showed
a grave want of forethought; for he ought not to have flouted
the daughter of a noble, and trifled with her in the matter of
marriage, and in the end have arranged for marriage with
another. The money at least he ought to have restored, and
made endeavour to propitiate with gentle speech a man like
the earl of March, of proved valour in the field. A thousand
times it has been shown, and in especial among northern
peoples and others of strenuous character, that they have
been ready to risk their wide domains, their lives, and all
they had, if so they might avenge an insult done to them.
In this matter, too, earl Archibald Douglas was no way without
blame ; but he dreaded a rival, and feared that through this
marriage his rival might become a greater than himself. And
he wished by any means, and lawfully or unlawfully, to maintain his position. Nor do I hold the earl of March without
sin ; nay rather, he acted most wickedly, in bringing a foreign
force against his country to avenge a private insult.

In the year fourteen hundred died Archibald Douglas, called

---

[1] Orig. ' Machlando '.   [2] Orig. ' Poxis ' ; F. ' Popil '.   [3] ? Mersehill.

the Grim or Terrible, the first earl of his name. He was a high-tempered man, and performed many notable feats in war. He it was who brought Galloway into subjection to the king, and for this achievement the king granted that territory to him in perpetuity, but unwisely as I think; for to confer immense domains on men of high position does vast harm to the commonwealth. This Archibald enlarged his borders greatly. He was a man faithful to his promise, and he held churchmen in all honour. He laid no burdens upon religious houses or churches [1]. The nuns of Lincluden he drove out, and founded there a college of clerics. It may be presumed that these nuns had not observed their vow of chastity, otherwise he would not have driven them out. For this act I praise him. He also founded the college of Bothwell, and sufficiently endowed the same.

Death of Archibald the Terrible.

In this same year king Henry entered Scotland. But this year, or at the least our record of the year, does not square with the statements of the English chroniclers. For our historians call this Henry son to the duke of Lancaster; he would in that case be the fifth Henry, and by consequence must have lived after these years. Henry the Fourth, on the other hand, duke of Lancaster, began to reign, according to the English historians, in fourteen hundred and seven, after Richard had been deposed. But there is ever a difficulty in the ascertainment of a date among authors who differ, and when the date has perchance been given at the first in rough and ready fashion. It was in any case about this time that Henry, as I think the Fourth, entered Scotland, and made his way as far as Edinburgh, to whose castle he laid siege. It was defended by the duke of Rothesay and Archibald earl of Douglas, the second of that name. The duke of Albany meanwhile, regent of Scotland, marched with a large army to Caldermuir ; but, by reason of certain jealousies betwixt him and the duke of Rothesay, he did not play the part of an honest and upright man, but suffered the English to depart in peace to their own country without striking a blow.

Henry, the English king, invades Scotland.

Henry the Fourth.

David duke of Rothesay then cast aside all prudent counsels,

---

[1] nec coenobia nec ecclesias alias oneravit.

Waywardness
of David of
Rothesay.

and began to follow his own wayward will, and do what seemed
good to himself; for which cause the third Robert sent his
brother to the duke of Albany, with instructions to make a
prisoner of the duke of Rothesay for a time, until he should
return to a saner mind ; and with the help of Archibald Douglas
the duke of Albany did this.   The story goes that John
Remorgenay[1] was at the bottom of this matter ; for that he had
first of all counselled the duke of Rothesay, whenever he found
an opportunity so to do, to seize the regent of the kingdom,
his father's brother, and put him to death—on the ground
that his place and reputation in the realm were higher than
his own.   Full of peril, in truth, are those counsels sometimes
which are given in the hope that thereby the adviser may be
raised to high place, and become the familiar friend of a prince.
But the Duke of Rothesay refused this offer, and said that he
had no mind to harm his uncle.   And when that same John
had gained his object[2], he urged the regent to make away
with the future king, who, he said, would otherwise compass
the death of the regent.   And the story goes that William
Lindesay was in the plot along with John Remorgenay, because
duke Rothesay plighted his troth of marriage to his sister, just
as he had done to that daughter of the earl of March whom he

Death of duke
Rothesay.

abandoned.   Not to enlarge further, I will say simply that
duke Rothesay was imprisoned in the castle of Falkland, and
there he died.   Whence may be seen how dangerous it was for
him to play false with the daughters or sisters of noblemen.

Revenge of the
earl of March
upon the Scots.

About the same time the earl of March and the English
together wrought vast injury upon the Scots ; for the eastern
border Scots, who in all that pertains to war are behind none
of their countrymen, loved their ancient lord now that he was
exiled from his native land, as indeed is the common way ; and
thus the other Scots suffered much at the hands of their
brethren.   Wherefore lord Archibald, captain of the castle of
Dunbar, sent summons to the lords of Lothian, calling upon
them to take each of them his turn in the invasion of England,
so that each in turn should have precedence of the rest ; and
all the rest, though they might have held higher rank than

---

[1] Sir John Ramorny of *The Fair Maid of Perth*.
[2] 'optatum assequutus est'.   Probably we ought to read 'optatum non
assequutus est,' since Ramorny had not gained his object.

himself, for that time obeyed him.   And first of all them that entered England was John Hamilton of Dirlton ; to him succeeded Patrick Hepburn younger of Hales to take command, for his father was now a man of eighty years.   Now this Patrick, when his turn came to make invasion, tarried in England one day beyond his appointed time ; for which cause did the earl of March and the earl of Northumberland pursue him, and on Nisbet moor they attacked him, and slew him.   Other stout Scots were likewise taken, and among them John and Thomas Haliburton, Robert Lauder of the Bass, John and William Cockburn, with many another valiant Scot, so that there perished at that time the flower of Lothian[1]. Patrick Hepburn. Capture of the Scots in England. Cockburn.

When Archibald earl of Douglas, who, like his forebears, was a man of high courage, though himself unskilled in war, came to hear of this, he went to the guardian of Scotland and sought from him assistance in attacking the earl of March and the English ; and the guardian sent with him Murdach, his first-born son.   These two noble men then invaded England ; and to meet them came Henry Percy, who had been a prisoner in Scotland, and George Scot, earl of March, and they met in a great battle at Milfield. Douglas took up his position on a hill which was called Homildon, where Percy desired to attack him ; but following the counsel of the earl of March, than whom no one was more skilled in warfare, they chose rather another and most destructive method of dealing with the Scots.   For they shot their arrows against Douglas, and plied him with missiles of war from their engines, and slew in this fashion very many of his men.   And when Douglas saw how the matter inclined, he came down from the hill and made a fierce assault upon the opposite side. Nevertheless, exhausted by his struggle for victory, he lost there many valiant warriors, of whom these that follow were the chief : John Swynton, Adam Gordon, John Livingston of Callander, Alexander Ramsay of Dalhousie, Walter Saint Clair, Roger Gordon, and Walter Scot.   Prisoners made in that battle there were : Murdach Stewart, eldest born of the regent, Archibald earl of Douglas, who also lost an eye, The rising of Archibald. The Scots are slain by engines of war. The Scots that were slain ; that were taken prisoner.

---

[1] As to the fighting at Nisbet-moor Major is thus mentioned by Edward Hall in his *Chronicle*, published in 1548 (p. 24, ed. 1809) : ' . . . the Scottes valiantly resisted, but after a long fight the victory fell on the Englishe parte, and as Ihou Mayer the Scot writeth, there wer slain the flower of all Loughdean . . .'

Thomas earl of Moray, George earl of Angus, Robert Erskine
of Alva, William Abernethy of Salton, James Douglas, master
of Dalkeith (the heirs or the guardians of noblemen are among
the Scots called 'master'), William Erth, John Stewart of
Lorn, John Seiton, William Saint Clair of Hirdemanston,
George Leslie of Rothes, Patrick Dunbar of Beil, Alexander
Home, Adam Forester of Corstorphine, William Stewart of
Angus, Robert Stewart of Durrisdeir, Walter Bikcartoun of
Lufness, Robert Logan of Restalrig[1], Ramsay of Greenock,
Helias Kenninmont, Lawrence Ramsay of Clat, John Ker of
Samelstoun, Fergus Macdoual of Galloway. And all this
calamity was wrought by the anger against the king of one
nobleman, George Dunbar, earl of March. Hence let kings
take a lesson not to trifle with men of fierce temper,—though
these be less powerful than themselves,—nor yet with their
daughters. Rather than this woman had been scorned,
it were better that the Scots had given her a dower of two
hundred thousand pieces of gold. And now let us turn our
narrative to the English.

CHAP. VIII.—*Of Henry the Fourth of England, who escaped plots
that were laid for him, and tamed rebellious men; and of the death of
Robert the Third of Scotland in sorrow at the captivity of his son.*

Henry the
Fourth escapes
certain plots.

HENRY the Fourth, of whose succession to the crown after
the deposition of Richard we have already spoken, kept the
feast of the Nativity in the first year of his reign at Windsor.
On the eve of the Epiphany[2] some of the nobles made known
to the king their wish to act a play along with him, disguising
their usual dress, as in a friendly way men sometimes do; and
these nobles were the duke of Surrey, the duke of Exeter, the
duke of Salisbury, and the earl of Gloucester. Now these men
designed under shelter of their masks to murder the king. But
when Henry the Fourth was told by the duke of Albemarle
what their intention was, he forthwith left Windsor and went
to London; and when these nobles saw that their treachery
was discovered, they fled to different parts of the kingdom;
but they were seized by the common people and, as was just,
suffered the punishment of their crime.

---

[1] Lestalrikus.   [2] In profesto Regum.

In the third year óf the reign of Henry the Fourth did The rebels
submit them-
selves to the
English king. Henry Percy, heir to the earl of Northumberland, being persuaded to that course by his father's brother, Thomas Percy, earl of Worcester, go forth with a strong army to fight against the king; and a battle took place at Shrewsbury. In this battle Henry Percy came by his end, and Thomas Percy was taken prisoner, and thereafter hanged, and his head was sent to London. Our chroniclers for this period tell that George Dunbar, earl of March, was along with the king of the English. For the Percys claimed that the king should either abdicate his kingdom or fulfil to them those conditions by which he had bound himself when he first assumed the crown. And inasmuch as the Percys had under them a great army, the king followed the cautious counsel of the earl of March, and told them that they should tarry for a little time, until he had considered the matter, whether, with a good conscience, he could lay down his crown. And thus it came to pass that many of Percy's men fell away. Along with Percy was Archibald Douglas, earl of the same, who had been made prisoner at Homildon, and who slew three sham[1] kings, for I may call them such, seeing that they were men who wore royal robes; and there he was sorely wounded[2].

In the eighth year of the reign of this same Henry the earl of Northumberland and the lord Bardolf came from Scotland, and their coming was fraught with danger and risk to the English king; but they were taken by the Northumbrians and put to death. In the fourteenth year of his reign died King Henry Death of
Henry. himself, that is, in the one thousand four hundred and twenty-first year of our Lord, according to the English chroniclers.

After the death of the duke of Rothesay, Robert the Third, Robert the
Third, the Scot
sends his son
into France,
and when the
latter was taken
by the English,
dies of grief. king of Scotland, sent his son James, then a youth of fourteen years, into France for his education, and perchance he also thought that he should thus be able better to secure his safety after the death of his brother; for he was now his only son.

---

[1] 'sophisticos'. Cf. for the incident Hall's *Chronicle*, p. 31 : 'The erle Douglas strake him doune and slewe sir Water Blonte, and three other appareled n the Kynges suite and clothyng saiyng : I maruaill to see so many Kynges so sodainly arise again.'

[2] 'In that flighte therle Douglas, whiche for hast fallyng from the cragge of a mountagnie brake one of his genitals and was taken, and for his valiantnes of t e Kyng frely and frankely deliuered.'—*Ib.*

He took ship at the island of the Bass along with the lord
Saint Clair, and at Flamborough-head he was made prisoner
by the English. Now they had not shown a proper caution
in thus sending the young man. It may be that some evil-
disposed Scots, moved by hope of reward, declared the matter
to the English—or perchance they were young kinsmen of his
own who were aspiring to the kingdom; or again, the English
may have had spies in Scotland, as their custom was. For the
king might have managed the business with such secrecy that
it should have escaped the knowledge of all men. Robert the
Third, when he heard of the captivity of his only son, died
suddenly of grief in the sixteenth year of his reign. Herein
the king made no proof of a lofty spirit. So far as regarded
the life of the young man, he seemed to be more secure with
the English than with his own people, for he might have been
ransomed or gained his liberty by way of marriage, as indeed
was proved by the event. A good man was this third Robert,
but no way a good king.

CHAP. IX.—*Of the achievements of Henry the Fifth, king of the
English, and of James the First, king of the Scots ; and of the good
faith kept by the Scots with the French ; of the various fortune in war
of both, and of the death of Henry the Fifth and his eulogy.*

Henry the Fifth
destroys
heretics.

To Henry the Fourth, king of England, succeeded Henry the
Fifth, who gained in war a great renown. In the first year of
his reign some heretics, whom they call Lollards, who spoke
wicked things of the church and the clergy, were burned ;
among them was burned one Roger Acton, a knight. In the
second year of his reign he made public statement to the

As he is making
for Normandy
a plot is formed
against him.

nobles of his kingdom of his title to Normandy, and besought
their help to make it good. And they promised to stand by
him, and for the purpose of his expedition taxes were raised
from the people ; but before he had taken ship at Southampton
water, some of the nobles of the kingdom laid a plot to slay
him, and they had been bribed to do this by the French with

Names of the
traitors.

a great sum of money. Of the chief conspirators these were
the names : the earl of Cambridge, brother to the duke of
York ; the lord Scrope, treasurer of England ; Thomas Gray,
knight, from the northern part of England. And all these

were condemned to death at Hampton. In the first year The expedition
of his invasion he took Harfleur, and fought the battle of Normandy.
Agincourt in Picardy. Of this battle the histories of the
French are full. But Caxton the Englishman reports one
thing concerning it, which you will not find in the French
chroniclers, and which is indeed hard of belief: to wit, that Victory of the
there fell in that battle of the English only twenty-six, of English.
whom two were the duke of York, captain of the first line of
battle and the vanguard, and the other the earl of Suffolk [1].

In the fifth year of Henry's reign John Oldcastle lord Heretics are
Cobham was burned at London for heresy. burned.

In the fourteen hundred and nineteenth year from the Scottish auxili-
Virgin's travail, the French king sent into Scotland the earl of aries are sent
Vindocinium, commonly called Vendôme, with a petition for into France.
help. At that time the king of the Scots was in the hands of
the English, for as a boy he had been taken prisoner on his
voyage to France, as we have related above. But the duke of
Albany, who was then guardian of Scotland, sent his second-
born son John Stewart earl of Buchan, and Archibald Douglas
earl of Wigton, the eldest-born son of Archibald Douglas earl
of Douglas, along with seven thousand men. In the French
chronicles where they deal with the life of Charles the Sixth,
you shall read how the English king carried James the First, James the First.
when James was a captive in his hands, to the cities and troops
in which Scots were to be found; for he thought in this way
to gain over to his own side the Scots who had come to the
succour of the dauphin; but the Scots, holding their king in
small esteem, followed the dauphin. This you shall find in
the history of Robert Gaguin [2].

In this matter I approve the conduct of the Scots; for The Scots in
they knew that the stability and permanence of the Scottish France keep their
kingdom did not depend upon their king, and that though allies.
the English king might make a prisoner of their king, he

---

[1] Caxton places the French loss at more than 11,000 : ' God and our archers
made them ryght soone to stomble, for our archers shotte neuer arowe amysse,
but it peryshed & brought to ye grounde bothe hors & man, for they shotte y^t
daye for a wager. And our stakes made them toppe ouer terue eche one ouer
ouer, y^t they laye on hepes two speres length of heyght.'

[2] ' Scotorum regem quem captivum habebat secum ducens, ratus Scotos qui
auxiliares dalphino venerant captivi regis miseraturos et cum eo in Scotiam
reversuros.'—Gaguin's *Compendium*, etc. fol. ccvi. ed. 1511.

could not for all that make a prisoner of the kingdom
of Scotland; and they had the mandate from the nobles of
Scotland to help to the uttermost the dauphin, and to pay no
respect to the dauphin's father who was upon the side of the
English; because, if the dauphin had been conquered by the
English, then would the kingdom of the French have been
utterly overthrown; and to give their lives in its defence they
held an honourable thing, bearing in mind the ancient amity
of the kingdoms. On a few Frenchmen and in his faithful
Scottish allies lay all the strength of the dauphin and all his
sinews of war. John Stewart earl of Buchan, son of the
guardian of Scotland, was chosen to be constable to the
dauphin, and this will be found quoted as a well-known fact in

The duke of
Clarence bears
rule over
almost all
France.

the French chronicles[1]. When Henry the Fifth had subdued a
large part of France he went into England, leaving his brother,
the duke of Clarence, a brave and strong soldier, as governor
in France. A battle was fought between him and the earl of
Buchan, the constable, who had with him Archibald Douglas
earl of Wigton, and both French and Scots. In this battle the

The duke of
Clarence is
slain.

duke of Clarence was slain. Gaguin tells how he had gone in
advance of his line of battle, wearing above his helmet a
wreath of gold adorned with precious stones[2], and for this
reason he was the rather recognised by the enemy. I condemn
his thoughtlessness; for thoughtless he was to wear such an
ornament as this to the end he should be known by the
enemy. The chronicles tell that John Swinton knight wounded
this duke of Clarence sorely in the face, and that the earl of
Buchan slew him after he had been laid low by a club[3].

Who of the
English were
missing or
taken.

On the English side there fell, besides the duke of Clarence,
the earl of Ryddisdale, the lord Ros, the lord Gray. There
were made prisoners the earl of Somerset, the earl of Huntingdon, and many other gentlemen. A short time thereafter the
earl of Buchan fought with the English and the men of
Burgundy at Crevant; and in this second battle, since he had
lost those that formerly aided him, he was taken prisoner by

---

[1] 'comitem bouscaudum scotum conestabilem creat.'—*Gaguin, u.s.*, fol. ccvii.

[2] 'super galeam sertum gemmis honestatum portantem'. These are also
Gaguin's very words.—*Ib.* fol. ccvii.

[3] See *The Swintons of that Ilk and their Cadets*, Edinburgh 1883, pp. 22, 23;
and Hume's *History of the House of Douglas*, there quoted, p. 125.

the enemy.   There fell at that time three thousand Scots Slaughter of fighting in the front of the battle.   This is all told by the Scots. Monstrelet the French historian[1].   About this time, as is told by Gaguin, the earl of Glasgow, a man of Douglas,—or, as he should have said, the Douglas,—went to the help of the French, with a following of five thousand Scots, at Rochelle[2], and from them had cordial welcome.   The dauphin bestowed upon him the dukedom of Tours, and he fell at Verneuil along with James his son and heir.   And in the same battle the earl Douglas and of Buchan, constable to the dauphin, lost his life.   The burden the earl of
Buchan are of the battle fell to the share of the Scots, for therein the slain. largest part of them lost their lives.   This you gather from Monstrelet the Frenchman, but Gaguiu attributes the loss of the battle in part to the men of Lombardy[3].   Another cause for this defeat is current amongst the Scots, for they say that two Scots fell to quarrelling as to which should bear the chief command, either striving to have pre-eminence over the other. Stewart was constable of France and son to the guardian of Scotland, and he was near of kin to the king, and bore the same surname ; on the other hand, lord Douglas was amongst the Scots regarded as equal in influence with his own father ; and the nobles of Britain do not lay such stress on royal blood as do the French.   Yet, beyond a doubt, it behoved the Douglas to yield the first place to the constable.   But, however this may have been, there fell in that battle the earl of Buchan, after he had performed many mighty deeds in behalf of the French, and along with him Stewart son of the Who of the earl of Lennox, a valiant warrior,—he was grandsire of that Scottish
nobility there lord Aubigny who is lately dead[4]—and Lindesay, and Swinton lost their lives. that was ever ready for the fight, and many other gentlemen of Scotland ; these came, all of them, in that battle by their end.   For they chose rather a glorious death than to be taken prisoners by the English.

---

[1] *Chronicles* : ed. Johnes's trans., 1845, vol. i. p. 500.

[2] ' Venit eodem tempore rupellam comes glascuensis scotus quinque armatorum milia ducens ut Carolo regi auxilians esset.'—*Gaguin, u.s.*, ccix.   Gaguin therefore does not say that the earl of Glasgow's 5000 men were Scots.

[3] ' Lombardi · · · prædæ avidi ad diripienda castra magis quam ad feriendum bostem operam navaverunt.'—*Ib.*

[4] ' Bernard lord d'Aubigny, famous in the Neapolitan war under Charles VIII. and Lewis XII. of France.'—Crawfurd, *u.s.*, p. 259.

Death of Henry and his praise.

Henry the.Fifth died, in the thirty-sixth year of his reign [1], at the wood of Vincennes, which is distant about one league from Paris. As a warrior he gained the highest renown, and must be ranked second to no one of the Edwards or Henrys (of whom some had gained much glory in the field). He was buried at London.

Henry the Sixth.

To the fifth Henry succeeded Henry the Sixth when he was a child of one year; and for the present I say naught of him, for I am about to deal with what had come to pass meanwhile in Britain.

CHAP. X.—*Of the restoration to his earldom of George earl of March; of the destruction of the castle of Jedburgh; and of the dispute that arose as to the legality of the imposition of new taxes. Of the battle at Harlaw, and the men who there lost their lives. Of the foundation of the University of Saint Andrew; of the death of Robert duke of Albany, and an estimate of his achievements.*

Restoration of George earl of March.

In the year of our Lord fourteen hundred and five George earl of March was restored to his earldom and to the charge of the castle of Dunbar: in such wise however that the earl Douglas still held the castle of Lochmaben with the whole domain of Annandale. In the same year was the castle of Jedburgh taken by the common people of Teviotdale. But inasmuch as this stronghold could not, save at great cost, be razed to the ground, it was determined by a general council of the Scots at Perth that a contribution of two pence should be made by every house for the destruction of the castle from top to bottom. Now its governor opposed himself to this determination, asserting that in all time of his governance no tax had ever been levied, nor should now be levied, lest the poor folk shall say evil things of himself as the man who had been the first to bring in such an abuse; and he provided the cost of the destruction of the castle out of the royal revenues.

The castle of Jedburgh is razed to the ground.

The governor shows respect to the poor.

Whether new taxes may be legally imposed,

The question of taxation in general seems here to offer itself for discussion, and we will conduct the argument for both sides. In the first place, as against the procedure of the

---

[1] Major no doubt meant to write (with Caxton) 'in the thirty-sixth year of his age.' Henry V. died in the tenth year of his reign.

governor, I state the argument thus: The commonweal had rightful precedence of him,—nay, it had rightful precedency of the king himself,—if we may suppose that the three estates had been duly summoned. Therefore he acted wrongly when he put aside their ordinance and preferred to it his own wish. You will say perchance,—True enough, if what be really to the advantage of the realm were made clear before any conclusion was taken in the matter of taxation. Thereto I argue thus: First argument: under what conditions, and in the second place, an evasion. The commonweal it was, as the chroniclers relate, that made this ordinance, and many eyes see more than one eye sees. Therefore this statute concerning taxes among the Scots was a lawful statute. In the third place, this argument may be Third argument. used: The English, who in civil polity are at least not less wise than we are—and to my thinking they are wiser—levy a tax; and the same custom holds in all other kingdoms; and the Scots practice therefore in this matter separates them from all other kingdoms. But the political practice of many kingdoms is likely to be safer than the political practice of one: *Igitur.* Fourthly, I argue thus: It is better, in time Fourth argument. of war and any urgent necessity, that the rich man and he who from any cause can perform no military service should contribute money, than that he and all the rest should go forth to war and leave the land untilled. And though two pennies, Fifth argument. which amount to one small white[1], neither more nor less, had been raised from every single hearth, that would have ruined nobody; but for him who can collect no more from the country at large to take the whole from the royal treasury is for the latter fraught with danger, when we consider that he does not draw from the people the greatest part of his income.

For the other side the argument runs thus: Let a small tax On the other side—First argument. be once admitted, kings would in the end make it a large one; wherefore it is well worth while to withstand beginnings. Kings Second argument. might even make pretext for a war, and feign urgent reasons therefor, which might end in present risk and long-lasting burden to their people. Therefore it is better sometimes to refrain from the imposition of a tax. But to this it might be answered: The answer. Without the consent of the three estates, as happens in

---

[1] qui parvum album præcise valent.

England, he will not be permitted to levy a tax, for in
England the people are more hotly jealous of their rights than
in many other kingdoms, and rise against their kings should
these make any unreasonable demand ; so that in this wise
the kings take fright, and for the most part draw back from
their proposal of a tax.   The increase of a tax need not therefore give cause for fear, and from the point of view of the poor
this consideration is of much weight.   Without intentional
injustice to the other side, there is scarce any one who can
make clear and determinative answer one way or the other ;
but my own private judgment on the whole matter (which I
leave to be discussed by persons of sense) an intelligent man
may gather from what I have just said.

The conclusion.

In the fourteen hundred and tenth year from the incarnation of our Lord, Patrick Dunbar, son and heir of George,
took Fastcastle, that is 'strong castle', and made prisoner of
Thomas Holden, who was at that time within the castle,—an
Englishman, who had wrought much harm in Lothian.   In
the year fourteen hundred and eleven was fought that battle,
far-famed amongst the Scots, of Harlaw.   Donald, earl of the
Isles, with a valiant following of Wild Scots ten thousand
strong, aimed at the spoiling of Aberdeen, a town of mark,
and other places ; and against him Alexander Stewart earl of
Mar and Alexander Ogilvy sheriff of Angus gathered their men,
and at Harlaw met Donald of the Isles.   Hot and fierce was
the fight ; nor was a battle with a foreign foe, and with so
large a force, ever waged that was more full of jeopardy than
this ; so that in our games, when we were at the grammar
school, we were wont to form ourselves into opposite sides, and
say that we wanted to play at the battle of Harlaw.   Though
it be more generally said amongst the common people that the
Wild Scots were defeated, I find the very opposite of this in
the chroniclers ; only, the earl of the Isles was forced to retreat ;
and he counted amongst his men more of slain than did the
civilised Scots.   Yet these men did not put Donald to open rout,
though they fiercely strove, and not without success, to put a
check upon the audaciousness of the man.   They slew his
drill-master[1], Maklane, and other nine hundred of his men, and

Fastcastle is
taken.

The battle of
Harlaw.

Battle betwixt
Donald and the
Scots.

The killed and
wounded.

---

[1] Campiductorem.   See *ante*, p. 235.

yet more were sorely wounded. Of the southerners six hundred
only lost their lives, of whom some were gentlemen, William
Abernethy eldest-born and heir to the lord Saltoun, George
Ogilvy heir to the lord of that name, James Skrymgeour,
Alexander of Irvin, Robert Malvile, Thomas Muref, knights;
James Luval, Alexander Stirling, with other gentlemen of
lesser fame.   But inasmuch as very few escaped without a
wound, and the fight lasted long, it is reckoned as hot and
fierce.

In the same year the university of Saint Andrews had its
beginning.   I marvel much at the negligence of the Scots
prelates, who were content up to that time to go without a
university in the kingdom. Foundation of the university of Saint Andrew.

In the year fourteen hundred and fifteen the earl of Northumberland restored Murdach Stewart, the regent's son, to Scotland, without exacting a ransom.   This was done in return
for the good service of the regent, who during the English
invasion had treated the earl's grandson kindly, and caused
him to be educated as if he had been his own son. Murdach is restored to his father without a ransom.

In the year fourteen hundred and nineteen died Robert,
duke of Albany, earl of Menteith, and guardian of Scotland,
after he had for eighteen years governed the kingdom. A just
man he was, and one who bent all his strength to the task of
ruling wisely.   Yet is he no way worthy to be placed by the
side of Thomas Randolph, guardian of Scotland.   But it is to
be wondered at that he did not labour in behalf of the son of
his brother, the rightful heir of Scotland, so that in his own
day he might have seen the sceptre in the hands of the rightful
king.   For had he worked with vigour and success to compass
this end, I should extol him yet more.   Perhaps you will tell
me : His son, lord Murdach, was a grown man, and, failing his
nephew James, the rightful heir ; and it might have been
better for the kingdom that James should tarry for a time in
England than that his return should involve the payment by
his kingdom of an enormous sum of money.   For all that, I
say that the regent might have aimed to bring about a marriage, so that the dowry might have gone to pay the ransom
that was needed. The death of Robert, duke of Albany, and a comparative estimate of him.

CHAP. XI.—*Of the return of James the First, the Scot, into his kingdom by way of the marriage that he contracted ; the author's opinion concerning the ransoming of kings ; and of the sins of kings against the state.*

The return of James the First to Scotland through his marriage.

In the year fourteen hundred and twenty-four James the First took to wife Joanna, grand-daughter of the earl of Somerset, and duke of Lancaster ; but he had not wherewith to meet the costs and his ransom, wherefore he left as a hostage for the remnant of his debt certain of those who were heirs amongst his nobility.

Thus, however, does Caxton tell the story of his marriage :— In the year fourteen hundred and twenty-two did the lord James Stewart, king of the Scots, take to wife the lady Joanna, daughter of the duchess of Clarence ; and it was to her former husband that the duchess of Clarence bore this lady Joanna, who became wife to James the First. But he had not wherewithal to meet his costs and the payment of his ransom ; and for the remnant of his debt he left behind him in hostage certain of the heirs amongst his nobles. When he was returned into Scotland, James the First was made king. In the same year did the king cause Walter, Malcolm of Cumbernauld, and Thomas Boyd of Kilmarnock, to be arrested.

Convention of the nobility in the matter of the king's ransom, and their decree as to the raising of the sum demanded.

And a little while after, in the same year, he summoned a parliament, wherein he proposed many things for the advantage of the state, and asked for a subsidy wherewith he might meet the cost of his ransom. And it was determined that he should be allowed to raise a tax for the two years immediately following : and its extent was this—a twentieth part of all moveables, spiritual as well as temporal ; and he appointed as collectors of that tax the bishop of Dunblane and the abbot of Saint Columba. Now I find that these men collected this money from the poor people only, and scarce one hundredth part instead of the twentieth part. And yet the common people murmured because of the collection.

The author's opinion in the matter of raising money for the king's ransom.

Here, however, I mean to express my own particular opinion, which I will leave for the consideration and judgment of sensible men. This tax ought to have been imposed upon the noblemen and gentry of the kingdom, and upon ecclesi-

astics, and also upon the common people, but on this wise :
from the nobles should have been asked as a favour a sixth
part, or a fifth part, of their annual revenues; from each
ecclesiastic a contribution should have been levied in proportion to the ability of each ; while every peasant who had eight
oxen to his plough should have paid two shillings. And I
know, beyond a doubt, that in this fashion the king would
have raised a sufficient, nay rather a superabundant, sum,
without the infliction of great hardship upon any single man ;
and that, I take it, would have been better for the nobility
than to leave their heirs as hostages for the payment of the
ransom. Of ecclesiastics what am I to say ? Their conscience
pricks them not when they bestow with prodigality church
property upon their own kinsfolk and connections ; but if in
the hour of need of their own king, when he is in captivity,
they are called upon to help him out of the funds of the
church, of that they make forthwith a matter of conscience[1].
Thus they strain out a gnat[2] and swallow a camel. For the
funds of the church, outside the supply of the necessities of
churchmen, ought to be devoted to the relief of the poor, and
to the ransom of those captives who may not otherwise be
easily ransomed, as was the case in this of the king ; and
ecclesiastics ought to do this gladly, inasmuch as taxation
shall thus be made to fall less heavily upon the poorest folk.

In this matter I praise our neighbours the English, who, when He praises
Richard, son to the second Henry, was unlawfully kept prisoner the English.
by the emperor, sold every other vessel, were it of gold or of
silver, and used its value in securing the liberation of their
king[3]. Hardly would our people have granted to their king
what the English granted to the third Edward that he might
regain his territory—for they granted him a fifth part of all
moveables, their whole wool, and the ninth stalk in every sheaf
of corn throughout the kingdom. I bring forward this instance,

---

[1] In the next century, and under the influence of Cardinal Beaton, in 1543,
'the clergy were called upon to tax themselves for war with England', and
'were ready in such a quarrel to sell their chalices, and, if need be, go themselves into battle'—a course of conduct that must have been abhorrent to Major,
who was still living at that time.—See Mr. Law's edition of Hamilton's
Catechism, p. xix.

[2] excolantes culicem.   [3] Cf. p. 154.

not as if it were right, or one which should be followed—for,
indeed, such a course of action is deserving rather of censure—
but because it shows the temper of these people toward their
king.

The author's
opinion regard-
ing the levying
of taxes.
As to the levying of taxes, I will limit my opinion to this
expression: that in no wise should the power be granted
to kings save in cases of clear necessity ; and that necessity
should further be one which has arisen without fault of the
king himself. And such, indeed, was the case with this James,
who was sent outwith the kingdom by his friends for his own
safety, and was made prisoner when he was no more than
fourteen years old. Further, it belongs not to the king, nor
to his privy council, to declare the emergence of any sudden
necessity, but only to the three estates. And thus no way
will be opened for the imposition of unprofitable taxes, while
no obstruction will be offered to the imposition of those
which are clearly necessary. I am aware that Aristotle, in
his second book of the *Politics*, says wisely that laws are not
to be changed ; yet in the judgment of the wise they may be
modified in accordance with the demands of equity[1]. Behold,
then, how it is in the power of a people to deal honestly or,
contrariwise, dishonestly by its king.

How the kings
of the Scots sin
against the
state.
On the other hand, the kings of the Scots sin against the
state when they punish with the utmost rigour any of the
nobility who may revolt against the government, to the end
that the rest may be restrained through fear of the like punishment ; and the lands of these men they confiscate to the
public treasury. Now, if the kings would keep the income of
their lands for themselves, they would have immense revenues ;
but most unwisely they bestow them upon courtiers and others
of the nobility who make petition for them. Thus acting—
when we consider that there is no regular taxation of the

---

[1] '*ἐπιείκειαν* pati debent'. In the original Paris edition it is printed in Roman
type—and thus : ' epikiian '; for the French did not confine their arbitrary dealing
with foreign words to those which Major calls 'British'. Cf. *ante*, p. 320. Major
puts Aristotle's view rather too strongly. The pas-age referred to is in ch. viii.
Bk. II. of the *Politics*: ' The habit of lightly changing the laws is an evil, and,
when the advantage is small, some errors both of lawgivers and rulers had better
be left.'—Jowett's translation, vol. i. p. 50.

people—they gravely sin against the state.　Further, they bestow upon members of their household pensions in money, but reason rather demands that they should give rich heiresses in marriage to their noble followers.　And if that should chance which does not often happen, namely, that they beget many children, they ought to cause their younger sons to be educated in letters and all rightness of conduct, and promote them to ecclesiastical benefices ; not that they ought to enjoy a plurality of such benefices, but because there are several in the country, whereof one alone would be a sufficient maintenance for the younger son of the king.

CHAP. XII.—*Of the marriage of Lewis the Eleventh, king of the French, and Margaret of Scotland.　Of the crime committed by James Stewart, and his banishment, and how he, with his fellow-conspirators, was punished.　Of trial by jury or assise of the nobles[1] of Scotland.　Of the rebellion of Alexander of the Isles and his petition for mercy.*

In the year fourteen hundred and thirty-six did James give his daughter Margaret, a fair maiden, and of proper nurture, in marriage to Lewis the Eleventh ; and that he might give with her a dowry he imposed a tax upon his people like to that other tax ; whereat the people murmured not a little.　And when the king came to hear of their murmuring he ceased from the tax, and caused the money that had been already collected to be restored to the common people.　In consistency with the opinion that I have already expressed, I affirm that the nobility, the ecclesiastics, and the whole people ought to have made a proportional contribution ; and notably the religious, who from land held in perpetuity, which was the grant of this king's predecessors, drew an annual revenue of three hundred thousand francs ; for all these lands held of the crown.　It was for this that king James said, as the story goes, of king David, that he was a saintly man indeed, but most unprofitable to the kingdom of Scotland [2]—the reason being that he had endowed out of the royal lands so many religious houses, as we have already told in the life of David.　There is no more likely way to extend the

Scottish Margaret marries Lewis the Eleventh the Frenchman.

---

[1] De assissio seu assessu procerum.　　[2] Cf. *ante*, p. 135.

renown of a kingdom and the increase of amity than an honourable marriage. This marriage was, in spite of these difficulties, accomplished; for the Scots had been in high favour with Charles the Seventh when he was dauphin, and of their number twenty thousand had lost their lives in France in defence of his right to the throne; wherefore, I take it, Charles was content to receive from them a moderate dowry for his son, holding that friendship between kings and their kingdoms was a far more precious thing than gold.

In this year did James hold, at Perth, his second parliament, wherein he caused arrest to be made of Murdach, duke of Albany, and the lord Alexander Stewart, his second son, <on whom, on the day of his coronation, he had placed the soldier's knightly belt; and likewise those whose names here follow, that you may understand the families of the men of old>[1]: Archibald, third of this name, earl of Douglas; William Douglas, earl of Angus; George Dunbar, earl of March; Adam Hepburn of Hailes; Thomas Hay of Yester; Walter Ogilvy; Walter Haliburton; David Stewart of Rossyth; Alexander Seton of Gordon; Patrick Ogilvy of

---

[1] 'quem in die coronationis suae equitem auratum militari balteo praecinxit; et hos etiam sequentes, ut veterum familias intelligas'. In a communication to the *Scotsman*, dated 12th July 1883, Sir J. H. Ramsay has pointed out that the statement of Scottish historians that James the First arrested twenty-six of the leading nobles of Scotland had its origin in mistaking 'an awkward parenthesis in the *Scotichronicon* for part of the text. The passage may be given in English as follows: "And on the ninth day he (King James) let arrest the Lord Murdach, Duke of Albany, and his younger son the Lord Alexander Stewart, whom, on his coronation day, he had knighted, with six-and-twenty others, namely, Archibald, Earl of Douglas," etc. In Goodall's text it will be seen that the parenthesis is made to include only the words corresponding to "whom, on his coronation day, he had knighted" (vol. ii. p. 482). That the parenthesis ought to include all the twenty-six appears from the text itself, which, after the close of the list, resumes thus [as also in Major]: "And on the same day he arrested the Lord Montgomery," etc. If the preceding list was that of the persons arrested, why should the writer begin again like that?'

I think it is just possible that Major was not misled in the same way as other historians, and that by his 'hos etiam' he means the knights and not the arrests to be enumerated, and I may refer as giving some colour to this view to ch. xiv., where Major speaks of James's affection for many of his nobles. But I confess that without the correction, to which my attention was called by an editorial note in the late Dr. John M. Ross's *Early Scottish History and Literature*, 1884, p. 137, I should have had no doubt that he included the names following (in his case twenty-two, not twenty-six) among the arrests.

Auchterhouse ; John Red-Stewart of Dundonald ; David Murray of Gask ; John Stewart of Carden ; William Hay of Errol ; John Skrimgeour, constable of Dundee ; Alexander Irvine of Drum ; Herbert Maxwell of Carlaverock ; Herbert Herries of Terregles ; Andrew Gray of Fowlis ; Robert Cunynghame of Kilmaurs ; Alexander Ramsay of Dalhousie ; William Crichton, lord of the same. On the same day the king made arrest of John of Montgomery of the same, that is, lord of the same ; and of Alan Otterburn, secretary of the duke ; and he sent incontinent and took the castle of Falkland, and Doune in Menteith, from which he caused to be removed duchess Isabella, daughter of the earl of Lennox ; and all these he intrusted to the charge of the keeper of the castle of St. Andrews ; but a short time thereafter John and Alan received their freedom. The duke was transferred to the castle of Carlaverock, and the duchess to Tantallon. And in the following year, on the festival of the Holy Rood, James Stewart, who alone of the duke's sons had escaped arrest at the hands of the king, set fire to Dunbarton, where he put to death *The crime of* the lord John Red-Stewart of Dundonald, otherwise of Burley, *James Stewart.* the king's uncle[1], and his own grandfather, and the lord Robert, uncle of the duke of Albany—with three and thirty other men. At all which the king was moved to righteous indignation, and banished the foresaid James from the kingdom. This James fled into Ireland along with Finlay bishop of Argyll, of the order of Preachers, who was his accomplice in crime, and neither one nor other returned ever to Scotland.

On the fifth day after the festival of the finding of the Holy *Punishment of* Rood, five of those who had been fellow-conspirators of the *his companions* foresaid James were brought before the king, and they were *in crime.* dragged at the tails of horses, and thereafter hanged on gibbets. In the same year, and on the eighteenth day of the month of May, the king held a parliament at Stirling, whereat Walter Stewart, heir of Albany, was convicted of treason and beheaded before the castle ; the like fate befel his brother

---

[1] F. 'regis patrui' ; Orig. rightly 'regis patruum' ; but the sentence remains confused : ' ubi dominum Joannem Red-Steuartum de Dundonald, alias de Burlei, Regis patrui, et avi sui dominum Roberti [? Robertum] ducis Albaniæ patruum . . . interfecit.'

Alexander, his father too, and his grandfather, the earl of Lennox—but this was on the following day. Those who sat in judgment upon these men were Walter Stewart of Athole, father's brother to the king; Archibald earl of Douglas, the third of the name, Alexander of the Isles, de Ross, Alexander Stewart of Mar, William Douglas of Angus, William Saint Clair of Orkney, George of Dunbar, earls, seven in all; likewise James Stewart of Bawane, Robert Stewart of Lorn, John de Montgomery of the same, Gilbert Hay of Errol, constable of Scotland, Thomas Somerwale of the same, Herbert Herries of Terregles, James Douglas of Dalkeith, Robert Cunynghame of Kilmaurs, Alexander Livingston of Callander, Thomas Hay Lochurquhart, William Borthwick of the same, Patrick Ogilvy, sheriff of Angus, John Forester of Corstorphine, Walter Ogilvy of Luntrethyn, knights. Now it is not likely that a great company of gentlemen such as these would condemn to death noblemen who were of the blood-royal, had these not been guilty of conspiring against the king. For a merciful disposition will not always incline a merciful man to remit the punishment due to crime; far rather will it compel him to punish the powerful where reason points that way, forasmuch as it is the part of sensible men to give well-weighed consideration to all the circumstances, and so to determine when punishment ought to be inflicted and when it may be mitigated. For when it is probable that indulgence shown to criminals will bring worse things upon the state, a grave peril to the state must ever be involved in allowing the criminal to escape unpunished.

So much concerning trial by jury: about which, since I have been led to say something in regard to it, you will observe that neither in the laws[1] nor in France shall you find aught of this trial by jury. This alone is what is called trial by jury: Where a question arises as to the guilt of a man who is accused of another's death, twelve of his neighbours, or it may be more, are summoned; and these men, making careful consideration of every doubtful point, either set the accused at liberty or

---

[1] 'in legibus'—which may be illustrated by the common use 'utriusque juris' —*i.e.* in civil and in canon law.

declare that he shall forthwith be put to death. The whole number of these men is called the jury. The accused is allowed to challenge any one of their number, on the ground of kinship by blood, or marriage, or by some other tie to him who has been slain, and in that case the judge will remove such an one from the jury. But it is only after a careful balance of every particular that these men will give their verdict; they will leave no suspicious point, no evidence, in a word nothing, unweighed, and in accordance with what they have heard they form their opinion. It is no small advantage, however, to the accused when his neighbours are able to bear favourable testimony to his character[1]. So much then it may suffice to say about the law of trial by jury among the Britons.

A power of excepting allowed to the accused.

In the year of the Lord one thousand four hundred and twenty-five the king passed an ordinance for the practice of archery under certain penalties[2].

The practice of shooting with arrows.

In the year one thousand four hundred and twenty-six he caused the castle of Inverness to be restored, and in the following year he held a parliament, in the course of which he invited Alexander of the Isles, earl of Ross, and the countess his mother, daughter and heiress of the once powerful earl Walter Lesly earl of Ross, and many others, men of mark,—all these he invited one by one to the tower, and there caused them to be kept in close custody. While he was showing in the presence of his friends the pleasure that he felt in this occurrence, he bent his face somewhat toward the ground, and then repeated before them these two verses which himself had made, and here they are ;—

---

[1] This refers to the earlier method of trial, when 'the accusers did not call witnesses cognisant of the facts', but when the accused 'was bound to find *compurgatores* to swear for him and with him that they believed him guiltless'; when, as we may say, witness was borne to *character* and not to *fact*.—Cf. Mr. Innes's *Lectures on Scotch Legal Antiquities*, p. 210.

[2] The Act in question ran thus :—
    ' That ilk man busk thame to be archaris.
'ITEM That al men busk thame to be archaris frá thai be xii yeiris of age, & that ilk x pundis worth of land thair be máid bow markis, and speciallie neir paroche Kirkis, quhairn (*wherein*) upone halie dayis men may cum and at the leist schute thryse about and have usage of archarie, and quhasá usis not the said archarie the Laird of the land sall rais of him a wedder, and gif the Laird rasis not the said pane the Kingis Schiref or his ministers sall rais it to the King.'

Ad turrim fortem ducamus caute cohortem ;
Per Christi sortem meruerunt hi quia mortem[1].

Rhymed verse was at that time the custom, amongst the French as amongst the Britons, and the king had had intercourse with both. He treated the last syllable of the adverb *cautè* as short, whereas it is long ; but some allowance may well be made for kings when they take to extempore verse-making.

Evil deeds and punishment of the Wild Scots.

There were also imprisoned in that fortress Angus Duff with his four sons—he was the chief of four thousand men in Strathnaver, Kenneth More with his son-in-law, John Ross, who was chief of two thousand, William Lesly, Angus of Moray, and Makmanke[2]—all these were Wild Scots. And many other Scots whose tempers were alike savage followed them, ever prone to do evil rather than good, and with no notion of a peaceful life. Many of these he put to death, and others he disposed in different castles, to be kept some here some there. I have nothing but praise for this spirited conduct of the king, and the desire that he showed to deal justice upon all. Those men, all low-born as they were, held in utter subjection some seventy or eighty thousand others ; and in their own particular tracts they were regarded as princes, and had all at their own arbitrary will, evincing not the smallest regard for the dictates of reason.

Revolt of Alexander earl of the Isles.

In the year one thousand four hundred and twenty-nine the lord of the Isles, at the instigation of the Wild Scots, and in contempt of the king's command, burned the town of Inverness, for all that the king had before then given him warning that he should not lend an ear to the designs of those wicked men. The king therefore collected an army, and in Lochaber routed Alexander of the Isles, who had with him of them of Ross and the Isles more than ten thousand men, for of all the Wild Scots this lord of the Isles was the chief and leader.

Tribes and factions of the Wild Scots and their extirpation.

Two of the wild tribes, clan Chattan, to wit, and clan Cameron[3], deserted Alexander of the Isles and attached themselves like honest men to the king. On the Palm Sunday following, their

---

[1] Let us carry that gang to a fortress strong,
          For by Christ's own lot they did deadly wrong.

[2] 'Makmaken' in Goodall's *Fordun*, xvi. 15.

[3] On these clan-names see *ante*, p. 334.

riotous conduct reached at last such a pitch that the tribe clan
Chattan put to death every mother's son of clan Cameron.
There is kinship of blood among these tribes; their possessions
are few, but they follow one chief as leader of the whole
family, and bring with them all their relations and dependants.
They lead a life of blissful ease; from the poor people they
take what they want in victual; bows they have, and quivers, The arms of
and they have halberts of great sharpness, for their iron ore is the Wild Scots.
good.   They carry a stout dirk in their belts; they are often
naked from the knee down.   In winter for an over-garment
they wear a plaid[1].

Alexander of the Isles sent various messengers to the king to
treat for peace; but to this the king would not consent, and he
said in anger that within a few days he would humble him yet
further.   But Alexander, when he saw the fixed purpose of the
king, went in secret to Edinburgh, and when he was got within
the king's palace went upon his knees, and so came to the
presence of the king and queen, carrying his sword by the
point, and so gave the hilt into the king's hands, as who
should say that he placed his head in the king's hands.
Whereupon the queen and those of the nobles standing round The supplica-
urgently besought the king that he would spare the life of tion of Alex-
Alexander; and the king sent him to the castle of Tantallon, Isles.
there to be safely guarded until he should determine what
should be further done concerning him.   His mother the
countess of Ross he sent to the island of St. Columba, there to
be kept.   And there she remained one year and two months.

CHAP. XIII.—*Of the twin sons that were born to the king, and of
the fresh institution in their case of the order of knights, after the custom
of Britain.   Of the making of a cannon, and in defence of engines
of war generally*[2]. *Of the rising of the nobles.   Of the conflict
between the Wild Scots.   Of the vain attempt that was made to seduce
the Scots from the French alliance; and of the disheriting of the
duke of March; of the death of Alexander Stewart, and of his heir.*

In the one thousand four hundred and thirty-third year from
the Virgin's travail, and on the sixteenth day of October, were

[1] Chlamys.   [2] de fabrorum defensione.

Twin sons are
born to the
Scottish king—
Alexander and
James.
born to the king twin sons, in the monastery of the Holy Rood
at Edinburgh. Alexander was the name given to the elder-born,
and the younger received the name of James; and on the day
of their second birth, in the font of baptism, their father made
They are
made knights
with the usual
ceremonies.
them likewise knights with those ceremonies which are of human
institution ; and the heirs of certain of his nobles he invested
likewise with knightly cincture. Such is the custom among
Death of
Alexander.
the Britons with the first-born of a king. Alexander died in
youth, and James survived him. In the same year the king
caused to be made in Flanders a huge cannon, which was named
Leo, and on its circumference were engraved in large letters these
words—

> Illustri Jacobo Scotorum principi digno,
> Regi magnifico, dum fulmine castra reduco:
> Factus sum sub eo, nuncupor ergo Leo[1].

And inasmuch as this Caxton contends that the craft and
skill that furnished such engines of war as these were of dia-
bolic origin, and that their first inventors were wicked men, let
me, as against him, use some such argument as this: Swords,
bows, spears, all weapons of this sort, though I grant you
that men may be killed by them, are counted good in so far
as they serve the commonweal either for lawful invasion or
The author
defends the
makers of
engines of war.
for lawful defence. But the case is precisely similar with the
engines now under discussion: *Igitur*. And this reasoning
receives confirmation when we consider that without these
engines many strongholds would be held against justice which
by these means are forced to surrender ; but this surrender is
profitable to the commonweal ; therefore the means is a lawful
means, since from no other source it contracts a stain of wrong.
Nor is it any valid objection to our argument to contend that
with these engines bad men may sometimes cause the death of
good men ; for that may happen just as well with sword and
bow, and all weapons of that sort, though I grant you that the
slaughter may be greater with these engines than with other
weapons. This in fine is our conclusion: that in a just war

---

[1] While with my bolts I throw stout strongholds down
For James, of Scots the king, a monarch of renown,
' Lion ' I'm called—when I was born he wore the crown.

these engines are the best weapons that can be used, and full
of advantage to the commonweal. No one who is acquainted
with the substance and the generation of lightning will doubt
that sulphurous mountains belch forth large stones; the same
effect you shall see when the exhalations which are pent up in
the bowels of the earth cause the earth to quake, and rend her
asunder, and throw aloft large fragments and stones,—whence
it may be said that this invention of man is made in imitation
of nature.

But to take up again the thread of our history: king James
the First in the year fourteen hundred and thirty-one caused
arrest to be made of Archibald earl Douglas, and placed him in
safe custody at Loch Leven; and the lord John Kennedy, the ^{A new imprison-}
king's nephew, he had placed in Stirling, and kept him there ^{ing of noble
men.}
up to the feast of Saint Michael; and in his parliament at
Perth, at the instance of the queen and some of the nobility,
he gave earl Douglas his freedom, but kept his own nephew
still in prison. I marvel that the historians have not told
us the reasons for putting those Stewarts to death, and for
the imprisonment of those others, for then we might be able to
form an opinion whether it were after a full and just consideration of every circumstance that men thus imprisoned were set
free, or whether this treatment of men so outstanding in the
state had its origin rather in some trifling cause, or in the
arbitrary judgment of the king.

It was at this time that Donald Balloch, a Wild Scot, son of ^{Rebellion of}
a man who was on the father's side uncle to the lord of the ^{Donald Balloch.}
Isles, bore down with his islesmen upon the territory of the
Gaels[1] at Lochaber, meaning to harry that country. And
against him went forth Alexander and Alan Stewart, earls of
Mar and Caithness, and with them a goodly number of soldiers.
But Donald slew Alan and many of his followers, and he put
the earl of Mar to the rout; and yet in numbers he was far
inferior to them. When he had done this he turned back and
went into Ireland.

In the same year took place a fierce battle between Angus ^{Conflicts}
Duff and Angus Moray at Strathnaver. These two men had a ^{between the
Anguses.}
short time before made their escape from the king's prisons, and

---

[1] de Galeis.

The savage
disposition of
the caterans. regained their liberty. Either leader had with him twelve
hundred caterans ('caterans' is the name given to the wildest
and most lawless of the Highlanders); and in such fashion did
those wild men fight that on both sides scarce one escaped with
his life; for the conflict was, as it were, by an equal number
of duels, and every man made an end of his antagonist, or
contrariwise.

The Carthu-
sians at Perth. James the First founded at this time a Carthusian house at
Perth, in which the religious of Saint Benedict have to this
day continued, and observe the rule of those fathers.

Mission of
Scrope to make
a treaty with
the Scots. The lord Scrope was sent about this time by the English
king into Scotland, to the end these two neighbour kingdoms
should establish a perpetual peace : that the Scot should agree
to help the Englishman, and conversely; that in every contingency and against every action they should succour each of
them the other; and, as to all parts of territory about which
there was any doubt whether these belonged to the English or
the Scots, the English were at once to give them to the Scots.
The Scots keep
faith with the
French king. Whereupon James summoned the nobles of his kingdom, and it
was with one voice concluded that their most ancient treaties
with the French king should not be broken.

At this same time it was that James sent William earl of
Angus, his chancellor William Crichton, and Adam Hepburn,
knights all of them, to take the castle of Dunbar. He retained in
his own custody George Dunbar, the second of the name, earl
of March, and gave strictest injunction to the keepers of this
castle that they three should hold it in their own hands. And
without consultation with the earl they yielded obedience to
the king, and intrusted the keeping of the castle to the foresaid
Adam Hepburn. In the following year, and on the seventh of
August, at the parliament held at Perth, he disherited the son
Disheriting of
Dunbar. on account of the sins of George his father. We have told in
an earlier part of this book how George Dunbar, in his anger
against the third Robert, father of this king James, had passed
into England, and with English help had wrought many and
no small injuries to the Scots. But that second George made
answer in parliament that he held a pardon for what he had at
that time done; and that is true, for he had been pardoned by
the duke of Albany, who was at the time guardian of the

kingdom; but this parliament counted that pardon as null and void. But the king exercised mercy towards him, and bestowed on George the earldom of Buchan; and after the king's death there was granted to George and his heir, by consent of the three estates, and in expectation of the good-will and ratification of James the Second, whom that earl had received at the sacred font, a yearly payment from the earldom of March of four hundred marks. For it is said that it is allowed by the whole community to the kings of the Scots that nothing done by them in childhood shall be counted for fixed and settled unless those same kings shall have ratified the same when they have reached the age of twenty years. Here then you may behold how an ancient, powerful, and in very truth high-tempered family, that had flourished through a succession of many earls, fell, for its sins, and suddenly, from its possession of the earldom of March! teaching thereby this lesson to all that have the sense to profit thereby, that though men may suffer injury at the hands of their king, they should bear themselves with equanimity, or at least dissemble their impatience, and least of all rise in war against their country. *The king's clemency. What constitutes authoritative action with the Scottish kings.*

In the year one thousand four hundred and thirty-five died Alexander Stewart earl of Mar. In his youth he had been an intrepid leader of the caterans; when he was thirty years of age he had become one of the most renowned and wealthy of men [1]; he bought many estates, and in the northern parts there was no one who could be named beside him. At the battle of Harlaw he had withstood the lord of the Isles; with the duke of Burgundy he had borne himself manfully against the men of †Liége. And notwithstanding that he had the goods of fortune abundantly, yet, since peace reigned *Death of Alexander Stewart and his eulogy. John of Burgundy. † Leodienses.*

---

[1] The Continuator of Fordun, whom Major is probably following, is more explicit : ' Hic fuit vir magni conquæstus, qui in juventute erat multum indomitus, et ductor catervanorum. Sed postea ad se reversus, et in virum alterum mutatus . . .' His most memorable achievement as a leader of the caterans was his seizure in 1404 of Isabel countess of Mar, and his extorting from her, under covenant of future marriage, a charter by which she bestowed upon him in free gift the earldoms of Mar and Garioch, with destination to his own heirs whatsoever—an arrangement of momentous consequence in the history of the earldom of Mar down to our own day. See Lord Crawford's *The Earldom of Mar in Sunshine and in Shade during five hundred years*, vol. i. pp. 201-217.

at home amongst his own people, his desire for warlike service
drove him to foreign shores. To all his possessions James
the First succeeded, for this valiant man was the bastard son of
Alexander Stewart earl of Buchan, who was son to king Robert
the Second. It hence appears that James gained for his own
purse various fair earldoms, the earldom of Buchan with that of
March. The battle that was fought at that time between the
English and the Scots was no great one[1]; for of English slain
and taken the sum was but fifteen hundred. On that day,
however, the Scots suffered the loss of one valiant gentleman
in Alexander Elphinston. The Scots commander was William
Douglas earl of Angus, with whom were Adam Hepburn of
Hailes and Alexander Ramsay of Dalhousie, knights. In this
year did James lay siege to the castle of Roxburgh, but without success. It was at this time too that James Kennedy,
nephew to the king by his sister the countess of Angus, was
promoted from the bishopric of Dunkeld to St. Andrews.

*James the First
is Alexander's
heir.*

CHAP. XIV.—*Of the murder of James the First, and the treason of
the earl of Athole. Of the outward aspect and the moral characteristics
of this same James the First ; the good faith that he kept towards the
French, and other his praises.*

In the year of the Lord one thousand four hundred and
forty-seven [2] was James the First, in the town of Perth, treacherously done to death, with thirty mortal wounds, on the twenty-
first day of February, and there in the Carthusian house of his
own founding was he buried, in the one-and-thirtieth year of
his reign, and of his age the forty-fourth. Now the occasion
of this treachery and murder was on this wise : the earl of
Athole, father's brother to the king, was a man grown old in
wickedness, and did not cease from his ambition to be king.
By his craft and guile it was that the duke of Rothesay, elder
brother to James, had perished ; and Murdach duke of Albany,
and his two sons likewise, who were next heirs to the kingdom

*The murder of
James the First.*

*Perfidy of the
earl of Athole.*

---

[1] The battle of Piperden, or, as the site is more particularly given by Rid-
path (*Border History*, ed. 1776, p. 401), 'Pepperden, on Brammish, not far
from the mountains of Cheviot'. This battle is said to have been the foundation
of the ballad of Chevy Chace.   [2] This should be 'thirty-seven'.

before himself. This man then won over to the perpetration of this crime his nephew Robert Stewart, who was the king's most familiar friend, and also one Robert Graham, a bold and crafty man, who had before that time been banished by the king, and from these he took assurance that of his own action in the matter naught should be brought to light, but that, by universal consent as it were, he should be chosen for guardian of the realm when the king was once removed; and thus he thought he should be able to do with James the Second, a boy of seven years, what he would, and perchance would even have killed him too, and so prevented his coming to the throne. For a certain witch is said once to have declared to him that before he died he should wear the crown; and to her prediction he trusted not a little.

Now the king showed herein much want of foresight, in that, waking or sleeping, he did not keep men by his side, seeing that he had for their ill deserts put to death many of his nobles. Nor can I approve of this: that he admitted to such familiarity of intercourse the nephew of the earl of Athole. It is no common practice with kings to admit to any close intimacy the next heir to the crown, or the next but one, unless these are direct descendants of their body. Such men they love and honour, but to their very bedchamber kings do not admit them, nor allow them to be their attendants, with a small following, to places that are fitted for the carrying out of a dangerous design. For blind lust of empire has driven many men to commit crime.

The author blames the imprudence of the king.

Our James was, if we may trust the chroniclers, short of stature, but robust and stout of body; and this which follows is his description by Aeneas Sylvius, afterwards Pope Pius, when he visited Scotland: 'James is square-set, of a full habit; he punished many of the petty chieftains of his kingdom, and in the end he was murdered by his own followers.' Among the Italians Britons are reckoned fat, just because they are of a large build; for men of the north eat plentifully of flesh, and indeed of very good flesh, wherein is no fat. This you may observe in the Germans, the Goths, and the Britons. Men of the south are thin from want of sap and a general dryness of body, and they reckon any man of a sanguine com-

The endowments of James the First, both in his person and in his character.

plexion to be fat. If you were to find in Italy men of the
same bodily habit as is in Scotland well-nigh universal, these
men would in very truth be fat—but that would not be so
with men of northern parts. The king was a man of the
finest natural gifts and of a very lofty spirit. He took in all
manly exercises a foremost place ; further than all could he put
a large stone or throw the heavy hammer ; swift he was of foot,
a well-skilled musician, as a singer second to none. With the
harp, like another Orpheus, he surpassed the Irish or the Wild
Scots, who are in that art pre-eminent. It was in the time
of his long captivity in France and England that he learned
all these accomplishments. When he wrote the language of
his own country he showed the utmost ability of that sort. He
left behind him many writings and songs, which are to this
day remembered amongst the Scots, and reckoned to be the
best they have. He wrote an ingenious little book about the
queen[1] while he was yet in captivity and before his marriage,
and likewise another ingenious ditty of the same kind, *Yas
sen*[2], etc., and that pleasant and ingenious poem *At Beltayn*[3],
etc., upon which other writers of Dalkeith and Gargeil laid
themselves out to make some change[4],—because he was at that
time kept a prisoner in the castle, where the lady dwelt with her
mother, or even in his own chamber.

Henry the Fifth,
the English
king, tempts
James in vain. Henry the Fifth, who held almost all of France, endeavoured
to entice him, with the promise of his freedom, to admit that
he held Scotland of the English king ; but this he magnani-
mously refused to do ; for he preferred, he said, in the fashion
of his ancestors, to go without his kingdom till he died, rather
than it should pass with aught of blemish to his successors.
Also, it was no business of his to place Scotland beneath the

---

[1] *The King's Quair.*

[2] The poem beginning 'Sen that eyne that workis my welfair '. Pinkerton
(as quoted in Irving's *History of Scotish Poetry*, p. 153) perceived signs of
mutilation in this line, and proposed to read ' Yas, sen that the eyne that workis
my weilfair '. Ritson conjectured that we ought to correct Pinkerton's text by
reading ' Sen yat '. Dr. Irving sees a tendency to rashness in both critics, but
Pinkerton's suggestion is strengthened by this passage in Major.

[3] *Peblis to the Play*, which begins with the words ' At Beltane '.

[4] That is, as it would seem, they wrote a parody on the poem. I have not
been able to find out anything about this parody, or to identify Gargeil.

English yoke. On the other part it must be said that his paternal uncle, the duke of Albany, who was at that time guardian of Scotland, took small pains to secure his ransom; —for he was himself next in line of succession. Now, according to that of Lucan—

> Place thou no faith in partners of thy rule,
> For power will ever chafe at partnership [1].

In the administration of justice he was not inferior to Thomas Randolph—nay rather, he excelled Randolph in this very thing; for Thomas found the country in a more peaceful state than did James. James tamed the Wild Scots, even the fiercest of them, and somehow led them to a gentler way of life; and though some birds, wild by nature, such as cranes and crows, and fowls of this sort, may be tamed, and it may be contended that, *a fortiori*, men endowed with reason, who are born near the poles, ought to be tameable, yet did he not fear also to execute the penalty of death upon certain of his nobles, such as Murdach duke of Albany with his sons. The earl of Douglas, too, he arrested, and placed in prison. In his time was no noble who dared to raise his sword against another; to his orders, written or spoken, every man alike yielded obedience. It is told how he said once to the queen that he would leave no man in Scotland save him who was her bed-fellow; and this can be no otherwise interpreted than that he had in mind to put to death his whole nobility. But indeed, so far as my memory serves me—and the chroniclers have many true stories to tell—he never dreamed of such a thing as this; for without his nobility he could not have protected the kingdom against his enemies, and many of his nobles too he dearly loved. These are mere inventions of his enemies, manufactured to excuse their own villanies. In such wise did he administer justice among his people, that when once the king was named, they yielded an absolute obedience. For once upon a time when a robber had seized two cows belonging to a widow woman, and she had said that she would tell the king what had been done, and would go to the king, unshod, with her tale, that scoundrel took two horse-shoes, and nailed them to the

Eulogy of James the First.

---

[1] Nulla fides regni sociis : omnisque potestas
Impatiens consortis erit.—*Pharsal,* i. 92.

soles of her feet, and said that she would not, as she said, go
unshod ; and to her he said further, ' Go then to the king,
and make choice whether thou shalt first complain of the hurt
done to thy body or of the theft of thy cows '.   And when she
was cured of the wounds in her feet, she went to the king, who
was then tarrying at Perth ; and he, when he understood what
had happened, made such search that the robber was sent to
Perth.   And he caused the woman to be clad in a white
garment, and then made her fasten those horse-shoes upon the
man, and so for two days caused him to be led about in the
town, and on the third day he was hanged.

   This man indeed excelled by far in virtue his father, his
grandfather, and his great-grandfather, nor will I give precedence over the first James to any one of the Stewarts, and there
have been of them only six, reckoning the boy who now is king.
Many Scots are accustomed, though not openly, to compare
the Stewarts to the horses in the district of Mar, which in
youth are good, but in their old age bad.   It is no hard
matter to disprove this vulgar saying about those kings.   The
second Robert and the third Robert, and likewise the first two
Jameses, united the fairest ending with a good beginning ; nor
do I reckon the fourth James, as will afterwards appear from
a consideration of his acts, to be inferior to the second of that
name ; and you shall find many a king, both at home and
abroad, who was worse than James the Third.   The Stewarts
preserved the Scots in all the blessings of peace, and maintained
the kingdom that was left to them by the Bruces in undiminished state.   This then let it suffice to have said about
James the First.

   CHAP. XV.—*Of the fearful but well-deserved punishment that was
inflicted upon the parricides of James the First, and of the marriage of
the queen his wife with a man of obscure condition, and the banishment
of her new husband.*

An exemplary
punishment of
parricides.

   AFTER the murder of James the First, the nobles of the
kingdom assembled themselves.   They made most diligent
search for the earl of Athole, for his nephew, for Robert

Graham, and for their accomplices ; and when these had been found they were sentenced to death in the royal palace at Edinburgh in manner following : the earl was stripped of every piece of clothing, that alone excepted which covered his private parts ; he was then dragged many times through the city with ropes that now swung him into the air, now permitted him to be trailed along the ground ; a red-hot iron crown was placed upon his head, whereby they would signify the fulfilment of that prediction of the witch that he should one day wear a crown, or, as Monstrelet observes [1], he was in this way declared to be king among traitors.   And on the following day they tied him to a horse's tail, and his fellow they made fast on a board, and so was he dragged by horses from village to village. On the third day they placed him upon a table, and while he was yet living his bowels were taken out and burnt before his face [2].   Now you need not marvel that a man should live after he has been disembowelled, for when any one has suffered a severe internal hurt the surgeon will remove the bowels and replace them all orderly as they were before.   Thereafter they took out his heart and flung it into the fire : and last of all was he beheaded, and his body was quartered, and a fourth part was sent to each of the four chiefest cities of the kingdom.

Robert Stewart, the earl's nephew, seeing that he had sinned by instigation of another, suffered a milder punishment.   For he was hung upon a gibbet, and then quartered.   Robert Graham, for he was murderer-in-chief, underwent a fearful punishment ; inasmuch as he was placed upon a carriage under a gallows, which was fixed upon the carriage ; and to this gallows they bound that right hand of his which had struck down the king, and so was he drawn throughout the city and

Punishment of Robert Graham.

---

[1] Monstrelet's *Chronicles*, vol. ii. p. 48, ed. 1845.

[2] I have been assured that this could not have been done while the victim yet lived.   But as an example of vitality under torture the reader may be referred to *A Calendar of the English Martyrs of the 16th and 17th Centuries* compiled by Mr. T. G. Law (London 1876), p. 9, where an eye-witness of the martyrdom of Hugh Green, who suffered at Dorchester in 1642, relates that after ' the butcher had cut his belly on both sides and turned the flap upon his breast '. . . . ' Whilst he was thus calling upon Jesus, the butcher did pull a piece of his liver out instead of his heart, and tumbling the entrails out every way to see that his heart was not amongst them, then with his knife he raked in the body of the blessed martyr, who even then called on Jesus.'

from village to village, and all the while were there three men
present to torture him by pricking him with pointed irons
made red-hot, and in such fashion that they should not kill
him outright, but that his punishment should last the longer.
Thereafter he was quartered. Christopher Chawmer and others,
who had been party to this wickedness, were put to an igno-
minious death. Monstrelet, indeed, reports that some of their
innocent kinsfolk were likewise put to death [1]. I confess that
these were fearful punishments; but the crime was of the
fearfullest, since these 'men sinned against the whole kingdom,
in slaying him who had been its most worthy head.

Graham's paltry excuse.
There is a story that Robert Graham said by way of excuse
for himself that since he had been proscribed by the king and
sent into banishment he was no longer the king's subject. It
was like that scoundrel, that man of Belial, marked with everlasting infamy, to snatch at this paltry exculpation ; for which
cause our people have made a rhymed proverb in the language
of the common folk :

> ' Robert Gramen
> that slew our King,
> God giff him schamen ' ;

that is, < they pray God to brand with infamy Robert Graham,
because he slew the king>[2].

The queen marries Stewart.
After the death of the king the queen married James
Stewart, a young man whose family was of the smaller gentry.
Among the Britons it is not held to be improper for queens
to enter a second time on the married state, nor is it in point
of fact improper ; for, according to the apostle, 'tis better to
marry than to burn. But she should have chosen for a husband the eldest-born son of one of the chief nobles, or a nobleman of high birth ; and because she did not do this, James the
Stewart is banished.
Second, as I have understood, banished the foresaid James
from Scotland ; and in doing so he showed his wisdom, for he
gave a lesson to those who should come after him to act more
Stewart's issue. warily. She bore to this James Stewart, however, three sons,
of whom one came to hold the earldom of Athole, though

---

[1] ' Such severe punishments were not remembered to have been ever before
inflicted in a Christian country.'—*Calendar, u.s.*

[2] In the original this is, of course, a Latin translation of the vernacular proverb.

shorn of its former state, and another had the earldom of
March; the bishopric of Moray was bestowed upon the third,
who died even in our own day [1].

We will now leave the affairs of Scotland for a time, and
turn our pen to deal with Henry the Sixth of England.

CHAP. XVI.—*Of the deeds of Henry the Sixth of England, and
the death at Orleans of Thomas Montacute. Of the French maid ;
Philip of Burgundy ; the ignoble marriage of the queen of England ;
the unhappy marriage of Henry with the Lotharingian. Of various
rebellions of the English nobles against the king.*

HENRY THE FIFTH had invaded a great part of France. To
him succeeded, as we have said above, his son, Henry the
Sixth, when he was still less than a year old ; and his uncles,
the dukes of Bedford and Gloucester, governed the kingdom
during his minority. Bedford was made regent of France,
Gloucester regent of England. It was in the fourth year,
after the battle of Verneuil [1], that Bedford came to England
and knighted Henry the Sixth at Leicester ; and soon thereafter Henry, now that he was himself a knight, made knights
likewise of those whose names follow: Richard duke of York,
the eldest son and heir of Norfolk, the earl of Oxford, the
earl of Westmorland, the eldest son of Northumberland, the
eldest son of Ormond, the lord Roos, James Butler, the lord
Maltravers, Henry Gray of Tankerville, William Nevyll, the
lord Falconbridge, George Nevyll, the lord Wellys, the lord
of Berkley, the eldest son of Talbot, Rodolph Gray of Werk,
Robert Weir, Richard Gray, Edmund Hungerford, John
Butler, Ronald Cobham, John Passheley, Thomas Tunstall,
John Chydiok, Rodolph Langeforde, William Drury, William
Thomas, Richard Carbonell, Richard Wydewyle, John Schredelowe, William Chayne, William Badyngton, John June, Gil-
bert Beauchamp.

It was in this year that Thomas Montacute, earl of Salisbury,
laid siege to Orleans, and during the siege he lost his life by a

Marginal notes: The things that happened in the days of Henry the Sixth. Names of those who were recently made knights. Thomas Montacute loses his life while besieging Orleans.

[1] Alexander Stewart, bishop of Moray, died in 1501. Keith's *Scottish Bishops*, ed. 1824, p. 146.

[2] The battle of Verneuil was fought in August 1424.

cannon-ball.   The English made small way in France after
his death.   In the same year a certain Briton, who had been
brought up by a widow woman for the love of God, killed that
widow, and after he had robbed her took refuge in a church ;
and when he had been signed with the sign of the cross he
took a vow to go to Jerusalem, but as he approached the place
where he had killed the widow he was stoned to death by the
women of the place.   I will here add that this thankless wretch
deserved his punishment, and even a heavier punishment than
this[1].

Henry was crowned at London in the seventh year of his
age, and at his coronation he made knights to the number of
seven-and-thirty.   Thereafter he passed into France, and on
the sixth of December of the same year was crowned king at
Paris in the church of Our Lady.   In the same year the maid
of France, who had helped to drive the English out of France,
was burnt at Rouen ; and in the following February Henry
the Sixth returned into England.

In the year fourteen hundred and thirty-four the duke of
Burgundy laid siege to Calais ; but when he learned that the
duke of Gloucester's army had set out from England he raised
the siege.   In this year died Katherine, the king's mother, who
was wife to Henry the Fifth and daughter to Charles the Sixth
of France.   After her husband's death she had made a secret
marriage, of which no one knew, with Owen, a gentleman[2] of
Wales.   The Britons call by the name of 'armiger' those who
stand next below knights in rank.   This man was of the lowest
sort of gentry, and to him she bore three sons and a daughter.
He was imprisoned in London by the duke of Gloucester for
having led the queen to marry him, as happened in the similar
case of her who was wife to James the First of Scotland and
queen of Scotland, as I have made mention above.

Of the sons one became earl of Richmond, another earl of
Pembroke, and the third became a monk.   Bear the eldest son
in remembrance in connection with the kings of England, for,
when I come to speak of these, I follow as far as I can the
English chroniclers.

A Briton's crime.

Henry the Sixth is crowned at London and Paris.

Punishment inflicted on the maid of France.

Philip of Burgundy lays siege to Calais.

The queen marries a plain gentleman.

The queen's issue by this gentleman.

---

[1] The story is taken from Caxton (fol. clii.) verso.   [2] armiger.

In the year fourteen hundred and forty-seven Eleanor The duchess[1] of Gloucester is banished. duchess of Gloucester, for having taken part in a conspiracy, was banished to the Isle of Man, and was placed in charge of Thomas Stanley, knight. About this time there were many Heretics in England. heretics in England, and when they persisted in this way they were burnt. In this year was the earl of Stafford advanced to be duke of Buckingham. In this year too did Henry the Sixth take to wife Margaret, daughter of the duke of Lorraine[2]. He Henry the Sixth marries her of Lorraine. had formerly made promise of marriage to the sister of Armagnac, and that he failed to keep his word is put forth by the English chroniclers as the reason that the English lost all the possessions that they held in France. Henry the Sixth was deposed, and the queen, with her son, took refuge in Scotland, Flight of the Lotharingian princess. and from Scotland passed into Lorraine, whence she had come.

In the year fourteen hundred and forty-seven[3] a parliament was held at Bury St. Edmunds, and a short time thereafter the A historical resumption. duke of Gloucester was arrested by the viscount Belmont, constable of England, and in his company were the duke of Buckingham and various others. On the following day the duke of Gloucester was found dead. Whether he had died of grief, or by the wicked plot of other men, is not clear. He was a very learned man, and a sensible man too, nor had he at any time sinned against his king or country; but through the jealousy of some of the nobility he lost his life; and the English earls grievously felt his loss. He is no good man who can view with equanimity the death of an innocent man who has deserved well of his country[4].

In the year fourteen hundred and forty-eight[5], in the time of king Henry, Francis of Arragon, who had embraced the Arragon attempts to succour the English. English cause, took Fougères[6] in Normandy, while there was a

---

[1] dux.

[2] Not duke of Lorraine, but earl of Provence, duke of Anjou and Maine, and king (in title only) of Naples and Jerusalem. See Powell and Mackay's *History of England*, Part I. p. 320. Even Caxton has nothing to say about a duke of Lorraine.

[3] Orig. and F. ' vigesimo sexto '. The true date is 1447.

[4] It is worth while to draw attention to the discrepancy between Major's estimate of Gloucester's character and that of our most competent modern historians. Cf. Mr. S. R. Gardiner's *Student's History of England*, vol. i. p. 317.

[5] Orig. and F. 'Anno 1427 '.   [6] Orig. and F. ' Fogiesium '; Caxton ' Fogyers '.

truce of arms between the French and English: Which deed
was the beginning of a mighty loss; for that was the occasion
of the loss of all Normandy by the English.

In the year fourteen hundred and forty-eight[1], in Henry's
reign, did the duke of Somerset and the earl of Shrewsbury
altogether abandon Rouen and Normandy; and inasmuch as
the duke of Suffolk was reckoned to be the cause of this action
of theirs, he was kept prisoner in the tower of London; and
when he had been there for one month he was set at liberty.
There was a mighty stir among the people at this and also at
the death of the duke of Gloucester. A parliament, however,
was continued to be held in the presence of the king, but the
place of its meeting was changed to Leicester, and the duke of
Suffolk was present at this parliament. The commonalty, however, did not cease from their murmurs and their complaints
against the duke of Suffolk, the lord Saye, and the bishop of
Salisbury; and to appease the people a decree of banishment
for a period was passed against Suffolk; but while he was on
board ship he was taken prisoner by some one and killed.

In the year fourteen hundred and fifty, the same when the
jubilee was held at Rome, the people of Kent rose against the
king, and, as they were drawing near to London, routed the
king's army which had been sent out to meet them. And
when the servants of noble families—for these men belong to
the common people—saw this, they too rose in rebellion, and
demanded that those who were traitors to the kingdom should
be slain, otherwise they too would join the Kentish mob in
their rising. They made petition too for sentence of death
upon the lord Saye, treasurer of England, the bishop of
Salisbury, and the baron of Dudley[2]; wherefore was the lord
Saye arrested and carried to the tower of London, in hopes to
appease the people. When the king's army had been defeated,
the mob, under its Irish leader[3], made for London, and there,
on the third day of July, did that same Irishman[4], in his own
name and the king's make proclamation of many things, and

---

[1] Orig. and F. 'Anno 1428'. The true date is 1448.
[2] Orig. and F. 'Doubly'; in Caxton 'Dudby'.   [3] *i.e.* Jack Cade.
[4] Orig. and F. 'Henricus', but read 'Hibernicus'.

this amongst the rest, that under pain of death no man should take for himself meat or drink or aught else without he paid for it[1]. Afterward they marched to the tower of London and demanded that the lord Saye should be handed over to them; and when this was done, and when he had been brought to trial before the mayor of the city and the leader of the common people, he refused to acknowledge their right to sit in judgment upon him, and declared that it was his due to be judged by his peers and the nobility, and not by the common people. And when the people heard these words, their rage had no bounds, and without further inquiry they ordered him to make his last confession, and before he got half way through they cut off his head.   He is beheaded.

Hereafter did that Irish leader of the common people begin to rob many wealthy merchants of London of their goods; and for this the sensible men amongst the common people held him in detestation, and the chief citizens, along with the lord Scales, captain of the Tower of London, gathered together a large number of the men of London, and went out against the Irishman and the rabble, who made a stubborn resistance. Round about London Bridge the fighting went on all night long, the rabble fighting outside the city, the London men within. And when the chancellor of England, who was a man of sense, saw how matters went, he sent to the Irish captain of the rabble and promised him for him and his a general pardon for all that he had done in the past; and forthwith the rabble dispersed, and every man returned to his own house. Proclamation was made a short while afterward that whoever should take that captain, John Cade the Irishman, living or dead, should be rewarded with one thousand pounds of sterling money. And without delay he was taken, and others along with him who had taken part in that conspiracy.   The Irishman is taken.

The evil deeds of the Irishman.

Rioting in London.

And here I may say that there is nothing more unprofitable than a rebellion of the common people and government at

---

[1] Caxton's account (fol. clvii.) is as follows: 'And as it was sayd they founde him wytty in his talkyng and in his request, . . . and there dyd make cryes in the kynges name and in his name, that no man sholde robbe, ne take no maner of goodes but yf he payed for it.'

their hands[1]; for they make a general unreasoning overturn of
everything: when they have to pass judgment or sentence upon
men, 'tis without discrimination that they do so. As well in
fact be governed by brute beasts as by them; and, to say
truly, they are but a beast with many heads. And this is
plain enough from a consideration of that thrice-damnable

A riotous
rabble.

rabble[2] which, when John the French king was a prisoner,
violated many noble women of France—whom afterward they
murdered[3]. There is nothing for it but the sword when the
common people rise in wanton insolence against the state;
otherwise they will confound in one common ruin themselves
and all else. For which reason Henry the Sixth went into
Kent, and at Canterbury did justice upon this pestiferous
people. After that he went into Sussex, and executed like

---

[1] Cf. Major's opinion in his Exposition of St. Matthew (1518) fol. xiv. recto 1:
'Taking the word "nobility" or "nobles" in its vulgar acceptation, the common
mass of nobles is to be preferred to the common mass of persons that are ignobly
born. I mean to say, those that are of noble birth are for the most part wiser and
better than those of ignoble birth. Well-born men have a certain care for the
education in right manners of their children; with the others this is not so. For
this cause I prefer an aristocratic to a democratic polity. If the Roman
patricians had ruled the republic and the common people had devoted themselves to their crafts, the republic in my opinion would have flourished better.
Whence I am wont to say (though I be myself ignobly born) that I prefer that
men of noble birth, and not men of ignoble birth, should govern.'

[2] Cf. Knox's phrase 'the rascal multitude'.

[3] The reference is to the peasants' rising, known as the Jacquerie, during the
two years' truce (1357-1359) when John the Second was a prisoner in England.
As Major quotes Robert Gaguin so freely throughout this book there is no doubt
that he had in his mind the terrible description of that historian: 'Insurrexit per
idem tempus in beluacensium territorio agricolarum insolens turba quae ex vicis
in nobilitatem duce guillermo calleto irrumpens caedem multam facit, com-
pendiumque usque atque siluanectum et suessionem grassata: arces complures
spoliauit deiecitque. Erat huic hominum pesti in nobilitatem praecipua con-
spiratio et execrabilis saevitia. Cuius ne per eius singula flagitia circumferar,
duo tamen praecipua immanitatis crimina memorabo. Inter plurimas caedes
haec debacchantium furia castellum quoddam irrumpens loci dominum cum palo
alligassent; eius uxorem filiamque in conspectu mariti stuprauerunt; stupratas
necauerunt viro mox crudeliter interempto. Alterum praeterea auratum equitem
a se trucidatum et veru transfixum igni assuauerunt (?) spectante equitis uxore,
quam a duodecim stupratoribus violatam impulerunt de mariti carne vesci,
miseram paulo post mulierem morte afficientes. Sunt qui memoriae prodiderunt
hos grassatores regem sibi instituisse iaqueum quemdam bellouacum, a quo ipsi
se iaquas volunt appellari.'—*Compendium*, etc. lib. ix. fol. cliv. ed. 1511.

judgment there. I have nothing but approval for the zeal for justice of this king, as he showed the same in curbing this unruly rabble and severely punishing them for their evil deeds, to the end that there should be less likelihood in time to come of such frivolous insurrections ; for facile pardon gives not seldom the occasion to offend.

In the thirtieth year of Henry's reign the duke of York, the earl of Devonshire, and the lord Cobham came from the Welsh marches, desiring to approach the king in hope of getting amendment of certain wrongs, and also to have justice upon certain lords that were about the king ; and they took the field at Brentheath [1], near to Deptford in Kent. And when Henry knew of this, he gathered a large army wherewith to oppose them. Among the number were some prelates, who made an attempt at mediation, seeking to persuade the king to put the duke of Somerset in prison, until he should answer certain of the charges brought against him by York, urging that when this had been done, the duke of York would disband his army and seek audience of the king. And to this the king assented ; and York disbanded his army forthwith, and went to the king. Thereupon the king and Somerset made him prisoner, and made as if they would take him captive to London ; and this they would have done had not a rumour got abroad of the arrival of the earl of March, son of York, with a great army ; wherefore York was set at liberty, and allowed to go whither he would.

Rising of the Welsh.

The duke of York is taken by a stratagem.

CHAP. XVII.—*Of the birth of Edward of England and the rebellion of the duke of York. Of the various fortune of King Henry. Of York's ambition of the crown ; and of the various chances of the war, and attempts of the nobles.*

In the year fourteen hundred and fifty-three queen Margaret gave birth to Edward heir of England [2]. But inasmuch as Somerset ruled both king and kingdom at his will, many among the nobles were filled with anger against the king, and most of all the duke of York, the earl of Warwick, with others many ;

Birth of Edward.

---

[1] Orig. 'Breuth' ; F. 'Brentheth', *i.e.* Blackheath.
[2] Angliæ hæredem.

New rebellion of the duke of York.

and when he had gathered a large force of soldiers he hastened to the king, meaning to remove from him Somerset and his other favourites. And when the king learned of their approach he left London and made for the western parts of the kingdom ; and he had with him Somerset, the duke of Buckingham, the earls of Strafford and Northumberland, the lord of Clifford, and many more. When York was aware of the road that the king took, he turned that way against him, and met him at St.

York gains a battle.

Albans on the twenty-third day of May. There was fought a battle in which York was the conqueror ; Somerset as well as Northumberland, Clifford, and many more of the king's side, lost their lives.

The king is carried to London as a prisoner.

When they had put the king's army to the rout at St. Albans, they carried the king to London, and there summoned a parliament, in the which York was declared protector of England, Warwick was made captain of Calais, and Salisbury chancellor of England, and some of the king's favourites were driven from court. It was in this year that some turbulent

The Longobards at London are ill-treated.

persons rose against the Lombards sojourning in London ; and of these the duke of Buckingham and the nobles put three to death ; but after they had thus dealt justice upon these men, they were not able to make a stand by reason of the insolence of the common sort, for many armed themselves secretly in their houses. When the unruly rabble of great cities rises in rebellion, it is to be with all care put down ; and the leaders of the revolt should be chastised with utmost rigour, to the end the rest should take a lesson by them and fear. Act otherwise, and you shall let loose upon the state a very pestilence of riot. In the days of Charles the Sixth you will find

The Capitiati.

a rising of the Capitiati[1] at Paris and in Flanders. In regard

---

[1] 'Hoc tempore Caroli sexti apud Parrhisios et in Flandria Capitiatos per seditionem invenies.' This refers, as to Flanders, to the defeat of Philip van Arteveldt by Charles the Sixth in 1382. But the name 'Capitiati' which Major gives to the insurgents, both of Paris and Flanders, seems to have a more special history. In the reign of Charles the Fifth of France (1364-1380) we read in Gaguin (*Compendium, etc.*, fol. clii.) of a rising of the Parisians in which the citizens wore as a 'signum civilis concordiae' a 'capuciola rubri blauiique coloris '—a little hood red and blue. Ducange has under CAPUCIATI 'factiosorum hominum cohors in Arvernia exorta ann. 1183 ' and also the Wicliffites, known as Hooded Men—' quod velato capite ad sacramenti participationem accederent '.

to this matter I hold Henry the Eighth worthy of praise, when Treatment of
in the year that is just past he put down with utmost severity evil-doers by
a rising against the Lombards and foreign merchants on the Henry the Eighth.
part of the Londoners; for of these Londoners he took fifteen,
and hanged them upon gallows that he put up in front of their
own houses[1]. In this year did Peter Brise [2], seneschal of Nor- Brise.
mandy, and those that were with him, take Sandwich, a town
of England, and when taken they plundered it, and carried
away captive its inhabitants. In this year too was Reginald [3] Heresy of
Pecock, bishop of Chester, accused of heresy, and many of his Reginald, a bishop.
books were burnt. A little while after this the lord Audley
attacked the earl of Salisbury near to Bloreheath[4]; but Audley Death of
was slain and many that were along with him. Audley.

In the year fourteen hundred and sixty-three the duke of York's rebel-
York, and Warwick and Salisbury, were filled with discontent lion.
at the manner of the government of the kingdom: for this
reason, that all was done at the nod of the queen, and that the
nobility were not summoned together; a report even was
noised far and wide that she had it in her mind to put them
to death. And that they might mend this state, these nobles
gathered a great army in the western part of England; and
Warwick summoned many of the men of Calais to take part in
the conflict. The king, on the other side, gathered likewise a
great army, and drew near to the enemy; and just at that
moment when it seemed that the battle would begin, Andrew
Trollop led off the men of Calais, and joined himself to the
king. When York saw this, he directed his course through York declines
Wales, and went over to the island of Ireland, leaving behind battle.
him the earl of March, who was his son and heir, and other
two earls; but these likewise soon left the field of battle, and
betook them to Calais, into the fortress of which town they
were received by a postern. Now the king created the duke

---

[1] See Lord Herbert of Cherbury's *King Henry the Eighth*, fol. 1672, p. 67
(about July 1517): 'Some Citizens and Apprentices of London of the poorer sort,
being offended that all their chief Customers were won from them by the Diligence
and Industry of Strangers, and (for the rest) pretending to have received from
them divers Contempts, Affronts, and Injuries, found some Occasions, and took
others, to make an insurrection against them.'

[2] *i.e.* Peter de Brezé.   [3] Orig. and F. 'Reynoldus'.

[4] Orig. 'Bkercheth'; Caxton 'Bloreheth'.

Somerset, who was already reported dead, is made captain of Dover.

of Somerset captain of Calais[1]; but when the duke came to Calais he found it already in the hands of the three earls; wherefore he turned aside to the fortress of Guisnes, which is held by the English in Picardy. To these men there came daily out of England more and more. Warwick borrowed a large sum of money from the merchants of Etaples, and passed into Ireland, for he wished to take counsel with York. Afterward he returned to Calais, and thence by way of Dover all three earls with a large force landed in England. They drew near to London, where they were joined by a large part of the population; for the common people are only too ready to follow at their own costs men that are of noble birth when these go to war. Everywhere they caused a report to be spread that they meant no harm to the royal majesty, but had it in view only to remove evil counsellors from the king, and were thus taking the best course for the welfare of the state. With a large force therefore they made for Northampton, where the king

A fierce battle. The king is worsted.

was then dwelling; and there a fierce battle took place, wherein the king was worsted. There fell on the king's side the duke of Buckingham, the earl of Shrewsbury, the viscount of Beau-

He is carried a prisoner to London.

mont, the lord Egremont, and many more. The king was carried prisoner to London, and a full parliament of the lords was soon summoned. Meanwhile York was returned from Ire-

York claims the crown.

land. He made claim to the crown of England, to which he asserted that his title was just. But the matter was on this wise settled: that for his life Henry should be king, but that York with his issue should succeed to him, and in the mean-

He is declared governor of the kingdom and heir to the crown.

while should be protector and regent of the kingdom; and if from this pact the king should depart, he should be deposed, and York should take his place.

But to the ordinance of this parliament the queen and her son Edward yielded no obedience, and they continued in the northern parts. Against them marched York, and in his company were the earl of Salisbury, Thomas Neville his son, and many more. The friends of the queen made a stand against them, and a battle was fought at Wakefield

York is slain.

in Christmas week. In that battle the duke of York

---

[1] 'ductor Itiorum'. See *ante*, p. 5.

was slain, and likewise the earl of Rutland and Thomas Neville; and the earl of Salisbury was taken. The earl of March, who was son to York, forthwith gathered an army, and on the feast of the Purification he gained a victory over the other side at Mortimer. And following thereon, the queen, and those that had stood by her, made for the southern part of the kingdom. And the duke of Norfolk, Warwick, and many others went forth against her near St. Albans; and along with them they carried king Henry. And there a battle was fought in which Warwick was worsted; and the queen and her son Edward set Henry his prisoner at liberty. After this, the duchess of York, who was in London, sent her sons George and Richard beyond sea. Thereafter did Warwick and the earl of March gather a large army out of Wales, and they made for London; and they created Edward earl of March, who was heir to Richard duke of York, to be king, in the fourteen hundred and fifty-ninth year of our Lord; and the whole people followed him. He afterward sought out Henry in the northern parts, and gave him battle at Towton, not far from York, and put to rout thirty thousand of the enemy, and came off victor. In this conflict there fell on Henry's side the earl of Northumberland, the lord of Clifford, John Neville, brother to the earl of Westmorland, Andrew Trollop, and many more. Henry, his queen, and their followers, fled into Scotland. Here then we will leave the sixth Henry, his kingdom lost, and turn once more to the affairs of Scotland.

The victory gained by his son.

Warwick having been worsted lost the king, whom he had taken prisoner.

Edward earl of March is created king, and gains a battle.

Those who were slain in that battle.

Flight of Henry into Scotland.

CHAP. XVIII.—*Of the marriage of James the Scot, the Second, who was called Red Face; of the struggle for power with the Douglases; and, in connection therewith, of the danger to the state which comes from the exaltation of powerful lords. Of the reign of this same James the Second, his issue, his death, and his praise.*

AFTER the murder of James the First, James the Second, or James of the Fiery Face, son to James the First, was created to be king[1]. He came by the name of Fiery Face because he had on one cheek a broad red mole. When he was come to

James the Second, named 'Burnt Face.'

---

[1] in regem creatus est.

He marries
a wife of
Guelders.
He seizes
certain lords
and condemns
them to death.

man's estate, he was strong and valiant; and he took to wife a daughter of the duke of Guelders. He laid hands on William earl Douglas, and David his brother, along with Malcolm Fleming, lord Cumbernauld, in the castle of Edinburgh; and on the highest point of that castle[1] he caused them to be beheaded. I have read in the chronicles that those men were not guilty, and that this deed was perpetrated at the instigation or by the craft of William Crichton, chancellor of Scotland.

The castle of
Edinburgh is
besieged.

In the year fourteen hundred and forty-five James the Second laid siege to Edinburgh castle. William Crichton was its keeper at that time.

In the year fourteen hundred and fifty, that is, in the year of jubilee, William earl Douglas went abroad to Rome, with a large number of noble lords.

The power of
the Douglases
draws suspicion
upon them.

In the year of our Lord fourteen hundred and fifty-one, on Quinquagesima[2], James the Second sent for earl Douglas. And the earl went to the king, who was then dwelling at Stirling. The king called him to a private audience, and proposed to him that he should abandon the league and party which he had made with the earl of Craufurd. A rumour went abroad among many that Douglas was aiming to usurp the royal crown; for he had two brothers that were earls, Archibald, to wit, earl of Moray, and Hugh Ormond; and besides, the earl of Angus bore the same surname and was his kinsman, and the earl of Morton likewise; and other powerful men there were of the same name; and he had made a wide-spreading league with other lords. The king feared therefore for himself and his kingdom, seeing what was the wealth of the Douglases and their following, and that these earls were men of a high spirit and ambitious, and warriors from their youth up. It is reported that the earl made ill-considered answer to the king, and, that

Douglas is
slain.

I may end the story without more words, he was slain by the king and those that were about him.

Acts of treason
by Douglas's
brothers in
Scotland.

After the assassination of the earl, his brothers behaved with so great insolence to all the king's men, that wayfaring men might reasonably doubt whether it were not better to

---

[1] 'in ejusdem arcis monte'; Buchanan, lib. xi. 17, 'in aream arci propinquam eductus'.   [2] 'in carnisprivio'. See *ante*, p. 231.

call themselves Douglas's men than king's men. The town of Stirling was burnt down by the lord Hamilton, one of the most obstinate adherents of the Douglases. But by the wise measures of James Kennedy, archbishop of St. Andrews, who was cousin to the king, the king was victorious, and the rest were either put to death or banished. For Scotland, as I see, the earl of Douglas was too powerful: he had thirty or forty thousand fighting men ever ready to answer to his call. The kings of Scotland found their occupation in the chase and in the administration of justice; and earl Douglas had time for the things of war; and for this reason a swarm of men ever ready for a fray attached themselves to him. Whence there was every reason why James the Second should fear him. It is related by many that from the beginning of his reign James the Second felt the burden of the Douglas power so strongly that he had it in mind to desert his kingdom of Scotland; but by the wise counsel of James Kennedy and the active help of this prelate he was enabled to form a loftier purpose. Kennedy so carried things that the earl of Angus, a Douglas by name, and his brother on the mother's side, and most of the other brothers of earl Douglas, were brought over to the side of the king.

I often say to my own countrymen that there is naught more perilous than unduly to exalt great houses [1], and most of all if their territory happen to lie in the extremities of the kingdom, and the men themselves are high-spirited; for these Borderers are constantly practised in active exercises, and the life of a soldier is natural to them, and so they come to place their hope in arms, and judge that they shall be able to find a means of escape from their enemies in time of need. For seventy years you may find a practical example of just this state in Scotland. The thing is plain from the case of that earl of March, whose name was Dunbar, and who, when he was warden of the eastern marches, and wished to avenge himself for a small injury done to him by Robert the Third, went over to the English [2]; and Edward the Second, when he had been put to flight by Robert Bruce,

The king is victorious. Why Douglas was so dangerous to the king.

The dangers that attend the exaltation of great families.

---

[1] Cf. *ante*, p. 188, on the family of Cumming. [2] See *ante*, p. 310.

was received, so they say, into the castle of Dunbar by another,
his predecessor; and for this cause he lost his earldom, as we
have told in the life of James the First. The same thing,
again, is plain from that of the earl of Douglas, who was
warden of the two other marches. In my own day[1] did James
the Third deprive the earl of the Isles and Ross of his territory,
for his scorn of the king. Not more than four years from this
present writing, we saw the lord Hume for a like cause lose both
his property and his life[2]. So long too as the dukes of Normandy
and Brittany and other very powerful families had their seats
within the circumference of France, the empire of the French
underwent but very small extension, and was far from peaceful.
And though those dukes in France were possessed of larger
revenues than are enjoyed by powerful earls in England or
Scotland, yet were they not capable of bringing on occasion
more warriors into the field; for the Britons are so kindly
affected to their lords that thirty or forty thousand men will
follow these at their own charges. But why wonder that they
should thus expend their money, when they are ready to risk life
itself for these men, though many among them never received,
whether from these lords or from their own parents, so much as
a single piece of Tours; but, led by habit, they walk in the
footsteps of those that have gone before them. Now when the
captains of the marches are not so powerful, the smaller
nobility will not follow them, nor by consequence the common
people; and though one very powerful lord may be better able
to withstand an enemy than one of the smaller nobles will do,
yet will that greater power of resistance turn in the end to the
ruin of their families, while it is profitless to the state. For
powerful nobles do not fear to engage in war on their own
authority, and a number of lords, when they get the common
people to join them, are strong enough, when they think fit to
do so, to make stand against the king.

When James the Second had gathered an army to oppose

---

[1] *i.e.* in 1474.

[2] It was on the 16th of October 1516, according to Crawfurd, *Peerage*, p. 221,
ed. 1716, that the first Lord Hume and his brother William lost their heads. It
appears from the statement in the text that Major's History was written leisurely;
for a part of it at least was written in 1518 (see *ante*, p. 309), and this part in 1520.

the Douglases, he found that the Douglases took the field with a force no whit inferior to his own, and with this force it was determined by Hamilton and most of the others to make war against the king. But the head of the house of Douglas avowed that he had no mind to fight against his rightful king ; and when the leading men of his faction heard this, they besought him that he would at least maintain a force in readiness wherewith to oppose the king, until with their own assistance a settled peace might be secured : for, with their army once routed or dispersed, there could be no thought of peace. And the lord Hamilton, more cautious than the rest, parted company thereupon with the Douglas chief, for he felt that he should never afterwards have such an opportunity of playing for the stake of a kingdom. Hamilton, indeed, soon secured not only a peaceful settlement from the king, but won the king's daughter to boot ; and after that the king consented to make peace with the whole house of Douglas. For God willed not that it should come to fighting, to the end that the Scots should ever enjoy their rightful kings. And though God could have brought this to pass by other means [1], yet did He choose this way, and so save the country from civil war. There is not a doubt that if Douglas had consented to Hamilton's proposition, a most fearful war would have ensued, for the Douglases were roused to fury by the slaying of their kinsmen, and were driven to desperation ; and, for the rest, they would have been fighting for kingship. Thenceforward, with the Douglases once subdued, James first began in truth to reign, and could impose laws upon his people as he would. He gathered an army, and in the year fourteen hundred and fifty-six invaded England. To him the English king sent an embassy, which made many promises ; but when James was returned home and saw no fulfilment of these promises, he again gathered a great army, and laid England waste with fire and sword, and then returned unscathed to his own country ; and in time of war he used in the field so great humanity, without distinction of person, that he was not so much feared as revered as a king, and loved as a father. His queen, Mary, bore to James the Second three sons—James, to

James, with the Douglases once subdued, has freedom to reign, and invades England.

---

[1] Cf. *ante*, p. 233.

wit, who succeeded him on the throne; Alexander duke of
Albany, and John earl of Mar—and two daughters, of whom
the elder, as I have said, became the wife of Hamilton.

Hereafter did James lay siege to the castle of Roxburgh,
which for a long time had been held by the English, in Scotland; and he was over-curious in the matter of engines of war.
For a wooden ball, which formed the charge of a large engine
of this sort, when it was shot forth, struck the king and killed
him, and wounded the earl of Angus—a lesson to future kings
that they should not stand too close to instruments of this
sort when these are in the act of being discharged. But the
besiegers did not suffer themselves to be hindered by the death
of the king, and they took the castle. On the third day then
of August, in the nine-and-twentieth year of his life, and of
his reign the twenty-fourth, was he killed; and he received
honourable burial in the monastery of the Holy Rood at Edinburgh; and at his death there was such sorrow and lamenta-
tion of his people as you may see in a private house on the
death of a dearly beloved father.

For vigorous kingship, most writers give the first place to
this monarch, seeing that he gave himself with all zeal to the
things of war, and to naught else; and in time of war he was
fellow to every private soldier. I, however, prefer before
him his father, the first James, alike for his natural endowment
and his fortitude in the field. But in energy of action the
second James followed his father closely. Both were alike
careless of bodily comfort, while in time of war the second
James would ride among his soldiers as one of themselves; and
in food or drink the soldiers would offer him of their own
provision. He called on no man to taste before him what he
would eat and drink, for he had that trust in his soldiers that
not one would try to poison him. And his confidence was
justified; yet in this matter I will not say that I deem him
prudent.

CHAP. XIX.—*Of the coronation of James the Third; of Henry the Sixth and the things done by him in Scotland and England. Of the death of the queen of Scotland and her incontinence. Of the capture and the restoration of the duke of Albany. The death of bishop Kennedy and his encomium.*

AFTER the death of James the Second, James the Third, then a child of seven years, was crowned at Kelso; and thereafter the Scots forthwith razed to the ground the castle of Wark in England. In the year fourteen hundred and sixty-one, Henry the Sixth, when he had been defeated by Edward of York, sought a safe-conduct from the Scots for a thousand horsemen; and when his request was granted, he went to Edinburgh, the royal seat of Scotland [1], which is but twenty leagues distant from England. There he had hospitable reception in the convent of the preaching friars, along with queen Margaret his wife and Edward his first-born son. There were likewise with them Somerset duke of Exeter and Gloucester and many other lords. But the queen, for she was a French woman, went thence with her son into France. Henry handed over the town of Berwick to the Scots; but the Scots made a fifteen years' truce with the new king, Edward, though I know not by what promises Edward bound himself to its observance. For the king was a child, and the whole government of Scotland was then in the hands of James Kennedy, archbishop of St. Andrews.

After this, and when he was urged thereto by many of the English lords, Henry returned into England; and he suffered defeat at the hands of Edward, and was put in prison. While this was happening, Peter Brise [2], who had been sent by the French king to carry succour to Henry, took some of the strongholds in the northern parts. But Edward laid siege to Alnwick castle, where Brise was, and when he was unable to make his escape, he sent to the Scots, praying them to raise the siege. George Douglas, earl of Angus and warden of the marches, led an army to the English borders; and of his whole force he made choice of thirteen thousand men, the best he

Marginal notes:
James the Third is crowned.

What Henry the Sixth did in Scotland.

The queen of England returns to France.

Return of Henry the Sixth into England. He is taken.

The deeds of Brise, and how he was besieged.

---

[1] Orig. and F. 'Scotiae reginam'; probably a misprint for 'regiam'. The distance from England (twenty leagues) is curious.

[2] *i.e.* de Brezé.

had, and with these he reached the besieged castle at noon, set
the Frenchmen free, and, all in sight of that mighty English
army, carried them with him into Scotland. For some of the
English had given their counsel in favour of fighting, but to
others (and these carried it) it seemed better to let the man
depart without striking a blow ; for though he had but a
small force, yet were they all picked men.

In the year fourteen hundred and sixty-three died the queen
of Scotland, at Edinburgh ; and she was buried in the college
of the Holy Trinity, which herself had founded. After the
death of James the Second she had not kept her chastity, but
had dealt lewdly with Adam Hepburn, heir to the lord of
Hales, who was a married man. Now, I say that this woman
was herein exceeding careless, for she should rather have taken
a lord who had no wife, or the heir of some lord ; and she thus
acted more wickedly than did the wife of James the First. In
the same year was Alexander, duke of Albany, and brother to
James, taken by the English at sea. I have nowhere found it
stated whither our people desired to send this boy ; but James
Kennedy obtained his liberty, with his ship and all his goods ;
for otherwise he would not have secured the truce that had
been made with the English king.

Death of the
queen and her
incontinence.

The duke of
Albany is taken.
He is restored.

In the year one thousand four hundred and sixty-six died
James Kennedy, and he was buried in that college of St.
Salvator at St. Andrews which he himself had reared and
richly endowed. I have found among our fellow-countrymen
no man who rendered more signal public service [1] than this
prelate. It was by the wise measures of his devising and the
skill with which he put them in practice that earl Douglas,
the most powerful of our Scottish nobles, was brought to
naught. In his time, too, the whole kingdom enjoyed tran-
quillity ; and the truce with the English king was kept inviolate. Beside St. Andrews he held no benefice—unless it were
that of Pittenweem, which amounted to no more than eighty
pieces of gold. Yet did he build at his own charges, and
richly endow it, a college at St. Andrews. His property he
held in that way in which in matters ecclesiastical a bishop
may hold property, in regard to which I have spoken more at

---

[1] præsentatiorem.

length in my work on the Fourth Book[1]. In addition, he built a huge and very powerful ship, and likewise for himself he prepared a splendid tomb, so that many men are apt to put the question on which of those three things he had spent the most. Two points in this man's conduct I cannot bring myself to praise: to wit, that along with such a bishopric he should have held a benefice *in commendam*, even though it was a slender one; nor do I approve the costliness of his tomb[2].

In the year of the Lord fourteen hundred and sixty-nine and on the tenth day of July, James the Third, then aged twenty years, was married at Edinburgh to Margaret, who was then twelve years old, daughter to the king of Norway. The dowry that he got with her was that right which had been claimed by the king of Norway to the Orkney islands, and the rest of the islands adjacent to British Scotland. We will now leave James the Third, and resume the affairs of England.

CHAP. XX.—*Of the character and the death of the duke of Clarence and the earl of Warwick. Of the deeds of Edward, Richard, and the Henrys, kings of England, and various occurrences. Of the wickedness of Richard and his miserable death, and of the marriage of Henry the Eighth and of his sisters.*

In the year fourteen hundred and seventy the duke of Clarence and the earl of Warwick left England from fear of

Flight of the duke of Clarence and the earl of Warwick.

---

[1] The reference is to *In Quartum*, Quest. 21 of Dist. 24, where the Second Conclusion is as follows : ' The beneficiary who possesses a patrimony sufficient for his needs would do well if he were to live upon his patrimony and serve God, and would thus act more meritoriously than if he lived upon his benefice, since he would be giving more to God without return [gratis]. Furthermore, charity ought to move him to succour his poorer brother, and it may be that he is not without sin when he himself holds a benefice, and a poor man, as competent as himself, remains without one.' Qu. 8 of Dist. 38 may also be compared : ' It may be argued in the third place : Bishops own wealth and property, and never. theless they are in a state of perfection, and, from what has been said above, in a higher state than that of religious, wherefore to have wealth does not argue a dangerous state. It is answered : Bishops do not own wealth for themselves ; for they are not lords of that wealth, but are held bound to apply it to pious uses in the manner of abbots.'

[2] The criticism of Buchanan upon this passage (lib. xii. 23)—' Quod tamen ei privatim de pluribus publice de omnibus optime merito malignitas hominum in. vidit '—is perhaps itself more open to the charge of ' malignitas ' in one sense of the word.

king Edward, along with their wives, and landed in Normandy,
meaning to dwell there for a time and, as it were, take breath,
until they should be in a way to make war against Edward.

But when this came to the knowledge of Charles of Burgundy,
who had to wife king Edward's sister, he was very wroth, and
wrote a letter to the parliament of Paris, wherein he called
upon king Lewis to send the Englishmen out of his kingdom
and make no delay.   And he added this, that if Lewis would
not do so, in whatever part of France the Englishmen might be
found he would make them his prisoners.   But no action was
taken in consequence of this threatening letter of Burgundy's.

At the same time the queen gave birth on the eleventh day
of June, in the castle of Amboise, to him who afterwards became Charles the Eighth, and the prince of Wales, that is, the
heir of Henry the Sixth, stood sponsor to the infant.

A short time thereafter the duke of Clarence and the earl of
Warwick left France and went into England, and at their very
landing they beheaded a certain baron[1].   Thence they made
for Bristol, a stately town of England, and were there made
welcome.   Afterward they made sail for London, and on their
way thither they were joined by sixty thousand men ready to
help them in what they had in hand.   O the marvellous fickle-

ness of that race!   They set Henry the Sixth at liberty, taking
him from the Tower of London, and restored him to his
kingdom, while Warwick took up the reins of government.
The same man who drove out Henry, and made Edward king,
now recrowns Henry who had been deposed.   Of him it was
said that he made kings, and at his pleasure cast them down.

Edward made his escape to him of Burgundy, who had married
Edward's sister.   He sought and received succour from him
toward the recovery of his kingdom.   Once more, therefore,

and with a large army, Edward made for England, in the year
fourteen hundred and seventy-one; and many Englishmen
gathered round him with what aid they could.   Against him

---

[1] Probably John Tiptoft, earl of Worcester, ' the most learned and best-read
noble in England ', and Caxton's chief patron.   He was beheaded by Clarence
and Warwick, though not ' in primo in terram descensu ', ' because when he was
constable under King Edward he had judged men to death by the law of Padua
[Roman law] '.—York Powell and Mackay's *History of England*, pt. I. p. 333.

then marched Henry the Sixth, his son the prince of Wales, and the earl of Warwick. A fierce battle took place, in which Edward was victorious[1]. In that battle the prince of Wales lost his life; Henry the Sixth was taken prisoner; and Warwick the king-maker perished. Whence men may learn that no trust is to be placed in fortune; for doubtful indeed is the issue of battle, and the sword devours now this man and now that.

After this the earl of Pembroke and Henry earl of Richmond, landed in Little Britain. In the year fourteen hundred and seventy-five, and on the twenty-ninth day of August, Edward went to France, whither he had been enticed by the promises of help toward the recovery of France that had been made to him by Charles of Burgundy and the count of Saint Paul[2], constable of France. But when he came there, these promises were not fulfilled. For which cause did English Edward send a herald to Lewis the eleventh, with this message: that he had certain secrets to disclose to the French king, and to this end sought to come to speech of him. And all this pleased Lewis mightily. The place chosen for this conference Conference of was Pecquigny in the neighbourhood of Amiens. Lewis had the kings. meanwhile borrowed from the people of Paris five-and-seventy thousand pieces of gold, which he promised to repay after the first of November. Thereafter Lewis marched at the head of a vast army to Amiens, and he caused two platforms to be raised upon the bridge of Pecquigny, on the one of which he should himself stand, while Edward should stand upon the other; and between these was a mutual partition, pierced with wide holes, so that through these holes the kings might have sight and speech one of another. The river Somme, which flows through Amiens, separated the English and French armies. The money The agreements which Lewis had borrowed of the people of Paris was then which were handed to Edward[3]. Whence we may understand that Lewis Conference. made at the had been told by Edward's ambassadors that he would have to

---

[1] Battle of Barnet, April 14, 1471.   [2] St. Pol.

[3] Cf. Gaguin (*u. s.* fol. cclxxiv) for an example of the use which Major has made of the work of that historian in dealing with French matters throughout Book VI. Even the verbal differences between the two accounts of this meeting are very slight.

make payment of this sum. A truce of arms was then made
upon this condition, that for five years from that time Lewis
should make annual payment to the English king of fifty
thousand pieces of gold. This done, Edward withdrew the
whole English force to Calais. And while Edward was still at
Calais, he received a letter from Lewis constable of Luxemburg, which taunted him with cowardice in that he was ready
to leave France without striking a blow. Whereat Edward
was very wroth, and all unknown to the constable he declared
the whole matter to Lewis.

The duke of
Clarence is put
to death. A short time hereafter the duke of Clarence, Edward's
brother, was put to death, in London, because of an attempt
which he made to carry succour to his sister, who was wife to
Burgundy, against Edward's wish; or because, as others have
it, and with more likelihood, he was ambitious of the English
crown; and it favours this explanation that he had to wife
a daughter of Warwick. During Edward's reign Henry the
Death of Henry
the Sixth. Sixth, who had been crowned at Paris, died in prison. It
was said by very many that Richard, duke of Gloucester,
brother to Edward, was the author of his death. This
same Henry, as the English writers report, was renowned for
the many miracles that he performed. His spirit was high,
and his disposition was towards clemency, as indeed the times
demanded; but he came by his end through that fickle temper
of the English, whose delight it is to get a new king. Three
sons and two daughters were born to Edward; and when he
Edward com-
mends his
kingdom and
his children to
his brother
Richard. was about to go the way of all flesh he commended his children
and his kingdom to his brother Richard, with the prayer that
he would place Edward's eldest son upon the throne. After
the death of Edward, Richard was declared regent of England,
and he began to use every craft to gain the kingdom for him-
Richard's
usurpation. self. That himself might reign he ordered the three fair sons
of Edward to be put to death; and yet he had no children of
his own. O the blind lust of empire! These nephews of
Richard's were in very truth his heirs; he might have kept
them and his kingship both; but, trampling under foot all considerations divine as well as human, he caused those three[1] bright
and innocent children of his brother, his own nephews, to be

---

[1] I have found no other mention of *three* children.

put to death, and after that placed the crown upon his own head; but not for long did he wear it. A multitude of Englishmen began to call for Henry earl of Richmond, who was at that time an exile in France. Inasmuch as he had been long a dweller in France, Charles the Eighth granted him an aid of five thousand men (of whom one thousand were Scots, but John, son of Robert of Haddington[1], was chief among them, and leader of the Scots), and he landed in Wales, where his army was forthwith increased greatly, for the English people welcomes ever a change of king. Against king Richard then they made war, and Richard was slain in battle; and thereafter Richmond went to London where he was declared king under the style of Henry the Seventh. His grandmother was that Katherine who had been wife to Henry the Fifth, and daughter to the king of the French. On the mother's side he was brother to king Henry the Sixth[2]; but he also entered into union of marriage with the eldest-born daughter of king Edward, who was then heiress to the kingdom, and thus he became indisputably king. The earl of Lincoln revolted against him; but he prevailed against this and every other rebellion. <This same Henry had dwelt for a long time at Rouen, where in the house of a man named Patrick King, a Scot, he took his daily victuals in penury. And Patrick was moved to compassion for him, and bestowed upon him a large part of his fortune>[3].

Henry earl of Richmond returns to England.

Richard is slain.

Henry the Seventh.

---

[1] This is probably a mistake either of Major's or of the printer (see *ante*, p. 320), for 'Coningham'. John de Coningham succeeded his father, Robert de Coningham, as captain of the Scottish Archers in 1478, and held that office until 1493. See Forbes Leith, *Scots Guards in France*, vol. ii. p. 56. I have been unable to trace any connection between the Cunningham family and Haddington that might have justified Major in claiming them as fellow-countymen. Drummond of Hawthornden says that Bernard Stewart (of Aubigny) was in command of the Scots at Bosworth.—*Hist. of the Five Jameses*, p. 106.

[2] It was his father, Edmund Tudor, who was half brother to Henry the Sixth.

[3] 'Hic Henricus fuerat diu Rothomagi, ubi in domo Patricii cognomine Regis Scoti commensalis in tenuitate steterat: cui Patricius commisertus magnam fortunae partem exposuit.'—I have found no record of this incident elsewhere. Major's translation of the surname 'King' is characteristic of him. A good example of his arbitrary rendering of British proper names into Latin will be found in the case of 'Gravesend', in his Exposition of St. Matthew (fol. lxxviii. verso 2): 'Via est periculosa inter hierico et hierusalem propter desertum: propterea conuenerunt ut esset cum multitudine, ut in loco periculoso facimus, ut videre est inter Londonias et finem sepulchri, quod grauis end vocant, transeundo per terram.'

In every action of his life Henry proved himself a most
sagacious man ; he showed much wisdom in the suppression of
rebellion, and he caused many nobles to be beheaded ; yet was
he given too much to avarice, for in all ways he could contrive
did he raise vast sums of money from merchants and other
wealthy men. He married his eldest son, Arthur, to the

Marriage of
Henry the
Eighth.

daughter of Ferdinand, king of Aragon ; and after the death
of Arthur he gave her to his second son Henry to wife. For
that two brothers should marry, one after the other, the same
woman is forbidden by human law alone, and is contrary
neither to the law of nature nor to the law of Moses [1]. For
rather was it specially enjoined by that law that the next
brother should raise up seed to his brother that was dead.
Now Arthur had no issue ; but his father had left two
daughters, of whom the elder, Margaret, married James the
Fourth, king of Scots, and Mary, the younger daughter, was
married to Lewis the Twelfth, king of the French ; but, on
the death of Lewis, she was given in marriage to the duke of
Suffolk.

This, then, so far ; the rest let others tell, or we in other place.

END OF THE HISTORY.

---

[1] This is interesting as having been written before the question of the divorce
arose.

ADDITIONAL NOTES

I.—*Population of Medieval Cities.*[1]

In the number of *La Normandie* (a monthly journal published at Rouen) for May 1891 there is a paper by M. Raoul Aubé, entitled 'La population rouennaise à travers les siècles'. From this special contribution to the difficult subject of the population of medieval cities we gather that the first authentic document on the population of Rouen dates from the year 1274, when a diocesan statistical report, known as 'le *Pouillé* d'Eudes Rigaud', which was published by M. Léopold Delisle in the collection of *Historiens des Gaules*, places the number of 'paroissiens' at 7,839. But as the word 'paroissien' (*parochinus*) does not there denote each several inhabitant, but a head of a household, we have a total population, on the basis of five persons to the family, of 40,000. The *Normandie* then refers to the startling computation of the inhabitants of Rouen which is to be found in M. L. Puiseux's *Siège et prise de Rouen par les Anglais en* 1418 (Caen ; 1867). M. Puiseux estimates the population at that time at no less than 300,000 souls. His argument is ingenious[2]. but his conclusions have not been accepted. M. Puiseux quotes the story of the conversation between the Emperor Charles the Fifth and Francis the First,—when the emperor asked the king which was the largest town in France and the most populous, and the king answered—'Rouen'. 'Why not Paris?' said the emperor. 'Because Paris is not a town, it is a province[3].' But the population of Paris even

---

[1] See *ante*, p. 22.

[2] *Siège et Prise*, pp. 13-18.

[3] Yet it was of this same Paris that Charles the Fifth said punningly—and not untruly—that he could put the whole of it into his 'glove' (*i.e.* Gant or Gand=Ghent). From a reference by Herr Jastrow (*Die Volkszahl deutscher Städte zu Ende des Mittelalters und zu Beginn der Neuzeit*, Berlin, 1886, p. 154) I learn that the emperor undertook an exact measurement of several large cities, from which it appeared that Ghent, Paris, Cologne, and Liége had nearly the same circumference, but that Ghent had the largest,—a fact which proves that the spacial extent of a city could be no measure of its comparative population without full knowledge of the manner in which its houses were constructed. Herr Jastrow quotes an '*Atlas des villes de la Belgique au* 16e *siècle*. Cent plans du géographe Jacques du Deventer exécutés sur les ordres de Charles-Quint et de Philippe II., reproduits en facsimiles chromogr. par l'Institut national de géogr. à Bruxelles. Livre I.' Brussels, 1884, fol.

in 1520 was probably no more than 230,000; and M. Aubé, following
M. Henri Martin, estimates the population of Rouen at the time of the
English invasion at probably 80,000, at certainly no more than 100,000.
From that date to the end of the seventeenth century all estimates of the
population of Rouen are approximate only; but we know that it must
have fluctuated largely, and on more than one occasion the city is said to
have lost nearly one-third of its inhabitants from the Black Death.
One visitation of this plague had taken place in 1512, *i.e.* within six
years of the date of Major's writing.

M. Beljame of Paris has kindly informed me that the population of
Paris in 1553, calculated on an estimate of the consumption of food in
the markets of the city at that date, may be reckoned at 260,000; and
he does not think that it can have been very different in the first quarter
of the century. Major is, I think, rather more doubtful that London
was larger than Rouen than that Paris was three times the size of London.
But his testimony may be taken on the whole as confirmatory of the
general belief, as indicated above, that Paris, in the first quarter of the
sixteenth century, had a population of 230,000, and London and Rouen
of about 75,000.

As to the population of London and of Paris at more recent dates,
Botero, writing about 1590, classes London with Naples[1], Lisbon, Prague,
and Ghent as having about 160,000 inhabitants, while he reckons the
population of Paris at 400,000. The late Professor Thorold Rogers, however, says in an article on ' The Population of England from 1259 to
1793' (*Time*, *N.S.* 3 March 1890), that 'in 1631 the entire population
of London and Southwark, a census being taken by the wards, was only
a little over 131,000. Sir Robert Dallington, as quoted by Weever
(*Ancient Funeral Monuments*, ed. 1631, p. 350) writes that ' Paris is the
greater, the fairer built, and the better scituate : London is the richer,
the more populous'. In 1683 we have one estimate of the population
of London at 696,000, and another in 1694 at 530,000. ' From about
this period London superseded Paris as the largest city in Europe' (*Encyc.
Brit.* Art. LONDON). The same authority places the population of Paris
in 1718 at 509,000.

The English towns besides London which are mentioned by Major are
York, Norwich, Bristol, Coventry, and Lincoln. Professor Thorold
Rogers, on an estimate based upon the poll-tax granted by Parliament to
the king in 1377, has reached the conclusion that the population of London
at that date was 35,000 ; of York nearly 11,000 ; of Bristol, 9,500 ; of
Coventry about 7,000 ; of Lincoln, 5,000. For the population of York,
Bristol, Coventry, and Lincoln, at the date of Major's history, it would
be difficult to give an approximate estimate ; but, in regard to Norwich,

---

[1] As to Rome, I am told by Count Ugo Balzani that its population in 1520
may be reckoned at 85,000 ; but this number was greatly diminished a few years
later in consequence of the siege and sack of the city in 1527.

I have to thank the Reverend Dr. Jessopp for a valuable communication. Dr. Jessopp writes : ' Nothing is more difficult than to arrive at even an approximate estimate of the population of large towns in the prehistoric ages which can at all be relied on.   Some years ago, however, I investigated the great plague in Norwich in 1579 . . .   Here are some rough notes made from a careful examination of the Registers of Burials of twenty-six of the Parishes in Norwich ; and these really embrace the *whole* city, for I left out only one or two very small parishes, which I could not conveniently get at : Sum total of deaths in 1579=**1761** ; average of deaths during three to five previous and succeeding years=**190**. Assuming the death-rate to be only ten to the thousand—(it *must* have been more, but let us take that average inasmuch as we must make *some* allowance for burials not entered and, I think, some allowance for *disorderly* burials)—the average would give us 19,000 as the *outside* population of the city in 1579.   The city at the beginning of the sixteenth century was, we know, in a very depressed state . . . My own strong opinion is that Norwich in 1510 could not have had 15,000 inhabitants.'

It may be of interest to quote Herr Jastrow's estimate of the population of German towns in the sixteenth century : Nürnberg, 40,000 to 50,000 ; Danzig and Augsburg more than 50,000 (Augsburg had at one time reached as high a mark as 60,000) ; Breslau, 40,000 ; Strassburg, 30,000 ; Leipzig, 15,000 ; Berlin, 14,000 ; Brandenburg and Frankfurt, 10,000 ; *u.s.*, pp. 156, 157).

II.—*Passage on* ' Nobility,' *from the Fourteenth Question of the Twenty-Fourth Distinction of the* In Quartum Sententiarum [1].

Second Conclusion: Ceteris paribus, nobles are rather to be dispensed with than men of low birth.   Against the second conclusion it is argued thus : No men are noble ; therefore the conclusion presupposes what is false.   The consequence is known.   And the antecedent is proved by supposing in your mind one proposition, that no man is noble unless both his parents, or one of them, be noble.   I speak of nobility vulgarly so called, for it is that which is universally understood.   This supposition premised, I argue as follows :—In the case of any noble person as commonly understood, if all his ancestors were noble, and there is no procession *in infinitum*, Adam and Eve were noble ; but their parents properly speaking were not noble, for they had no parents save God who created them.   If you say : it behoves us to reach the first noble, then there is some noble whose father was not noble—contrary to the supposition.   In the same manner I can argue that in the case of any given noble nobility will be the mark of all his progeny, supposing that the sons of

---

[1] See *ante*, p. 46.

any noble you will are noble—always speaking of nobles as commonly
understood.   And this reasoning is confirmed by the answer of Ulysses to
Telamonian Ajax in the thirteenth of the Metamorphoses, where he says:
'Nam genus et proavos et que non fecimus ipsi Vix ea nostra voco.'
❧ It is answered: Noble [nobilis] is so called from 'nosco' as it were
'noscibilis', whether for evil or for good.   For of the former use of the
word [i.e. for evil] we read in Cicero in the Second Book of the Offices,
where he says: 'Testis est Phalaris cuius est preter ceteros nobilitas et
crudelitas.'   Of the meaning of the word in its good sense it is not
needful to bring forward examples.   Or 'nobilis' has its origin (as is preferred by some) from 'notabilis' by syncope, because a certain thing is
marked [notatur] with pre-eminence beyond others.   This agrees with
the use as to the brutes, and in speaking of other things.   For we call
falcons and dogs for the chase and swift greyhounds and fertile land
'noble'.   About the two first [falcons and dogs] this common use of the
word is patent.   As to the third, we have that of Virgil: 'Est locus
Italie medio sub montibus altis Nobilis.'   ❧ Secondly, let it be observed
that nobility is twofold.   There is a certain nobility of the soul; and
that is the virtue by which a man obeys God and reason; and that
alone is, rightly speaking, nobility.   And, on the contrary, the vicious
are ignoble, even Scripture bearing witness in the second chapter of
the First Book of the Kings: 'Qui contemnunt erunt ignobiles.'
Another kind of nobility there is as that appears in the case of him
whom we call noble because the common people so call him, though
he be not noble in mind.   And that man is thus called because his
progenitor or he himself has been ennobled, without taking heed of the
manner in which this nobility of his had its origin.   Very often, however,
it is through a man's wealth that he derives his nobility; whence says
Aristotle in the first part of his Rhetoric: 'Nobility is ancient wealth,
whether that wealth have been gained by theft or plunder'; like as those
most powerful emperors of the Assyrians had their origin from that
mighty hunter Nimrod who had gained all he held by rapine.   For himself was notable for wickedness; but noble, as the word is commonly understood, up to that time he could scarce have been called.   His posterity,
however, and ever the more the further they were distant from his original
ignobleness, were in common speech called noble.   Signally too (on this
side of ignobleness), for nothing is more certain than that some who are
now shepherds and peasants are descended from kings.   Some men have
attained to nobility by strenuous faculty in war, others by outstanding
corporeal beauty.   As Porphyry says of Priam: 'The face of Priam is
worthy of empire.'   And Saul, who excelled all other men in stature from
the shoulders up.   Others have become noble from their splendid virtue;
and one part of their immediate issue or of their grandchildren has
enjoyed the same nobility, as was the case with David the second king
of the Hebrews, who was chosen for king 'de post fetantes', and his
posterity likewise, for his descendants Hezekiah and Josiah were worthy
rivals with him in true nobility of soul.   And though some of his descend-

ants were evil, yet all were in common speech called noble. But in what manner the noble condition of this man or of that had its first emergence is uncertain. But such a man ought to think shame to act unworthily, and if the deeds of his ancestors have been praiseworthy, by that fact he ought to be inflamed to virtuous action, as is indeed not seldom the case. Take that of Ovid when he writes: 'Pyrrhus Achilleides animosus imagine patris', and Sallust, in his Jugurtha, thus speaks: 'For I have ofttimes heard that Q. Maximus and P. Scipio, illustrious citizens of our own, were wont to say, that when they looked upon the likenesses of their ancestors, they felt the fire of virtue kindle within them'; and Baptista likewise in the First Book of Alphonsus. Add this, too, that to hear the praises and noble acts of our fathers moves the soul and stirs up the generous hearts of us their descendants, and carries with it, as it were, a spur, and puts all slothfulness to flight; and Virgil, in the Twelfth of the Aeneid, brings forward Aeneas as animating his son Ascanius to the exercise of valour by the example of Hector his uncle—

> O thou, my child, do learn, thus I thee pray
> Virtue and very labour to assay
> At me, who am thy father as thou wot.
> Do thou likewise, I pray thee, mine own page,
> As fast as thou shalt come to perfect age,
> Remember this, and revolve in thy mind
> Thy lineage, thy forebears, and thy kind;'
> Examples of prowess in thee stir friends before,
> Both father Aeneas and thy uncle Hector.[1]

Nay more, by instinct, by nature, good sons are born of good parents, as Aristotle has it in the fourth chapter of the first book of the Politics. For they hold that just as a man is generated of men, and a brute of brutes, so too the good is generated by the good, after that saying: 'The sap that flourishes in the leaves comes from the root.' For all this there is a reason of nature, for sons follow in their bodily constitution the natural bents of their parents, and by consequence also in the constitution of their souls, as by skiey influence, yet not so that in the exercise of their free will they may not turn and choose what is contrary. For no other cause than this is it enjoined by the common law that those that are born of fornication are not to be admitted to the priesthood, since it is presumed that, like as with their parents, they will not preserve their chastity. Wherefore it is easier for one that is born of good parents to act aright than for one that is born of bad parents. Parents ought therefore to give utmost diligence to stir up their children, while these are young, to right conduct, and then will these children excel their parents even in virtue. ❡ Whence it follows that the suppositions which I have admitted are to be denied, and inasmuch as we have treated the substance of the argument with some prolixity, and the formal part is easy, I do-

---

[1] Gavin Douglas's translation, with modernised spelling.

not answer them. But from a gathering together of what has been said it is plain that it is virtue of the soul alone which ennobles a man. And any other accidental nobility is of small moment, coming as it does from whom you will, but ever from without. Besides this, it is necessary to posit some first noble in a family, and a last noble in another family just as in that, as, in his invective against Sallust, M. Tullius says : 'That which hath surcease in thee shall have its beginning in me.' For Ptolemy, son of Lagus, was, from a common soldier, made king of Egypt, but those that are his descendants are now without a kingdom and perchance beg their bread. Further, it is plain that it is more glorious for a man to be illustrious for virtue, albeit he was begotten by a father of ignoble birth, than to be stained with low vices and sprung from what king you will. According to that of Juvenal in his eighth satire :—

> I 'd rather, so thou sought'st Pelides' fame,
> That thou wert cursed with vile Thersites' name,
> Than that Achilles should have given thee life.[1]

And though that vulgar nobility is not to be recognised, by a person otherwise ignorant, either in the performance of those acts which are common to noble and to plebeian alike, or by the bodily habit whether in life or after death—though Diogenes did indeed say, jester fashion, to Alexander, son of Philip, that he wished to separate among the bones of the dead the heads of kings from the rest—yet this manner of speech in regard to nobles is a common one, both in the sacred histories and in other chronicles, and we are not to hold cheap the common mode of speech (though it be an arbitrary mode) ; for even in the Gospel we read, Luke xix. : 'A certain nobleman went into a far region to receive a kingdom' ; and, in the seventeenth of the Acts, 'Certain among them believed and were joined to Paul and Sylla.' And afterward Paul : 'Noble women not a few.' And Ecclesiasticus xvi. : 'Blessed is that land whose king is noble.' Historians are full of examples bearing upon this proposition, thanks to which we have made a digression, partly in jest, about these nobles. In saying, however, that men of noble birth may rather be dispensed with than men of ignoble birth, I speak of the highest nobility and not of the lowest nobility, who are, as it were, the boundary line of both. But not much respect is to be had to what is vulgarly called nobility as compared with nobility of soul, unless greater advantage to the common weal is to be had that way. And although my own origin was from those who were not of noble birth, and I seem to have intercourse with those whose birth is noble, I ought not to be a person suspect, for assuredly it is my intention, not only here but everywhere, to proclaim that view which I judge to be more consonant with reason.

---

[1] Badham's translation.

APPENDICES

COMPILED BY

THOMAS GRAVES LAW

2 c

BIBLIOGRAPHY OF JOHN MAJOR
AND HIS DISCIPLES

	PAGE
JOHN MAJOR, . . .	403
Logic and Philosophy, . .	403
Scripture, ...	410
History, ...	411
Chronological Index, . .	411
DAVID CRANSTON, . .	412
GEORGE LOKERT, . . .	414
WILLIAM MANDERSTON, . .	415
ROBERT CAUBRAITH, . .	417

II
PREFACES TO MAJOR'S WORKS

Illustrations

Reduced facsimile of the title-page of Major's Commentary on Matthew, Edition 1518, . . . at 403

Reduced facsimile of an old engraving of the 'Assembly of the Saints,' printed by Major in the Commentary on Matthew, ... at 450

TITLE PAGE OF MAJOR'S COMMENTARY ON MATTHEW

BIBLIOGRAPHY

The following Bibliographical lists originated in an attempt to correct and complete the imperfect 'Librorum Major quos scripsit Catalogus' prefixed by Freebairn to his edition of the 'Historia'. It was thought well, in further illustration of Major's work at Paris, to add a list of the books produced under his eye by his countrymen and disciples, Cranston, Lokert, Manderston, and Caubraith. The lists, which have increased beyond expectation at the last moment, cannot pretend to be exhaustive, and the compiler will be glad to receive any additional information.

T. G. L.

JOHN MAJOR.

Logic and Philosophy.

1. Exponabilia magistri Johannis maioris. Paris, 1503.
   Colophon : *Exponabilia . . . Impressa parisii [sic] opera iohannis lamberti impensis Dyonisii Roce mercatoris sub divi martini ymagine vici sancti iacobi morā tenētis. Anno dni millesimo quingētesimo tertio in Kalendis Augusti. Finiunt feliciter.*
   Aberdeen University Library.

2. Acutissimi artium interpretis magistri Johannis maioris in Petri Hyspani summulas cōmentaria. Lugd., Franc. fradin. 1505. fol.
   (See Prantl, *Geschichte der Logik*, iii. 40 ; iv. 247.)
   Trinity College, Dublin.

3. Joannis maioris in Petri Hispani summulas Commentarius. Venetiis, per Lazarum de Soardis die xxviii Julii, anno 1506. 4to.
   Panzer, viii. p. 382.

4. Medulla dyalectices edita a perspicassimo artium preceptore Hieronymo Pardo . . . de novo correcta et emendata cum tabula notabilium . . . per honoratos magistros magistrum Johannen Major' in sacra theologia baccalaurium necnō per acutissimū virum magistrum Ortiz qui postremo ipsam cum augmento castigavit eique tabulam supradictam apposuit.
   Per Guillermū anabat impensis durādi gerlieri alme universitatis bibliopole iurate. Paris, 1505. fol.
   British Museum.

5. Magister Johannes Majoris Scotus. Inclitarum artium etc. Venundantur vero a Dyonisio Roce, cive Parisiensi, in vico Sancti jacobi sub Divo Martino degente. Paris, 1506. fol.

At the end of the second part : *Impressa Parisiis, per johannem Barbier, pro Dyonisio Roce sub Divo Martino in vico S. Jacobi sedente, A.D. 1506, sole vero junii vicesimam claudente.*

At the head, letter of the author to 'Nynianus Humme' followed by a letter from the editor Antony Coronel to his brother Louis Coronel.

Bibliothèque Nationale, Paris ; Cambridge Univ. Lib.

6. Inclitarū artiū ac sacræ paginæ doctoris acutissimi Magistri Johannis Maioris scoti Libri quos in artibus in collegio Montis acuti Parisiis regētādo cōpilavit hoc in volumine cōtinent' :

Primo. questio de complexo significabili.

Primus liber terminorum cū figura.

Secundus liber terminorum.

Summule eiusdē : videlʒ figura quatuor p'positionū et earū c'versionū.

Predicabilia : cum arbore porphyriana.

Predicamenta : cum sua figura.

Sillogismi.

Posteriora : cum textu Aristo. primi et secūdi capi. libri primi ac eiusdem propositionibus.

Tractatus de locis.

Tractatus elenchorum.

Tractatus consequentiarum.

Abbreviationes parvor' logicalium.

Parva logicalia.   Exponibilia.

Insolubilia.   Obligationes.

Argumenta sophistiça.

Propositum de infinito.

Trilogus int' duos logicos et magistr'.

Venūdātur Lugduni ab Stephano queygnard. In vico Mercuriali. Prope sanctum Antonium.

In the same volume with new pagination but no separate title ː Exponabilia prestantissima J. M. olim artiū luculentissimī interpretis, iam sanctarum quidem litterarū fidelissimi ac facile peritissimi lectoris omnem argutiarū labyrinthum admussim enodantia et enucleātia felici aruspice incipiunt. Lyons, 1508. 4to.

Letters of Major to Ninian Hume.

Colophon ends : *Imp'ssi lugd. per Johannem de vingle. Anno nostre salutis Mccccc. octavo. die xix mensis Octobris.*

Advocates' Library.

7. Magister Joannes Majoris Scotus. Inclitarum artium, etc. *Venundantur vero Lugduni, in intersignio Quinque plagarum Salvatoris J. C. & Tholose in eodem intersignio, in vico Portarietis.* 1513.

At the end of the second part : Impressi Lugduni, anno nostre salutis 1513, die vero prima mensis octobris.

Same preliminary pieces as in the edition of 1506.

Biblioth. Nat., Paris.

8. Inclytarum artium ac Sacre pagine doctoris acutissimi M. J. M.
Scoti libri quos in artibus . . . regentando in lucem emisit . . .
Venundantur Lugduni . . . a martino boillon. 1516. 4to.

The title inside woodcut, on the top of which, in red, Magister
Joannes Maioris Scotus.

Colophon : *Inclytarum atq; argutissimarū artium,* etc., *hoc in
volumine feliciter expliciunt. Impressi lugd. Anno nostre Salutis*
M.CCCC. *decimo Sexto, die vero decima mēsis.*

In two parts, with separate foliation : pt. I. title and table, 8 foll.
and clviij foll. ; pt. II. table, 8 foll. and clx. foll.

Bodleian Library.

9. Commentum Johannis Dorp super textu summularum Johannis
Buridani nuperrime castigatum a Johanne Majoris cum aliquibus
additionibus eiusdem. Paris, 1504. fol.

Prantl, *Geschichte der Logik,* iv. p. 14.

10. Johannes Dorp recognitus et auctus. Summule Buridani. Cum
expositione praeclari viri interpretis, nominalium terminorum,
Johannis Dorp. Recognitus a magistro nostro Johanne Majore.
Cum annotationibus. Et postillis in margine libri de novo
insertis. Lugduni, 1510. 4to.

Described by Prantl, iv. p. 237.

11. Expor.ibilia magistri Johannis Maioris [Device of Denis Roche].
(59 leaves). Paris, 1513. 8vo.

a. ii. Incipiunt quedā questiones in . exponibilibus disputatæ a
joh. Mair Hadingtounen.

Colophon : . . . *Impressa Parisii opera iohannis Lamberti impensis
Dyonisii Roce mercatoris, etc.,* A.D. 1513. *in kal. Augusti.*

Univ. Aberd.

12. Termini magistri J. M. cum abbreviationibus parvorum logicalium,
etc., s.l. a et n. typogr. (*Parisiis Denis Roce,* c. 1500 [?]). 4to.

From Harrasowitz's *Antiquar. Catalog.* (176), 1892.

13. Insolubilia Johannis Maioris nunq. prius impressa. *Venundat' parrhisiis a Johane Grājon ejusdem civitatis bibliopola in claustro brunelli
prope scholas decretorum e regione dive virginis Marie. Cum priuelegio.*
Sequitur tractatus Obligationum ejusdem J. M. 1516. fol.

Brit. Mus.

13*. Tractatus de insolubilibus et obligationibus. *Impress. Parrhisiis
sumptibus Io. grantion bibliopolæ commorantis in claustro brunello
sub intersignio magnorum iuncorum.* 1516 [?]. fol.

From the Catalogue (171, No. 305) of Harrassowitz of
Leipzig. (Is this a second impression in the same year ?)

14. Aureum opus moraliū . . . iacobi almain S.T.D. . . . . a doctissimo
viro mag'ro Jobañe Maioris sacre sophie p'fessore nup' studiosissime revisū q'd bisce diebus nouissimis ij. recognitū oībusq; mēdis
tersum. Jobēs frellon inter diligētes bibliopolas diligētissimus
. . . imprimi curavit.
Venales habētur in domo dicti Johannis Frellō in vico mathuri-
norum. Paris. 8°.
No colophon. Printer's dedication, ' F. Guillermo Hueto', dated
Parisiis, xii kal Julii, 1518.
Univ. St. Andrews.

15. Summule Majoris Parhisiis ab eodem composite et revise, quibus
per eundem adjecti sunt duo tractatus insolubilium scilicet et
obligationum. . . . *Venalia reperiuntur in edibus johannis Parvi
sub intersignio Lilii.* . . . Paris, 1520. 4to.
At the end : *Que omnia voluit honestus vir Michael, civis Cadmeus,
diligentissime & emendatissime Cadomi per Laurentium Hostingue,
formularium vigilantissimum imprimi, anno salutis humanæ
MCCCCCXX, finiri autem die xii Octobris.* [Compare Delisle
L'Imprimerie à Caen, p. 42.]
Biblioth. Nationale, Paris.

16. Introductorium in Aristotelicā dialecticen totāque Logicē M. Joānis
Maioris, nuper ab eodem summa diligentia repositum & in duo-
decim libellos qui a tergo huius explicabuntur, digestum : atq;
prelo Ascensiano excusum. Venūdatur cum gratia et priuilegio
ab eodem Ascensio. Paris, 1521. 4to.
Engraving of Printing Press on title-page with date 1520.
Colophon : *In Officina Iodoci Badii Ascensii ad Calendas
Maias MDXXI·*
Adv. Lib.

17. Introductorium perutile in Aristotelicam dialecticen, duos Ter-
minorum Tractatus, ac Quinque Libros Summularum complectens,
M. Johannis Maioris Philosophi, ac Theologi Parisiensis : denuo
ab eodē summa vigilātia repositū.
Venundantur in edibus Joannis Parvi, & Aegidi Gormontii biblio-
polarū, via ad diuum Iacobum. Cum Gratia & Priuilegio, ad
Biennium. M.D.XXVII. Paris, 1527. fol.
Fo. 2. Johannes solo cognomenti Maior acutissimo theologo Petro
Chaiplane rectori Dunneuñ. S. P. D. *dated* ex Monte acuto—16
cal. Decemb. 1527.
Colophon : *Foelicem optatumq; finem Sortitum est hoc in Aristo-
telicā dialecticen ītroductorium nusquā antehac impressum Anno
virginei partus.* XXVII. *super* M.D. XVI. *Kalendas Decembris.*
Univ. Cam.; St. Andrews.

18, 19. Other editions of the same : *Paris* [*Jehan Petit ?*], 1508, referred
to by Prantl (iv. 248), or *Parisiis apud Joannem Lambert*, 1509,
cited in Watt's *Bibliotheca.* Also *Lugduni apud Antonium Ryum*,
1514, mentioned in Freebairn's list.

20. Octo libri physicorum cum naturali philosophia atque metaphysica
J. M. . . . *venundantur Parrhisiis in vico sancti jacobi a jo.*
Paruo sub intersignio Lilii aurei et ab Ægidio Gormōtio scuto trium
coronarum Colonie indice, Kal. Decemb. Paris, 1526. fol.
Epistle to Jean Bouillache.
Cam. Univ.; Edin. Univ.

21. Questiones Logicales M. J. M. Hadyngthonani, jam primo in lucem
missæ cum ejusdem literali expositione succincta in veterem
Aristotelis Dialecticē Joanne Argyropilo interpraete.   *Vænun-*
dantur Parisiis apud Joann. Parvum ac Ægidium Gormontium.
Via jacobæa, 1528 fol.
Dedicatory epistle of Major to Dr. John Weddel.
Univ. Cam.; Adv. Lib.

22. Ethica Aristotelis Peripateticorum principis.   Cum Jo. Maioris
Theologi Parisiensis cōmentariis.   [Device of the *Prelum Ascen-*
sianum.]   *Venundantur, cuius prelo impressa sunt Iodoco Badio, &*
in societatem accepto Io. Paruo.   [Paris], 1530 fol.
Prefatory epistle of Major to Cardinal Wolsey ; dated, Ex collegio
literario Montisacuti in Parrhisiorum gymnasio ad Cal. Junias,
1530.
a ii. *Tabula*, 14 folios. Fo. 1. Aristotelis Ethica . . . opus ab
Ioanne Argyropylo Byzantio traductum & ab I.M. Had. elucidatum.   Colophon (Fo. clxx), dated *Pridie Nonas Junias*, 1530.
Brit. Mus. ; Signet Lib.

Commentaries on the Sentences.

23. Quartus Sētētiarum Johannis Maioris [mark of ' Ponset le Preux'].
Venundantur parrhisiis a Ponceto le preux, eiusdem ciuitatis
bibliopola : ad signum poti stagnei ī vico sancti Jacobi prope
diui yuonis edem commorante. Paris, 1509. fol.
Ded. letter to Alexander Steuuard, abp. of St. Andrews & primate
of Scotland, dated prid. Kal. Jan. 1508 ; followed by :
Dialogus inter duos magistros Johannem formam precentorem
glasguensem et Petrum Sandelands rectorem de calder.
Impressum . . . etc. *per me Philippum Pigouchet commorantem in*
vico cythare Anno dni millesimo qu'gētesimo nono : die penultīa
mēsis Junii (leaf 228 *b* marked ccxxiii).

David crenston in sacra pagina bacchalarius ad lectores.
[Mark of Philippe Pigouchet.]
Table (fol. 229 *b*-248 *b*).
Brit. Mus.; Univ. Cam.; St. And.

24. Quartus sententiarum Johannis Majoris ab eodem recognitus denuo-
que impressus.
Venundatur Parrhisiis a Ponceto le Preux, ejusdem civitatis bibliopola, in vico Divi Jacobi sub Potti Stannei signo. Paris, 1512. fol.
Colophon : *Impressum atque exaratum est hoc opus Parrisiis*
per Johannē barbier impressorem Impensis vero honestorum virorum
Johannis petit Johānis grātō et pōceti le preux huius almc parisiēsis
academie bibliopolarum. Anno dni millesimo qugētesimo duodecimo
decimo kalēdas junii.
The same preliminary pieces as in the edition of 1509.
Aberd. Univ. ; Biblioth. Nat. Paris.

25. In Quartum Sententiarum. . . . suprema ipsius lucubratiōe
enucleatæ : denuo tamen recognitæ : et maioribus formulis
impressæ : cum duplici tabella : videlicet alphabetica materi-
arum decisarū in fronte : et Questionum in calce.
Robertus Senalis J. Maiori Præceptori suo.
In Chalcographia J. Badii Ascensii [Paris], 1516. fol.
Brit. Mus.

26. In Quartum, etc. Venundantur a sui impressore Iodoco Badio.
Paris, 1519. fol. Date in colophon, *Anno salutis humanæ sesqui-*
millesimo decimo nono ad Idus Augustas.
The *Tabula alphabetica* by Mag^r Georgius Lokert, Scotus.
Preface addressed to Gawin Douglas bishop of Dunkeld and Rob.
Cockburn bishop of Ross.
Brit. Mus.; Bodl. Lib.; Univ. Cam.; Adv. Lib.; Glasgow ;
St. And. ; Aberd.

27. I. M. . . . in Quartum Sententiarum quæstiones utilissimæ, etc.
Venundantur Parrhisiis in ædibus Joannis Parui in vico sancti
Jacobi, etc. Paris, 1521. fol.
Colophon . . . *quæ rursus ab erratulis tersa est, et maioribus*
characteribus impressa. In Officina Jacobi le Messier. Anno 1521
die vero xiiii mensis Octobris.
Univ. Cam.; St. And.; Signet Lib.

28. Joannes Maior in primū Sententiarum. Paris, 1510. fol.
I. M. to George Hepburn, Abbat of Arbroth, dated 7 cal. Jan.
1509 (fol. 1 *b*).
Dialogus . . . inter Gawin. douglais. ecclesie b. Egidii edinburg.
prefect. et M. Davidem Crenstonem in sacra theosophia baccalaureum formatum . . . (fol. 2 *b*).

Colophon : *Impressum et exaratum est hoc opus Parisiis per Henricum stephanum impensis* . . . *Jodoci ḥadii ascensii, Joannis parui, et magistri Constantini leporis. Anno* . . (1510 *Apr.* 29).
Tabula . . . J. Maioris, eiusdem singulariora dicta continens extracta per M. Alexandrum Couan Scotum hadyngtonensem (fol. 126 *a*).

Brit. Mus.; Univ. Cam.; St. And.

29. Joannes Maior in secundum sententiarum [mark of J. Petit].
Venundatur in edibus J. Parui ct Jod. Badii Ascensii. Paris, 1510. fol.
I. M. magistro nostro Natali Bede primario collegii montisacuti . . . etc. (sub natalem dñicum 1510).
Tabula . . . collecta raptim per M. Antonium Coronel Hispanum (fol. 2 *a*).

Colophon : *Finis decisionum variarum questionũ magistri nostri Joannis Maioris theologi parrhisieñ. natione scoti : in secundum sententiarum : in edibus ascensianis In vigilia Natalis dominici* 1510.

Brit. Mus.; Univ. Cam.; St. And.

30. In primum Sententiarum. Paris, 1519. fol.

Colophon : *Impressum est rursum hoc opus Parisiis sub recognitione et impensis Jo. Badii Ascens. ad idus Octobris anni Redemptionis humanæ, MDXIX.*

Bodl. Lib.; Adv. Lib.

31. Io. M. Hadingtonani scholæ Parisiensis Theologi, in Primum magistri Sententiarum disputationes et decisiones nuper repositæ . . . *Venundantur Jo. Parvo et Jodoco Badio.* Paris, 1530. fol.
Preface by Major to his namesake John Major Eckius.

Univ. Cam.; Univ. Edin.

32. Editio secunda J. M. . . . in secundum librum Sententiarum nunquam antea impressa. *Veneũt apud preclar. bibliopolã iohannem grátion : in claustro brunello in signo magni iunci adpendente.* Paris, 1519. fol.
I. M. magistris Natali Bede et Petro tempete . . . primariis, etc.

Colophon : *Expensis Jo granion bibliopolc, etc.*

Bodl. Lib.; Univ. Cam.

33. In secundum Sententiarum disputationes denuo recognitæ et repurgatæ. *Venundantur Jo. Parvo et Jod. Badio.* Paris, 1528. fol.
Preface of Petrus Peralta, the reviser of this edition, to Dr. Ortiz.

Univ. Cam.

34. Editio Jo. M. doctoris Parisiensis super Tertium Sententiarum : de novo edita. *Veneunt Parrhisiis cum gratia et priueligio a jo. Grãion bibliopola apud Clausũ brunellum, etc.*

Imprimatur: *faict en parlemēt le quatrieme jour Daoust Lan Mil cinq centz dixsept.* 1517. fol.
J. M. Matheo Galthero.
Univ. Cam.; Adv. Lib.; St. And.

35. In tertium sententiarum disputationes . . . denuo recognitæ et repurgatæ. *Vænundantur Jod. Badio et Jo Parvo.* Paris, 1528. fol.
Univ. Cam.; Univ. Edin.; Aberdeen.

36. Adamus Goddamus, Super iv libros Sententiarum, etc. *Parrhysiis, per J. Barbier,* 1512. (52 leaves.) fol.
Edited with Preface and Life of the author, 'De Vita Ade,' by Major.
Brit. Mus.; Bodl. Lib.; Univ. Cam.

37. Reportata super primum [secundum, tertium, quartum] sententiarū fratris Johannis duns Scoti : ordinis minorum, doctoris subtilis Parisien nunq; antea impressa. *Veneunt Parhisiis . . . a Joanne Grāion bibliopola,* etc.   Paris, 1517-18. fol.
Edited under the direction of Major by two licentiates of theology, James Rufin, minorite, and Brother Peter Du Sault.
Dedicatory epistle addressed by Major to Franciscus de Bellavalle, Guardian of the Reformed Convent of Friars Minor at Paris.
The four parts have separate title-pages, foliation, and *tabulæ.*— Super Primum is dated in the Colophon Apr. 1517 ; Super Secundum, Feb. 1517 ; Super Tertium, Jan. 1517 ; Super Quartum, Sept. 1518.
Major's Preface to the first book is repeated in the fourth.
Adv. Lib.; Signet Lib.

Scripture.

38. Io. M. . . . in Mattheū ad literam expositio, vna cum trecentis et octo dubiis et difficultatibus ad eius elucidationem admodum conducētibus passim insertis, quibus perlectis peruia erit quatuor euangelistarum series.
In florentissima Parrhisiorum vniversitate Anno saluatoris n'ri M.cccc xviii. Jehan Grāion.
Veneūt apud præclarum bibliopolam Ioañem grāion apud clausum brunellū in signo magni Iunci appēdēte. 1518. fol.
Preface to James Beaton, archbishop of Glasgow.
Univ. Cam.; Univ. Edin.; St. And.

39. Io. M. Hadingtonani Theologi in quatuor Euangelia expositiones luculente et disquisitiones et disputationes contra hereticos plurime, premisso serie literarum indice, et additis ad finem operis quatuor questionibus non impertinentibus. *Venundantur a quo impressæ sunt Iodoco Badio.* Paris, 1529. fol.

Matthew is dedicated with a new preface to James Beaton, archbishop of St. Andrews; Mark to Jean Bouillache of Nevers,
professor and parish priest of St. James at Paris; Luke to Gavin
Dunbar, archbishop of Glasgow; John to Robert Cenalis, bishop
of Vence.

Brit. Mus.; Bodl. Lib.; Univ. Cam.; Adv. Lib.;
Univ. Edin.; Glasgow; St. And.

History.

40. Historia Majoris Britanniæ tam Angliæ q. Scotiæ per J. M. nomine
quidem Scotum professione autem theologum e veterum monumentis concinnata. *Venundatur J. B. Ascensio.*   Paris, 1521.
4to.

Brit. Mus.; Adv. Lib., etc.

41. Historia Majoris Britanniæ . . . Editio nova mendis quam
plurimis in antiqua Jodoci Badii Ascensii editione Parisiis
edita MDXXI extantibus repurgata. *Edimburgi apud Robertum
Fribarnium Typographum Regium.*   1740.   4to.

Brit. Mus.; Adv. Lib., etc.

An excerpt from the commentary on the Fourth Book of the
Sentences, under the title ' Disputatio de Ecclesiæ Monarchiæ
episcoporum et parochorum auctoritate' was published in the
edition of Gerson's works printed at Paris in 1606, and Lyons in
1706 (Opera auctiora cum aliquot opusculis P. de Alliaco et Jo.
Majoris), Vol. i. In the same volume was re-edited another
excerpt, from Major's Commentary on S. Matthew, under the
title ' De Ecclesiæ et concilii auctoritate.'

Both excerpts were reprinted in the ' Vindiciæ doctrinæ majorum
Scholæ Parisiensis . . . contra defensores Monarchiæ universalis
et absolutæ Curiæ Romanæ.   Liber Quartus continens Scripta
Jacobi Almaini et Joannis Majoris . . . Authore Edmundo
Richerio, Doctore ac Socio Sorbonico' Coloniæ, 1683.   4to.

The *Magnum Speculum Exemplorum*, originally published anony-
mously by John Major, a Belgian Jesuit (*d.* 1608), has been
erroneously attributed (by Mackenzie, Freebairn, Dupin, and
others) to our author, whose writings have also been sometimes
confused with those of yet another John Major, a German Protestant.

Chronological Index.

1503. Exponibilia.
1504. Commentum J. Dorp.   Ed. J. M.   (Prantl.)

1505. In Petri Hisp. summulas.
,, Medulla dyalectices of H. Pardus. Ed. J. M.
1506. Inclitarum artium . . . Libri, etc.
,, In Petri Hisp. Summ. *New edit.* (Panzer.)
1508. Inclitarum artium, etc. *New edit.*
,, Introd. in Aristot. dialect. (Prantl.)
1509. In iv. Sent.
,, Introd. in Aristot. logic. (Watt, *Bibliotheca.*)
1510. (Apr.) In i. Sent.
,, (Dec.) In ii. Sent.
,, J. Dorp, recognitus a J. M. *New edit.* (Prantl.)
1512. Goddamus in iv. Sent. libb. Ed. J. M.
,, In iv. Sent. *New edit.*
1513. Inclitarum artium, etc. *New edit.*
,, Exponibilia. *New edit.*
1514. Introd. in Aristot. *New edit.* (Freebairn.)
1516. In iv. Sent. *New edit.*
,, Inclitarum artium. *New edit.*
,, Insolubilia, etc.
1517. In iii. Sent.
,, Reportata Duns Scoti. Ed. J. M.
1518. In Matthæum expositio.
,, Moralia J. Almain. Ed. J. M.
1519. In i. Sent. *New edit.*
,, In ii. Sent. *New edit.*
,, In iv. Sent. *New edit.*
1520. Summulæ Majoris.
1521. (May). Introd. in Aristot. *New edit.*
,, (Oct.). In iv. Sent. *New edit.*
,, Historia Brit.
1526. Octo libri physicorum.
1527. Introd. in Aristot. logic. *New edit.*
1528. In ii. Sent. *New edit.*
,, In iii. Sent. *New edit.*
,, Questiones Logicales.
1529. In iv. Evangelia.
1530. In i. Sent. *New edit.*
,, In Ethica Aristot.

DAVID CRANSTON.

1. Positiones phisicales magistri dauid Cràston. [Device of Denis
   Roce.] Venales reperiuntur in vico sancti iacobi ad intersigniũ
   diui martini in domo Dyonisii roce. (38 leaves.) Paris. *s.a. 8vo.*
   Univ. Edin.; Univ. Aberd.

2. Tractatus insolubilium et obligationum magistri Davidis Cranston de
novo recognitus et correctus per magistrum Guillermium Man-
drestou et magistrum Anthonium Silvestri, ejus discipulos, cum
obligationibus Strodi . . . incipit feliciter.
*Venum exponuntur ab Oliverio Senant in vico Divi jacobi sub signo
beate Barbare sedente.* sig. a-i. *no date.* Paris. fol.
On the back of title-page two pieces of verse :
De immatura magistri nostri Davidis Cranston Scoti morte hujus
voluminis autoris carmen elegiacum.
Theobaldus de Pontavice Cenomanus ad dialecticarum artium
cultores.

Biblioth. Nat., Paris.

3. Questiones morales M. Martini magistri [Le Maistre] . . . de fortitudine novissime . . . limate adiecta tabula alphabetico ordine
contexta per Dauid Cranston . . . Uenundantur Parisiis a Johanne
granion eiusdem ciuitatis bibliopola : in claustro brunelli : prope
scholas decretorum sub signo sacratissime dei genitricis marie.
Egidius delfus ad lectorem (fol. 101).
Colophon : *Impressum parisius* [sic] *per Guillermi Anabat* . . .
Questiones additæ in librũ de Fortitudine Magistri Martini de
magistris per Davidem cranston scotum in theologia baccalaureum.
Venundantur parrhisius a Joanne granion eiusdẽ, etc., as before.
Colophon : *Has præclaras & admodum ingeniosas questiones in
magistri Martini de magistris Librum de Fortitudine addidit littera-
tissimus vir magister Dauid Cranston Pro Johanne Granion almæ
parrhisiensis academiæ Librario iurato . . . Quas quidem impressit
diligenter Nicolaus de pratis in vico olearum apud magnum ortum
moram trahens. M.D.X. Idibus Maij.*   Paris, 1510. fol.

Brit. Mus.; Bodl. Lib.; Univ. Cam.

4. Martini Magistri Questiones morales de Fortitudine adjecta Tabula
alphabetica per D. Cranston. Paris. *J. Petit. s.a.* fol.
Questiones additæ . . . per D. Cranston. Paris. *J. Petit. s.a.*
fol.

Catalogue of D. Laing's Library (1st Sale, 2359).

5. Moralia acutissimi et clarissimi Doctoris . . . Jacobi Almain cũ
additionibus eiusdem et David Cranston Scoti non ante hac
impressis neq; in aliis appositis . . .
Venundantur Parrhisiis ab Claudio Chevallõ. s.a.

Univ. St. Andrews.

6. Aurea . . . Jacobi Almain opuscula, omnibus theologis perquam
utilia, cum additionibus Davidis Cranston, ex recensione Vincentii
Doesmier. Parisiis, per Egidium Gourmont, 1517. fol.

Panzer, viii. 41.

7. Moralia acutissimi Theol. Prof. M. Jacobi Almain Senonensis . . .
   cum additionibus M. Dauid Cranston Scota . . . Paris, 1525. 8vo.
   Colophon : *Parisiis in edibus Claudii Cheualto, anno domini
   MCCCCCXXV. mense Maio.*
   Univ. Cam.

8. Acutissimi viri M. Jacobi Almain . . . Moralia que vocāt cū ipsius
   authoris et D. Cranston additionibus . . . adjectus est et libellus
   de auctoritate ecclesiæ contra Thomam de vio. . . . *J. Petit.*
   Parisiis, 1526. 8vo.
   Brit. Mus.; Bodl. Lib.

9. Ramirez de Villascusca (A). *Incipit :* Si diligenti navatione, etc.
   ends : Finem hic capiunt Parva Logicalia cum tractatu terminorum, additionibusque D. Cranstoni, [1520 ?]   4to.
   Brit. Mus.

   Also, along with Gavin Douglas, Cranston compiled the
   Tabula for Major's commentary *In Quartum Sent.* (1509). See
   his Preface (*infra,* p. 424) and his Dialogue with Douglas (p. 425).
   He is said to have written 'Orationes,' 'Votum ad D. Kentigernum,' and ' Epistolæ.' (T. F. Henderson in *Dict. Nat. Biog.*)

GEORGE LOKERT.

1. Scriptum in materia noticiarum. [Mark of Denis Roche.] Venun-
   dantur Parrhisiis in vico sancti Jacobi sub intersignio diui
   Martini.
   Colophon : *Finit scriptura . . . Georgii Lokert ayrensis Scoti.*
   Parrhisiis impressū opera Nicolai de pratis pro Dionysio Roce.
   Anno 1514 *die vero xxiv men' Novembris.* [On the next and last
   page two verses : Finis.] 1514. 8vo.
   Adv. Lib.; Univ. Edin.

2. Scriptum in materia noticiarum Georgii Lokert. [Mark of Bernard
   Aubry.] Venundantur Parrhisiis ī vico sancti iacobi . . .
   Colophon: *Finit scriptura super quibusdam noticiarum diui-*
   sionibus G. L. ayrensis Scoti. Parrhisiis impressa : op'a michael
   leslancher p' Bernardo Aubry. Anno 1518. *Die vero xiiii men'*
   augusti. 1518. 8vo.
   Sig. Lib.

3. Scriptum in materia notitiarum Georgij Lokert. [Device of Pierre
   Gaudoul.] Venundantur Parisiis a Petro Godoul commorātē : ī
   clauso brunello sub intersignio diui Cyrici.
   36 leaves. 1ᵇ. woodcut, ihs.   36 . Joannis Vaccei ad condiscipulos
   exhortatoriū Carmen. Ejusdem henecasyllabon.
   Colophon : *Finit Scriptura. . . . Parisii impresssa o j*

*Joannis du Pre p'Petro Goudoul.   Anno dñi. MDXX.   Die vero
.xxij mensis Julii* 1520.   4ᵗᵒ.
Univ. Cam.

4. Aureus notitiarum libellus.   *Caen, M. et G. Angier,* s.a. [8° ?].
   Delisle *L'Imprimerie à Caen.*

5. Questiones et decisiōes physicales insignium virorum . . . Alberti
   de Saxonia in Octo libros physicorum.   Tres libros de celo et
   mundo . . . Recognitæ rursus et emendatæ . . . accuratione et
   iudicio . . . G. Lokert . . . a quo sunt tractatus proportionum
   additi.   2 pt. [Paris] 1518.   1518.   fol.
Brit. Mus.

6. Tractatus exponibilium multo alijs lucidior Georgij Iokert scoti &
   artium & sacræ paginæ professoris acutissimi.   [Mark of De
   Marnef.]   Venundantur Parisius in vico Iacobeo sub intersignio
   Pellicani Ab engleberto et Ioanne marnefio bibliopolis ad aedem
   diui Yuonis commorantibus.
   ❡ Cum priuilegio biannij vt liquido p₃ instrumento.
   No date on title and no colophon.   Preface : Thomas de Cueilly
   Auditoribus suis S.D. *dated* ex nostro Marchie gymnasio prid.
   nonas junias 1522.
   Title and preface, 2 + 35 foll.   4to.
Univ. Edin.

7. Termini Magistri G. Lokert, etc. a Johanne Grāion, parrhisiis
   [1523?].   4to.
Brit. Mus.

8. Sillogismi Georgii Lokert sacre Theologie professoris.   [Mark of
   De Marnef.]   Venūdātur Parisiis ī vico Iacobeo sub signo Pelli-
   cani etc.
   Preface : Thomas de Cueilly Parrisinus suis discipulis Salutem . . .
   Ex Marchiano gymnasio 12 Kal. Sept. 1527.   (2 + xliv. foll.) 4to.
Univ. Edin.

Lokert also compiled the *Tabula alphabetica* for Major's *In Quartum
Sent.* 1519.   See above, p. 408.

WILLIAM MANDERSTON.

1. Bipartitum in morali philosophia opusculum ex variis autoribus
   per Magistrum Guillelmum Manderston Scotum nuperrime collectū . . .
De virtutibus in generali.

   Bipartitum.)
De quatuor virtutibus cardinalibus in speciali.

   Veneunt in ædibus Ioannis Gormontii ad insigne duarum Cipparum.
   A ii. figure of St. Andrew with bishop kneeling, and six lines of

verse, followed by Dedication to Andrew Forman, archbishop of
St. Andrews.

Colophon: *Explicit opusc. in mor. philos. bipartitum à mag.
G. M. Scoto diocesis S. Andreæ nupcrrime collectū dum regeret
Parisiis in famatissimo diue Barbare gymnasio. Anno 1518, 14 kal.
Aprilis.*

Verso. Iohannis Haye Scoti Diocesis Glascuensis super sui preceptoris Encomio. (22 lines of verse.) 1518. 4to.

Adv. Lib.; Univ. Glasgow.

2. Bipartitum in Morali.Philosophia opusculum . . . [Device of Virgin
and Child in a ship.]
92 leaves. 1[b]. Letter of Manderston to Forman. 2[a]. Verses of Th.
Morellus Campanus. 2[b] Cut of 'Tree of Philosophy.' 92. Letter
of Morellus to Nicholaus Buatius.

Colophon (91[b]): *Explicit opusculū in famatissimo diue
Barbare gymnasio.* [no date].

Univ. Cam.

3. Bipartitum in Morali Philosophia . . .
Vænundantur in ædibus Gormontianis ·sub gratia & prævilegio vt iň
sequenti patebit pagina.

a i. *verso.* Vilelmi graym Scoti de fĭtre exhortatoriū carmē ad iuuenes
vt moralibʒ īcubāt.

a ii. Guillermus Manderston . . . Iacobo Beton sancti Andree archipresuli . . . xvi Kal. Feb. anno (calculo Rōano) 1523.

a iii. *verso.* Robertus Gra. medicinæ amator præceptori suo vilelmo
Manderstō apollonie artis professori peritissimo . . . Parrhisiis
ex collegio bone Curie, 1253 [sic] calculo Romano.

foll. cclx. Colophon: *Explicit opusculum . . . Parhisiis* 1523, 24
Jan. 8vo.

Univ. Edin.

4. Tripartitum epithoma doctrinale et cōpendiosū in totius dyalectices
artis prīcipia a Guillelmo Māderstō Scoto collectū et secūdo
revisum cū multis additionibus necnon questione de futuro contingenti insignitum.

❧ Tripartitum epithoma
❧ Principia communissima dyalectices
Tractatulus terminorum. Parua Logicalia
❧ Questio de futuro contingenti.

[No printer's mark, date, or place on title page.]

Verso. Guillelm' Monderston medices professor . . . Andreæ
formā: Sancti Andree archipresuli . . . Ex Lutecia Parisiorum.
Anno 1520, 14 Kal. Dec. 4to.

Adv. Lib.

5. Tripartitum epithoma. Doctrinale and compendiosū in totius
Dyalectices artis principia a G. M. Scoto nuperrime collectum.
Principia communissima dyalectices.
    ¶ Tripartitū epithoma
    Tractatulus terminorum
    Parua logicalia
[Device of Virgin and Child in a ship.]
Uenūdantur Parisius ī Clauso brunelli a Petro Gaudoul sub
intersignio diui Cirici commorantis. 70 leaves, 4ᵗᵒ. 1520.
    Colophon (70ᵃ) : *Explicit in totius dialectices principia opus-
culum . . . in lucem editum dum cursum artium pro tertio Parisius
regerit in famatissimo collegio diue Barbare. Anno Domini millesimo
quingentesimo vigesimo. iiij. die Augusti.*
                        Univ. Cam.

4. The Bodleian Library Catalogue has an edition of the Tripartitum,
    Lugd. 1530, 8vo, with the note, ' Liber iste ascribi debet Hieron.
    Angesto ut notavit Raymundus.'

5. Guillelmi Manderston compendiosa Dialectices Epitome ab authore
    recens emendata et ab innumeris quibus undique scatebat mendis
    liberata. Item et eiusdem quæstio de futuro contingenti. Par-
    rhisiis, 1528.
The preface repeated from the first edition (1520).
                        Prantl, iv. p. 257.

6. Termini, etc. *Cadomi, M. Angier*, s.a.
    Delisle, *L'Imprimeric à Caen*, p. 42.

ROBERT CAUBRAITH.

1. Quadripertitum in Oppositiones, Conversiones Hypotheticas et
    Modales magistri Roberti Caubraith omnem ferme difficultatem
    dialecticam enodans. *ex off. Ascensiana*, 1510. fol.
                        Bodl. Lib.

2. Quadripertitum in Oppositiones . . . diligenter recognitum et labe-
    culis tersum. Vænundatur Parrhisiis in ædibus Iodoci Badii : &
    Edmundi Fabri. 1516. fol.
    At end : *Ex officina Ascensiana rursus ad Nonas Octobris, MDXVI,
    calculo Romano.*
                        Univ. Glasgow.

II

PREFACES TO MAJOR'S WORKS

[*Inclitarum artium . . . Libri etc.* 1508]

JOHANNES MAIORIS nyniano hume tum natalibus tum litteris
amplissimo Salutem dicit.

Dum in erudiendis artistis quorum presentem gero provinciam aliqua-
tenus laborarem, mi Nyniane, sæpius ab eis flagitatus sum et potissimum
a Ludovico coronel et Antonio eius germano, Baspardoque lax hispanis,
et Roberto caubrath compatriota tibi et mihi communi, ut commentarios
in petri hyspani summulis cuderem, argumentum assumpsere in medium
quod david craston conterraneo, et Jacobo amnayn senonensi, Petro
crokart bruxellensi, Roberto cenalis parisiensi in primo cursu existen-
tibus prædicabilia, exponabilia, obligationes cum insolubilibus scripto
dederam, inferentes pro eis rationem æquam surgere. Ratio tamen contra
pugnabat tamen propter meam inertiam, tum propter hominum linguas
ad male loquendum et potissimum de viventibus proclives, tum propter
alienum genus studii ab artibus humeris assumptum, scilicet in legendis
sententiis, libuit tamen lectionem lente proferre ut qui vellet lectionem
scripto mandaret. Quocirca non mireris si interdum succincte dissuteve
quæ dedi protulerim immediate post prandium et cœnam tempore repara-
tionum hæc scriptitarunt me memoriter : ut sciunt omnes et tu ipse :
proferente si hosce libros in tot hominum ora vagari opinatus fuissem
aliter iove propicio insudassem. Sed eos iam revocare nescirem et quando
hæc in bibliotheca excogitatæ [?] ipse exarassem, propter mei ingenii parvi-
tatem facile erat delirare non dubito : scribimus indocti doctique poemata
passim. Viris nobilitate sanguinis vel virtute micantibus sua munimenta
scriptores creberrime dicare solent. Cum te ex antiqua nobilium domo
ortum in nodosis artium dyaletice meandris vigilantissimum considero
ut amplius circa artes capescendas elaborares tibi hos commentarios
utcunque scriptos dicare proposui hoc munusculum non te dignum
accipias sed offerentis animum aspicias. Robertus valterson hading-
tonensis in hoc collegio montis acuti conregens et noster Johannes
zacarias censis te saluere iubent. Vale.

[*Ibid.* fol. clxx.]

JOHANNES MAIOR ingenua indole iuveni et discipulo semper amato.
Niniano Hum. S. D.

Dum crebrius mecum ipse tacitus revolverem cuiusnam nomine quos olim
meis dyaletice artis tyrunculis codicellos de parvis logicalibus vocitatos

tribueram improcessioni mandarentur, multis de causis quæ meum animum
exangebant, tum propter gravissimum illum febrium morbum quo fere
mea vita extincta est, tum etiam propter impestrivas[?] et improvisas im-
pressorum assiduaq. deprecationes : quæ hinc illicque me auxium reddebant, an videlicet imprimendi venirent : cum a tempore illo quo sunt
emissi ipsos non viserim, nec in ipsis ab omnibus mendis corrigendis
Horatii consilio plures annos vacuerim propter infinita pæne quæ nosti
impedimenta.   Alia ex parte instabant artis impressoriæ magistri :
rationibus nostrum animum obruentes.   Tum propter ipsorum codicel-
lorum commoditatem quod si qui his pueri infundent brevi proculdubio
nodosas complurium argutiarum huiusce artis dyaletice difficultates dissolvent.   Et cum non solum nobis ipsis nati simus, sed etiam propinquis,
dicebant me quoddammodo ad hoc iure divino et humano astringi. Hac
potissimum ratione parum eis adhærens, et adhuc me inscio, eorum
aliquid impressioni demandarunt.   Tandem tot victus rationibus cessi :
et codicellos tradidi imprimendos, supposito tamen quod nunquam nostro
aspectui afferentur, propter continuas mihi lectiones faciendas. Scilicet
quempiam comperirent qui ineptas eorum mendas extergeret.   Et a me
expetito uni tribui Magistrum philippum de clermont quem nosti qui
ipsos reviseret.   Cum igitur hasce curas in me revolverem, in mentem
subiit : Ille tuus circa palestram litterariam et precipue artem dyaleticam
nodositatesque eius discutiendas dissolvendasque animus.   Quamobrem
tibi soli commode dicandum putavi.   Hos ergo codicellos ad te velut eorum
patronum mitto quos semper apud te habeas ; non enim solum uni studio
insudandum est, sed uni vacans alterum non omittas.   Et cum te leges
fastidierint hos codices nonnunquam vises.   Quoniam facile tibi præbe-
bunt methodu[m] ad leges multo facilius capiundas.   Me apud Magistrum
Georgium tournebulle commendatum facies.   Vale meque ut soles ama.
Ex ædibus nostris parisiacis decimaquinte kalendas Junias.

[*In Quartum Sent.* 1509.]

    ❡ GENEROSISSIMO nec minus erudito et imprimis obseruando domino
    Alexandro Steward diui Andree archipresuli et Scotie primati :
    Iohannes Maior theologorum minimus cum omni veneratione
    salutem dicit.

    Cum annis hiis preteritis aliquas lucubratiunculas in sententiis nostro
auditorio tradiderimus et aliquas penes nos domi seruauerimus, plusculos
dies volutabam, eruditissime presul, an eas impressas lectum iri sinerem,
tandem expandimus vela ventis, sed quia aurum argentum et cetera id
genus in gazophilatium domini offerre nequiuimus pro virili cum muliere
cananea micas de mensa domini cadentes, et cum cleoabitide spicas manus
messorum effugientes simul colligere gestiebamus et omnia in taberna-
culum domini secundum talentum nobis traditum offerre.   Uerum cui
vigiliolas dicarem post longam explorationem te aptior occurrebat nemo,
tum opus ipsum propter te partim excudimus tum ut tibi in studiis

currenti calcaria ocius currendi ministrarem et ad theologiam (que pro-
uincie tibi imposite maximopere conducit) incenderem, tum quia conterraneus et in lauacro tue dyocesis regeneratus sum et ut apud Tullium
primo officiorum preclare scriptum est non solum nobis nati sumus sed
partem patria vendicat et amici. At nescio qua natale solum dulcedine
cunctos ducit et immemores non sinit esse sui. Et si hec sub verborum
lenocinio ad mulcendas tuas aures delicatissimas non dedimus, non
demirabere, michi satis erit more patrum et neothericorum nostre professionis omne illud quod venit in mentem memoria dignum sub verbis
theosophie primo occurrentibus raptim committere calamo, nec fucatorum
verborum indiga est theologia, domus marmorea superficietenus, non
querit dealbari, ymo si dealbetur nitorem amittit et terminos peculiares
quelibet scientia sibi vendicat, nostros viros quos barbaros appellitant
in venere dicendi non ille pidus iohannes picus legere et adamussim
relegere non erubuit, quorum partes contra hermolaum barbarum (ut in
quadam eius epistola tibi peculiari liquet) elaborat tueri. Rursus si a
veritatis tramite me labi contigerit canere palinodium (sicut par est)
studebo. Sed hiis qui nos minus probabiliter in materia ancipiti opinari
censent dictum velim velle suum cuique est domus que apud forum
extructa est quod editior sit vel depressior (quam equum videatur) sepe
contenditur que dicunt medulitas excoquant antequam nos a tergo feriant
maledicorum censuras aspernamur iudicium proborum non declinamus
dummodo sit lusco qui possit dicere lusce loripedem rectus deride at
ethiopem albus. Sed nobis consolationi erit paucissimis scriptoribus non
canonicis multa frabricantibus [*sic*] in nullo aberrare concessum est, nichil
est ex omni parte beatum et quandoque bonus dormitat homerus sancte
matris ecclesie et sacre facultatis theologie parisiensis et ubiuis gentium
doctorum determinationi omnia committo. Nec stupendum est quod ego
homuncio crassa minerua preditus ancer inter olores obstripens dauus non
edippus nunc titubem condimentum cibo per aduerbium dubitandi ap-
ponens nunc ieiune et aride tricas nodosas pertransio circa immensum
opus nostris humeris impar et legendo et scribendo insudamus. Quo
circa multa tangere ad perpendiculum non poteramus, aliis occasionem
indagande veritatis enucleatius impartiuisse sufficiat, e dumo leporem
exiguus canis venaticus exitat quem ad iugum montis concendentem
magnus cum oblectamento capit ac filum unus facit et telam alius orditur.
Accipe igitur hoc munusculum accipe quantillum sit tuo faustissimo
nomini nuncupatum. Vale. Ex collegio montis acuti pridie kalendas
Januarias. Anno domini Millesimo quingentessimo octauo.

> I liber haud ullo decoratus pumice gressum
>   Flecte celer nostra carbasa solue domo
> Curre per occeanum te mitto videre britannos
>   Andree sacri limina tutus adi
> Hic manet antistes humili quem voce salutes
>   Eius custodes sintque precare deos
> Qui cum maiore referet tibi gaudia vultu
>   Una dies mecum quam tibi mille darent.

[*In Quartum Sent.* 1509.]

⁋ Dialogus inter duos magistros Johannem formam precentorem glasguensem et Petrum sandelands rectorem de calder.

Iohannes. quas nudiustertius accepi litteras de patria michi periocunde fuerunt domine rector quare remigrare in patriam ocissime urgeor, ut michi comes sis itineris te exoratum facio. Pe. lares nunc patrios visere recuso, aurelium vel andegauos propediem sum petiturus ut legibus vacem. Jo. probe agis ut te cura quam habes dignum reddas. Pe. ad hoc si fata sinant enitar nec in hac parte magistri nostri consilio acquiescere institui qui studium theologicum michi suadens ad kalendas grecas persuadebit humilis sortis tantum viros theologie se dedere intueor. Jo. nec voto viuitur uno, mille hominum species et rerum discolor vsus, nullum caput omnis homo habet opinetur ut volet, tecum assentior studium Iegum nobilibus et hiis qui ad honorum apicem conscendere anhelant inprimis'petendum. Sed cum inter loquendum de viro illo incidimus cedo nonnulla que de eo sum indagaturus inter mortales quid mente gerat optime nosti dum sub eo manum ferule subduximus in artibus et meum discessum diu moram traxistis familiariter mutuo. Pe. Licet ei‘ modus sit ut melius me nosti fido amico archana sue mentis detegere tamen quo ad aliqua est coopertus. Sed venare in hiis que intellexi et respondere (si conducat) curabo. Jo. Quare non proficiscitur in natale solum hercule mirandum est pro eius aduentu in patriam pia mater flagrat et dum de eo sermo habetur suspiria cum singultibus ab imo pectore trahit genas lacrimis frequenter irrorans. Pe. causam sue more michi hactenus occuluit amphibologice suo more me querente ad hoc ruent ipsum vigesimum annum nunc intrare asserit peregrinationis sue extra patriam et cum illum compleuerit unam medietatem in patria alteram extra patriam absoluisse putat laborem numerus quadragenarius representat ut in . xv . disti. inferius in eo considerabis si spiritus inquit suos regat artus illo curriculo extincto lucidius quid dicere velit explicabit. Si aliud exoptes oraculum apolinis consulito ad locum sue originis nisi interim intereat suapte natura salmo tendit. Jo. Cum tua responsio in hac parte sit tenebrosa aqua in nubibus aeris eam missam facientes quid in ocio litterario faciat aperias. Pe. Quartum sententiarum olim ab eo conflatum calcographis dat imprimendum unam partem adhuc habet in incude et id cause fuit dum unam partem imprimendam daret non ab re mutant propositum ab exordio questiones nonnullas solum in materiis scholasticis tractauit nunc autem super singulas distinctiones questionem unam vel plures scribere satagit et potissimum in. xv. distinct. xxiiii. et xxxviii. ne opus mancum in potioribus membris appareret. Jo. Proth iupiter opus contortum et inconcultatum ex hiis liquet emittere necesse est cum nunquam integrum exemplar simul pre manibus haberet. Pre. [*sic*] Hoc vehementer veretur. Sed postquam ipse librum publice ut proponit legerit secundum exemplar tertius euadet. Jo. Ut te cum familiariter colloquar

a plerisque recta putatur sententia comia nichil dictum de nouo. Si mel
ab aliis apibus mellificatum colligat earum surda aure pertransiens iniuria
earum diues putabitur. Pe. De dicto terentii modica est danda fides qui
dixere aliqua de nouo venemur et quando fuit status noua dolandi et
quare citius illo tempore quam alio. Ex isto nec euangelium nec ethnicum
aliquem in prophanis scribentem nec ecclesie doctores post id temporis
aliquid in auditum fabricare concludes quod non minus est absonum
quam falsum. Aliud obiectum eneruare non est difficile per modum inter
non in celebres viros vulgarem cum ab emulis quod homerum ad litteram
nonnunquam mutaretur mantuanus vates carperetur magnarum dicebat
esse virium clauam de manu herculis surripere et cum priori de equali
palma dimicabat secundum illud iuuenalicum conditor iliades cantabitur
atque maronis utrinque ambiguam faciencia carmina palmam sic a grecis
marcus tullius latine lingue parens repetundarum accusatur identidem in
predicamentis architam et pithagoram in primis libris problumatum hypo-
cratem philosophorum princeps insequi non erubuit eorum nomina
silentio pertransiens a quibus multa frugifera colligerat. Hoc ipsum
sue professionis fecere viri semel in quarta parte raymundi mentionem
facit alexander alensis quem irrefragabilem appellitant quotiens reminis-
citur altisiodorensis contemplaberis sic albertus, aquinas, noster conterraneus, et innumeri heroici (quos ciere longum foret) factitarunt et haud
iniuria aliorum id actum putes non ideo quia maiores sic rati sunt dixere
sed quia vel eis probabili ratione vel auctoritate aliunde constabat aliis
adinuentionibus cunclusiones obstipantes et eas acrius oppugnantes et
illud luce meridiei est splendidius cum aliorum mendis emunctis bene-
dicta sumpsere. Rursus opinationem aliquam ob elencum sophisticum
primus ponit quam validiori argumentatione secundus munit paucis
tamen rationibus et quidem tenuibus quatit sed eam solidius tertius
roborat argutiis magne molis ferit quas medullitus eneruat tunc palam
est hanc opinionem non magis primo quam secundo secundo quam tertio
ascribendam fore huius tempestatis viris quare non dabis veniam faciendi
quod sapientibus ubiuis gentium concessum est. Ceterum magistrum
nostrum auguror positiones maiorum nominatim recensere si ei occurrant
nec ulli hominum extra ea que fidei sunt in opinando esse addictum
argumenta quedem [sic] vulgaria que nodosiora esse solent nulli hominum
merito attribuit licet a multis doctorellis qui ea eluere nequibant assu-
mantur sicut in rerum possessione quod in nullius hominis est potestate
licet sit apud alium animantem id occupanti conceditur ut puta de talibus
de dilectione dei antea instans de ablatione successiua granorum de
voluntate innumeros homines interimendi et ceteris id genus et si a
theologie primoribus huiuscemodi argumentationes pretermisse sunt non
vicio dandum putaverim sed necessarium eas colligere ideo eas preteriere
nolentes a precipuis obsenticosa argumenta impediri. Forte etiam suam
famam que magna erat et merito apud vulgus exponere discrimini pro
enodatione talium tricarum nolebant. Dic sodes mi iohannes quas fabri-
casti obiectiones baculo arundineo inituntur [sic]. Io. Hac lege cuilibet

facile erit librum ioui dignum posteritati tradere optima queque deser-
pendo posthabitis erroribus. Pe. Illationem e uestigio eo inficias erit ne
ignanus [*sic*] censor inter vera et tenebrosa falsa qua via zizaniam a tritico
enucleabit cum quedam falsa multis viris non refert esse probabiliora est
enim via que videtur homini recta et nouissima eius ducunt ad mortem
hanc rationem in calce ethices aristoteles diluit. Jo. Et si tuas respon-
siones equitati consentaneas admittam tamen satius fuisse auguror magistrum nostrum ob dicaculos nugigerulos nasutos et sussurones tacuisse
debere illotis sermonibus hii omnia fedant ut docti apud vulgus emineant.
Pe. Non me fugit optime precentor nasum renocerotis habens more pice
blacterans se coturnicem credens omnia sinistre interpretabitur nec eam
ob rem nomen docti viri sed inuidi nanciscetur scite apud iuuenalem
legitur inuidet figulus figulo etc. lingua eius manifestum eum facit et a
fructibus eius eum cognoscetis ideo maledicit quia benedicere nescit pro
pane lapidem et pro ouo dans scorpium in oculo fratris festucam a
remotis in proprio egre trabem contemplatur nimirum secundum fic-
tionem esopi aliorum errata a fronte et nostra a tergo ferimus amplius
aliorum vultus per lineam rectam nostros solum per reflexam et in
corpore leni contemplamur talibus canibus os marcialicum rodendum
damus qui ducis vultus et non vides ista libenter omnibus inuideas liuide
nemo tibi propter tales grunientes porcos maiores nostri non tacuerunt
quare quos ex suo dolatorio libros viri presentes fabricant in lucem
emittere propter zoilos verebuntur qui considerat ventum nunquam
seminat et qui nubes formidat non metet. Jo. Perbelle facis amici
partes in re honesta tutans nec peruicaciter obloquor ut virum a scriptura
deterream eum rei publice prodesse velle reor et non segniter vitam
degere dii cepta secundent perpetuo nexu amoris nos iunctos esse nosti
verum si non sim tibi tedio mi suauissime petre edissere cur diui andree
archipresuli hunc librum deuouere instituit quia apud nostras aures sic
rumor increbruit. Pe. Dii boni gratissima sunt michi tua quesita colloqui
de rebus amici communis est voluptuosum ea propter libens respondebo
rationibus non aspernendis opinatione mea ducitur cui librum citius nun-
cupare debeat quam illi cuius gratia illum conflauit amplius antistitem
magno adiumento ecclesie scotice futurum si vitam protrahant superi
existimat cum stematibus maiorum ad virtutem inflammabitur cum ab
unguiculis et a teneris annis sub circunscripta tutela et litteratissimis
preceptoribus religiosissime educatus sit sic quod in angusto temporis
curriculo omnium iudicio qui nouere in virum opido eruditum euasit
potissimum in romana lingua greca et legibus reliquum est theologie et
altioribus studiis suo officio congruentibus sese accomodare. Et cum
supremo britannorum sanguini de quo noster primas satus est, multam
doctrinam et morum probitatem (que indies coalescit) adiecerit cui eo
neglecto sine iniuria primitias sui laboris in theologia dicare poterat. Jo.
Ingenue fateor rationibus non caducis ducitur et meis rogationibus
medius fidius ita scite respondisti ut tedium foret ulterius obiicere et quia
domino meo me vocante per litteras ut nosti citissime discedere cogor

verum si librorum aut pecunie egeas michi resera et mea omnia sicut
propria accipias. Pe. Quamuis scolasticorum morbus ut aiunt peculiaris
sic egestas habentibus beneficium pecunie raro aut nunquam desunt ad
votum et pecuniam et libros meo studio sufficientes habeo sed de tua
liberalitate immensas gratias habeo sed si vestes aut alia munuscula
parisii vel rothomagi ut moris est empturus es ut domi in nouo aduentu
largiaris amicis si non satis pecuniarum habes expete audacter et non
negabo. Jo. michi deest nichil sed tibi regratior. vale petre vita longa
et bona nestoreos petre tibi iupiter errogat annos. Si non sufficiant
mathusalem superes. Pe. Et bene valeas mi iohannes caram matrem
amicos et magistrum Robertum watterson magistro nostro amicissimum
meo nomine et suo salutem dices.

[*In Quartum Sent.* 1509.]

    DAUID CRENSTON in sacra pagina bacchalarius ad lectores.

    Et si diis parentibus preceptoribusque (ut ille nature prodigium
aristoteles testatur) eque ualens reddere valemus minime. Id tamen
equum ducere non dubitaui : si aliquantulum benefaciendi occasio olim
oblata foret, pro virium tenuitate meo preceptori obsequium prestare
valerem. Cum igitur michi preclarum elaboratumque opus in quartum
sententiarum ingeniosissimi preceptoris mei de me apprime meriti ac
conterranei magistri nostri Maioris, sub cuius vexillo primis pueritie
stipendiis merui in manus deuenerit nostras : quo profecto nunc practice
modo speculatiue sententiam examinatam septuplo probatam purgatam-
que singulis super materiis eiusdem quarti depromptam curauit : quo nulla
alta me ingratitudine accusare valeret : pro virili mea lectoris manuduc-
tioni consulens tabulam alphatico [*sic*] ordine contextam putassem adiici,
si temporis angustia regentie prouincia (qua profecto plurimum distrahor)
viriumque debilitas non a voto animum cohibuissent. Uerum id partim
consulto faciundum censui : si non quod necessitas exigit tamen quod
administrant vires exequi cupierim. Quoniam librum raptim lectitando
non ad amussim castigatum ab omnique erroris labe expurgatum comperii,
nouam castigationem expectantes temporis habita ratione alium indicem
paulo strictiorem, distinctiones, questionesque certo tenore enucleantem
adiiciendum curauimus qui nempe lectoris directioni conducere poterit :
cum singulis in questionibus doctoris resolutionem sub paucis detegere
non neglexerimus : folium columnamque certis quotationibus assignare
studuimus haud secus nostrum dirigere processum valuimus ubi calchographorum incuria alphabeticos caracteres (qui ceterorum librorum mar-
ginibus et § exordiis adiungi solent) iniectos inuenimus minime. Proinde
alphabeticam tabulam libro paulominus fuisse aptam ambigit nemo.
Attamen secundum virium oportunitatem castigationi operam dantes
necessarium quid (annuentibus superis) imposterum omittemus nusquam.
Hanc ergo tantarum rerum copiositas cui minus nostre sufficiunt vires
exigit opellam. Quod si minus digestum exactum ve quid notauerimus
benignus lector lectori veniam dabit.

[*In Primum Sent.* 1510.]

EPISTOLA.

IOANNES MAIOR professorum Theologiæ minimus : domino Georgio
Hepburnensi laudatissimi cœnobii de Arbroth abbati dignissimo :
& serenissimi Scotorum regis a secretis prudentissimo ac fidelis-
simo cum observantia S.

Quoniam anno superiore, pater cum primis venerande, elucidatiunculas
quasdam & ab auditoribus nostris quotidiano ferme convicio efflagitatas
in quartum magistri sententiarum cum earum qualibuscunque decisionibus
quæstiunculas emisimus, emissas explanavimus, explanatasque studiosis
theologiæ alumnis in honestissimo Montisacuti apud Parrhisios collegio,
domo mihi tutrice semperque cum veneratione nominanda, sub magistro
nostro Natale Beda, eiusdem collegii primario & vigilantissimo & doctissimo, vel eo absente sub magistro Nicolao Trevero, viro sane docto,
fructiferæ disputationis examine discutiendas subministravimus, eorun-
dem aliorumque qui meas non nihili faciunt lucubratiunculas, & oppor-
tunis & importunis hortationibus & precibus, evictus. Primum præfati
magistri sententiarum nostra theologica Minerva utcunque elucidatum
exire permisi in tuum, pater honorande, optatissimum & tutissimum
sinum, quem ut tuæ venerationi nuncupatum benivole suscipias maiorem
in modum obsecro. Non enim est cui mea quantulacunque sunt dicare &
præscribere aut lubentius velim aut iustius possim, tum propter incu-
nabulorum nostrorum coniunctionem arctissimam ; vix etenim ab Halis,
domo celsitudinis tuæ altrice, ter mille natus & educatus sum passibus.
Sines igitur hanc quoque opellam nostram præclare bibliothecæ tuæ acce-
dere : nosque dignaberis dedititiorum tuorum consortio ascribere. Vale.
Ex Monteacuto ad septimum calendas Ianuarias : Anno salutis nostræ
Millesimo Quingentesimo Nono.

[*Ibid.*]

DIALOGUS DE MATERIA THEOLOGO TRACTANDA.

DIALOGUS inter duos famatos viros magistrum Gawinum Douglaiseum
virum non minus eruditum quam nobilem : ecclesiæ beati Aegidii
Edinburgensis præfectum : & magistrum Davidem Crenstonem in
sacra theosophia baccalaureum formatum optime meritum.

[D.] Salve præfecte dignissime. G. Salve & tu vir charissime. Sed
quæ te huc afflavit aura ? Sæpe enim oratum ut de re literaria tecum com-
miniscat exorare ut nos visas non potui. D. Non voluntas : sed facultas
parendi defuit : verum eam ob rem nunc ultro advenio. G. Optata
loqueris, hoc triduo primum sententiarum magistri nostri Maioris legi
quem iamiam emisit in auras : quem permonitum velim ut relictis
scholicis exercitiis natale solum repetat : atque illic vineam dominicam

colat: & concionando semina evangelica: unde optimos fructus animæ
fidelium demetant late longeque dispergat.   D. Id quidem se alioquin
facturum proponit: sed interea temporis ob hoc munere non segniter
desistit.   Nam quæ prædicanda decenter scribunt: non suo tantum ore:
sed omnium quos erudierunt prædicant: nec uno tantum sæculo, sed quot-
quot eorum doctrina steterit.   G. Accipio, sed ut Flaccus ait, Mortalia
facta peribunt.   Debemus morti nos nostraque.   Et Aeneas Sylvius
(postea Papa Pius dictus) de situ minoris Asiæ loquens: Aristotelis
scripta inquit aliquando temporis edacitate absumenda sunt: ideoque
bonum fuerit eum operari cibum quod non perierit.   D. Quo tempore
peritura sint Aristotelis aliorumque scripta nec definitum est a Pio:
neque si definitum fuerit omnino pro concesso recipiendum fuerit.   G.
Totum assentior: sed tanta est nunc librorum congeries, ut quorsum se
divertat ignoret quodlibet.   D. In quolibet libro aliquod frugiferum
invenies: & opus ab aliquibus neglectum in magno precio est apud alios
propter varias materias occurrentes, unde ut ecclesiastes ait, scribendi
libros nullus est finis.   G. Contra illud non multum reluctabor: sed de
isto genere scribendi plerique obloquuntur: & rugata fronte theologos
apparenter subsannant.   & id causæ est quod pluries Aristotelem in
physico auditu & prima philosophia cum eius commentatore allegatum invenies, quam doctores ecclesiæ.   D. Secundum materias occurrentes nunc
philosophum nunc doctores ecclesiæ scribentes introducunt: unumque
facientes aliud non omittunt: ut theologiam scientiarum deam a vera
philosophia non deviare ostendat: & parvulos per manuductiones in fide
alant: secundum beati Petri eloquium: parati semper ad sanctificationem
omni poscenti vos rationem de ea quæ in vobis est spe.   G. Pace tua non
satisfacis. videre enim nequeo quantum theologiæ conducat tot frivolas
positiones de relationibus intensione formæ an sint ponenda puncta in
continuo: & de cæteris id genus prodigaliter pertractare. siquidem
aditum ad theologiam hæc non ministrant: sed obfuscant & obtenebrant.
Non sic autem ad Spartiatas Ionathas, & Machabæi scriptitarunt. libros
enim sanctos quos præ manibus habuere, sibi solatio esse affirmarunt.
Et Timotheo apostolus inquit.   Tu permane in his quæ didicisti & credita
sunt tibi: sciens a quo didiceris: & quia ab infantia sacras literas nosti
te possunt instruere ad salutem.   Hoc ipsum ad Titum scribit.   In pro-
logo quarti illius sententiæ noster Maior (ut in lumine patet) erat: nunc
suorum dictorum immemor ad ea quæ tunc floccipendit utriusque oculi
aciem convertit.   D. Hunc modum scribendi in sententias a trecentis
annis scriptores observavere: et si præter rationem id factum esse censeas
ius (ut vulgari ter aiunt) communis error facit. bibliam & faciliores
theologiæ partes nonnulli exoptant. absconsas & intricatas calculationes
alii: modo (secundum apostoli sententiam) Græcis & Barbaris debitor est
theologus.   Eæ autem quas existimant quæstiones futiles crebro scalam
intelligentiæ ad sacras literas capessendas præstant   Quinetiam in fronte
huius primi Maior noster eiusdem est mentis cum exordio quarti. sicut
frequenter ab eius ore accepi, & accipio.   Quae vero aliorum opinationes

peregrinas nonnulli recensent : & eas multiplici genere argumenti exu-
beranti verborum dicacitate confutant : nunquam approbavit. talium
enim caducarum positionum succincta recitatio, earundem est sufficiens
explosio. In materiis vero utrinque, apparentibus maiori mora opus est :
& hunc modum tenere ratus est magister noster. G. A theologo hæc
præsupponi habent : et prius in philosophia videnda : & si ita factum
fuerit compendiose non improbaverim. D. In theologia hæc consulto
scribentes interserunt. Tum primo ut philosophos ad hoc sanctum
studium more Origenis inducant & alliciant : Tum secundo quia vix
iactis in philosophia solidis fundamentis provectæ ætatis viri ad theologiam
advolant : qui manum supponere ferulæ in artibus erubescerent : &
tamen hi sub theologiæ umbra minutatim hæc colligunt : et si in his
eruditi fuerint sapientiores evaserint. quia secundum sapientem, audiens
sapiens sapientior erit. Rursus non ab re relicto aratro oblectamenti
gratia murem arator nonnunquam prosequitur. & in vitis patrum memoriæ proditum est plerosque nulla spe lucri perlectos : sed vitandi ocii
causa rebus mechanicis operam navasse non modicam. G. Non sic institutum istud laudas : sed errores sub quodam velamine veri tueri satagis &
id paucis tibi detegere enitar. Postquam enim magnam partem ocii
literarii in philosophia aristotelica sententiarii consumpsere : non modo
eius scripta : sed & modum scribendi usurpant ut in præludio primi libri
dialectices Laurentius Vallensis quæ res an plura quam alius quispiam
Aristoteles composuerit, sic inquit. Sed & plura compilavit : in quo
improbitatem eius licet cognoscas : quod quæ compilat non illis refert
accepta a quibus sumpsit : sed sibi vendicat : & eosdem ubicunque pec-
casse opinatur citius ardentem flammam ore continere posset quam non
nominare. Sicut Aeneas Sylvius de palestepsi minoris Asiæ de Aristotele
loquens sic asserit. Sed melius cum eo actum est quam cum reliquis :
quorum opera funditus periere : & ipse causa extitit cur multa perirent :
quod aliorum gloria ad se traxit. Sicut in secundi libri capite de logica
Valla recitat : sic de theologia sententiarum invenies. Cum rursus ait,
quicquid infinitis libris tradiderunt, id ore paucissimis tradi præceptis
potuisse animadverto. Quid igitur aliud causæ tantæ prolixitatis credas
fuisse nisi inanem arrogantiam eorum quod dum vites longe lateque dif-
fundi sarmentis gaudent uvam in labruscam mutaverunt? Adde, quod
indignissimum est, cum captiones cavillationes calumnias video quas &
exercent a quibus sumpsit : non possum eis non succensere, quasi pyraticam non
navalem rem : sive (ut mollius loquar) palæstræ pro militia disciplinam
tradentibus. Erat enim dialectica res brevis prorsus & facilis, id quod
ex comparatione rhetoricæ diiudicari potest. & paucis interiectis dicit.
Nulla doctrina mihi brevior faciliorque quam dialectica videtur, ut quod
aliis maioribus servit : quam non intra plures quis menses quam gramma-
tica intra annos perdiscet. Sed videlicet huius puellæ parens dum timet
ne filia sua quæ fusca quæ strigosa quæ pusilla est nullos inveniat pro-
cos, magnæ dotis specie & ambitu commendandam putavit : ut multos
sollicitaret ad contubernium eius. Multi itaque sine dubio spe divitiarum

concurrunt, sed non fere alii quam plebei, obscuri, ignobiles, omnium rerum inopes : & quod alias facultates ad veras divitias desperarent. Id idem rectissime modo nunc theologicam tractanti contingit, optimatum & locupletum liberi & logica & theosophia relicta ad leges ocyssime post auditas summulas ruunt. Magnam affluentiam ad summulas in Navarræ collegio vel Burgundiæ facile est reperire, sed ob penuriam licentiandorum in fine cursus cum bursa vacua regentes discedunt, & totus error est quoniam tritico relicto ad paleas curritur. Quid de theologicis neotericis in dialogo de libero arbitrio idem Valla dicat quæso considera. D. Fallaciam non causæ ut causæ in medium affers dignissime præfecte. multa veritati consona recitasti. quam in iuvenili ætate quæ studio accommoda, omnes finem statuunt ut in maturioribus annis tranquille vivat : optimatum filii omni studio prætermisso favore parentum ad honores passim conscendunt. De te tuique similibus minime loquor, sed de iis quos vulgo videmus. Non enim multi Parisienses de opulenta domo orti ad gradum in artibus vel theologia ascendunt, sed legibus operam raptim navant, ut demum palatini evadant. & qualitercunque theosophia tractaretur, id idem fieret. Ad dicta Laurentii respondere inopportunum est. nulli hominum generi (ut nosti) vir ille pepercit : et in eius dialecticæ (potius in deliramentis philosophiæ) plura errata inseruit quam maculæ in pardo reperiantur. quia modum theologorum in dialogo quem recitas imitari noluit : omnem libertatem ab animo inscite eripuit. præ eo cum Pogio consulito, ad alia de Aristotele in præsentiarum subticeo. G. Hæc igitur missa faciens ad aliud me converto. xxiiii. distinctione noster Maior modum illum menti Aristotelis conformem putat : quod minus idoneo beneficium conferens perperam agit. id multipliciter oppugnavi, sed responsionem habui ab eo nullam. D. Hoc ab ipso intellexi. succincte & subtiliter in quodam codicello a te misso hoc impugnasti. sed ipsius negligentia codex ille amissus est proculdubio : quocirca (si placeat) veniam dabis amico. In materia enim problematica utramvis partem vt nosti tueri sciret si vellet : sed illam rationi conformiorem putavit. G. Pro eo veniam implorare noli. quam enim coniunctus est mihi patria : tam coniunctus est amicitia. Intervallum inter Tentalon & Glegornum de quo oriundus est bene nosti opinor. D. Optime novi : iter sabbati in lege Mosaica vix hæc intercapedo suscipit. G. Temporis angustia me premit : discedere operæ precium est. bene valeas : & me nostro Maiori commendatum facito. D. Bene valeas generose præfecte, faciam id ac lubens.

[*In Secundum Sent.* 1510.]

LUDOVICO CORONEL Antonius coronel. S. .P. dicit.

Non possum ego, studiosissime frater, non magnopere lætari summum rerum opificem, deum potiusquam fortunam, nobiscum tam prospere tam clementer egisse, ut nobis commodam opportunitatem faceret adeundi huiusque celeberrimi omnium litterarum emporii parisiensis : ad quod ingenti concursu a remotissimis quibuscunque mundi regionibus tanquam ad bonarum artium mercaturam cuiuslibet sortis homines profisciscuntur : quo sitim ardoremque doctrinæ ac eruditionis ebibendæ expleant. Nusquam enim alibi disciplinarum fluenta uberius quam in hac parisiorum achademia scatent, nusquam emanant profusius, nusquam abundantius emergunt, adeo ut rivis inde profluentibus xpianus ager undiquaque fœcundissime irrorent. Quæ etenim est gens tam semota, tam extrema natio, in quam non procurrant flumina vivacissimæ aquæ doctrinæ parisiensis. Ex hoc igitur tam præclaro parisiorum gymnasio quam plurimi fontes scaturiunt inter quos omnium limpidissimas atque illimes aquas emittit is qui a monte acuto exoritur. Qui instar fontis paradisum deliciarum irrigantis suauissima quadam in morum disciplinarumque aspergine totam parhisiensem achademiam fœcundissime alluit hic siquidem mons dei mons pinguis mons coagulatus mons in quo beneplacitum est deo habitare in eo, cui non absurde illud psalmi accommodari poterit firmamentum in summis montium. Sapientissimum quippe colonum dominus deus olim huic fœcundissimo feracissimoquo monti præfecit ioannem standonk, qui iam non apparet quia tulit eum dominus : qui tanto studio tam vigili cura, ut præparat agricolationis divinæ studiosus, sic montem illum excoluit ut non solum triticeas segetes in amplissimam messem, verumetiam plantas cuiusquam generis et varii fructus iugiter continuoque producat. Cum ergo multa sint parhisius gymnasia in quibus litteralis pallestra quam accuratissime atque ferventissime exercetur, gymnasium montis acuti nomen gloriosum adeptum est. Ex cuius grege non inferiorem sibi locum iure vendicare potest Joannes maioris præceptor noster, quem remotissima abditissimaque et philosophiæ et theologiæ doctrina non solum posteritati, verum etiam æternitati, commendabunt, unius plane viri non a quovis sed ab eloquentissima [?] tamen laudes efferendæ veniunt. Quocirca eloquii latini penuria sermonisque tenuitas me cogit quæ ad illius immortalem gloriam spectare videntur supprimere, hoc tamen unum silentio non involvam, eum in arte dyalectices inter huius ætatis viros solum constituisse in qua complura scripsit non mediocriter profecto utilia, quæ cum iniuria quin potius inscicia calchographorum tot erratis tot mendis obtenebrata essent ut vel legentibus confusionem ingenerarent vel constare posset ex tanti viri officina eiusmodi libros minime prodiisse : quantumcunque potui operam impartitus sum ut hi solito emaculatiores in manus studiosorum adolescentium venirent. erasis ergo abstersisque erroribus adiecto præter hoc certo . . . orum indice ac tabula hanc opellem et tenuem lucubratiunculam nostram me . . . quam tibi, frater amantissime, dicare constitui : quo tibi persuadeas non maio. . fraternitatis quam studii litteralis necessitudine nos pariter esse connexos.   Vale.

[*In Secundum Sent.* 1510.]

JOANNES MAIOR Magistro nostro Natali Bede primario collegii montisacuti vigilantissimo : et communitati theologorum eiusdem
collegii S. D.

Forsitan labe ingratitudinis apud Persas teterrima vel merito nota-
rer : si nostrarum lucubrationum, qualescunque sunt ad te et ad theologicum cetum cui prees, nihil dicatum destinarem. Multis enim
nominibus tibi debeo. Nam cum artes liberales in collegio Barbare sub
Magistro Joanne Bulliacho in theologia (ut aiunt) licentiato (cui plurimum obnoxius eram et qui nunc habenas grammaticorum regalis collegii
Nauarre circumspectissimi moderatur) audiuissem auspiciis tuis Beda,
etiam venerabilis, ad magistrum nostrum Standoncum Mechlinianum
adductus sum : vt quo nomine tibi non parum debeo. Magni enim estimaui
atque estimo sub umbra talis ac tanti viri quiescere : vtpote cuius vite
celebritas et integritas ad meothidem usque paludem et ad ultimam
thylen vagata est. Et inter theologos quos tunc primum instituere
ceperat : unum annum te cum militaui, quo completo ad regentie, quod
vocant, munus, in artibus et ad communitatem aliam, etiam te ei apud
quem omnia poteras : vt id faceret persuadente, accersitus sum. Ubi
quindecim annos sub ipso et te permansi. Et cum post visas artes fluctu-
aret animus desyderio natalis soli, quo nihil dulcius, tandem visendi, tu
et prolixioris more isthic trabende et regentie subeunde et litterarum
discendarum, que licet in me parue sint per te tamen non stetit quin
maiores essent : mihi causa eras. Ingratissimi igitur hominis esset hec
tanta beneficia non recognoscere. Quocirca tibi et utriusque communi-
tatis theologis sub te militantibus, quorum consocius sum, hanc nostram
in Secundum sententiarum opellam et dico et dedico ut ceteros ad theologie studium incenderem : et pignus perpetui in omnis studiosos amoris
nostri inter confratres relinquerem. Uale.

Ex preclaro Montisacuti apud Parrhisios collegio sub Natalem domi-
nicum M.D.X.

[*Goddamus in libb. Sent.* (*fol. A.* 1. *v°.*) 1512.]

JOHANNES solo cognomento maior theologorum minimus eruditissimo
viro Mattheo galtero doctori theologo in maioris monasterii
abbatem electo S. P. D.

Ego eam ne dicam fortunæ sed ethereæ cuiusdam sortis electione cum
ipse reputarem, prudentissime virorum, demiratus sum qua in pastorem
& via quidem honestissima, quam spiritus sancti dicunt, assumptus fueris,
non multorum more violenter intrusus es, sed ingenuus conuentus filius
& cænobita integerrimus, ita quod sicut in apostolorum actibus super
Matthiam sors apostolatus cecidit sic super Mattheum archimandritæ
sors requievit, non potui non tibi gratulari, gratulari doctis omnibus,

gratulari nostro seculo, ita ut fortuna prius ceca in te uno oculos re-
cuperasse videatur, quæ toties indignos promovere solet ; & quid mirum
cum amicorum precipuum, cum quo in summulis amicitiæ & charitatis
iecerim fundamenta, quæ viginti annos coaluit, ad honorem sublimem
more Aaron vocatum contemplar ; attamen cum in præsentiarum, desin-
ente nostri laboris fœtura, impressioni Adæ inuigilaremus, quæ hactenus
calcographis nondum erat præsentatus, placuit ipsum nomini tuo dicare.
Si vero inter legendum quidam ungue & obeliscis emaculanda comperiant,
non id mirum videatur, cum inter multa exemplaria vix duo visa sunt
conformia, nec sedulum castigatorem me fuisse permiserunt quotidiane
lectiones nostri quarti emunctum re & tumultuaria quæ intercedere solent
negocia : tamen ut cunque est hoc munusculum accipito. Vale felix.

ELEGIACUM CARMEN.

Qui fuerat tenebris perfusa latentibus olim
Clarior igniuomo lima nitore micat.
Qui fuerat quondam mendis fallacibus asper :
Splendicat ex omni sorde politus Adam.

[*Here follows the printer's privilege.*]

[*Ibid. fol. A. 2.*]

DE VITA ADE.

Vitam autoris nusquam me legisse memini : aliqua tamen quæ per
eius & aliorum monimenta innotescunt scribere enitar. Nostra ex insula britannia ea in parte quam angli colunt oriundus est. cognomento
goddam alias voddam, professione minoritanus, Oxoniensis achademiæ
(quæ ea in tempestate viros celebres emisit), doctor Londonijs anglorum
regia, Oxonie & Norwici plurimum moratus, quibus in locis duas sententiarum lecturas peregit, Okam & Catonis contemporaneus. Utrumque in
scholis respondentem audiuit. Materias positiuas & faciles & necnon
præcedentium nexus intricatos inutiles aspernatus, theoricas theologas
pertractat, interserendo secundum sententiæ oportunitatem philosophiam
moralem & naturalem utilem, acriter perspicue succincte & solide omnia
prosequens. Sententias ab eo scriptas nullibi offendi : earum succum &
medullam Henricus oyta a centum & viginti annis abhinc extraxit, quem
sententias Adæ appellamus. Eum nonnunquam abbreuiauit ut in quarto
in materia de quantitate videre est. In omnibus librariis & in caracteribus
optimis Adam inuenimus quod viro erat magnæ laudi ; si eius librum
habuissemus lubenti animo eum calcographis tradidissemus, sed illustris
viri & eruditi Petri menenes lusitani in theosophia bacchalarii exemplar
procurauimus mediocriter castigatum, quod imitari pro maiori parte ele-
borauimus [*sic*], curantes ut tabula alphabetica ad folia & columnas
adderetur. Et si pro secundo aut tertio loco inter angliæ literatos
certauerit duobus sic ei resistit ut quotum locum inter eos optinuerit a

musis nondum accepi. Primam sedem iam diu venerabilis beda pacifice adeptus, tum quia Oxoniam (sicut athenas homerus) antecessit, tum quia in scriptis bibliacis commentarios, annales patrias, calculationes, temporumque supputationes studiosissime composuit, & si sedem secundam, septuaginta annis Alexander halensis iure quidem optimo vendicauerit, ab Okam & Adamo pro eadem dimicatum esset ob veterum maiestatem & ut lite pendente nihil innovetur. Secundo adhuc loco gaudeat. Okam & Adam accedunt in logica & utraque phisophia [*sic*] pares : in sententiis Okam ampullosus & diffusus, Adam digestus & resolutus ; si Guillermi dyalogus non obstiterit palmam a priore surriperet posterior. Sublimi ingenio & audaci Guillermus, excelso & solido Adam. Ille rugosa fronte dimisso supercilio micantibus oculis tanquam vir bellator ab adolescentia suadendo dissuadendo seriose disputat ; hic serena fronte eleuato supercilio ridendo singulis gratus ; omnia diluit ; quocirca neutrum alteri præferam. Hec sunt quæ de autore & vicino in presentiarum scribere libuit.

[*In Quartum Sent.*, 1516.]

Robertus Senalis Ioanni Maiori Theologo Doctori Maximo Praeceptori suo aeternum vivere.

Nulla re apertius (meo quidem cogitatu) divinam sapientiam (et si alioqui plurimum admirabilem) clarescere arbitror preceptor suavissime : quam cum tanta sit rerum quæ in hunc nostrum orbem suo nutu (qui vice habetur imperii) prodierunt vasta congeries : tanta hominum atque omne genus ferarum ab ipso mundi nascentis exordio ad hanc usque nostram senescentem (quæ etiam prope interitum est) ætatem extra omnem numeri aleam multitudo neque tamen unquam neque usquam locorum videre quis (etiam oculatissimus) potuit animantia in toto rerum acervo duo (qui minimus est numerus) quæ sese paribus formis typisque similibus demonstrarent. At neque ova quidem duo simillima undecunque quæsita reperias : de quibus proverbium tamen exiit cum rerum duarum similitudinem exprimere volumus sic eas esse similes ut nec ovum ovo similius esse possit. Hæc tantum in tanta rerum vastitie inter se discrepans varietas dei optimi maximi sapientiam thesaurosque nulla arte comprehensibiles apertissimis declarat argumentis. Hinc mille hominum species : hinc rerum discolor usus. At ne quis molem solum corpoream ista quam diximus amictam putet varietate est etiam ipsis spiritibus sua discriminata species vultus dissidens ac diversa effigies. Quod eum non latuit qui ait. Velle suum est nec voto vivitur uno. Hæc diversitas sive corporis sive animæ iam in confesso habetur : idque adeo ut si quos maiorum monumentis reppererimus sibi fuisse admodum similes illos miraculi atque ostenti vice posteritati commendarit antiquitas : ut non sit ulla res tam admirabilis ex omnibus quæcunque sub orbe admiranda traduntur quam duos spectare qui sese omnibus partibus: lineamentis omnibus perfecta similitudine presentent.   At contra si nostri conatus imbecillitatem attendas, vix alteram aut tertiam ingenii feturam ex una atque eandem [*sic*] officina prodire intelliges: ubi non sit altera alteri persimilis.   Id in orationibus aliisque id genus humani intellectus fetibus deprehendere non sit admodum operosum.   Nam ubi duas aut tris in vulgum quis ediderit orationes: illas si invicem conferas: sibi cognatæ adeo adeoque videbuntur et attiguæ: ut unam in altera vel olfacias vel certe manifesto argumento deprehendas.   Tu vero præceptor humanissime mihi iam maxime si unquam alias visus es eas divinæ sapientiæ partes assecutus (quantum divina conferre licet humanis) in his tuis qui in Quartum Sententiarum in lucem prodeunt commentariis: quos iam æneis formulis excusos atque in exemplaria plus mille propagatos totus orbis non sine plausu obviis manibus excipiet.   Tanta est enim (absit dicto invidia ut abest assentatio) amenissimi ingenii tui fecunditas ut duos commentariorum fetus veluti fratres uterinos tam inter se dissimiles licet consentaneos edideris: ut e diversis natos qui unius esse parentis non norit autumet: et cum priores fuerint optimi: posteriores tamen sint longe meliores: usque adeo ut æquo jure de gemellis istis pronunciari possit: maior serviat minori.   Tanta enim bona pepererunt continuata in diversa facultate studia: quæ quia quamprimum me mittes: consules partim tuorum auditorum insignium sed defunctorum memoriæ inter quos præcipui fuerunt Iacobus Almain Senonensis.   David Craston tuus conterraneus: et Petrus Bruxelleus ordinis prædicatorum: partim viventium qui plurimi sunt utilitati.   Neque est quod formides tot charissimorum in ocio litterario desurdantium fultus patrociniis.   Nihil est inquam quod ora loquentium formides. hi nempe sunt invidiæ mores: semper ut antiquos præferat illa novis.   Sic sua riserunt sæcula Maonidem.   Nam si quis ista tua fetura operosa offendatur ipse secum agat iniuriarum: utpote qui neminem lædat præter seipsum.   Nempe quod palatum: quos oculos: quem tandem vultum sibi assumat: qui tam utili tam suavi tamque grata re offendatur?   Hi quicumque illi fuerint si in speculo suis coloribus sese pictos contemplentur: se primum rideant alios deinde admirentur necesse fuerit.   Iuvabit te potius illud Petrarchæ scitu dignissimum: præstare odiosum esse quam miserabilem nam quis unquam insignis: quis literarum studio clarus hoc invidiæ iaculo caruit?   Non defuit Homero suus homeromastix. habuerunt insignes poetæ suos zoilos. percurre animo omnes terras omnia secula cunctas historias evolve: vix unquam insignem unum quempiam hac peste immunem reperies.   Et ubi plerosque tui similes invidiæ fluctibus agitatos deprehenderis gloriandum tibi erit magis quam dolendum: utpote quod tam insigni illustrium virorum ascribaris consortio.   Hinc Themistoclem ferunt tum maxime nihil a se splendidum factum coniectare solitum: cum invidos nullos haberet.   Sola enim miseria est quæ invidia caret: nec ferunt [*sic*] nisi magnos fulgura montes. hinc et lucerna sacri eloquii Hieronymus ita loquitur: fiscelam iunco texerem: si canistrum lentis

2 E

iungerem viminibus : si servile aliquid humile angustum ocio delitescens
meditaret : nemo morderet : invideret nemo. Tolerandus est igitur invidiæ morbus et is quidem morbus quo sint peior a remedia miseria
videlicet atque ingenii hebetudo sive inertia. Quod Socrates aptissime hac
ironia ostendit percunctanti cuipiam qua arte invidiam abs se depellere
posset : si vixeris (inquit) ut Thersistes [*sic*] : quem virorum novissimum
in Iliade Homerus appellat. Qua re cum nihil fedius aut dici aut cogi-
tari possit hoc uno te admonitum velim (absit arrogantia verbo) Tu ne
cede malis : sed contra audentior ito. Vale itaque atque æternum vive
venerabilissime preceptor.

Ex fecunda Augusta nostra Suessonum. xiiij. Calendos [*sic*] Decembres
Anni MDXVI.

[*Reportata Duns Scoti*, 1517-18.]

JOANNES solo cognomento maior religioso patri francisco de bellavalle
doctori theologo ac reformatissimi conventus minorum Parisius
gardiano meritissimo. S. D.

Non parva ducor admiratione, vir circumspectissime, quidnam causæ est
cur doctoris subtilissimi theologiæ percunctatores in re litteraria minorum
vexilliferi opera quæ reportata vocant Parisii impressioni non demanda-
rentur. Qua propter bibliothecas anxius Parisienses adprime voluminum
fecundas perlustravi : ut exemplar aliquod lectione dignum invenirem.
Verum enim vero duo presertim in manus occurrerunt corrupta quidem
undequaque et scabrosa ac portentuosa ab ipsaque crebro veritate theologica prorsus aliena : quæ tamen non sine animi dolore quod opus ipsum
toties ab omnibus desideratum situ veternoso oblitteraretur perlegi : et
ut tandem theologiæ sititoribus satisfacerem impressione dignum censui
necnon oxoniensi lecturæ longe anteferendum. Nimirum dum oxonie
scriberet baccalaureus in nostra dumtaxat theologia erat. Dum vero
Parisiis legeret professor et multa topice et interdum tumultuarie in sua
oxoniensi lectura discussa peritissime resolvit : et multorum veterum
opiniones methaphisices disciplinam concernentes ad theologiam nullius
frugi reliquit ; ita ut vix solidum aut theologicum quid in oxoniensi
lectura quin id idem in hac lutecie luculenta professione offendes : immo
sane illam hæc dilucidat enodat et enucleat. Castigationi tamen aliunde
prepeditus vacare nequivi. Quare duobus baccalaureis recenter tamen
licentiatis, fratri videlicet Jacobo Rufin minoritano ac fratri petro du
sault, hunc nostrum montemacutum nobiscum incolenti curam huius
codicis emaculandi commisi. Quo fit ut hoc opus diu neglectum improbo
labore in lucem emissum a mendisque purgatum hilari fronte suscipias
velim studiosissimisque tuis religiosis commendabis. Vale.

[*In Tertium Sent.*, 1517.]

EPISTOLA.

IOANNES solo cognomento maior Matheo galthero doctori theologo perspicacissimo : necnon maioris monasterii abbati vigilantissimo S. P. D.

Sæpiuscule ratus sum, oculatissime vir, ingratitudine (qua scelus nullum est fedius) me notatum iri si lucubrationum mearum (qualecunque sint) ad te dicarem nichil. Et id causæ est in litterario ludo Parisii tam in artibus quam in theosophia a multis retro actis annis tecum familiaritatem et amicitiam contraxi non vulgarem : sed talem quod omnium iudicio chariorem te habuerim neminem. In cuius rei argumentum nostro in collegio et passim inter nostrates cum de te sermo incidebat, dicere solent prior aut abbas maioris, si ex tali loquutione augurari liceat, fortasse non abs re dicetur fuisse omnem maioris monasterii te futurum pastorem. sed quocunque spiritu ducti illi communius abbatem maioris te appellitarunt : sive fortuna sive pneuma ne divum ita protulere : tua virtute caudam scilicet monasterium adiecisti. quo circa ut a me hanc tetram ingratitudinem aboleam : et ut antiquæ nostræ amicitiæ pignus qualecunque apud te repositum sit. Hunc sententiarum tertium de novo excussum tibi nuncupo et devoveo. Accipe ergo hoc opusculum ea fronte qua tibi offertur. Vale. Raptum ex monte acuto pridie Kalend. Decembris.

[*In Matthæum*, 1518.]

OPPIDO quam Reverendo nec minus famigerabili in christo patri & domino domino Iacobo Beton archipræsuli glasguensi cordatissimo & Scotie cancellario oculatissimo Ioannes solo cognomine maior cernua cum veneratione in eo qui mandat salutes Iacob eviternam fœlicitatem.

Aegiptiorum olim famigerabilis propago Osirim (quem solem autumabat) vano delusa idololatritio venerabatur, illique mirandæ venustatis sceptrum insculpebat in quo oculi effigies depingebantur. Quo significaret eos qui sunt et prothomiste et antecellani sacros codices celestiave charismata linceis argi luminibus et altissima cogitatione circumspicere oportere utpote qui sunt aliorum ideæ et imagines. Qua propter non abs re instituit prudens mundi archetypus divina mysteria dumtaxat ab iis pertractari qui sapientiæ deosculatores essent. Proinde hebræorum vates et essei sapientiæ non minus quam sacerdotio vacabant. Quo fit ut librili mentis acumine obductus cui nostram hanc elumbem feturam devoverem primus obviis (ut aiunt) ulnis occurristi ut pote quæ singula in tua veneranda dominatione cernere perspicuum est archiantistes augustissimæ & candidatæ cancellariæ qui evangelicæ tubæ clepsidra existis, indeficiens ecclesiæ columem doctrinæ promptuarium. passim omnium in

ore haberis predicaris. Aquila summi dei paulus apostolus sobrietatem,
prudentiam, continentiam, sanctitatem, sanamque doctrinam in archi-
præsule prædicat quæ omnia & longe maiora in te uno affatim redundare
meridiana luce clarius conspiciuntur. Pauperibus delphicus es gladius
omnibus, tuam insignem mansuetudinem chameleontis instar ac commodam exhibes. Teque non solum stemmata in illud honoris cacumen
erexere, sed sacra religio doctrinæ maritata & mens sacrarum adapalibus
doctrinarum saginis pinguescens quæ effecerunt ut patriæ parens &
ecclesiæ nomenclator britannicæ dicaris iure & quidem optimo. Perge
igitur perge & sinuosi pectoris archivis mystica hæc recondas tragemata,
reconditaque omni poscenti rationem de ea quæ in te est fide spe &
charitate hubertim effunde. Quandoquidem in non vulgari laude habentur
Alexander Macedonius & Romanus quod ille homeri rapsodias, iste andinum
poema sicuti Cyripediam affricanus & yvo britonum confessor bibliæ canones
pulvino supposuerunt. In vero longe huberiores commendationis titulos &
spolia ampla referes si ut cœpisti cum sapientissima abigail & pulcherrima
rachel tua in dies magis atque magis incalescant pectora. Porro si ociari
velis delectabit domi, si rusticaberis peregrinabitur tecum hæc sponsa
innumeros degustaturus cœlestium charismatum lectulos, modo ipsam sin-
cipitis capillo comprehenderis. Verum enim vero (quarum trium charitum
penicilli mortales omneis beneficia recognoscere debere satis superque
effectim demonstrarunt due nempe connexe primam insequebantur porri-
gentive unum duo reddebant aurea poma) ideo tuæ sanctissimæ paternitati
quam obnixissime obstrigilatus hos commentarios non calabrij hospitis
munera devoveo quos clara (ut assoles) suscipias fronte eisque contra
blaterones murus ahenus existas. Epaminundas exercitum sine duce
cernens video (inquit) belluam sine capite, sic sine tuo numine & auspitio
nostra hæc tantilla editio investis & acephala exiret in proscenium. Vale.
Raptim exaratum in Academia glasguensi, x. cal. Decemb. Anno a
virgineo partu. ccccc. xviii. supra millesimum.

[*In Secundum Sent.*, 1519.]

JOANNES MAIOR magistris nostris Natali Bede et Petro tempete :
collegii Montisacuti vigilantissimis primariis salutem dicit.

Reliquit memoratu dignum portius ille Latho [Porcius Latro] censorius
non minus ocii quam negotii reddendam esse rationem. Qua percelebri
sententia admonet nos ipsa litterarum ocia nervis anhelis amplecti, ex
quibus uberior emanat fructus quam ex tumultuosis temporalium rerum
occupationibus. Quid enim excogitari possit litteraria quiete iucundius?
quid suavissima scripturarum amenitate dulcius? qua corporei recreantur
spiritus et ieiune mortalium mentes pascuntur. Tibi illa animi operatio
secundum virtutem in vita perfecta consistit : ubi summa illa ociandi
voluptas reperitur, quam plerisque ut gratissimo scientiæ fruerentur
oblectamento expetierunt. Ergo itaque preclarum Lathonis secutus

documentum ocii mei rationem hoc brevi epistolio vobis reddere decrevi,
prestantissimi Montisacuti moderatores, quibus acutissima ingenii acies
nedum nature dotibus insita, verumetiam laboriosa lima contemplationis
adeo polita est ut non sit qui limpidius perspicatiusque intueri possit
hanc nostram secundam in secundum sententiarum editionem : quam
non immerito vobis dedicavimus, que licet haud preclaris ac maximis
vestris in me beneficiis correspondeat : illam tamen obviis voluntarius
suscipite : Valete litterarum presidium.

[*In Quartum Sent.* 1519.]

IOANNES MAIOR : Venerandis in Christo Patribus ac præsulibus :
Gauuino Douglas episcopo Dunkeldensis [*sic*]: & Roberto Cokburn
episcopo Rosensi salutem.

Hisce diebus nuperque exactis circumspectissimi præsules lucubrationem secundum ingenioli mei tenuitatem in Sententiarum Quartum
ad Ariophanis [*sic*] lucernam edidi : quam chalcographis emunctissime
insculpendam curavi. Et quoniam mos est antiquus longum servatus in
ævum : qui nec apud neotericos exolevit : ut scriptores suas lucubratiunculas ni aut pluribus dicent morem illum observare mihi volupe fuit :
ideoque monumentum hoc qualecunque meæ in vos necessitudinis pignus
consecrandum nuncupo : his rationibus persuasus : quod non solum
uterque vestrum est mecum Scotus Britannus : sed et patriæ finibus pro-
pinquissimus.   Natalitii siquidem soli unius intercapedinem dialogus in
exordio Primi enucleat : Alterius origine Hadingthona plenius gaudet :
quæ mei studii primitias dulcibus amplexibus fovens : suavissimoque
grammaticæ artis lacte me neophitum enutriens : et ad longiusculam
ætatem provexit : et vix a Glegorno viculo (unde ipse sum oriundus)
quinquies mille passuum intervallo discriminatim se iungitur : sic ut
complures me Hadingthonensem appellitent : haud iniuria : tum quod
utriusque vestrum contubernio tam domi quam Parisiis amice et familiariter usus fuerim : tum propter vestrarum laudum præconia : de quibus
plene paucis dicere nequeo : quocirca ut Sallustius de Carthagine : malo
tacere quam parum de eis loqui. His itaque de causis hanc lucubratiunculam vobis dicandam censui.   Hanc igitur nostram opellam non severis
ac elatis superciliis sed benignis et modestis (ut soletis omnibus adesse)
suscipite precor. Valete. Actum Parisiis in Collegio Montis acuti.   Anno
domini sesquimillesimo decimo sexto.   Octavo Calendas Decembres.

IOANNIS MAIORIS in exordio praelectionis lib. quarti sententiarum ad
auditores propositio.

In huius lectionis principio, studiosi viri, aliqua dicere institui. Fortasse
multis apprime placebit non amplius in sententias scribendum esse : cum
iam in eas scriptum sit. Quod argumentum si efficaciam habeat ullam a

diebus Magistri Sententiarum, in sententias finem scribendi imposuerit :
cum tamen constet plerosque post ipsum resolutius et clarius materias
quas collegit explicasse.   Multas enim quæstiones sub eisdem titulis
movere scriptores et creberrime diversis modis respondent ac eruditiorem
ineruditior nonnunquam castigat.   Dicite Pierides non omnia possumus
omnes.   Contradictione namque et exercitatione exploratur veritas, et
hominum malitia ingenioque vario casus ancipites in medium prodiere
in quibus est tenebrosa aqua in nubibus aeris sententiam ferre.   Novis
etenim supervenientibus causis novo opus est remedio quod Ecclesiastes
innuit dicens : Faciendi plures libros nullus est finis.   Et ut alter inquit :
Laudamus veteres sed nostris utimur annis.   Præterea unius monumentum magis quibusdam placet ob ordinem et venam discurrendi
quam alterius fortasse doctoris ; et ita is illo utilior, sicut cibus minus
digestibilis a peritis physicis admittitur, si cum maiore aviditate sumatur.
Insuper nominalium adhuc vidi neminem qui opus in Quartum ad umbilicum calcemque perduxerit : quod in eos tanquam probrosum alii retor-
quent dicentes nominales logice et philosophie sic implicari ut theosophiam
negligant : et tamen varia sunt theologica quæ metaphysicam præsup-
ponebant.   Conabor ergo nominalium principiis adhibitis in singulas
distinctiones Quarti unam quæstionem vel plures scribere quas et reales
si advertant facile capient.   Utrinque enim viæ theologia (circa quam
præcipue versabor) erit communis.   Et quia iam innumeri a trecentis
annis scripsere : materiis quas alii minus discusserunt (si eas utiles
consuero) iuxta temporis exigentiam prolixius insistam communiorem
præteriens nisi quatenus conducent ne opus mancum et præsuppositum
ab aliis videatur.   Communia enim et necessaria omnes acceperunt et
tamen nullus ab aliquo : quia illa in nullius potestate sunt : sicut de aqua
Sequanica et communi omnes accipiunt sed de aqua sui putei solus dominus
fundi.   In re prolixa paucis totam materiam epilogabo cum nonnullis
obiter inter summandum occurrentibus ut quilibet facilius quæ dicere
volumus memoriæ mandet.   Invidiæ iacula aspernabor.   Licet enim
Martinus Magister quæstione penultima de temperantia dicat seniores
iunioribus in re scholastica invidere : non sum de numero iuniorum nam
hoc libro absoluto quadragesimi noni anni fimbrias aggredior.   Etiam non
est facile credere in theologis qui concionando ad populum et legendo
semper invidiam carpunt damnant et pessundant quod invideant nec
aliarum professionum viri nobis invidebunt : siquidem solum invidet
singulis singulo et poeta poetæ, et si aliqui tetrici illo monstro feriantur :
sententiæ Salomonicæ non sum nescius dicentis qui observat ventos non
seminat.   Propterea censeo non esse timendum.   Cæterum quod secundo
scribam non est (ut aliqui falso putant) me opus prius in Quartum emissum
castigare : licet non turpe ducam (ubi par est) canere palinodiam, nam bis
vel ter aliam editionem publice legi et tamen nec ego nec auditorum
aliquis quicquam offendit quod non putaretur probabile. nunc tamen ratus
sum post lecturas crebriores me opus maturius completiusque edere posse :
an id fecerim (cum quilibet sibi plus æquo afficiatur) aliorum sit iudicium.

Nam ut ait Flaccus, Scribimus indocti doctique poemata passim. Intentionis meæ est mihi et aliis proficere : mihi quidem ne ingenium in morem ferri in terra absconsi, rubiginem contrahat, et ut veterum omnium virorum fomentum evitem, de aliorum particulari commodo eorum sit judicium. Rursus si singulas materias quas tango non ita exacte cribraverim ut expedit : lector consideret aliorum librorum materias quas ad sua loca propria reservavi et non unam habui quæstionem terminandam. Modo vetus est proverbium : Pluribus intentis minor est ad singula sensus; et Davus sum non edipus. Nec humanam opem habui nisi calcographi qui vigilantissime insudavit : ut commata virgulæ periodi non deessent : licet variis manibus exemplar scriberentur. Famulus enim meus interdum lectionibus quibus intererat impediebatur : et scriptura mea erat cæteris difficulter legibilis. ❡ Cæterum si in hoc opere vel in alio in lucem emisso vel emittendo erraverim sacrosanctæ Romanæ ecclesiæ et aliis facultatis theologiæ Parisiensis matris meæ acquiesco iudicio : et quod ille approbant vel reprobant hoc ipsum approbo vel reprehendo.

Dixi.

[Introd. in Aristot., 1527.]

Johannes solo cognomento Maior acutissimo theologo Petro Chaiplaine rectori Dunneun. S. P. D.

Nosti, eruditissime vir, theosophiæ professores in Scotia Britanniæ liberales profiteri artes. Illud rei theologice conducibile non ab re suspicantur, questionarii in sententias nunc dialectices ceratinas & soritas interserunt, nunc philosophiæ abdita elucidationis gratia annectunt, ipse hoc institutum probans utrique facultati pro ingenioli ruditate genitali solo his paucis exactis annis operam impendi, nec destiti quousque stellifer athlas solarem orbem octies ab occasu eoam plagam versus complete circumtor queret, qua circumgiratione octonos volubiles compleui annos. Summulas (quas abhinc triginta annos Parisiorum leutitia cudimus) auditorio perlegimus, antiquo genere studii partim delectatus in Aristoteles stragerite logicam iuxta ac philosophiam interea quæstiones absoluimus, necnon introductiones summularum vice edidimus. ❡ Cæterum cui hanc opellam dicarem circumspicienti precipuus occurrebas, nec fluxis rationibus tractus id operis tibi nuncupaui. In primis lucubrationum mearum studiosum te vidi, idemtidem artium inuolucra haudquaquam spernentem. In earum spinosis ac cornutis elenchis non parum oblectamenti capis, diuinam paginam cum aliis scitu dignis cum otium suppeditat misces. Denique es mihi conterraneus nedum genere Scotus Britannus verum etiam Laudoniensis. Sumus enim ambo sub feracis Laudonie meditullium creti, his atque aliis argumentis haud frigidis allectus tuæ eruditioni hosce labores deuoui. Duas vias extremas in logicalibus sum contemplatus, aliqui sophismata ac cornutos sillogismos in totum reiiciunt, contra vero alii illos in immensum producunt, sophistarum meras præstigias auide pertractantes, quos pseudo dialecticos nec iniuria multi appellitant, in talibus quisquiliis cuiuslibet hominis & alterius angeli uterque asinus currit totos dies inutiliter conterunt. Inter hos lapsus interstes mediare laboraui. ❡ In super Hugoni spens omnium bonarum litterarum promptuario meo nomine salutem dices. Est enim venerabilis tui collegii sancti Saluatoris prefectus vigillantissimus, omnium horarum vir, centoculus Argus, nulli mortalium (quos nouerim) mansuetudine ac comitate secundus, hæc animi placabilitas Atropos fatale stamen prorogat, ac senilem longeuitatem parit. octoginta annos citra mineruæ dispendium natus est, nec adhuc memoriæ armarium est illi contractum. Tanta ingenii dexteritas rarissima est inuentu, lanificas sorores ardescens bilis præpropere‚inuocat, & inexorabilum pacarum [sic] filum rumpere coadiuuat, hoc uno superciliosum eum iocose dixeris, suam molem iactans Johanne maiore‚sese altiorem præconisauit. Verum enim vero nostræ proceritatis abiectæ me pudet, breuicole admodum sumus stature, plus ab Og rege Basan & staterosis quam pomilionibus elongamur, hæc inter iocandum carptim litterarum monumentis commendaui, dum mei Hugonis sermo incidit paucis diuelli nequeo. ita illius insita urbanitas, ac vitæ, candor meo in sinu amicitiæ imaginem iecit, ut antequam humanis validixero neutiquam oblitterabitur. ❡ Nec Thomam Ramsay frugi doctrinæ officinam silenter præteribis, mei causâ illum pleno ore salutabis, de eius alterna febricula decennio continuata lubens commentarer, sed vereor ne suum in Johannem sales recitantem stomachetur. Attamen sua benigna cum venia hoc unum dixero, diem illum quo prospera valitudine fruitur albo lapillo notet, eo colloquium atque irrequietum motum subduplet, alteram partem crastinam in lucem seruet, fausto ac infausto die æqualiter est atque bibit, verum hoc cubiculo necnon taciturnitate gaudet, illo vero turturis‚silentio utitur, vicatimque motatur. Guilermum Guyndum & Johannem Annandum cenobitica vita & scientia conspicuos infestat, noua quæ circumferuntur locupletat, discrasiam acrasi sola taciturnitas tita [sic] despescit. Hisce cum solicitudinibus vix feruidum ingenium litterario ludo relaxat, ebdomadatim doctoris subtilis placita explanat. Signa originis intricata, naturas communes formalitates, nexibus lororum gordii tenebrosiores aperire magno molumine conatur, sane magne est acrimonie sterilia & captu difficilia ditare. Vale, ex Monte acuto Anno virginei partus sesque millesimo vigesimo septimo, Sexto decimo Kalendas Decembris.

[*In Secundum Sent.* 1528]

JOANNES MAIOR Hadyngtonanus, Natali Bedæ et Petro Tempeste contheologis, et collegii scholasticorum Montisacuti primariis vigilantissimis, S. D.

Reliquit memoratu prorsus dignam M. Portius Cato ille Censorius sententiam: non minus ocii quam negocii reddendam esse rationem: Qua nos admonet, adhortaturque ipsa literarum ocia neruis anhelis amplecti : quippe ex quibus uberior emanat fructus quam ex tumultuosis temporalium rerum occupationibus. Quid enim excogitari possit literaria, quiete iucundius? Quid suauissima scripturarum amœnitate dulcius? qua corporales recreantur spiritus et ieiunæ alioqui mortalium reficiuntur mentes, ubi videlicet illa animi operatio secundum virtutem in vita perfecta consistit, ubi summa illa ociandi voluptas reperitur, quam plærique ut gratissimo scientiarum fruerentur oblectamento, vehementissimo expetierunt studio. Ego itaque præclarum hoc Catonis documentum secutus, et ocii mei rationem hoc epistolio vobis reddere conatus præstantissimi Montisacuti moderatores, quibus acutissima ingenii acies non solum naturæ dotibus insita, verumetiam sedula contemplationis lima, adeo polita est, ut non sit qui theologica præsertim limpidius perspicaciusque intueri possit : hanc in secundum sententiarum disputationem pridem vobis dicatam, diligentius reposui, et cribro theologico ab alienis inquisitionibus repurgaui. Duobus enim ferme seculis iam transactis theologiam tractantes, quæstiones mere physicas, metaphysicas, et nonnunquam mathematicas, suis scriptis inserere haud sunt veriti : quorum vestigiis tametsi inuitus, illorum tamen exemplo innixus, similia in disputationibus nostris pertrectare non erubui : siquidem ea tempestate theologiæ studentes alia rudimenta tanquam protrita et captu nimis quam facilia contempserunt. Verum abhinc decem, plus minus, annos, magna pestilentium hæreticorum cohors cortice sacrorum fulta, quamquam abominabilia delyria inuexit : hoc tamen boni (domino sic volente, qui quorundam vitiis ad uniuersi utitur decorum) suos inter errores attulit, ut sacris literis et illarum illustrationi theologiæ professores syncerius insudarent, et aliena studia reiicerent. Quocirca (ut iam dixi) multa huic ætati minus grata in his disputationibus stili parte illa delebili expunxi, relictis duntaxat quæ præ cœteris desideranda lectoribus sunt visa. Quam lucubrationem vobis denuo nuncupatam pro veteri inter nos amicitia et charitate obuiis (ut aiunt) ulnis suscipite. Valete, firmissima eloquiorum morumque castorum præsidia. Ex Montisacuti collegio literis et moribus decorato ad quintum Kalendas Septemb. M.D.XXVIII.

[*Ibid.*]

PETRUS PERALTA Petro ab hortis doctori theologo eruditissimo S. P. D.

Recognouit hos in secundum librum sententiarum commentarios superioribus diebus Joannes Maior (doctor, tam vere theologus, quam vere doctor,) quos a se olim editos ideo ad seueriorem censuram reuocauit, quod animaduertisset in illis esse nonnulla, suum in aliis habitura locum, quæ tamen hic haud dubie superfluerent : et contra pleraque his addi posse quæ illi grauior ætas et maturior eruditio suggessissent. Neque enim veritus est, vir ad ostentationem minime compositus, ne ab improbis vitio detur, id opus ad incudem reuocasse, quod tot ante annis in lucem a se emissum agnoscat : quin hoc potius nomine theologiæ candidatos se

demereri putat, quos neque plerisque rebus iam recisis ut huic argumento
non ita conuenientibus detinuerit, neque aliis pluribus huius loci propriis
quæ adiectæ sunt defraudauerit. Iussit itaque mihi is, ut quæ in hoc
volumine obseruatione digna viderentur (quæ plurima sunt atque optima,
diligenter annotata) in alphabeticum indicem redigerem, quod in eiusdem
operis editione prima Antonius Coronellus magna vir eruditione sed
maiori ingenio fecerat · sic enim fieri ut rebus ipsis studioso lectori obuiam
factis atque expositis, indagandi molestia neminem ab his legendis auer-
teret. Reliquum est ut quando ego eius viri authoritate impulsus, cui
quicquam denegare nephas esset, quod imperatum est utcumque præsti-
terim, nostri laboris partem non exiguam præstantiæ tuæ cui omnia debeo,
nuncupem. Tu igitur qua nos nostraque soles fronte, diligentiolam
nostram boni consulens suscipe, et in hortos istos admitte : in quibus sunt
omnis disciplinæ præsertim theologicæ et fontes irrigui et arbores proceræ
amœnissimis studiorum et naturæ fructibus decoratæ : de quibus quia
alias plenius loqui constituimus consultius nunc tacere, quam parum
dicere ducimus. Vale igitur decus et præsidium nostrum dulcissimum.
Ex Monteacuto ad Calendas Septemb. MDXXVIII.

[*Quæst. Logic.* 1528.]

IOHANNES MAIOR Hadyngtonanus Ioanni Vueddel bonarum artium
doctori. S. D.

Dum Iuniores essemus Aristotelis Strageritæ logicen nostra pro virili
elucidavimus, necnon quæstiones de moræ[?] literæ explanativas inter-
servimus.   Hisce diebus veterem dialecticam tipographis tradidimus,
quam operam tibi velut amicorum uni nuncupamus, ut veteris nostræ
amicitiæ non currax sit pignus.   Roberto banerman, atque gawino logy,
in artibus vigilantissimis præceptoribus meo nomine salutem dices. Vale.
Ex monte acuto, anno salutiferi partus duodetrigesimo supra sequimilles-
simum undecimo Kalen. octobris.

[*In Evangelia.* 1529.]

IOANNES cognomento Maior lectori salutem.

In nonnullis te admonitum lector esse cupimus : ante omnia si in
bibliaca scriptura aliqua variatio evenerit id præter meam opinionem
contigisse arbitreris : receptissimum enim ecclesiæ usum in contextu
bibliaco mutare alienum censui, hoc non semel in commentariis insinuo.
Iussi ut nihil illic variarent, verumtamen circa illud non oppido insudavi,
præsupponens illud facile factu per alios, non tamen eadem vocabula
in commentario assumpsi ut verbi causa docilis pro docibilis scripsi :
ecclesiam pro hominum consessu, et non pro æde sacra cepi. Ita enim

Valla et ornatioris eloquii homines faciunt. Semper tamen potius sententias quam sermonis politiam assequi curavimus ; aliorum est eloquentiæ
fiumine sua asserta ornare, nobis sat est venere dicendi neglecta bar-
bariem utcunque devitare. Qui in oratorum pigmentariis, studii partem
multo maximam consumpsit splendore currentis stili auditorum animos
illicit. In Aristotelica doctrina et scholasticorum processu assuetus per-
politis verbis posthabitis rem ipsam comminus attingere curat. Aliquibus
placet hic aliis placet ille, uniusquisque [sic] pro suo palato escas inquirit.
Cæterum neque miretur doctus si non viam illi gratiorem usquequaque
imitor, diversa sunt hominum ingenia, nec in paradoxis ubique est
concordia, plusquam in ciborum sectatione : verbi causa aliquis festum
conceptionis deiparæ nullo modo putat ad corpus virgineum referendum,
aliter tamen scripsi, et ut paulo fusius id explanem, Magister sententiarum distinctione trigesima secundi libri ait : quod est qualitas morbida
in carne genitorum ab Ada quæ animam primo momento quo est in rerum
natura inficit, hanc morbidam .qualitatem fomitem appellitant. Hoc
Henricus a Gandavo, Ockam tertio quolibeto, et Gregorius ariminensis
insequitur, dicens tortuosum serpentem suo sibilo et inflatu corpora
protoplastorum infecisse. Ad hoc Augustinum libro quarto contra
Iulianum capite trigesimo sexto introducit : sive fomes hoc modo pona-
tur sive alio, dico deiparam illam fomitem nunquam habuisse. Nam
sicut anima eius primo puncto temporis quo erat in rerum natura gratia
erat referta, ita eius corpus primo momento quo extitit fuit fomitis ex-
pers. Itaque suo modo sanctum, non per gratiam gratificantem cuius est
incapax. Anologiam [sic] accipito: nonne oleum exorcizatur et consecratur
atque in chrisma sanctificatur : sic aqua lustralis benedicitur, templa
polluta reconciliantur et sanctificantur. Ita erat de massa illa ex
qua corpus palestinæ virginis est factum. Decentia manuductionis ad
propositum applica, indecentia obliterato : utpote corpus eius nunquam
erat pollutum, siquidem pollui almam virginem dedecet, sanctificari ei
congruit. Hoc accipe, illud vero abolito. Itaque quia præ tacta via corpus
omnis infectionis exors erat, animam inficere nequibat : fomes non est
homini naturalis : primis enim parentibus ante lapsam non infuit :
proinde decuit illum a virgineo corpore removeri : quas ob res ecclesia
festum conceptionis Christiferæ tam corporis quam animæ sexto idus
decembris annuo ritu celebrat : nam ex corpore non ex anima Christus
portionem accepit. Præterea in Ioannis sextum : dico hominem rem
divinam audientem annis senescere, nec rogantem divos semper releva-
men morbi impetrare, eius enim saluti fortasse obest : deus tamen præro-
gativas sanctis largitur ut variis hominum laboribus succurrunt, quin [?]
expedire norit. Sanctorum in hoc cultui minime detraho, sum enim
severus osor vitiorum eorum qui suis ineptiis in sanctos temere blacterant.
Commentariusque noster sexti decimi capitis in Ioannem hæc aperte
pronunciat. Quædam ex libro sententiarum quasi manifestaria iam non
repeto : utpote in Ioannis nonum, ubi dico quod perpauci erant parvu-
lorum Sodomæ et Gomorræ non purgati ab originali, illic enim prætereo

duo paradoxa quæ ad primam distinctionem quarti sententiarum recito :
quomodo parvuli ab originali labe purgabantur. Unum theologorum
placitum tenet exterioribus sacrificiis amicorum ad parvulos relatis.
Verum hæc præmonitio in immensum cresceret si singula speciatim
explicaremus. Gratus autem et humanus lector boni consulet : et anci-
pitia in meliorem partem interpretabitur : nec siquid ad stomachum non
facit, statim expuet, memor illius gallorum adagii : qui sine hospite expen-
sarum calculum ponit, nihil agit. Ego pro virili Christianam modestiam
tenui, neminem qui in gremio ecclesiæ se continet nominatim taxo,
cuiuslibet dicta minus placentiam modeste impugno : æquissimo animo
laturus, si de meis minus accurate scriptis benigne me quispiam admoneat.
Hoc præmonitum volui. Vale lector bone.

[*Ibid. ad init. Marci.*]

IOANNES MAIOR Hadingtonanus Ioanni Boluaco Nivernensi theologiæ
professori acutissimo et amico integerrimo, nec non gregis dominici
apud divum Iacobum in Parrhisiorum Lutetia pastori vigilantissimo
S. P. D.

Quandoquidem lucubratiunculas nostras in Aristotelicam philosophiam
emissas, tibi, vir doctissime, ut in artibus illis liberalibus quondam præceptori optimo, nuncupavimus : e re atque officio fore duximus, si com-
mentariolorum nostrorum in sacrosancta evangelia partem saltem
aliquam eidem ut contheologo et perpetuo amico, dicaremus. Accipe
igitur quas in divi Marci evangelium mox impressori Badio daturi sumus
expositiunculas, ea quidem lege, eaque stipulatione ut quæ inter legendum
tibi occurrent a nobis errata, corrigas, et reposita atque emendata mox
nobis remittas : ut studiosi lectores non minus argutissimæ limæ tuæ
debeant quam meo huic præcipitanter scribentis calamo. Vale. E
Monte acuto ad Idus Martias sub Pascha hoc MDXXIX.

[*Ibid. in Lucæ Ev.*]

REVERENDO in Christo patri ac domino, Gawino Dumbar, Glasguenn
archiepiscopo dignissimo, Ioannes Maior Hadingtonanus cum
omni observantia fœlicitatem.

Cum hisce diebus in sacrosanctum divi Lucæ evangelium commentarios
nostros novitios typographo excudendos committere festinarem, anxie
mecum disquirere cæpi, cuinam, iuxta veterem eorum qui lucubrationes
novas emittunt consuetudinem, eos ut præsidi honorifico et vindici
potenti nuncupatos dedicem : tandemque id sedulo actitanti una atque
eadem amplissima dignitas tua, Archiepiscope præstantissime, sub oculos
meos omni ex parte observata est, visaque iustis nominibus, cui eos
dicarem dignissima. Et quod in eadem Parrhisiorum academia philo-

sophiæ operam navavimus auctoramentumque cepimus. Et quod opera novitia recensendi et in ordinem, si ita visum, redigendi summam potestatem adeptus es: in præclaro siquidem Andegauorum gymnasio ad utriusque iuris apicem evectus es: idque magno tuo merito, totiusque musæi facile celeberrimi mirifico applausu. Non enim Minervam istam, ut plerique alii, ab limine duntaxat salutasti: nec ex isto amplissimo et inexhausto utriusque iuris fonte, ut canis Ægyptius Crocodilum veritus ex Nilo parce et anxie bibens statim aufugisti: sed ut Bithias ille Maronianus, impiger hausit spumantem pateram, et pleno se proluit auro: ita divini seu pontificii, et humani seu cæsarei iuris, nectareos latices non summis modo labris, sed pectore capacissimo et sagacissimo imbibisti amplissime, illicque condidisti ubi nec tiniæ corrodere, nec fures demoliri, nec piratæ eos deprædari valeant. Istis itaque et artium bonarum et legum canonumque thesauris honustus, ut tutus ita securus altricem navibus petisti patriam, nihil illorum nomine piratas Oceanum infestantes veritus. Negociatorum enim illi extrariis bonis arcis fragilibus inclusis inhiant non mentium thesauris, in quos neque fortuna neque prædo potestatis habet quicquam. Quæ enim solo studio et virtute acquiruntur casu auferri nequeunt: proinde talia sunt sola vere bona et vere nostra: quod quia tibi, viro sapientissimo, perspectissimum etiam tunc erat, potuisti cum Biante illo a Marco Tullio celebrato, vere dicere, omnia mea mecum porto. Istis igitur ornamentis præter naturæ dotes amplissimas et dumbariæ domus nobilissimæ natales clarissimos in patriam vere inclytam receptus, mox ad Glasguensem archiepiscopatum omnibus punctis et pleno suffragio evectus es, nihil insolentior ex tanta cathedra effectus: quocirca cum tua laude de te quoque dici potest, quod a Pitaco Mityleneo dictum Aristoteles, ut nosti, Ethicorum quinto celebrat, Magistratus virum ostendit. Illinc enim me quoque respicere tua comitas et generosa humanitas dignata est: qua de causa, ut occœpi dicere, hanc novitiam editionem iustis nominibus tuæ excellentiæ debitam dicamus, et ut eam benevole accipias, precamur. Vale.

Ex Parrhisiorum academia Anno sesquimillesimo vicesimo nono ad calendas Aprilis.

[Ibid. in Joannem.]

REVERENDO in Christo patri ac domino Roberto Senali doctori theologo et episcopo Vendesino, meritissimo, Ioannes Maior Hadingtonanus. S.P.D.

Quo sæpius attentiusque mecum considero rationem huius nostri propositi, quo enarrationes in divi Ioannis evangelium, spectabilissimæ sapientiæ tuæ, præsul doctissime, ab invidulorum morsiculis protegendas dicare constitui: eo concinnius appositiusque (deo, ut facile credo, sic volente) hoc facinus pium quidem sed audacius susceptum molitus videor. Plurima siquidem quæ in ipso Ioanne et miratur et veneratur ecclesia mihi in te quoque et mirari et venerari datum est. Primum (ut hinc

incipiam) Ioannes peculiari quadam nuncupatione etiam a se non semel
dictus est, discipulus ille quem dilexit dominus. Deinde cum esset
plurimorum iudicio inter apostolos natu minimus, diu tamen vivendo id
gloriæ nactus est, ut vulgata iam agnominatione diceretur senior. ˙ Tum
licet piscatoriæ artis professor esset, et in nulla præterquam Christi et
spiritus sancti academia institutus, apposito tamen nomine supra cæteros
vocatus est theologus. Demum cum vero simile sit primum multa scrip-
sisse, ac ex magistri et domini dictantis ore plurimos præsertim sermones
excepisse, ultimus tamen evangelium edidit : eaque circumspectione
temperavit, ut plurima quia ab aliis bene scripta, prætermiserit, et non
omnia quæ scribere potuisset, si expedire censuisset, conscripserit. Unde
et ipse in evangelii calce : sunt autem, inquit, et alia multa quæ fecit
Iesus : quæ si scribatur per singula, nec ipsum arbitror mundum capere
posse eos qui scribendi sunt libros : ob quod et temperanter docentis
domini et circumspecte scribentis discipuli in nos beneficium, immensas
debemus omnes supremæ providentiæ gratias. Nam quæcunque a domino
tradita discipulus nobis scripta reliquisset, etiam cælestia illa arcana
quam capere vix possumus, omnia et credere si non capere, et meminisse
si non perficere debuissemus. Parcius ergo ne nostram capacitatem
obrueret, et magister ille summus cælestia docuit, et discipulus iste
divinus scripsit : qui tamen sic evangelium ut hæreticos confunderet
exorsus est ut si quo altius, ut aquila evolasset, aut sublimius ut filius
tonitrui intonuisset, totus eum mundus comprehendere nequisset. Verum
ut facti mei rationem ad divi Ioannis elogia applicem : ut ipse domini
discipulus et dictus est et fuit charissimus : ita (quod verecunde exalta-
bunde tamen repeto) omnium discipulorum inventus est mihi et ob
ingenii bonitatem, doctrinæ excellentiam, et quæ merito secuta est digni-
tatem maxime observandus. Deinde ut ille senior ob morum gravitatem
est peculiariter dictus, ita tu Senalis, non senili modo maturitate, quam
ante canos præ te tulisti, sed etiam senatoria, quasi divino præsagio id
cognominis sortitus. Tu ut ille Theologus, quia de divinis præter cæteros
locutus vulgo est nuncupatus, ita quod verecunde vere tamen dico, inter
paucos meruisti et esse et vocari theologus : et, quod amplissimum est,
etiam verus episcopus : nam quod episcopi quasi peculiare est officium,
divini verbi seminare semen, id ita deples, ut neque frequentius neque
felicius quisquam. Demum ut ille novissimus evangelium edidit, tametsi
fortasse primus scripsit, ita ego has novissimas in evangelia lucubratiunculas tuæ dexteriti quam primam suspicio et observo, et nuncupo et dico ;
ut quæ in eis offendes aut rudius aut negligentius dicta aut scripta, pro
solita tua in me clementia admoneas ut saltem, si iterum emisero a nobis
reposita castigatoria et emunctiora exeant. Hoc te rogatum volui. Vale.
Ex Acuto monte ad Calendas Maias. M.D.XXIX.

[*In Matth. ad init.*, 1529.]

Longe Reverendo in Christo patri, natalibusque splendido domino Iacobo Betoun Sancti Andreæ Archiepiscopo, Scotiæ primati & legatonato, Ioannes Maior Hadingtonanus, Theologorum minimus cum omni observantia Salutem.

Iuxta ingenii studiique tenuitatem et divinam gratiam, exposuimus, Præsulum dignissime, bisce diebus, Evangelistas quatuor : conati pro virili nostra ipsorum ubique synceram demonstrare symphoniam non solum diversorum inter ipsos, sed etiam uniuscuiusque in se, ut quod uno in loco dixerit alteri concordare noscat per omnia : antiquam præterea servare tralationem, & catholicas iuxta Romanæ ecclesiæ doctrinam per Doctores receptos traditiones. Quocirca Theophilacti Bulgarorum episcopi evangeliorum explanationes, ubi ab orthodoxorum sententia aberrare visæ sunt, repellimus. Wicleuitarum item et Hussitarum et eorum sequacium Lutheranorum pestiferas zizanias e bono dominici agri semine, quantum potuimus, evellimus : cæterorum quæ humano casu lapsi sunt, errata quidem fratri dicere. Denique ut summatim dicamus, nullum locum vel mediocriter docto ambiguum indiscussum prætermisimus, intermiscentes subinde breves quæstiunculas ; et earum, si amor studii nos non fallit, non pœnitendas decisiunculas, interim etiam prolixiunculas, præsertim quatuor, quas post enarrationem Evangeliorum, quia ad eorum elucidationem visæ sunt accommodatissimæ, adiecimus. In harum itaque salutis nostræ quadrigarum aurigam primum Mattheum directiones nostras celeberrimo nomini tui tuo, archiepiscope dignissime, iustis rationibus præscripsimus : et quod studiorum nostrorum bonam partem celsitudini tuæ debemus, & quod huiusmodi lectiones, nomini, professioni, generi, studio, moribusque tuis vel maxime conveniunt. Nomini quidem, nam et Jacobus nobis supplantatorem significat : tua autem præstans virtus Lutheranam hæresim, ut mox apertius docebo, ita in Scotia supplantavit, ut sperare liceat eam nunquam istic repululaturam : et Betonia, ut physici nobis tradunt, nobilis est hærba, in tertium usque gradum calida & sicca, animalis venenati morsui si superponatur præsentissimum præbens remedium : sicque circumspectissima tua sapientia nuper viperinæ Lutheranorum infectioni æternum peperit e Scotia exterminium. Professioni vero et dignitati tuæ, qui et Archiepiscopus es, et primas, et legatus (ut dicitur) natus Scotiæ, maxime convenit et lectitare et prædicare evangelia, iuxta sententiam illius cuius dignitati archiepiscopi succedunt, væh mihi est si non evangelizavero ; generi autem tuo, cui ut illustrissimo cuique semper fuit primum et antiquissimum, ecclesiæ sanctæ iura protegere et integræ fidei patrocinari. Porro studio tuo qui a teneris unguiculis sacris incubuisti lectionibus, ab evangeliis indivulsus, testimonio sunt priores nostræ in Matthæum expositiunculæ, quæ licet minus quam hæ posteriores accurate essent emissæ, in tuis tamen manibus visæ sunt, dum istic agerem fere semper. Denique moribus maxime

tuis, nam ut dicere occœpimus, non sine plurimorum invidia nobilem in
primis sed infelicem Lutheranæ hæreseos et perfidiæ sectatorem viriliter
sustulisti : ut secundum nomen tuum sit et laus tua. Nec ab re : nosti
enim ab illo, cuius successorem te diximus, ¦pronunciatum : si adhuc
hominibus placerem, Christi servus non essem. Hisce itaque de causis
ut boni consulens hanc lucubratiunculam et nuncupationem in partem
accipias bonam rogamus. Vale. Ex Monteacuto apud Parrhisios Musæo
illustri, ad octavum Kalend. Iulias. MDXXIX.

[*Arist. Ethic.* 1530.]

    REUERENDISSIMO in Christo Patri ac domino, domino Thomæ Vulsæ
        Sanctæ Romanæ Ecclesiæ titulo Sanctæ Cæciliæ presbytero Car-
        dinali, Eboracensium Archiepiscopo, Angliæque Primati, atque
        Apostolicæ sedis ab latere Legato, Ioannes Maior Hadyngtonanus
        cum omni obseruantia, Salutem.

    Sæpe multumque mecum decreui animoque concepi, Præsulum am-
plissime, lucubratiuncularum mearum (qualescunque sunt) primitias,
Anglorum cuipiam dicare nuncupareque Principi. idque iustıs (ut mihi
quidem visæ sunt) rationibus. Quarum primum (ne longus fiam) sibi
addicit locum communis patriæ, omnibus animantibus innatus amor ;
una enim Britannia, insularum in tota Europa celeberrima, quasi in navi
quadam, Oceano magno, parvo interstitio concludimur. Alterum siue
proximum locum, religionis et studiorum occupat consensio. A susceptæ
enim pietatis Christianæ primordio, multi et magni fuerunt in utroque
regno illustres in omni, sed præcipue in diuina sapientia viri : qui et
plures sunt, quam ut eos hac epistolari angustia complecti valeam, et
notiores quam ut debeam. Tertium, eumque ne multis agam, postremum
et tamen potissimum locum sibi vendicat, ingrati animi, quæ vel Persis
semper odiosissima labes fuit, etiam minimæ notæ, fuga. Tam enim
frequenti hospitio, tam humano comique colloquio, et tam amico com-
mercio ab Anglis acceptus dignatusque sum, ut sine immemoris animi
labecula diutius tacere nequeam. Abhinc enim quadraginta annos,
si iusto calculo supputaui, paternos primum egressus lares, cum per
Angliam Parrhisios iter facerem, tanta Anglorum humanitate retentus
et acceptus sum, ut annum integrum in celeberrimo Cantabrigiæ musæo,
nunc Christi nomenclatura illustrato, prima artium bonarum rudimenta
acceperim : atque ex illo quum per mare perpetuum potuissem, fere per
Angliam profectionem reditionemque fecerim : atque quod et recenti
memoria teneo perpetuaque, dum spiritus hos reget artus, tenebo, iam
quartus agitur annos, quo tua, Legate longe Reuerende, maiestas inter
ecclesiasticas totius Angliæ dignitates amplissima et facile princeps,
exiguitatem meam istac rursum iter habentem veteri Christianorum
hospitalitate susceperit : et ad literarium gymnasium tunc recentius a
magnifica beneficentia tua Oxoniæ institutum, præsentia et doctrina mea

utcunque illustrandum, oblata etiam splen[di]dissima mercede, inuitarit: verum tanta me tenuit matris iam meæ Parrhisiorum academiæ, et studii sociorum ac cœptorum librorum quos perficere affectabam, amor, ut ultro oblatam tam honorificentissimam conditionem accipere non potuerim : nunc igitur ne penitus immemor tanti arguar beneficii, et ut tot annos quod parturiuerim aliquando pariam, tibi tali tantoque in ecclesiastico ordine principi, ac theologorum, immo literatorum omnium Mecœnati, Aristotelis complurium iudicio philosophorum principis, moralium traditionum opus laudatissimum meis utcunque expositum commentariis et dico et dedico.   Quippe in quo opere, ut in reliquis alios, ita sese, id est naturæ vires superasse visus est : nam in omnibus fere sententiis, cum syncerissima catholicæ ac vere Christianæ persuasionis integritate concordat.   Liberum enim hominis arbitrium constanter asserit.   Manum sibi inferre ac necem consciscere ob rerum tristium deuitationem non vere fortis animi, sed potius meticulosi grauissime definit.   Voluptatem honestam et bonis expetibilem a spurcissimis illecebris quas Turcæ sibi proponunt, seiungit.   Felicitatem bomini in hac vita contingentem in heroicarum virtutum operatione constituit : duplicemque vitam et utramque laudabilem, actiuam dico et contemplatiuam, Iudæis olim in Rachele et Lya, nobis nunc etiam in Martha et Magdalena sororibus figuratam, miro iudicio prosequitur : nam hanc etiam superis, illam tum mortalibus accommodat.   Denique in tanto et tam multiiugo opere vix placitum unum Christiano homine indignum, si ut a nobis explanatum est legatur, offendas.   Proinde, Pater magnificentissime, ut qua humanitate et beneuolentia me nuper suscepisti, hanc nouam fœturam, tuæ dignitati etiam si longe (quod vellem) melior esset multo ante debitam et nunc ex animo dictatam, accipias rogamus.   Vale.   Ex collegio literario Montisacuti in Parrhisiorum gymnasio ad Calendas Iunias M.D. XXX.

[*In Primum Sent.* 1530.]

IOANNES MAIOR Hadingtonanus D. Ioanni Maiori Eckio Sueuo, cognomini ac contheologo, fideique orthodoxæ protectori strenuo, in fide ac charitate Christiana dilectissimo Salutem.

Abhinc annos ferme viginti, virorum optime, quæstiunculas complures in primum Magistri Sententiarum emisimus, in quibus multa quæ liberales concernunt artes, de formarum intensione et similia placita pro virili nostra discussimus, multaque refellimus.   Hic enim fere mos scribendi tunc theologis erat.   At quamquam bonam ætatis illius partem in Aristotelica doctrina exponenda transegi, tamen (quod ingenue fateor) mos ille scribendi parum mihi placuit, cum viderem eum auditoribus meis nec gratum nec iucundum.   Quando enim quartum sententiarum profitebar, auditores ad me numerosi confluebant: dum vero in primum Sententiarum scripta conterranei mei Ioannis Duns, aut Anglicani Guil-

helmi Okam, aut Gregorii Ariminensis, prælegerem, mira erat antequam
opus ipsum perlegerem, auscultatorum paucitas. Accessit præterea a
duodecim (si rite recordor) annis fidei catholicæ noua et detestanda
calamitas, Martini Luteri, et qui ab eo os ponendi in cælum temeritatis
ansam acceperunt, execranda hæresis : ad quam confutandam, omnes
theologiæ studiosi Luteciæ ad sacras sese literas, neglectis sententiarum
definitionibus, accinxerunt, ita ut nostra Academia Sorbonica obtutum
mentis omnem ad materias cuilibet captu faciles fixerit, positionesque
Sorbonicas ingeniosis animis dignas, in materias maiorum ordinarium
(ut vulgato more loquar) commutarint. Quod videns sacra nostra facultas,
ac verita ne sic multorum ingenia torperent, et in crassam degenerarent
Minervam, Baccalauriis (qui sunt theologicis sacris initiati) indixit, ut in
Sorbonicis et tentatiuis (ut dicimus) disputationibus, scholastica et
argutiora placita more maiorum nostrorum tractarent ac sustinerent, per-
mittens tamen eis thesim unam interserere cum corollariis facilioris et
minus theoricæ farraginis. Quocirca stilum tempori accommodaui, non
immemor illius Aristotelici dicti, Sæpius redeunt opiniones ; hoc est, mos
scholasticarum disputationum variatur crebrius : de extremo enim in
extremum transeunt, et rursus dum unum extremum est multitudine
tædiosum in alterum, quasi neglecto medio, recurrunt. Quare non osci-
tanter perspecta nonnulla in prologum olim a me disputata, quæ Aristotelica posteriora sapiunt, paucis percurri, et pauca physicalia quæ rem de
qua agitur patefaciunt carptim exaraui. Hunc autem primum librum sic
repositum observandæ et omnibus honorandæ præstantiæ tuæ nuncupaui,
cum propter nominis cognominisque ac studiorum inter nos communionem,
tum ob singularem obseruantiam nominis tui, quam non sólum apud
commilitones tuos theologos Parisienses, verum apud omneis boni nominis
Christianos meruisti, ob egregiam istam fidei Christianæ adversus impios
defensionem. Vale. Ex conclaui nostro in collegio Montis Acuti ad
Calendas Septemb. 1530.

'THE ASSEMBLY OF THE SAINTS'

Illustration used in Major's *In Matthæum Expositio*. 1518.

This woodcut was used by Notary in 1503, and at Paris by Hopyl in 1505-7 for his Dutch edition of the Golden Legend.

INDEX

INDEX

ABELARD, lxiv *n.*
Abercorn, 65.
Aberdeen, 36, 181, 278, 316, 348.
—— university, 28 and *n*, 29.
Aberdeenshire rivers, 33.
Abernethy collegiate church, 108.
—— Hugh, 187.
—— William, of Salton, 340, 349.
Abington (Aberton), sir Thomas, 323.
Achaius, king of Scots, 100 ; alliance with Charles the Great, 101, and *n.*
Acton, sir Roger, 342.
Ada, countess, 135, 165.
Adam of Ireland, 23 and *n.*
Adam of Kilconquhar, 188 *n.*
Adelbert, king of Kent, converted by St. Augustine, 90.
Adelstanfurd. *See* Athelstaneford.
Adelston. *See* Athelstan.
Aegidia. *See* Giles.
Aeneas Sylvius. *See* Pius II.
Aesop, 330.
Africa, 90.
Agarenes, 269.
Agincourt, 343.
Agned. *See* Edinburgh.
Agnes of Dunbar. *See* March, countess of.
Aidan, king of Scots, 87.
—— St., 37, 92-94, 97, 102.
Ailly, Peter d', bishop of Cambray, lvii, 411.
Airth, William, friar, cvi-cvii.
Akirkirre, son of Ecchach Audoch, 185.
Alain de Lille, 81 *n.*
Alan of Galloway, 168, 180, 189.
Alban, St., 60.
Albanac, son of Brutus, 50.
Albanactus, first king of Scots, 287.
Albany, Alexander, duke of, 211 *n*, 212, 386, 388.
—— John, duke of, 211 *n.*, 212.
—— Murdach, duke of, 339, 343-349, 354, 364, 367.
—— Robert, duke of, 355, 337, 338.
Albemarle, earl of, 180.

Albemarle, duke of, 340.
Alberic, bishop of Ostia, 135.
Albertus de Sax, 415, 422.
Albine, daughter of Diocletian, king of Syria, 1, 2 *n.*
Albinus, 102 *n.*
Albion, origin of the name, 1.
Alcaris, Antony, cxxv.
Alcluyd, 65.
Alcock, John, bishop of Ely, xxxvii *n*, xciii *n*, 26 *n.*
Alcuin, 102 and *n.*
Aldhame, 86.
Aldrey, king of Little Britain, 60.
Ale, 13.
Alertoun. *See* Northallerton.
Alexander of Macedon, 83, 264 and *n*, 270, 436.
—— VI., pope, cvii.
—— I., king of Scotland, 126, 132, 133, 210 *n.*
—— II., 167, 169-172, 179-181.
—— III., dispute regarding coronation of, 182 ; his coronation and genealogy, 184, 185 ; marries the daughter of Henry III., 186 ; taken by the earl of Menteith and carried to Stirling, 187 ; his death, 189 ; eulogy, 191.
—— son of Alexander III., 188, 189.
—— son of James I., 360.
—— lord of the Isles. *See* Ross, earl of.
—— of Argyll surrenders Dunstaffnage castle to Robert Bruce, 231.
Alexandria, 90.
Alfred, king of the West Saxons, 114.
Alinclud or Alclid. *See* Dumbarton.
Almain, James, lii, liv, lviii, 10 and *n*, 409, 411-414, 418, 433.
Almond, the river, 118.
Alnwick, 130, 186 *n.*, 387.
Alphin, king of Scots, beheaded by the Picts, 103.
Alpin, son of Ethach, 185.
Altisiodorensis, 229 and *n.*
Alured, king of Suffolk, 111.

Amberkeleth, king of Scots, killed by the Picts, 99.

Amboise, castle of, 390.

Ambrose, St., in Tours and Milan at the same time, 87 *n.*

Ambrosius Aurelius, 67, 69; lands with an army at Totnes, crowned king in London, kills Vortiger, enters into a treaty with Constantius, 78; defeats and slays Hengist, perishes by poison, buried in Stonehenge, 79.

Amiens, 391.

Anabat, William, ci.

Anacharsis the Scythian, 7 and *n.*

Anatolius, bishop of Laodicea, 92 and *n*, 96.

Andegavia, 146 *n.*

' Andium '. *See* Anjou.

Andrew, St., his relics brought to Britain by Regulus, receives gifts from Hungus, king of the Picts, 63; held in honour by Picts, 108.

Anglia, origin of the name, 72.

Anguischel, king of Scots, 84.

Angus, 279.

—— brother of Fergus II., 64.

—— a chieftain of Galloway, becomes a monk, 162.

—— countess of, treacherously murders Kenneth II., 118.

—— earl of, 295.

—— George Douglas, earl of, 340, 387.

—— William Douglas, earl of, 354, 356, 362, 364, 383, 386.

Anjou, 41, 146 and *n*, 153, 157, 445.

—— Geoffrey, earl of, 144, 170.

Anna, sister of Aurelius, 82.

—— queen of Richard II., 302.

Annabella, queen of Robert III., 332.

Annand, John, li, 440.

Annandale, 189, 293, 346.

Anselm, dean of Laon, compiler of the *Glossa Interlinearis*, 75 *n.*

—— archbishop of Canterbury, banished by William Rufus, 129; returns to England, 143.

Antoninus, archbishop of Florence, 52 and *n.*

—— Verus, 59.

Aquinas, Thomas, lxiii and *n*, lxiv *n*, cxxii *n*, cxxvii, 174, 184 *n*, 229 *n*, 422.

Aquitaine, 41, 146, 153, 253.

Arbroath, 165 and *n*, 169, 278.

Arbuckle, a friar, cviii.

Arcadius, emperor, 64.

Archery, 357 and *n.*

Aremorica in Gaul, 4, 17, 6c.

Argadia, 37 and *n.*

Argentolium, 8.

Argyll, 37, 38, 221.

Aristotle, lxx, cxxiii, 15 and *n*, 40, 72 and *n*, 75, 79, 115, 119, 352, 426-428, 439, 442-445, 449, 450.

Armagnac, 373.

Arran, island of, 37, 93.

Arteveldt, Philip van, 378 *n.*

Arthur, king, how he came to be king, his character, wars, armour, etc., 81-83; killed in battle, 84, buried in Glastonbury, 85.

—— son of Henry VII., 394.

Arthur's O'on, 58 *n.*

—— Seat, Edinburgh, 82 and *n.*

Arundel, earl of, 251, 254, 280, 307.

—— Thomas, archbishop of Canterbury, 307, 308.

Asahel, 112 and *n.*

Ascelin, founder of Montaigu college, xlvi.

Asslingith, Fechelmeth, son of Enegussa Buchyn, 185.

Assouan, 90 *n.*

Assyrian empire, foundation of the, 56.

Astrology, 183, 184 and *n*, 248.

Asturia, 54.

Athelstan of England, 108, 111 and *n*, 314.

Athelstaneford, 111 and *n.*

Athole, 221.

—— earl of, conspires against James I., 364; his execution, 368, 369.

—— David, earl of, 211 and *n*, 274-278.

—— Patrick, earl of, burnt to death, 181.

—— Robert, earl of, 365, 369.

—— Walter, earl of, 311, 331, 356

Aubert, Charles, 165 *n.*

Aubigny, Bernard, lord d', 345 and *n.*

Audley, lord, 379.

Audoch, Ecchach, son of Fiachrach Catinall, 185.

Augsburg, 397.

Augustine, St., 90, 91, 443.

Aurelius Commodus, 59.

Auvergne, 212.

Avignon, 306.

Avon or Sanda. *See* Sanda.

Awyna island, 37 and *n.*

Ayr, 194, 195, 196, 242.

BADELESSEMOR, BARTHOLOMEW, 251.

Badius, Jodocus, lxx, lxxix, xciv, c-cii.

Badyngton, William, 371.

Baldred, St., buried in three different places, 86, 87 *n.*

Balfour, Alexander, cxix.

—— Martin, rector of Duninoch, cxxi.

Baliol, Edward, 211, 269-279, 287, 293, 296.
—— Henry, 271.
—— John, 180, 192-194, 207, 211-215, 224 and *n*, 287, 291.
Balloch, Donald, rebellion of, 361.
Balmerino, 180, 278.
Balnaves, Henry, a lord of session, cvii.
Bamburgh, 147.
Bane, Donald. *See* Donald.
Banister, William, 223.
Bannerman, Robert, li, 442.
Bannockburn, 221; origin of the name, 232; position of the armies, 233; the battle, 239-241.
Barclay, David, of Aberdeen, slain by Douglas, 293.
—— Thomas, cxxi.
Bardolf, lord, 341.
Barley, 7, 13.
Barnet, battle of, 391.
Barry, Thomas, first provost of Bothwell, 328 and *n*.
Bartane or Bertane cloth, 28 *n*.
Bartholomew's *De Proprietatibus Rerum*, 45 and *n*.
Bass Rock, 34 and *n*, 342.
Bassianus, a Roman general, 61, 62.
Baston, William, his verses on the battle of Bannockburn, 242 and *n*.
Baugy, battle of, 88 *n*.
Bayeux, bishop of, created earl of Kent, 127; defeated by Malcolm, 128.
Beaton, David, archbishop of St. Andrews, cx-cxi, 351 *n*.
—— James, archbishop of St. Andrews, lviii, lxxi, xci-xcii, civ, cx, 410, 411, 416, 435, 447.
Beatrice, daughter of Malcolm, 120, 185.
Beauchamp, Gilbert, 371.
Beaumont, lord Henry de, 274, 275, 279.
—— viscount of, 380.
Beauvais, 229 *n*.
Becket, Thomas, archbishop of Canterbury, 143, 144, 146, 147, 150.
Beda, Natalis, xxxviii, lxxxviii, lxxxix, 409, 425, 430, 436, 440.
Bede's *Ecclesiastical History*, lxiii, cxxxiv, cxxxv, 4, 12, 37, 45, 50, 54, 56, 59, 60, 66,78, 92, 94-96, 98, 99 and *n*, 102, 107, 108, 287.
Bedford, 289.
—— duke of, 371.
Beigheland. *See* Byland.
Beil. *See* Dunbar, Patrick.
Bel, founder of Assyria, 56.

Belgium, 5.
Bellavalle, Franciscus de, 410, 434.
Bells in England and Scotland, xxxiv, 110; in Paris, xliv.
Belmont, viscount, 373.
Benedict, xii, 137 *n*.
Benedictine monastery founded at Newcastle, 135; Germany, 100 and *n*.
—— monasteries at Perth, 362.
Benefeld, Roger, 252.
Berengarius, xciii.
Bergamo's *Chronicles*, 85 and *n*.
Berkeley, lord, 371.
—— castle, 262.
Berlin, 397.
Bernard, St., 98.
—— —— convent of, Haddington, 165.
Bernicia, 66, 72, 113 *n*.
Berquin, his martyrdom, lxxi, lxxxviii.
Bersson, Reginald, 150.
Berta, 217 *n*.
Berwick, 16, 135, 164, 171 *n*, 192, 204 *n*, 221, 224, 225, 227, 244, 250, 271-273, 275, 281, 287, 295, 296, 336, 387.
—— castle, 271, 312.
Biel, Gabriel, xlv *n*.
Bieland. *See* Byland.
Bikcartoun, Walter, of Lufness, 340.
Bilenus, king of Britain, 72.
Bishops, ordination of, 66 and *n*.
Bisset, William, 181.
Black parliament, 245, 269.
Blackheath, 377.
Blonte, sir Walter, 341 *n*.
Bloreheath, 379.
Boarhills, near St. Andrews, 133 *n*.
Boars, 7.
Bodin, Jean, 184 *n*.
Boece, Hector, xlix, lxxv.
Bohun, Humphrey de. *See* Hereford, earl of.
—— William. *See* Northampton, earl of.
Boillon, Martin, ci.
Boisil, St., 98.
Bokingham (Bokinham), John, 23 and *n*.
Bolingbroke. *See* Henry IV.
Boluacus, Joannes, 444.
Bonaventure, St., 174, 229 and *n*.
Bonet, Etienne, xxxviii and *n*.
Boniface VIII., 147.
Bordeaux, 301.
Borlier, J., ci.
Boroughbridge, 251.
Borough moor, battle of, 277.
Borthwick, lord, 299.

Borthwick, sir George, cx.
—— William, of Borthwick, 356.
Bosworth, battle of, 393.
Bothwell, 279.
—— college, 337.
—— James, earl of, 305 *n.*
—— Patrick, earl of, 323 *n.*
Boucard, John, cxxvi.
Boulac or Bouillache, John, xxxviii, xci, 407, 411, 430.
Boulogne, 5.
—— Eustace, count of, 132.
Boyd, Robert, an adherent of Wallace, 196.
—— Thomas, of Kilmarnock, 350.
Bradwardine (Bravardinus), Thomas, 23 and *n,* 26.
Braganza, 51.
Brandan's serving-men, 276.
Brandenburg, 397.
Bravardinus. *See* Bradwardine.
Braxy, 13 and *n.*
Brechin, David, lord, execution of, 245.
Bred, Robert, 278.
Brek, Donald, son of Occabuid, 185.
—— Simon, 52, 56.
Brentheath. *See* Blackheath.
Breslau, 397.
Breton, William, 150.
Breuil, 88 *n.*
Brezé, Peter de, seneschal of Normandy, 379, 387.
Bricot, Thomas, cxxii and *n,* cxxvi and *n.*
Bridgenorth, 20.
Bridget, St., 108.
Brintel, 293 and *n.*
Brise. *See* Brezé.
Bristol, 20, 22, 71, 390, 396.
—— castle, 145.
Britain, origin of the name, 2-14.
Britannicus, 58.
British names, peculiar spelling of, 320, 321.
Brittany, 28 *n.*
—— duke of, 135.
Brotherton, Thomas, 289.
Broughton, Edinburgh, 28 *n.*
Brown, Richard, executed for treason, 245.
Bruce, Alexander. *See* Carrick, earl of.
—— —— beheaded at Carlisle, 221.
—— Christiana, 274.
—— Edward, defeats Donald of the Isles, 231; his siege of Stirling castle, 232, 233; subdues a large part of Ireland, 243; killed at the battle of Dundalk, 244.
—— Nigel, 221.

Bruce, Robert, 174; marries the daughter of the earl of Carrick, 188.
—— —— king of Scotland, his advice to his successors, 38; at the battle of Falkirk, 200; his speech to Wallace, 201; claims the throne of Scotland, 207; stabs the Red Cumming, 208; crowned at Scone, his descent from Malcolm Canmore, 209, 211, 212; the justice of his claim to the throne, 213-220; defeated by Odomar de Valence, 220; his wife carried prisoner to England, 221; takes Inverness castle, 222; Merlin's prophecy, 224; gains a victory near Stirling, 225; excommunicated, 226; subdues Alexander of Argyll, 231; takes Perth, 231; and the Isle of Man, 232; his speech to the army before Bannockburn, 236; disposition of the army, 238; kills an English knight, 239; declared king, 242; his expedition to Ireland, 243; invades England, 246; speech to the army, 247; defeats the English, 249; sends an army into Northumberland, 256, 263; marriage of his son to Joanna, sister of Edward III., 263; his death, 264; his last testament, 264, 265; defence of, against Caxton, 287.
—— Thomas, beheaded at Carlisle, 221.
Brude, king of the Picts, 86, 108.
Brutus, 2, 3, 50.
Bryangen. *See* Jay, Frere Bryan.
Buatius, Nicholaus, 416.
Buchan, 275.
—— earl of, 180.
—— earldom of, 364.
—— Alexander, earl of, 187.
—— —— Stewart, earl of, 331, 364.
—— John Stewart, earl of, 298, 343, 345.
Buchanan, George, xl, xliii, lxxii-lxxiv, civ, cv, cix.
—— Thomas, of the Moss, lxxii.
Buchyn, Enegussa, son of Fechelmeth Romaich, 185.
Buckingham, Humphrey Stafford, duke of, 373, 378, 380.
—— Thomas Woodstock, earl of. *See* Gloucester, duke of.
Budæus, lvii.
Bullock, William, keeper of Cupar castle, 283.
Burgundy, John, duke of, 363, 372.
Buridan, John, lxii and *n,* lxiii and *n,* cxxii and *n,* cxxviii *n,* 405.
Burley, Walter, 228 and *n,* 230.

Bury St. Edmunds, 110 and *n*, 373.
Bute, island of, 37.
Butler, James, 371.
—— John, 371.
Bygot, lord Hugh, 145.
Byland (Beigheland), 247, 252, 253.

CADE'S REBELLION, 374, 375.
Caen, 128.
Caermarthen, 74 and *n*.
Caithness, 5.
—— bishop of, 167, 179.
—— Alan, earl of, 361.
—— John, earl of, 179, 180.
Cajetan, Thomas, cardinal, lii *n*, lviii, 414.
Calais, 5, 292, 307, 372, 378, 379, 380, 391.
Caldermuir, 337.
Caledonian forest, 36.
Calibur, the sword of Arthur, 83.
Callum More, 37.
Calvin, John, xc.
Camber, son of Brutus, 50.
Cambrai, college of, xlvii.
Cambria. *See* Wales.
Cambridge, xxxiii, 25 and *n*, 110, 448.
—— earl of. *See* York, duke of.
Cambridgeshire, 71.
Cambuskenneth monastery, 135.
Cameron clan. *See* Clan.
Campbell of Lochaw, 276.
Candida Casa founded by St. Ninian, 66.
Cannon made in Flanders, 360.
Canterbury, 157, 180, 306, 376.
—— archbishop of [Walter Reynolds], 226, 286.
Canute, king of England, 111, 115, 120.
Capitiati, the rebellion of the, 378 and *n*.
Carausius, 61, 62.
Carbonell, Richard, 371.
Cardross, 264.
Carham (Carra), 311.
Carinthia, 100 *n*.
Carlaverock, 298, 303, 355.
Carlinlyppos (Carlops), 293 and *n*.
Carlisle, 19, 59, 135, 146, 147, 156 *n*, 172, 221, 256, 258.
Carmalin. *See* Caermarthen.
Carmelites arrive in Scotland, 188.
Carnarvon, 225.
Caron, Alexander, standard-bearer to Alexander I., 133 and *n*.
Carrick, 167, 222, 276.
—— countess of, 188.
—— earl of, dies on an expedition to the Holy Land, 188.

Carrick, earl of, taken prisoner at the siege of Dunbar castle, 192.
—— Alexander Bruce, earl of, 270, 271, 273.
—— David, earl of. *See* Rothesay, duke of.
—— John, earl of, son of Robert II., 329.
—— Thomas, earl of, 276.
Carron, 58 and *n*.
Carruther, William, 276.
Carthusian monastery founded at Perth, 362, 364.
Cassibellaunus surrenders to the Romans, 57.
Castile, 243.
—— king of. *See* Ferdinand of Aragon.
Catalonians' observance of Lent, 97 *n*.
Catholic faith accepted by the Scots, 61.
Catinall, Fiachrach, son of Echad Ried, 185.
Cato, 436.
Cattle, 7 ; in the Highlands, 36 and *n*.
Caubraith, Robert, li and *n*, cxxv, 409, 418 ; bibliography of, 417.
Cawood, 22 *n*.
Caxton's *Chronicle*, 1, 3, 57, 127, 143, 145 and *n*, 146, 147, 160, 191, 194, 201, 224-226, 228, 255, 287, 288, 343 and *n*, 350, 360.
Celestine, pope, sends St. Palladius to Scotland, 65 ; consecrates St. Patrick and sends him to Ireland, 66.
Cenalis or Senalis, Robert, liv and *n*, xcii, 408, 409, 411, 418, 432, 445.
Ceylon, 6, 243 and *n*.
Châlus, 155 *n*.
Chaplain, Peter, li, 406, 439.
'Chapter of Mitton.' *See* Myton Upswale.
Charles the Great, 83 ; alliance with Achaius king of Scots, 101 and *n* ; patron saint of the 'English Nation', 110 *n*.
—— the Bald, 113.
—— of Burgundy, 85, 390, 391.
—— IV., emperor, 110 *n*.
—— V., of France, xl, 378 *n*, 395 *n*.
—— V., emperor, 395 *n*.
—— VI., of France, 216, 378.
—— VII., of France, 44, 216, 354.
—— VIII., of France, xxxviii-xxxix, lviii, 390, 393.
Chastel-Neuf, in Bearn, 327.
Chattan. *See* Clan.
Chawmer, Christopher, one of the murderers of James I., 370.

Chayne, William, 371.
Chester, 71.
—— earl of, 167, 309.
—— Ralph, earl of, 145.
Christ's church college, Cambridge,
  xcvi and n, 25 and n, 110 n.
Christianity in Britain, 59, 61.
Chrysanthus, 116 and n.
Chydiok, John, 371.
Cicero quoted, 6, 420, 422, 445.
Cistercians, cix.
Clan Cameron, 344 n, 358-359.
—— Chattan, 334, 358-359.
—— Kay and clan Quhele, combat
  between, 333 and n, 334.
Clare, Gilbert. See Gloucester, earl
  of, 251.
—— Thomas, 174.
Clarence, duke of, 344, 389, 390, 392.
Claudius Cæsar invades Britain, 58.
Clemangis, Nicholas, lvii.
Clement sent to France, 102 and n.
Clergy and lay jurisdiction, 147.
Clermont, Philippe de, 419.
Cleveland, 189.
Clifford, John, lord, 378, 381.
—— Roger, 174, 250-252.
—— sir Thomas, 324, 331.
Clyde, the, 33.
Clydesdale, 276.
—— Maurice de Moray, lord, 282
  and n, 283.
Coal, 39.
Cobham, lord, 377.
—— John Oldcastle, lord, burned for
  heresy, 243.
—— Ronald, 371.
Coccio, Marcantonio. See Sabellicus.
Cockburn, John, 339.
—— Robert, bishop of Ross, xxxi-
  xxxii, l and n, 408, 437.
—— William, 339.
Cockburnspath, 293.
Coldingham, 98, 132.
Coldstream nunnery, 36 n.
Colet and the relics of Thomas Becket,
  152 n.
Colluthy. See Ramsay, William.
Colman, St., 96, 97, 100 n, 102.
Cologne, 60, 100, 126, 207, 230 n,
  395 n.
Colquhoun, Adam, canon of Glasgow,
  lxvi, cxvii.
Columba, St., 86, 88 and n, 96, 98,
  100 n, 108.
Comet seen at the death of Aurelius
  Ambrosius, 79 and n.
Coner, son of Mogolama, 185.
Coneremore, son of Etherskeol, 185.
Confectioners, 9 and n.

Confrey, Rodolph, 202.
Congal, king of Scots, 78, 102.
Coningham, John de, 393 n.
Conor-o-Bryan, king of Munster,
  100 n.
Constance, 101 n.
Constantine, king of Scots, treacherously slain at Inverdovat, 112.
—— the Bald, 118.
—— son of Eth, succeeds Donald as
  king of Scots, invades England, 114;
  becomes a religious at St. Andrews,
  115.
Constantius, king of the Britons, 60,
  67, 78.
—— son of the preceding, after having
  become a monk, is crowned king,
  murdered by Picts, 68.
Copeland (Colpedupe), sir John,
  323.
Corfe castle, 262, 290.
Cornubia, 313 and n.
Cornvalia, 313 and n.
Cornwall, 5, 83.
—— earl of, 81.
—— duke of, 309.
—— Richard, earl of, 174.
Coronation stone brought by Fergus
  from Ireland, 56.
Coronel, Antony, liv, lv n, lvi, cxxv,
  404, 409, 418, 428, 442.
—— Louis, liv, lv and n, 404, 409,
  418, 428.
Couan. See Cowan.
Couchi, Ingelram de, 180 and n.
Couplant, John, takes David II. pri-
  soner, 293.
Coventry, 22, 396.
Cowan, Alexander, 409.
Crabs in Scotland, 33, 34.
Cranston, David, xlix, l, lii, liv, cxxiv,
  10 and n, 408, 409, 424, 425, 433;
  bibliography of, 412-414.
—— William, civ.
Crawford moor, 6 and n.
Crayfish, 33 n.
Cressingham, Hugh, 193, 196.
Crevant, battle of, 344.
Crichton, William, lord of, 355, 362,
  382.
Crockert, Peter, Dominican friar, lii
  and n, liv, 10 n, 409, 418, 433.
Cromarty harbour, 35 and n.
Cronan. See Cryninus.
Cross, ancient, discovered at Peebles,
  188.
Crossecarne, 293.
Crumgring, Corbre, son of Dare-
  diomore, 185.
Cryninus, abthane of Dul, 118 and n.

Crystyclok eats human flesh, 283 and *n*.
Cudlington, 26 *n*.
Cueilly, Thomas de, 415.
Culinus, king of Scots, 117.
Culross, 177.
Cumbrae, Greater (island), 37.
Cumbria, 114, 117.
Cumberland, 127, 128, 134, 162, 216, 312.
Cumming, John, 187, 192, 194, 203, 207, 208, 211 and *n*, 222, 237.
—— Walter. *See* Menteith, earl of.
—— William, 221.
—— family, 187, 188, 199-202, 208, 221, 237, 275.
Cumnock church, 298.
Cunningham, 276.
Cunynghame, Robert, of Kilmaurs, 355, 356.
—— *See* also Coningham.
Cupar, 278, 279, 283.
Currie, Walter, 283.
Curthose, Robert, 128, 143.
Cuthbert, St., 98, 132.
Cynimond, 95.

DALARY, 221.
Dalkeith, 28 *n*, 366.
Dalswinton, 298, 300.
Dammory, Roger, 251.
Dandale, Hugh, 251.
Danes invade Northumberland, 109, 111.
Danube, the, 20 and *n*.
Danzig, 397.
Darediomore, son of Corbre Findmor, 185.
Dares, James, 295.
Daria, 116 and *n*.
Darvargilla, 210 *n*, 211.
David, king of Israel, 83.
David I., lxviii, 126, 145, 210, *n*; defeats Stephen, king of England; gains possession of Northumberland and Cumberland; treaty with Stephen, 134; builds a castle at Carlisle, founds monasteries, taunt of James I. at his tomb, 135; his upright life, 138; and regard for the poor, 139; his death, 140; founder of nine bishoprics, 141.
David II., 263, 286, 289, 304; flies to France, 270; returns to Scotland, 285; invades England, taken prisoner, 292; his ransom, 298, 299; gains possession of the tithes, 303; divorces Margaret Logy, 305; his death, 306.
David, brother of Llewellyn, prince of Wales, 175.

David of Huntingdon. *See* Huntingdon, earl of.
Davidson, Thomas, xcix.
Davil, Joslin, 250, 251.
Dearndil, son of Mane, 185.
Debateable land, the, 19-20.
Dechath, son of Sin, 185.
Dee, the, 33, 231.
—— near Chester, 71.
Deer, monastery of, 87 *n*.
Demonology, 75 and *n*, 170 and *n*.
Denbigh, 175.
Derby, earl of, 281, 307.
Devonshire, earl of, 377.
Devorguilla, 189.
Diocletian, king of Syria, 1, 2 *n*.
Dionoth, father of St. Ursula, 60.
Dionysius' *De Situ Orbis*, 43.
—— the Carthusian, 113 and *n*.
Dirlton. *See* Hamilton, John.
Divorce in Scotland, 305.
Doesmier, Vicentius, 413.
Domesday survey, 129 *n*.
Dominicans. *See* Preaching friars.
Dompnach, 108.
Don, the, 33.
Donald, king of Scots, 112, 114.
Donald Bane, 121; invades Scotland, but is defeated by his nephew Duncan, 131; again becomes king, 131; crown taken from him by Edgar, 132; his death, 166.
Donald of the Isles, 231, 348.
Doncaster, 156 *n*.
Donibristle, 244.
Dorp, John, cxxii and *n*; 405, 411.
Douglas, Archibald, guardian of Scotland, 270, 272-73.
—— —— third earl, 298-99, 313-16, 329-30.
—— —— fourth earl, 335-37, 339, 341, 343-44.
—— —— fifth earl, 343-45, 354-56, 361.
—— David, 382.
—— Gavin, bishop of Dunkeld (third son of fifth earl), xxxi-xxxii, l, lxi, lxv, lxxv, 408, 414, 425, 437.
—— James, lord, 11, 226, 231, 233, 241, 243, 252, 255, 256, 260, 261, 265, 269.
—— James, second earl of, 279, 313-314, 316-17, 321-22, 329.
—— James, of Dalkeith, 329, 340, 354.
—— John, cxx.
—— —— of Dalkeith, 293.
—— Marjory, daughter of Archibald, fourth earl of, 335.
—— sir William, 272, 277, 278, 281, 291, 294.

Douglas, William, first earl of, 282-
285, 293, 294, 297, 309, 312, 313.
—— —— sixth earl, beheaded at Edin-
burgh, 382.
—— —— eighth earl, 382.
—— —— of Nithsdale, 315, 331.
Douglasdale, 293.
Doune, in Menteith, 355.
Dovengard, son of Fergus the Great,
185.
Dover, 172, 380.
—— Straits, 5 and n.
Dragons, 77, 80.
Dronstan, St., 87 and n.
Drury, William, 371.
Drusco, king of the Picts, 105-107.
Dryburgh, 314.
Dublin, marquis of. See Oxford, earl
of.
Dudley, baron, 374.
Duels condemned, 332.
Duff, Angus, 358, 361.
Duffus, son of Malcolm, reigns over
the Scots, 117.
Dullart, Johannes, cxxv.
Dumbarton, 59, 72, 274-76, 309, 355.
Dumfries, 208, 211, 300.
Dunbar, 28 n, 171.
—— castle, 190, 192, 194, 241, 279,
281, 336, 338, 346, 362, 384.
—— Agnes of. See March.
—— Elizabeth, 335.
—— Gavin, archbishop of Glasgow,
l, 411, 444.
—— George, earl of, 356.
—— James, archbishop of Glasgow, xci.
—— Patrick. See March, earl of.
—— —— son of the earl of March,
340, 348.
Duncan, grandson of Malcolm, king
of Scots, 120.
—— succeeds to Malcolm Canmore,
131.
—— son of Beatrice, 185.
Dundalk, battle of, 244.
Dundark, 275.
Dundas, George, xlix.
Dundee, 33, 39, 133 and n.
—— castle, 196.
Dundonald castle, 331.
Dundrennan, 135, 180.
Dungal, king of Scots, 103.
Dungard, brother of Constantius, 78.
Dunglas bridge, 331 and n.
Dunfermline, 28 n, 130, 132-33, 163,
185, 203, 268, 278.
—— monks in St. James's monastery,
Ratisbon, 101 n.
Dunhowm castle, 276.
Dunkeld, 108, 118 n.

Dunkeld, Richard, bishop of, 188.
Dunpier, in France, 291.
Dunnottar castle, 279.
Duns, 311.
Duns Scotus, John, lxii, lxiii and n,
lxxviii, cxxvii, cxxviii, cxxxv, 23
and n, 206 and n, 213 n, 229 and n,
230 n, 311, 410, 412, 449.
Dunstaffnage castle, 231.
Dunstan, St. See Dronstan.
Dunstanburgh, 251.
Dunstane, 206 n.
Dupplin, 211, 269.
Durham, 99, 130, 132 and n, 134, 225,
313, 316.
—— bishop of, 130 n, 324-326.
Durrisdeer, 300.
Dury, abbot of Dunfermline, cx.
—— Andrew, cxvii.
Du Sault, Peter, 410, 434.
Duthac, St., miraculous powers of his
shirt, 273 and n. See also Tain.

Easter, celebration of, 95, 96.
Ebro, the, 51, 185.
Ecclesiastical polity of Scotland, 30.
Echadius, 64 and n.
Echdach, son of Donald Brek, 185.
Edaim, son of Gobram, 185.
Eck, Dr. John Major, xcix n, 409,
449.
Edana, an Irish nun, 16 n.
Edelstan, son of Constantine, 114.
Edgar, son of Malcolm Canmore, 126,
131-32, 210.
—— Atheling, 126, 131.
Edinburgh, xliv, 28 and n, 29 n, 59,
82, 246, 297, 306, 313, 387.
—— castle, 15 and n, 17, 164, 180,
232, 278, 283, 309, 339, 382.
Edmund, king of England, 117.
—— Ironside, 111 and n.
—— St., 109, 110 n.
Education neglected among the gentry.
48 and n; education of children,
115, 116.
Edward, king of the west Saxons, 114.
—— son of Alured, 111.
—— St., king of England, murdered
by his stepmother, 111.
—— the Confessor, 115, 116 and n;
125.
—— son of Malcolm Canmore, 126.
Edward I., 36 n, 174, 210 n, 287-288,
290; invades Wales, drives the Jews
from the kingdom, 176; decides in
favour of John Baliol, invades Scotland, 192; wins the battle of Falkirk, subdues Scotland, 193; true
version of Falkirk battle, 199-202;

declares Baliol king of Scotland, 207; his death, 222; judged worthy of censure, 223; Merlin's prophecy, 224.

Edward II., 203; defeated by Robert Bruce, 225; raises an army for the relief of Stirling castle, 233; his address to the army before Bannockburn, 235; defeated at Bannockburn, 241; sends another army into Scotland and is again defeated, 243, 244; makes his way to Edinburgh, 246; speech to the army, 248; defeated by Bruce, 249; revolt of the barons, 250; defeats the earl of Lancaster, 251; invades Scotland; defeated by Randolph and Douglas, 252; exiles his wife and son, imprisoned in Kenilworth castle, 254; confined in Berkeley castle, removed to Corfe castle, his murder, 262.

Edward III., ii, 231, 275, 277, 278; exiled, returns to England, proclaimed king, 254; marches towards Scotland, 256, 259; his vain pursuit of the Scots army, 259, 260; sends an embassy to Scotland, 263; marches towards Scotland, but disbands his army, 268; besieges Berwick, 271, 272; invades Moray, and razes Aberdeen, restores various strongholds in Scotland, 278; puts his brother John to death, 279; returns to England, 279; treaty with Scotland, 286; his achievements in France, 291; leaves France and leads an army against the Scots, 296; burns Lothian, Edinburgh, etc., 297; his death, 301.

Edward IV., 377, 379, 381, 386, 390, 391.
—— son of Henry VI., 377, 380.
Egremont, lord, 380.
Egyptian or unlucky days, 182-183.
Eichstadt, 101 n.
Ekin, Robert. See Montgomery, lord.
Eleanor, queen of Henry III., 173.
Eldred, king of England, 111.
Eleutherus, pope, 59.
Elga, brother of king Govan, 60.
Elgin, 120, 278.
Elinand. See Helinand.
Eliphat, Robert, 23 and n.
Ella, king, slain by Danes, 109 and n.
Ellela, son of Jair, 185.
Ellis-Croft, 109 and n.
Elphinston, bishop, founder of Aberdeen university, 28.
—— Alexander, 364.
Elstonenfurd. See Athelstaneford.

Emergarda, 167, 180.
Emonia. See Inchcolm.
Engist. See Hengist.
'English Nation', 110 and n.
Engusafith, son of Fechelmeth Asslingith, 185.
Enoch, St., 82 n.
Eochodius. See Eugenius.
Erasmus, xlvii-xlviii, lxxxviii, cxxvi, 27 n, 152 n.
Erfurt, 101 n.
Eric, son of Ethach, 62.
Erigena, John Scotus, lxiv n, lxxviii and n, cxxxv and n, 100, 101 and n, 113 and n, 114 and n.
Erskine, lord, 309.
—— Robert, of Alva, 340.
Erth, son of Echeach Munremoire, 185.
—— William, 340.
Essex, 71.
Etaples, 380.
Ethach, brother of Eugenius, 62.
—— son of Ethafind, 185.
Ethafind, son of Echdach, 185.
Etheldred, son of Malcolm Canmore, 126.
Etherskeol, son of Ewan, 185.
Etholach, Lugtagh, son of Corbre Crumgring, 185.
Ethus, king of Scots, 112.
Ettrick forest, 293, 294.
Eugenius, king of the Scots, slain by Picts, 62.
—— son of Fergus II., 65, 85, 87.
—— IV., 98.
—— V., 99, 114.
Euphemia, wife of Robert II., 331.
Ewan, son of Ellela, 185.
Excommunication, lxxx, 172.
Exeter, duke of, 340, 387.

FALAISE CASTLE, 164.
Falconbridge, lord, 371.
Falkirk, battle of, 193, 199, 200.
Falkland castle, 279, 338, 355.
Fast castle, 348.
Fasts, xlvii, 96, 97 n.
Felix, St., stabbed to death by cobblers' awls, 114.
Ferdinand of Aragon, 190 and n, 394.
Feredech, 185.
Fergus, son of Ferchard, 56, 63, 64, 141, 185, 213.
—— son of Erth, 64-65, 141, 185.
—— of Galloway, 164.
Festivals, 151.
Feu-ferm, 31 n.
Fiacre, St., 88 and n.
Fife, Duncan, earl of, 269, 270.

Fife, Macduff, earl of, killed at Fal-
  kirk, 200.
—— Malcolm, earl of, founder of the
  monasteries of Culross and North
  Berwick, 177.
—— Robert Stewart, earl of, 314,
  316.
—— sheriff of, defeats the English at
  Donibristle, 244.
Finan, successor of bishop Aidan,
  95, 96.
Findachar, son of Akirkirre, 185.
Findmor, Corbre, son of Coneremore,
  185.
Finlay, bishop of Argyll, 355.
Fires in Scotland, 181.
Firth of Forth, 64 n, 65, 67.
Fish in Scotland, 31 and n, 32, 33;
  in Iceland, 34.
Flamborough Head, 342.
Flanders, 53; bells in, 111; cannon
  made in, 360; rebellion in, 378.
—— earldom of, 128.
Fleming, David, 316.
—— Malcolm, 274, 275, 382.
Floods in Scotland, 169.
Foix, count de, 327 and n.
Foresta, Jacques-Philippe de.   See
  Bergamo.
Forester, Adam, of Corstorphine, 340.
—— John, of Corstorphine, 356.
Forestham, 293.
Forfar, 181, 194.
Forman, Andrew, archbishop of St.
  Andrews, 415, 416.
—— John, precentor of Glasgow, li,
  407, 421.
Forth, the, 33, 57, 232, 244, 254.
Fougères, in Normandy, 373.
Fradin, Francis, c, ci.
Francis I. of France, xxxix, lxxxviii,
  lxxxix.
—— St., order of, cix, 174 n.
—— a man of Arragon, 373.
Franciscans, 206, 207.
Frankfurt, 397.
Fraser, Alexander, 269.
—— Andrew, 273.
—— James, 270, 273.
—— Simon, 203; executed in Lon-
  don, 222.
—— —— 270; killed at the battle of
  Halidon, 273.
—— Walter, 283.
Frideswide's, St., nunnery, 23 n.
Frillon, Johannes, ci.
Froimont of Citeaux, abbey of, 113 n.
Froissart's Chronicles, liii, 11, 28, 256-
  261 and n, 295, 315, 328.
Fulda, 75, 126.

Fulk the Black, 171 n.
Furd castle, 313 and n.

GABRIAN, ST., 78, 79 and n.
Gaguin, Robert, lxxv, 343 and n, 344,
  345, 376 n.
Galgacus, lxxxii.
Gall, St., 100 n, 102 n.
Galleston.   See Keith, William.
Galloway, 79, 162, 167, 180, 293, 298,
  337.
—— Alan, earl of, 211 and n.
Galterus, Mathæus, 410, 430, 435.
Galvort, in Ettrick forest, 294.
Gant, John.   See Lancaster, duke of.
Garancières, Eugene de, 294, 295.
Gargeil and Dalkeith, writers of,
  parody Peblis to the Play, 366.
Garnard, king of Picts, 108.
Garrenter.   See Garancières.
Gascony, 146, 176, 192, 203, 233.
Gateshead, 127.
Gathelus, son-in-law of Pharaoh, lxxvi;
  settles in Portugal and founds Bra-
  ganza, 51.
Gaul, 5.
Gaul cisalpina, and Gaul transalpina,
  8 n.
Gaunora, queen of Arthur, 84.
Gavaston, Peter, 225.
Gawain, 84.
Gelecolne.   See Gillecolum.
Geller, duke of, 277 and n.
Genoa, 99.
Geoffrey of Monmouth, lxxv, 3 and n,
  83.
George of Brussels, cxxiv.
Gering.   See Guerinck.
Gerlier, Durand, ci.
'German Nation', 110 n.
Germany, 5, 14; Benedictine monas-
  teries in, 100.
Gerneth castle, 78 and n.
Gerson, Jean Charlier de, chancellor,
  lvii, lviii, 214 n, 411.
Ghent, 395 n.
Giffard, John, 251.
Gilbert, son of Fergus of Galloway,
  164.
—— of Malerb, executed for treason,
  245.
Giles, daughter of Robert II., 315.
Gillecolum, 167 n.
Gillenus, St., famous for his miracles,
  87 and n.
Gilloschop invades Moray, and is put
  to death, 180.
Glamis, 118.
Glasgow, lxviii, 65, 72, 86, 203.
—— university of, lxvii, 28 and n, 29.

Glastonbury, 85, 111.
Gleghornie, xxix, xxx, xxxii, 34, 86, 93, 217 *n*, 428, 437.
Glossa Interlinearis, 75 *n*.
—— *Ordinaria*, 75 *n*.
Gloucester, 20.
—— Eleanor, duchess of, 373.
—— Gilbert Clare, earl of, 251.
—— Humphrey, duke of, 371-373 and *n*, 374, 387.
—— Richard, duke of, 392, 393.
—— Robert, earl of, 145.
—— Thomas Woodstock, duke of, 286, 289, 290, 302, 307.
Gobram, son of Dovengard, 185.
God's house, Cambridge, xxxiii.
Goddam (Godham), Adam, lxii, lxiii and *n*, lxiv, 230 and *n*, 410, 412, 431.
Godfrey of Boulogne, 83.
Gold found in Crawford moor, 6 and *n*.
Gonville hall, 26 *n*.
Gordon, Adam, 339.
—— lady Jane, 305 *n*.
—— John, 310, 311.
—— Roger, 339.
Gormund, an African, lands with an army in Ireland, crosses to Britain and establishes paganism, 89; his followers join the Danes, 111.
Gouran the Scot, son of Dongard, 80.
Gourmont, Giles, lxx, ci.
Gournay, Thomas, 262, 290.
Govan, king, 60.
Gowry, 279.
—— earl of, 132.
Graham, George, 19 *n*.
—— John, an adherent of Wallace, 196; killed at Falkirk, 200.
—— Patrick, 192, 281.
—— Richard, of Netherby, 19 *n*.
—— Robert, 416.
—— —— murderer of James I., 365, 369, 370.
—— William, 416.
—— —— chief of the clan, 19 *n*.
Graham's dyke (Gramysdyk), 65 and *n*, 72.
Grame. *See* Graham.
Gratian, a Roman, claims the British crown, 60.
Grandjon, John, c, ci.
Graunston, Othes, 174.
Gravesend, 393 *n*.
Gray, lord, 344.
—— Andrew, of Foulis, 355.
—— Henry, of Tankerville, 371.
—— Richard, 371.
—— Rodolph, of Werk, 371.
—— sir Thomas, 295, 342.

Green, Hugh, martyrdom of, 369 *n*.
Greenside, 28 *n*.
Greenwich, 21.
Gregorian chant, xxxiv *n*, 30 and *n*.
Gregory of Ariminum, 87 *n*, 443, 450.
—— of Tours, lxxv.
—— son of Dongal, rebels against Ethus, 112 and *n*; crowned at Scone, 113 and *n*.
—— pope, 89.
Greygown, Geoffrey, 171 *n*.
Gryme claims the sovereignty of Scotland, but is defeated by Malcolm; his adherents murder Malcolm near Glamis, 118.
Gualo, legate apostolic, 172, 173.
Guelders, duke of, 382.
Guerinck or Gering, Ulric, ciii.
Guerne's wife violated by Osbricht, king of Northumberland, 109.
Guernsey, 19.
Guian. *See* Vienne.
Guisnes, fortress of, 380.
Guynd, William, li, 440.

Haco. *See* Hangovan.
Haddington, xxxi-xxxii, 165 and *n*, 171, 181, 296, 297, 313.
Hadrian, emperor, 139 *n*.
Hadrian's wall, 27 *n*, 60 *n*.
Hagarenes, 245 and *n*.
Hailes. *See* Hepburn, Patrick.
—— castle, xxix, 336.
Hainault, 233.
—— John of, 254-256.
Hales, Alexander, lxiii, 23 and *n*, 174 and *n*, 229 *n*, 422, 432.
Haliburton, John, 295, 316, 339.
—— Thomas, 339.
—— Walter, 354.
Halidon, battle of, 272.
Hamilton, abbot of Kilwinning, cx.
—— lord, 37, 211 *n*, 212, 383, 385.
—— John, of Dirlton, 339.
—— Patrick, martyr, lxxi, lxxii, lxxxi.
Hampshire, 17, 71.
Hampton, 343.
Hangovan (Haco), 189.
Hannibal, 62, 84.
Harbours of Scotland, 35.
Hardicanute, 115, 122.
Harfleur taken by Henry V., 343.
Harlaw, battle of, 348, 363.
Harold I., his body cast into the Thames and afterwards buried in the church of St. Clement, 115.
Harold II., 116, 117, 127.
Harundel. *See* Arundel.
Harvey, John, xxxviii and *n*.
Hastings, Henry de, 210 *n*.

Hastings, John de, 191, 207, 210 *n*.
Havering in Essex, 116 *n*.
Hawthornden, 284.
Hay, Gilbert, of Errol, 356.
—— John, 416.
—— Thomas, of Lochurquhart, 356.
—— —— of Yester, 354.
—— William, of Errol, 355.
—— —— King's college, Aberdeen, l.
Hazel rods, 14 and *n*.
Hearth-cakes, 11 and *n*.
Heather, 39.
Hector of Troy, 83.
Helinand, 113 and *n*.
Helton (Helcon), lord of, 32.
Hengist lands in Britain, 17; defeats the Scots and Picts, and places Vortiger on the throne, 69; is driven out of the kingdom, returns with an army, and takes Vortiger captive, 70; destroys churches, etc., and bestows seven kingdoms among his followers, 71; Saxon army defeated, and Hengist slain, 79.
Hengist's [Engist's] land, 71, 72.
Henricus a Gandavo, 443.
Henry the minstrel, 205.
—— son of David I., 135, 185.
—— v., emperor, 143.
—— I. of England, 128, 143, 144.
—— II., 146, 150, 153, 162, 164, 170 and *n*.
—— III., 164 and *n*, 173, 174, 180, 186.
—— IV., 302, 304, 308, 337, 340, 341.
—— v., 88 *n*, 342, 344, 346, 366, 371.
—— VI., 25 *n*., 371, 381, 387, 390-393.
—— VII., xl, 212, 213, 289 *n*, 391-393.
—— VIII., xl, cix, cxi, cxii, 149 *n*, 213, 379, 394.
Hentisbery or Heytesbury, William, 23 and *n*.
Hepburn, Adam, of Hailes, 354, 362, 364, 388.
—— George, abbot of Arbroath, l, 408, 425.
—— John, bishop of Brechin, lxix.
—— Patrick, cvi, 316, 318, 319, 323.
—— —— younger of Hailes, 339.
—— family, 323.
Hereford, earl of, 251, 252, 256; [*misprinted* Norfolk] 308.
—— bishop of, 286.
Heriot, James, of Traprain, lxxii.
Herkelay, Andrew, 252, 253.
—— Maurice de, 262.
Hermann, Christian, cxvi.
Hermitage castle, 292, 293.

Herries, Herbert, of Terregles, 355, 356.
Herring, price of, in Scotland, 32.
Hert, sir Robert, 321.
Hertford, 174.
—— duke of, cxi-cxii.
Hertfordshire, 71.
Hesperiæ, 8 and *n*.
Heth, king of the Picts, 16 *n*, 59.
Heytesbury. *See* Hentisbery.
Hiberus, a Spanish soldier, 51.
Highlanders of Scotland, their manners, dress, arms, etc., 49 and *n*, 238, 240.
Hii, island of. *See* Iona.
Hinds, 7.
Hinguar, 108 *n*, 109, 111.
Hircanus, John, 331 *n*.
Holden, Thomas, 348.
Holinculstramen. *See* Holmcultram.
Holkot, Robert, 23 and *n*, 24.
Holland, Lincolnshire, 109 and *n*.
—— count of, 135.
Holmcultram monastery, founded by David I., 135.
Holonde, John, created earl of Huntingdon, 302.
Holyrood, xliv, 135, 162, 306, 314, 360, 386.
Home, Alexander, 340.
Homer quoted, 422, 433, 434, 436.
Homildon hill, battle of, 339.
Honorius, emperor, 64.
Hood, Robert, robber, 156 and *n*.
Horace quoted, 72, 116, 330, 419, 426, 439.
Horsa. *See* Hengist.
Horses, 38; of Ireland, 53 and *n*; of Mar, 368.
Hubba, 109, 111.
Huet, Guillermus, 406.
Hugh, a Christian boy crucified by Jews, 186 and *n*.
—— of St. Victor, 113 *n*.
Humber, the, 20, 71, 72, 128.
Hume, lord, 384.
—— Ninian, l, liv, lvi, 404, 409, 418.
Hungerford, Edmund, 371.
Hungus, king of the Picts, 63, 108, 111.
Huntingdon, 162, 165 *n*, 216.
—— earl of, 344.
—— David, earl of, 135, 164-167, 189, 210 and *n*, 211 and *n*, 213.
—— Henry, earl of, 209, 210 *n*.
—— Isabella, countess of, 211 and *n*.
—— Valdeof, earl of, 135.
—— earldom of, 135, 166.
Hussites, 447.
Hy. *See* Iona.

ICELAND, 32, 34, 37.
Ignatius, St., lxii n.
Iles Oonæ, 8 n.
Images in churches, xciv.
Inchcolm, 133, 359.
Indulphus, king of Scots, 117.
Ingham, Oliver, 286.
Innisboffin, 97, 98 n.
Innocent III., 157.
'Sensus compositus' defined, 76 and n.
Inverbervy, 285.
Inverdovat, 112 n.
Invergowry, 132.
Inverness, 180, 358.
—— castle, 222, 357.
'Invincible ignorance', 136 and n, 223.
Iona, 37 n, 93 n, 96, 113, 120.
Ipswich, 156 n.
Ireland, 5, 8 n, 37, 41, 51, 62, 83, 153, 169, 379, 380.
Irish, language spoken in Scotland, 48-51; the Irish descended from the Spaniards, 50-52; relation of the language to the Spanish, 53.
Irvine, Alexander, of Drum, 349, 355.
Isabella, daughter of William, king of Scots, 168.
—— queen of Edward II., 225, 253, 263, 286, 289.
—— queen of Richard II., 302.
Isidore of Seville, 148.
Isigny-pain-d'aveine, 8 n.
Isius, 5 and n.
Isla, 37.
Isle of Man, 37, 232, 307, 373.
—— of Wight, 19, 71.
Ivo, 436.

JACQUERIE, THE, 376 and n.
Jair, son of Dechath, 185.
James I., 135, 211 n, 212, 341-343, 350, 353-370.
—— II., 42, 211 n, 212, 360-365, 368, 381-386.
—— III., 211 n, 212, 368, 384, 386, 388.
—— IV., 85 and n, 211 n, 212, 289 n., 368, 394.
—— V., lxxvii, civ, cix, 42, 212.
—— St., of Ratisbon, 100 n, 101 n.
Jarrow, 99 n.
Jay, Frere Bryan, 193 and n, 200.
Jeanne of Navarre, lvi.
Jedburgh, 135, 163, 188, 316.
—— castle, 346.
—— staves, 240.
Jerome's charge of cannibalism against the Scots, 44.
Jersey, 19.
Jesus college, Cambridge, 26.

Jews and usury, 176; Jews put to death for crucifying a Christian boy, 186 and n.
Joan of Arc, burnt at Rouen, 372.
Joanna of Tours, 263, 285, 286, 289, 300, 304.
—— queen of James I., 350, 370.
John the evangelist and king Edward's golden ring, 116.
—— king of England, 157-160 and n, 168-171.
—— brother of Edward III., 278, 279.
—— II., king of France, 298, 375.
—— son of Robert II., his name changed to Robert, 331 and n.
—— king of Castile, 331 n.
—— de Fidenza. See Bonaventure, St.
—— of Salisbury, 213 n.
—— of Saxony, 114 n.
—— of the Towers, 328.
—— de Trevisa, 45 n.
—— the Briton. See Richmond, earl of.
—— the Scot. See Erigena, John Scotus.
—— the Voiwode, 331 n.
—— XXII., pope, 225 and n.
Johnston, John, 311.
Jonson, Christy, chief of clan Quhele, 333.
Joshua, 83.
Jovius, Paulus, lxxv.
Judas Maccabæus, 83.
Julius Cæsar, 57, 58, 83.
Julius II., pope, xxxix, lviii.
Julius Hoff, 58 n.
June, John, 371.
Juvenal quoted, 16.

KATHERINE, QUEEN OF HENRY V., 372, 393.
—— of Aragon, 394.
Kay. See Clan.
Keith, Robert, 270.
—— William, of Galleston, routs the English under Talbot, 281; at the siege of Perth, 282.
Kellheim, 101 n.
Kelso, 19, 28 n., 135, 387.
Kenath, son of Alpin, 185.
Kenilworth, 174, 254.
Kennedy, James, archbishop of St. Andrews, lxix, lxxxiv, 28, 364, 383, 387, 388.
—— lord John, 361.
Kenneth I., 103-107.
—— II., 118.
Kennimont, Helias, 340.
Kent, 70-71, 90, 145, 374.
—— earl of, defeated by Malcolm Canmore, 128.

Kent, Edward Woodstock, earl of, 254, 289.
—— Thomas Woodstock, earl of, 289.
Kentigern, St., lxviii ; baptized by Servanus, 66 ; buried in Glasgow, 86.
Ker, John, of Samelstoun, 340.
Kesteven, 109 *n.*
Kiev, 101 *n.*
Kilblene, 278.
Kildrummie castle, 221, 274, 278.
Kilian, St., 87 *n*, 100 *n.*
Kilpatrick. *See* Kirkpatrick.
Kilrimont, 133.
Kinboc, 124 and *n.*
King, Patrick, 393 and *n.*
King's college, Cambridge, 25 and *n.*
King's hall, Cambridge, 25 and *n.*
Kinghorn, 189, 207.
Kinloss monastery founded by David I., 135.
Kinnear (Kyneir), Thomas, cxxi.
Kinross, 187.
Kirkby, sir Richard, 271.
Kirkpatrick, 65, 72.
—— Roger, lord, 208, 298, 303.
Knoth. *See* Canute.
Knox, John, lxvii, cvi-cvii, cxi, cxiv.
Kruithlind, son of Findachar, 185.
Kyle, 195, 276.
Kyneir. *See* Kinnear.
Kynnef castle, 279.

LABANA, wife of Diocletian, king of Syria, 1, 2 *n.*
Labienus, Roman tribune, 57.
Laing, James, civ.
Lakes containing islands, 38.
Lambert, John, c, ci.
Lamp of Lothian, 297 and *n.* *See* also Haddington.
Lanark, 181.
Lancaster, 147.
—— Henry, earl of, 255, 286, 289.
—— John Gant, duke of, 302, 312, 313.
—— Thomas, earl of, 225 ; invades Wales, 250 ; banished, besieges Tikhil castle, defeated by Edward II., 251 ; executed, 252 and *n.*
—— William of. *See* Derby, earl of.
—— earldom, 252.
Landlord and tenant, 30, 31 and *n.*
Langeford, Rodolph, 371.
Langle, Edward. *See* York, duke of.
Langley, Climiton, 23 and *n.*
Langton, Stephen, archbishop of Canterbury, 157.
Languages spoken in Scotland, 48, 49, 50.

Laon, dean of. *See* Anselm.
Lapide, Johannes a, cxxvi.
Latimer, William, 193.
Lauder, Robert, 316, 339.
—— Thomas, keeper of Urquhart castle, 274.
Launoi, lvii, lviii.
Lauriston castle, 279.
Lax, Gasper, liv, cxxv, 409, 418.
Lazarus de Soardis, ci.
Leadhills, 6 *n.*
Leicester, 371, 374.
—— earl of, 254.
Leipzig, 397.
Leith, 28, 33.
—— axes, 240.
Le Maistre, Martin, 413, 438.
Le Messier, James, ci.
Lennox, Stewart, earl of, 211 *n*, 212.
—— John, earl of, 355.
Leo, a cannon made in Flanders, 360.
—— X. makes over the monastery of St. James, Ratisbon, to the Scots, 101 *n.*
Lepus, Constantine, ci, 409.
Leslie, George, of Rothes, 340.
—— Norman, cxi.
—— Walter. *See* Ross, earl of.
—— William, 358.
Lewes, 174.
Lewis VIII., 159, 161, 172, 173.
—— XI., 353, 390, 391.
—— XII., xxxix, liii, lviii.
—— constable of Luxemburg, 392.
—— island of, 16, 38.
Lichtoun, Walter, 332.
Liége, 363, 395 *n.*
Liff, 132.
Lilborn, sir John, 311, 323.
Lile, Alan, 276.
Lincluden, 337.
Lincoln, 22, 109 and *n*, 145 *n*, 156 *n*, 186, 396.
—— earl of, 393.
Lindesay, Alexander, 316.
—— sir David, cvii, 333.
—— sir James, 303, 316, 322, 324-326.
—— lord John, 208.
—— William, 316, 338.
Lindisfarne, 93.
Lindsey, Lincolnshire, 109.
Lindores monastery, 165, 278.
Linlithgow, 309.
Lintown, 336.
Lionverius. *See* Oxford, earl of.
Lismore, 38.
Little Britain, 68, 391.
Little John, 156

Livingston, Alexander, of Callander, 356.
—— John, of Callander, 339.
Llewellyn, prince of Wales, 175.
Lobsters, 33 *n.*
Lochaber, 277, 358.
—— axes, 240 and *n.*
Loch Ard, 38.
—— Awe, 38.
Lochbanquhar. *See* Loch Vennacher.
Lochgowane, 120.
Lochindorb, 275, 278 and *n.*
Lochleven castle, 274, 361.
Lochlomond, 38.
Lochmaben castle, 285, 313, 346.
Lochris, 278 and *n*, 279.
Lochryan, 221.
Loch Tay, 38.
—— Vennacher, 38.
Locrinus, son of Brutus, 50.
Logan, Robert, 269, 340.
—— Walter, 222.
Logy, Gavin, rector of St. Leonard's, li, 442.
—— John, executed for treason, 245.
—— Margaret, 305, 306.
Lokert, George, li, 408 ; bibliography of, 414-415.
Lollards, 342.
Lombards, ill-treatment of, 378, 379.
Londe, William, 328.
London, 17, 20, 21, 80, 222, 225, 230 *n*, 374, 378, 390, 396.
—— bishop of, 68, 91.
—— bridge, 21, 194, 203.
Longueville, duke of, 328.
—— Thomas, pirate, 204.
Lorn, brother of Fergus II., 64.
Lorraine, 373.
Loth, lord of the Lothians, 82, 83.
Lothian, 67, 93, 275, 297, 303, 439.
Louis. *See* Lewis.
Louvain, college of, xlvii.
Loyola, Ignatius, xc.
Lucan quoted, 367.
Lucius, king of Britain, 59.
Lulach, crowned at Scone by Macbeth's adherents, put to death by Malcolm, 123.
Lumphanan, 123.
Lusitania, 51.
Lussy, sir William de, 324.
Luther, Martin, lx, 450.
Lutherans, xcii-xciv, 447.
Luval, James, 349.
Lylaw, Edmund, 243 and *n.*
Lyn, John, 204.
Lyons, lviii, 165 *n.*, 229 *n.*
Lyra, Nicholas de, author of the *Postilla*, 75 *n.*

MACBETH murders Duncan, 120 ; oppresses adherents of Malcolm Canmore, seizes the possessions of Macduff, 122 ; slain by Malcolm, 123.
Macdoual, Fergus, of Galloway, 340.
Macdowel, Donald, 298.
Macduff, thane of Fife, 31 *n*, 122, 123 and *n*, 124.
MacMadach. *See* Orkney, earl of.
Mactrevers, John, 262.
Macwilliam. *See* Donald Bane.
Madeleine, daughter of Francis I., cx.
Magdalen college, Oxford, 25 *n.*
Maidens' castle. *See* Edinburgh castle.
Maitland, Robert, 336.
Major, John, his birth, xxix ; native place, xxx ; school at Haddington, xxxi ; Cambridge, xxxiii, xxxiv ; at Paris, xxxvii-liii ; encomium on, by Coronel, lv ; doctor of theology, lix ; criticised by Melanchthon, lx : visits Scotland, lxi ; regent in Glasgow, lxvi ; regent in St. Andrews, lxvii-lxix ; returns to Paris, contrasted with Buchanan, lxxi-lxxiii ; title of the *History*, lxxvi ; its dedication to James v., lxxvii ; its scheme, lxxviii ; his views on church and state, lxxix ; on taxation, lxxxi, 346-348, 352 ; on nobility, 46-48, 376 and *n*, 397-400 ; on a union between England and Scotland, 41, 42 and *n* ; on the divine right of kings, 213-215, 219, 220 ; on divorce, 305 ; on the early history of Scotland, lxxxv ; commentaries on Aristotle and Scripture, xci ; letter to Wolsey, xcv-xcviii, 448 ; Major and the Parisian press, c-ciii ; returns to St. Andrews, ciii ; his declining years, cvi-cxii ; his character, cxiii ; characteristics of his *History*, cxiv ; notices of Major in French and Scottish records, cxvi-cxxi.
—— —— a Belgian jesuit, 411.
—— —— a German protestant, 411.
Makardy. *See* Mamgarvy.
Makerel, John de, 319.
Makkesone, George, cxx.
Maklane, drill-master to Donald of the Isles, 348.
Makmanke, 358 and *n.*
Makwilliam, Gothred, his rebellion and death, 169.
Malcolm I., king of Scots, 117.
—— II., 118.19.
—— III. (Canmore), 121-123, 126-130, 185, 186 and *n*, 210.
—— IV., 135, 140, 162, 163, 210 *n.*

Malcolm of Cumbernauld, 350.
Malduin, king of Scots, 98.
Malet, Louis, sieur de Granville, xlvi.
Malmesbury monastery, 113.
Maltravers, lord, 371.
Malville, sir Robert, killed at Harlaw, 349.
Mamgarvy, 166 *n.*
Manderston, William, civ, cxix, cxxv, 413; bibliography of, 415-417.
Mane, son of Fergus I., 185.
Manners and customs of the Scots, 40; of the Highlanders, 49.
Mar, Alexander Stewart, earl of, 348, 356, 361, 363 and *n.*
—— Donald, earl of, governor of Scotland, 269.
—— Garthen, earl of, 211 *n*, 212.
—— John, earl of, 211 *n*, 212.
—— Isobel, countess of, 363 *n.*
—— John, earl of, 386.
—— William, earl of, 187.
—— earldom of, and Garioch, 363 *n.*
March (Berwickshire), 293.
—— earl of, 190, 273.
—— Agnes, countess of, 280, 281.
—— Edward, earl of. *See* Edward IV.
—— George Dunbar, tenth earl of, 309, 310, 313, 327, 335-39, 341, 346.
—— —— eleventh earl, 354, 362.
—— Patrick Dunbar, earl of, 269, 277, 278, 282.
—— Roger Mortimer, earl of, 241, 251, 255, 256, 262, 286, 288-290.
—— earldom of, 363, 364.
Marches, earl of the, 271, 294.
Marchmont castle, 134.
Margaret, daughter of William, king of Scots, 168.
—— queen of Malcolm Canmore, 126; her holy life, 130, 185.
—— queen of Alexander II., 209.
—— queen of Alexander III., 186.
—— daughter of Alexander III., 188.
—— the maid of Norway, 189 and *n.*; her death, 191.
—— of Anjou, 25 *n*, 289 *n*, 373, 379-381, 387.
—— queen of Louis XI., 353.
—— of Navarre, xc.
—— queen of James III., 389.
—— queen of James IV., 394.
—— daughter of Henry VII., 211 *n.*
Marianus Scotus, 126 and *n.*
Marjory, mother of John Cumming, 210 *n*, 211 and *n.*
—— daughter of Robert Bruce, 243.
Marne, the, 20.
Marshal, earl, 286, 289, 329, 330.

Marsilius of Inghen, cxxiii and *n*, cxxviii *n.*
Martin, St., 66, 87 *n.*, 140.
Mary, daughter of Malcolm Canmore, 126, 132.
—— of Guelders, queen of James II., 211 *n*, 212, 382, 385, 388.
—— of Guise, civ, cx.
—— queen of Louis XII., 394.
Matilda, queen of England, 126, 132 and *n*, 135, 143, 145.
—— daughter of Henry I., 143, 144.
Maurus, Rabanus, 75 *n.*
Maximus, a Roman general, 62, 65.
Maxwell, Herbert, of Carlaverock, 355.
Mayence, 126.
Mayo, 97 *n*, 98 *n.*
Mayor, election of a, 21.
Mearns, 279.
—— Malpet, earl of, 131.
Mechlin, college of, xlvii.
Mecklenburgh, 100 *n.*
Media Villa. *See* Middleton.
Melanchthon, lx.
Melch, on the Danube, 100 *n.*
Mellitus, bishop of London, 91.
Melrose monastery, lxi, 98 and *n*, 135, 181, 313, 314.
Melville, Andrew, lxviii.
Memmingen, 101 *n.*
Menenes, Petrus, 431.
Menteith, earl of, 183, 316.
—— John, 203, 204.
—— Walter, earl of, 271, 278.
Mercian kingdom and its divisions, 71, 72.
Merkil, 336.
Merlin's prophecies, 74, 77, 80, 81, 175, 224, 254.
Meroe, 90.
Mersey, the, 71, 72.
Methven, battle of, 220.
Metro (Metaurus), the, 20.
Michaelstow, Cornwall, 5.
Middleton, Richard, 23, 206 and *n.*
Milan, lviii.
Milfield, 339.
Minorite church, Haddington, 297.
—— friars. *See* Franciscans.
Miracles, lxxxiv, 141 and *n*, 293, 297, 312, 392.
Mirandola, John Picus de, 420.
Mitton, Gilbert, beheaded for robbing two cardinals, 225.
Modred, 82, 84.
Mogolama, son of Lugtagh Atholach, 185.
Molossian hound causes strife between Scots and Picts, 61, 104.

Monasteries on the continent, 100 *n*; in Scotland, 165, 177. *See* also Religious Houses.
Monenna, St., 16 *n*.
Monstrelet's *Chronicles*, 345, 369-370.
Montagu. *See* Salisbury, earl of.
Montaigu college, xxxii, xxxviii, xliii, xlvi-l, lxxi.
Montfort, Simon de, 174, 175.
Montgomery, lord, 316, 323.
—— John de, 355, 356.
—— family, 323.
Montrose, 181.
Moray, 162, 180, 331.
—— firth, 35 *n*.
—— Andrew of, 271, 275, 277-279. 281.
—— Angus of, 358, 361.
—— Archibald, earl of, 382.
—— David, of Gask, 355.
—— John Randolph, earl of, 270, 284.
—— Maurice de. *See* Clydesdale, lord.
—— Thomas Randolph, earl of, 11, 225, 231-234, 244, 252, 256, 261, 266-268, 276, 277, 309, 316, 318, 321, 327, 333, 340, 367.
More, Kenneth, 358.
Morellus, Thomas, 416.
Morgan, John, 26 *n*.
Morlay, lord Robert, 145.
Mortimer, battle of, 381.
—— Roger. *See* March, earl of.
Morton, 300.
—— earl of, 382.
Morvil, Hugh, 150.
Mount Breigh, 73, 77.
Mountains in Scotland, 36 and *n*.
'Mounth of Scotland', 36 and *n*.
Mowbray, Alexander, 274, 275.
—— John, 222, 250, 251, 271.
—— Philip, governor of Stirling castle, 232.
—— Thomas, created earl of Nottingham, 302.
Multure dues, 276 and *n*.
Munich, 230 *n*.
Munremoire, Echeach, son of Engusafith, 185.
Münsterberg, dukes of, 101 *n*.
Mure, Adam, 211 *n*, 212, 331.
—— Elizabeth, queen of Robert II., 331.
Muref, sir Thomas, 349.
Murray. *See* Moray.
Musgrave, Thomas, captain of Berwick, 311.
Music in Britain, 27 and *n*; in England, 110; in Scotland, 30 and *n*, 50.

Musselburgh, 268.
Myton Upswale, 228 and *n*, 250.

NAMES of places and persons, peculiar spelling of, 320, 321.
Navarre, college of, xxxviii, xlv, lvi.
Nealus, king of Greece, 51.
Neville (Nevyll), George, 371.
—— John, 381.
—— Robert, 243.
—— Thomas, 380, 381.
—— William, 371.
Newark, 160 *n*.
Newbattle, 135, 314.
Newcastle, 135, 140, 147, 204 *n*, 256, 258, 316, 324.
New college, Oxford, 25 and *n*.
New Forest, 129 and 130 *n*.
Nichol. *See* Lincoln.
Nicol or Nicolai, 145 and *n*.
'Nine just men', named, 83.
Ninian, St., 66, 67, 79, 293.
Ninus Nembrothides, 56.
Nisbet moor, battle of, 295, 339.
Nithsdale, 298, 315.
Nobility, 397; of Scotland, 46-48.
Nominalists, the, 229.
Norfolk, 6, 71.
—— duke of, 307, 381.
Norham, 171.
Normandy, 8, 14, 41, 143, 146, 153, 157, 342, 373, 374, 390.
—— Robert, duke of, 120.
—— William, duke of. *See* William I.
Northallerton, 134, 252.
Northampton, 156 *n*, 169 *n*, 286, 288, 380.
—— William Bohun, earl of, 284.
North Berwick, 177.
Northumberland, 66, 72, 109, 131, 134, 135, 140, 162, 163, 171, 217, 225 and *n*, 256, 257.
—— earl of, 378, 381.
—— Henry Percy, earl of, 293, 311, 339, 341, 349.
—— earldom of, 135.
Norway, 62, 83.
Norwich, 22, 156 *n*, 230 *n*, 396.
Nottingham, 109.
—— earl of, 302.
Nunland, 165 *n*.
Nunneries, disorders in, 26 and *n*.
Nuns, seclusion of, 177-179.
Nürnberg, 101 *n*, 397.

OATEN BREAD, xxii, xxx, lii, 7, 8 and *n*, 11, 257.
Oats, 7; preparation of, 8 and *n*.
Occabuid, son of Edaim, 185.
Ochta, son of Hengist, 79, 80.

Ockham, William, lxii-lxiv, cxxvii, 23 and *n*, 24, 228, 230 *n*, 431, 432, 443, 450.
Odam, 314, 315 and *n*.
Oels, in Silesia, 101 *n*.
Ogill, Alexander, 295.
—— sir Robert, 323.
Ogilvy, Alexander, sheriff of Angus, 348.
—— George, 349.
—— Patrick, of Auchterhouse, 354.
—— —— sheriff of Angus, 356.
—— Walter, l, 332, 354.
—— —— of Luntrethyn, 356.
Oldcastle, John. *See* Cobham, lord.
Olivier de Castille, 165 *n*.
Oresme, Nicolas, lvii, 184 *n*.
Orkney islands, 5, 14, 36, 58, 389.
—— earl of, mutilates the bishop of Caithness, 167, 168.
—— Henry, earl of, 342.
—— William Saint Clair, earl of, 356.
Orleans, siege of, 371.
Ormond, Hugh, 382.
Ortiz, Jacobus, lxii and *n*, c., cxxii *n*, 403, 409, 441.
Osbricht or Osbert, king of Northumberland, 109.
Oseney, chime of bells in, xxxiv, xxxv, 26 *n*, 110 and *n*.
Ossa, son of Hengist, 80.
Ostade, 22 and *n*.
Ostia, 135.
Oswald, king of the Bernicians, sends to the Scots for a bishop, 91; a church in Lothian founded in his honour, 93; his arm and hand miraculously preserved from decay, 94.
Othobona, legate, 174.
Otterburn, 315, 317-323, 329, 330.
—— Alan, secretary of Murdach, duke of Albany, 355.
Ouse, the, 20.
Ovid quoted, 301.
Owen of Wales, 372.
Oxen, 13.
Oxford, 22, 25 and *n*, 145, 174, 206, 230 *n*, 448.
—— earl of, 154, 302, 371.
Oysters in Scotland, 33.
Oyta, Henry, lxii and *n*, 230 *n*, 431.

PAIN D'AVEINE, 8 and *n*.
Palladius, St., 65, 66.
Panther, Patrick, secretary to James IV., l.
Pardus, Jerome, lxii, c, cxxii and *n*, cxxvi and *n*, 403, 412.
Paris, xli, 22, 207, 378, 395 and *n*.
—— university, xxxv, xxxvii, xxxviii, xli-xliv, 101 *n*, 110.

Passheley, John, 371.
Patrick, St., 66, 108.
Paul II., 173 *n*.
Paulus Mantuanus, cxxiv and *n*.
—— Venetus, cxxiv and *n*.
Pease, the river, 331 and *n*.
Peat, 39 and *n*.
Pecock, Reginald, bishop of Chester, accused of heresy, 379.
Pecquigny, 391.
Peebles, 188, 336.
Pelagius denies the grace of God, 63·
Pembroke, earl of, 180, 203, 220, 251, 372, 391.
Penrith, 312 and *n*.
Penwichstreit, 5 and *n*.
Pepin, king of France, 214.
Peralta, Peter, 409, 441.
Percy, Henry, 286, 316-18, 323, 327, 330, 336, 339, 341.
—— Ralph, 316, 327.
—— Thomas. *See* Worcester, earl of.
Perth, cxi, 29 and *n*, 33, 39, 162, 169, 181, 194 *n*, 231, 269, 270, 274, 277-279, 282, 354, 361, 362, 364, 368.
Peter of Brussels. *See* Crockert.
—— Lombard, liv, lix, lx, lxii, cxxii, 438, 443, 449.
—— the Spaniard, lii *n*, liv, lvi and *n*, ci, cxxii *n*, cxxiii, 403, 412, 418.
Peter's pence, 158.
Petit or Parvus, John, ci.
Petrarch quoted, 433.
Pharaoh's son-in-law builds Braganza, 51.
Philip Augustus, 159.
—— the Fair, lvi.
—— of Valois, 291, 292.
Picardy, 53.
—— place, Edinburgh, 28 *n*.
Pigouchet, Philip, c.
Pike in Scotland, 33.
Pilgrimages, 306 and *n*.
Pinkie, battle of, cxii.
Piperden, battle of, 364 *n*.
Pisa, council of, lvii, lviii.
Pittenweem, 388.
Pius II. (Æneas Sylvius), 16 and *n*, 39, 365, 426, 427.
Plato quoted, 116, 217 *n*.
Pliny quoted, 8.
Pluscardin monastery founded, 180.
Poggio Barcciolini, 428.
Poissi, 177 and *n*.
Pole, Michael de la, created earl of Suffolk, 302.
Polypods in Scotland, 33 and *n*, 34.
Ponset le Preux, c.
Pontavice, Theodorus de, 413.

Pontefract, 251-2, 308.
Population of London and Paris, 22 ; of mediæval cities, 395.
Portugal, 51.
Portus Salutis, 36 *n.*
Poverty, evangelical, cxxviii.
Preaching friars in Scotland, 173 and *n.*
Preston, 86.
—— Lawrence, 280.
Preth, William, 145 and *n.*
Priests as warriors, 322.
Printers, early, xcix-ci.
Provence, count of, 173.
—— earl of, 373.
Proverbs, 43-45, 55, 57, 84, 92, 106, 107, 137, 146, 187, 198, 204, 274.
Ptolemy's *Geography*, 6.
Pythagoras, 422.

QUEENS' COLLEGE, Cambridge, 25 and *n.*
Queensferry, 28 *n.*
Queygnard, Stephen, c, ci.
Quhele. *See* Clan.

RABBITS, 7.
Rabelais, Francis, xc.
Rademan, sir Matthew, 325-326.
Ramorny (Remorgenay), sir John, 338 and *n.*
Ramsay of Greenock, 340.
—— Alexander, 277, 280-285, 291-292, 294, 316, 339.
—— —— of Dalhousie, 355, 356.
—— Lawrence, of Clat, 340.
—— Thomas, canon of St. Salvator, li, 440.
—— William, of Colluthy, 298.
—— —— of Dalhousie, 295.
Randolph. *See* Moray, earl of.
Ratisbon, monastery of St. James in, 101 *n.*
Reading monastery, 144.
Redesdale, 56, 65.
—— [Ryddisdale] earl of, 344.
Red kirk, 19 and *n.*
Regensburg. *See* Ratisbon.
Regulus, abbot, brings into Britain relics of St. Andrew, 63.
Religious houses, 137 and *n.*
Renfrew, 163.
Rether, king of Scots, 56 and *n*, 185.
Retherdale. *See* Redesdale.
Reuda, a chief of the Scots, 55.
Rheims, 79.
Rhine, the, 60.
Richard of Chester, 143 *n.*
—— of St. Victor, 142 and *n.*
—— I., 154-55 and *n*, 166.

Richard II., 301, 302, 307, 308, 314.
Richerius, Edmund, 411.
Richmond, Edmund, earl of, 372.
—— Henry, earl of. *See* Henry VII.
—— John the Briton, earl of, 252 and *n.*
—— and Derby, countess of, 25 *n.*
Ried, Echad, son of Coner, 185.
Rivers of England, 20 ; of Scotland, 33 and *n.*
Robert of Sorbonne, lix.
—— I. *See* Bruce, Robert.
—— II., 211 *n*, 212, 244, 276, 277, 281, 282, 309, 329-331, 368.
—— III., 211 *n*, 212, 329, 331, 332, 341, 342, 368.
Roce, Dyonysius, c, ci.
Rochelle, 345.
Rochester, 91.
—— bishop of, 91.
Roddam, 314, 315 and *n.*
Rodington, John, 23 and *n.*
Roger, archbishop, 164 *n.*
Roland, suppresses a rebellion in Galloway, 167, 180.
Romaich, Fechelmeth, son of Senchormach, 185.
Roman wall, 60 and *n*, 65 and *n.*
Romans, invasion of Britain by the 57.
Rome, 16, 374, 382, 396 *n.*
Ron, the lance of Arthur, 83.
Ronan, 96 and *n.*
Ronovem, daughter of Hengist, 69, 70.
Rosin, son of Ther, 185.
Roslin, 202.
Ross, 169.
—— Alexander, earl of, 37, 356-359.
—— countess of, 357, 359.
—— Hugh, earl of, 273.
—— John, 358.
—— Walter, earl of, 357.
—— William, earl of, 282, 11, 331, 344, 356.
Rothesay, 38.
—— David, duke of, 312, 335, 337, 338, 364.
Rotholand. *See* Roland.
Rouen, 21, 372, 374, 393.
—— population of, 395.
Rough, John, minister of St. Andrews, cvii.
Round table, 83,
Rous, John, 286.
Rowen, son of Dearndil, 185.
Roxburgh, 134, 164, 181, 278, 291, 293, 310.
—— castle, 231, 313, 314, 364, 386.
Roygny, Jean, cii.

Rufin, James, 410, 434.
Rukby, Thomas, keeper of Stirling castle, 283.
Russel, John, 187.
Rutland, earl of, 302, 381.
Ryddisdaile. *See* Redesdale.

SABELLICUS, his description of the Scots, 42 and *n*, 45, 46.
St. Albans, battles of, 378, 381.
St. Andrew of Kilrimont, church of, endowed by Alexander I., 133.
St. Andrew's parish, Cambridge, 25 and *n*.
St. Andrews, xxx, lxvii, lxviii, cvii-cxii, 28 and *n*, 29, 30 *n*, 113 *n*., 115, 278, 279, 349, 355, 388.
St. Bernard, convent of, Haddington, 165.
St. Clair, Henry. *See* Orkney, earl of.
—— —— John of, 316, 322 *n*.
—— —— Oliver, cxi.
—— —— Walter, 339.
—— —— William, 269.
—— —— bishop of Dunkeld, 244.
—— —— of Hirdemanston, 340.
St. Clement, church of, 115 and *n*.
St. Colmoc, island of, 38.
St. Columba's isle. *See* Inchcolm.
St. David's, 5.
St. Duthac. *See* Tain.
Sainte Barbe, college of, xxxvii.
St. Edmund's fosse, 71.
St. Edmundsbury. *See* Bury St. Edmunds.
St. John's, Smithfield, burned, 301.
St. John's town. *See* Perth.
St. Leonard's college, St. Andrews, lxix, 30 *n*.
St. Margaret's Bay, 126.
St. Martin's of Cologne, 126.
St. Ninian or Whithorn, 37.
St. Oswald, church of, Nastley, 132 *n*.
St. Paul, count of, 391.
St. Radegunde's nunnery, xciii *n*, 26 *n*.
St. Salvator's college, St. Andrews, xxx, lxix, ciii, cxv:ii, cxix, 247.
St. Victor of Paris, cloister of, 142.
Salisbury, 70.
—— bishop of, 144 and *n*, 374.
—— John, duke of, 340.
—— Richard, earl of, 378-381.
—— Thomas, earl of, 371.
—— William, earl of, 279, 281, 284.
Sallust quoted, xxxii, 64, 437.
Salmon, price of, in Scotland, 32.
Sanda, island of, 37 *n*.

Sandilands, Peter, rector of Calder, li, 407, 421.
Sandwich, 379.
Sark, battle of, 29.
Sarmatia, 15.
Saxo Grammaticus, lxxv.
Saxon kingdoms and their boundaries, 71.
—— soldiers called into Britain, 69.
Saye, lord, 374, 375.
Scales, lord, captain of London-tower, 375.
Scandinavia, 14.
Scarborough, 156 *n*.
Sceachbeg, chief of clan Kay, 333.
Schredelowe, John, 371.
Scone, 36, 56, 107, 113, 123, 209, 245, 270, 286, 309, 331.
Scota, daughter of Pharaoh, lxxvi, 51.
Scotisgilmor, 100 and *n*.
Scots descended from the Irish, 50, 52.
Scottish students in Paris, l, li.
Scotus. *See* Duns.
Scrope, lord, treasurer of England, 342 *n*, 362.
Scythia, 7, 54, 107.
Seasons in Britain, 15.
Segrave, John de, 204 *n*.
Seine, the, 20.
Senalis. *See* Cenalis.
Senchormach, son of Kruithlind, 185.
Sens, 10.
Serpents die near Irish soil, 53 and *n*, 54.
Servanus ordained bishop by St. Palladius, is sent to the Orkneys, 66 ; baptizes St. Kentigern, 66.
Seton, Alexander, lord, 271-273, 316.
—— —— of Gordon, 354.
—— John, 340.
—— Thomas, hanged by the English at Berwick, 272.
Severn, the, 20, 71.
Severus, 27, 59, 60 and *n*.
Shaw, Henry, cxx.
Sheep, 13, 36 and *n*, 38.
Shetland, 36, 37.
Shrewsbury, 20, 71, 341.
—— earl of, 374, 380.
Siligo, 7 *n*.
Silvester, Antony, 413.
Sin, son of Rosin, 185.
Sinclair. *See* St. Clair.
Siward, earl of Northumberland, 121, 135.
Skrymgeour (Skyrmengeoure), Alexander, 133 and *n*.
—— sir James, 349.
—— John, constable of Dundee, 355.

Skye, 16, 38.
Socrates quoted, 434.
Sodor, 37.
Solan geese on the Bass Rock, 34, 35 *n.*
Solinus quoted, 6.
Solway, the, 19, 20, 314.
—— moss, battle of, cxi.
Somerset, duke of, 344, 374, 377-380, 387.
Somerwale, Thomas, 356.
Somne, the, 391.
Sorbonne, the, xlv, lvii, lix, 10 and *n*, 450.
'Sortes', an imaginary person, 217 and *n.*
Southampton, 342.
Soutra, 293 and *n.*
Spain, 269.
Spaniards, haughtiness of, 43, 44 and *n.*
—— settle in Ireland, 51.
Spens, Hugh, principal of St. Salvator's college, li, ciii, 440.
Spenser, Hugh, chamberlain of Edward II., 250, 251, 253, 254.
Spey, the, 33 and *n*, 132.
Stafford, earl of, 373, [*misprinted* Strafford] 378.
Stags, 7.
Standard, battle of the, 134 and *n.*
Standish, Henry, bishop of St. Asaph, 149 *n.*
Standonk, John, xxxviii, xlvi, liii, lv and *n*, 429, 430.
Stanhope in Weardale, 255.
Stanley, sir Thomas, 373.
Stanmore, 198, 246.
Stapylton, Walter, bishop of Exeter, 254.
Stephen, king of England, 134, 135, 144-146.
—— Henry, cii.
—— Robert, cii.
'Sterling', origin of, 232 and *n.*
Stewart, Alan, killed at the battle of Halidon, 273.
—— lord, killed at Falkirk, 199, 200.
—— Alexander. *See* Buchan, earl of.
—— —— archbishop of St. Andrews, lxxxviii, 407, 419.
—— —— bishop of Moray, 371.
—— lord Alexander, 354-356.
—— Bernard, of Aubigny, 393.
—— David. *See* Rothesay, duke of.
—— —— of Rossyth, 354.
—— Duncan, son of the earl of Buchan, 332.
—— James, rector of Glasgow university, lxviii, cxvii.
—— —— killed at the battle of Halidon, 273.

Stewart, James, of Bawane, 356.
—— —— son of Murdoch, duke of Albany, 355.
—— —— marries the widow of James I., 370.
—— John. *See* Buchan, earl of.
—— —— killed at the battle of Halidon, 273.
—— —— of Carden, 355.
—— —— of Lorn, 340.
—— —— lord John, of Dundonald, 355.
—— Murdach. *See* Albany, duke of.
—— Robert. *See* Robert II.
—— —— of Lorn, 356.
—— —— of Durrisdeir, 340.
—— Walter, 355, 356.
—— William, of Angus, 340.
Stirling, 82, 164, 181, 193, 197, 204 *n*, 225, 232-234, 278, 283, 309, 355, 361, 382, 383.
—— Alexander, 349.
Stonehenge, 79.
Story, John, xcix.
Strabo quoted, 45.
—— Walafridus, compiler of the *Glossa Ordinaria*, 75 *n.*
Strassburg, 397.
Strath, 112 and *n.*
Strathbogie, 123.
Stratherne, countess of, imprisoned on a charge of treason, 245.
—— earl of, 162, 192, 312, 331.
Strathnaver, 358, 361.
Straton, Edrich de, 111 and *n.*
Strawe, Jake, 301, 302 and *n*, 312 and *n.*
Strode, Ralph, 23, 24 *n*, 413.
Strongholds in Scotland, 30 and *n.*
Strozzi, admiral, cxi.
Stuart. *See* Stewart.
Stubbs, a doctor in theology, xxxvii and *n*, 26 and *n.*
—— Edmund, D.D., master of Gonville hall, 26 *n.*
—— Lawrence, 26 *n.*
Stute, Carolus, xcix.
Suarez, Francis, xlv.
Succession, order of, to the Scottish throne, 112, 243; the question of, debated, 212-220.
Suffolk, 71.
—— duke of, 302, 343, 374, 394.
Suiset, Roger, 23 and *n.*
Sullage, William, 252.
Sumerled, a chieftain of Argyll, 162.
Superstition as to building of a fortress, 73 and *n.*
Surrey, 71.
—— duke of, 340.

Sussex, 376.
Sutherland, Kenneth, earl of, killed at the battle of Halidon, 273.
Sutra. *See* Soutra.
Swans on the Thames, 22.
Swave, Peter, 98 *n.*
Sweetheart abbey founded, 189.
Sweyn of Denmark, 111 and *n.*
Swinton, John, 328 and *n*, 339, 344, 345.
Swynesheid monastery, 160.
Swynton. *See* Swinton.
Syene, 90 and *n.*
Sykkersand, 36 and *n.*
Syria, 1.

TAILS, CHILDREN BORN WITH, in Rochester, 91.
Tain, 221, 273.
Talbot, Richard, 274, 275, 281.
Tantallon castle, xxix, 355, 359, 428.
Tartary, 15.
Tataretus, Petrus, 207 *n.*
Taxation, lxxxi, 346-352.
Tay, the, 33, 169.
Tees, the, 127.
Tempest, Peter, 409, 436, 440.
Terence quoted, 422.
Tetbury castle, 251.
Tethford. *See* Thetford.
Teviot, the, 19.
Teviotdale, 19, 20, 281, 291, 293, 313, 346.
Thames, the, 20, 60, 71.
Thenew, 82 and *n.*
Theophylact, archbishop of Bulgaria, xcii and *n*, 447.
Ther, son of Rether, 185.
Thérouenne in Belgium, 315.
Thetford, 109.
Thirlwall, 27 and *n.*
Thomas the rhymer, 190.
—— William, 371.
Thomson, John, superior of St. James's monastery at Ratisbon, 101 *n.*
Thule, 37.
Tikhil castle, 251.
Tiler, Walter, 301.
Tinctor, Nicholas, cxxii and *n.*
Tiptoft, John. *See* Worcester, earl of.
Tolbooth, the, xliv.
Totnes, 78.
Tournaments, 281, 282.
Tournay, 28.
Tours, 66 ; coinage of, 33 *n*, 38, 384.
—— dukedom of, 345.
Towton, battle of, 381.
Tracy, William, 150.
Trajan, 139 *n.*
Transubstantiation, the doctrine of, xciii.

Traprain, 336.
Trays, Henry, 251.
Trent, the, 20.
Treschel, Jean, cii.
Trever, Nicholas, 425.
Trial by jury, 356, 357 and *n.*
Trinity college, Cambridge, 25 *n.*
Trollop, Andrew, 379, 381.
Trout in Scotland, 33.
Tuda, successor of Colman, 97.
Tudor, Edmund, 393 *n.*
Tulibard, Andrew of, taken prisoner and executed, 270.
Tullilum, 188.
Tunstall, Thomas, 371.
Turbot in Scotland, 33.
Turgot, bishop of Durham, 130 and *n.*
Turnberry castle, 188.
Turnbull, sir James, killed at Nisbet moor, 295.
—— George, li and *n*, 419.
Turstan, archbishop of York, 134.
Tuscany, 229 *n.*
Tweed, the, 19, 33, 98, 171.
Tweeddale, 293.
Tyburn, 203 *n.*
Tyne, the, 28, 128, 258.
Tynemouth, 186 and *n.*
Tyninghame, 86 and *n.*

UCHTRED, 167 *n.*
Union between England and Scotland desirable, lxxix, 41, 42 and *n*, 186, 217-219, 289.
Universities of England, 22 ; of Scotland, 28 and *n.*
Urquhart, 274.
Ursula, St., 60.
Urthid, Thomas, keeper of Perth, 282.
Usury, 176 and *n.*
Utha, 95.
Uther, son of Constantius, 67, 69, 78, 80, 81.

VAIRE, THOMAS, 316 and *n.*
Valance, Aldomar. *See* Pembroke, earl of.
Valdeof. *See* Huntingdon, earl of.
Valenciennes, xlvii, 28, 111.
Valerius Maximus, cxxxiv.
Valla, Laurentius, 427, 428, 443.
Valvanus, 82, 85.
Varia Capella, 199 and *n*, 205.
Vascosanus, Michael, cii.
Vendôme, earl of, obtains assistance for France, 343.
Venice, 307.
Verdon, John, 174.
Vergil, Polydore, lxxv.
Verbal. *See* Wirral.

Verjuice, a wine of Britain, 12 and *n*.
Verneuil, battle of, 345, 371 and *n*.
Vessi, John, 174.
Veypont, Alan de, keeper of Lochleven castle, 274.
Victor, pope, 61.
Vienna, 100 *n*, 101 *n*.
Vienne (Guian), Jean de, admiral of France, 313, 314 and *n*.
Villacrusca, Ramirez de, 414.
Vincennes, 346.
Vincentius Bellovacensis, 52 and *n*.
Vine, the, 12 and *n*, 14.
Vingle, John de, c, ci.
Vio, Thomas de. *See* Cajetan.
Virgil quoted, 37, 62, 134.
Virgilius, apostle of Carinthia, 100 and *n*.
Viridalia. *See* Weardale.
Vortiger, 68-78 and *n*.
Vortimer, 70.

WAKE, THOMAS, 286.
Wakefield, battle of, 380.
Wales, 5, 6, 17, 41, 50, 146, 169, 175, 379, 393.
—— prince of, 175, 309.
Wallace, William, Caxton's account of Wallace, 193; his origin and military genius, 195; defeats the English at Stirling, 196; takes Dundee castle, marches into England, 197; defeated at Falkirk, 200, 201; his betrayal and death, 203 and *n*; review of his conduct, 204.
Walled cities, 29 and *n*.
Wallingford, 145.
Walsingham (Walsington), sir William, 323.
Walterson, Robert, l and *n*, liv, cxvi, 409, 418, 424.
War, evils of, 218.
Wardlaw, Walter, cardinal-bishop of Glasgow, lxix, 312.
Wark castle, 186, 313, 387.
Warren, earl of, 135, 193. 286.
Warwick, Guy, earl of, 225.
—— Richard, earl of, 377, 380, 381, 389-392.
—— Thomas, earl of, 307.
Water of Leith, 28.
Wauchope, Robert, bishop of Armagh, lxxiii.
Waynflete, William, bishop of Winchester, 25 *n*.
Weardale, 255, 263.
Weddel, Dr. John, 407, 442.
Weir, Robert, 371.
Wellys, lord, 371.
Wessex, earl of. *See* Vortiger.

Westminster, 21; Westminster hall built by William Rufus, 129.
Westmorland, earl of, 371.
Wetherby, 244.
Weyh St. Peter, 101 *n*.
Wheat, 7.
Whitekirk, 297.
White ship, the, 143 and *n*.
Whithorn. *See* St. Ninian.
Whittingham church, lxxxv; founded in honour of Oswald, king of the Bernicians, 93.
Wick, 5, 224.
Wicliffe, John, 25 *n*.
Wicliffites, 447.
William the Conqueror, 120, 127, 129 and *n*.
—— II., 128, 129.
—— the Lion, king of Scotland, 135, 140, 163-169 and *n*, 185, 210 *n*.
—— the Scot, founder of monasteries in Germany, 100 and *n*.
—— of Auxerre. *See* Altisiodorensis.
—— of North Berwick, 321.
—— of Soulis, 245.
Winchelcombe, abbot of, 149 *n*.
Winchester, 25, 30 *n*, 68, 80, 145, 156 *n*, 175.
—— bishop of, 286.
—— John, cxx, cxxi.
Windsor, 231, 340.
Wine imported, 12 and *n*; wine of Gascony, 203.
Winram, sub-prior, St. Andrews, cviii.
Winton, Roger, earl of, 180.
Wirral, 71 *n*.
Wishart, George, xxxiii, cxi.
Wissent or Witsand, 5 *n*.
Wolsey, Thomas, cardinal, xcv, xcvii, 407, 448.
Wood abundant in Britain, 7.
Woodham. *See* Goddam.
Woodstock, Edward. *See* Kent, earl of.
—— Thomas. *See* Gloucester, duke of.
—— *See* Kent, earl of.
Woodville, Elizabeth, queen of Edward IV., 25 *n*.
Wool, 7; wool trade, 22 *n*; wool weavers, 28 and *n*.
Worcester, 20.
—— John Tiptoft, earl of, 390 and *n*.
—— Thomas Percy, earl of, 341.
Worstead, 22 *n*.
Würzburg, 101 *n*.
Wydewyle, Richard, 371.

YARMOUTH, 6.

York, 16, 22 and *n.*, 79, 109, 111, 156 *n.*, 228, 246, 252, 396.

—— archbishop of, 226, 286.

—— duchess of, 381.

York, duke of, 302, 342, 343, 371, 377-380.

Young, John, cxx.

Yla. *See* Islay.

Zacharias, John, lv, 409, 418.

CORRIGENDA

P. cxxviii, last word of note ², *for* purity *read* poverty

308, l. 5 : *for* Duke of Norfolk *read* Duke of Hereford

302, l. 8 : *for* grandson *read* nephew

339, l. 19 : *for* George Scot *read* George the Scot

370, l. 2 from foot, for *Calendar* read *Chronicles*

378, l. 6 : *for* Strafford *read* Stafford

373, second-last line of text, *for* Francis of Arragon *read* a man of Arragon named Francis

Printed by T. and A. CONSTABLE, Printers to Her Majesty,
at the Edinburgh University Press.

𝔖cottish 𝔥istory 𝔖ociety.

THE EXECUTIVE.

President.
THE EARL OF ROSEBERY, LL.D.

Chairman of Council.
DAVID MASSON, LL.D., Professor of English Literature,
Edinburgh University.

Council.

J. R. FINDLAY, Esq.
P. HUME BROWN, M.A.
G. GREGORY SMITH, M.A.
J. FERGUSON, Esq., Advocate.
Right Rev. JOHN DOWDEN, D.D., Bishop of Edinburgh.
ÆNEAS J. G. MACKAY, LL.D., Sheriff of Fife.
JOHN RUSSELL, Esq.
Sir ARTHUR MITCHELL, K.C.B., M.D., LL.D.
Rev. GEO. W. SPROTT, D.D.
Rev. A. W. CORNELIUS HALLEN.
W. F. SKENE, D.C.L., LL.D., Historiographer - Royal for
    Scotland.
Colonel P. DODS.

Corresponding Members of the Council.

OSMUND AIRY, Esq., Birmingham; Professor GEORGE GRUB,
    LL.D., Aberdeen; Rev. W. D. MACRAY, Oxford; Professor
    A. F. MITCHELL, D.D., St. Andrews; Professor J. VEITCH,
    LL.D., Glasgow; A. H. MILLAR, Esq., Dundee.

Hon. Treasurer.
J. T. CLARK, Keeper of the Advocates' Library.

Hon. Secretary.
T. G. LAW, Librarian, Signet Library.

RULES

1. The object of the Society is the discovery and printing, under selected editorship, of unpublished documents illustrative of the civil, religious, and social history of Scotland. The Society will also undertake, in exceptional cases, to issue translations of printed works of a similar nature, which have not hitherto been accessible in English.

2. The number of Members of the Society shall be limited to 400.

3. The affairs of the Society shall be managed by a Council, consisting of a Chairman, Treasurer, Secretary, and twelve elected Members, five to make a quorum. Three of the twelve elected Members shall retire annually by ballot, but they shall be eligible for re-election.

4. The Annual Subscription to the Society shall be One Guinea. The publications of the Society shall not be delivered to any Member whose Subscription is in arrear, and no Member shall be permitted to receive more than one copy of the Society's publications.

5. The Society will undertake the issue of its own publications, *i.e.* without the intervention of a publisher or any other paid agent.

6. The Society will issue yearly two octavo volumes of about 320 pages each.

7. An Annual General Meeting of the Society shall be held on the last Tuesday in October.

8. Two stated Meetings of the Council shall be held each year, one on the last Tuesday of May, the other on the Tuesday preceding the day upon which the Annual General Meeting shall be held. The Secretary, on the request of three Members of the Council, shall call a special meeting of the Council.

9. Editors shall receive 20 copies of each volume they edit for the Society.

10. The owners of Manuscripts published by the Society will also be presented with a certain number of copies.

11. The Annual Balance-Sheet, Rules, and List of Members shall be printed.

12. No alteration shall be made in these Rules except at a General Meeting of the Society. A fortnight's notice of any alteration to be proposed shall be given to the Members of the Council.

PUBLICATIONS

Works already Issued

1887.

1. BISHOP POCOCKE's TOURS IN SCOTLAND, 1747-1760. Edited by D. W. KEMP.

2. DIARY OF AND GENERAL EXPENDITURE BOOK OF WILLIAM CUNNINGHAM OF CRAIGENDS, 1673-1680. Edited by the Rev. JAMES DODDS, D.D.

1888.

3. PANURGI PHILO-CABALLI SCOTI GRAMEIDOS LIBRI SEX. — THE GRAMEID : an heroic poem descriptive of the Campaign of Viscount Dundee in 1689, by JAMES PHILIP of Almerieclose. Translated and Edited by the Rev. A. D. MURDOCH.

4. THE REGISTER OF THE KIRK-SESSION OF ST. ANDREWS. Part I. 1559-1582. Edited by D. HAY FLEMING.

1889.

5. DIARY OF THE REV. JOHN MILL, Minister of Dunrossness, Sandwick, and Cunningsburgh, in Shetland, 1740-1803. Edited by GILBERT GOUDIE, F.S.A. Scot.

6. NARRATIVE OF MR. JAMES NIMMO, A COVENANTER. 1654-1709. Edited by W. G. SCOTT-MONCRIEFF, Advocate.

1890.

7. THE REGISTER OF THE KIRK-SESSION OF ST. ANDREWS. Part II. 1583-1600. Edited by D. HAY FLEMING.

8. A LIST OF PERSONS CONCERNED IN THE REBELLION (1745). With a Preface by the EARL OF ROSEBERY and Annotations by the Rev. WALTER MACLEOD.
   Presented to the Society by the Earl of Rosebery.

9. GLAMIS PAPERS: The ‘BOOK OF RECORD,’ a Diary written by PATRICK, FIRST EARL OF STRATHMORE, and other documents relating to Glamis Castle (1684-89). Edited by A. H. MILLAR, F.S.A. Scot.

1892.

10. JOHN MAJOR's HISTORY OF GREATER BRITAIN (1521). Translated and Edited by ARCHIBALD CONSTABLE, with a Life of the author by ÆNEAS J. G. MACKAY, Advocate.

To be issued in 1892.

THE RECORDS OF THE COMMISSION OF THE GENERAL ASSEMBLY, 1646-1648. Edited by the Rev. JAMES CHRISTIE, D.D., with an Introduction by the Rev. Professor MITCHELL, D.D.

COURT-BOOK OF THE BARONY OF URIE. Edited by the Rev. D. G. BARRON, from a MS. in possession of Mr. R. BARCLAY of Dorking.

THE JACOBITE RISING OF 1719. Letter Book of James, Second Duke of Ormonde, Nov. 4, 1718—Sept. 27, 1719. Edited by JOHN RUSSELL.

' THE HISTORY OF MY LIFE, extracted from Journals I kept since I was twenty-six years of age, interspersed with short accounts of the most remarkable public affairs that happened in my time, especially such as I had some immediate concern in,' 1702-1754. By Sir JOHN CLERK OF PENICUIK, Baron of the Exchequer, Commissioner of the Union, etc. Edited from the original MS. in Penicuik House by J. M. GRAY.

In preparation.

THE DIARY OF ANDREW HAY OF STONE, NEAR BIGGAR, AFTERWARDS OF CRAIGNETHAN CASTLE, 1659-60. Edited by A. G. REID, F.S.A. Scot., from a manuscript in his possession.

SIR THOMAS CRAIG'S DE UNIONE REGNORUM BRITANNIÆ. Edited, with an English Translation, from the unpublished manuscript in the Advocates' Library.

THE DIARIES OR ACCOUNT BOOKS OF SIR JOHN FOULIS OF RAVELSTON, (1679-1707), and the ACCOUNT BOOK OF DAME HANNAH ERSKINE (1675-1699). Edited by the Rev. A. W. CORNELIUS HALLEN.

PAPERS RELATING TO THE MILITARY GOVERNMENT OF SCOTLAND, AND THE CORRESPONDENCE OF ROBERT LILBURNE and GENERAL MONK, from 1653 to 1658. Edited by C. H. FIRTH.

A SELECTION OF THE FORFEITED ESTATE PAPERS PRESERVED IN H.M. REGISTER HOUSE.

CONTINUATION OF THE RECORDS OF THE COMMISSION OF THE GENERAL ASSEMBLY, 1648-1662.

In contemplation.

DIARY OF COL. THE HON. JOHN ERSKINE OF CARNOCK, 1680. From a MS. in possession of HENRY DAVID ERSKINE, Esq., of Cardross.

ALBEMARLE PAPERS, 1746.

SD - #0002 - 270122 - C0 - 229/152/33 - PB - 9781330247358 - Gloss Lamination